TRANSCENDENT MASTERY

ALBERT GRAEFLE (1807-89): BEETHOVEN PLAYING FOR HIS FRIENDS.
Heliograph by Franz Seraph Hanfstaengl (1804-77). Beethoven-Haus, Bonn.

Transcendent Mastery

Studies in the Music of Beethoven

Bathia Churgin

NORTH AMERICAN BEETHOVEN STUDIES 4

Pendragon Press
Hillsdale, New York

NORTH AMERICAN BEETHOVEN STUDIES SERIES
William Meredith, Series Editor

1   *Beethoven's Compositional Process,* ed. William Kinderman

2   *Letters to Beethoven and Other Correspondence,* tr & ed. Theodore Albrecht (3 vols.)

3   *The Critical Reception of Beethoven's Compositions by His German Contemporaries,* ed. Wayne Senner, Robin Wallace, and William Meredith
    (Vols. I and II available)

4   *Transcendent Mastery. Studies in the Music of Beethoven* by Bathia Churgin

Cover art: *August von Klöber (1795-1864): PORTRAIT OF BEETHOVEN. Pencil drawing. 1818. Beethoven-Haus, H.C. Bodmer Collection.*

Library of Congress Cataloging-in-Publication Data

Churgin, Bathia.
   Transcendent mastery : studies in the music of Beethoven / Bathia Churgin.
      p. cm. -- (North American Beethoven Studies ; 4)
   Includes bibliographical references and index.
   ISBN 978-1-57647-122-7
   1. Beethoven, Ludwig van, 1770-1827--Criticism and interpretation. 2. Music--19th century--History and criticism. I. Title.
   ML410.B42C48 2008
   780.92--dc22
                              2008035629

Copyright 2008 Bathia Churgin

To Hannah Abrahamson
connoisseur of art and music

Contents

Frontispiece	ii
Preface	ix
Acknowledgments	xiii
Abbreviations	xv

Chapter 1: Violin Concerto in D major, Op.61

Background	1
Unifying Elements Throughout the Concerto	9
First Movement: *Allegro ma non troppo*	13
Second Movement: *Larghetto*	39
Third Movement: Rondo	50
The Sketches	70
The Original Sources: the Autograph	72
The Piano Arrangement of Op. 61	80
List of Editions	84

Chapter 2: Piano Sonata in D major, Op. 10, No. 3

Background	86
First Movement, *Presto*	100
The Sketches	118
Sketches for the First Movement	120
Second Movement: *Largo e mesto*	127
Sketches for the Second Movement	149
Third Movement: Menuetto, Trio, *Allegro*	154
Trio	157
Sketches for the Third Movement	159
Fourth Movement: Rondo, *Allegro*	161
Sketches for the Fourth Movement	179
Integration of the Cycle	181
List of Editions	183

Chapter 3: Violin Sonata in G major, Op. 96
    Background   185
    First Movement: *Allegro moderato*   198
    Second Movement: *Adagio espressivo*   222
    Third Movement: Scherzo, *Allegro*   235
        Trio   241
    Differences in the Draft and Autograph   245
    Fourth Movement: *Poco Allegretto*   247
    Three Earlier Versions of the Theme   256

Chapter 4: String Quartet in A minor, Op. 132
    Background   285
    First movement: *Assai sostenuto-Allegro*   293
    Second Movement: *Allegro ma non tanto*   317
        [Trio]   321
    Third Movement: *Molto Adagio, Andante*   334
    Bartók and the "Heiliger Dankgesang"   353
    Fourth Movement: *Alla marcia, assai vivace*   357
    Fifth Movement {Recitative]   360
    The Instrumental Recitative in Beethoven   362
    Op. 132 and Mendelssohn's String Quartet
        in A Minor, Op. 13   365
    Sixth Movement: *Allegro appassionato*   368
    Integration of the Cycle and Cyclic Form   385

Selected Bibliography   395

Index of Beethoven's Works   409

General Index   411

Preface

The purpose of the four long chapters in this volume is to consider widely and deeply four of Beethoven's most excellent works. Each work represents a different genre and each comes from a different period of Beethoven's stylistic development. Thus, the Piano Sonata, Op. 10, No. 3 (1797-98), represents the early period; the Violin Concerto, Op. 61 (1806), and Violin Sonata, Op. 96 (1812), the middle period (though with several later traits in Op. 96); and the String Quartet, Op. 132 (1825), the late period. In this way, the reader becomes acquainted with the special character of each genre as well as the overall development of Beethoven's style—including a large range of structural types and unique forms. Each work is given a comprehensive analysis rarely applied to single compositions of Beethoven.

Beyond the necessary historical background and references to the critical reception, comparisons have been included with other works by Beethoven in the same genre and period. This wider context combines with an effort to view Beethoven's music not only in terms of the heritage of Haydn and Mozart, but also his relation to the long development of Classic style and its procedures from the early Classic period onward, starting in the 1730s. My close study of the music by G. B. Sammartini (1700/01-75) has greatly aided my close study of the music by Beethoven (1770-1827). Beethoven's use of convention—and his departures from it, are basic themes in the analysis of these four compositions.

The main emphasis in this book is on analysis of the music itself, analysis that reflects especially the approaches of Jan LaRue's *Guidelines for Style Analysis* (1970; 1992) and Leonard G. Ratner's basic survey *Classic Music: Expression, Form, and Style* (1980). The focus, therefore, is on Beethoven's treatment of the various musical elements: growth (formal aspects), sound (including texture, dynamics, and timbre), harmony, melody, and rhythm.[1] Depending on the emphases found in the music, the order of the elements after growth may differ in each movement. Subdivisions of growth that are considered in all relevant movements are discussions of the coda sections and continuity.

A sixth element, expression, has been added with respect to the conventional dance types and styles of the period. These "topics" (topoi) conveyed a host of associations to the listener, many of the topics having a long history. Ratner emphasized this aspect as a fundamental consideration with regard to Classic music, and many other musicologists have followed his lead in further

---

[1] For a discussion of these elements see the chapters in LaRue, *Guidelines for Style Analysis*.

exploring and refining the subject.[2]

Beethoven's powerful expressivity and his large range of moods mark all the works here, though differently in each one. In the early Piano Sonata one thinks of the deeply melancholy *Largo e mesto* on one hand and the humorous *finale* on the other. We are moved by the singing allegros so evident in the Violin Concerto, Violin Sonata, and refrain of the Quartet's impassioned *finale*. Many other topics make their effect, like the pastoral and sensibility in the Violin Sonata, and the topical panorama of the Quartet, with its somber learned style combined with a fragile lyricism in the first movement, the waltz, musette, and allemande in the second movement, and the chorale, march, and recitative in movements III-V. These works do not embody the heroic style in any significant way, reminding us that Beethoven's range of expression goes far beyond the heroic. Some stormy passages in the developments of the early Piano Sonata and *finale* of the late Quartet represent another topic often associated with Beethoven's music, though not dominant in any work discussed here.

In analyzing the music I have used analytical symbols introduced by LaRue, and they are included in the List of Abbreviations. These symbols are increasingly being adopted by musicologists and analysts. The symbols save many descriptive words and identify with perfect precision musical functions, phrases, subphrases, and motives, the very essence of the musical language. Ideally suited to Beethoven's style, the symbols assist in identifying motivic and other variants, as well as derivations and developmental processes on various hierarchic levels. It has been my experience as a teacher after using these symbols for many years that one becomes quickly accustomed to both seeing and applying them. Students have invariably expressed enthusiasm for being given a logical method that provides the tools for interpreting musical events as they unfold.

Furthermore, I have supplied timelines for each movement discussed. Another LaRue invention, the timeline, contains the interpretation of structure with the LaRue symbols placed on a horizontal line, together with indications of the basic keys, cadences, and derivations for the movement. Some of the timelines are simplified and some more complex, depending on the movement and genre. I believe all are helpful to the reader, particularly the reader with score in hand.

The frequent references in my analysis to articulations concern the way Beethoven has joined phrases, periods, and sections in a movement. The basic types are listed and briefly defined following the List of Abbreviations. These articulations are not new but the point is to see how they operate in Beethoven's music as it evolves. Concern with articulations is related to the subject of continuity and the achievement of a more and more intensive musical flow in Beethoven's compositions.

---

[2] For explanations of the topics, see the references in Ch.1, n. 26.

The compositional process is an essential subject in the discussion of the music. For each work there occur some references to Beethoven's sketches, alterations in the autograph, or borrowings from earlier drafts. For the Sonata, Op. 10, No. 3, I have considered all extant sketches. These analyses have led to some surprising revelations, like the early emergence of coda ideas and thematic resolutions in the Op. 10, No. 3 sketches, and Beethoven's brilliant use of the old technique of the *ars combinatoria* in the Trio of the Quartet, Op. 132. In the chapter on Op. 132, the reader will find lists of Beethoven's instrumental recitatives and cyclical forms, with brief discussions of each example. The same chapter deals with the influence of the "Heiliger Dankgesang" on Bartók's Third Piano Concerto and the recitative style of the Fifth Movement on Mendelssohn's String Quartet, Op. 13.

Undoubtedly, my choice of works was influenced by the fact that I have played the violin most of my life and so I am drawn to string music. The neglect by analysts of Beethoven's Violin Sonatas led to my selection of his remarkable Op. 96 sonata, and my choice of the Violin Concerto occurred in the early 1990s, when the only meaningful analysis was the brief though profound assessment by Tovey. The Concerto is placed first as the sole orchestral work in this study.

I have tried to include some references to performance practices, though I could not attempt a large-scale treatment of the subject. Thus, I have given the suggested metronome marks by Carl Czerny, Ignaz Moscheles, and Karl Holz, as well as comments on performance style by Czerny and Holz. References have been made to Beethoven's notation of staccato marks, the meanings of some unusual performance terms, and some textual problems. The best editions for each work have been cited, since these are essential for a full understanding of the music.

I have done little, however, with the sound and construction of musical instruments during Beethoven's lifetime, a period of constant change and improvement. I refer the reader to the information on Beethoven's pianos in the studies by William S. Newman and Sandra P. Rosenblum, and the book on violin technique and performance practices in this period by Robin Stowell. For Beethoven's orchestra and orchestra players, there are helpful articles by Joachim Braun, Clive Brown, and Theodore Albrecht. All these studies are listed in the Bibliography.

The chapters may be read singly or consecutively. Each chapter is largely self-sufficient, and much can be gained by careful study of the information and analysis found there. Those reading the four chapters consecutively will find that the book as a whole is integrated by common analytical procedures and concerns. It is through the parallel analysis of each work that the constant and variable features of style emerge. The examination of the same musical elements and use of the same analytical approaches insure long-range connections from one chapter to the other. Many cross-references integrate the various discussions and guide the reader along the way. The cumulative result reveals Beethoven's transcendent mastery of all facets of musical composition.

These chapters assume a knowledge of harmony and counterpoint on the reader's part. They are aimed at musicians of all persuasions, as well as educated music lovers, who wish to penetrate more deeply into Beethoven's music than briefer studies permit. Despite the length of the chapters, there is always more to engage the mind and ear with music of such immense richness and power.

Readers interested in further details regarding Beethoven's life can consult one of several recent biographies in English. These include the Beethoven articles by Joseph Kerman and Alan Tyson in the *New Grove Dictionary of Music and Musicians*, 1st and 2nd editions (1980, 2001; in the 2nd ed. with Scott G. Burnham), and the books by Maynard Solomon (2nd ed., 1998), Barry Cooper (2000), and Lewis Lockwood (2003). All these and others are listed in the Bibliography. For the older standard and more detailed biographies by Thayer-Deiters-Riemann (in German) and Thayer-Forbes (in English), the reader is referred to the List of Abbreviations. Since this book was written in 1995-2003, most later studies relevant to these chapters could not be incorporated in my discussions.

Acknowledgments

I wish, first of all, to express my warmest gratitude to Sieghard Brandenburg, retired Director of the Beethoven-Archiv, Bonn, for reading the entire manuscript and offering valuable comments and suggestions, as well as providing sketch transcriptions for Chapters 3 and 4. My grateful thanks go to Floyd Grave and William Meredith, original readers of the first chapter, for their detailed and thoughtful observations. I also profited from the reading of single chapters by my former students at Bar-Ilan University and the University of North Carolina, Chapel Hill, Martha Frohlich, Jae Morgenroth, and Adena Portowitz.

I gained much from conversations on analytical matters with Jan LaRue, which contributed significantly to the content of the book and even to its title. My discussions on this music with Janet Levy were, as always, clarifying and enriching. I wish to thank my old friend, Leonard G. Ratner, for valuable insights and ideas over many years. My dear friend Ellen Rosand played a key role in this publication, for which I am ever grateful. For their encouragement and interest in the progress of these studies I warmly thank Joanna Biermann, Floyd and Margaret Grave, Edith Kraus-Blödy, Marian LaRue, Marina Ritzarev, Sandra Rosenblum, and Judith Schwartz. I wish to recall here the inspiring friendships of the conductor Max Rudolf and Alan Tyson.

I am most grateful to Bar-Ilan University for generous financial assistance covering both large and small needs. For indispensable help over the years I am indebted to Lydia Ashri, Fritzi Schul, Adi Tsarfati, and Efrat Mor, music librairians at Bar-Ilan University, and Elizabeth Davis, music librarian of Columbia University. I have been most fortunate in having Claire Brook as my highly expert and supportive editor. My excellent typist, Efrat Ashkenazi, made the preparation of the manuscript as pleasant as possible, and Sergei Ritzarev worked with special care on the many musical examples and figures in this book. Morel Koren, director of the computer laboratory of the Music Department at Bar-Ilan, gave generously of his time and expertise. Rachel Lowenstein, assistant to the Music Head, and the Music Department secretary, Dorit Buchman, were always there when needed. My sister, Naomi C. Miller, provided a haven for work on the book in her beautiful New York home. Hannah Abrahamson, with Benjamin and Rose Sklarz, generously devoted many hours to computerizing the bibliography, and Arlene Gordon gave essential assistance in printing the manuscript. I am also particularly indebted to Hannah Abrahamson for vital moral and practical support during the final preparation of this book.

I am grateful for permission to publish the following: several diagrams from Leonard G. Ratner, *Classic Music,* and Gail Nelson Johansen's D. M. A. thesis, "Beethoven's Sonatas for Piano and Violin, Op. 12, No. 1 and Op. 96: A Performance Practice Study" (Stanford University, 1981); Sieghard Brandenburg's transcription of the continuity draft for Op. 96/ III, from his article, "Bemerkungen zu Beethovens Op. 96," *Beethoven-Jahrbuch* 9 (1973-77): 21, and two transcriptions for Chapters 3 and 4; and many musical examples from the new Beethoven *Werke* published by G. Henle Verlag, Munich. I also wish to thank the Scarecrow Press for permission to cite material from my article "Recycling Old Ideas in Beethoven's String Quartet Op. 132," first published in *Essays in Honor of László Somfai on His 70th Birthday*, ed. László Vikárius and Vera Lampert (Lanham, Maryland, 2005), 249-65.

Kiron, Israel
March, 2008

Abbreviations

AmZ	*Allgemeine musikalische Zeitung,* Leipzig: Breitkopf & Härtel, 1798-1848.
Anderson	Emily Anderson, ed. and trans. *The Letters of Beethoven.* 3 vols. London: Macmillan, 1961. References to letters follow Anderson's numbering.
BGA 1-7	Ludwig van Beethoven, *Briefwechsel Gesamtausgabe.* Im Auftrag des Beethoven-Hauses Bonn. Ed. Sieghard Brandenburg. 7 vols. Munich: G. Henle, vols. 1-6, 1996; vol. 7, 1998. References to letters follow Brandenburg's numbering.
B-J	*Beethoven-Jahrbuch,* second series, 1953- . Published by the Beethoven-Haus, Bonn.
CM	Leonard G. Ratner. *Classic Music: Expression, Form, and Style.* New York: Schirmer, 1980.
GSA	Jan LaRue. *Guidelines for Style Analysis.* 2nd ed. Warren, Michigan: Harmonie Park Press, 1992.
Hess-Green	Willy Hess. *Verzeichnis der nicht in der Gesamtausgabe veröffentlichten Werke Ludwig van Beethovens.* Wiesbaden: Breitkopf & Härtel, 1957; James F. Green, ed. and trans. *The New Hess Catalogue of Beethoven's Works,* with a new foreword by James F. Green and a new introduction by Sieghard Brandenburg. West Newbury, VT: Vance Book Pub., 2003.
JAMS	*Journal of the American Musicological Society.*
JM	*Journal of Musicology.*
JTW	Douglas Johnson, Alan Tyson, and Robert Winter. *The Beethoven Sketchbooks: History, Reconstruction, Inventory.* Ed. Douglas Johnson. Berkeley and Los Angeles: University of California Press, 1985.
KH	Georg Kinsky. *Das Werk Beethovens: thematisch-bibliographisches Verzeichnis seiner sämtlichen vollendeten Kompositionen.* Completed and ed. Hans Halm. Munich-Duisburg: G. Henle, 1955.
MGG	*Die Musik in Geschichte und Gegenwart.* Ed. Friedrich Blume et al. 17 vols. Kassel: Bärenreiter, 1949-86. Zweite neubearbeitete Ausgabe. Ed. Ludwig Finscher. Sachteil 9 vols., Personenteil, 17 vols. Kassel: Bärenreiter, 1994-2007 .
MQ	*Musical Quarterly.*

N I	Gustav Nottebohm. *Beethoveniana*. Leipzig and Winterthur, 1872. Reprint, with a new Introduction by Paul Henry Lang. New York and London: Johnson Reprint Corporation, 1970.
N II	Gustav Nottebohm. *Zweite Beethoveniana: nachgelassene Aufsätze*. Leipzig, 1887. Reprint, New York and London: Johnson Reprint Corporation, 1970.
NGA	Neue Gesamtausgabe *Beethoven Werke*. New edition of Beethoven's complete works. Published for the Beethoven-Haus, Bonn, in Munich: G. Henle, 1961-.
NGD	*The New Grove Dictionary of Music and Musicians*. Ed. Stanley Sadie. 20 vols. London: Macmillan, 1980. Second ed. Ed. Stanley Sadie. Executive ed. John Tyrrell. 29 vols. London: Macmillan, 2001.
TDR	Thayer-Deiters-Riemann. A. W. Thayer. *Ludwig van Beethovens Leben*. Continued by Hermann Deiters and completed by Hugo Riemann. 5 vols. Vol. I, 3rd ed., 1917; Vol. II, 3rd ed., 1922; Vol. III, 3rd-5th ed., 1923; Vol. IV, 1907; Vol. V, 1908. Leipzig, Breitkopf & Härtel. Reprint, Hildesheim: Georg Olms, 1971.
Thayer-Forbes	*Thayer's Life of Beethoven*. Rev. and ed. Elliot Forbes. Rev. ed. Princeton: Princeton University Press, 1967.
WoO	Werke ohne Opuszahl (works without opus number) as listed in KH.

La Rue Symbols (see *GSA*, 145-60)

P	Primary themes in the primary key
T	Transitional themes connecting the main key areas
S	Secondary themes in the secondary key
K	Cadential or closing themes in the secondary key
PT	A transitional unit from P to T or S
ST	A transtional unit within or from S
KT	A transitional unit within or from K
N	A new theme introduced after the exposition
RT	Retransition (my symbol)
a, b, c	Phrases
x, y, z	Subphrases
m	Motive
o, O	Opening or introductory element or section
h	Accompaniment
r	Rhythm of a theme, phrase, or motive
( )	Derivations are shown in parentheses.
$1P^1$	Superscripts indicate a varied form of an idea. Themes are numbered as: 1P, 2P, etc.

Other Indications

V_9^0	This symbol, introduced by Walter Piston, indicates a vii^7 chord.
m. 45^1	A superscript attached to a measure number identifies the beat. Thus m. 45^1 refers to the first beat in m. 45.
d, D	When keys are listed in a series, and sometimes in the text, lower-case letters represent minor keys and capital letters major keys.
i, I	Lower-case Roman numerals indicate a minor, diminished, or augmented sixth chord; capital Roman numerals indicate a major chord.

Octave Designators

c^1	middle c
c^2, c^3, c^4	consecutive octaves above middle c
c, C, C_1	consecutive octaves below middle c

Types of Articulations (Punctuations): see *GSA*, 125-32.

1. <u>open</u>: Refers to phrases, periods, and sections that are not interlocked (as in articulations 2-5) and are often separated by rests. A homophonic punctuation.
2. <u>overlapping</u>: Occurs at the ends of phrases, periods, and sections, where "one or more parts . . . reach over the articulative boundary established by the other parts," producing a layered or contrapuntal effect.
3. <u>elision</u>: A single measure serves as the conclusion and beginning of a phrase, period, or section. Not contrapuntal.
4. <u>anticipation</u>: Refers to upbeats and accompaniments anticipating the start of a theme.
5. <u>truncation</u>: "The complete elimination of the final measure of a phrase by too early intrusion of the following phrase."

CHAPTER 1
Violin Concerto in D major, Op. 61

Background

In his maturity Beethoven composed seven complete concertos, five for Piano (Opp. 15, 19, 37, 58, 73), one for Violin (Op. 61), and one for Piano, Violin, and Cello (the "Triple" Concerto, Op. 56). In addition, the Violin Concerto exists in a piano arrangement (see Table 1.1)[1].

Table 1.1 A Chronology of Beethoven's Completed Viennese Concertos

Work	Date	First Published	Key	Instrument
Op. 19	c. 1788; rev. 1794-95, 1798	Leipzig, 1801	B♭	Piano Concerto No. 2
Op. 15	1795, rev. 1800	Vienna, 1801	C	Piano Concerto No. 1
Op. 37	?1800-03	Vienna, 1804	c	Piano Concerto No. 3
Op. 56	1804-07	Vienna, 1807	C	"Triple" Concerto for Piano, Violin, and Cello
Op. 58	1805-06	Vienna, 1808	G	Piano Concerto No. 4
Op. 61	1806	Vienna, c. 1808	D	Violin Concerto
Op. 61	1807	Vienna, 1808	D	Arrangement of Violin Concerto for Piano
Op. 73	1809	London, 1810	E♭	Piano Concerto No. 5

---

[1] For fuller information about the concertos, see the Work-list by Douglas Johnson and Scott G. Burnham, article "Beethoven, Ludwig van," *NGD*, 2nd ed., 3: 115-16. After this chapter was completed, two studies of the Beethoven Violin Concerto appeared. These are: Robin Stowell, *Beethoven: Violin Concerto* (Cambridge: Cambridge University Press, 1998) and Leon Plantinga, *Beethoven's Concertos* (New York: Norton, 1999), Ch. 10. Naturally there is common material between these studies and my chapter, but also different approaches and analyses. In general, my discussion contains more analytical detail than the later studies. Stowell includes a chapter on the cadenzas for the concerto and a Select Discography (that strangely omits the great Heifetz-Toscanini recording). Stowell also presents as Table 5.2 (70-73) a representation of the various rhythmic patterns connected to the pervasive tapping motive in the first movement that closely parallels my own Table 4 (see pp. 17-18), formulated in 1995. My table, however, is organized according to the principles of multistage variance as proposed by Jan LaRue (see n. 28), while Stowell's gives the patterns as they unfold from measure to measure throughout the movement. Plantinga's study of the Violin Concerto is especially valuable for its treatment of all the Beethoven concertos, thus affording the reader an overall context for the Violin Concerto.

Beethoven's interest in the concerto goes back to his Bonn years. His first concerto for Piano, WoO 4, in E♭, was written in 1784 when he was 13. Only the piano part survives, however, in the hand of a copyist, together with orchestral cues and Beethoven's corrections. Also associated with the Bonn period is a lost oboe concerto (Hess-Green 12), sketches for a piano concerto in A, *Adagio*, and fragments of two concerto movements: an incomplete *Romance cantabile* in E minor (Hess-Green 13) for piano, flute, bassoon, and orchestra (dated 1786), and about half of the first movement for a violin concerto in C, WoO5 (dated 1790-92; see the discussion later in this chapter).[2] The earliest version of the Piano Concerto in B♭ Op. 19, was also conceived in Bonn and its original *finale*, a rondo in B♭ WoO 6, is extant (dated 1793).[3] Sketches for another concertante (1802) and a late piano concerto in D (1814-15) also exist.[4] Fifteen piano cadenzas were composed by Beethoven for the six piano concertos (including Op. 61) in c. 1809.[5] Thus, Beethoven's interest in this genre was more considerable than we generally think. The mature concertos span the early and middle periods, from the mid 1790s (excepting Op. 19) to 1809.

All the concertos, of course, have three movements in the usual tempo sequence: fast-slow-fast. Only one concerto is in minor, the Third Piano Concerto in C minor, very different from the Romantic obsession with the minor mode.[6] A comparison of the concertos (including the completed WoO 4) shows that all the first movements are in ¢ meter (also true for WoO 5); the meters of the slow movements are the most varied; and most of the *finales* are either in 2/4 or 6/8 (one in 3/4, in Op. 56, is entitled "Alla Polacca"). While the early concertos specify a fast tempo for the first movement (*Allegro con brio*, also found in WoO 5), the last four concertos require moderate tempos (*Allegro, Allegro moderato*, or *ma non troppo*). This moderate tempo also appears in the Bonn piano concerto. Beethoven prefers slower tempos for his middle movements than Mozart

---

[2] Sketches for the oboe concerto's second movement in B♭(¢ meter) are found in Joseph Kerman, ed., *Ludwig van Beethoven: Autograph Miscellany from circa 1786 to 1799 . . .* (the "Kafka Sketchbook") (London: The Trustees of the British Museum, 1970), Vol. I, Facsimile, fol. 150v, Vol. II, Transcription, 126-27, as well as sketches for an Adagio in D (meter also ¢) intended for a piano concerto in A major, fol. 154, transcription, 127-28.

[3] For discussions of the complex dating and sources for Op. 19, see Geoffrey Holden Block, "The Genesis of Beethoven's Piano Concertos in C Major (Op. 15) and B-flat Major (Op. 19): Chronology and Compositional Process" (Ph.D. diss., Harvard, 1979), 2 vols.; and Douglas Johnson, *Beethoven's Early Sketches in the "Fischhof Miscellany," Berlin Autograph 28*, vol. I (Ann Arbor: UMI Research Press, 1980), 364-85.

[4] See especially Richard Kramer, "An Unfinished Concertante of 1802," in Alan Tyson, ed., *Beethoven Studies* 2 (Oxford: Oxford University Press, 1977), 33-65.

[5] See the volume of cadenzas in the NGA, Abt. VII, Bd. 7, ed. Joseph Schmidt-Görg (1967).

[6] For example, all the concertos of Chopin, later Mendelssohn, and Schumann (both Robert and Clara) are in minor. Beethoven's preference for the major stands out in contrast even to G.B. Viotti, with 10 concertos of 29 in minor.

(*Largo, Adagio*), with only one *Andante* (Op. 58) and one *Larghetto*, close to *Andante* (Op. 61). *Finales* are mainly in a moderate tempo, two inscribed simply as *Allegro* (Opp. 37, 73). The longest first movements occur in the last two concertos, Op. 61 (535 mm.) and Op. 73 (582 mm.), while the longest and certainly most complex *finale* belongs to Op. 58 (600 mm.). The *finale* of Op. 61 is actually next to the shortest of the concertos (360 mm.).

Typically, all *finales* are rondos. Connections between movements II-III appear in three of the last four concertos, Opp. 56, 61, and 73, reflecting a middle-period trend toward intensifying continuity in the latter portion of a work.[7] Even in the Fourth Piano Concerto, movement II connects with movement III via a common melodic tone, e^2, and a linking C-major chord that reaches G major only at the end of the primary theme. Connections to the last movement mark other middle-period compositions, including the String Quartets Op. 59, Nos. 1 and 3, and Op. 74, the Piano Sonatas Op. 27, No. 1, Op. 57 ("Appassionata"), and Op. 81a ("Das Lebewohl"), as well as the Fifth and Sixth Symphonies, all dating from 1802 to 1809.

The Violin Concerto was composed in 1806, the date found on the autograph score. It was the last major work in a remarkably fertile year, which saw the completion of the Fourth Piano Concerto, Op. 58, and the composition of the *Leonore* Overture No. 3, "Rasumovsky" String Quartets, Op. 59, Nos. 1-3, Fourth Symphony, Op. 60, and the C-minor Piano Variations, WoO 80, as well as the finishing touches of the "Appassionata" Piano Sonata, Op. 57. According to latest information, the Violin Concerto (first version) was written in November-December 1806.[8] It was first performed at the benefit concert for the violinist Franz Clement (1780-1842) on 23 December 1806 at the Theater an der Wien. On the rich program of this concert the concerto was preceded by an overture of Méhul and followed by music of Mozart, Handel, and Cherubini, though it closed with a fantasy by Clement and his sonata for one string, played by holding the violin upside down.[9]

---

[7] Such connections occur in music by other composers of the period. Boris Schwarz, "Beethoven and the French Violin School," *MQ* 44 (1958): 436, points out that connections between movements II and III are found in concertos by French composers writing in the late 18th and early 19th centuries (with reference to works by Rode, Kreutzer, and Baillot). Connected movements are fairly frequent in the music of Boccherini, as the connection to the *finale* from the preceding *Andantino* in the late String Quartet Op. 58, No. 4 (1799).

[8] For the dating and sources of the concerto, see the *Kritischer Bericht* for the Violin Concerto, NGA, Abt. III, Bd. 4 by Ernst Herttrich (1994), 5-12 (hereafter cited as *KB*). The dates of composition are considered on 8-9.

[9] See the reproduction of the concerto poster in the *Kommentar* by Franz Grasberger accompanying the concerto facsimile (hereafter abbreviated as Facs. Ed.), *Ludwig van Beethoven, Konzert für Violine und Orchester, D-Dur, Opus 61* (Graz: Akademische Druck u. Verlagsanstalt, 1979), 20.

Beethoven's score is inscribed with a typical pun, "Concerto per clemenza pour Clement." Clement was the orchestral director of the Theater an der Wien and had close connections with Beethoven in the early years of the 19th century. In his previous benefits, Beethoven's Symphonies Nos. 1-3 received their first public performances, and Clement led performances of Beethoven's works at the semi-public concerts sponsored by the bankers Würth, Fellner, and von Häring. Clement was a child prodigy and a brilliant violinist in his early years. His style of playing was opposed to that of Viotti and Rode in remarks in the *AmZ* as follows: "It is not the marked, bold, powerful playing, the gripping, striking Adagio, the power of bow and tone which characterizes the Rode/Viotti School: but an indescribable delicacy, neatness, and elegance; an extremely delightful tenderness and cleanness in playing which indisputably places Clement among the most perfect violinists." His memory was legendary.[10]

According to Carl Czerny, Beethoven composed the concerto quickly and it was premiered barely two days after completion.[11] A contemporary even remarked that Clement performed the concerto at sight, without previous rehearsal.[12] Czerny described this work as "perhaps [Beethoven's] greatest and most beautiful [concerto]" and wrote that the concerto was produced "with greatest effect." The earliest review, of 8 January 1807 in the Viennese *Zeitung für Theater, Poesie, und Musik*, both praised and criticized the concerto. On one hand, the concerto was "received with exceptional applause because of its originality and abundance of beautiful passages." On the other hand, "the verdict of the connoisseurs is unanimous: they concede that it has much beauty, but maintain that the coherence is often completely broken, and that endless repetitions of some commonplace passages might easily prove wearisome." They preferred that Beethoven continue to write in a style like that of his First and Second

---

[10] For Clement, see especially Grasberger, *Kommentar*, 16-22. For Beethoven's high praise of the youthful Clement ("delightful, splendid playing"), see his statement in Clement's album of 1794 translated in Anderson, I, No. 13. The description of Clement's performing style was published in the *AmZ* 7 (1805): col. 500. The translation comes from Clive Brown, "Ferdinand David's Editions of Beethoven," in *Performing Beethoven*, ed. Robin Stowell (Cambridge: Cambridge University Press, 1994), 119. However, in a letter dated before 30 January 1808 Beethoven expressed his displeasure regarding a performance of the concerto by Clement at his benefit concert of 23 December 1807 at the Theater an der Wien. He refused to allow Clement to perform the concerto at a forthcoming concert. See *BGA*, 2, No. 316 and Anderson, I, No. 180 (Anderson's suggested date of November 1808, though, is incorrect). I am grateful to Sieghard Brandenburg for this reference.

[11] Paul Badura-Skoda, ed., Carl Czerny, *Über den richtigen Vortrag der sämtlichen Beethoven'schen Klavierwerke* [*On the Proper Performance of all Beethoven's Works for the Piano*]; Ch. III, 115, n., also the source of the Czerny quotation below. Cited hereafter as *On the Proper Performance* (for the full citation, see the Bibliography).

[12] TDR, II, 558.

Symphonies, Septet, and spirited ("geistreich") Quintet in C.[13] The reference to excessive repetition could refer to repetitions in the ritornellos in the first movement and refrain in the last, as well as to passages in the first movement of the solo violin part that were later varied (see below, "The Two Main Violin Lines").

After Clement played the concerto again the following year,[14] in Dresden in 1815, and Vienna in 1833, performances followed by some of the greatest violinists of the time, such as Baillot in Paris (1828) and Vieuxtemps in Vienna (1834).[15] It was only later, with the renowned performances of Joseph Joachim (1831-1907), starting in 1844 with Mendelssohn conducting, that the concerto's high place in the violin repertory was assured. However, an enthusiastic review by the often critical musicologist F.J. Fétis of the Baillot performance shows that the concerto's worth was well recognized earlier.[16] Fétis described the concerto as "one of the most

---

[13] Part of the translation is taken from Alan Tyson's edition of the Violin Concerto, p. I (see the list of editions at the end of this chapter), and from Wayne M. Senner, ed. and trans., *The Critical Reception of Beethoven's Compositions by his German Contemporaries*, musicology eds. Robin Wallace and William Meredith (Lincoln and London: University of Nebraska Press, in association with the American Beethoven Society and the Ira F. Brilliant Center for Beethoven Studies, San Jose University, 2001), II, 68-69. For the original text, in Jg. 2, 27, see Stefan Kunze et al, eds., *Ludwig van Beethoven, Die Werke im Spiegel seiner Zeit* (Laaber: Laaber-Verlag, 1987), 80. The review was signed by J.N. Moser, a well-known critic in the Viennese literary world (see also TDR, II, 538). The German text runs as follows: "Der vortreffliche Violinspieler Klement spielte unter andern vorzüglichen Stücken, auch ein Violinconcert von Beethofen, das seiner Originalität und mannigfaltigen schönen Stellen wegen mit ausnehmenden Beyfall aufgenommen wurde. . . . Ueber Beethhofens Concert ist das Urtheil von Kennern ungetheilt, es gesteht demselben manche Schönheit zu, bekennt aber, dass der Zusammenhang oft ganz zerrissen scheine, und dass die unendlichen Wiederholungen einiger gemeinen Stellen leicht ermüden könnten." The complete review mistakenly refers to Beethoven's Quintet in D rather than C major.
[14] Mary Sue Morrow, *Concert Life in Haydn's Vienna* (Stuyvesant, NY: Pendragon, 1989), 346.
[15] Christoph-Helmut Mahling, "Violinkonzert D-Dur, op. 61," in *Beethoven: Interpretationen, seiner Werke*, eds. Albrecht Riethmüller, Carl Dahlhaus, and Alexander L. Ringer (Laaber: Laaber-Verlag, 1994), I, 465-66. The concerto was also performed by Luigi Tomasini Jr. in Berlin, 1812. (Mahling, p. 465). In George Grove, "Beethoven's Violin Concerto," *Musical Times* 46 (1905): 471, the editor of the *Musical Times* reports that the first performance of the concerto by the Philharmonic Society in London took place on 9 April 1832 with a Mr. Eliason. The performance was "not very cordially received by the critics. . . ."
[16] See the review in Kunze, ed., *Die Werke im Spigel seiner Zeit*, 56, from the *Revue musicale* (1828), 202-06, of the concert in the Paris Conservatoire on 22 March 1828. The translation partly draws on that in Stowell, *Beethoven: Violin Concerto*, 34. The French text runs as follows: "Ce concerto . . . s'est trouvé à coup une des plus belles conceptions musicales qu'on puisse imaginer. Admirable par le plan comme par les penseés, ce morceau a été pour l'auditoire un enchantement continuel. Phrases charmantes, modulations inattendues, effets piquants d'orchestre, tout s'y trouve réuni. Mais pour produire tout l'effet que l'auteur s'était promis, il fallait un virtuose du premier ordre, un homme qui réunit au plus haut degré le mécanisme parfait de l'instrument à une ame passionnée, et au sentiment le plus exquis; tout cela s'est trouvé dans M. Baillot . . . . aussi personne ne se souvenait qu'un concerto de violon eût produit un pareil effet."

beautiful musical conceptions that one could imagine. Admirable in structure ["plan"] as in ideas, this work was a continual enchantment for the audience. Charming phrases, unexpected modulations, piquant orchestral effects, all are gathered together in this work. But to produce all the effect intended by the author requires a virtuoso of the first rank, a man who combines to the highest degree perfect technique on the instrument with a passionate soul and the most exquisite feeling; all this is found in M. Baillot. ... In addition, no one could remember a violin concerto that had produced such an effect."

When the famous pianist Muzio Clementi (1756-1832) visited Vienna in April 1807 he became acquainted with the concerto, which he described as "wonderful" in a letter to his London associate F. W. Collard of 22 April 1807.[17] He not only asked for publication rights in London but also commissioned Beethoven to make a piano arrangement of the concerto as well. In addition, Clementi bought the rights to Opp. 58-62 on 20 April 1807, but he only published Op. 61.[18] In the end, both versions of Op. 61 were published in Vienna and London, though with some differences in the violin part in London. The orchestra parts are the same for both concertos (for further details on the prints and the piano concerto, see below).

The two concertos were published by the Bureau des Arts et d'Industrie in Vienna, which put out all of Beethoven's works from Op. 52 to Op. 62. While the piano arrangement was announced in the *Wiener Zeitung* on 10 August 1808, it may have been in print even earlier. However, the earliest announcement of the Violin Concerto only appeared in the *AmZ* of 19 April 1809, despite the fact that the concerto was mentioned as being in press as early as August 1807. The Viennese print may have been published late in 1808. In the end, Clement did not receive the official dedication of the concerto, but Beethoven's old and close friend from Bonn days Stephan von Breuning (1774-1828), and the piano arrangement was dedicated to his wife Julie (1791-1809), the dedications perhaps a wedding present to the pair, who were married in April 1808.[19]

As in most of Beethoven's concertos, the composer specifies a smaller orchestra for the second movement. This reduced scoring omits the flute, trumpets, and timpani. All of Beethoven's concertos include

---

[17] KH, 148, Thayer-Forbes, 418.
[18] The text of Clementi's contract (in French) is given in Anderson, III, Appendix F, No. 3. The contract also mentions the commission of three piano sonatas or two piano sonatas and a fantasy, to be provided at an unspecified date, perhaps the inspiration for Beethoven's Piano Fantasy, Op. 77 (1809).
[19] Tyson edition, II. Julie was an excellent pianist as well.

Table 1.2 The Violin Concerto: Gross Form

Scoring (orchestral): 1 flut, 2 oboes, 2 clarinets in A (in C, Mvt. II), 2 bassoons, 2 horns in D (in G, mvt. II), 2 trumpets in D, timpani in D, A, strings (2 violins, viola, cello, double bass)

Mvt.	Key	Tempo/Heading	Meter	Length (mm.)	Form
I	D	*Allegro ma non troppo*	c	535	concerto-sonata
II	G	*Larghetto*	c	91	synthesis of theme and variations, and rondo
III	D	Rondo	6/8	360	sonata-rondo

Cadenzas: Movement I, before the coda; Movement II, at the very end of the movement, an "Eingang" (leadin), followed by the indication *attacca subito il Rondo* , connecting movements II and III; Movement III, before the first return of the refrain (also called an "Eingang") and before the coda.

only one flute, except for the more monumental Third and Fifth Piano Concertos. In this respect, Beethoven follows Mozart, most of whose Viennese concertos also call for only one flute.

BEETHOVEN AND THE VIOLIN

By the time Beethoven wrote the D-major Violin Concerto, he had composed a large repertoire of music involving the violin. Besides Symphonies Nos. 1-4, this repertoire includes a sizable portion of the first movement of an early violin concerto in C, WoO 5, two *Romances* for solo violin and orchestra, Opp. 40 (1802) and 50 (c. 1798), the Triple Concerto, Op. 56, with extensive violin solos (1803-04), and a large amount of chamber music: 9 string quartets, 5 string trios, 4 piano trios, one original string quintet, and 9 violin-piano sonatas, the last being the brilliant "Kreutzer" Sonata, Op. 47 (1802-03). In addition, Beethoven played the viola in the Bonn orchestra in 1788-92, and took violin lessons from Franz Ries in the 1780s, and probably from Ignaz Schuppanzigh in Vienna in 1794 as well as Wenzel Krumpholz in 1796 or later.[20]

Thus, one should not give credence to the oft-repeated remarks that Beethoven found it difficult to write for the violin since he was a pianist,

---

[20] Thayer-Forbes, 82, 95-96, 146. For Krumpholz, see *Beethoven Remembered: Biographical Notes of Franz Wegeler and Ferdinand Ries,* trans. Frederick Noonan, (Arlington, VA: Great Ocean Publishers, 1987),106; first published as *Biographische Notizen über Ludwig van Beethoven* (1838, 1845).

or that he wrote awkwardly for the violin in this concerto. In actuality, the final version of the work is not technically difficult except for the few high passages, and the figuration falls gratefully into the hand. Beethoven certainly rejected some difficult passagework found as alternatives on the autograph, notably the more virtuosic retransition of the first movement. Some such passages were used instead for the piano arrangement. Whether Clement helped Beethoven shape the final version as some writers suggest cannot be known since no evidence has been found on this subject. There is no evidence either that the refrain of the finale might be Clement's, as suggested by Boris Schwarz in an otherwise valuable article.[21] Indeed, the first phrase of the theme appears on the only sketch page for the concerto.

When Beethoven wrote this concerto, the French violin school had become predominant. Strongly influenced by the great Italian violinist G.B. Viotti (1755-1824), the school was led by such brilliant performer-composers as Rodolphe Kreutzer (1766-1831), Pierre Baillot (1771-1842), and Pierre Rode (1774-1830).[22] Beethoven had personal contact with all three, though Baillot valued his music the most. Beethoven dedicated his most brilliant Violin Sonata, Op. 47, to Kreutzer, who came to Vienna in 1798 and won Beethoven's admiration (though Kreutzer disliked Beethoven's music). Baillot was in Vienna in 1805 and Rode in 1812, and it was for Rode that Beethoven wrote the exquisite last Violin Sonata, Op. 96.

Schwarz points to some types of figuration found in Beethoven's concerto that resemble figurations in French violin concertos of the period. These include passages in broken octaves (as in I/*O and 1T—see the timelines for the thematic functions in Tables 1.3 and 1.8), and elaboration of the melodic line in triplets and sixteenths (as in I/2S, 1K, and the development).[23] On the other hand, the concerto places far less emphasis on technical brilliance than in the French style, and makes much less use of double stops (found only in III/S and K). One important feature held in common is the occasional connection of movement II to movement III in French concertos. The French preference for national color in the *finale* and the use of connected movements are both present in the Triple concerto, with a *finale* entitled "Rondo alla Polacca." Beethoven's violin writing in this concerto is not so different from that in the Violin Concerto, written a few years later, except for the lower tessitura.

---

[21] Schwarz, "Beethoven and the French Violin School," 447.

[22] See Boris Schwarz, *French Instrumental Music Between the Revolutions (1789-1830)* (New York: Da Capo Press, 1987), Ch. IV, "The French Violin Concerto," 163-222.

[23] Schwarz, "Beethoven and the French Violin School," brings forward many comparative examples on 443-45.

We can find some common elements between the first movements of Beethoven's concerto and Viotti's famous Violin Concerto No. 22 in A minor (London, c. 1792-97), a work greatly admired by Brahms.[24] Viotti's first movement has a similar lyrical orientation, uses larger rhythmic values, and even incorporates a scalewise S theme. The solo is integrated in the tutti reprise of 1P, as Beethoven first intended in Op. 61.

Many differences between the movements exist, however, such as the use of a more remote key for the S area (E major), and a highly revised recapitulation that deletes S and much of P, 1P returning near the end of the movement. The orchestral background is also primarily accompanimental.

Unifying Elements Throughout the Concerto[25]

Expression: The Singing *Allegro*

A larger integration of the concerto stems from the intense lyricism (singing style) of movements I and II, a lyricism resumed in the new theme of the second episode in the *finale*. The lyrical first movement is continued in the 19th century after Beethoven in the greatest violin concertos of the period by Mendelssohn, Brahms, and Tchaikovsky.

The first movement is a magnificent example of what musicologists have termed the "singing *allegro*," which, in instrumental music, normally refers to the first fast movement with a lyrical primary theme and other lyrical ideas, usually including the secondary theme. Here most of the S area and new theme area in the development are also in the singing style.

This style is only occasionally present in Beethoven's early works (as the first movement of the Cello Sonata, Op. 5, No. 1, dated 1796). Strikingly, several such first movements mark the start of the Middle Period in works composed 1800-01, such as those in the Violin Sonata, Op. 24 ("Spring"), the Piano Sonata, Op. 28 ("Pastoral"), and the String Quintet, Op. 29. To this group we can add the lyrical slow first movements found in the same years

---

[24] Seven performances of Viotti's violin concertos occurred in Vienna before the composition of Beethoven's Op. 61; they took place between 13 April 1791 and the summer of 1805. Two of the performances were given by Clement and two by Ignaz Schuppanzigh (1776-1830), leader of a string quartet associated with Beethoven. See Morrow, *Concert Life in Haydn's Vienna*.

[25] See the seminal article by Michael C. Tusa, "Some Factors for Cyclic Integration in Beethoven's Early Music," *International Journal of Musicology* 2 (1993): 153-92. I have used the basic categories cited by Tusa partly independently of his article. From the article I have drawn on the categories of "Tonal Cross-Reference," "Structural Parallels," and "The Cyclic Finale Coda." Some further remarks regarding similarities among the movements appear within the specific discussion of each movement and the concluding section, "Integration of the Cycle."

in the Piano Sonatas, Opp. 26 and 27, No. 2 ("Moonlight"). In 1802, the opening passages of the Violin Sonata Op. 30, No. 1 and Piano Sonata Op. 31, No. 3 also reflect the lyrical impulse of these years. This remarkable group of compositions was succeeded by the great lyrical beginning movements in the Fourth Piano Concerto, the Violin Concerto, the String Quartet Op. 59, No. 1 (all completed or written in 1806), the Cello Sonata Op. 69 (1807-08), the Piano Trio Op. 97 ("Archduke," 1810-11), and the Violin Sonata Op. 96 (1812), as well as the shorter example in the Piano Sonata Op. 78 (1809). All these works remind us that the Middle Period has a far greater range of expression than that suggested by the rubric "heroic style," which has been so emphasized in recent years. Beethoven was not always shaking his fist at the world!

The singing *allegro*, of course, is a type that goes back to the early Classic period, though it was more common later on. Early examples can be found in Haydn's Symphonies Nos. 12 (1763) and 29 (1765), both in E, and Boccherini's Symphony in C, Op. 12, No. 3 (1771). The best known examples are probably the first movements of Mozart's symphonies Nos. 39 and 40, and several later Mozart piano concertos, such as the concertos in A, K. 414 (1782) and K. 488 (1786), K. 453 in G (1784), and K. 595 in B♭ (1788-91). Nor should one forget the lyrical cello concerto in D by Haydn, Hob. VIIb (1783), and the very lyrical orientation of many first movements in the popular concertos of Viotti, such as Concerto No. 22 in A minor.

In the first movement of Beethoven's Violin Concerto, lyricism is coupled with the tapping motive introduced at the very start of the concerto by the timpani. The motive recurs throughout the movement (see below), suggesting the usual march topic of the concerto style. This topic emerges dramatically in the great *tuttis* presenting transformations of 2S in the second ritornello, and 1P and 2P in the recapitulation. The joining of march and aria is also found in the *Adagio* of the Fourth Symphony, composed just before the Violin Concerto.[26]

THE SYMPHONIC CONCERTO

The symphonic concerto, developed by Mozart, is even more weighted toward the orchestra in this work. The orchestra carries the main thematic material to an unusual degree in the first and second movements, against which the violin contributes an *obbligato* that partly doubles the melodic line in the orchestra. This occurs especially in movement I/2S, 1K, and the development; movement II, the solo variations; and movement III, N. In the first movement the unusually long ritornellos 1 and 2 also emphasize the orchestra, as does the fact that Beethoven withholds from the solo a

---

[26] For these and other topics, see the pioneering discussion in Leonard G. Ratner, *CM*, Part I, "Expression," 1-30, and Wye Jamison Allanbrook, *Rhythmic Gesture in Mozart: Le Nozze di Figaro and Don Giovanni* (Chicago and London: University of Chicago Press, 1983).

complete presentation of the haunting 1S theme until the coda. Finally, the pervasive tapping motive in the first movement appears most often in the orchestra, as background and as theme. Thus, the display element in the concerto is limited mainly to the transitions, cadential areas (I/K, III/K), retransitions, and cadenzas. And even these written sections are restrained.

SOUND

The sound aspect further integrates the concerto in various ways. Both the first and second movements exploit the high register of the violin, and, in addition, significant registral contrasts in the thematic material occur in all movements: in the high-low (coda) location of I/1S; the high-low contrast of the violin variations with the rondo episodes in the *Larghetto*; and in the low-high contrast of the violin refrain in the *finale*. Beethoven's exploitation of sound values finds its fullest expression in the varied orchestral rescorings of P in the second movement (six different settings), ending with a rare use of muted horns.

TONAL CROSS-REFERENCES

As in so many works of Beethoven, recurring keys or key relationships also integrate the various movements of a cycle. Here, it is the subdominant major and minor found in each movement. In the first movement, the new theme of the development starting in G minor is echoed by the new theme in G minor in the *finale*'s second episode. While G major pervades the slow movement to an unusual degree, it appears as well in the more conventional functions in the T section of the recapitulations in both movements I and III. The subdominant emphasis contributes much to the mellow mood of the concerto.

The major-minor contrast in the subdominant areas is paralleled by the major-minor contrast in the repeat of 1S in both movements I and III, and the largely minor 2T and *3T in movement I, another integrating feature. The key of D minor recurs in the *finale*'s first retransition, with a stress on Bf(V^9), a note so important in the first movement (III/85-88). D minor also returns in the retransition from N in the *finale* (mm. 158-66), and in the coda's N3K, with its twice-repeated emphasis on fVI (mm. 342^2-43, 346^2-47).

Further tonal relationships relate to the famous Ds in I/2P. In the sketch for this theme, the note is Ef, the Neapolitan, which became the key to which N modulates from g in the development. This flat key is also connected to the bold tritone modulations in III/K, to ef (in the exposition) and af (in the recapitulation), and to Af major in the return of the refrain after the cadenza in the *finale*, a key reached via enharmonic modulation. Another enharmonic modulation in movement I occurs to the key of B minor just after the start of the development (end of *0^1) in C major, which becomes the Neapolitan of B minor. C major itself is reached via an enharmonic modulation from A.

Structural Parallels

Use of chromatic lines for transitional or connective purposes in movement I (see Melody below) finds an echo in similar lines and functions in the *finale*: the retransition from N, 3RT (mm. 167-73), and the retransition to the final cadenza, 1RT¹ (mm. 263-69). The chromatic coda progression, N3K (mm. 341-49), repeated twice, is not connective, however, though it is obviously integrative in effect (see "The Cyclic Finale Coda" below).

Phrase structure, symmetry, and repetition also pertain to the use of structural parallels. The lyricism of the concerto as well as its special mood of tranquility are bound up with an unusually balanced phrase structure in the first movement. There, both 1P and 1S are eight-measure units (Ex. 1.1). The rondo refrain is built the same way, though it contains a two-measure extension always ending on V, a witty ploy (see Ex. 1.12). Balance stems, too, from the dialogues between the solo and orchestra in both fast movements, as in K in the coda of the first movement; S, as well as N2K and N3K in the coda of the rondo. The large-scale repetitions in both the first and last movements, and more local repetitions in movements II and III, both literal and varied, contribute to the more relaxed character of the concerto.

The Cyclic *Finale* Coda

The long coda (mm. 280-360) acts in many ways as a coda for the entire concerto, especially with respect to its repeated cadencing in the very last part (mm. 329-39) and concluding tonic pedal (mm. 349-59).

A brief thematic connection is made in this coda, where its first part ends with a similar rhythmic-thematic cadence to the cadence of 1P in the first movement coda. Compare measures 521-23 in movement I and measures 311-15 in the rondo, melodically: B-G-E-A-D versus G-E-B-C♯-D.

Example 1.1 Parallel period structure of 1P and 1S, first movement (mm. 2-9, 43-50)

VIOLIN CONCERTO

Both cadences stand out because of their augmented rhythmic values, half notes in the first movement, dotted halves in the finale (Ex. 1.2 on p. 15). There are two other connections between the coda and first movement: one is the turn to D minor with a cadential progression featuring a rising chromatic bass to the chord of B♭ (N3K); the other is the dramatic enharmonic modulation to A♭ after the cadenza (KT), which ties in with the dramatic use of such modulations in the first movement. We may add the long trill in KT, which recalls the long trill in I/2K, both associated with areas of harmonic suspense.

The Resultant Cyclic Form

Though there are almost no intermovement thematic quotations in the concerto, the unifying elements give the work an integrated character that goes beyond mere compatibility of general style and affect. To these elements we should add the *attacca* connection of movements II and III, which intensifies the overall continuity, and brings a greater sense of the whole work as indivisible.

The First Movement: *Allegro ma non troppo*

Table 1.3 Timeline: Movement I

Key: D   Meter: c

Ritornello 1—Exposition 1

	(Pmh)	(Pm)	(Pmh)	(1T)	(1Pr, Pmh)	(1S)		(2P)	(1Sr, 1Pr)
Po=m	1P	2P	|1T	2T	|1S	2S		3S	|1K
1	2	10	18	28		43	51	65	77	86³
D				(B♭)-d–D:V D		d/F-d	D		D:V
				(♭VI)					

Solo 1—Exposition 2

(1Kb)					(Pm)				
*0	|1P¹	2P¹	|1Ta¹	1T²	*3T	|1S¹	2S¹	3S¹	|⁽*⁾1K¹a
89²	101⁴	110	118	122	134	144	152	166	178
V	I			d-F-a	A:V A		a/C-a	A	

			(Pm)	(Pm, 2P)	
a¹ -	b¹ -	b² - *c -	*d	*2K	
182	186	191 195	201	206	
				(C)-A:V	

Ritornello 2—Central Tutti

2T	|1S	2S²	3S²	|1K		
224	239	247	261	272	281³	
F-	a	A	a/C-a	A-C	C	C:V
(♭VI)						

Table 1.3 Timeline: Movement I (cont.)

Solo 2—Development

(Pm)		(+Pmh)	(+Pmh)	(1P, 1Tr, 3S, Pmh)		(0, 1K*c, *2Ka, Pm)	
*0¹	₁1Pa²	Pay dev.	y² dev.	₁*N		*N¹	₁*RT
284²	301	309	315	331		339¹,⁴	357
C-b	b-e	-G	g	g-E♭		E♭-d	V ped.

Ritornello 3—Solo 3--Recapitulation

Po¹	1P³	2P²	₁1Ta¹	Solo:	1Ta²	b¹	b²	1Ta dev.*3T¹₁
365	366	374	382		386	392	396	400 408
D					G		e-d	d-D:V
(Exp. 1)								(Exp. 2)

1S²	2S³	3S³	₁(*)1K²	*2K¹₁
418	426	440	452	480
D	d/F-d	D		(F)-D:V

Ritornello 4

2T¹	₁CADENZA₁
497	510
B♭-d-D:I$^6_4$	ends V

Coda

1S¹	ext.	₁1Ka³-b³ ‖	
511	518	523	total: 535 mm.

Length of Sections
Rit. 1   1-88   88 mm
Solo 1   89-223   135 mm
Rit. 2   224-83   60 mm
Solo 2   284-364   81 mm
Rit. 3   365-85   21 mm.
Solo 3   386-496   111 mm.
Rit. 4   497-510   14 mm.
Coda   511-35   25 mm.

N.B. A star next to a function or phrase indicates it is first found in the solo sections. Functions are numbered consecutively from Rit. 1 through Solo 1. Keys indicated as d/F alternate as d-F-d-F.

EXPRESSION

This is the only opening movement of a Beethoven concerto without an overt march-like rhythm, especially dotted rhythm--so common in the Classic concerto--somewhere in the movement, though the association of the tapping motive with the timpani and brass instruments may suggest the march. As mentioned earlier, the climactic presentations of 2S and the

Example 1.2 Rhythmic-thematic connection between the codas of movements I and III; recurring cadential phrases (I/mm.521-23; III/mm. 311-15.

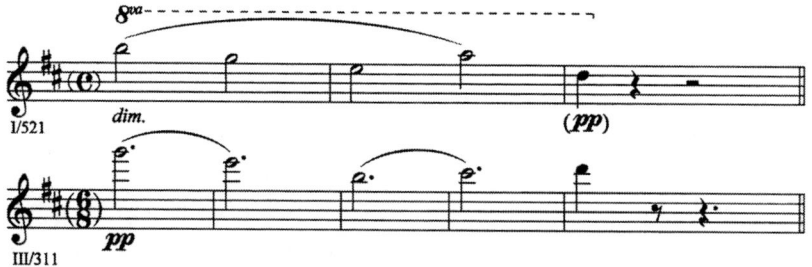

start of the reprise create more of a march-like effect. Brilliant style, as usual, marks the solo transition, 3S cadence, 1K, and *2Kc, as well as the opening solo cadenza-like passage (*O) of the exposition and development, and the first part of the development after the presentation of *O and 1P. Other topics are suggested by the various styles here: the *Sturm und Drang* in 2T, with its agitation and heightened activity; sensibility in 3Sa, with its chromaticism; *ombra* in *2Ka and the approach to the retransition in the development (mm. 351-54), with their mystery and suspense; and the learned style in the *obbligato* counterpoint in 2S and the development.

GROWTH

The Tapping Motive

Themes with repeated notes have a long history. Think of the Baroque canzona and canzona-like fugue subjects, as in Bach's fugue in D, *Well-Tempered Clavier*, Book II. In Classic sonata form, Haydn would seem to be Beethoven's most significant predecessor in the use of tapping motives in themes and accompaniments in several works, like the String Quartet in f, Op. 20, No. 1 (formerly No. 5), as accompaniment, Symphony No. 103/IV, P, and the Piano Sonata in E♭, CL No. 59/1 (Hob. XVI: 49), K area. Another striking example occurs in Clementi's Piano Sonata in g, Op. 34, No. 2/I, O and P, and, of course, the P theme in Mozart's overture to *The Magic Flute* (drawing on Clementi's Piano Sonata Op. 24, No. 2). Then there is the long Classic tradition of starting overtures and symphonies with repeated tonic notes or chords, a tradition with which we are familiar from the openings

---

[27] An early Classic example of an entire movement based on repeated-note motive is the first movement of Haydn's Symphony No. 28 in A (1765). A typical example of a repeated-note beginning occurs in Pergolesi's overture to his oratorio *San Guglielmo* (1731), with four repeated tonic notes followed by a fifth as part of the next phrase. For such repetitions Ratner, *CM*, uses the French term "premiers coups d'archet." I am indebted to my student Moshe Davidovitch for the analogy between the opening of Op. 61 and the Italian overture.

of Mozart's Symphonies Nos. 31, 38, and 41.[27]

Use of a motive involving repeated notes occurs in five major works by Beethoven completed in 1805-08: the Piano Sonata, Op. 57 (mainly composed 1804-05), the Piano Concerto Op. 58, the String Quartet Op. 59, No. 1, the Violin Concerto Op. 61, and the Fifth Symphony Op. 67, sketches for which appear together with sketches for Op. 61 (see the discussion of the Op. 61 sketchleaf below). All movements concerned are first movements except for Movement II in Op. 59, No. 1, and in the Opp. 59, 61, and 67, the motive pervades the movement, though in partially different ways. In each case, however, the motive is used both as theme and accompaniment, and is presented in the opening of the movement in 1P, or, as in Op. 61, as both introduction (Po) and punctuation.

In fact, in Op. 61, the five opening taps on the tonic D by the timpani *piano* constitute a unique and extraordinary beginning, creating mystery and surprise where we expect a straightforward musical statement. We may add that having a unique start to the first movement marks each of Beethoven's last three concertos (Opp. 58, 61, and 73); the piano concertos open with either a solo passage (Op. 58) or a solo plus orchestra (Op. 73).

The tapping motive in Op. 61 is found in three basic rhythmic forms: quarter-note (1m), eighth-note (2m), and sixteenth-note (3m); the quarter-note version is also modified as an eighth-and eighth-rest ($1m^1$; see Table 1.4). The motive ends in several different rhythmic values as well. It can begin on the strong or weak beat; it is altered from five notes to four and three notes, or expanded also as a tremolo to nine or more notes. The various versions embody the Haydn-Beethoven technique of multistage variance: making variants on variants, as 2m and 3m in relation to 1m, plus variants of these versions as well.[28] The motive functions as both theme and accompaniment but mainly as accompaniment in the orchestra, and it appears in all functions except 1Ka-*c and *3T in the solo sections.

As theme, the motive appears in a three-fold progression, moving from the four mysterious unharmonized d-sharps in 2Pa (m. 10) to a chromatic harmonic setting as a diminished seventh chord ($\sharp vi{}^{4}_{3}$-V^2) in 3Sa (m. 64) and a simple diatonic harmonization (I-V^7) in *2Kb (m. 213). The harmonic clarification coordinates with a rise in the melodic line, the initial descent becoming a rising second and third. This is a typical Beethoven progression, spanning two entire expositions (216 mm.) and moving, as it were, from darkness to light (Ex. 1.3 on p. 19). The rhythm of 1m is also embedded in the melodic line of 1Pay, 1Sz, and the development of 2Sy, nearly identical to $1Pay^1$ (mm. 57-62; see Ex. 1.4 on p. 19).

---

[28] Jan LaRue, "Multistage Variance: Haydn's Legacy to Beethoven," *JM* 1 (1982): 265-74; reprinted with clearer examples in *JM* 18 (2001): 344-60.

Table 1.4 The Tapping Motive: Multistage Variance

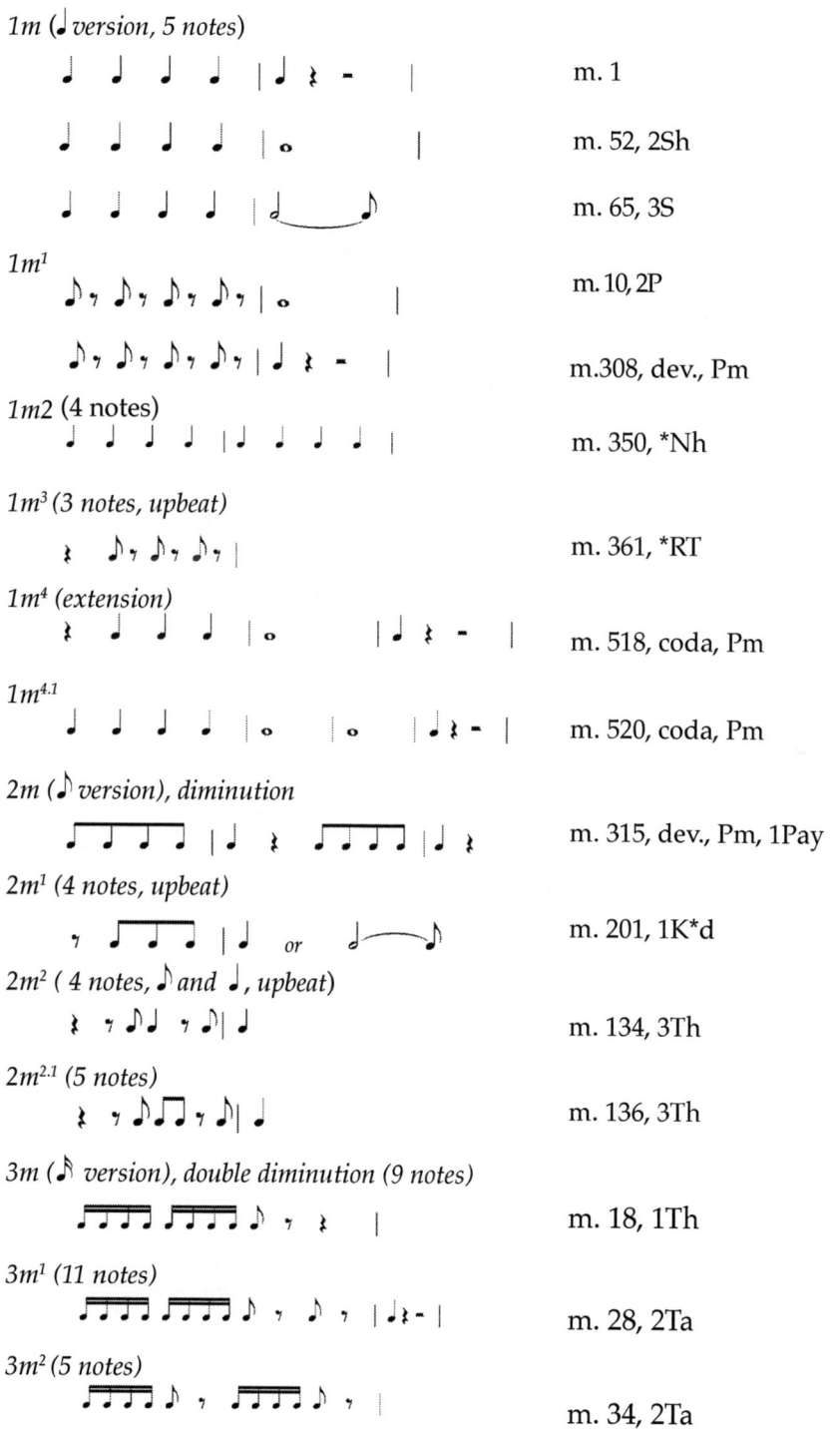

The Tapping Motive (cont)

$3m^{2.1}$ (upbeat)

♪♪♪♪ ♪ , ♪♪♪♪ | ♪ ,   m. 35, 2Tb

$4m$ (♩ version), augmentation

♩ ♩ | ♩ ♩ | ♩ 𝄽 - | m. 521, coda, vn. cadence (Stowell)

Note: The measure number indicates the first appearance of the motive.

1m or $1m^1$ acts as an introduction, not only to 1P but also to 1S, 2S, and *N in the development, connecting the main lyrical ideas of the movement. For the sake of variety, however, the accompaniment is omitted to 1S and 2S in the solo sections, so that its appearance with the solo in *N is unique. Further, in the buildup to the retransition, $1m^2$ steadily repeats seven times in the trumpets and timpani until the dominant pedal is reached. Effective in the retransition is the fragmentation of 1m to only three notes, starting on beat two ($1m^3$; see the discussion on the retransition). The last appearance of 1m (as $1m^4$ and 4m) occurs in the coda, where it twice accompanies the extended cadence of 1S, at first starting on beat 2, as in the retransition, but now "resolved" by completion of the pattern, making a two-measure phrase. Its second appearance is extended to five beats, both presentations coordinated with the violin phrases. Finally, the motive recurs mainly in half notes in the broadened violin cadence of the section (see Ex. 1.2).

The eighth-note form, 2m (1m in diminution) occurs in the orchestra only in the development, intensifying both expression and rhythmic drive in the key of G minor, the main key of the development and the key of *N to come. The bassoons, with Pay, dialogue with the strings, first presenting 1m (mm. 307-14) and then 2m (mm. 315-24). Against the orchestra, the violin weaves its triplet figuration (recalling 2S), first *legato* and then non-*legato* as 2m is heard. The triplets then mix with the more active ♩♪♪ pattern as tension increases toward the cadence and the entrance of *N. 2m is anticipated in the violin and orchestra in 1K*d, the motive starting on the upbeat with an eighth rest ($2m^1$).

3m in sixteenths, the fastest surface rhythm (double diminution), predominates in 1T as a tremolo accompaniment, and in 2T as a tremolo theme with an extension to 9, perhaps 11 notes (the last three notes being eighths with eighth rests). In fact, 3m occurs in three versions in the melodic line of 2T, the second and third only as a rhythmic pattern; the motive is melodized in both downbeat ($3m^2$) and upbeat ($3m^{2.1}$) forms, leading to $1m^1$ and 1S. The tremolo version recurs in the melody of the cadence to 3S (mm. 73-74, only in ritornellos 1 and 2). It seems natural that the fastest versions of the motive coordinate with T and the 3S cadence, functions that usually require increased motion, while the slowest form of the motive coordinates with the lyrical themes.

VIOLIN CONCERTO

It should be noted that the basic motive is found in both upbeat and downbeat patterns. Though 1m or 1m¹ begin on beat 1, the first four notes of the motive have an upbeat character, the fifth note often being a longer value, with the effect of a downbeat, as in the accompaniment to 1S, 2S, and *N. In its appearance in *2Kb, the upbeat feeling is reinforced by a *crescendo* to a *sf* on the fifth, whole note, making a strengthened downbeat. The same *sf* on the fifth note is applied to Po at the start of the recapitulation. While 2m has both rhythmic positions, 3m is mainly downbeat. The basic motive also occurs in varied dynamics (from *pp* to *ff*) and in varied scoring, especially in the brass and timpani.

Example 1.3 Evolution of the tapping motive as a thematic idea, first movement (mm. 10-13, 65-68, 213-16)

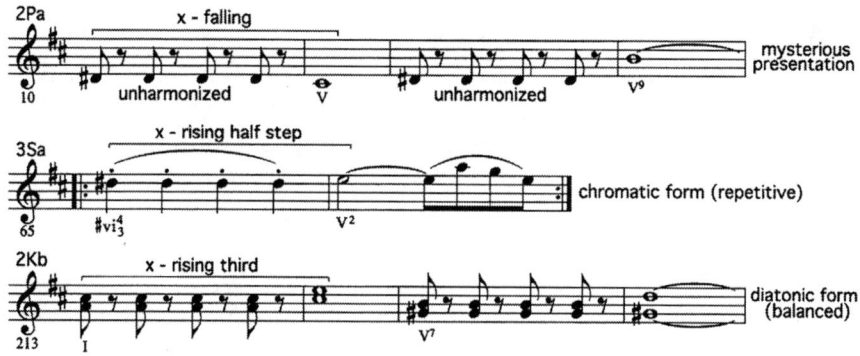

Example 1.4 Interconnection between 1P, 1S, 2S, and 1K, first movement

a. Rhythm of m in 1P

b. 1Pr in 1 Sa and 1 Ka

Some Thematic Interconnections

Besides the pervasiveness of Pm, Beethoven has connected his main themes rhythmically, harmonically, and melodically (see also Ex. 1.4b on p.19).

1. The rhythmic pattern of 1P, mm. 8-9 recurs in 1S and 1K.
2. Surprisingly, the lyrical *Nax (mm. 331-33 and repetitions) draws on the rhythmic pattern of 1Tax (mm. 18-19 and repetitions).
3. 1Ta, 1Sa, 1Ka, and 1*Na all balance two measures of I going to two measures of V.
4. Scaleline motion connects 1P, 1T, 1S, and 1K.

Treatment of Concerto-Sonata Form

As is well known, the first movement of the Classic concerto synthesizes the *tutti*-solo contrasts of the late-Baroque concerto with sonata form in an evolution that has still not been fully traced.[29] In general, the ritornello-solo structure of the first movement follows the late Classic model of concerto-sonata form as established by Mozart (see timeline, Table 1.3). There are a total of four ritornellos and three solos (not counting the cadenza and coda) that together make a large sonata form. Ritornello 1 and solo 1 comprise the exposition in two presentations (exposition 1 and 2); ritornello 2 acts as the central *tutti* (this *tutti* has no parallel in non-concerto sonata form); solo 2 is the development, ritornello 3 and solo 3 comprise the recapitulation, and ritornello 4 the final ritornello. We might call the cadenza solo 4 and the coda solo 5, since it is the solo that closes the movement together with the orchestra. This device occurs in all the Beethoven concertos from the Third Piano Concerto onward (for its appearance in Mozart, see below).

Neither the latest description of first-movement form by H.C. Koch in his *Musikalisches Lexikon* of 1802, nor the description of Carl Czerny, Beethoven's student and friend, in his *School of Practical Composition*, Op. 600 of ?1848, fully cover the ritornello-solo structure of this concerto, not to say others by Beethoven and the previous concertos by Mozart.[30] Koch, unlike Czerny, does not include ritornello 3, which starts the recapitulation in this concerto, nor does he refer to a modulation away from the second key in the second ritornello, as we find in all Beethoven concertos except

---

[29] For important discussions of concerto-sonata forms, see Jan LaRue, *GSA*, 191-93, 281; and Ratner, *CM*, 283-307. For sonata form itself see especially the discussions in Ratner, *CM*, 217-47, and LaRue, *GSA*, 187-91. I have used the terms "ritornello" and "solo" in my analysis, following the concerto descriptions of H. C. Koch. Other theorists like Vogler, Galeazzi, Kollmann, and Czerny use the term "tutti," rather than "ritornello." See the article by Stevens cited below in n.30. For the best short discussion of this movement, indeed of the entire concerto, see Donald Francis Tovey, *Essays in Musical Analysis*, m vol. III: Concertos (London: Oxford University Press, 136) 87-96 on movement I.

[30] See Jane R. Stevens, "Theme, Harmony, and Texture in Classic-Romantic Descriptions of Concerto First-Movement Form," *JAMS* 27 (1974):38-41 (Koch) and 46-50 (Czerny).

VIOLIN CONCERTO

Opp. 19 and 58, a point explicitly made by Czerny. Though Czerny's basic formal layout is closest to the plan we find in Beethoven, he deemphasizes the orchestral *tuttis* after the first, and the role of the orchestra in general. Neither Koch nor Czerny deal with the problem of reorganizing the two expositions into one recapitulation. For Czerny, the solo following the third *tutti* "is only a repetition of the first part in the original key, but furnished with new and more brilliant passages, and a coda, in which the performer can display all his execution." "The more modern concertos," states Czerny, "discard the cadenza, which is replaced by a brilliant coda."[31]

LENGTH OF SECTIONS

Most unusual here are the great lengths of ritornello 1 (88 mm.) and ritornello 2 (60 mm.). While solo 1 is 135 mm., solo 3 is only 111 mm.; put together with ritornello 3 (21 mm.) it is nearly the same length as solo 1 (132 mm.; see Table 1.3). 1T becomes progressively longer: in ritornello 1, 8 mm., solo 1, 16 mm., solo 3, 22 mm.

RELATIONSHIP OF THE MAIN SECTIONS

In relation to ritornello 1, solo 1 adds *0, *3T, and most of 1K and *2K. In solo 2, *N and *RT are new. The recapitulation omits *O and 1P from solo 3, and develops 1T. New treatment and extensions of 1S and 1K occur in the coda. Beethoven reserves 2T for the ritornello, and it opens ritornellos 2 and 4 on bVI (and even the cadenza for the piano version on the same chord; see also *Continuity* below). Ritornello 2 duplicates ritornello 1 starting from 2T, though changes are made in dynamics, scoring, and key, modulation occurring from A/a to C within 3S. Very striking and dramatic is the change to loud dynamics from 2S on. The recurrence of ideas from 2T means that 1S, 2S, 3S, and 1Kab are heard four times during the concerto, a unique example of such repetition in the Beethoven concertos. In addition, 1S and 1K return for a fifth time in the coda.

THE RECAPITULATION

In concerto-sonata form, one must always consider how ritornello 1 and solo 1, comprising two expositions, are joined together in a single recapitulation. In this movement, several changes occur in this closing section:

1. In ritornello 3, 1Po, 1P, 2P, and 1Ta return *ff* or *f*, and are rescored for a much bigger sound. The opening constitutes a triumphant reprise and the whole ritornello acts as <u>the</u> climax area of the movement. Such climactic returns of the main primary theme are especially characteristic of middle Beethoven (and found less extensively in all the concertos). They occasionally appear earlier as well, besides Opp. 15 and 19, in such works as the Piano Sonata Op. 2 No. 1/I (1793-95), the String

---

[31] Carl Czerny, *School of Practical Composition*, Op. 600, trans. John Bishop, vol. I (London: Robert Cocks & Co., 1848?), 160.

Quartet, Op. 18 No. 1/I (1799-1800), and the First Symphony, Op. 21/I (1799-1800). Po becomes a tutti unison and 1P is simplified so that the parallel phrase structure and inverted start of 1Pb are clearer than in the very opening of the concerto, where Pa is ornamented by an appoggiatura in measure 2 (Ex. 1.5). This simplified version of Pa, in fact, is anticipated in the development (m. 305-06).

2. Solo 3 omits *O and 1P, which had appeared at the start of solo 2, and therefore begins with 1T as a continuation of ritornello 3, a function that Beethoven recasts and expands (another typical device). After the orchestral Ta is heard, cut from eight to four measures, the expanded solo section contains further development of 1Tb-a (in that order), with passing modulations to the traditional subdominant of G, and then to e. The avoided cadence to e and V→VI cadence in D mirror such earlier types of cadences. In the orchestral development of Tax, the solo picks up the descending leap of a tenth ending x, and expands and inverts it as a counterpoint to 1Tax, the only development of this motive in the movement.

3. While the material from *3T on follows solo 1, there are several alterations in register, figuration, melodic direction, length of ideas, and surface rhythm. In the 1T and S areas especially, the violin tessitura is higher than in solo 1 and thus produces a greater intensity. This shift recalls the higher tessitura in the recapitulation often found in Mozart's first movements.[32] The presentation of 1Sb by the violin an octave higher than the orchestra, reaching d^4, is simply ethereal. Other differences are summarized below (see also Ex. 1.6).

*3T: changes direction from high-low to low-high and rises three octaves, climaxing on a^3; beginning of trill lengthened a measure by the descent to a^1.

Example 1.5 $1P^3$ *at the start of the recapitulation, first movement (m. 366-73)1.*

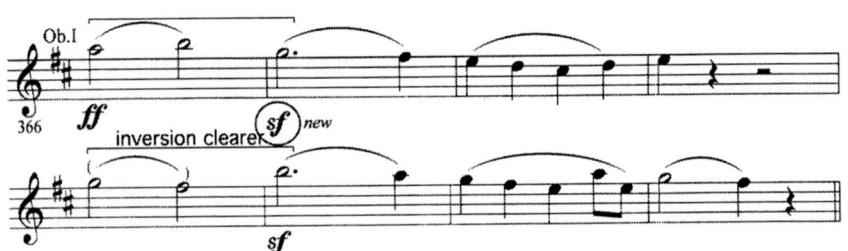

---

[32] See Adena Portowitz, "Mozart's Early Concertos, 1773-1779: Structure and Expression" (Ph.D. diss., Bar-Ilan University, 1995), and her article, "The Recapitulation as Climax in the First Movements of Mozart's Early Concertos," *Ad Parnassum* 2 (2003): 7-20. See also her "Innovation and Tradition in the Classic Concerto: Mozart's K. 453 (1784) as a Model for Beethoven's Fourth Piano Concerto (1805-06)," *The Beethoven Journal* 12 (1997): 65-72.

Example 1.6 Some changes in the thematic material of the recapitulation, first movment (mm. 134-36, 408-10 , 195-99², 469-73²)

*2Kc: another reversal of direction, here in the figuration within the measure from down-up to up-down, thus emphasizing the rising melody in the approach to ritornello 4. The rising line compensates for the lower tessitura.

2S: changes in figuration; rise to 3S lengthened by two beats.

3S: x^1 varied an octave higher; Beethoven builds a new rhythmic acceleration to the cadence. Most of the melodic line is new over the same harmony.

1Ka: enters on the downbeat, not upbeat, 1-½ measures later; first two measures and their broken chords integrate with material that follows.

1K*c: in measures 469-72, the first two are higher in range, to b^3, the next two have sixteenths, not triplets; the phrase ends lower; an upbeat is added to m. 472 making the melody more continuous.

While changes in figuration are motivated by transposition problems, they are turned to good effect, as always. The changes in general strengthen important points of arrival and produce greater stability, while achieving intensity and variety.

THE CODA

The relatively brief coda of 25 measures has a beautiful simplicity and calm, ending the movement by juxtaposing 1S and 1K. It thus highlights the rhythmic relationship between them. 1K also appears in its closing function, as in ritornellos 1 and 2.

Beethoven finally gives all of 1S to the solo violin (rather than just the second phrase). The violin plays the melody in the lower octave, never heard before (the D and G strings are specified), accompanied by *pizzicato* strings. The soloistic texture and hushed dynamics contribute to the sublime effect of this moment in the work.

The final subphrase of 1S is extended as the violin makes the cadence three times, each an octave higher, and the last in augmentation, a typical "slowdown" found in several concertos before the final rush to the cadence (which here, however, is postponed). A similar augmented cadence recurs in the rondo's coda before the concluding sections in the tonic, as noted above. Po makes its final appearance in the first two extensions of S as well. 1K follows in dialogue with the violin as it mounts up four octaves against a recall of 1Kb to some of its highest notes (see Melody below). The harmony of the coda consists of tonic and dominant chords only except for a ii^6 at the cadence of S.

SOME DIFFERENCES BETWEEN THE FIRST MOVEMENT OF OP. 61 AND THE FIRST MOVEMENTS OF MOZART'S LATER PIANO CONCERTOS

1. <u>Sheer length</u>. While the length of Beethoven's first movement in general goes beyond Mozart's standard practice, Beethoven did have a Mozartian model in this respect. It is the C-minor Piano Concerto, K. 491 (1786), whose first movement of 523 measures is the longest of Mozart's first movements, nearly equaling the 535 measures of Op. 61. Beethoven knew and admired K. 491 and learned much from it (see also the remarks in point 6 below).[33]

---

[33] See Michael C. Tusa, "Beethoven's C Minor Mood: Some Thoughts on the Structural Implications of Key Choice," *Beethoven Forum* 2 (1993): 7-8.

2. <u>The thematic status of *O</u>. The length of *O and its recurrence at the start of the development in a remote key (C major, ♭VII) have no parallel in Mozart.

3. <u>The treatment of ritornello 2</u>. In Op. 61, ritornello 2 parallels ritornello 1 starting with 2T to the end of the section. Such parallelism is found neither in Mozart nor in Beethoven's other concertos, which usually contain shorter and more cadential material in this ritornello. In Op. 61, ritornello 2 is modulatory, a preference in all the Beethoven concertos except Nos. 2 and 4; however, it occurs in only a few of Mozart's later concertos (such as K. 467). Another unique feature is the dramatic shift to loud dynamics in ritornello 2, sustained from 2S to the end.

4 <u>Developmental intensity.</u> This occurs especially in the solo K area, usually a harmonic-brilliant section in Mozart, the first part of the second solo (Po), and in the multistage variance of Po in general.

5. <u>The triumphant return of the P area</u> starting the recapitulation (ritornello 3), an effect absent in Mozart.

6. <u>The coda.</u> The solo returns after the cadenza to end the movement. This occurs in all the Beethoven concertos starting with the Third Piano Concerto and may have been inspired by the return of the solo in Mozart's K. 491, first movement. It also occurs in the *Andante* of Mozart's early G-major Violin Concerto, K. 216 (1775) and the Piano Concerto K. 271 (1777). It is doubtful, however, that Beethoven knew Mozart's early works. In the Mozart examples, the main material comes from P or final K ideas, not 1S and 1K, as in Op. 61 nor do we find the device of withholding the complete 1S from the solo until the coda.

7. <u>An even greater prominence of the orchestra</u>. This is reflected in the great lengths of ritornellos 1 and 2, the power of the big *tutti* in ritornello 3, and the development of Po, most of which is orchestral.

CONTINUITY

The lyric flow of the movement is greatly enhanced by the strong continuity achieved by the artful treatment of cadences at the end of periods and those linking the ritornello and solo sections. Critics always point out the intensive continuity found in Beethoven's late works, but many of the same devices occur in the middle period and even earlier. The immediate background for such devices can be found in the music of the mature Haydn and Mozart, but the techniques were developed from the early Classic period on and occur in works by many other Classic composers as well (such as G.B. Sammartini).[34]

---

[34] For Classic techniques of continuity, see Ratner, *CM*, "Disturbances of Symmetry; Period Extensions," 37-47, with a reference to the deceptive cadence to 2T, 42-43.

In this movement, except for the open cadence after 1P, all material thereafter is linked by elision, postponed or avoided cadences, and anticipation (the last examples comprising the introductory function of Po before 1S, 2S, *N, and elsewhere, or the trill in solo 1 and 3 before 1S and 2K).

Most outstanding is the dramatic use of the deceptive cadence to ♭VI, resulting in elision, which occurs four times: connecting 1T to 2T within ritornello 1; the connection of solos 1 and 3 to ritornellos 2 and 4 respectively (also moving to 2T); and in solo 3, the development of 1T in the recapitulation (mm. 405-06; see above. p.23). Except for the last example, all occurrences are major events, eliding a function or the solo to the ritornello and with a ff on ♭VI, as well. The latter type also stands out in Mozart's piano concerto K. 453 (1784), where Mozart elides ritornello 2 to solo 2 and solo 3 to ritornello 4 in a movement full of harmonic tension. Use of ♭VI relates to the introduction of tonic-minor contrast in 2T and later 2S (interchange of mode, as Ratner points out).[35]

Another deceptive effect includes the resolution of G:V to the minor tonic in the development (mm. 314-15), which initiates a section of increased development using 1m^2. Avoided cadences occur in the resolution of b:V to V^7/iv (e:V^7) in the development (mm. 304-05), leading 1P^2 to further development; and in the resolution of G:V^7 to e:V$^6_5$ in the recapitulation (mm. 399-400), connecting 1T to new development of 1Tax.

Postponement of resolution adds great breadth and tension to the structure. These examples include the long postponed cadence of 1K at the end of ritornellos 1 and 2. 1K ends on V followed by *O, with its extended dominant pedal delaying the tonic resolution for 13 measures in solo 1 (including the measure of resolution), and 26 measures at the start of the development, with a series of dominants of C, b, and e, the harmony finally cadencing on the tonic of e (see mm. 89-101, 284-309). Postponement of resolution occurs extensively with the deceptive cadences on ♭VI, where the resolution of V to the expected tonic is delayed for as much as 16 measures (mm. 28-43, 224-39), and 15 measures plus the cadenza (mm. 497-511). If we look for a V-I cadence in solo 1, 1K, after m. 190, we must wait far longer, a total of 49 measures (191-239), to the entrance of 1S in ritornello 2. A remarkable early example of a massive delay appears in the String Quartet Op. 18, No. 2/IV, between the presentation of S and start of K (mm. 64-112), a delay that also exploits an enharmonic resolution, there D-F.

THE *N THEME (IN THE DEVELOPMENT SECTION, MM. 331-56)

While much has been made of the N theme in the development of the *Eroica* Symphony/I, little attention has been given to Beethoven's use of

---

[35] An example also occurs in G.B. Viotti's A-minor Violin Concerto, No. 22/I, which elides solo 1 to ritornello 2 via a deceptive cadence as in Opp. 56 and 61.

this old device in many other works, with the exception of Tovey's acute observation regarding N themes in Beethoven's codas.[36] We should note the following important points regarding *N here (see Ex. 1.7 on p.28):

    1. The theme provides relief from the intensive motivic development of $1m^2$ that precedes it, and deepens the lyricism of the movement while shifting the spotlight away from the orchestra to the soloist. It is certainly one of the great moments in the concerto.

    2. Though I call it a theme, as often in Beethoven's music, it is really an N <u>area</u> lasting 26 measures, in which a new theme is introduced, extended, varied, and fragmented. The theme is heard after a formal cadence with a trill of two measures, an old Classic device underlining important articulations and points in the form.

    3. The *N theme is accompanied throughout in the orchestra by 1m, as 1S and 2S in the ritornellos. Embedded in the preceding development of those five notes, 1m eventually repeats without pause as tension heightens toward the retransition.

    4. Like many of Beethoven's N themes, the theme enters in minor, here G minor, the same key as the lyrical N theme in the rondo finale. It also emphasizes the subdominant key, so important in the concerto.

    5. Typically, the theme is modulatory, moving from G minor to Ef major, the Neapolitan, a favorite key in Beethoven's N themes, and from there to D minor, used as a foil for the brilliant return to the recapitulation in D major.

    6. Though the theme seems new, it characteristically contains some ties with earlier material. The rhythmic pattern of its first two measures (mm. 331-32) duplicates the pattern found in 1T (mm. 18-19); the prominent half steps stem perhaps from 3S (mm. 65-68); and the poignant sigh motives echo such motives in 1P.

THE RETRANSITION (MM. 357-65)

The retransition is often one of Beethoven's most imaginative and carefully calculated passages and this example is no exception. Though the retransition is short, being only eight measures, it still has several features characteristic of Beethoven, especially in the middle period, as enumerated by Beth Shamgar:[37]

    1. The dominant pedal point, divided into two units, V and V^7.

    2. Certain additional processes of intensification: (a) increase in vol-

---

[36] For an extensive survey of this device in Beethoven, see my article "Beethoven and the New Development-Theme in Sonata-Form Movements," *JM* 16 (1998): 323-43. The remarks in this section partly draw on the text of this article. Such themes actually go back to the early Classic period.

[37] See Beth Shamgar, "Dramatic Devices in the Retransitions of Beethoven's Piano Sonatas," *Israel Studies in Musicology* 2 (1980): 63-76.

Example 1.7 *The N theme (phrase a and b), first movement (mm.331-43)*

ume; (b) big shifts of register, often reaching a melodic peak; (c) anticipation of P (here Po); (d) production of one of the main climaxes of the movement.

Taking each point separately, certain special features create great suspense and drama.

1. The unison A pedal in the strings intensifies to an implied minor ninth and V^7 only in the last three measures.

2. The section is *pp* and Beethoven holds back the *crescendo-forte* until the last three beats, creating extraordinary tension. This brief but explosive *crescendo* reminds us of the two-measure *crescendo* to the reprise in the *Eroica*, first movement.

3. The violin line consists of steady triplets, making an active surface rhythm. It contains a broken octave figure (1-3-8), related to *O, that mounts up chromatically from a-a^1 to $c\#^2$-$c\#^3$ in m. 361^2 and then moves diatonically up notes 2-4 of the V^7 chord. It reaches a climax on g^3 and the widest spacing of the basic figure--an octave and a seventh.

4. Anticipation of Po is also withheld until m. 361^2 where $1m^3$ appears, the shortest, three-note version of m, starting on the offbeat. It is given a hocket-like *pizzicato* setting, going down the string group with dissonant intervals of the major and diminished seventh. Finally, in the last measure $1m^3$ occurs on V in the oboes, horns, and timpani, the last beat fortified by a string chord *forte*. The entrance of the timpani on V makes the perfect connection to the magistral *fortissimo* setting of Po on I at the start of the recapitulation.

The long delay of the *crescendo*, despite the rising and climactic violin line, and the late entrance and setting of $1m^3$ are some of the strategies used by Beethoven to make this passage one of the most dramatic in the entire concerto.

Melody

Though no large-scale study has been made of Beethoven's phrase structure as yet, we can offer a few observations on this subject for the first movement.

1P and 1S, as well as *Na on the phrase level, are "classic" examples of the parallel period, a format that became more common in the later 18th century and that we know from such examples as 1P of Mozart's Symphony

---

[38] See the study of this pattern by Robert O. Gjerdingen, *A Classic Turn of Phrase* (Philadelphia: University of Pennsylvania Press, 1988). An early example of the parallel-period structure for P can be found in Sammartini's symphony in D, J-C 14 (c. 1735). See also Ratner, *CM*, "Periodicity," 33-47, and remarks in Roger Kamien, "Phrase, Period, Theme," in: Glenn Stanley, ed. *The Cambridge Companion to Beethoven* (Cambridge: Cambridge University Press, 2000), 64-83. For the Classic background to Beethoven's phrase organization, see the outstanding dissertation by Judith L. Schwartz, "Phrase Morphology in the Early Classic Symphony," (c. 1720-c. 1765) (New York University, 1973), UM 73-19, 967.

No. 41/I and Haydn's Symphony No. 104/I.[38] While this format is used for the opening of Beethoven's early Violin Concerto in C, WoO 5 (1790-92; see below), and first two piano concertos, it does not appear for 1P in the later concertos besides Op. 61.

This balanced arrangement, as is well known, consists of an eight-measure period divided into two four-measure phrases as follows: a (4)+a¹(4), phrase a cadencing on V and phrase a¹ on I. Both phrases begin with the same material though the cadential subphrase may differ. Here 1Pa¹ starts with a free inversion of ax (a relationship that is clarified in the reprise), and ends with a variant of the cadence of ay. 1S is simpler than 1P--only the cadence in a¹ differs from Sa though the descending fifth of measure 4 is picked up in measures 7-8 (see Ex. 1.1). Introducing 1P with Po adds an asymmetrical one-measure start so that 1P becomes 1+8 rather than simply eight measures. 1S in solo 1 has an "extra" anticipatory measure of the violin trill that accompanies 1Sa in the winds.

Most of the melodic material is organized in four- and eight-measure phrases and periods, even when the phrases are developmental or contrasting. Some eight-measure periods are produced by elision. A good example is 2P that actually cadences in its ninth measure, which becomes the first measure of 1T. This period contains contrasting a and b phrases of four measures, but the melodic peak of 2Pa is held over for the start of 2Pb so that no melodic or rhythmic break occurs between phrases. Other such "contrast" periods appear in 1T (6+4) and 3S, with three distinct phrases. The start of 3S is an example of more subtle phrase treatment. Where does it begin in ritornello 1? According to the dynamics it starts in measure 65, with a four-measure phrase. But the ending measure of 2S in measure 64 duplicates the last three notes of measure 66. Is measure 64 a whole measure elision with 3S, which therefore becomes a five-measure phrase? Certainly, measure 64 can be heard as both the conclusion of 2S and an anticipation of 3S, thus closely binding the periods. Adding to the cohesion are the pedals in the horns here (and in other winds in solos 1 and 3), starting in m. 63^4 (five beats earlier) and going right through 3Sa proper (see Ex. 1.8 on facing page).

Another special case is the structure of 1K in ritornello 1 (m.77). This theme begins with a balanced dialogue between violin I and the cello/bass parts. 1Ka is repeated an octave higher in the violins, but the upper strings enter in measure 8, beat 3, starting a new, overlapping cadential phrase based on 1Ka. The twelve-measure theme thus divides 4+3½+2½+2 in shorter and shorter units. These few examples reflect a mastery and care in phrase and period organization that profoundly support the musical flow.

Stepwise motion in many of the themes has been mentioned in relation to thematic interconnections. This motion includes not only diatonic melodies but chromatic lines that are mostly linking in function

VIOLIN CONCERTO

Example 1.8 An ambiguous approach to 3Sa (mm. 63⁴-65), promoting continuity, first movement

or building a cadence, as between 1S and 2S in solo 1 (m. 151), 1K*d (mm. 199-200), *2Ka (mm. 209-13), solo 2 before *N (mm. 325-26), and the retransition (mm. 357-61^2).

Another melodic aspect concerns the treatment of the highest notes, which the listener certainly perceives. The very highest note is e^4, reached in the cadenza-like extension of 1K*d in solo 1 just before *2K (m. 204). However, solo 3 exploits a higher tessitura than that in solos 1-2, especially in T and S with b^3 in 1T and 1K*c, $c_{\natural}^4$ in 2S and 3S, and d^4 in 1Sb. The high d^4 (the tonic note) is first present only in solo 3 and it recurs in the penultimate measure of the movement together with the leading tone $c\sharp^4$, which finally replaces $c_{\natural}^4$, with its subdominant association.

Sound

Beethoven's organization of dynamics is a prime feature of his style, as Miriam Sheer has demonstrated.[39] A special effect here is the dynamic variation of many of the main themes of the movement, which are heard on two levels--p and $f(f)$. Thus, there is a shift to *ff* and *sempre forte* in ritornello 2 from 2S to the end, except for the p in the last two measures leading to *O and the start of the development.[40] The same process takes place in ritornello 3, where the first two functions and part of the third return in *ff* for 1P, and *f-ff* for 2P and 1Ta. These high dynamic levels in a full orchestral sonority enclose a development that is almost entirely on a soft dynamic level in a small orchestral sound, another example of Beethoven's long-range effects.

While the orchestral texture does not include imitation or fugato, it is enriched by dialogue arrangements (as in 1K and the coda) and especially *obbligato* counterpoint, where brilliant violin passagework accompanies thematic material in the orchestra (as in 2S, 1Kab, the development, the coda). These *obbligatos*, found in all three movements, mix doubling or outlining the orchestra's melodic line with independent figuration. Though the violinist as soloist has fewer purely solo passages than usual in a concerto, it nevertheless carries the most sublime moments--the *N area and the coda presentation of 1S, and in about half the movement it is the dominating line.

Beethoven introduces some special effects in the orchestration, starting with the use of the timpani to open the movement in a *piano* dynamic. Placing 1P in the winds is also exceptional for all the concertos. Though brass instruments and timpani typically play in loud passages within a movement, Beethoven scores the tapping motive in the horns, trumpets, and timpani in 2S *pianissimo* (ritornello 1), and the trumpets and timpani also *pianissimo* with $1m^2$ in the development, leading to the retransition.

---

[39] See Miriam Sheer, "The Role of Dynamics in Beethoven's Instrumental Works" 2 vols. (Ph.D. diss., Bar-Ilan University, 1989).

[40] 3Sc and 1K were ff in ritornello 1 as well.

Harmony

Besides the overall effects and connections indicated in the general remarks, we should stress the use of third relationships in this movement, so typical of the Middle Period. These appear in the modulatory ritornello 2 as F-A-C. The start of this ritornello introduces a tonization of F major in 2T, occurring by way of a deceptive cadence to VI, which then returns to a/A. An enharmonic modulation moves the harmony to C major, the key in which the ritornello ends. The modulation is achieved by reinterpreting the diminished seventh chord in 3Sa, #VI $^{0}_{3}$ (m. 263) as V$^{0}_{2}$ of F (a#=bb), which resolves to F: V^7-I, the F chord becoming IV of C, so that the cadences of 3S and K are presented in C (mm. 268-83). The broad contrast is between A (major and minor) and C (A: bIII), the connection to C made smoother by the area in A minor in 2S. The start in F, therefore, can be considered as a harmonic parenthesis since only three measures of I and V are heard, both coming from A and moving directly back to a/A. However, F major is first heard as a tonicization within 2S in ritornello 1 (within the tonic minor, d) and it returns in the enharmonic modulation to C, which is made via F. The key of F major, therefore, has a stronger presence than the two chords in mm. 224-26 seem to imply. It also returns briefly in the secondary dominant progressions of *2K in solo 3. The parallel tonicization of C in 2S and *2K in solo 1 and ritornello 2 prepare the strong modulation to C near the end of ritornello 2.

The keys of the development are also significant. They are organized as follows:

$$\overline{C\text{-}b}\text{-}e\text{-}G\text{-}g\text{-}\overline{E\flat\text{-}d}$$

The Neapolitan relation, a favorite of Beethoven's, occurs as C-b and Eb-d, thus framing the section. The most emphasized keys, however, move upward in fifths: C-g-d, while a circle-of-fifths progression descends from b to g, an old Classic and Mozartian device.

Besides the major-minor contrast of 1S-2S, frequent in both Mozart and Beethoven, 2S itself is additionally unstable in harmony, with a tonicization of its third degree being heard twice during the expansion of the theme: d-F in ritornello 1 and solo 3, and a-C in the first solo and second ritornello. As indicated, both F and C become important keys in the second ritornello. Thus, 2S introduces a characteristic tonal-harmonic instability in the second key area, as S and K do in the rondo finale.[41] Here, the chromatic start of 3S sustains the harmonic tension, resolved only by its strong diatonic cadence.

---

[41] See my article, "Harmonic and Tonal Instabiliy in the Second Key Area of Classic Sonata Form," in *Convention in Eighteenth- and Nineteenth-Century Music. Essays in Honor of Leonard G. Ratner*, eds. Wye J. Allanbrook, Janet M. Levy, and William P. Mahrt (Stuyvesant, NY: Pendragon Press, 1992), 23-57.

Parallel unstable harmony occurs in the K area, especially in the typically Beethovenian suspense section in *2K (mm. 205-23), intensified by the long trill in the solo. Here, the I ending of 1K resolves to V only in *2K, linking these two long periods. The mysterious F♮ in the bass (it could be the minor ninth of V) becomes the seventh of C major (the key ending ritornello 2), as the harmony moves up more rapidly to V/ii-ii and finally, the augmented sixth to wind chords of I_4^6 and V, the latter sounded for nine measures before resolving to ♭VI. The slow moving progression, the sense of digression and holding back, the clarification at the end, synchronized with the clarification of the 2Pax motive, all combine to create one of Beethoven's most remarkable passages.

Beethoven's powerful organization of harmonic rhythm has been most comprehensively documented by Jan LaRue.[42] The large range of harmonic rhythm reaches from the long dominant pedals in *O, *2K, and the retransition (solos 1 and 2 thus framed by long V pedals), to increased motion at cadences (end of 1K). 2T (mm. 28-42) moves in an accelerated pattern to its arrival at 1S. It shifts from one chord per two measures (mm. 28-29) to one chord per measure (mm. 30-33), two chords per measure (mm. 34-39), and a suggestion of four per measure over an implied V pedal (mm. 40-41), before broadening out to an implied V for one measure (m. 42). 3T maintains a fast surface rhythm in sixteenths together with a steady fast harmonic rhythm of two chords per measure in its drive to 1S in solos 1 and 3, speeding up to four chords per measure just before the long V pedal ending the period. In contrast, harmonic rhythm is <u>decelerated</u> in solos 1 and 3 from 1K*b¹, with two chords per measure, to slow moving chords in 1K*c,*d, and the start of *2K, which has a rest-motion-rest pattern, ending with a nine-measure pedal. In general, the first movement has a fairly slow harmonic rhythm, producing a spacious effect fundamental to the music.

Rhythm

The use of larger rhythmic values, especially quarters and halves, or basic movement on these levels in most of the main thematic functions, such as 1P, 2P, 1S, 2S, 3Sa, and 1Ka, creates a broad and relaxed effect. These larger values coordinate with a slower harmonic rhythm as well.

The rhythmic implications and shifts of accent in the tapping motive were discussed earlier. A special effect in the treatment of surface rhythm can be seen in 1T of ritornello 1. Phrase a intensifies the surface rhythm to eighth notes (with accompaniment in sixteenths), as one would expect in a transition, but phrase b surprisingly and mysteriously decelerates the surface rhythm to quarters and halves. This "negation" of Ta, however, throws the active 2T period in relief (as well as the deceptive cadence to 2T).

---

[42] See Jan LaRue, "Harmonic Rhythm in the Beethoven Symphonies," *The Music Review* 18 (1957): 8-20; reprint *JM* 18 (2001): 221-48.

It is only in 2T that the surface rhythm is activated to include sixteenths in the melody, though steady sixteenth-note motion is reserved only for the cadence in 3Sb. In solos 1 and 3, most of the sixteenth motion, as one would expect, occurs in T and K.

A unifying rhythmic element is the motion in triplets. This first appears in the counterpoint to 2S in ritornello 1, then in the violin *obbligato* to 2S in solos 1 and 3, as well as the cadenza-like passage in 1K*c, and most extensively in the violin *obbligato* to 1P and the tapping motive in the development.

Two further examples of manipulation of surface rhythm should be cited. One is the clear acceleration pattern in *O, which moves from quarters to triplets (at first, tied half to triplets), to sixteenths. Another example is the large-scale deceleration in solos 1 and 3 in the K area. 1K decelerates from sixteenths to triplets to eighths (at first after a tied half). In *2K, though the violin has long trills, an active surface rhythm, the orchestra gives out the tapping motive in quarter- and whole-note motion. The trill connects this quiescent section to the brilliant passage in sixteenths leading to ritornello 2, a passage certainly dramatized by the deceleration that precedes it.

THE EARLY VIOLIN CONCERTO IN C MAJOR, WoO 5: A FRAGMENT OF THE FIRST MOVEMENT

Composed: 1790-92
Source: Autograph score with a few corrections in Vienna, Gesellschaft der Musikfreunde, A5
Scoring: 1 flute, 2 oboes, 2 bassoons, 2 horns, strings with two violas
Tempo and meter: Allegro con brio; c meter
Length: 259 mm. (up to 15 mm. of solo 2 in the development)
Edition: Willy Hess, ed., *Supplement zur Gesamtausgabe*, III, vol. 1, with editorial notes. [43]

This imposing fragment belongs with the Joseph Cantata, WoO 87, the Righini Piano Variations, WoO 65, and the Wind Octet, Op.103, all of the period 1790-92, as one of Beethoven's most ambitious pre-Vienna compositions. The movement was apparently finished but the rest of the

---

[43] The original text of the concerto was first published by Ludwig Schiedermair in *Der junge Beethoven* (Leipzig: Quelle & Meyer, 1925), after having been published in Vienna in 1879, edited, elaborated, and completed by Josef Hellmesberger. The best edition was made by Willy Hess, ed. *Beethoven, Supplemente zur Gesamtausgabe*, 2nd ed., vol. III (Wiesbaden: Breitkopf & Härtel, 1971), 44-69, with *Revisionsbericht*, 75-76. For further details regarding this work, see *KH*. The concerto is copied on Bonn paper, as shown by Hans-Günter Klein and Douglas Johnson, "Autographe Beethovens aus der Bonner Zeit: Handschrift-Probleme und Echtheitsfragen," in: Kurt Dorfmüller, ed., *Beiträge zur Beethoven-Bibliographie* (Munich: G. Henle, 1978), p. 116. The first page of Beethoven's autograph is reproduced in Joseph Schmidt-Görg and Hans Schmidt, eds., *Ludwig van Beethoven* (Bonn and Hamburg: Beethoven-Archiv and Deutsche Grammophon Gesellschaft, 1969), 50.

Example 1.9 WoO 5, functions and incipits

VIOLIN CONCERTO

score was lost and remains lost. The fragment was completed by Wilfried Fischer, keeping as much as possible to the original, and a good recording was made of it by Gidon Kremer.[44]

A Comparison with the D-major Violin Concerto, First Movement

1. Large-scale Conception
Ritornello 1 and solo 1 are together actually longer than the corresponding sections in Op. 61 (see Table 1.5)

Table 1.5. WoO 5 and Op. 61 Number of Measures in Ritornello 1 and Solo 1 Compared

	Ritornello 1	Solo 1	Total
WoO5	96	131	227
Op. 61	88	135	223

---

[44] The Fischer score was published by Bärenreiter in 1972 in association with Breitkopf & Härtel, Wiesbaden, but it is available only for rental. The least characteristic features of his completion are the brief development of 47 measures and the incorporation of the solo in the final ritornello after the cadenza, a device not found in the first two piano concertos. Kremer's recording was made for Deutsche Grammophon with the London Symphony Orchestra conducted by Emil Tchakarov, and was released in 1979, first as a cassette (No. 3301193), then as an LP (No. 2531 193). For details regarding the completions of Hellmesberger, Juan Manén (Vienna, 1933 and 1943), and Fischer, see Willy Hess, "Beethovens C-dur-Konzertsatz und seine Ergänzungen," *Schweizerische Musikzeitung* 115 (1975): 233-36. Hess compares the rich thematic content to the *Eroica* Symphony, first movement.

2. <u>Some Other Similar Aspects of Structure</u>
a. 1P is also a parallel period.
b. In ritornello 1, 1S is unstable harmonically, as in most of the later concertos (2S in Op. 61). The theme starts in G and then modulates to C and A♭before returning to C minor and C:V.

Ritornello 1 is 8 measures longer in WoO 5 and solo 1 only 4 measures shorter than the later concerto. Filling out this large frame are a great number of themes, as in Op. 61, here 14 distinctive units (Ex. 9): 1P (m. 1)-2P (m. 9)-1T (m. 19)-2T (m. 39)-1S (m. 57)-1K (m. 73)-2K (m. 80)-*O (m. 96)-*3P (m. 102)-*3T (m. 131)-*2S (mm.163-64)-*ST (m. 188)-*3K (m. 207)-N (m. 227) (solo 2, of course, contains old and new material).

c. The solo violin does not enter wih 1P but with new cadential material, delaying the final cadence and start of solo 1. This differs from the style of *O in Op. 61, but even there *O postpones the tonic cadence of the orchestral ritornello until its end.
d. Ritornello 2 is modulatory, as in Op. 61 and most of the later concertos, moving from G to the dominant of d minor.

3. Range and Style of the Solo Violin
As in Op. 61, the violin part is wide-ranging, with much E-string writing. It goes even higher than the highest note of Op. 61, e^4 (K), reaching g^4 in the cadence before the end of the first solo. The figuration includes triplets (*ST) as well as sixteenths, and the violin has a sixteenth-note *obbligato* against the development of 1Px in the orchestra in *3K, resembling the texture of 1Kab^1 in Op. 61. Still, the violin part is far more soloistic than in Op. 61.

4. Importance of the Orchestra
The orchestra is emphasized not only in its imposing ritornello 1, but also during solo 1, as it dialogues with the solo in *3T (based on 1Px) and develops 1Px in *3K. One should note too the brilliant unison opening, recalled in 2K of ritornello 1, the chordal texture near the close of 2T and 2K, and the importance of the winds, especially in 1K and 2K. Typically the bass carries the important thematic material in 2T and 2K (based on P).

5. Dynamic Contrasts
Frequent dynamic contrasts heighten the dramatic style, ranging from *pp* to *ff*, with considerable use of dynamic extremes and *sf* accents.[45]

---

[45] Strangely enough, no dynamics are included in the solo violin part, and the fact that there are stretches without dynamic marks, as in *3K, suggests that the finishing touches were not yet completed on the score.

Some Mozartian Feaures

1. The withholding of 2S until solo 1 (as in the Piano Concerto, K. 467).
2. The introduction of an N theme at the start of ritornello 2, the theme picked up by the soloist at the opening of solo 2 (resembling the Piano Concerto, K. 488).
3. An unusual number of lyrical themes (2P, 1T, 1S, *2S, 1K, N).
4. Extensive melodic chromaticism and more frequent parallel period structures, especially 1P (as in the first two piano concertos and Op. 61). However, most such periods undergo long extensions or truncation, as in solo 1, 1S. Both the chromaticism and extensions create considerable instability, which, together with unstable harmony, is more Beethovenian than Mozartian, however.

Harmonic Aspects

The harmonic style supports the melodic chromaticism with many secondary dominants, major-minor shifts, and frequent use of diminished sevenths. Very striking is the developmental 2T in ritornello 1. Largely in A minor, it opens on a dramatic E-major chord, a third below G, the preceding dominant of C. The ritornello is thus modulating, as in the first three piano concertos and the Triple Concerto: 2T ends in G and S starts there but modulates back to C.

The Second Movement: *Larghetto*

The meditative heart of the concerto, the *Larghetto* has been described by Tovey as embodying a "dream-like state of repose," which can only end with a "dramatic interruption."[46] The "sublime inaction" here resembles the variation movements of the "Appassionata" Piano Sonata, Op. 57 (essentially completed in 1805) and the "Archduke" Piano Trio, Op. 97 (1810-11) in the "strict treatment" of the variation form, and unchanging mode, key, and tempo. The "dramatic interruption," in this case is the final *fortissimo tutti, senza sordino*, with double dotted rhythm, and an ending on d:V. It is followed by the solo "Eingang" to the rondo.

Growth

The form of the movement has posed a problem to most critics. Their reluctance to call this movement a theme and variations (with the usual exception of Tovey) may be ascribed not only to a lack of understanding of Classic procedures, but also to the fact that the movement is not a straightforward variation set.[47] It is instead a hybrid form, synthesizing a

---

[46] Donald Francis Tovey, *Essays in Musical Analysis*, III, 93, here and later quotations.
[47] See the summary of formal descriptions by Fiske, Deane, H.J. Moser, and Grove in Owen

theme and variation structure on two themes with the five-part rondo.[48] The alternation of P and 1S, and the variation of 1S on its second appearance recall Haydn's frequent type of variation on two themes, designated as "alternating variations" by Sisman.[49] This is a type that Beethoven explored in four great later examples, the slow movements in the Fifth, Seventh, and Ninth Symphonies, and the late string quartet Op. 132, as well as the "Prometheus" Piano Variations, Op. 35 (1802), and the finale of the *Eroica* Symphony (1803). We can specify two important differences from the Haydn prototype:

    1. Instead of a direct alternation of themes, Beethoven first presents three variations of the P theme before the appearance of S (this recalls the start of the Op. 35 variations and the *Eroica finale*).

    2. Beethoven introduces a brief third theme, 2S (ignored by most analysts), that encloses the variation of 1S, thus suggesting a rondo episode. Further, 2S is slightly varied on its return.

Other examples of this typical Beethovenian synthesis of two formal procedures can be found in the finales of the "Appassionata" Sonata and the Seventh symphony, where Beethoven combines sonata form and rondo elements, but not in the format of the sonata-rondo.[50] A synthesis of theme and variations with rondo in a gigantic five-part structure plus introduction and coda occurs in the *finale* of the Ninth Symphony. The basic formal pattern in the *Larghetto* is A-B-A-C-A, but without the usual tonal contrasts in the episodes (see the timeline on facing page). In the synthesis here, A stands for the variation of the main P theme, and the episodes B and C containing 1T, 1S, and 2S, offer both contrast and connection with A and each other.[51] This is the only concerto movement by Beethoven using these two forms. Precedents for both forms appear in Mozart's later piano concertos (as in K. 456/II, theme and variations; and K. 491/II, five-part rondo).

The P Theme

Much is unique in this movement, starting with the theme for the variation set. Its style combines the hymn and the march, the latter forcefully emerging in the third variation, while the dotted rhythm of Pa and b is

---

Jander, "Romantic Form and Content in the Slow Movement of Beethoven's Violin Concerto," *MQ* 69 (1983): 159-60.

[48] In Tovey's *Beethoven* (London: Oxford University Press, 1944), 132, he modifies his description of this movement as a simple theme and variations by noting "two episodic themes which intervene between the later variations."

[49] For the alternating variation in Haydn, see Elaine R. Sisman, *Haydn and the Classical Variation* (Cambridge, MA: Harvard University Press, 1993), 152-63. The most familiar Haydn examples of this form are the slow movement of Symphony No. 103 and the late F-minor Piano Variations.

[50] See Martha Frohlich, *Beethoven's "Appassionata" Sona*ta (Oxford: Clarendon Press, 1991), 36.

[51] All references to numbered variations, as Variation 1, 2, etc., are to the variation of P.

Table 1.6 Timeline: Movement II

Key: G   Meter: ¢

A				B		A¹
	(Var. 1)	(P)			(P)	
P	|Var. 1	Var. 2	Var. 3	|1T	1S	|Var. 4 |
1	10⁴	20⁴	30⁴	40³	45	55⁴
G						

C				A²			
(Pr, P)				(Var. 1, Pax)	(Pr)		
2S	1S¹	2S¹	2T	|Var. 5	|KT	Leadin to Rondo	
65³	71	79⁴	83²	86⁴	88⁴		D:V total: 91 mm.
					mod to d		

dramatized by double dotting at the end of the movement. The march association connects with the tapping motive in the first movement as well.[52] The theme starts on the upbeat, in contrast to the largely down-beat themes of the first movement.

Rather than the standard binary melody with repeats of each part, we find a unitary ten-measure period. This period contains three phrases, organized as follows: a-4 measures; b-3 measures; c-3 measures. Each phrase has a contrasting harmonic setting as well as the unexpected asymmetry of phrases b and c (see Ex. 1.10, p.43). Pa surprisingly cadences on the dominant of iii (B minor) rather than the home dominant (though the tonic of b is never heard). This suggestion of b, which Beethoven emphasizes with brief cadenzas on b:V in variations 1 and 2, perhaps echoes the B-minor presentation of 1P near the start of the development in movement I, and it injects a hint of minor in the strong major color of the movement.

Pb, which resembles the X (i.e. modulatory) section of a binary melody, is the most active and richest harmonically. First, V/iii resolves deceptively to a B⁷ chord (V⁷/VI). The major VI--E--then becomes minor in a direct major-minor contrast as the harmony continues its movement in fifths, the complete pattern being: F♯-B-E/e, A-D-G. Arrival on G coincides with the elided c phrase. Pb also contains a strong, delayed, and we might say, misplaced arrival on V. This chord is enriched by rising chromatic motion in the inner parts, which relates to the later chromatic lines in the solo part. In Pc, the harmony becomes quiescent, as it makes a simple cadence in the key, inflected by an opulent appoggiatura of the ninth over IV.[53]

---

[52] Again one thinks of the slow movement of the Fourth Symphony respecting this combination of topics. See "The Singing *Allegro*" with regard to the first movement.

[53] Jander,"Romantic Form," 65-72, stresses the outlining of the descending tetrachord ("chaconne bass") in phrases a, b--bass notes G-F♯-E-D--ending with the cadential bass notes B-C-D-G. He thus subdivides the theme as 8+2 measures (actually 7-1/2+2-1/2).

Pa and b start off like parallel phrases of a parallel period. They present similar upbeat motives at the start and continue with a similar broad movement in quarter notes, though such movement is extended in Pb, partly in the inner voices. Surprisingly, the melodic climax on g^2, approached by a large skip of the sixth, occurs early in the theme, in measure 3 of Pa; the melodic line then slowly descends to the tonic by measure 8. A second rise to d^2 produces a lower climax in measures 8-9, the line descending more quickly to the tonic a second time. Melodically, measures 9-10^1 decorate measures 7-8^1.

Tension produced by the structure and harmony is enhanced by syncopated harmonic rhythm in Pa and b, reflected in the syncopation in the melody and Variation 4. Further, the upbeat motive opening phrases a and b is reinforced in the solo variations 1 and 2 by their offbeat motives and phrases. Following the declamatory rest and repetitions at the start of Pa and b are five continuous measures containing a general acceleration in surface rhythm, from the tied dotted half in measures 6-7 to nearly steady eighths leading to the cadence.

At least five motives in P recur in the variations and episodes. These are the dotted rhythm in Pa and b (Pr=1m), the sigh motives in measures 1 and 2 (2m), the large skip of a sixth (3m), the rising chromatic line (4m), and the rising broken chord (5m; see Ex. 1.10).

STRUCTURE OF THE VARIATIONS

The many-sided beauty of P and its careful construction make possible its literal repetition as a *cantus firmus* four times plus phrase a of a fifth time designated as Variation 5. Variation 4 acts like a recapitulation, as almost the entire theme appears in the violin for the first time as well as in the orchestra. The withholding of the theme from the solo recalls the device in the first movement. Variation 5 is a coda-like recall of the start of Variation 1, thus rounding off the variations of P.

Section A is organized in an a-b-b^1-a^1 pattern, the orchestral setting of the theme (a) framing the solo variations 1 and 2 (b,b^1). The second variation is a variation of the first (like a double variation) in smaller values (see Rhythm). The second episode parallels the framing device with its b-a^1-b^1 form, 2S (b) framing 1S (a; see below). A novel and purely soloistic effect are the cadenzas added at the end of Pa in the solo variations 1 and 2, emphasizing as well the remote F♯ major chord. The second cadenza is much longer than the first in the piano arrangement of the concerto,

---

He relates the use of the descending tetrachord to Beethoven's examples in the "Waldstein" Piano Sonata, Op. 53 (1803-04) and the Thirty-Two Variations for Piano in C minor, WoO 80, also composed in 1806. One may agree or disagree with his interpretation of the bass line, but the existence of three phrases in P, rather than two, is clear to this writer.

VIOLIN CONCERTO 43

Example 1.10 The P theme and the start of Variation 1, second movement (mm.1-13)

suggesting that such freedom was also granted the violin soloist, despite the specific notes indicated.

The technique of variation in the solo variations 1, 2, and 5 is again that of an *obbligato* melody, partly independent and partly duplicating P in ornamental figures. Very little ornamentation is found in Variation 4, where P appears in the solo in a largely rhythmic variation close to the original melody and rhythmic values. The ornamental figures in Variations 1, 2, and 5 are not only similar, but they incorporate motives from P (see below).

THE VARIATIONS OF P

A key element in this movement is the treatment of sound.

1.Sound

The orchestral violins are *con sordino* (often a sign of an especially expressive movement since the *Sturm und Drang* symphonies of Haydn). Since the solo is not muted, it stands out in color, melody, and rhythm.[54]

2. Dynamics[55]

While the theme and variations are largely *pianissimo* and *piano*, Variation 2 ends with a *crescendo* to *fortissimo*, linking to Variation 3, which is entirely *forte*, except for the > *piano* in the last two measures. Variation 4 is played as a long *diminuendo* marked *perdendosi* from Pay to the *pp* of Pc. The *ppp* subclimax of the movement comes only with Pax in mm. 86^4–88^3. It should be noted that *ppp* is Beethoven's softest level and is always a special effect (the third *p* was added later--see the remarks on the autograph below).[56] The spell is broken by the *fortissimo*, *senza sordino* in the final, connective orchestral *tutti*.

3. Scoring:

A smaller orchestra omits the flute, oboes, trumpets, and timpani, making a much thinner and more delicate sonority. The variations have a different orchestral scoring for each unit:

P Strings alone

Var. 1 Theme in the upper choir: the horns and then clarinet I, supported by the upper three strings.

---

[54] Muting of the violins also occurs in the slow movements of the Triple Concerto and Piano Concerto No. 5.

[55] Experimentation with dynamics in a variation set can be found in the String Quartet Op. 74/IV, where the variations alternate *forte* and *piano*, and in Op. 96/IV. See Chapter 3, 265-67.

[56] For a survey of Beethoven's "Association and Locations of *ppp*," see Sheer, "The Role of Dynamics in Beethoven's Instrumental Works," 452-55. She found only 20 such indications in the works she surveyed. She points out that "this softest level almost always appears as an ending or a simulated one," (452) and that "melodically, *ppp* is mostly characterized by fragmentation, often through the insertion of . . . a shortened motive" (453).

Var. 2   Theme in the lower choir: the bassoon is supported by the viola and cello, with punctuation in *pizzicato* by the remaining strings.
Var. 3   *Tutti*: The theme is in the strings with an echo-like punctuation with Pr in the winds, plus wind doubling and background in Pby and especially Pc. While some analysts may wonder whether this is a variation, the changes in dynamics and scoring certainly constitute types of variation procedures.
Var. 4   Theme and accompaniment in the strings, *pizzicato*.
Var. 5   (Pax only) Theme in the horns *con sordino*, a rare use of this device by Beethoven, repeated by violins 1 and 2.

THE SOLO VIOLIN IN THE VARIATIONS

While the full range of the violin is used, from g to e^4, Variations 1 and 2 are again placed mostly in the high register on the E-string, reaching e^4 and d^4 in Pb, and $c\sharp^4$ in Variation 2. Variation 4 is also basically played on the E-string but has a lower tessitura, reaching only g^3. Variation 5 presents Pax an octave higher than in Variation 1, thus restoring the earlier high tessitura and reaching d^4. The high violin writing in the variations recalls similar high passages in the first movement and has the same ethereal effect.

RHYTHM

The solo *obbligato* in Variations 1 and 2 contrasts with and outlines the theme in mostly smaller rhythmic values--sixteenths and thirty-seconds, creating considerable local motion. Variation 2 varies Variation 1 by accelerating the rhythmic values to sixteenth sextolets and triplets, and thirty-seconds. In Variation 1 the thirty-seconds appear only in the second measure of Pc, while in Variation 2, they appear in measure 3 of Pa, driving up to the cadenza, and then predominate in Pc, which ends with a sweeping G-major scale rising three octaves in thirty-second notes. The acceleration of surface rhythm in Pc of the variations reflects the acceleration in the theme itself.

As mentioned earlier, the upbeat rhythm of Pa and b is taken over into the solo variations, where each measure starts with a sixteenth, eighth, or quarter rest, except for the cadenza ending Pa and the final measure. Quarter notes end the one-measure modules on beat 3, while a syncopated quarter leads to the cadenza and appears at the start of Pc, as a point of departure for increased motion. Small, one-beat modules occur at the end of Pb and Pc, intensifying the rhythmic impetus to the cadence, together with thirty-second-note figures. Very special are the fermatas on long notes--a half and quarter framing the cadenza, the first with a trill. These totally stop the motion forward.

By contrast, the solo melody in Variation 4 is mostly syncopated in large values against the orchestra, in a clear example of a written-out *rubato*. In fact, the upbeat and syncopated figures in the previous solo variations produce a similar *rubato* effect.

THE EPISODES

While the orchestra carries the theme in the variations (plus the solo in Variation 4), the two episodes focus exclusively on the solo violin with orchestral accompaniment, in the most intimate passages of the movement. Even here, however, the accompaniment is varied in sound: strings in Episode 1, but strings with horn background in Episode 2 for 2S, juxtaposed with sustained clarinets and bassoons in $1S^1$. The solos are also placed in the lower register of the violin, contrasting with the high register of the variations. The total range for Episode 1 is d^1-b^2, rising to e^3 in the extension back to Variation 4. A larger range in Episode 2 extends from the open G-string to d^3.

The cadenza-like approach to 1S and leadin to $1S^1$, the use of *tirate* including as many as 22 notes in measure 77, and ornamental style after the opening of 1S produce the effect of improvisation as opposed to the systematic variation process. Yet, the second episode, with its ornamental variation of 1S and 2S, does fall in line with the idea of variation that underlies the movement.

Just as P contains irregular phrasing, so do the units in the two episodes. They become more regular upon their recurrence in the second episode, and shorter as well, since the extensions at the end of the themes are omitted. The themes become closed rather than open and connective. The lengths are:

1T	4½ mm.	
1S	10¾ mm.	(4+6¾)
$1S^1$	8½ mm.	(4+4½)
2S	5½ mm.	(2+3½)
$2S^1$	3½ mm.	(2+1½)

The larger and smaller irregularities support the improvisatory style of the themes. Similarly, the slow harmonic rhythm in the episodes, often one chord per measure, and simple, sustained-note accompaniment give the soloist a necessary freedom in the performance of these ornamental and expressive melodies.

In episode 1, the rhythmic values extend from the half to sixteenths, but in episode 2, the rhythmic vocabulary enlarges to include triplets and ornamental passages in thirty-second notes, an increase in motion that one would expect in the variation process. It should be noted, too, that 1S is the only theme in the movement that starts on the downbeat.

DERIVATIONS IN THE VARIATIONS (A) AND EPISODES (B, C)

Several motives from P recur in the variations and episodes, integrating the structure more deeply.

The Variations

The variations incorporate four motives from P--1m, 3m-5m:

1m (Pr) The basic dotted rhythm, attached to three repeated notes and mainly on beat 2, appears in the wind punctuation in Variation 3, phrases a and b.

3m   The rising sixth in Pby, Variation 1; the falling sixth in Pby, cadenza, Variation 2.
4m   The rising chromatic line in Pby, Variation 2.
5m   The rising broken chord at the start of Variations 1, 2, and 5.

In addition, phrases b and c are connected by a common ornamental figure as found in mm. 15-17, further ornamented in m. 19 and Variation 2.

The Episodes

These include all the motives from P, thus connecting the episodes not only to P but the variations of P.

lm (Pr) The basic dotted rhythm recurs in Episode 2, where it appears as background in the horns to 2S and $2S^1$ on beat 2 (see Ex . 1.11). This procedure recalls the use of Po as background to the lyrical themes in the first movement, with similar anticipation. The reappearance of the motive links 2S and Episode 2 with Variation 3.

2m   Prominent sigh motives intensify both 1S (mm. 48, 50) and 2S (mm. 66, 67, 68)--and recurrences, an important expressive gesture.

3m   While the rising sixth itself is not present, 1S features large rising leaps increasing in size: an octave, m. 47, a tenth, m. 49, and two octaves and a fifth, m. 75. All are emphasized and related to the profoundly moving expression of 1S.

4m   Rising chromatic lines occur in connective passages: the extension of 1S (mm. 54-55^1) and 2S (m. 70).

5m   This is the most important motive in 2S, which contains rising and falling broken-chord figures, the rising form related directly to Pc and Variations 1, 2, and 5 of P.

CONTINUITY

How to achieve continuity was a challenge that Beethoven met in several ways. First, there is the unitary structure of the theme itself, without sectional repeats, and its irregular phrase structure, as well as the irregular phrasing in the Episodes. Second, there is a continuity of structure from the end of Variation 2 of P to the end of the movement. This comes about with the following means (as the movement unfolds):

   1. Dynamic connection (end of Variation 2 to Variation 3; end of Variation 3 to 1T).
   2. Elision (1T to 1S).
   3. Postponement of tonic resolution; surface-rhythmic continuity (1S to Variation 4).
   4. Harmonic continuity; anticipation (Variation 4 to 2S, which starts with the anticipation of Pr).
   5. Avoidance of open cadences (Episode 2).
   6. Harmonic continuity ($2S^1$ to 2T).
   7. Overlapping (2T to Variation 5).

Third, devices for variety and intensity include the harmonic color of P itself; the variation process in sound as well as melody; and rhythmic dissonance--the syncopations and offbeat placements, as well as surface rhythmic accelerations at the end of P, in successive variations 1 and 2, and in 1S and $1S^1$.

Harmonic Aspects

First, we should note the sharp contrast between the richly harmonized P and simple diatonic harmony of the transitions, 1S, and 2S, with the basic chords of I, IV (ii), and V. Both 1S and 2S end on dominant chords when first heard, but tonic chords on their recurrence, an example of large-scale harmonic resolution. The sense of repose and stasis so poetically evoked by Tovey is not only produced by the absence of tonal and modal contrast, but also by the unusually static harmony in measures 40-88 in 1T, 2T, and the S themes. Here, 24¼ measures out of 49 (practically one-half) are on a tonic pedal with or without harmonic change above the pedal, the most static harmony being in the transition passages and 2S (this statistic includes the unharmonized m. 86, beats 1-3). While the rich harmony of P sustains the momentum of the movement in its first part, the more static harmony of the episodes dominate the latter part, increasing its quiescence and inwardness.

The Romance Thesis

Owen Jander[57] has suggested that this movement is actually a *Romance* in five respects:

> (1) in its use of an essentially strophic form; (2) in its pastoral atmosphere; (3) in various musical details, [such as the chaconne bass] that suggest the "goût un peu antique;" (4) in its quasi narrative character; and (5) in its touching and extremely Romantic final experience.

These qualities are related by Jander most closely to the definition of the vocal *Romance* in Rousseau's *Dictionnaire de musique* (1768), certainly a very old source by Beethoven's time. The vocal term "strophic form" is applied to the theme and variation set since, he asserts, the theme itself is not varied. However, this is not really true. The theme is partly varied in the violin *obbligato* in Variations 1, 2, and 5, and in rhythm in Variation 4. Further, the theme is varied in the orchestra by changes in orchestration and dynamics. Such *cantus firmus* variations are found, for example, in Haydn's string quartet Op. 76, No. 3/II (on Haydn's "Kaiser" hymn), and in the finale of Beethoven's Ninth Symphony. The "touching" ending, too, occurs in several slow movements with no

---

[57] Jander, "Romantic Form," 161-65. The *Romance* is usually referred to by its Italian name *romanza* or the German *Romanze*. However, Beethoven used the French term.

Example 1.11 Use of Pr as background to 2S, second movement (mm. 61-69)

connection to the *Romance*, as in the *Eroica* Symphony/II, mentioned by Jander, as well as the String Quartet Op. 18, No. 3/II and String Quintet, Op. 29/II.

However, Jander's thesis is reinforced by the basic rondo form of the movement and duple rhythm, both found in the three instrumental examples of the *Romance* by Beethoven, references to which are omitted in Jander's discussion. The earliest is the fragmentary "Romance cantabile" in E minor, Hess-Green 13 (1786) for piano, flute, bassoon, and orchestra (with 2 oboes).[58] This work has ¢ meter and gavotte rhythm in P. The formal layout is A-B-A¹-C (only a start in E major); the remainder of C and return to A are lacking.

The two *Romances* for violin and orchestra, Op. 40 in G (1801-02, pub. 1803) and Op. 50 in F (c. 1798;? performed 7 November 1798 and published

---

[58] Reprinted in Hess, *Supplemente*, III, Bd. 1.

1805),⁵⁹ follow the early model by using ¢ meter and gavotte rhythm in P of Op. 40, as well as the five-part rondo form--A-B-A-C-A-coda. The rondo form, specified as typical by Koch for instrumental *Romances*,⁶⁰ occurs in many other such works of the period, including Mozart's, which also feature the gavotte rhythm (Piano Concerto, K. 466/II, *Eine kleine Nachtmusik*, K. 525/II).⁶¹ However, the "naive" character referred to by Rousseau and Koch (quoting Sulzer)⁶² is most assuredly not found in the *Larghetto*.

The scoring for both violin *Romances* resembles the *Larghetto* but includes a flute, plus 2 oboes in place of clarinets. Other similar features comprise the slow tempo (*Adagio cantabile* in Op. 50; no tempo specified for Op. 40); variation of the refrain in both accompaniment (especially Op. 40) and melody (only Op. 50); presentation of P an octave higher in the final refrain (Op. 40); the presence of a dotted, march-like rhythm in several ideas; and emphasis on the high register (Op. 50).⁶³ While Op. 40 ends *fortissimo*, the conclusion in Op. 50 is inscribed "*calando*," as the music gently fades away on a broken tonic chord. The earlier *Romance* is far more developed, adventurous (with its modulation to D♭ major in section C), and more brilliant than the later example. It should be noted that Jander proposes a detailed program for the *Larghetto* as a dialogue between the orchestra and solo.⁶⁴

The Third Movement: Rondo

> The *Finale* generally takes the well known form of the Rondo. It may begin either solo or *tutti*, and in the course of the same the orchestra receives single *tutti* passages, which must not last too long. In respect to character, it must differ from the first movement, in the same proportion as that of the Sonata. In bravura, brilliance, and vivacity, however, the *Finale* must be nothing inferior to the first movement, but rather surpass all that has preceded it, where this is practical.⁶⁵

Czerny's description of the concerto rondo *finale* is in general relevant for this movement, which, on the whole, is more brilliant than the first movement, and shorter and more popular in style, as one would expect from a rondo. The tension built up in the previous movements is

---

⁵⁹ New edition, together with Op. 61, in *NGA*, Abt. III, Bd. 4.

⁶⁰ Jander, "Romantic Form," 161. The reference is to H.C. Koch's *Versuch einer Anleitung zur Composition*, vol. III (Leipzig, 1793; reprint Hildesheim: Georg Olms, 1969), 340.

⁶¹ For other 18th-century examples, see Roger Hickman, "Romance," *NGD*, 2nd ed., 21: 575.

⁶² The citation is to J.G. Sulzer's encyclopedia *Allgemeine Theorie der Schönen Künste*, vol. II (Leipzig, 1774; reprint of the 1792/94 ed. in 4 vols., Hildesheim: G. Olms, 1967).

⁶³ The new theme in Op. 40, section C, is also structured like Op. 61/III, N.

⁶⁴ Jander, "Romantic Form," 172-79. Jander uses the dialogue arrangement in the *Andante* of the Fourth Piano Concerto as a model for the *Larghetto*, where the violin is ultimately "won over" by the Romance in the orchestra, "swayed by the Power of Song."

⁶⁵ Czerny, *School of Practical Composition*, I, 164.

characteristically relaxed with a clear structure and attractive themes. As Tovey put it: "With all its lightheartedness and comparative simplicity of form, the finale is the truthful outcome of its sublime antecedents."[66]

Inscribed simply as a "Rondo" without a tempo mark (for Czerny's tempo, see "Performance Practice" below), this movement is in sonata-rondo form, a common formal type for the concerto *finale* in the late 18th century. Beethoven wrote such *finales* for all his concertos, as did Mozart for most of his Viennese concertos. But the form also occurs in Beethoven's solo sonatas, chamber music, and symphonies, sometimes with great complexity, as in the Piano Concerto No. 4 and Eighth Symphony. The form disappears in Beethoven's music after the Piano Sonata Op. 90 (1814), with the exception of the beautiful finale of the String Quartet, Op. 132, written eleven years later (1825).[67]

As is well known, the sonata-rondo combines the key-area structure of sonata form with the refrain form of the rondo, so that the refrain returns after the exposition as well as the start of the recapitulation. It may return after the recapitulation as well. The familiar paradigm of the sonata-rondo in major is given here:

Table 1.7 The Sonata-Rondo Form (in major)

A	B		A	C	A
Refrain	Episode 1		Refrain	Episode 2	Refrain
P	T S K R T		P	N and/or dev.	P
I	mod. V mod. back to I		I	mod.	I

B¹	A or **Coda (A)**
Rec.-Episode 1	
T S K RT	P ‖
I	I
(mod.)	

As Cole points out,[68] the danger of monotony is great with the four-fold repetition of the refrain. Thus, various changes were usually made, the most familiar by Haydn, Mozart, and Beethoven. The second return of the refrain was often curtailed, as in this concerto, and the final return

---

[66] Tovey, *Essays in Musical Analysis*, III, 94.

[67] For the rondo and sonata form, see Malcolm S. Cole's article "Rondo," *NGD* 16:172-77; and Ratner, *CM*, 249-55. Ratner starts the first episode with the S theme, while H.C. Koch, *Introductory Essay on Composition*, trans. Nancy K. Baker (New Haven and London: Yale University Press, 1983), 174, and Cole, "Techniques of Surprise in the Sonata-Rondos of Beethoven," *Studia Musicologica* 12 (1970): 233-62 (and other writings) starts the episode with T, which is followed here. Also of great value are such Cole articles as "The Rondo Finale: Evidence for the Mozart-Haydn Exchange?" *Mozart-Jahrbuch* (1968-70): 242-56, and "Sonata-Rondo, The Formulation of a Theoretical Concept in the 18th and 19th Centuries," *MQ* 55 (1969): 180-92.

[68] Cole, "The Rondo-Finale," 244-45.

"telescoped" with the coda (as is also the case here; see the timeline below, Table 1.8). In fact, because of the special repetitive structure of the refrain in the Violin Concerto, its final appearance is limited to its first phrase in the remote key of A♭ Another preference found here is for a new theme in episode 2 rather than a development section, as in sonata form.

EXPRESSION

The basic topic is the hunt, a typical rondo finale type in 6/8 gigue rhythm. Since Pax outlines a broken tonic chord, it can be given to the horns, reinforcing the association of the hunt, in the tutti as well as with wind background (as in mm. 21-22, 25-26, 319-21). Further hunting calls in the horns and winds occur in T and the massive *tutti* based on T just before the main cadenza, using the typical descending horn progression 3rd--5th--6th (as in Domenico Scarlatti's well known sonata in C).

In the coda, the long tonic pedal, wind melody and background, and sing-song transformation of 1P (mm. 315-22) project a pastoral atmosphere found also at the very end of the movement, with its repeated broken triads over a tonic pedal (a bagpipe effect; see mm. 352-57). The many repetitions of themes, phrases, and motives also reflect the pastoral topic.

Table 1.8 Timeline: Movement III

Key: D   Meter: 6/8

A
                   (1Pm) (1P)   (1Pay) (T)   (1Pax)
*1P *1P¹ 1P² 2P |To   T |S |*K |1RT | LEADIN
1   11   21   31 43²   45   58² 68   81   92
D | mod. to A   A-a   A-A/e♭ mod. to D:V⁷

A¹
                   C
                   (1Pax)   (N)   (1Pax)
*1P *1P¹ |1Pa |NT |*N | 2RT   3RT |
93   103   113 117   126²   158   168
                d-E♭-F-g:V   g/d-(B♭)/g   g-d:V   d-D:V⁷

A   B¹
                                                              (T)
*1P *1P¹ 1P² 2P |To¹ T¹ |S |*K |1RT¹   4RT|
174 184   194 204 216² 218   233² 243   256   269
                       mod. to G-D   D-d   D-D/a♭ D-g-D

          CODA (A²) Part 1   Part 2   Part 3
          (1Pax)   (1Pax)   (1Pax) (1Paxm)(1Pax=1P⁴)
CADENZA |KT |*1Pa² |*5RT |1P³ |1P³ ext. |N2K   N3K   N4K ‖
279   280   293   297   315   323   329   341   349   360
D:I   D-A♭   A♭   A♭-D D: I ped.   d/D   D: I ped.

N.B. If a theme begins on an eighth upbeat, it is placed on the next beat or measure.

In contrast to the first movement, the *finale* contains far more passagework in brilliant style, found in the T, K, N *obbligato*, and coda sections (and far more difficult passages were abandoned in the final version). The lone example of singing style in the N theme creates one of the most memorable passages in the entire concerto. Other topics include the dialogue (S, 1RT, 3RT, coda), *ombra* (KT, perhaps Kb), fanfare (coda, mm. 349-52), and *Sturm und Drang* (coda, mm. 341-49). Learned style is represented by the violin *obbligato* in 1RT, where 1Px is developed in the orchestra, as it is in the coda (mm. 81-88; 323-28).

Aspects of Growth

The rondo, in contrast to the first movement, is more concentrated on the opening refrain (1P), from which 1Sa, most of the retransitions, and the coda are derived. The other striking idea is the beautiful N theme in the second episode, which stands out as the only lyrical theme of the movement. S and K are fairly brief and less distinctive. Fewer basic themes also occur, a total of only six: 1P, 2P, T, S, K, and N (not counting the many retransitions, NT, and new cadential units in the coda). The first movement contains twelve (excluding the retransition).

The proportions in the rondo differ from the first movement as shown by the sectional lengths. Most of the sections range from 42-1/2 measures to 63-1/2 measures, creating a more balanced effect. The large A section (42-1/2 mm.) is not much smaller than the B section (49-1/2 mm.) or second episode (58 mm.). Three of the last four sections, however (C, B^1, the coda), are the longest and reflect an expansion in the latter part of the movement, culminating in the very long coda of 81 measures (see below).

The Refrain: 1P

The main theme of the movement is 1P, the theme presented in the solo at the start of the movement, which occurs in all the Beethoven concertos. The *tutti* repeats this theme, which is followed by 2P, a purely *tutti* theme in the tonic that ends the section. 2P features dotted rhythm, not found elsewhere in the movement.

The refrain is a typical rondo theme in its symmetrical layout as a parallel period, a+a^1, 4+4 (Ex. 1.12). However, a two-measure extension to V is added in the solo and a three-measure extension to I in the *tutti*, thus introducing a witty asymmetry in the theme. The open-ended solo refrain is complemented in a larger dimension by the orchestral version, V being answered eventually by I. Within the four-measure phrases, we find a Mozartian type of balanced contrast:

    x: triadic, on the tonic chord, rising within an octave; repetitive, 2 x 1.
    y: conjunct, with skips of thirds; a smaller range of a diminished fifth or minor sixth; falling and rising without repeats; supported by a quick harmonic rhythm.

Example 1.12 The rondo refrain (1P), third movement (mm. 1-10)

Pax starts with a descending fourth, d-a, which is ultimately answered by a-d at the end of 2P (mm. 41-43¹), picked up for the link to T which opens with these notes, another typical long-range effect. The rising broken triad of Pax recalls the opening of Variations 1, 2, and 5 in the second movement, which begin with similar rising broken triads. Since Variation 5 appears at the very end of the *Larghetto*, the connection with 1Pax in the rondo is certainly heard.

Very characteristic are three transformations of 1Pa in the coda: (1) a less driving version, where x starts on the downbeat, and y has an initial repeated note and falls to the cadence (1Pa² in A♭, mm. 293-96); (2) the main transformation in a sing-song, pastoral style at the start of the second half of the coda (1P³, mm. 315-22); and (3) its concluding appearance as a fanfare, Pax mounting up the notes of the tonic triad (mm. 349-51, 357-59), with a falling, triadic, hurdy-gurdy effect in between, fading away (1P⁴, mm. 352-56) (Ex. 1.13).

The transformation as sing-song—a relaxed and simplified version of 1P, is the most radical, though typical of many Beethoven codas.[69] Here, Beethoven reduces the parallel period to a four-measure unit and replaces

---

[69] Some other examples of simplified, balanced evolutions of P themes occur in the codas of the Piano Sonata Op. 10, No. 3/I and the *Eroica* Symphony/I. Reduction of a P theme to a fanfare on the tonic occurs, for example, in the codas of Symphony No. 1/I and Symphony No. 5/IV.

Example 1.13 Transformations of the refrain, third movement

1Pay by a free inversion of 1Pax on V, thus making the subphrase parallel rather than contrasting. The phrase then repeats to fill out the eight-measure paradigm. The chords of I and V alternate over a tonic pedal in two-measure groups. Beethoven first introduces this oscillation with 1Pax in 1RT (mm. 81-84). A dialogue with the oboe on I and the solo on V heightens the balanced effect (the horn joins the oboe in the repetition). Earlier dialogues in 1RT and 3RT occur in one-measure modules rather than two, which is more fitting for that less stable function (see mm. 81-88, 167-73).

Quite intensively developed is 1Pax, in wonderful demonstrations of Beethoven's developmental power. This one-measure idea is given many forms in the transitions, retransitions, and coda. Alterations include the omission of the upbeat (a typical device, also found in 1Pa²); changing the chordal outline from the original major I^6_4 to a triad, sixth, seventh, and diminished-seventh chords; replacing the literal repetition of x by rising chromatic movement; revising the descending fourth between notes 1-2 to a sixth, fifth, diminished fifth, third, and second (most dramatic in mm. 341-42); repeating notes 1-2; inverting notes 1-2 to rise up a second or third; and fragmenting the subphrase to three and two notes (Ex. 1.14).

Example 1.14 Alterations of 1Px in the transtions, retransitions, and coda, third movement

THE NEW (N) THEME IN THE SECOND EPISODE

Beethoven replaces a possible development section with a completely symmetrical, self-contained new lyrical theme in rounded binary form, 8+8 measures, each part repeated, making a total of thirty-two measures. The basic structure is outlined below.

Part I: a-4; a^1-4. Part II: b-4; a^2-4

In the written-out repeats, the bassoon takes the theme two octaves below the violin, against a sixteenth-note *obbligato* in the solo. Though the theme is basically new, it shares the upbeat start and initial broken chords with 1Pax and the rising scaleline especially with Ka. The *obbligato* draws on the neighbor-note figure in Na^1, as well as broken chords and scale figures that link it with Na. Far more than the *obbligatos* in the first movement, this one closely outlines and varies the melody, and is like a formal variation.

The key of G minor connects N with the N theme of the first movement and the subdominant major of the *Larghetto*. The minor mode makes a striking contrast in the movement, which is deepened by the modulation to D minor at the end of Part I and the emphasis on C-minor chords in the a and b phrases (iv-of-iv). A brief reference to B♭ major in Nb brightens the harmonic effect. The theme thus has considerable harmonic color for such a relatively short section. It moves back to the tonic minor via 2RT, which draws on N, the violin part based on the obbligato to N and the orchestra part deriving from Nb, so that N material continues on for nine measures (a tenth overlapping with 3RT, based on 1P).

New themes in the second episode, usually dynamic, rhythmic ideas, occur in most of Beethoven's concertos, the exceptions being the Fourth and Fifth Piano concertos, which have completely developmental episodes. The N theme closest to Op. 61 is the one found in the Third Piano Concerto. There, a new lyrical theme appears in A♭ (Ex. 1.15). This theme too is in rounded binary form but 24 measures long, and 48 measures if we add the written-out repeats of both parts:

Part I: a-4; a^1-4. Part II: b-4; b^1-4; $a^{2(1)}$-4; a^3-4.

Each part is repeated with variation. Part I is presented by the clarinet (later the bassoon) and repeated in variation by the piano. Part II, b,b^1 are first heard in the clarinet (and later the bassoon) and the return of phrase a occurs in the piano, based on its variation of a^1 in Part I. In the repeat, b,b^1 still appear in the clarinet and bassoon (and strings), while a^2 and a^3 remain in the clarinet and bassoon, joined by the piano in a strengthened concluding phrase. Though the division between the solo and orchestra is more complex than in Op. 61, we still find a basic division between a solo wind instrument and the soloist. As in Op. 61 all phrase are four measures long--rigidly symmetrical, but unlike N in Op. 61, there is little harmonic color. All phrases end on the tonic except b^1 ending on V, and only a few secondary dominants inflect the harmony. This harmonic simplicity is undoubtedly intentional since the theme is followed by a *fugato* on the refrain and then a return of the refrain in E major, the key of the slow movement and extremely remote from the tonic of C minor. It is reached by another return to A♭, but in unison, a♭ becoming g♯ enharmonically. The key of E could thus be heard as ♭VI of A♭ also in relation to the large area of A♭ in the N theme.

Beethoven's model for the introduction of such a lyrical theme in the second episode may have been the beautiful lyrical N in the second episode of Mozart's C-major Piano Concerto, K. 503 (1786), *finale*, a work that Beethoven knew (see mm. 163-93).[70] The theme, in F major, enters as

---

[70] Czerny said he played this concerto for Beethoven when he was brought to him by Krumpholz at the age of ten. See the excerpts from Czerny's "Memoires" in *On the Proper Performance*, 4.

Example 1.15 Start of the N theme in the Third Piano Concerto, third movement (mm. 182-92)

2N, after a dramatic 1N in A minor. It is in binary, not rounded binary, form:

Part I: a-4; a¹-4. Part II: b(a)-4; c(b)-4.

The solo plays each part alone, which is then repeated by the oboe (the flute in c), with a simple piano accompaniment and almost no change, though the piano background accelerates from sixteenths in Part I to sixteenth triplets in Part II. However, the last phrase is extended, after a deceptive cadence to vi in the repeat of Part II, leading to development of both Nc and Nax (the sigh motive). Here too we find rigid four-measure phrasing and the alternation between the solo and a wind instrument in the repetition of each part. As in Op. 37, no modulation is found and all phrases end on the tonic except the first (resting on ii$^6_5$). The more varied texture, scoring, and rich ornamentation in the piano in Op. 37 stand in contrast to the simpler Mozart example. Mozart's melody, however, is more lyrically intense and therefore closer to Op. 61.

To return to Op. 61, N, we can now understand the richer harmonization of N. Since this is the central material, without further modulation and development as in K. 503 and Op. 37 (except for the retransition back to d), the theme of necessity had to contain some modulation and less stable harmony.

THE CODA

Whether the section I have labeled as A² constitutes the coda, as Tovey suggests,[71] or a last return before the coda[72] is a moot point. Malcolm Cole, in his detailed study of Beethoven's *finales* in sonata-rondo form, indicates that the coda "usually opens with a portion of the main theme" and that "the beginning of the coda is another point at which Beethoven throughout his career occasionally stated a portion of his reprise in an unexpected key area."[73] Cole's remarks seem to fit the situation here admirably. They also remind us of so many Beethoven codas in sonata form that start in another key or are modulatory before returning to an extended tonic affirmation. Leonard Ratner has made several significant observations in his consideration of the coda. A lengthy coda can have three elements in the following order:

(1) "A harmonic digression . . .
(2) A firm return to the tonic, generally with the opening theme
(3) A set of emphatic cadential gestures."[74] Further, the "opening digression create[s] a harmonic 'whiplash' that prepares the final tonic with increased force, a supreme effect of periodicity."[75]

---

[71] Tovey, *Essays in Musical Analysis*, III, 95-96.
[72] Mahling, "Violinkonzert, op. 61," 464.
[73] Cole, "Techniques of Surprise," 258-60.
[74] Ratner, CM, 230.
[75] Ibid., 231.

Ratner's description well fits the coda in Op. 61. On one hand, the coda can be subdivided into two parts tonally, as shown on the list of sectional lengths (Table 1.9 below). The first part is modulatory and the second part firmly grounded in the tonic. On the other hand, the coda can also be subdivided into three parts, following Ratner (and shown on the timeline). In the first part (mm. 280-314)[76] a modulation takes place to and from A♭ the key of the tritone, in which Pa appears in varied form in a kind of false recapitulation. Similar coda appearances of all or part of the refrain in a distant key occur in the first three piano concertos: modulation to the key of B in Op. 15, the key of G in Op. 19, and the key of D♭ in Op. 37.[77] In the coda's second part (mm. 315-28), the most important transformation of 1P appears on a tonic pedal, with the effect of recapitulation, followed by a connection to the main cadential area. In the third part (mm. 239-60), three new K units, all based on Pax, or smaller fragments, make a strong and brilliant conclusion to the entire concerto (see above, "Unifying Elements"). There is no doubt that the coda is also the most developmental portion of the *finale*, containing as it does the three transformations of 1Pa and several new motivic forms of 1Pax. The movement is thus powerfully end-oriented, with its culmination in its final portion. The coda also contains several allusions to the first movement (see above, "The Cyclic *Finale* Coda".)

Table 1.9 Sectional Lengths

A	P, solo and tutti	1-43^1:	42-1/2 mm.
B	T-S-K-1RT	43^2-92:	49-1/2 mm.
A^1	P, solo and tutti (cut)	93-116:	24 mm.
C	NT-N-2RT-3RT	117-73:	57 mm.
A	P, solo and tutti	174-216^1:	42-1/2 mm.
B^1	T^1-S-K-1RT^1-4RT	216^2-79:	63-1/2 mm.
cadenza			
coda: (A^2)	KT-1Pa^2-5RT	280-314	35 mm.
	1P^3 and ext. –N2K-N3K-N4K	315-60	46 mm. (14+ 32 mm.)

[76] The measure numbers exclude elisions.

[77] Cole, "Techniques of Surprise," 258, places the examples in Opp. 15 and 19 in Table XIV, "False reprise in retransition to final reprise statement or coda." However, both examples have much in common with Op. 61, the modulation to B occurring in Op. 15 after the main cadenza.

The Larger Structure and Continuity

Another relaxed aspect concerns the many literal repetitions in the movement, repetitions that must have particularly inspired the complaint by the reviewer of the first performance. 1P is heard complete eight times, phrase a twice more, though with slight variation in A^2. Further, repetitions occur in Kb, the two parts of N (though varied by an *obbligato*), 4RTx (four repeats), $1P^3a$, N2K, and N3K. Such repetitions were associated with the pastoral style, as we see in Beethoven's own "Pastoral" Symphony (1808). The repetitions also connect with the large-scale repetitions in the first movement. Somehow, they do not disturb us today because of the ebullience, beauty, and growth in the movement.

More open cadences occur in this movement than in the first movement, as one would expect in the more relaxed rondo style. These occur especially after the solo 1P and the end of the retransitions before the return of the refrain after episodes 1 and 2, which are major points of articulation, the first with a leadin. In addition, a new open cadence appears between T and S in the recapitulation, which had been overlapped in the exposition. A special effect here is the connection of sections via the same notes, happening between 2P and T, NT and N, and finally between the post- cadenza trill and KT. The trill on e never resolves to the tonic but continues as part of an extraordinary suspense section moving to the tritone key of A♭, the e^2 enharmonically becoming $f♭^2$. An intensive continuity occurs between the remaining sections, with either elision (S-K, 2RT-3RT, $1RT^1$-4RT, the coda, sections II-III, N1K-2NK), overlap (T-S, exposition, K-1RT, the coda, sections I-II, N2K-N3K, entry of the last solo phrase, m. 356), or anticipation (N and 2RT).

Sound

What is special here are the register contrasts in the solo 1P and its orchestral background. First, the refrain appears on the G-string (specified by Beethoven), accompanied by cellos alone. This rich sonority is contrasted with the bell-like repetition of the theme two octaves higher on the E-string, accompanied by just the two violins (it is inscribed *delicatemente*). The high register on the E-string also connects with other high E-string passages in the previous movements. A sheer play on color, this contrast resembles the register contrasts in the theme and variations of the *Larghetto*. The *tutti* violins then fill in the register gap by presenting the theme in the octave in between. While 1P exploits a low-high registral contrast, N reverses direction as the theme alternates in the violin and the bassoon two octaves *lower*.

A characteristic variation in slurring occurs in 1P, measures 1-2, beat 1 (see Ex. 1.12). Notes 2-3 are slurred in the G-string performance but all other recurrences are unslurred, note 3 being *staccato*.[78] Curiously, a *staccato*

---

[78] In the autograph, note 2 was originally *staccato* in the G-string presentation as well, and was then changed.

mark on the upbeat to 1Pax appears in the autograph only at the start of the first three presentations (mm. 1, 10, 20). Though omitted in the repetitions in the *NGA* they were surely intended.[79] On the other hand, the upbeat to 1Pay never receives a *staccato* mark. Besides the use of double stops in the solo (S and K), Beethoven specifies a brief but distinctive *pizzicato* effect (always performed by the left hand) at the start of T in the recapitulation (m. 218).

DYNAMICS

The dynamics in the movement both resemble and differ from the earlier movements. The resemblance concerns the treatment of the refrain, 1P, which is heard on both the *piano* (solo violin) and *fortissimo* (orchestra) levels. Such dynamic contrasts for the refrain are typical of Beethoven's concerto rondo themes, but they also relate to most of the themes in the first movement and P in the *Larghetto*.

An outstanding difference concerns the many *diminuendo* and *crescendo* passages, as well as the long *piano* passages--the last unusual for a fast movement. These carefully marked places lend a special dynamic character to the *finale*.

The *diminuendo* from *f* to *p*, and *crescendo* from *p* to *f* are found especially in NT, the retransitions, and the KT units. For example, NT, connecting the *tutti* to N and modulating from D to g, starts with a six-measure *fortissimo* and quickly moves to *piano*: *ff*--6 mm.; *f*--1 m. (solo); *dim.*--1 m. (solo); *p*--2 mm. (solo). The two units that follow N move first to *pp* and then to *ff*; 2RT (mm. 158-66): *dim.*--7 mm.; *pp*--2 mm.; 3RT: (mm. 167-73): *cresc.*--5 mm.; *ff* 2 mm. (solo). The dynamic plan of KT (mm. 280-97), which is a suspense passage like 2K in movement I, is very dramatic. It moves from D to A♭ via an enharmonic modulation, cutting the module from two measures to half a measure, and the motive from five notes to two. These events are thereby supported by the following dynamic plan: *f*--5 mm.; *dim.*--2 mm.; *p*--2 mm; *sempre più p*--2 mm., *pp*--2 mm. The *pianissimo* coordinates with the clarification of the modulation to A♭ in a typical example of concinnity.

The transition between the *tutti* P area and S is mainly *piano*, despite the solo's passagework, S here being *forte* rather than the usual *piano*. A very long transition of eighteen measures moving from 1Pa in A♭ back to D is entirely soft, being marked *sempre pp* and even *ppp* in the winds in measures 308-11, again despite a very active solo part. This transition is part of a long area of soft dynamics that precedes the mostly loud portion of the coda (mm. 287-322), a total of 36 measures. An earlier, even longer area of quiet dynamics occurs before and after N (mm. 125-66), a total of 42 measures, except for a rare *cresc.-p* (mm. 150-51).

---

[79] The later repetitions are not written out in the autograph. The Tyson edition includes the *staccato* in the repetitions.

Like the *Larghetto*, the Rondo makes use of the special dynamic indication *"perdendosi."* In the *Larghetto*, it was applied to Variation 4 as *"sempre perdendosi,"* starting in its second measure and ending in its eighth measure, where *pp* is inscribed. In the Rondo, we find it in N3K, near the end of the coda, for the final dying away of the sound before the concluding *ff* chords. It occurs after a *diminuendo* to *p*, lasts for only two measures (mm. 353-54), and ends again with *pp*. The term is defined in the Koch Lexikon as "losing itself" and the equivalent of *perdendo* and *diminuendo*.

HARMONY

The striking harmonic effects are the modulation to G minor in the second episode (see the discussion of N for the harmonic details); the major-minor contrasts in S and the RT, NT, and KT units, together with chromatic progressions; and the tritone relation in Kb and the start of the coda.

The tritone relationship established in Kb (A-e♭, D-a♭) is dramatized at the start of the coda with the actual presentation of Pa² in A♭ major. In these tritone relationships, enharmonic modulation occurs at some point. In Kb (mm. 73-76 and repetition; mm. 248-252 and repetition), the modulation is to the minor mode of the diminished fifth, even more shocking than the major would be. The key of the tritone is reached via the Neapolitan chord altered as a dominant seventh of the tritone. Thus, in the exposition, the tonic chord A, proceeds to the V⁷ of e♭ (on B♭), and the return to A occurs via b (e♭:vi=Aii) and the enharmonic equivalence of B♭and A♯. At the start of the coda (mm. 280-96) the tritone is reached via the enharmonic interpretation of the diminished seventh of D: C♯-E-G-B♭, which becomes the diminshed seventh of A♭: G-B♭-D♭-F♭. The new meaning of the chord coordinated with the *pp* and the descent of the trill on e² to e♭² (e acting as f♭; see m. 291 and 289, where the F♯ in the trill is changed to f♮ (ec. 1.16).

A brief major-minor contrast in S (in A/a, and D/d in the reprise) introduces some instability, which greatly increases in K. Even Ka emphasizes V⁷/IV, followed by the tritone-minor in Kb. This function is the most unstable of the movement (excluding most of the connective units), and, in general, S and K make a sharp contrast to the diatonic simplicity of the P and T areas.

Major-minor contrast in S is magnified in the retransitions, NT, and KT, all of which feature the minor mode in part or entirely, as well as chromatic bass lines or harmony. Thus, they function as the main repository of chromaticism in the movement. Each transitional unit differs in its choice of harmony, however. Four incorporate mainly rising chromatic basses or keys (NT, 2RT, 3RT, 1RT¹) and one a descending chromatic bass (5RT--A♭-d/D). Both types are directional, pointing to a main cadence on V or, as in the case of 2RT, to the newly restored tonic key. The minor and chromatic movement returns for one last time in the coda's cadential area in N3K.

Example 1.16 Enharmonic modulation from D to A♭, in KT, the coda, third movement (mm. 280-93)

Many of these harmonic effects relate to similar effects in the first movement: the major-minor contrasts, the use of the subdominant minor, the chromatic transitions, and the enharmonic modulations. All these were noted in the section "Tonal Cross-References."

As in the first movement, we find significant variation in harmonic rhythm. 1Pa is a typical example of a speedup of harmonic rhythm for emphasis of the cadence, the rhythmic pattern of both a phrases being:

Figure 1.1 Harmonic Rhythm of Pa

The contrast in harmonic rhythm coordinates with the change of melodic style and surface rhythm in 1Pay. Other such examples of rest-motion patterns appear in Kb and 2NK in the coda.[80] The reverse pattern of motion-rest occurs in 1RT, where a long-held dominant of 8 measures ends the function (mm. 85-92).[81] Another common pattern, rest-motion-rest, marks 3RT, with the harmony moving in two-measure units at the beginning and end, and one-measure units in between, providing drive to the concluding dominant chord (mm. 163-73).[82] An acceleration of harmonic rhythm (a

---

[80] See LaRue, "Harmonic Rhythm in the Beethoven Symphonies," 12; repr. 226-28.
[81] Ibid., 13; repr. 229-30.
[82] Ibid., repr. 231.

typical Beethoven effect also found in the first movement), propels 1RT¹ into the fanfare-like 4RT before the cadenza (mm. 256-68). The chords here move from two- and four-measure units to mostly one-measure and half-measure speeds (the inflection of the V^0_9/IV in mm. 261, 263 is not shown). Despite the acceleration, the dynamics are mostly *p* and *diminuendo*, leading to *pp*, the *crescendo* delayed until 4RT.

Figure 1.2 Acceleration of Harmonic Rhythm, mm. 256-68

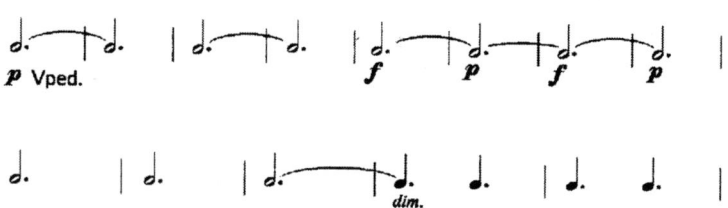

The three sections of the coda together make a pattern of harmonic rhythm in the larger dimension, another argument for starting the coda with KT:[83]

    Part I: rest-motion-rest
    Part II: rest
    Part III: rest-motion-rest

Part I starts with the suspense section, KT, where one basic harmony holds for 11 measures before the enharmonic modulation to V^6_5 of A♭ (mm. 291-92). Harmonic motion in the variant of 1Pa¹ (only 4 measures) is followed by a deceleration of harmonic rhythm in 5RT. Basic motion in this chromatic passage of 10 measures (sometimes ornamental) is in one-measure units, followed by a I^6_4 in D for two measures and V^7 in D heard and implied for 6 measures. This grand slowdown articulates the end of the first, modulatory part of the coda (mm. 293-314).

Part II, which presents the transformation of 1P in sing-song, contains unchanging two-measure chordal units over a tonic pedal, thus stabilizing the tonic after the tritone modulation in Part I. This steady, slow harmonic rhythm overlaps Part III, where it continues in the first four measures of N2K, changing to one chord per measure only at the cadence. Syncopated, chromatic harmony emphasizing the minor mode produces the more rapid as well as more dramatic harmony in N3K. The final section of Part III, N4K, rests entirely on tonic harmony, being the concluding tonic stabilization for the entire movement if not for the entire concerto. The last 12 measures contain only one V chord--for the final brief and snappy V-I cadence in eighth to quarter notes.

---

[83] For other large-scale patterns of harmonic rhythm, see ibid., 15-20; repr. 235-48.

Melody

The pattern of high notes differs from the preceding movements. The highest note d^4 is reached only once, in measure 329, at the top of a rising climactic scale eliding with the start of the final cadential area of the coda. Otherwise, the highest note is only a^3 in both the exposition and recapitulation, with the trill on a^3 before the cadenza including b^3 (mm. 270-71). Actually, the general tessitura of the recapitulation is lower than the exposition, probably in order to throw into relief the higher register of the extensive coda to come, where a^3 is heard several times, three times in measures 344-59. In addition, the repetition of 1P high on the E-string is placed between a^2 and a^3, and occurs in the three solo presentations of the refrain.

Though the melodic style was analyzed in the discussions of 1P and N, we should note that both themes feature initial broken-chord ideas, unlike the largely conjunct themes of the first movement. They connect instead with most of the solo variations in the *Larghetto*. Descending thirds delineate the S theme, in its upbeat and y subphrase. This theme has contrasting x and y units, the balanced contrast of the response type of melody, as in 1P. Since the retransitions (except 2RT) and KT as well as N2K and N4K in the coda are based on the broken-chord motive of 1Pax, this motive is highlighted throughout the movement and indeed it ends the movement.

The phrase symmetry generally associated with the rondo style appears here but with considerable modification. In fact, the first movement has greater symmetry in its phrase organization than the rondo, the reverse of our expectations! If we search for completely symmetrical periods, we find only 4: 1RT, N, the transformed 1P in the coda (1P³), and N3K. Otherwise, the periods feature additions, extensions, and fragmentations that lead to overall asymmetry, which helps explain the vital flow of the music. Thus, 1P is a 4+4 period, but contains an extension of 2 measures. Though 2P is 12-1/2 measures, it subdivides 6+6-1/2. All other functions contain some asymmetrical phrases, as the following table indicates.

In examining Table 1.10, we are reminded of the phrase irregularities we associate with Haydn.[84] What we find is the frequent fragmentation of the module so that shorter units and repetitions often occur at the end or middle of a period. This makes for an acceleration or "stretto" (to use Ratner's term), an effect called modular compression by Schwartz, that drives the period forward toward a cadence or a new thematic function (see 1P¹, T exp., NT, 2RT, 3RT, 1RT¹, 4RT, KT, N4K). We also find typical combinations of both even- and odd-numbered phrases (as in S and K);

---

[84] For the most valuable analysis of Haydn's early phrase structure and types of asymmetries, see Judith L. Schwartz, "Thematic Asymmetry in First Movements of Haydn's Early Symphonies," in *Haydn Studies*, eds. Jens Peter Larsen, Howard Serwer, and James Webster (New York: Norton, 1981), 501-09.

six-measure phrases composed of two-measure subphrases (P³ extension, N2K); and even-numbered periods with asymmetrical subdivisions (like the 12 measures of N2K and N4K). All these types are characteristically Classic and appear in Haydn's earliest symphonies.

Table 1.10 Asymmetry in the Rondo's Thematic Functions

Function	Measure Total	Subdivision
1P	10	4 +4 +2
1P¹	10	4+3+3 (3x1/2 sequence +3x1/2)
2P	12-1/2	6+6-1/2 (2x2+2 and 2x2+2-1/2)
T (exp.)	15-1/2 (16)	2-1/2+4+2+5+(2x2+1)+2-1/2 (final half is overlap)
T (rec.)	17-1/2	2-1/2+4+4+2+3 (2+1)+2
S	9	4+5
K	13	5+2x4
NT	9-1/2	6+3-1/2 (1/2+6x1/2)
2RT	9	4+5 (2+1+2x1)
3RT	7	2+3(1+1+1)+2
1RT¹	13	4+3 (2+1)+6(1+1+1+3)
4RT	11	4x2+3 (4x1/2 sequence +1)
KT	13	2+3+2+2+2+2(4x1/2)
5RT	18	10+4+4 (harmonically, last 8 mm. 2+6)
P³ ext.	6	2+2+2
N2K	12	2x6 (2-measure units)
N4K	12	2-1/2+3-1/2 (7x1/2)+2(4x1/2)+4(3x1 varied +1)

A few examples deserve brief discussion (see Ex. 1.17). In the extension in 1P¹, the one-beat cadential motive in measure 8 of the period (ym) is spun out in sequence (up in thirds) and then repeated three times at the

Example 1.17 Irregular phrase structure in 1P¹ and NT, third movement (mm. 21-31¹; 117-26¹)

end, driving into 2P. The final three measures are organized in one-half measure modules, 3 x 1/2 repeated in sequence and 3 x 1/2 in literal repetition. In NTa, the sequence occurs in two-measure groups; measure 6 is then repeated by the solo and its second beat is further repeated five times (5 x 1/2) before the upbeat to N, a good example of modular halving (another Schwartz term): 2-1-1/2-measure modules. The same type of halving occurs at the end of 2RT (two measures cut to one). The best example of modular compression appears in KT, where the initial larger units are followed by smaller ones, ending with a seven-fold repetition of a half-measure module before the entry of 1Pa² in A♭. The first three half-measure modules echo the preceding two-measure subphrase and are seemingly part of a two-measure repetition, but the continued repetition of the motive draws in the preceding repetitions in retrospect (see Ex. 1.16).

Rhythm

The strong rhythmic drive of the rondo partly stems from its irregular phrasing and use of modular compression. Three other major rhythmic aspects should be emphasized. One concerns the surface rhythm, so different from the first movement and including big contrasts.

Three basic types of rhythmic motion occur. One is the 6/8 gigue rhythm, with its typical trochaic pattern ♩ ♪, with or without an upbeat. The long note accentuates the downbeat and indeed, there is a strong downbeat feeling throughout the movement, with none of the rhythmic ambiguities of the first movement. Trochaic rhythm is featured in 1P, S, NT, and in the orchestra in most of the retransitions, KT, N2K, and N4K (conclusion in the solo).

A second type of rhythmic motion is the fast surface rhythm in largely steady sixteenths in the brilliant violin part. This appears in T, K, the retransitions, *obbligato* to N, the 1P^3 extension, and Part III of the coda. A third type is the smooth motion in eighths and other longer values in the lyrical N theme; indeed the trochaic rhythm is avoided in N. Similar steady eighth-note motion appears in the hunt fanfares in T, and some of the extensions of 1Pax (as in N4K).

In addition to these three basic types, other important rhythmic effects merit our attention. One is the persistent upbeat orchestral accompaniment to 1P (see Ex. 1.12), offsetting the strong downbeat emphasis in 1P. The accompaniment recurs in 5RT in twelve of its eighteen measures, set against the solo figuration in sixteenths outlining 1Pax as well as free figuration. Another type of upbeat accompaniment punctuates Sy. When the transformed 1P^3 is heard in the coda, significantly the accompaniment becomes downbeat, actually trochaic, in the clarinets and bassoons, producing a sense of resolution and tranquility (see Ex. 1.13).

Another, less frequent effect is the use of syncopation in Kb (mm. 73-74) and most strikingly in N3K (mm. 341-42 and repetition), where it appropriately coordinates with the minor and a *Sturm und Drang* topic. Special rhythmic patterns include the gigue-like dotted rhythm, associated only with 2P, and the longest values in the melodic line of the movement, dotted halves, in the four-measure cadence ending part one of the coda (mm. 311-14). This phrase, heard without accompaniment and so additionally highlighted, recalls the similar cadence in the coda of the first movement (see above, "The Cyclic *Finale* Coda"). Coming after twelve measures of almost steady sixteenths, this sudden calm, *pp*, prepares us for the tranquil and transformed 1P^3 that follows in the coda's second part.

In conclusion, if we consider this movement with respect to Beethoven's "techniques of surprise" in the sonata-rondo, as summarized by Malcolm Cole, we can find the following categories of surprise:

1. "Rondos with unusual main themes." Here the surprise is the contrast in registers and large range of 1P, as well as its three-fold repetition, altered only at the end of the third, orchestral presentation. Perhaps we should add its open ending on V in the solo.

2. "Rondo reprises with irregular phrase and period structure." 1P has an extension of two measures so that it is ten rather than eight measures, and on its third appearance, the theme ends with two three-measure phrases (still making ten measures).

3. "Themes of the first couplet [with] harmonic surprise." S includes major-minor contrast in its phrase repetition and extension, and K a tonicization of IV and the tritone minor, reached enharmonically.

4. Retransitions "filled with the unexpected." This applies to the introduction of the minor mode and especially chromatic harmony in 1RT, 3RT, 1RT¹, and 5RT.

5. "Unexpected harmonic areas in the central couplet [episode 2]." The episode is in G minor, rather than the usual subdominant major, and it tonicizes degrees distant from D, such as B♭ and C minor.

6. The lack of variation in the refrain on its third return after the second episode, since some kind of change or variation is the norm in Beethoven.

7. "Codas with a statement of the main theme in an unexpected harmonic area." The start of the coda contains an enharmonic modulation to A♭ ending with a variant of 1Pa.

The Sketches

The sketchbook for this concerto, if it ever existed, is lost. It may have contained the sketches for the orchestral works written or completed in 1806: the Fourth Piano Concerto, the Fourth Symphony, and the Violin Concerto, as well perhaps of the *Coriolan* overture, written in early 1807 and first performed in March 1807.[85]

What has remained for Op. 61 are two pages of sketches. The first and more important is page 64 in the sketch miscellany Landsberg 10. The second page is contained in the sketch miscellany Aut. 28, f. 11 recto and verso, with rejected sketches for the cadenza in the third movement of the piano arrangement of the concerto (between mm. 279-80). Both leaves are located in Berlin, Staatsbibliothek zu Berlin-Preussischer Kulturbesitz (see Plate 1.I on facing page).[86]

The leaf in Landsberg 10 has the same watermark as the main paper in the autograph of Beethoven's "Appassionata" Piano Sonata, Op. 57, which was completed by the second half of October 1806.[87] The same watermark (three half moons and the letters FS) appears in the autograph of the first "Rasumovsky" String Quartet, Op. 59, started on 26 May 1806, indicating that this paper was used by Beethoven in the spring to the fall of 1806.[88]

---

[85] *JTW*, 161

[86] See the sketch index by Hans Schmidt, "Verzeichnis der Skizzen Beethovens," *B-J* 6 (1965-68): 7-128; and the catalogue of the former West Berlin Beethoven collection by Hans-Günter Klein, *Ludwig van Beethoven, Autographe und Abschriften* (Berlin: Merseburger, 1975), with a description of the content of the leaf in Landsberg 10 on 135. The leaf in Aut. 28 is designated as Hess-Green 85 and the cadenza is reproduced in the Hess-Green catalogue between 56-57. The cadenza probably dates from 1809.

[87] See Op. 61, *KB*, 9; Frohlich, *Beethoven's "Appassionata" Piano Sonata*, 127-29.

[88] Alan Tyson, "The 'Rasumovsky' Quartets: Some Aspects of the Sources," *Beethoven Studies* 3, ed. A. Tyson (Cambridge: Cambridge University Press, 1982), 109-12

PLATE 1.I (MVT. I) OP. 61. SKETCHLEAF IN THE MISCELLANY LANDSBERG 10, CONTAINING EARLY SKETCHES FOR THE CONCERTO ON STAVES 2-12. Berlin, Staatsbibliothek zu Berlin-Preussischer Kulturbesitz, Musikabteilung mit Mendelssohn-Archiv, Mus. ms. autogr. Beethoven Landsberg 10, p. 64.

On the twelve-stave paper, staff one, written in thick dark ink, presents nearly the final version of measures 1-13 of the Fifth Symphony, first movement. Staves 2-12, in much fainter ink and pencil, seem to contain the earliest ideas for the Violin Concerto. While most concern the first movement, there is a concept sketch for a 3/8 *Andante* in G (staff 7), and a notation of the final version of 1Pa of the rondo (staff 8). Staves 2-6 present perhaps the first continuity draft for the opening ritornello, ending with an indication of the solo entry. The material was partially transcribed by Nottebohm.[89] Staff 9 bears the indication "in diesen beständige die Violin s[timme] mit Nachahmung (?)" [in this continuation, the violin part with imitation]. Below this is a *cantus firmus*-like succession of half notes, the bass clef implied, barred in 2/4 and ending with two whole notes. Staff 11 has clear references to 1T and 2T, and staff 12 suggests 2K (ending in A:V), and the cadential rise of 3Sb (also in A major).

The first continuity draft establishes several essential ideas. We find the opening tapping motive on d followed by 1P and 2P (Ex. 1.18). Though 1P seems distant from the final version, it still holds several features in

[89] N II, 532-33.

Example 1.18 Early sketches of 1P and 2P of the first movement (N II)

common: length--8 mm.; form--a parallel period, with cadences on V (m. 4) and I (m. 8); the same beginning and ending notes; and primarily conjunct motion, the descending scale of 1Pa closely related to the final version. Also related are the large rhythmic values; the rhythmic pattern in measure 3 of the theme nearly the same as measure 7 of the final version, and related to 1S and 1K; and the three-beat rest in measure 4. On the other hand, the range is considerably larger (a twelfth versus a seventh), and both melody and rhythm are far less varied.

This rather simplistic theme, typical of Beethoven's first jottings, has almost direct descending scalelines from a^2 to a^1 in the first phrase and e^3 to $f\#^2$ in the second phrase. In the final version, Beethoven dropped the predominant dotted rhythm except for measure 6, and instead emphasized rhythmic variety. In measures 5-7, the featured skip of a third expands to rising and falling fourths, while a rising third leads to the new expressive *appoggiatura* cadence. This cadence also fills in most of measure 8 and contrasts with measure 4. The simpler scale idea, both ascending and descending, was transferred to 1S.

2P, however, appears in nearly final form, the tapping motive on $e\flat^1$ rather than $d\#^1$ implying a Neapolitan chord. The final choice of d♯ connects with the harmonization in 3Sa. The remaining material transcribed by Nottebohm has much less in common with the final version except for the implied two-measure sustained harmonies at the start of 1T and 1K, and the ending on V, the final measure resembling measure 86.

The Original Sources for the Concerto: The Autograph

The autograph manuscript of Beethoven's Violin Concerto is in the Austrian National Library in Vienna (Österreichische Nationalbibliothek, Mus. Hs. 17.538); it was issued in a sumptuous facsimile edition in color in 1979. Even more than many autographs, the manuscript shows Beethoven at work during the autograph stage, and still considering alternatives, especially regarding the solo violin part, where the final version of some passages still does not appear. In addition, notations were made by Beethoven in movements I and II, largely in pencil and usually on the bottom staff, for the piano arrangement, particularly for the left hand. The orchestral parts also contain many changes but appear in final form except for certain omissions that Beethoven overlooked (see the section below on textual problems).

The Violin Lines

The autograph contains the original solo violin line often written in a faint brown ink of the same color found in the orchestral score. This part is complete and includes many corrections, both within the part and below it, with connective *Vi=de* signs. In addition, below the original part, and often on staff 15 of the sixteen staves, alternatives to certain passages are written in a thinner, darker ink, the original passage or figure marked with an X as well as the alternative (see Plate 1.II on p.76). Most of these alternatives are found in the first and last movements. Whether the alternatives were notated before or after the first performance is unknown. The supposition has been that the original part is the one played at the first performance and the alternatives were written later.[90] They seem to stem mainly from musical considerations, though they also simplify some difficult passagework, like the original retransition in the first movement.

The two and more lines on the autograph have been transcribed and published in two editions, one by Willy Hess in his supplement to the old collected edition (Vol. X, Bd. 2, 1969); and one by Ernst Herttrich in his *Kritischer Bericht* for the concerto (1994). Hess also supplies a list of variants that specifies and often gives in musical notation further alternatives that he omitted on the score, while all of these and some others are presented on the score by Herttrich.[91]

Most striking of the crossouts is the violin *obbligato* in high register to measures 365-81 of the first movement at the beginning of the recapitulation. Here, Beethoven thought of following some of the procedures used at the same point in the structure of the Fourth Piano Concerto, where after a forceful solo presentation of *1Pa, the orchestra continues with its ritornello in measures 258-66 together with a soft broken-chord background in the piano. However, in the violin concerto, Beethoven deleted the violin

---

[90] Shin Augustinus Kojima, "Das Solovioline-Fassungen und-Varianten von Beethovens Violinkonzert op. 61—ihre Entstehung und Bedeutung." *B-J* 8 (1971/72): 103; *KB*, 9.

[91] Both transcriptions contain some errors and omissions. The following examples are from Herttrich, movement I: mm. 113-15 were originally crossed out and then restored with the word "bleibt," but this is not indicated; mm. 148-50 in the final version have a single slur, not one per measure; in m. 159, note 1 is not c♯ but c♮ and there is no need for an editorial c♮ sign at the end of the measure; in m. 162, beat 2, though note 2 is written as f^2, e^2 was certainly intended (the omission of a natural sign for the note f also indicates that e was meant).

obbligato, probably because the *fortissimo tutti* would have drowned out the soloist (see Ex. 1.19).

THE TWO MAIN VIOLIN LINES

When we compare the two main violin lines from the first movement, as in Examples 1.20 and 1.21, we can see how the final version, if present, synthesized portions of both lines. In Example 1.20 (p. 77), from 2S in the exposition (mm. 152-64), choices for the final version were made for several reasons:

> (1) to emphasize the inversion of the theme in the orchestra with broken octaves (m. 152);
> (2) to coordinate the line with fast harmonic rhythm (the sixteenths, found only in the final version, not here, in m. 154);
> (3) to maintain a parallelism of subphrases between measures 153 and 155, which also introduce hemiola, integrated as well in measure 159;
> (4) to achieve a greater variety of figures (mm. 157,160,161);
> (5) to keep a higher register so that the violin can be heard more easily (mm. 158-59);
> (6) to support the *crescendo* with broken octaves in the high register (rejection of inverted broken octaves in m. 162);
> (7) to reach a high climax on g^3 (mm. 162-63);
> (8) to sustain the intensification produced by the violin climax (m. 164).

A preference for variety of figuration is a most important general consideration in the process of revision. We thus find several passages where rhythmic sameness and exact repetitions or sequences are replaced by varied rhythms and melodic contours.

Example 1. 21 (see p. 78) shows the alternatives in the first part of the N theme and area. First, there was a problem concerning the use of the high register. In the end, Beethoven reserved it for two intensifications, a brief one in the octave leap upward in measure 337, 6th eighth (making a more sweeping descent not found on the score) and a more extensive intensification, for contrast in the varied repeat of the theme, measures 341^4-43^2. Second, there was a structural consideration. The contrasted subphrase of Na (x and y) was changed to a varied repeat (x-x^1), as in 1P and 1S, thus linking the three lyrical themes of the movement in this way. Also, Nay (mm. 333^3-35^2) seems somewhat awkward and we might describe its cadence as sentimental. Finally, in the variation of x^1 (mm. 341^4-43^2), Beethoven eventually preferred rhythmic variety, featuring larger rhythmic values, rather than a replication of the sixteenths already used. In this way, he started a new buildup of surface rhythm, leading to triplets and finally sixteenths for the cadence. The triplet upbeat to measure 342 was later changed to eighths, a smoother effect that fits in more naturally with

Example 1.19 The deleted violin obbligato *at the start of the recapitulation, first movement*

the larger values that follow. The triplet upbeat was retained, however, in measure 343⁴, where it initiates a series of triplet figures.

The autograph contains many other kinds of corrections and repays close study. Three alterations may be mentioned here: the addition to the first movement's tempo mark of *"ma non troppo"* in red crayon, probably after the first performance; the addition of a second *p* in red crayon to the opening of the *Larghetto*; and the addition of a third *p* in darker ink to the *pp* in violin I and II at the subclimax of the end of the *Larghetto*, measure 87 (this replaced a specification of only one violin per part).

PLATE 1. II: *Op. 61. Autograph score of the concerto, first movement, fol. 19v, 2S (mm. 152-54), with alternatives to the solo line.* Vienna, Musiksammlung der Österreichische Natonalbiblothek, Sign. Mus. Hs. 17.538. Compare the page with Example 1.20 on p. 77.

The Remaining Sources and Textual Aspects

The most important discussions on this subject have been published by Alan Tyson and Ernst Herttrich.[92] There are four main sources for the concerto, three of prime importance. The first is the autograph (see above). The second is the copyist's score (*Abschrift*) in the hand of copyist D, one of Beethoven's main copyists in the period 1807-08.[93] This score was originally presented by Beethoven to the English musician Charles Neate in 1816 and

---

[92] Alan Tyson, "The Textual Problems of Beethoven's Violin Concerto, *MQ* 53 (1967): 482-502, and Tyson's edition of the concerto; Herttrich, *KB* (1994). Remarks on the sources are drawn from these discussions and Tyson's edition. The *KB* agrees with Tyson on most factual aspects. However, Tyson did not know about the oboe part (see below) and the dedication copy of the Vienna first edition to Stephan von Breuning in the Österreichische Nationalbibliothek. In this copy, the solo violin followed the printer's marks in the Stichvolage, but not in a second issue of the part, examined by Tyson, where the layout was changed.

[93] See Tyson, "Notes on Five of Beethoven's Copyists," *JAMS* 23 (1970): 456-60.

VIOLIN CONCERTO

Example 1.20 Different versions of 2S, Solo 1, in the autograph (final version in center)

Example 1.21 Different versions of N Solo 2, in the autograph

is now located in the British Library.⁹⁴ It contains the final version of the violin part and the piano arrangement, both copied from a now lost source; the orchestral parts stem from the autograph. Beethoven checked over the score more than once, and entered corrections in pencil (gone over in ink by the copyist) and in red crayon during the proof stage. This manuscript served as the engraver's copy (*Stichvorlage*) for the first editions, published in two sections, the piano arrangement in August 1808 and the violin concerto in c. 1808. In the violin concerto, some changes and errors were made in the edition, and some slurring returns to the autograph version. Many corrections were made on the plates of this edition. Clementi's edition of both concertos date from the late summer of of 1810. In this publication, the orchestra parts derive from the autograph and the solo parts from the Vienna editions, though Clementi sometimes transferred the piano version to the violin part in the belief, according to Tyson, that the piano part contained the "true" version. The last source is a frragment of the Oboe I part for the first movement (mm. 465-535), used for the first performance of the concerto.⁹⁵

    The most authoritative modern editions of the concerto are those made by Alan Tyson in 1967 and Kojima in 1973. While Tyson discusses several problematic passages in his article and presents over a four-page list of variants, Kojima did not do so, nor did he publish an editiorial report. Rather, he left notes for the *Kritischer Bericht*, which are cited and amplified by Herttrich. The bowings in Kojima's edition follow the autograph and the *Kritischer Bericht* does not give the alternatives in the other two main sources. Tyson tends to follow the copyist's score and first edition, but includes the alternatives in his list of variants. The later sources have in general shorter slurs in certain passages than those found in the autograph report. Thus, in the first movement, the solo violin's presentation of 1Pa in the first solo (mm. 102-05) has one long slur for the entire phrase, surely meant as a phrase slur by Beethoven, while Tyson gives one slur per measure, with mm. 104-05 slurred. Other decisions differ in the two editions, like the slurring of the very opening presentation of 1Pa in the winds (mm. 2-5), where the markings are unclear in the sources. As Tyson observes, expressive indications and dynamic marks in the *Stichvorlage* are generally given to all the instruments, while in the autograph they appear for only one or a few instruments. Tyson feels some of these added indications are not advisable and omits them, though Beethoven apparently accepted them. The original markings, however, are noted in the variant list.

    Several errors were made in the Vienna edition, some of which entered the standard scores until corrected by Tyson and Kojima. These

---

[94] A microfilm of the *Stichvorlage* is in the music library of Columbia University.
[95] The part is in Washington, D.C., The Library of Congress (*KB*, 6).

include the omitted cello melody in I/525-27 and 529-30; the omission of *senza sordino* in the last orchestral *tutti* of the *Larghetto* (this was corrected in the early scores), and an omitted measure in the *finale*, following measure 216. One characteristic inconsistency in the sources concerns the length of ending notes in 2T/29, 31 and recurrences, given as both eighths and quarters (in mm. 31, 500). Tyson alters the quarters to eighths but Kojima retains the quarters. Should the *sf* on the quarters be added to the string motive in sixteenths in I/35-38 (not in the autograph but the *Stichvorlage*)? What about the strange rests in I/308, cello, and 313-14, viola? Shouldn't these instruments double the bass line? They are corrected by Tyson and Kojima. In I/190^4 the wind chord is not resolved in the next measure as it is in the parallel passage in m. 465. These few examples represent the kinds of problems found in many sources of Beethoven's works. One major problem is whether to resolve the inconsistencies found in all the sources-- were these intended or accidental?

The Piano Arrangement (Op. 61a)

The arrangement of the violin concerto for piano was commissioned by Clementi in April 1807 when he acquired Beethoven's latest works for publication in London (see above, p.6). In Clementi's letter of 22 April 1807 to his colleague F.W. Collard in London, he stated that Beethoven would make this arrangement "for the pianoforte with and without additional keys."[96] Since the treble line follows the violin concerto it reaches beyond the high note of the period, c^4, to $c\#^4$, d^4, and e^4, as the violin version, while the left hand goes down only to A_1, and usually only to D, the left hand often being in the treble clef.

Jottings for the piano version, mostly for the left hand, appear occasionally on the autograph score's bottom staff for movements I and II, many of the figures used in the arrangement, which is found only in the copyist's score with the final version of the violin part (see Plate 1.II). There have been various speculations about the arrangement: was it actually made by Beethoven or by someone else under Beethoven's supervision, as Nottebohm and Tyson have suggested; and why did Beethoven include some of the rejected first version in the arrangement? With respect to authorship, both title pages of the Vienna and London editions ascribe the arrangement to the composer. On the other hand, the simplicity of the arrangement may suggest that a lesser musician was at work rather than Beethoven, despite the fact that many of the simple left-hand figures were notated by Beethoven on the autograph, like the very simple accompaniment in measures 331-36 (N theme, first movement).

---

[96] See *KH*, 148, and the entry for the piano concerto on 148-49. A review of the background and various evaluations is given in Grasberger, *Kommentar*, Fac.Ed., Op.61., 43-48.

While much of the melodic line remains the same, Beethoven sometimes incorporates the first version later replaced in the violin concerto. This led Nottebohm to argue that Beethoven actually preferred these versions and sought to preserve them in the piano arrangement.[97] Oswald Jonas, on the other hand, believes that such passages are more pianistic and sound more convincing on the piano than on the violin.[98] This strong argument would explain Beethoven's use, for example, of most of the original line for I/N, since the high register and flowing sixteenths sound more natural on the piano, though the violin version is musically preferable. The *finale* especially turns to the early version where more difficult figuration, rejected for the final version, is incorporated in the piano arrangement. Most striking is the use of the rejected octave figuration in III/297-306. In other passages, Beethoven replaces the original version with new figuration more natural for the piano, as in the triplet *obbligato* to I/2S (Ex. 1.22 on p. 82). Tyson suggests that the earlier versions are found because the final version had not yet been written.[99] To all these observations, one could add that Beethoven might have chosen some early versions to give more variety to the piano arrangement, considering the fact that the orchestra part had to remain the same, thus allowing little leeway for making changes.

THE CADENZAS FOR THE PIANO CONCERTO

In c. 1809, Beethoven composed 15 cadenzas for piano concertos 1-4 and the piano arrangement of Op. 61.[100] The four cadenzas for Op. 61 exist in autograph in the Beethoven-Haus in Bonn. They comprise a very long cadenza of 125 measures for movement I: a shorter cadenza for the connection of movements II-III, identified as an "*Eingang* [leadin]; another *Eingang* before the return of the solo refrain (m. 92) in the *finale*; and a cadenza for the *finale* (m. 279).[101]

The first-movement cadenza includes the timpani playing Po, and contains other references to 1P, 2P, and 2K, starting with 2T in B♭. It changes tempo and introduces a two-part march "*Più vivace*" in the key of A, which makes explicit the implicit march association of Po. Other tempo changes occur in this multisectional, virtuosic, Lisztian fantasy.

---

[97] N II, 587; Alan Tyson, review of the Willy Hess edition of the piano concerto, *Musical Times*, III (Aug., 1970): 827.

[98] Oswald Jonas, "Das Autograph von Beethovens Violinkonzert,"*Zeitschrift für Musikwissenschaft* 13 (May, 1931): 443-44.

[99] Tyson review. See also Robert Forster, "Zur Klavierfassung des Violinkonzerts op. 61 von Ludwig van Beethoven," *Die Musikforschung* 36 (1983): 1-15.

[100] For the cadenzas, see n.5.

[101] Facsimiles of the cadenzas can be found in Ludwig van Beethoven, *Sämtliche Kadenzen*, ed. Willy Hess (Zurich: Eulenburg, 1979).

Example 1.22: New triplet obbligato in 2S, piano arrangement, first movement (compare with Example 20)

References to the opening rhythm of III/Pa start the *Eingang* to the *finale*, which ends by anticipating notes 1-2 of the rondo refrain (unlike the ending notes indicated in the violin part). The second *Eingang*, actually in ¢ meter, is motivically unified, while the main cadenza echoes the preceding orchestral fanfare, though it is obvious that scales and trills dominate.

These cadenzas pose an aesthetic problem, since their brilliant pianism, especially in the first, seems entirely alien to the style and expression of the concerto. An arrangement of these cadenzas for violin has been made by Wolfgang Schneiderhan, and they sound even more bizarre because of their pianistic source. The best cadenzas, of many that have been written, seem to be those by Joseph Joachim and especially Fritz Kreisler, whose cadenzas relate far more closely to the spirit of the concerto.

PERFORMANCE PRACTICE

While Beethoven did not leave metronome marks for the concertos, they are given such markings in Carl Czerny's Op. 500. Czerny includes the piano arrangement of Op. 61 and suggests the following tempos: I ♩ = 126, II ♩ = 60, III ♩. = 100.[102] Most important, the tempos do not drag as in most modern performances, since the metronome marks left by Beethoven for his works indicate lively tempos for the most part.[103] That the *Larghetto* should not be too slow is also indicated by the fact that Beethoven called it an *Andante* (not an *Adagio*) when he identified the cadenza connecting movements II and III as an "Eingang von dem Andante zum Rondo." In fact, Koch in his *Musikalisches Lexikon* (1802) states that the tempo of a *Larghetto* "is usually the same as that of the *Andante*."[104]

Both the copyist's score and first edition show that the soloist was expected to play in all the tuttis except the tutti before I/1K in the solo section, and in III/1S and the coda of the finale (after m. 329), where there are dialogues between the solo and orchestra. This is indicated in the first edition by giving the solo part the orchestral first-violin part in large notes throughout the tuttis.[105] In the copyist's score, the solo piano also plays the main line in the *tuttis* and adds accompaniments in broken intervals or doubling the bass. The piano also sometimes fills out the main line with chords.

---

[102] Czerny, *On the Proper Performance*, 114-15.

[103] For the tempos chosen by various soloists from Kreisler to Tetzloff, see Mahling, "Violinkonzert, op. 61," 469. Only Tetzloff reaches Czerny's tempo for the first movement. See also the discussion of tempo, 468-69, and Robin Stowell, "The Violin Concerto Op. 61: Text and Editions," in *Performing Beethoven*, 187-89.

[104] "Die Zeitmass is dabey gewöhnlich dem das Andante gleich."

[105] See the *KB*, 12, which indicates that the same kind of doubling is also found in the *Romance*, Op. 40.

The autograph shows Beethoven's usual notation of staccato marks: a staccato line for a sharper, non-*legato staccato*, and dots below slurs for a softer staccato effect. There is no modern edition of the concerto that includes this differentiation (see the discussion in Chapter 2, p. 97).

A survey of various editions of the concerto since the first edition is given by Robin Stowell. He refers to editions made by such renowned violinists as Joachim, Ferdinand David, Wilhelmj, Hubay, and Szigeti, or teachers such as Dont, Auer, and Flesch. These editions have no authentic value but shed light on the performance style of the period and the editor. It is difficult to agree with Stowell's assertion, however, that the edition of the Viennese teacher Jakob Dont, published in Berlin c. 1880, preserves early 19th-century Viennese practice.[106]

List of Editions

1. Facsimile of the autograph. Ludwig van Beethoven. *Konzert für Violine und Orchester, D-Dur, Opus 61. Kommentar*, Franz Grasberger, Vorwort, Wolfgang Schneiderhan. Graz: Akademische Druck- u. Verlagsanstalt, 1979.

2. Revised edition by Alan Tyson. London: Edition Eulenburg, No. 701, 1967. With critical notes.

3. Edition in the *NGA*. Ed. Shin Augustinus Kojima. Abt. III, Bd. 4, 1973.

4. Ernst Herrtrich. *Kritischer Bericht* for the Kojima edition in the *NGA*, 1994. The most extensive critical report. Includes the various readings of the violin part in the autograph, occasionally differing from the Hess transcription. Contains previously unpublished critical notes by Kojima.

5. Edition by Willy Hess. *Beethoven. Supplemente zur Gesamtausgabe*, X, Bd. 2. Wiesbaden: Breitkopf & Härtel, 1969. The original version of the solo part with alternative versions. With detailed critical notes.

---

[106] Stowell, ed. *Performing Beethoven*, 154.

VIOLIN CONCERTO

6. The Arrangement for Piano
a. Edition in the *NGA*. Ed. Hans-Werner Küthen. *Klavierkonzerte*. Abt. III, Bd. 5, 2004.
b. Willy Hess, ed. *Beethoven. Klavierkonzert nach dem Violinkonzert. Op. 61*. Piano part with cadenzas. Wiesbaden: Breitkopf & Härtel, 1970.
c. The cadenzas for the piano arrangement. *NGA. Kadenzen zu Klavierkonzerten*. Ed. Joseph Schmidt-Görg. Abt. VII, Bd. 7, 1967.
d. Ludwig van Beethoven. *Sämtliche Kadenzen*. Ed. Willy Hess. Zurich: Eulenburg, 1979. Facsimile edition with commentary in German and English.

7. The Early Violin Concerto in C, WoO 5: Fragment of the First Movement
a. Willy Hess, ed. *Beethoven. Supplement zur Gesamtausgabe*, III, Bd. 1, 2nd ed. Wiesbaden: Breitkopf & Härtel, 1971. With critical notes.
b. Edited by Ludwig Schiedermair in *Der junge Beethoven*. Leipzig: Quelle & Meyer, 1926, pp. 427-78.

CHAPTER 2
Piano Sonata in D major, Op. 10, No. 3

> His pianoforte works so far surpass all which were previously written for this instrument, that even to the present day they remain unequalled, and the complete collection of them forms a store of imperishable masterpieces for all time.
>
> Carl Czerny[1]

Background

Of the main instrumental genres of Beethoven's compositions—the piano sonata, the string quartet, and the symphony—the piano sonatas have received the most critical attention by scholars, analysts, and performers. The reasons for this overwhelming critical interest are many. Among them are the large number of sonatas, 32 from Beethoven's Vienna years, their great range of expression and style, and their excellence, power, and often radical character.

Beethoven composed piano sonatas over the entire span of his creative life. The earliest three sonatas (WoO 47) were composed in Bonn and published in the fall of 1783 when the composer was twelve. These substantial youthful works, however, are not included among the canonical 32 piano sonatas. Nor is a brief two-movement sonata in F (WoO 50) composed by Beethoven before c. 1790-92 for his good friend in Bonn, Franz Gerhard Wegeler. The piano composition from the Bonn years that best reflects Beethoven's early maturity and brilliance are the 24 Righini variations (WoO 65) of c. 1790-91.

The Vienna sonatas may be grouped as follows:[2]

Early Period: 13 sonatas from 1793-95 to 1800: Op. 2, Nos. 1-3, Op. 7, Op. 10, Nos. 1-3, Op. 13, Op. 14, Nos. 1-2, Op. 22, Op. 49, Nos. 1-2

Middle Period: 14 sonatas from 1800-01 to 1814: Op. 26, Op. 27, Nos. 1-2, Op. 28, Op. 31, Nos. 1-3, Op. 53, Op. 54, Op. 57, Op. 78, Op. 79, Op. 81a, Op. 90

Late Period: 5 sonatas from 1816 to 1822: Op. 101, Op. 106, Op. 109, Op. 110, Op. 111

Three of these sonatas are "easy" sonatas, composed for near beginners. These are the two sonatas Op. 49, No. 1 (?1797) and No. 2 (1795-96), and Op. 79 (1809). The early pair were first published in 1805, hence the high opus number.

---

[1] Czerny, *On the Proper Performance*, Ch. II, 30 of the English translation.
[2] For editions of the Viennese piano sonatas, see the list at the end of this chapter.

The first sonatas for the modern piano, a set of 12, were published in Florence in 1732 by Lodovico Giustini. From that time on, the keyboard sonata gained in popularity with first Italian and then German composers especially. The sonatas were widely published in Paris, London, and many other centers, and most were written for amateur pianists.[3] While the earlier keyboard sonatas were intended for the harpsichord and clavichord as well as the piano, by the later eighteenth century the piano had become the main keyboard instrument and it underwent constant modifications and improvements.[4] Of Beethoven's predecessors, most important are C. P. E. Bach, Haydn, Mozart, and Clementi. Indeed, in piano style and some other musical features, Beethoven's sonatas have most in common with those by Clementi (1752-1832), and far more study of Clementi's sonatas is needed from this point of view.[5]

There are many descriptions of Beethoven the pianist. By the age of twelve, Beethoven was described by his teacher Christian Gottlob Neefe as playing "the clavier very skillfully and with power." He added that Beethoven "reads at sight very well and . . . plays chiefly the *The Well-Tempered Clavier* . . . [and connoisseurs] will know what this means."[6] Beethoven's virtuoso years lasted until the early 1800s, when his deafness and intense compositional activity led to less polished performances. His last public performance occurred when he accompanied the singer Franz Wild in 1816 in his songs "Adelaide," Op. 46, and "An die Hoffnung," Op. 94.[7]

---

[3] For a survey of the Classic sonata, see the monumental study by William S. Newman, *The Sonata in the Classic Era* (Chapel Hill: University of North Carolina Press, 1963; 2nd and 3rd editions; New York: Norton, 1972, 1983).

[4] For a helpful brief survey of the "Invention and Gradual Acceptance of the Piano," see Sandra P. Rosenblum, *Performance Practices in Classic Piano Music* (Bloomington and Indianapolis: Indiana University Press, 1988), 2-8.

[5] For Clementi, see Leon Plantinga, *Muzio Clementi, His Life and Music* (London: Oxford University Press, 1976), and Newman, *The Sonata in the Classic Era*, 738-59. A basic reference is Alan Tyson, *Thematic Catalogue of the Works of Muzio Clementi* (Tutzing: Schneider, 1967). For a valuable Beethoven-Clementi comparison, see Miriam Sheer, "A Comparison of Dynamic Practices in Selected Piano Sonatas by Clementi and Beethoven," *Beethoven Forum* 5 (1996): 85-101. It is surprising that a chapter on Clementi's sonatas is lacking in the survey *Eighteenth-Century Keyboard Music*, ed. Robert L. Marshall (New York: Schirmer Books, 1994). Newman, *The Sonata in the Classic Era*, 89, points to Clementi's sonatas, Op. 2 (1779) as anticipating the brilliant piano writing in Beethoven's piano sonatas.

[6] For a summary of these descriptions, see William S. Newman, *Beethoven on Beethoven: Playing His Piano Music His Way* (New York: Norton, 1988), "Beethoven as a Performing Pianist," 76-82. For Neefe's remarks, see 76. For another study regarding the performance of Beethoven's piano music, see George Barth, *The Pianist as Orator: Beethoven and the Transformation of Keyboard Style* (Ithaca and London: Cornell University Press, 1992). Barth, 86-97, points to the many changes of Beethoven's markings of slurs, staccato, and dynamic marks in the incipts of Czerny's *On the Proper Performance*, though many fewer such changes were made in Czerny's editions of the sonatas. The long slurs in *On the Proper Performance* seem to be mainly phrase slurs.

[7] Thayer-Forbes, 641.

Beethoven's activity as pianist extraordinary in Vienna in the 1790s is reflected in the composition of 13 piano sonatas in the short period of seven years, 1793-1800, as well as nine variation sets (1795-1800) and several important chamber works with piano: two Cello Sonatas, Op. 5 (1796), two sets of variations for cello and piano, WoO 45 and Op. 66 (1796), three Violin Sonatas, Op. 12 (1797-98), the Horn Sonata, Op. 17 (1800), three Piano Trios, Op. 1 (1794-95), the Clarinet Trio, Op. 11 (1797), and the Piano Quintet, Op.16 (1796). To these must be added Beethoven's first two Piano Concertos, Op. 15 (1795, rev. 1800) and Op. 19 (c. 1788, rev. 1794-95, 1798).

Of the many descriptions of Beethoven's style of performance, those left by his pupil and friend Carl Czerny are the most revealing. Newman has brought together several remarks by Czerny, some of which are cited below.[8]

> Nobody equaled him in the rapidity of his scales, double trills, skips, etc.—not even Hummel.... He made frequent use of the pedals, much more frequent than is indicated in his works.... Beethoven ... enriched the Piano-forte by new and bold passages, ... by an extraordinary characteristic manner of execution, which was particularly remarkable for the strict Legato of the full chords, and which therefore formed a new kind of melody;—and by many effects not before thought of. His execution did not possess the pure and brilliant elegance of many other Pianists; but on the other hand it was energetic, profound, noble, with all the charms of smooth and connected cantabile and particularly in the Adagio, highly feeling and romantic. His performance, like his Compositions, was a musical painting of the highest class, esteemed only for its general effect.... Whereas Beethoven's playing excelled in extraordinary strength, character, and unprecedented bravura and fluency, Hummel's performance was the model of the highest purity and clarity, the most ingratiating elegance and delicacy.

Before discussing the sonata Op. 10, No. 3, it would be well to add several of Czerny's comments concerning the performance of Beethoven's sonatas.[9] Czerny emphasizes that the sonatas "are written for good and well-cultivated pianists" and not for those with limited pianistic ability. He states that "the general character of Beethoven's works is fervent, grand, energetic, noble, and replete with feeling; often also humorous and sportive, occasionally even eccentric, but always intellectual; and though sometimes gloomy, yet never effeminately elegant or whiningly sentimental." Czerny stresses that each piece "expresses some particular and well supported idea or object" which pervades the music, including embellishments and passagework. Brilliance should never be the object. Czerny further insists that Beethoven's works cannot be altered—no additions or deletions are permitted. Even the limitations of the five-octave piano range in the early works must be respected. In Czerny's "Concluding Remarks," he emphasizes three "important conditions which are indispensably necessary and upon which everything else depends." These are: the correct

---

[8] Newman, *Beethoven on Beethoven*, 78-79.
[9] These remarks are found in Czerny, *On the Proper Performance*, 31-32.

tempo; the "observance of all the marks of expression, which Beethoven particularly in his later works, has very carefully indicated"; and "the thorough mastery of all difficulties."[10] Though these admonitions seem obvious, performances of Beethoven's sonatas and indeed of his works in general still suffer from ill-chosen tempos and the lax observance of performance indications.

Numerous studies of Beethoven's 32 piano sonatas have been written. Newman mentions more than fifty in his chapter on the sonatas included in *The Sonata in the Classic Era*. These studies began appearing in the nineteenth century, the most famous being that by Wilhelm von Lenz, *Beethoven et ses trois styles* (1852), with further details on the sonatas in Lenz's *Kritischer Katalog* (1860). Among the more recent analytical books are those by Donald Francis Tovey (1931) and Jürgen Uhde (1974), Tovey's measure-by-measure analysis remaining a classic. Some books on single sonatas are the important publications by Martha Frohlich on two sonatas, Op. 28 and Op. 57 (the "Appassionata"), both containing transcriptions and analyses of the sketches and autographs as well as the final version; and the famous analyses of the last five Beethoven sonatas by Heinrich Schenker. Two indispensable major studies regarding the performance of Beethoven's piano music have been written by William S. Newman and Sandra P. Rosenblum.[11]

On the Op. 10, No. 3

On 7 July 1798 the piano sonatas Op. 10 were announced for subscription in the Wiener Zeitung as "3 very beautiful clavier sonatas" by the Viennese publisher Joseph Eder. The print itself was advertised on 26 September 1798 in the *Wiener Zeitung*. It was dedicated to one of Beethoven's patrons, the Countess von Browne (1769-1803), to whom Beethoven also dedicated two sets of piano variations, WoO 71 (1797) and WoO 76 (1799).[12] Perhaps because of her early death on 13 May 1803, Beethoven dedicated his set of six Gellert *Lieder*, Op. 48 (1802) to her husband, the Count von Browne, also a Beethoven patron and the dedicatee of four Beethoven works, including the String Trios, Op. 9 and the Piano Sonata, Op. 22.[13]

The sonatas Op. 10 were composed in the order of publication. No. 1 in C minor has been dated ?1795-97, No. 2 in F major 1796-97, and No. 3 in D major 1797-98.[14] The title (in French) states that the sonatas were intended "pour

---

[10] Ibid., 118.

[11] See n. 4 and n.6.

[12] For the facts about this publication, its reprints, arrangements for other media, etc., see the entry in K-H.

[13] Kinsky-Halm states that the Gellert *Lieder* were composed by Beethoven in response to the death of the Countess. However, recent research has shown that the song cycle was completed by March 1802. See Joanna Cobb Biermann, "Cyclical Ordering in Beethoven's Gellert Lieder, Op. 48: A New Source," *Beethoven Forum* 11 (2004): 162-80.

[14] For the dates of the piano sonatas see the Work-list by Douglas Johnson and Scott G. Burnham in the article "Beethoven," *NGD*, 2nd ed., 3: 119-20.

le Clavecin [harpsichord]ou Piano Forte," despite the clearly pianistic idiom of the music. This designation, which was certainly added for commercial purposes to reach the greatest number of buyers, appears in the titles for most first editions of Beethoven's piano sonatas until Op. 28, excepting Opp. 14 and 22. The sonatas were reprinted in Vienna, many German cities, Paris, London, and even Stockholm (No. 2/II in a music journal). Most of the arrangements of these works were made for string quartet, No. 3 arranged by Beethoven's pupil, friend, and early biographer Ferdinand Ries (published in 1835).

Gross Form

Of the three sonatas Op. 10, Nos. 1 and 2 are the first mature Beethoven sonatas in three movements, the preceding four sonatas being in four movements, as well as Op. 10, No. 3. While Op. 10, No. 1 is standard in its fast-slow-fast succession, No. 2 already deviates in replacing the usual slow movement with an extended minuet-like movement plus trio, a format repeated in Op. 14, No. 1.

The four-movement plan for the Beethoven sonatas appears to be an innovation, applying to the sonata the broader plan associated with the string quartet and symphony, and thus making the sonata a more imposing work.[15] The same transfer was made in Beethoven's Op. 1 Piano Trios, another innovation since piano trios were normally in three and even two movements. There are seventeen such four-movement piano, violin, and cello sonatas, and five piano trios (see Table 2.1).

Table 2.1 Chronological List of Beethoven's Four-Movement Piano, Violin, and Cello Sonatas, and Piano Trios

Op. 2, Nos. 1-3	1793-95
Op. 7	1796-97
Op. 10, No. 3	1797-98
Op. 22	1800
Op. 24 (violin)	1800-01
Op. 26	1800-01
Op. 27, No. 1	1801
Op. 28	1801
Op. 30, No. 2 (violin)	1801-02
Op. 31, No. 3	1802
Op. 69 (cello)	1807-08
Op. 96 (violin)	1812

---

[15] Two very early Haydn keyboard sonatas in four movements should not be considered as precursors of Beethoven's four-movement plan. There are two sonatas in G, one with very short movements (Hob. XVI: 8 and Christa Landon [CL] No. 1), and another with substantial movements (Hob. XVI: 6 and CL No. 13). Both sonatas are dated ?1760. In both cases the minuet (with trio in CL No. 13) is the second movement and the slow movement is third. Somfai considers these examples to be influenced by the suite and calls them "partita" sonatas. See László Somfai, *The Keyboard Sonatas of Joseph Haydn* (Chicago and London: University of Chicago Press, 1995), 156-57. Undoubtedly other scattered four-movement sonatas exist in the later eighteenth century as well. Clementi wrote his sole four-movement Piano Sonata, Op. 40, No. 1, only much later in 1802. See Alan Tyson, *Thematic Catalogue of the Works of Muzio Clementi*.

Op. 101	1816
Op. 106	1817-18
Op. 110	1821-22
Piano Trios	
Op. 1, Nos. 1-3	1794-95
Op. 70, No. 2	1808
Op. 97	1810-11

Most examples fall into the early and early middle periods, but three occur within the five late piano sonatas. The late cello sonata in C, Op. 102 (1815) is an anomaly, since it contains two fast movements, each preceded by a slow movement or introduction, the second recalling and varying the first. However, its experimental arrangement reflects the many changes Beethoven made in the cycle, and especially the four-movement cycle in the middle and particularly late periods. One change, placing the Scherzo as the second movement, has a precedent in the placement of the minuet as movement II in string quartets and quintets in earlier years by Haydn and Mozart, though it does not occur in late Haydn quartets. This reversal appears in Op. 26, Op. 27, No. 1, Op. 69, Op. 97, Op. 101, Op. 106, and Op. 110 (and it is found in most of the late quartets, including Op. 132 (see Ch. 4). Several works also join two of the movements via half cadences or modulation, a feature of the late quartets as well: Op. 27, No. 1, Op. 96, Op. 97, Op. 101, with a recall of the opening of the first movement, and Op. 106, with a fantasy-like section connecting the slow movement with the fugue *finale*. Most works bind the slow with the final movement, though in Op. 96 the slow movement links with the Scherzo (see the discussion in Ch. 3). Such connected movements become a feature of Beethoven's string quartets from Op. 59 onward (1806). Other special features include the recall of the slow movement before the coda of Op. 27, No. 1/IV, and the intertwining of the slow *Arioso* and fugue *finale* in Op. 110 (see Ch. 4, Table 4.24).

Several other aspects of Op. 10, No. 3 depart from standard Classic practice (see Table 2.2). The *Presto* tempo of the first movement is a most unusual choice since the fastest movement was usually the last. Certainly few sonatas start at such a high rate of speed. As a result the sonata opens with an unusual burst of energy. This very fast movement in cut time is then followed by a very slow movement: *Largo e mesto*. Considerable tension therefore comes from the juxtaposition of these extreme tempos. In the eleven tempo lists given by Neal Zaslaw that date from 1756 to 1828, all but two place *Largo* as slower than *Adagio*.[16] According to Koch's *Musikalisches: Lexikon* (1802), the term *Largo* "indicates the most familiar slow tempo, which accommodates itself only to those

---

[16] See Neal Zaslaw, "Mozart's Tempo Conventions," in *International Musicological Society, Report of the Eleventh Congress Copenhagen 1972*, ed. Henrik Glahn, Søren Sørensen, and Peter Ryom, vol. 2 (Copenhagen: Wilhelm Hansen, 1974), 720-33.

Table 2.2 The Piano Sonata, Op. 10, No. 3: Gross Form

Movement	Key	Tempo	Meter	Length in mm.	Form
I	D	*Presto*	c	344	sonata form, exposition repeated 124+220 (59/114/47)
II	d	*Largo e Mesto*	6/8	87	non-repeating sonata form 29+58 (14/21/23)
III	D, G	*Menuetto Allegro*	3/4	54-32	large A-B-A *da capo* "senza replica" Menuetto: rounded binary, A-B-A^1 16+39 (8/19/11) Trio: A-A^1 16+16
IV	D	*Rondo Allegro*	c	113	multicouplet rondo A- B- A- C- A^1-D- A^2-Coda 8 16 8 23 8 20 8 22

*In sonata-form and rounded-binary movements, the measures indicated for part II refer to the lengths of the development, recapitulation, and coda sections.

sentiments that should be expressed with solemn slowness."[17] At the end of his his remarks Koch asserts that pieces in this tempo should be short, because it is hard for the listener to sustain concentration on the music, advice that Beethoven clearly ignored. On the other hand, Koch described an *Adagio* as "moderately slow" (*mässig langsam*). Four other early *Largo* movements, all in major, appear in the Piano Trio, Op. 1, No. 2, the Piano Sonatas, Op. 2, No. 2, and Op. 7, and the First Piano Concerto, Op. 15. In later instrumental works, only five *Largo* markings occur: for the brief opening phrase in the D-minor Piano Sonata, Op. 31, No. 2; the slow movements of the Third Piano Concerto, Op. 37, and Triple Concerto, Op. 56, and the Piano Trio, Op. 70, No. 1; and the initial section of the fantasy-like transition to the fugue *finale* of the Piano Sonata, Op. 106. As we see, most appearances of this tempo are fairly early and in major keys. However, the appearances in minor occur strangely enough in D minor, the other full movement being the *Largo* in Op. 70, No. 1 (1808), the "Ghost" trio, and there the tempo is even slower, a *Largo assai*. The standard slow movement in Beethoven's instrumental music is some kind of *Adagio,* not *Andante* , which was most common in Classic music before Beethoven.

The choice of the tonic minor for the slow movement here and in the later Piano Trio is also unconventional. The use of the tonic minor for slow movements often occurred in the early Classic period, but in later Classic music, the

---

[17] Translation from Ratner, *CM*, 183.

minor was a fairly rare option for a slow movement, and, if used, was the relative minor, not tonic minor (as in Haydn's Symphony No. 103, 1795). Most composers preferred to retain the major, the key of the subdominant or dominant.[18]

In Beethoven's early piano sonatas, however, most slow or middle movements already show a preference for tonic minor or third relationships—the mediant or submediant keys. Of the eleven early piano sonatas only three utilize the subdominant major key for slow movements (Op. 2, No. 2, Op. 14, No. 2, Op. 22), and the last such examples can be found only in the piano sonatas Op. 31, Nos. 1 and 3 (1802). So far as third relationships are concerned, the composer who served as Beethoven's model was Haydn, in many of his works of the 1790s.[19]

The forms of each movement also require some comment. The first movement, in sonata form with a repeat of the exposition, constitutes a standard first movement type. The slow movement in 6/8 has a non-repeating sonata form, the omission of the exposition repeat undoubtedly due to its very slow tempo and considerable length. Examples of this formal type go back to the early Classic period in both fast and slow movements. Only one other early slow movement in the piano sonatas has this organization, the *Adagio con molto espressione* of Op. 22, also in compound meter, there 9/8. The fact is, most slow movements in Beethoven's piano sonatas are not in sonata form but rondo form, exposition-recap form (sonata form without development, as in Op. 2, No. 1, and Op. 10, No. 1), ABA form, and theme and variations. After Op. 22, the next slow movement in non-repeating sonata form in the piano sonatas appears in the extraordinary *Adagio* of Op. 106, also in minor and 6/8, as in Op. 10, No. 3, although much longer and far more complex.

The third movement here is a lyrical minuet, a special type in Beethoven's largely early piano sonatas, found as well in Op. 7 (though not called a minuet), Op. 22, and Op. 31, No. 3. While the minuet is a typical two-reprise rounded binary form, it is the Trio in G major that is uniquely treated. It comprises only the first part of a binary form, repeated in slight variation. This musical joke, rarely mentioned by analysts, exemplifies Beethoven's often freer treatment of the minuet/scherzo-trio movement.[20]

Another unexpected format appears in the rondo *finale* of Op. 10, No. 3. Six of the eight *finales* in the early piano sonatas are sonata-rondos (found in Op. 2, Nos. 2 and 3, Op. 7, Op. 13, Op. 14, No. 1, and Op. 22). Two rondos are multicouplet, containing three, not two couplets, and in Op. 14, No. 2, without a sonata-form exposition or recapitulation. These movements, the *finales* of

---

[18] This tendency has been thoroughly documented for the Viennese symphony in Eliyahu Greenzweig, "A Survey of Keys in Symphonies and Slow Movements in the 18th-century Viennese Symphony, *Min-Ad* (2006), II: 112-41 (electronic journal).
[19] See Douglas Johnson, "1794-1795: Decisive Years in Beethoven's Early Development," in Alan Tyson, ed., *Beethoven Studies* 3 (Cambridge: Cambridge University Press, 1982): 1-28.
[20] See especially the discussion in Chapter 4 of the Trio in the String Quartet, Op. 132/II.

Op. 10, No. 3 and the less complex example in Op. 14, No. 2, make the overall pattern A-B-A-C-A-D-A-coda. Four additional multicouplet rondos appear in works of the Bonn and earlier Vienna years. These are the rondo in the keyboard sonata WoO 47, No. 1/III (?1783), the A-major rondo WoO 49 (1783), the famous "Rondo a capriccio," Op. 129 (1795, with six couplets), and the rondo in the Horn Sonata, Op. 17/III (1800).[21] For Beethoven's sonata-rondos in the middle and late periods, see the discussions in chapters 1 and 4.

A final consideration of the cycle concerns the succession of movements and moods. The cycle has sometimes been criticized as unbalanced: two long, well developed and dramatic movements followed by two movements of lesser complexity and lighter expression. Most insistent on this point was the nineteenth-century commentator Ernst von Elterlein, especially in the 1875 English translation of his book on the Beethoven sonatas, first published in 1857, which seems to have exaggerated his ideas about the movement.[22] In the English translation, Elterlein is quoted as saying that regarding the Minuet and Trio,

> granting that psychological correctness requires that brightness and light should follow the night . . . still it seems to me that the movement . . . has too much of this light . . . I miss the working up of the ruling thought.

About the finale, Elterlein complained that

> the tone and . . . whole . . . appear to me too light and fleeting and the humour too shallow to feel that there is any conclusive inward unity, or to find in it an adequate conclusion of the whole.

In the earlier German edition, he was less critical of the finale, finding that it was "especially original" as is the "first motive," and "extremely lively" [*höchst lebendig*]. However, he still complained that the sonata lacks "unity of expression" and the "organic development of a basic mood" [*Der Sonate fehlt nach Allem Einheit des Ausdrucks, organische Entwicklung Einer Grundstimmung*]. He felt that the sonata broke into two parts, movements I-II and III-IV. Both developed a unity "but not in their combination."[23]

A. B. Marx, in his 1859 study of Beethoven's *Life and Works*, considered the sonata to be a great work. He wrote:

---

[21] See Malcolm S. Cole, "The Development of the Instrumental Rondo Finale from 1750 to 1800" (Ph. D. diss., Princeton University, 1964), 234-35. See also his discussion of the Beethoven rondos until 1800, 232-47. Cole, 244, incorrectly lists the rondo of Op. 10, No. 3, as a sonata-rondo despite the lack of a sonata-form recapitulation. He considers the third episode to be an extension of the recapitulation despite its modulatory and developmental character, probably because of the return of T in the tonic. The movement is also listed as a sonata-rondo in Cole's valuable article, "Techniques of Surprise in the Sonata-Rondos of Beethoven," 237. For other articles on the rondo by Cole, see Ch. 1, n. 67.

[22] Ernst von Elterlein [pseud. for Ernst Gottschald], *Beethoven's Pianoforte Sonatas Explained for the Lovers of the Musical Art*, trans. Emily Hill, Preface E. Pauer (London: W. Reeves, 1875), 45-46.

[23] *Beethoven's Clavier-Sonaten für Freunde der Tonkunst eiläutert*, Zweite Auflage (Leipzig: Heinrich Matthes, 1857), 47-48.

According to meaning and significance we have here the first grand sonata of Beethoven before us, even if it is not so called, a creation from a master's hand and poet's spirit.[24]

Marx's observations on the movements of the sonata give the greatest number of details about the first movement but Marx treats each movement with sympathy, emphasizing the moods of movements II-IV. In the second edition of his book, published only four years later, however, Marx altered some of his discussion of the sonata. He includes new remarks, stating that there is a harsh break between movements I and II, and that the *Largo* does not belong with movements I, III, and IV. The first and second movements in Op. 10, No. 2 "stand in a clear psychological relationship," but this is not true for Op. 10, No. 3.[25]

Wilhelm von Lenz, in his study of the Beethoven piano sonatas, *Beethoven et ses trois styles* (1852), has mostly praise for Op. 10, No. 3, which he rightly describes as one of Beethoven's most symphonic sonatas; this is especially true of the *Largo*. Lenz highly values the *finale* as one of Beethoven's "most extravagant" movements, one that has the "character of the second manner." However, he feels the Trio does not seem to belong to the Menuetto.[26]

A few years later, in his *Kritischer Katalog* (1860),[27] Lenz quotes a communication from Anton Schindler of 1856, claiming to convey "Beethoven's purpose concerning the number of movements" in Op. 10, No. 3. Schindler maintains that "according to Beethoven's teaching" the Largo and fourth movement "stand in an inner relationship." He implies therefore that the Menuetto is actually unnecessary because it "weakens the effect of the fourth movement that comes too late." However, since Schindler was in contact with Beethoven from only1822, and he is a proven liar, it is doubtful that this conception stems from the composer.[28] Schindler also sent a detailed description regarding the performance of the finale. Lenz then goes on to quote a letter from a friend, Hugo Dingelstädt in Odessa, of May 1856, which defends the inclusion of the Menuetto and offers a long description of the sonata's expressive program, ending with the following expressive summary for each movement:

I Life's high spirits [*Lebensübermuth*]
II Presentiment of death [*Todesahnung*]

---

[24] A. B. Marx, *Ludwig van Beethoven, Leben und Schaffen* (Berlin, 1859; facs. reprint Hildesheim: Georg Olms, 1979), 134-36, quotation on 134.

[25] A. B. Marx, *Ludwig van Beethoven, Leben und Schaffen*, rev. ed., vol. I (Berlin: Otto Janke, 1863), 160-63. The text of this edition was reprinted several times.

[26] Wilhelm von Lenz, *Beethoven et ses trois styles*, new ed. by M. S. Calvocoressi (Paris: Legouix, 1909), 159-61, quotations on 160, 159.

[27] Wilhelm von Lenz, *Beethoven, eine Kunst-Studie. Kritischer Katalog sämtlicher Werke Ludwig van Beethovens mit Analysen derselben*, Erster Theil, 2nd rev. ed. (Hamburg: Hoffmann & Co., 1860), 120-25. Cited hereafter as *Kritischer Katalog*. "Die blaue Schleife" seems to refer to youthful love (see 123-24).

[28] For a recent study of the Schindler problem see Helga Lühning, "Das Schindler- und das Beethoven-Bild," *Bonner Beethoven-Studien* 2 (2001): 183-99.

III The blue ribbon (*Die blaue Schleife*)

IV Fresh blossoms, fresh life (*Frisches Blüthen, frisches Leben*)

Most other discussions and analyses of the sonata by well-known writers do not consider at all the sharp expressive contrasts of the movements. Czerny (1846) describes the sonata as "grand and significant" (*gross und bedeutend*) and makes no mention of problems regarding the cycle as a whole.[29] Even in the late nineteenth-century commentary by the distinguished pianist and composer Carl Reinecke there is no mention of this aspect.[30] Similarly, no such discussion occurs in analyses by Tovey, Rosenberg, and Uhde.[31] Only a passing remark can be found in Riezler: the third movement "seems like sunshine after clouds."[32]

We may consider that the third movement has a bridging function. The Menuetto still connects via its lyricism and rich harmony with the *Largo*, while the rollicking Trio anticipates humorous elements in the rondo, both sections asserting the life force by making a steep ascent away from the gloom of the *Largo*. In several later examples of tragic slow movements in minor, such as the *Adagios* in the String Quartet, Op. 59, No. 1, and the Piano Sonata, Op. 106, the *scherzando* or scherzo movement comes before, not after, the slow movement. In fact, the late sonata fugues follow and resolve the tragic expression in preceding slow movements, as we see in the Piano Sonatas Opp. 106 and 110, and the Cello Sonata, Op. 102, No. 2. In works after the early period, final movements in cycles with tragic slow movements are substantial and serious. We need not refer to all examples to see that a cycle with this kind of slow movement posed a special problem to which Beethoven gave various solutions. In the String Quartet, Op. 132, how to follow the great meditative *Adagio*, the "Heilige Dankgesang," though it was not a movement in minor also presented a considerable challenge to the composer (see Ch. 4).

Aspects of Performance Practice

We know more about performance practice with relation to Beethoven's piano music than to any other genre. Two remarkable studies cover the subject in great depth—the studies by William S. Newman and Sandra P. Rosenblum.[33]

---

[29] Czerny, *On the Proper Performance*, 41-42, quotation on 41. Czerny, of course, takes for granted the excellence of Beethoven's music and is concerned primarily with aspects of performance (see my comments below on performance practice).

[30] Carl Reinecke, *Beethoven'schen Clavier-Sonaten* (Leipzig, 1895; 2nd ed. Leipzig: Gebrüder Reinecke, 1897), 26-29.

[31] See Donald Francis Tovey, *A Companion to Beethoven's Pianoforte Sonatas* (London: Associated Board of the Royal Schools of Music, 1931); Richard Rosenberg, *Die Klaviersonaten Ludwig van Beethovens*, vol. 1 (Olten and Lausanne: Urs-Graf Verlag, 1957); and Jürgen Uhde, *Beethovens Klaviermusik*, vol. 2 (Stuttgart: Reclam Jun., 1974).

[32] Walter Riezler, *Beethoven*, with an introduction by Wilhelm Fürtwängler, trans. G. D. H. Pidcock (New York, 1938; reprint New York: Vienna House, 1972), p. 118.

[33] These are the most comprehensive and reliable studies yet published.

The following remarks pertain largely to the notation of staccato marks and to early metronome marks that specify tempo preferences for all movements from the generation after Beethoven.

Staccato Marks

Beethoven's autographs show a simple type of notation for staccato marks. The composer uses staccato lines for unslurred staccatos or staccatos found at the end of a slurred figure. The lines indicate a sharper, shorter type of staccato effect. In contrast, staccato dots are notated with slurred groups of notes to indicate a softer, longer, portato effect. Many of the contemporary printed editions do not reflect Beethoven's notation. However, the first edition of this sonata follows Beethoven's preferences, though it uses staccato wedges rather than lines.[34] That Beethoven consciously differentiated the staccato marks is shown by his comments in a letter of 15 August 1825 regarding the importance of this differentiation to Karl Holz and the copyist Rampl, who were copying the parts for the String Quartet, Op. 132.[35] This system of notation began early in Beethoven's career. It can be found c. 1790-92 in the autograph of Beethoven's *Variationen über ein Schweitzer Lied*, WoO 64.[36] In examining many Beethoven autographs, I have not found any great confusion in the notation of staccatos as many commentators have mentioned. One exception, however, where Beethoven does notate staccato dots for unslurred passages, occurs in a soft staccato passage in the Fourth Symphony, first movement, development, mm. 245-47.[37]

No autograph has survived for Op. 10, No. 3. The earliest extant autograph of a piano sonata is that of Op. 26, published in a facsimile edition in 1895. If we examine the first edition of Op. 10, No. 3 in all movements except the *Largo*, only staccato strokes appear, the Trio of the Menuetto being a good example of the slur ending with a staccato stroke (here a wedge). It is the *Largo* where both types of staccatos are printed, sometimes within the same measure, as in measure 10 (see Plate 2.II, p.130). The unslurred staccato dots in m. 16 are an enngraver's error and were corrected in the recapitulation (m. 55) as wedges.

Metronome Marks

Beethoven was greatly concerned in his later years with establishing the correct tempo for his works. He embraced the possibilities of Mälzel's metronome with enthusiasm and published metronome marks for all his symphonies, the

---

[34] The edition I have used, reproduced in the Tecla collection of first editions, comes from the Nationalbibliothek, Vienna, Musiksammlung, Hoboken collection, S. H. Beethoven 46.

[35] See Ch. IV, p. 287, and n. 9 regarding the letter and its contents. For a survey of theoretical sources and their confusion on this subject, see Rosenblum, *Performance Practices*,183-89, and Newman, 139-46, with several reproductions of autograph passages.

[36] See the reproduction of the theme in the autograph given in Robert Bory, *Ludwig van Beethoven, His Life and Work in Pictures*, trans. from the French by Winifred Glass and Hans Rosenwald (New York: Atlantis Books, 1960), 42.

[37] See my new edition of the Fourth Symphony (London, Mainz: Eulenburg No. 414/6820, 1998).

string quartets through Op. 95, and for several other works. However, he left metronome marks for only one piano sonata, the "Hammerklavier," Op. 106.[38] Thus, with regard to the piano sonatas, musicians can only turn to metronome marks left by Beethoven's friends after his death, Carl Czerny (1791-1857) and Ignaz Moscheles (1794-1870). Czerny studied piano with Beethoven in 1801-02. He remained in Vienna all his life, active as a performer, teacher, theorist, arranger, and composer. He therefore had the opportunity to hear Beethoven perform his piano music and to play various sonatas for the composer himself. He also gave one of the early performances of the Fifth Piano Concerto, Op. 73, in 1812.[39] Moscheles was a brilliant pianist as well as a composer and an important conductor of Beethoven's music. He was in Vienna in 1808-14, and in 1814 was commissioned for a piano-vocal score of Beethoven's newly revised opera *Fidelio*, a score he made under Beethoven's direction. After leaving Vienna, Moscheles concertized widely but settled in England from 1825, moving to Leipzig in 1846. He remains a significant figure in the history of Beethoven performance and reception.[40]

There are six sets of metronome marks for most of Beethoven's piano sonatas published by these musicians, sets that date c. 1828-c. 1868. The tables below list the sources for each and the various metronome marks for each movement.[41]

Table 2.3 Sources of Metronome Marks for the Beethoven Piano Sonatas

A.   Carl Czerny: in *Sämtliche Werke von Ludw. van Beethoven*, published in Vienna by Tobias Haslinger, announced December 1828; first state published by 1831

B.   Czerny: as above, second state, mid-late 1830s-1842

C.   Czerny: *On the Proper Performance*, 1846

D.   Czerny: edition of Beethoven's piano sonatas published by Simrock in Bonn, 1856-68

E.   Ignaz Moscheles: edition of Beethoven's piano sonatas published by Cramer in London between c. 1834 and 1838-39

F.   Moscheles: edition of Beethoven's sonatas published by Hallberger in Stuttgart between 1858? and 1867

---

[38] For a summary of Beethoven's involvement with the metronome, see Rosenblum, *Performance Practices*, "Beethoven and the Metronome," 323-29. See also Newman, *Beethoven on Beethoven*, Ch. 4, "Tempo Rate and Flexibility," 83-120.

[39] A relevant portion of Czerny's "Memoirs" (*Errinerungen aus meinen Leben*) and his "Anecdotes and Notes about Beethoven" (*Anekdoten und Notizen über Beethoven*) are available in German and English translation in the editions of *On the Proper Performance*.

[40] See the articles on Moscheles in *NGD* and *MGG*, and *Recent Music and Musicians as Described in the Diaries and Correspondence of Ignaz Moscheles*, edited by his wife and adapted from the original German by A. D. Coleridge (New York, 1873; reprint New York: Da Capo Press, 1970).

[41] The sources and sets of metronome marks come from Rosenblum, *Performanc Practices*, 329-33 and 356. Her Appendix (Ch. 9, 355-61) lists all the available metronome marks for all the piano sonatas established by Czerny and Moscheles.

Table 2.4 Metronome Marks for Op. 10, No. 3, by Czerny and Moscheles

SOURCES			A	B	C	D	E	F
Presto	¢	𝅗𝅥 = 152		132	126	132	132	132
Largo e mesto	6/8	♪ = 66		76	72	76	72	72
Menuetto, Allegro	3/4	𝅗𝅥. = 84		80	76	84	84	84
Allegro	c	𝅗𝅥 = 160		152	152	152	152	152

Newman refers to modern recordings of the sonata, in which the *Largo* is slower than the tempo indicated by Czerny and Moscheles. He remarks that the tempo in a performance by Anton Kuerti (1976) is ♪= 54 and other recordings of the movement average ♪= 60, including a recording by Alfred Brendel.[42]

This writer compared the performances of Malcolm Bilson on a rebuilt Schantz piano of c. 1800 to that of Artur Schnabel on a modern piano.[43] Both pianists have a large range of tempo in each movement. As expected, Schnabel's eloquent *Largo* is extremely slow, mainly ♪ = 40s, though the suggested tempo in Schnabel's edition of the sonata is ♪= 63, still lower than the early sets except for Source A. Both performers speed up at the end of movements I and IV and rush the opening phrase of the first movement. Bilson also performs the *Largo* with considerable *rubato*, following too literally Czerny's advice that "the effect must be also increased by a well directed *ritardando* and *accelerando*."[44]

AN EARLY REVIEW OF THE SONATA

An anonymous review of the three piano sonatas Op. 10 was published in the *AmZ* 2 (9 October 1799: 25-27).[45] This is the earliest review of Beethoven's piano sonatas in the famous music journal published by Breitkopf & Härtel in Leipzig, a journal that Beethoven read and commented on in his letters. While the reviews of many other early works by Beethoven, such as the piano variations and the Violin Sonatas, Op. 12, were quite negative, this review mixes negative with primarily positive remarks.

---

[42] See Newman, 107. The Brendel recording is on Philips 6500 417. Kuerti's recordings of all the 32 piano sonatas and the Diabelli variations were issued by Don Mills (Ontario), Acquitaine Records, 1976.

[43] The Bilson recording was made in 1996, and the Schnabel recording on 12 December 1935. Bilson's recording belongs to a set of 10 CDs with performances of all the Beethoven piano sonatas (including WoO 47) by Bilson and his students on contemporary instruments. The set was issued in 1997 by Claves CD 898125.

[44] See Czerny, *On the Proper Performance*, 42. Czerny suggests *accelerandos* in the second half of mm. 23 and 27, all of m. 28, and in mm. 71-75. He gives no specific references to *ritardandos*. For remarks concerning the use of the pedal in this sonata, see David Rowland, *Early Keyboard Instruments: A Practical Guide* (Cambridge: Cambridge University Press, 2001), 107-08.

[45] *The Critical Reception of Beethoven's Compositions by His German Contemporaries*, Wayne M. Senner, general ed., compiler, and trans., Robin Wallace and William Meredith, musicological eds., vol. I (Lincoln and London: University of Nebraska Press, in association with the American Beethoven Society and the Ira F. Brilliant Center for Beethoven Studies, San José State University, 1999), 142-44.

In the unfavorable comments, the reviewer makes the usual objections to Beethoven's

> abundance of ideas . . . [which] too often still causes him to pile up ideas without restraint and to arrange them by means of a bizarre manner. . . .

The critic complained about harshness of harmony, and writing for the piano occasionally in organ style. On the other hand, he starts his review by calling Beethoven "a man of genius, [who] has originality and goes entirely his own way." He ranks Beethoven as "among the best keyboard composers and performers of our time." He finally speaks about the Op. 10 set and praises it for

> good invention, [an] earnest, manly style, well-ordered and connected thoughts, well-maintained character in every part, difficulties not carried to excess, and an entertaining treatment of harmony. . . .

The reviewer observes that in the "fundamentals of feeling . . . this manly style bears a certain similarity to the characteristics of Phil. Em. Bach's style," though "our present manner of writing . . . departs much from Bach's choppy style."[46]

The only reference to a specific sonata is to the coda of Op. 10, No. 3, *finale*; though the sonata is not identified, the key signature indicates to the reader that it is No. 3. The reviewer starts from mm. 99-101 with a quotation of the basic motive in G major and minor, and follows it with the next passage in harmonic reduction (without barlines), described as the "important harmony in syncopated motion" that "brought him much joy." A description of the final measures of the coda concludes the review.

On the whole, the reviewer is remarkably perceptive regarding Beethoven's achievement in his early compositional phrase.

The First Movement: *Presto*

Growth

The overall proportions of the movement reflect both Beethoven's early preferences and later features. The large scale of 344 mm. makes the movement one of the longest in the early period and illustrates the tendency toward expansion found in many works throughout Beethoven's lifetime. Typical of the early period, however, is the relatively short development section of 59 mm., less than half the length of the exposition of 124 mm., and the same proportion as the development section of the *Largo*. This proportion is closer to Mozart than to Haydn. While the recapitulation is only slightly shorter than the exposition, 114

---

[46] Beethoven knew well Bach's treatise *Versuch über die wahre Art das Clavier zu spielen* (1753, 1762), and admired and copied his music. In a letter to Breitkopf & Härtel of 26 July 1809, he requested copies of Bach's music, noting "I have only a few samples of Emanuel Bach's compositions for clavier; and yet some of them should certainly be in the possession of every true artist, not only for the sake of real enjoyment but also for the purpose of study"(Anderson, I, No. 220; see also *BGA* 2, No. 392).

PIANO SONATA

mm., the movement contains a long and significant coda of 47 mm. In fact, all the main movements have large codas, a Beethoven hallmark and a unifying element in the sonata as a whole (see also p. 182). The length and richness of the movement give it a symphonic cast.

This rich monothematic movement contains an exposition of thirteen

Table 2.5 Timeline: Movement I

Key: D   Meter: c

	(a)			(Pa)		(2m,1m^5)			(1Ta^1, 1m^5)		
exp.	Pa	b	b^1	PT	1Ta	a^1		2Ta		a^1
	0^4	4^4	10^4	16 16^4	22 22^4	26^4		30 30^4		35
				D:I	b:V			f$_s$: i		mod.- A

(1m^5)	(3T. 1m^5)	(1m^5, 1T, 4T)	(2m)				(1m)	(2S, 1m)	(a)
3T	4T	1Sa	b	a^1	b^1	2S	STa	b
38$^{1.5}$	45	53 53^3	56^3	60^3	63^3	65 66^4	70^4	74^4
		A:I	a		a:V	A	A,D	C, d,Bf

(1m)				(1m)		(1m)		(3K,1m)	
c	1Ka	a^1	a^2	2Ka	a^1	3Ka	ax	KT	:‖
85^3	93$^{1.4}$	97$^{1.4}$	101$^{1.4}$	105^1 105^3	109^3	113$^{1.4}$	117^4	119^4	
A	A:I ped.			A:I		A:I ped.		D:V	

					(3m)	(4T)				(1Tm)
dev.	KT^1	Pa^1	1Kar	1Kar^1	Par	Nb	Par	Nb^1	Par^1	Nc
	124^4	128^4	133	137	141	145	149	153	157	161
	d	V	fVI=Bf			mod.-g g		mod.-Ef Ef -d	d	

(Par, Pa)		(1m^1)		
RTa	a^1	b		
167	171^2	175	183	
V ped.- 176		D:V ped. 179-83^3	V$^6_5$	

		(Pb^1)							
rec.	Pa b	NPTa	a^1	b		1T^1	2T	3T^1	4T^1
	183^4 187^4	193^4	197^4	201	204	204^4	212^4	220$^{1.5}$	225 233
		mod.-e		e:V ped. V		e-b	b-D		D:I

1Sa	b^2	a^1	b^3	2S	STa	b	c	1K^1	2K^1	ext.
233^3	236^3	240^3	243^3	246 247^4	251^4	255^4	266^3	274$^{1.4}$	286^1 286^3	294
		d		d:V D	D,G	F-g-Ef	D	D:I ped. D:I		mod.-G
					(1m)	(1m^{10})	(1m^{11})		(b^2)	

coda	3K^1	KT^{2}a	a^1	a^2	KT^{3}a	b	Pa^1	b^2	b$^{2.1}$	c ‖
	298$^{1.4}$	305^4	309^4	313^4	316^4	320^4	327$^{1.4}$	333$^{1.3}$	337^3	341 344mm.
	G:I ped.	G	g		Ef:V^7	V ped.	D	D:I ped. to end		

functions (see the timeline, Table 2.5). The longest sections comprise the transition (30-1/2 mm.), the developmental episode between S and K which I call ST (23 mm.), and the closing, K section needed to stabilize the key after the tonal excursions of ST (26 mm.). Several special features of the movement as a whole comprise the lyrical 1T, the developmental episode between S and K, and the continuity of exposition-development and recapitulation-coda.

The lyrical 1T appears in the relative minor, B minor, ending in F♯ minor (the keys are a fifth below in the recapitulation). As the only lyrical element in the movement, it must have confused Beethoven's early listeners (see Ex. 2.1g). Some analysts have even called this theme a secondary theme, despite its "wrong" key and tonal instability.[47] Other such lyrical 1T themes occur in the first movements of Beethoven's early piano sonatas, Op. 2, No. 3, and Op. 14, No. 2. A precedent for lyrical T themes may be found in Mozart, as in the piano sonatas K. 457/I (mm. 23-30^2) and K. 570/I (mm. 23-34).

The lyricism of 1T in this movement is enhanced by its presentation in a texture of melody and accompaniment, with a fast-moving left hand in eighths offsetting the formal melody above. Further, the regular phrase structure of 4+4 measures supports its theme-like status. The theme appears almost in final form in Beethoven's early continuity draft of the exposition (where it is even repeated; see the discussion of the sketches below). It is thus an essential part of Beethoven's conception of the movement.

Another essential component, the developmental episode, is also notated in condensed form in the early draft. Though it would seem to be a rare device, other tonally unstable periods occur between S and K in such works as the Piano Sonata, Op. 7/I (mm. 81^2-92), the Violin Sonata, Op.12, No. 1/I (1798; mm. 58-96), and the first Symphony, Op. 21/I (1800; mm. 77-87). Some precedents can be found in Haydn and Mozart, as in Mozart's Symphony No. 40, K. 550/I (1788; mm. 58-66^1), a work Beethoven knew well.[48] A last extraordinary example occurs in the third movement of the late String Quartet, Op. 130. None of Beethoven's other early examples have the developmental intensity of ST in Op. 10, No. 3. Just as in Op. 130/III, we may describe this section as a parenthesis, a "detour" in the normal succession of thematic functions and the expected behavior of the tonal layout.[49] Using the basic four-note motive of the start of P (1m) in the bass and then in a mirror setting between the bass and an upper voice, the section is spun out in the keys of A-D-C-d-B♭-A. Of the non-tonic

---

[47] Rosenberg, *Die Klaviersonaten*, 99, falls into this trap. Janet Levy explains the norm in her searching article, "Texture as a Sign in Classic and Early Romantic Music," *JAMS* 35 (1982): 490, "... the beginning of a regular accompaniment pattern cues us to what we will *not* hear. The passage is not likely to be the beginning of a transition, for example...."

[48] In early 1808 Beethoven copied a part of the development section, mm. 148-76, from Mozart's K. 550/IV. See my article, "Beethoven and Mozart's Requiem, A New Connection," *JM* 5 (1987): 476.

[49] See my article, "The *Andante con moto* in Beethoven's String Quartet Op. 130: The Final Version and Changes on the Autograph," *JM* 16 (1998): 232-33. Here, the parenthesis has features of an S theme in chromatic third relationships.

keys most significant in relation to the movement as a whole are D minor and the Neapolitan B♭ though we should note the use of the key of C major, which is ♭III, a distant third relation. After the key of B♭ ending in the high register, the motive is extended down in the left hand from $b♭^2$ to A, and doubled in octaves as the tonic returns dramatically. The thick chords in the right hand, each *sf*, the *crescendo*, and the *ff* dynamic at the cadence make the conclusion of this section the climax of the exposition.

A third special feature concerns the continuity between the exposition and development, the recapitulation and coda. Thus, 3K, featuring a dialogue of the bass and treble with 1m and its variant in the treble, modulates back to the tonic with 1m on V in *pp* and a one-voice texture. This KT unit both connects back to the start of the exposition and makes a bridge to the development that starts with Pa in the tonic minor, creating a V-I progression in both cases. Such transitions from the end of the exposition using P material are common in Beethoven's works. Two obvious examples occur in the early Piano Sonata, Op. 14, No. 1/I (1798-99) and the first movement of the *Eroica* Symphony (1803). Another more daring and ambiguous connection occurs at the end of the recapitulation. Beethoven extends the chordal 2K theme into G major, together with a four-measure *crescendo* ending *forte*. 3K then follows in G major, *pp* as in the exposition. Thus, the recapitulation material concludes in the subdominant. Where does the coda begin, with 3K in G or with the extension of 2K? In my timeline, the coda begins with 3K in G since Beethoven has left the tonic key only to return to it near the end of the section. This deliberate ambiguity, a thematic but a non-tonic return of 3K, joins the recapitulation and coda indissolubly. Tovey starts the coda in m. 294, at the start of the extension of 2K to G. However, I believe that the strong cadence in G, m. 298, articulates the division between the sections.[50] The subdominant, of course, has a long history as a closing harmonic effect, here expanded to a long tonicization.

Let us consider how intensifications of various SHMRG elements support Growth aspects in the movement. We will discuss each function, the development, and the coda. Most of these intensifications go beyond the Haydn-Mozart style, even in such an early work. P itself has many remarkable traits (see Ex. 2.1a). The most traditional aspect concerns the organization of its three phrases in the format a-b-b¹, an old melodic design that goes back to the early years of the Classic style and forward into the 19th century and even P of Beethoven's Eighth Symphony/I (1812). While Pa contains four measures, Pb and b¹ extend to six measures, another typical Classic device. Pa, however, makes a shocking beginning with an extremely steep rise, moving down at first from d^1 to a and then ascending rapidly two octaves to a fermata on a^2. Beethoven enhances and intensifies the b phrases somewhat as in the P area of the String Quartet, Op. 18, No. 1/I. He alters the range, texture, surface articulation, dynamics, and contours of the b phrases. Each phrase in P starts an octave higher: d^1-d^2-d^3.

---

[50] Tovey, 58.

Example 2.1 Treament of motives in P and pa

    a. The primary theme, its motives and inner motivic development (mm. 1-16)

    b. Linear extension in STc (mm. 84^4-91^1)

    c. Countermelody texture in 2S (mm. 66^4-68)

d. Mirror inversion in STb (mm. 74^4-78^3)

e. Dialogue texture and intervallic variation in 3K (mm. 113-17^3)

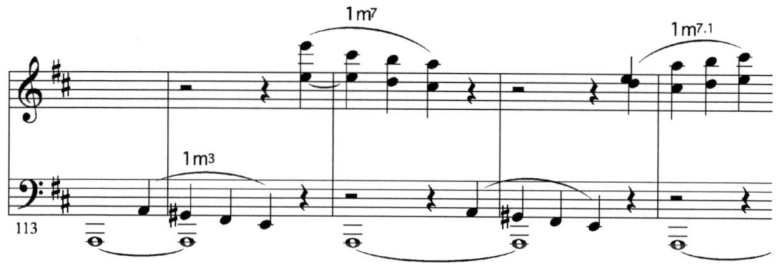

f. Phrase variants of Pa (mm. 93^4-97^1, 133^4-37; 141^4-45^1)

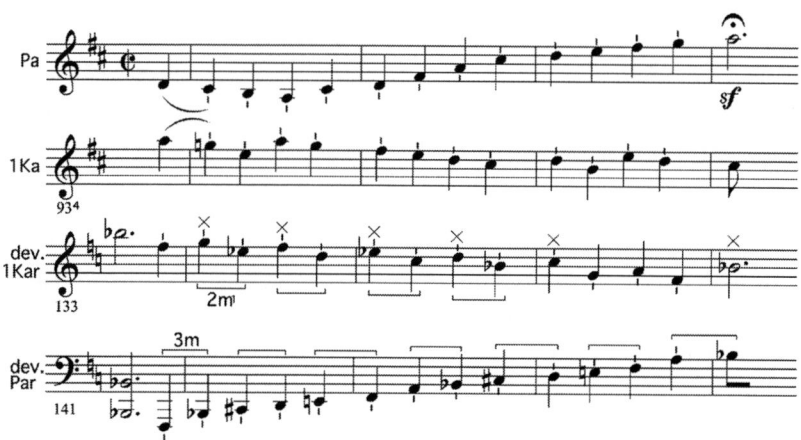

g. Use of 1m in diminution and 2m in 1T and 1Sa (mm.22^4-26^3; 53^3-56^2)

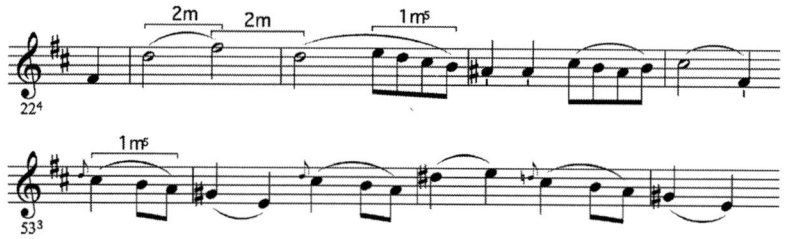

h. Final transformation of 1m as a descending scale and descending interlocking tetrachords in partial mirror inversion and augmentation (mm. 326⁴-41¹)

While Pa is entirely in unison, Pb is harmonized and develops 1m sequentially in an enriched and speedy harmonic texture largely in sixth chords. The surface articulation changes from mostly staccato to mostly legato. It is Pb¹ that finds greatest enhancement in the highest range, *forte* dynamic, fastest surface rhythm in eighths until the cadence. The melodic line, largely in broken sixths, is supported by a rhythmically varied, low bass line in octaves, making a partial mirror with the treble. So much is happening at every moment in this theme, and the changes continue with PT. This function returns to Pa, but it too is extended to six measures with a sudden modulation to B minor ending on V. PT sustains the rhythmic intensification in Pb¹ with an off-beat echo of the bass in the right hand, broadening only for the final cadential measures. The melodic range rises to e³, the highest note of the P area and an implied f#³, unavailable on many pianos of the time. While a *crescendo* was withheld from the rise in Pa, which was *piano* throughout, the *crescendo* here is 2-1/2 measures long, reaching a *ff* for the last three cadential notes. Thus, in both the end of P and in PT major intensifications take place.

The much more extensive T area builds its specific climax more gradually. The entire section contains a greater drive forward in perpetual eighth-note motion in the accompaniment or melodic action. Greatest rhythmic intensity occurs in 4T, when both hands move together in eighths, as in the 5-3/4 mm. approach to the final cadence in the new tonic of A major (mm. 45²-50). After imitation, a probable *crescendo*, and *sforzandos* in 3T, ending in F# minor, 4T starts *ff* but with an immediate long *diminuendo* to *piano* together with a two-octave melodic descent. This descent makes possible a long rising scale of three octaves before the final cadence. In this highpoint of rhythmic intensity, Beethoven reaches the lowest bass note of the section, C# (m. 49), introduces a two-measure *crescendo* together with a rising chromatic line to *forte* (mm. 49-51), and moves to the highest note of the section, e³ (m. 51³), a striking example of concinnity, as so many elements coordinate to make the climactic effect. The cadence itself broadens in rhythm, the formal trill preceded by the largest melodic leap of the section, a descending twelfth. Thus, in the last 8-1/2 measures of T, Beethoven activates rhythm, heightens dynamics, and expands the melodic range and leap to mark the end of the modulatory section.

After the high activity of T, 1S and 2S are necessarily quiescent. The surface rhythm in 1S, a new gavotte pattern, returns to a basic quarter-note movement, with descending eighths in 1Sa recalling the diminution of 1m found in 1T. In a way, these eighths maintain a link with T, so that the slowdown does not occur too abruptly. The theme repeats an octave higher in the tonic minor and then breaks off in a long dramatic rest of five quarters that separates 1S from 2S and its continuation as ST. The great buildup in ST to the strongest cadence in the exposition has already been discussed. The long S and ST areas feature largely quarter-note motion for nearly 40 measures.

1K has its own intensifications and in many ways serves as the brilliant ending of the exposition. It revives the active eighth-note surface rhythm for 12-1/2 mm. as its thrice-repeated phrase variant of Pa descends three octaves against a rising line in eight-notes and double counterpoint—all against a tonic pedal. The rising scale line recalls the linear motive of 1m, each note moving however on the half-note level elaborated in eighths. After closing the musical space in 1Ka, Beethoven expands it over four octaves to its highest note e^3 before the cadence. The last phrase reaches *ff* after a 1-1/2 measure *crescendo*.

The larger rhythmic values that follow in 2K, 3K, and KT—motion in halves and then quarters—constitute a low point at the end of the exposition in order to highlight the intensification of the development. This ending too departs from Classic norms where the exposition usually ends strongly and loudly, as in the close of Mozart's Piano Sonata, K. 332/I.[51]

After four measures of KT descending three octaves, *pp*, the development starts with the return of Pa in D minor, with an added *crescendo* to *ff*. As we know, there was an old tradition going back to the late Baroque of starting Part II of a binary or sonata form with P in the second key. Here, the appearance of Pa in the tonic minor is a shocking transformation of this old procedure.[52]

---

[51] Other such quiet endings to the exposition appear in Op. 2, No. 2/I (*pp*), Op. 10, No. 1/I (*p*), and Op. 14, No. 1 (*pp*, with KT).

[52] Francesco Galeazzi, in his description of sonata form (published in 1796), notes that beginning the second part of a movement with "the same Motive (i.e. subject) as the first transposed to the fifth of the key" is in "disuse . . . since it does not introduce any variety into the compositions, which is always the purpose of all the skills of genius." Rather, Galeazzi recommends starting Part II with the final K in the second key or with a new theme in a "related key, but separated and unexpected." Starting Part II with the final K (called the "Coda" by Galeazzi), occurs, for example, in the Beethoven Piano Sonatas, Op. 2, No. 3/I and Op. 10, No. 2/I, as well as Beethoven's last Violin Sonata, Op. 96/I (see Ch. 3). There is no comprehensive study of this aspect of Beethoven's treatment of the sonata form. See my article, "Francesco Galeazzi's Description (1796) of Sonata Form," *JAMS* 21 (1968): 195. For a slightly revised translation, see Oliver Strunk, ed., *Source Readings in Music History*, rev. ed., Vol. 5, *The Late Eighteenth Century*, ed. Wye Jamison Allanbrook (New York: Norton, 1998), 85-92.

Following the cadence of Pa on V, Beethoven changes the key signature with two natural signs, writing in b-flat throughout; the D-major key signature returns only with the start of the recapitulation.[53]

The relatively short development makes a dramatic effect through its highly unified character in rhythm, modulatory plan, thematic material, and dynamics. Following Pa, which functions as an introduction, the development gets underway with a deceptive cadence to ♭VI or B♭. Eighth-note surface rhythm in the accompaniment in either hand produces an exciting rhythmic propulsion for fifty measures, the longest stretch of eighth-note motion in the movement. The keys descend in thirds from the tonic minor, a choice found also in some middle-period works, as in the developments of two movements in minor, the Violin Sonata, Op. 30, No. 2/I in C minor (1802) and the Piano Sonata, Op. 57/I (the "Appassionata") in F minor (1804-06). Here, the keys after the tonic minor spell out the notes of the Neapolitan chord: B♭-g-E♭ before moving to D minor and then D major. The number of measures in each key are indicated below, starting with D minor (see Table 2.6).

Table 2.6 The Keys in the Development Section

key	d*	B♭	g	E♭	d	D
scale degree	i	VI	iv	♭II	i	I
number of mm.	8	13	6	7	16	7

*includes KT

The keys of iv and ♭II appear in ST and the coda, thus linking the three sections, and they recur with B♭ in the *Largo* and *finale* as well. In fact, the only movement without a Neapolitan chord or key is the Menuetto. Harold Thompson, in his essay on Beethoven's use of "Neapolitan formations" in his piano sonatas states that "the first use of the ♭II-iv-♭VI region as the harmonic basis of a principal section in Beethoven's piano sonatas is in the development section of the first movement of Opus 10, No. 3. . . ."[54] The return in d/D consists of a long dominant pedal of 21 mm. (mm. 161-83), interrupted in mm. 177-78 by the major IV^6 shifting the harmony to D major.

---

[53] Such changes of key signature for the development also occur in the Piano Sonata, Op. 2, No.2/I, and the Violin Sonata, Op. 12, No. 1/I. In the Piano Sonata in F, Op. 10, No. 2/I, a change in the key signature to two sharps appears near the end of the development for a false recapitulation of the entire P theme in D major (mm. 117^2-29), followed by a modulation back to F.

[54] Harold Thompson, "An Evolutionary View of Neapolitan Formations in Beethoven's Pianoforte Sonatas," *College Music Symposium* 20 (1980): 145. Other sonatas discussed are Op. 27, No. 2/III ("Moonlight"), Op. 57/I, III, and briefly Op. 106.

Thematically, the development relates essentially to Pa, by presenting phrase variants of 1Ka (descending form) and then of Pa (rising form), the latter featuring the rising half-step in notes 5-6 of Pa (see Ex. 2.1f). The regular four-measure rising phrases are contrasted with a new b phrase that modulates to the next key. It breaks the persistent quarter-note motion in Par with syncopations and a descending eighth-note scale driving into the new tonic. The third such phrase develops the initial skips and expands to six measures as it leads into the retransition. While the descending phrases at the start are in the right hand, the rising phrases appear in the left-hand bass register, and in the RT, in both bass and treble with crossed hands as the harmonic rhythm speeds up from one chord per three or four measures to one chord per two measures. The faster, steady harmonic rhythm starts in the approach to the RT and characterizes much of the function (mm. 161-78).

In order to sustain the tension of the development to the very end, Beethoven concludes the section with a rising bass in quarter notes highlighted by *sforzandos*: A-B-c♯-C♯, mm. 175-83 (the last four *f* signs are probably a shorthand for the continuation of the *sf* marks). These notes occur in wide spacing of 2 mm. and 1-1/2 mm., coming on the weak measures of the four-measure phrase, and then with metrical displacement on V^7, mm. 179-83. Beethoven cuts m. 179 in half so that the third quarter functions as the first of the measure, with the bass and soprano notes starting on that beat until the fermata on V^6_5 ending the development. The phrase terminates with a 2/4 measure before the fermata. The crossed hands, the left hand playing both the soprano and bass, add to the excitement of the passage, while the soprano notes, three octaves and more above the bass, move in parallel tenths for the most part. The rising bass, of course, is a thematic reference to 1m in inversion. Ending the development with a fermata relates Beethoven more to Haydn than Mozart, and in the middle and late works such an open cadence is rejected in favor of a continuous connection to the reprise. One thinks of the dramatic retransitions in the Piano Sonatas, Op. 53/I ("Waldstein"; 1803-04) and Op. 57.[55]

Two further intensifications take place. One consists of maintaining a loud dynamic level for most of the development: *ff* from m. 141, with *sf* marks and a brief *crescendo* mm. 179^3-80. To prevent the *ff* level from weakening, Beethoven repeats the *ff* mark in mm. 149, 157, 167, and after the *crescendo* in m. 181. A second intensification is the exploitation of the full range of the five-octave piano, from $F^1{}_s$ (m. 149) to f^3 (m. 155), the highest note of the instrument.[56]

---

[55] Three other first movements of Beethoven's early piano sonatas end the development with a fermata on V^7 or rests after the V^7 chord: Op. 2, No.2/I, Op. 7/I, and Op. 22/I. In addition, the development section in three fast movements from Beethoven's early string quartets, Op. 18, also end on V^7 with a fermata: Op. 18, No. 2/IV, No. 5/IV, and No. 6/I.

[56] The $F♯_1$ appears in the exposition and recapitulation as well and the f^3 briefly in the recapitulation. In general, Beethoven makes frequent use of the lowest and highest registers of the early piano.

Some intensifications occur in the recapitulation, though on the whole the section follows the exposition with only occasional changes, most of them a result of adjustments caused by transposition. Most dramatic is the alteration in Pb^1 and PT, which are fused, becoming therefore NPT, a new PT. The unit makes a modulation to E minor, a fifth below the B minor of the exposition, the modulation featuring a new rising chromatic bass and dominant pedal of E minor before the entry of 1T. Another striking difference is the elimination of the active bass in eighth notes in 4T, except for the final two measures, thus lessening the rhythmic intensity of the passage.[57]

All movements except the Menuetto contain substantial codas, another forward-looking aspect of the sonata. In this first movement, Beethoven makes the coda largely a low point that soars at its end with a climactic passage finishing the movement *ff*. Most of the coda is *pianissimo* as the section takes off from the subdued 3K and KT^1. Suspense comes from mysterious gradual harmonic changes with KT^1 from G major to G minor, used as a pivot to V^7 of E♭ major, the Neapolitan key, whose tonic chord, however, is withheld. Once again, as in the development section, the Neapolitan appears as the most distant key before the final strong swing back to the tonic. The rich harmonic passage, from m. 316^4 to m. 320^3, still based on KT^1 with its variation of 1m from 3K but with a partial mirror in the inner parts, sits on the dominant of E♭ until a♭ is respelled as g♯. The enharmonic modulation back to D major is effected by the augmented iv$^6_5$ that replaces V^7 of E♭, moving to D:V^7 and with other cadential chords leading to a strong cadence in the tonic, a cadence strengthened by a long four-measure *crescendo* to I (Ex. 2.2). Such harmonic digressions characterize the first part of many Beethoven codas, as in Opp. 61/III and 96/II, and as we will see also the codas of the second and fourth movements. Thus, the intensification here is at first harmonic.

The second intensification occurs in the closing portion of the coda. First, the low dynamic level of *piano* returns with the transformation of 1m as a long descending D-major scale. Then a passage featuring the augmentation of 1m rises with the longest *crescendo* of the movement—seven measures—to a *fortissimo* climax two octaves higher (see Ex. 2.1h). Both transformations of 1m are sustained with tonic pedal points to the end of the movement in a necessary stabilization of the key after the long harmonic digression. The first pedal is elaborated in the bass, alternating the leading tone and tonic note in a kind of dissonant written-out trill (mm. 327-32). The second pedal alternates in the left hand with the descending interlocked tetrachords derived from the sequential expansion of Pb; the notes are B-F♯, G-D. The start on B and its B-minor harmony clearly connect with the special role of B minor in the movement (see below). This version of 1m is combined with a free mirror in the right hand that ascends an octave and a sixth to the final cadential measures on d^3. The tonic also rises as the top note of the right hand for the final measures (mm. 339^3-43).

---

[57] A fine detail is the surprising extension of the descending thirds in $1Sb^1$ by a measure.

Example 2.2 The modulatory passage in the coda (mm. 316^4-27^1)

Giving further intensity to this passage is the return of eighth-note motion, first in the bass (mm. 327-32), then in both hands for the final rise (mm. 333-40), and then in the right hand alone in mm. 340-41 for the climax on *ff*.[58] Two tonic chords in the penultimate measure on the two main beats end the sounding portion on the weak beat. However, they are followed by a measure of silence, with a fermata on the third quarter of the measure that fills out the four-measure phrase ending the movement. Thus rhythm, dynamics, and melodic transformation combine to intensify the very ending of the movement. A long rise to the concluding chords is an unusually dramatic effect, one occasionally used by Beethoven in later works, for example in the endings of the Violin Concerto, the Fifth Piano Concerto, the Violin Sonata, Op. 96, and, most unforgettably, at the end of the fugue *finale* of the late Piano Sonata, Op. 110 (1821-22).

---

[58] We should note too the chromatic thirds on the first eighths in mm. 341 and 342, pushing the melodic line forward to the final chords.

Joseph Kerman, in his discussion of Beethoven's codas, refers to two aspects that we find in this unusual coda.[59] First, the sense of resolution that occurs with the relaxed descending scale version of 1m. Here, the descending fourth from d to a continues down to the tonic in a scale descending two and a half octaves from d^3 to a, the tetrachords d-a- g-d divided between soprano and alto in the right hand. The tetrachord no longer turns upward to the tonic in order to rise to the dominant. It is startling to discover that the descending scale form of 1m was one of Beethoven's earliest ideas for the coda (see my discussion of the sketches). Kerman refers to the fact that in the middle period "the feeling of consummation [is] achieved by upward linear motion in [Beethoven's] codas."[60] He then points to a rare middle-period example in the coda of the Piano Sonata, Op. 81a ("Das Lebewohl"), which combines both a descent in the left hand and a steep rise in the right hand. He remarks that

> Something similar is perhaps to be detected in an unusually extended coda from the first period, that in the first movement of the Sonata in D major, Op. 10, No. 3.

The feeling of resolution in the treatment of 1m at the end of the coda makes one think of the resolved, balanced form of the primary theme at the end of the coda of the *Eroica* Symphony, first movement, and the change in the cyclical minor half step, in particular e-f, in the String Quartet, Op. 132, to its major form of e-f♯ in the coda of the *finale*. Such simplifications and resolutions usually concern the P theme.

Another special detail in the coda pertains to an harmonic aspect pointed out by Douglas Johnson.[61] This is the play on the enharmonic equivalence of the notes a♯ and b♭ throughout the movement, a♯ associated especially with B minor and b♭ with D minor. Johnson points to the bass movement a-a♯ in Pb^1, PT in the modulation to B minor, and NPT in the recapitulation's modulation to E minor. On the other hand, a-b♭ is the basic motion from V of D minor to the deceptive cadence on VI at the start of the development. Both notes return significantly in the coda, b♭ as the dominant of the Neapolitan key of E♭, and then in m. 323^4 as a♯, the leading tone of B minor, now vi of D major, the tonic key being fully asserted (see Ex. 2.2). As Johnson further observes, such long-range play on enharmonic reinterpretation of chromatic notes continues in Beethoven's later works, most famously with relation to the treatment of the notes c♯-d♭ in the first movement of the *Eroica* Symphony.

Monothematic Sonata Form and Op. 10, No. 3/I

The history of monothematic sonata form in Classic music is yet to be written, though it was a common type of sonata form in the period. Since the term "monothematic sonata form" has been applied to various types of structures,

---

[59] See Joseph Kerman, "Notes on Beethoven's Codas," in *Beethoven Studies* 3, 149.
[60] Kerman, 151, here and for the following quotation.
[61] Johnson, "1794-1795: Decisive Years in Beethoven's Early Development," 27.

some analysts dislike it and prefer not to use it at all. The term has been applied to a movement like this *Presto*, where all the material of the movement can be traced to the primary theme. There are many movements like this, a type that goes back to the 1730s, as in the first movement of G. B. Sammartini's early symphony in D, J-C 14/I.[62] Other such structures occur, for example, in Haydn's Symphony No. 30/I (1765), Symphony No. 44/IV (c. 1771), and his Piano Sonata in C♯ minor, H. XVI: 36 (? c. 1770-75). In other cases of so-called monothematic sonata form, more contrast occurs though P is predominant. In one type, associated with Haydn, the primary theme returns as the secondary theme in the second key area, though it may be somewhat altered. The remaining material may be partly derived from P but contrasting material occurs as well, as in the first movements of Haydn's Symphonies Nos. 85 (1786) and 104 (1795) or in the String Quartet, Op. 77, No. 1/I (1799). Other examples can be found in the *finale* of Mozart's Symphony No. 39 (1788) and in Mozart's Piano Sonata K. 570/I (1789). Though this type may seem especially Haydnesque, several examples also occur in symphonies by G. B. Sammartini, as the third movement of his early symphony in G, J-C 39 (dated probably in the late 1730s), and some middle-period symphonies of the 1740s and an overture of early 1751.[63] Undoubtedly many other examples exist by other composers.

For Beethoven, Haydn's various models seem to have been the most influential. A variety of procedures may be found in Beethoven's music, from completely unified movements to various degrees of integration. In the first movement of Beethoven's first mature piano sonata, Op. 2, No. 1, a Haydnesque integration includes S as a free inversion of P and the derivation of all functions from P except 2S. A hint of the recurrence of P as S can even be heard in the Piano Sonata, Op. 57/I. A more personal device of Beethoven's is the use of a basic motive that not only pervades much of the melodic material but also functions as background accompaniment in the bass or middle of the texture. A good example in this volume is the first movement of Beethoven's Violin Concerto, with its pervasive tapping motive. An earlier example is the ubiquitous turn motive in the first movement of the String Quartet, Op. 18, No. 1 (1799-1800).[64] The most famous of Beethoven's monothematic movements is, of course, the first movement of the Fifth Symphony (1804-08), which, despite its extraordinary motivic concentration, contains a long contrasting S, as in the first movement of Op. 18, No. 1. Repeated-note motives are a favorite with Beethoven since they

---

[62] The symphony can be found in my edition, *The Symphonies of G. B. Sammartini. Volume I: The Early Symphonies* (Cambridge, MA: Harvard University Press, 1968), score 3.

[63] See the score in Giovanni Battista Sammartini, *Il Pianto delle pie donne* (J-C 118), ed. Marie Marley, "Recent Researches in the Music of the Classical Era," vol. 34 (Madison: A-R Editions, Inc., 1990), Introduzione.

[64] See Janet M. Levy, *Beethoven's Compositional Choices: The Two Versions of Opus 18, No. 1, First Movement* (Philadelphia: University of Pennsylvania Press, 1982). As Joseph Kerman pointed out, Beethoven actually reduced the number of occurrences of the turn motive from 130 in the first version of movement I to 104 in the second version. See Kerman, *The Beethoven Quartets* (New York: Norton, 1966), 32.

can easily fit into the texture and harmony. Besides such examples as the first movements of the Violin Concerto and Fifth Symphony, one thinks of the scherzando second movement of the String Quartet, Op. 59, No. 1 ("Rasumovsky," 1806) and the scherzo of the Ninth Symphony, with its basic rhythmic motive ♩．♪♪ together with its octave skip (a variant of the repeated-note idea).

The *Presto* of Op. 10, No. 3 is Beethoven's first monothematic movement of broad scope and the only such example in the piano sonatas and indeed of the solo sonatas (Op. 2, No. 1/I is only 152 measures long). It seems that in the late period Beethoven's most important monothematic structures were not in sonata form but theme and variations and the fugue.

In Op. 10 the *Presto* is unified by a descending scale motive of a fourth found in notes 1-4 of P in the very opening of the movement. This was recognized by Czerny who stated:

> The first four notes of the theme are carried through the whole piece and must therefore be rendered distinguishable in all modes of performance.[65]

It is typical of Beethoven to use such a simple, even primordial idea on which to build his movement. The motive moves down from d^1 to a, tonic to dominant notes, and is identified here as 1m. A secondary motive of the skip of a third appears in the second measure in a series of rising thirds, identified as 2m. Another motive, 3m, is the opening half step between notes 1-2 and is found mainly in the development section. However, most of the material in the movement derives from 1m and the motive appears in every function and section of the movement (see Ex. 2.1).

Table 2.7 Development of P Elements

1m	Pa: m. 1^{1-3} with upbeat, descending scale from I-V
$1m^1$	inversion: Pa, PT, 2T-4T, STb, 3Km (free inv.), KT^1
$1m^2$	linear extension of 1m and $1m^1$: Pa, PT, 3T-4T, STc, 1Kh, NPT, $a-a^1$
$1m^3$	legato, not staccato: Pb, 1T-4T, 1Sa, 2S, STab, 2K, 3K, KT
$1m^4$	minor, not major: 1T, 2Ta, $1S^1$, in STb, KT^1, Pa in dev.
$1m^5$	diminution (8th-notes): 1T, 2T, 3T (+ inv.), 4T (+ inv.), 1Sa, a^1 (in minor), NPTb (in minor)
$1m^6$	augmentation (half and whole notes): 2T (+ inv.), 1Kh (+ inv.), 2K (outline of 3 descending notes), 1Kar (dev.), RTb (wider spacing), syncopated enharmonic passage (coda)
$1m^7$	intervallic variation: with initial skip (also inv.): 3K, KT^2
$1m^8$	sequential expansion: Pb, b^1, 2T
$1m^9$	chromatic version: 4T (+ inv., ext.)
$1m^{10}$	transformation as a descending octave scale in D (coda)
$1m^{11}$	interlocked descending tetrachords in partial mirror (coda)
2m	skip of a third; 1Ta (partly inv.), 1Sab (inv.)

---

[65] Czerny, *On the Proper Performance*, 42.

3m   half-step from Pa, notes 1-2: in dev., Par, Par^1, Par^2
Phrase variants of Pa: 1Ka; dev.: 1Kar, Par, Par^1, Par^2
Varied textural settings, such as: unison (Pa), harmonized (Pb, b^1), chordal (2K), melody and accompaniment (1T), countermelody (2S, 1K), mirror (STa,b), partial mirror (1m^{11}), imitative (3T), dialogue (3K), monophonic (KT)

As Table 2.7 shows, Beethoven uses many devices for varying the basic motive and these produce perpetual variety. Even within P, as indicated earlier, we find 1m inverted and extended (Pa). a change from unison texure to harmonization (b, b^1), sequential treatment (b), a shift from staccato to legato (b), changes in octave location, and changes in dynamic, from *p* to *f* (b^1). Thus intensive growth occurs from the very opening. Several examples of 1m in diminution and augmentation are inverted as well. Beethoven connects the lyrical 1T with 1S via 1m in diminution and legato, and 1S actually starts with the same notes as Pa. On the other hand, both functions are linked to the presence of 2m—the skip of a third—especially at the start of 1T and 1Sb. All scaleline motives can be related to 1m, including the scales in 3T-4T, the long extension at the end of ST, the countermelody in 1K, the scale outline of 2K, and the rising bass ending of the development. The varied textural settings enrich the movement, especially the mirror combinations, as in ST and the final period of the movement, the countermelody texture in 1K, and the dialogue arrangement in 3K.

Quite unusual is Beethoven's use of phrase variants of Pa. The first of these is the basic phrase in 1K, which represents a free inversion of Pa heard three times. Phrase variants of P dominate the development and feature mainly the rising form after the first descending version (derived also from Ka). The introduction of the striking simplified and resolved forms of 1m (1m^{10}, 1m^{11}) at the end of the coda, brings the movement to a most satisfying close.

Articulations and Continuity

Like many early works of Beethoven, the first movement has numerous open articulations between thematic functions and phrases. Ten of the thirteen functions end with open articulations, most of them with rests following the cadence. In P itself, each phrase ends with an open articulation, Pa with a fermata on V, and Pb and b^1 with strong cadences on the tonic followed by rests in both hands (see Ex. 1a). Further, both the exposition and development end with such articulations. The exceptions deserve comment, however. In the transition, 3T elides with 4T, strengthening the rhythmic drive in the most active part of the section. The cadence of 2K ends with an elision and anticipation of the tonic pedal of 3K. Beethoven avoids a formal cadence in 3K, modulating back to D near the end of the theme (m. 120, with the upbeat), which is then extended via KT, based on 1m featured in the left hand of 3K. In the repeat of the exposition, the first note d^1 can be heard as completing the downward scale of KT—a, g, f♯ e, though it appears in a high register.

This kind of linking device, despite separating rests and articulations, occurs in six functions: 2T inverts the descending three-note scaleline outlined at the end of 1T; 4T continues the rapid eighth-note scales introduced in 3T; 1S varies the descending octave leap in the bass of 4T's final cadence for its left-hand accompaniment (an observation by Jan LaRue); ST continues the repetition of 1m in the left hand found in 2S; while ST ends with a descending scaleline, 1K that follows contains a countermelody that rises by step four octaves; and KT takes off from 3K as discussed above. The same concern for continuity applies to the linking of the end of the retransition and start of the reprise. On one hand there is an open cadence with a fermata on a V_5^6 chord closing off the development. On the other hand, the rising scaleline in the bass ending the retransition A-B-C♯ elides with the tonic d starting the reprise, the rising tetrachord an inversion of the descending tetrachord opening P.

Rhythm

If we consider the basic surface rhythmic patterns of the movement, what may be called its rhythmic spine,[66] the use of equal rhythmic values stands out as the norm. Beethoven alternates phrases and sections based on predominantly quarter-note and eighth-note motion, and occasionally half-note motion, as in 2K. Whole sections are blocked out by one basic type of surface rhythm, as we can see in the exposition:

    Quarter-note: Pa-b, 1S-2S-ST, 3K-KT
    Eighth-note: Pb¹-PT, 1T-2T-3T-4T, 1K
    Half-note: 2K

The K section has the most contrast in this respect, and 1K itself combines four types of surface rhythm: quarter notes in the melodic line, eighth notes in the countermelody, half notes in the highest notes in the countermelody, and a long tonic pedal point of four measures in each of the second and third repetitions. Some exceptions naturally occur in these block rhythms. Thus PT decelerates in its last two measures for the cadence in B minor, and 1Sa includes the eighth-note motive found in the melody of 1T.

As indicated earlier, the surface rhythm of the development is mainly in eighth notes. The coda, in contrast, features mainly quarter-note motion (mm. 299-326) but ends with eighth-note motion, at first in the bass and then in both hands (mm. 327-42), as the movement drives to its conclusion. Surface rhythm in eighth notes is clearly associated with areas of intensification: Pb¹ through T, the start of K, the development, and the very end of the movement.

Most of the thematic functions in the movement begin on the upbeat quarter note or second half of the measure (1S, 2K), further integrating the thematic ideas. 3T also starts on an upbeat, but the second half of the first quarter note. Only 4T enters on beat one, but with an elision. This location on the

---

[66] This term was suggested to me by Jan LaRue.

PIANO SONATA

downbeat is picked up in the phrase variants of the development, all of which precede their upbeat placement with a long dotted half on the tonic, a shift emphasized by dynamic marks of *ffp* and *ff*.

We have already noted the metrical displacement at the end of the development. Another example of rhythmic dissonance occurs in 3K, between the tonic pedal point and theme. The pedal precedes the theme by three quarters. The clash comes about from the reiteration of the pedal in two-measure units placed nearly a measure earlier than the start of the melodic line so that the beginning of the pedal and ending of the melodic subphrase occur at the same time (see Ex. 2.3 and mm. 113-15). Such examples of rhythmic dissonance become more frequent and complex in middle and late Beethoven, as in the treatment of the *Allemande* in the trio section of the quartet Op. 132.

Example 2. 3 Rhythmic dissonance in 3K (mm. 113-15)

Sound

The large range of dynamic marks from *pp* to *ff* sets Beethoven apart from Haydn and Mozart. It has more in common with the music of Clementi and contemporary French opera composers such as Cherubini and Méhul.[67] Beethoven's sensitivity to dynamic levels and their relation to structure and expression can be seen in all his works, from early to late, in all the movements of this sonata, and in all works discussed in this volume. Here, Beethoven uses nine types of dynamic marks and accents: *pp, p, f, ff, cresc.>, sf, fp, ffp*. The dynamic extremes highlight significant portions of the movement: *ff* as the main level of the development, and *pp* for the close of the exposition and recapitulation, and surprisingly for most of the coda.

The *sforzando* has many functions. It strengthens syncopations in 2T (left hand) and 2S (melody); it accents the quarter-note upbeat of 1m and its dominant harmony in ST, and it underscores rising scalelines in the bass, stemming from 1m, at the end of the RT and in the new bass of NPT of the recapitulation. As expected, *sforzandos* are applied to notes and chords that Beethoven wishes to emphasize, like the final note of Pa, and the full chords ending 3T, ST, and the movement itself.

---

[67] See Sheer, "A Comparison of Dynamic Practices" and her Ph. D. dissertation "The Role of Dynamics in Beethoven's Instrumental Works," Ch. II, "Dynamic Usages in Works by Beethoven's Older Contemporaries: Haydn, Mozart, and Clementi"; and Ch. III "Dynamic Treatment in Works of Beethoven's Early and Middle Periods."

Beethoven considered his dynamic plan very carefully and usually left it for the end of the compositional process.[68] This is why, for example, the autograph of the String Trio, Op. 3, is complete except for the dynamics. Many special dynamic effects were late thoughts of Beethoven, like the *ppp* in the second violins against the *pp* of the horn solo just before the recapitulation of the *Eroica* Symphony's first movement (m. 394), and the *ppp* in the strings just before the end of the *Larghetto* of the Violin Concerto.

Expression

Much has been said of the high degree of contrast in this movement, though the music is so tightly unified. These contrasts embody various topics that would have been easily recognized by the performer and listener.[69] The phrases starting with a quarter-note upbeat in ¢ meter recall the *bourrée*. The singing style of 1T and its extension in 2T is followed by brilliant style in 3-4T. Imitation also in 3T is associated with the learned style of counterpoint, a style that characterizes a block of three functions with countermelodies and mirror writing: 2S, ST, and 1K. Frustrating our expectations, 1S has a gavotte rhythm, its phrases starting on the second half of the measure, and it turns out to be more scherzando than singing, despite its slurs and eighth-note motive from 1T. The final two K functions contrast strongly with 1K; the block chords of 2K suggest the hymn style while 3K concludes the exposition with a dialogue between the bass and treble. Most of the development suggests the *Sturm und Drang* in its minor mode, high activity, wide range, and loud dynamics.

Some astute observations by Carl Dahlhaus touch on the seeming paradox of intense unity and variety in this movement. His statement deserves extensive quotation. Dahlhaus refers to

> the ambition on one hand, to accomplish a grouping of thematic characters which is as richly contrasted as can be imagined, and, on the other hand, nevertheless, to weave a dense network of motivic relationships which spreads itself over virtually the entire movement. Opposing extremes of divergence and unification were to be compelled to combine, and it is no exaggeration to claim that the exposition of the D major Sonata is a composed-out contradiction. That, and nothing less, is its "underlying idea."[70]

The Sketches for Op. 10, No. 3

Most of Beethoven's early sketches, including the surviving sketches for Op. 10, No. 3, are found in two large sketch miscellanies. The MSS originally belonged together in one large collection that contained material from the Bonn and early Vienna periods that became divided after Beethoven's death. The collection

---

[68] See Paul Mies, *Textkritische Untersuchungen bei Beethoven* (Bonn: Beethoven-Haus, 1957), 96.
[69] For the topics, see the references in Ch. 1, n. 26.
[70] Carl Dahlhaus, *Ludwig van Beethoven: Approaches to his Music*, trans. Mary Whittal (Oxford: Clarendon Press, 1991), 147

was bought by the Viennese music publisher Domenico Artaria at the auction of Beethoven's estate. Between 1830 and 1835, the Viennese musician and collector Joseph Fischhof (1804-57) purchased part of the collection. Of the original 66 leaves and bifolios, 56 survive. In 1859, the collection was acquired by the Königliche Bibliothek in Berlin (later renamed the Preussische Staatsbibliothek). It was given the library number Mus. ms. autogr. Beethoven 28. Today the collection is housed in the Staatsbibliothek zu Berlin-Preussische Kulturbesitz, Musikabteilung mit Mendelssohn-Archiv (the former East Berlin library). The collection has been studied, the MSS dated, and all leaves transcribed by Douglas Porter Johnson in his outstanding two-volume monograph, *Beethoven's Early Sketches in the "Fischhof Miscellany:" Berlin Autograph 28*.[71] It should be noted that both the Fischhof as well as the Kafka miscellanies contain many unidentified sketches, and some works in autograph, both complete and incomplete. Sketches for many works appear in both miscellanies.

The second, much larger part of the original collection was purchased in the early 1870s by the composer and collector Johann Nepomuk Kafka (1819-86)—no relation to the famous writer though he too was born in Bohemia. The collection of 124 leaves and bifolios was then bought by the British Museum (now the British Library) in 1875. It bears the library number Additional Manuscript 29801, ff. 39-162. The entire contents were published in a lavish edition in facsimile and transcription in 1970, edited by Joseph Kerman.[72] It is to be regretted that a facsimile edition has not been published as well for the Fischhof miscellany. In the later nineteenth century, Gustav Nottbohm transcribed some sketches for Op. 10, No. 3 from both miscellanies.[73] Johnson has dated the sketches for Op. 10, No. 3 from early 1797 to the first half of 1798.

All these sketches are incomplete and many are fragmentary. This is also true of the sketches for Op. 10, No. 3, though more sketches survive for this sonata than for most of the previous sonatas. Only the sketches for Op.14, No. 1 are more extensive. For more comprehensive sketch material that allows us to follow many more steps in the compositional process we must turn to the integral sketchbooks, the first of which is Grasnick 1 (1798-99).[74]

---

[71] Douglas Johnson, *Beethoven's Early Sketches in the "Fischhof Miscellany,"Berlin Autograph 28*, 2 vols. The transcriptions are in Volume II. The first volume contains studies of Beethoven's musical handwriting and the Bonn and Vienna papers, a history and description of the collection, and discussions of the sketches according to opus and WoO numbers, and unfinished works. These discussions offer remarks about dating and present analytical observations. Comparison is also made with additional sketches in the Kafka Miscellany, the second part of the original collection. Johnson's consideration of the sketches for Op. 10, No. 3 appears in Vol. I, 335-39.

[72] See Kerman, ed., *Ludwig van Beethoven, Autograph Miscellany from circa 1786 to 1799.*

[73] *N II*, 35-40.

[74] For a monumental study of the sketchbooks, see JTW. For a helpful and authoritative introduction to Beethoven's sketches, see Alan Tyson, "Sketches and Autographs," in *The Beethoven Companion*, ed. Denis Arnold and Nigel Fortune (London: Faber and Faber, 1971), 443-58.

The following abbreviations are used in the discussion:

CD (continuity draft), st. (staff), sts. (staves), and f. v. (final version). Beethoven's frequent indication "usw" is rendered as "etc."

Sketches for the First Movement

Sketches in the Fischhof Miscellany: f. 45v, sts. 1-16. Transcriptions: Johnson, II, 37-38.

The sketches in Fischhof comprise what is probably the first CD of the entire exposition on sts. 1-10. On the remaining sts. 12-16 there occur eight sketches, six of which seem to be sketches for the K section and two for 2T (see Plate 2.I on facing page).

The exposition draft, excluding crossouts but including rests, contains 89-1/2 written measures as against 124 measures of the f. v. An "etc." after m. 53 in the transition indicates additional measures not yet written out. Still, the CD is far shorter than the f. v., a characteristic of the first continuity drafts in many other works.[75] Also typical is the absence of a tempo mark and meter as well as dynamics and staccatos; only one slur appears in a sketch on st. 12. With one exception, the sketches are monolinear.

Material used in the f. v. occurs for P, PT, 1T, 2T, 3T, $1S^1$, and ST; 1Ka appears on staves 14 and 15. The latter part of T as well as K in the CD differ from the f. v. For the lengths of functions, see Table 2.8.

Table 2.8 Lengths of Functions in the Fischhof CD and Final Version of the Exposition

Function	CD (no. of mm.)	Final Version (no. of mm.)
P	12	16
PT	13	6
1T	16	8
2T	12 -etc.	7
3T	9	15
4T	-	8-1/2
1S	-	7
$1S^1$	6-1/2	6-1/2
2S	2	4
ST	9-1/2	23/22 (elision)
1K	9-1/2	12-1/2
2K	-	8-1/2/7-1/2 (elision)
3K	-	7
KT	-	5

---

[75] See, for example, the transcription of the first CD of the exposition, first movement, for the String Quintet, Op. 29 (1801), given in my article "Beethoven's Sketches for His String Quintet, Op. 29," in: *Studies in Musical Sources and Style, Essays in Honor of Jan LaRue*, eds. Eugene K. Wolf and Edward H. Roesner (Madison: A-R Editions, Inc., 1990), 463-65.

PLATE 2.1 *Op. 10, No. 3/1: Sketches in the Fischhof Miscellany, Mus. ms. autogr. Beethoven 28, f. 45v, with a continuity draft for the exposition on sts. 1-10.* Staatsbibliothek zu Berlin-Preussischer Kulturbesitz, Musikabteilung mit Mendelssohn-Archiv.

The most striking thematic material of the movement can already be found here: P, 1T, and SK, and in nearby sketches the phrase variant for 1K. The sketches show that from the start Beethoven intended to compose a movement infused with scale motives derived from the very opening four notes. In fact, the draft reveals that after the beginning with Pm, Pa simply went up the scale from d^1 to d^2, descending to a^1 with a fermata. This was evidently deemed too simplistic. Beethoven crossed it out and replaced it with the more varied rise by skips of thirds to d^2, as in the f. v. However, the scale does reappear in descending form as one of the ultimate resolved versions of the motive, $1m^{10}$, near the end of the coda. The cadence of the nearly f. v. of Pa, however, does not continue the rise to a^2 but negates the strong rise by skipping down a seventh to $g\sharp^1$-a^1. Pb features Pm but only by simple repetition for two measures followed by a cadence used in Pb in the f.v. The repetition of Pb, however, is an octave lower and has a different, simple bass cadence IV-V-I.

The a-b-b^1 form of P thus appears in this draft as well as the overall cadence pattern V-I-I ending the phrases. Besides lacking the extension of the b phrases to 6 mm., the original conception places the theme in the middle-low registers rather than ascending in octave placement to the highest register. There is no hint, either, of intensifying the b phrases.

While P is shorter than the f.v., PT is far longer, using Pa to modulate to b via e, ending with a fermata on f♯^{1} as in the f.v. but an octave lower. Both P and PT are much less dramatic in effect than the f.v. The f♯ does not come as a surprise, as in the f. v., but at the end of a phrase in the key, the three-measure rest before the cadence evidently meant for further exploration of the modulation to b. The modulation to e, however, recurs in NPT and IT in the recapitulation.

Significantly, the transition begins with the lyrical 1T in b in nearly final form, thus highlighting the key to a greater extent than in the f.v. An harmonic ambiguity, however, marks the cadence as the turn figure occurs a third higher, ending on a^1. Another difference is the exact repeat of 1T, implying perhaps a reharmonization of its cadence. The theme is twice as long via repetition than the f.v. As in many early versions of Beethoven themes, the melody lacks the upbeat of the f. v. that will link it with the other melodic ideas of the movement.[76] The upbeat does appear in the Kafka draft, however.

In response to 1T, 2T has some melodic connection to the f. v. but differs in tonality. It surprisingly returns to the tonic, D, for 8 mm. rather than continuing the modulation toward A, as in the f. v. Only in 2Tb does Beethoven introduce a chromatic passage suggesting a move to A though with some distant chromatic movement that peters out with an "etc." Both phrases, however, feature scaleline movement that rises from a to e^3 before descending with chromatic thirds. A much shorter 3T appears to be in A (mixing g♮ and g♯), and 3Ta unexpectedly anticipates 1Sa and b in major, before cadencing on a^2. Only a hint of the brilliant scales of the f. v. can be found in the rising scale from a^1 to d^3 before the cadence. Obviously, the transition section after 1T required much work tonally, thematically, and rhythmically. Still, not counting the repeat of 1T, the section is nearly as long as the f. v., 29 mm. (plus the "etc."), as against 30 mm. of the f. v. Beethoven often has the rhythmic feel for the length of ideas or sections even if the material itself differs.

The formal 1S theme here is in the dominant minor and became 1S^1 in the f. v. Its appoggiatura appears on the following beat one rather than at the opening of the theme. The descending phrase, mostly in eighths, is more active than 1S of the f. v. and less contrasting to the end of the transition. The phrase repeats x-x^1-x-x^1, x^1 being in the higher octave. In the f. v. the motive is melodically and rhythmically varied. 1Sb is the same as the f. v. though in major and an octave lower.

What follows is basically a briefer version of ST, but it is preceded by a two-measure unit based on the half-step motive of Pa—3m, alternating A-G♯ in quarters. In the f. v. this motive appears in the tenor of 1Ka, and ends up in the coda as a melodic pedal point in the bass on c♯-d, supporting the first trans-

---

[76] See Paul Mies, *Beethoven's Sketches: An Analysis of His Style Based on a Study of His Sketch-Books*, trans. Doris L. Mackinnon (London, 1929; reprinted New York: Dover, 1974), Ch. I, "The Melodic Line," (a) Up-beat and "curtain," 5-16.

formation of 1m (mm. 327-32). ST develops 1m as in the f.v. The descending sequences in A-D-C are the same, but they conclude with a descending and then rising chromatic bass to A: V, not related to the f.v. The cadence on V also contrasts with the powerful tonic cadence at this point in the f.v.

Only a single repetitive closing theme (essentially 2 x 4 mm.) ends the exposition in eighth-note motion and a wide, two-octave range, e^1-e^3. This theme was omitted from the f.v., though its y idea contains a long descending scale that relates to earlier ideas. On the lower staves, we find Beethoven trying out various K ideas, of which three are connected to the f.v. Closest to 1K is the sketch of melody and bass on sts. 14 and 15, which includes the rising bass line and indication of the eighth-note accompaniment. The first measure of the bass has the only indication of the murky bass type, transferred to 3T and the development section of the f.v. A slurred melody of four measures on st. 12 resembles 1Ka to a lesser degree. The three-fold repetition of 1Ka appears in two sketches without a melodic connection to 1K on st. 11 and st. 16. Two chromatic phrases on st. 11 and st. 12 seem related to 2T since they start in f♯ but they were not used for the f.v.

Though this draft remains far from the f.v., it reveals Beethoven's basic conception of a movement integrated primarily by the scale motive of P, but with strong contrasts and a multiplicity of functions. The contrasts in surface rhythm also have a start here with eighth-note activity mainly in 2-3T and the single K.

Sketches in the Kafka Miscellany: f. 102v, sts. 1-10; f. 157v, sts. 8-12.
Transcriptions: Kerman, 19-20.

Two shorter drafts in the Kafka miscellany have little in common with the material in Fischhof. Though Johnson (I, 335) suggests that the briefer Kafka drafts preceded the drafts and sketches in Fischhof, the evidence indicates that they may have followed Fischhof because they contain ideas for the later sections of the movement—the development, recapitulation, and coda. Indeed, the appearance of 1S with an upbeat in the last CD indicates an advance over Fischhof, not an earlier version. Still the Kafka drafts reflect an early stage in the composition of the movement.

The first CD on f. 102v, sts. 1-4, contains only 31 mm. and is inscribed "Sonata Terza." Kerman and Johnson suggest this draft is an exposition, but the modulation and motivic development indicate it is a development draft. At the opening, rapid descending scales in eighths move from D to b (mm. 1-5). The keys thereafter descend sequentially—b, a, G—and go to an implied V pedal in D, followed by what seems like the start of the recapitulation. Emphasis on b remains important in the f. v., though the key is excluded from the development. Beethoven stresses sharp keys in the development, not flat keys as in the f. v.

The material of the development is based first on the final version of Pa in b, a version not found in Fischhof. Starting the development with Pa in minor also occurs in the f. v. but there in d, not b. After Pa, the development features treatment of 1m and its variants. There appears a dialogue of 1m between the bass and soprano with its inversion ($1m^1$) and intervallic variation, as in 3K ($1m^7$). The dialogue idea, but within a stable harmonic framework, was in fact transferred to 3K in the f. v. Over the implied V pedal, the soprano further develops 1m, suddenly leaping from b^2 to e^1 with a fermata, thus ending the development with a fermata, as in the f. v. An X here indicates a revision, which Kerman believes may be a series of whole-note leaps starting on b^2 and ending on the leading tone, $c\sharp^1$, as in the f. v. (st. 9). Similar large leaps end the f. v. of the development, though most are metrically displaced and on V harmony. In summary, the draft so far contains several ideas that were incorporated in the f. v., though not all of them in the development.

The start of the recapitulation that ensues (only 3 mm.) opens with 1m but follows it with repeated quarters plus a turn motive in eighths on the main note, making a new idea (that I call N). This seems to be another conception of P, using 1m as upbeat to N, which is repeated in sequence. It is found in all three Kafka drafts. The turn motive itself was not discarded by Beethoven but incorporated in mm. 3 and 7 of 1T and in the development (mm. 162, 164, and 166). The draft then breaks off with an "etc." and "sim:".

Another CD on sts. 5-10 appears to be for the coda. Beethoven often makes coda sketches and drafts in the early stage of composition as he tries to establish the framework for the movement. Examples include the sketches for the slow movements of the Piano Sonata, Op. 28 (1801) and the "Kreutzer" Violin Sonata, Op. 47 (1802).[77] Here, in about 16 mm., Beethoven first develops N in the bass against a running counterpoint in eighths in the right hand. A cadence on the tonic leads to the most astonishing event in the coda, the appearance of the resolved 1m ($1m^{10}$) as a descending scale in almost final form, together with its ornamented tonic pedal (see Ex. 2.4).

A third, longer draft appears on f. 157, sts. 8-12, and contains 53 mm. This draft has many puzzling features, though Kerman describes it as "an abbreviated draft from the end of the exposition to the conclusion." What do we find:

1. An extension of N around the key of A, with a long descending A-major scale ending with a fermata on a and double bar with repeat marks for the second part. This would seem to be the end of the exposition.

2. The start of 2K (first three notes) in A, with an "etc." This is the only appearance of the theme in the extant sketches. Its function in this context is unclear, however. According to its placement, it would be the start of the development, despite its cadential character.

---

[77] See the draft and analysis in Martha Frohlich, "Ideas of Closure, Derivation, and Rhythm in the Sketches for the Andante of Beethoven's 'Pastorale' Sonata, Op. 28," *JM* 16 (1998): 350-53. See also Martha Frohlich, ed., Ludwig van Beethoven, *Piano Sonata Op. 28, Facsimile of the Autograph, the Sketches, and the First Edition*, with transcription and commentary by Frohlich (Bonn: Beethoven-Haus, 1996). For the example in Op. 47, see Peter Cahn, "Aspekte der Schlussgestaltung in Beethovens Instrumentalwerken," *Archiv für Musikwissenschaft* 39 (1982): 20-21.

PIANO SONATA

3. An harmonic progression from a c♯-minor chord to a pedal point on A (D: V) ending with a fermata on V. Repeated quarters probably derive from N. The phrase could be the retransition.

4. After a "d. c.", suggesting the start of the recapitulation, Beethoven notates a chromatic bass line that resembles the chromatic bass of NPT of the recapitulation's f. v. (notes 1-6 are the same as the f. v., as is the general rhythmic style). However, the bass modulates to b, not e, and ends on b: V.

5. 1T then follows in b, as in the exposition, but after a measure, Beethoven writes "etc." and presents 1Ta in the bass in f♯ minor. Measures 1-2 of the phrase are then spun out in a rising sequence by step until the tonic is reached, the sequence shifted to the soprano making a climax on g^2. A long descending scale ends with another "etc."

It is hard to explain the two-fold sequence of 1T in b and f♯ (the key is e, a fifth below b, in the f. v.). The theme is therefore strongly emphasized, as in Fischhof, and even developmental. In the f. v. 1T does not repeat and its extension in 2T evolves more subtly from the end of the theme, not the beginning as in this draft. Though there seems to be some confusion in

Example 2.4 A comparison between the final version of $1m^{10}$ and its appearance in Kafka, f. 102v, sts. 7-10

this draft, we do encounter for the first time 2K and the bass of NPT. The sweeping scales, as in the first coda draft, tie in with 3T especially.

6. The most striking reference comes at the end of the draft, after Beethoven's inscription "Ende." Here again is an attempt to complete the coda. Beethoven has noted down the idea and texture of the second resolved form in the f. v. ($1m^{11}$), the augmentation of 1m, which starts in the bass on B as in the f. v. The phrase, however, lacks the final descent to F♯ and turns back to A. This phrase includes the pedal on D, but in the bass, not in the tenor voice of the figuration. Here, the treble is static against the bass but then it rises 5 mm. to d^3 and the movement's end. The final presentation appears here *in nuce*, needing only expansion and elaboration (see Ex. 2.5).

Most remarkable in these early drafts is the emergence of the two resolved forms of 1m ending the coda in the f. v. before the movement is fully

Example 2.5 A comparison between the final version of $1m^{11}$ and its appearance in Kafka, f.157v. sts/ 11–12.

PIANO SONATA

conceived and worked out. Thus, the end results of the motivic development appear before the development itself has barely taken place. Something similar occurs as well in the early CD of the *Largo* in Fischhof, and the early Kafka sketches for the *finale*. These coda examples call to mind Beethoven's statement of 1814, that when composing, he "keep[s] the whole in view."[78]

The Second Movement: *Largo e mesto*

GROWTH

The movement, as stated earlier, is a full sonata form but without repeat marks for the exposition, and thus an example of non-repeating sonata form. This form occurs in Beethoven's music not only for certain long, even tragic slow movements, but also for some fast movements, such as the first movements of the Piano Sonatas, Opp. 57, 90, 101, 109, and 110, the String Quartet, Op. 59, No. 1, and the Ninth Symphony. For the *Largo* of Op. 10, No. 3, besides the very slow tempo, the formality of repetition goes against the mood and structural growth of the movement.

The larger structural proportions are indicated below (see also the timeline, Table 2.9, p. 128):

exp., mm. 1-29:	29 mm.
dev., mm. 30-43:	14 mm.
rec., mm. 44-64:	21 mm.
coda, mm. 65-87:	23 mm.
exp. + dev.:	43 mm.
rec. + coda:	44 mm.

The short though dramatic development is contrasted with a long coda, far longer than the development and even the shortened recapitulation. As a unit, the exposition plus the development almost exactly balance the recapitulation plus the coda. The coda itself stands out as the climax section of the movement.

Unlike the exposition of the first movement, the *Largo*, as one would expect, has fewer functions and all themes are memorable except for the brief K unit (see Plate 2.II on p. 130 for P, T, and S). In addition, the development introduces two new themes, 1N and 2N, both with significant roles in the movement.

P remains one of Beethoven's most individual conceptions. In order to convey the sad and melancholy mood of the movement Beethoven starts his theme in the low register of the piano, with a deep tonic chord spanning two octaves and seven notes in close position. Besides this unusual opening the theme embodies many other special features that lend the theme a special intensity:

---

[78] See Ch.4, n. 161 for the full citation.

Table 2.9 Timeline: Movement II

Key: d   Meter: 6/8

		(a)	(P4m)	(a)		(P4m)	(Tar)				
exp.	Pa	b	|Ta	b		|Sa	b		S¹a¹	b¹	|
	1	5	6	9^{1,4}	13^{4,5}	17¹	17³	19⁴	21¹	21³	23⁴
	d	d:iv		d:i	– C	C:I	a		a:i		

(P4m,Tb)		
K		|
26^{1,5}	29	
	a:i	

	(P4m, Tb)		(y, P2m)					
dev.	1Nx	y	|z	2Nx	1Nz	|2Na	a¹	|
	30^{1,4}	32⁶	35	36	37	38	41	
	F		mod.	g	mod.	d:V ped.	unacc.	

		(Pb)					
rec.	Pa¹	NPT	|Tb		|S¹		S$^{1.1}$	|
	44	49	52^{1,5}	56¹	56³	60¹	60³	
	d	mod.	B♭	B♭:I	d	d:i		

coda	P1m, 2m¹		|2N¹		|P3m		|2m	|
	65		72	76¹	76⁴	81¹	81⁴	
	d, mod.: rising chrom. bass		d:V ped.	d:i		d: V		

4m	2m	||	
84	86³		87 mm.
d:i ped.	unacc.		

1. In harmony, the saturation with diminished seventh chords of d especially, and also of the dominant in m. 7; an intermediate cadence surprisingly on the tonicized subdominant, G minor, rather than on the usual dominant.

2. In melody, the asymmetrical phrases of 5+3 (1/2) mm., Pb eliding with the accompaniment of T. Suspenseful, mysterious repeated notes on b¹ bridge the two phrases. The longer Pa is developmental and includes dissonant melodic intervals, especially of the diminished fourth and fifth. Its melodic line is tortuous, twisting and turning within a small space of a diminished fifth in the first four measures of the theme. The melodic curve, after hovering around d¹ and c¹, rises from the end of m. 4 to a high note of g² in Pb (m. 6), though f² in the next measure receives stronger emphasis as climax, with its repetition, *sf* accent, arpeggiation, and sheer length.

Beethoven follows the gloomy, tense P theme by an exceptionally beautiful, aria-like transition, making a parallel with the lyrical 1T of the *Presto*. Like that theme as well is the broken-chord accompaniment, here in flowing sixteenth-note motion that recurs in K, though in a more linear fashion.

The transition has a large range of over two octaves, climaxing on e^3, its remarkable expressivity also produced by a series of sigh motives (mm. $10^{1,4}$, 12^1, 13^1, and 15^1). T starts in the tonic, d, but moves surprisingly to C major and cadences there. It is thus associated with the only portion of the exposition in major. The implication of the modulation to C (fVII of d), as Tovey remarks, is that C major appears as the dominant of F major, the expected relative major key for S and K.[79] Instead, however, after the cadence in C Beethoven turns to A minor, the dominant minor, a surprise as he maintains the minor mode for P, S, and K. The indirection itself has expressive import as Beethoven avoids conventional expectations here and in the recapitulation. However, a resolution of c to f in the bass does take place, not to I of F but the augmented sixth of A minor. Resolution to the key of F major is postponed until the start of the development, in an early example of Beethoven's long-range effects.[80]

S also poses strong contrast to T though like T it begins with a descending fourth, here a diminished fourth, derived from P. The most dramatic theme in the movement, and harmonically the most tense, S hovers around V, cadencing on the tonic only at the end of its fourth measure, while exploiting both the augmented sixth chord and a bitter cross relation of d^2 against $d\#^1$ (m. 18^6) within that chord. The varied repetition of S (S^1) is almost explosive, as S^1a^1 is transferred to the low tenor, with an added countermelody in the right hand. S^1b^1 then extends into the high register with mounting diminished-seventh chords accented by *ffp* effects. Its tonic cadence comes almost as a relief. S, too, has an extremely large range of three octaves and a diminished fourth. This theme is a typical example of the unstable S of the Classic period, which does not exhibit the expected tonal clarity and stability of the second key area, a task that is shifted to the closing theme of the exposition.[81] Extension of S^1b^1 lengthens the theme by a measure to nine measures but the full measure is cut short by an elision with K. The brief K idea, derived from Tb, both brings this remarkable exposition to a lyrical close and acts as a preparation for the soft opening of the development.

---

[79] Tovey, *Companion*, 59. In the discussion of the *Largo*, beats will be identified on the eighth-note level unless otherwise indicated.

[80] For other examples, see Ch. 3, p. 281. For the use of the dominant minor, see Joseph Kerman, "Beethoven's Minority," in Sieghard Brandenburg, ed., *Haydn, Mozart, and Beethoven: Studies in the Music of the Classical Period, Essays in Honour of Alan Tyson* (Oxford: Clarendon Press, 1998), 153-54. However, Kerman does not include on his list slow movements in minor within cycles in major, such as this *Largo*. He deals mainly with works in C minor, and only first and last movements. Regarding Kerman's list of secondary key areas in minor-mode works other than C minor, we may add some nuances to his choice of keys. In the "Kreutzer" Violin Sonata, Op. 47/I, S first appears in the dominant major and then in the dominant minor; and in Op. 132/VI (see Ch. 4) v minor is preceded by its relative major, fVII of A minor, the keys returning as III (not iv)-i. Most of the examples of S in v minor occur in the middle period.

[81] See my article "Harmonic and Tonal instability in the Second Key Area of Classica Sonata Form," 23-57.

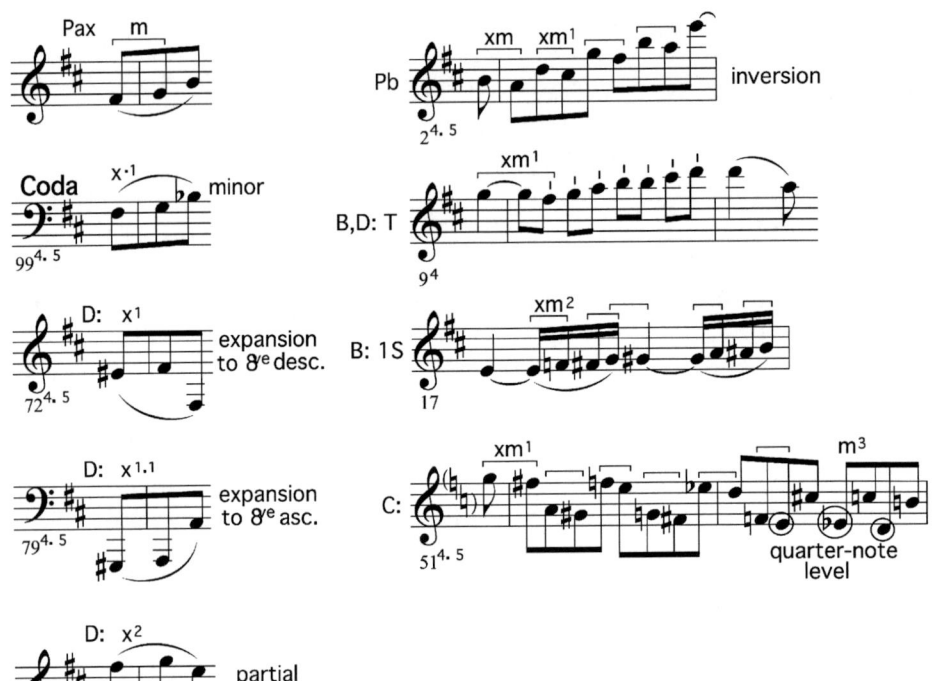

PLATE 2.II *Op.10, No.3/II: First edition, p. 35, second movement, mm.1-26³. Vienna: Musiksammlung der Osterreichischen Nationalbibliothek, S.H.Beethoven 46.*

The new themes of the development introduce further contrast. Because of its new themes, the section is sometimes called an episode.[82] However, a long history exists of the use of new material in this section from the early Classic period onward, and it was a device favored by Mozart as well. Beethoven utilized it in all periods of the composition. While in the Beethoven piano sonatas new material appears only in the early works, the procedure persists in the quartets and other genres. A striking example occurs in the Violin Concerto (see Ch. 1) and the most famous instance of all in the development of the *Eroica* Symphony/I.[83] Significantly, Beethoven introduces long new themes in the first-movement developments of the preceding Op. 10 sonatas, making this device a special feature of the set as a whole.

---

[82] See Tovey, *Companion*, 59. Tovey considers all new themes in the development as episodes. Christopher Wintle also describes the development as a "Trio" or "Episodic Development" in his long analytical article, "Kontra-Schenker: *Largo e mesto* from Beethoven's Op. 10, No. 3," *Music Analysis* 4 (1985): 150.

[83] For a survey of this device in Beethoven's music, see my article "Beethoven and the New Development-Theme," 323-43. For examples of developments consisting entirely or almost entirely of new material, see Mozart's "Paris" Symphony, K. 297/I (1778) and Beethoven's String Quintet, op. 29/IV (1801).

1N is a consoling lyrical theme in the much postponed key of F major, establishing only the second area in major in the movement. Set in a rich tenor-bass register, it recalls the low sonority of P, thus establishing a degree of parallelism between the two larger parts of the movement, a parallelism connected with the traditional melodic rhyming of the two parts in a binary or earlier sonata-form movement. The parallelism occurs in the *Presto* as well, but with the more traditional P theme though in the very untraditional tonic minor key.

The theme begins on the second larger beat of the measure, as in S and K (see 144-45), and like many new themes borrows some motives from earlier themes, here the scaler rise and fall from P and the turn motive from T. Simple I and V harmonies, conjunct melody, and balanced phrase structure contribute to its special tranquility. This tranquility, however, is soon broken by a brief *crescendo* leading to a transformation of 1Nz (mm. 33^{1-3}) harmonized by a diminished seventh chord on F♯ as the bass rises chromatically F-F♯-G to G minor. The *ff* accents introduce a stormy confrontation with 2N, as the bass continues to rise to G♯ and A/a, bringing the dominant pedal of D minor and the sole spotlight on 2N, destined to return in the coda as well.

Unlike 1N, 2N is at first high in register and developmental. The theme consists of brief three-note scale motives, mainly descending, with expressive variations and initial thirty-second rests, which could be called sighs.[84] Certainly the theme evokes the pathetic style in mm. 36, and 38-40. Each measure contains a melodic curve with a partial rise of an eighth and then a long fall. The top notes rise at first to d^3, e^3, and f^3, the highest note of Beethoven's piano, before falling to $b♭^2$ and continuing down to c♯, so that the entire range covered is over three octaves.

The last three measures are unique in Beethoven's sonatas. The melodic line descends *smorzando* without accompaniment and thus the rhythmic beat is totally lost due to the initial rests of the motive in addition to two eighth rests starting at the end of m. 41 through m. 42 (eighths 5-6, 2-3, 5-6). After a final *pp* in m. 42^4, the motive repeats *forte*, leaps a diminished seventh on a *sf* and descends largely chromatically and *decrescendo* to the reprise and return of P (Ex. 2.6 on p. 132).

The absence of the accompaniment has an even greater dramatic effect because a regular eighth-note accompaniment occurs from the start of the development, present either in the bass or inner voices in the left hand. Even when the inner voices have an initial eighth rest, the bass strikes the beat so the steady pulse continues for eleven measures of the fourteen-measure development. Rosenberg derives this steady beat from the repeated notes in P, m. 5.[85] Once again we find an analogy with the development of the first movement and its unified character due to pervasive eighth-note surface rhythm.

---

[84] I have borrowed the term "sighs" from Miriam Sheer, "Dynamics in Beethoven's Late Works, A New Profile," *JM* 16 (1998): 373.

[85] See Richard Rosenberg, *Die Klaviersonaten Ludwig van Beethovens*, vol. 1, 105.

Example 2.6 The collapse of 2N at the end of the development (mm. 40-43)

Absence of an accompaniment in the left hand and consequent rhythmic vagueness and low dynamics produce a subclimax before the recapitulation, an early example of this special effect. Similar low points, though far more extensive, appear some years later in first-movement development sections of Beethoven's middle symphonies Nos. 3, 4, and 5 (1803-08). In No. 4/I (1806), the subclimax appears before the retransition, which is built on a long *crescendo* from ***pp*** to ***ff***. A striking case is the retransition in the "Appassionata" Piano Sonata/III (1804-06), organized as a long rhythmic deceleration and dynamic decline from ***ff*** to ***pp*** before the reprise resumes its style of perpetual motion.

Both characteristic and surprising changes occur in the reprise. Pa itself returns in a richer and more active texture, with enhanced dynamics intensifying its expression via new emphases (two *rinforzandos*) and a longer *crescendo* to its cadence on iv. Additional dominant enhancement in mm. 44^5 and 45^5 and imitation of its important descending scale motive in mm. 46-47 increase the quality of movement in the phrase, while the vertical presence of nine notes in m. 45^1 darkens the sonority even more. The intensification or variation of P at the start of the recapitulation occurs in many Beethoven works from the early Vienna period onward. It is one of Beethoven's most characteristic procedures that makes the point of return a dramatic event in the movement. Examples appear in all the other works in this volume as well, in Op. 61/I, Op. 96/I and II, and Op. 132/I, II, and VI.

In this *Largo* P is also abbreviated as Beethoven replaces Pb by a modulatory phrase developing Px, like the omitted Pb, and ending in B♭ major. It thus functions as a new transition from P (NPT; mm. 49-52^1). Again we find a parallel with the first movement where in the recapitulation Pb^1 is also transformed into a PT function, modulating from D to e for the start of T. The progression is extremely indirect, however, starting as it does on E♭ major and minor chords, the Neapolitan harmony so important in the sonata. These chords function as

IV/iv of B♭ the ultimate destination, but V⁷ of B♭ moves not to its tonic but V$^0_9$ of vi to vi, ending on a g-minor chord, a deceptive resolution on the same bass note on which the phrase began.[86] The static, though coloristic chords are countered by the steeply rising melodic line: $b♭^1$-$e♭^2$-a^2-$e♭^3$, resolving with a final *crescendo* to a *fp* and the start of the transition.

Beethoven omits Ta and limits the transition to Tb, starting in a new high register reaching f^3. The phrase is set in the unexpected key of B♭ major rather than F, a fifth below the key of C in the exposition, since F major had already been given prominence at the start of the development. S, in the tonic key, returns with alterations in register as well, S being a fifth lower than in the exposition and S^1 being a fourth higher, and again reaching the highest note on Beethoven's piano, f^3. S^1 thus makes an even stronger contrast with the coda that follows, as Beethoven deletes K to move directly into his most dramatic section. Altogether the recapitulation is eight measures shorter than the exposition, omitting two lyrical ideas so that the section focuses on the darker P and S themes.

Unlike movements I and IV, which are intensely monothematic, Beethoven here stresses contrast of ideas and feeling within an overall somber expressive world. Yet, P can be divided into five motives which appear in various passages, usually rhythmically altered (see Ex. 2.7 on p. 134). The half step starting the movement (2m) is heard often as a sigh motive, both descending and ascending (as in T, S^1b^1, 1N). It appears at the very end of the coda where the opening d-c♯ becomes c♯-d, leading tone-tonic, rounding off the movement (mm. 86-87). This inversion of the motive is heard three times earlier as $g♯^2$-a^2 (mm. 81^4-83), the leading tone of V to V, thus making broad V-I melodic gestures. In this way, the very opening notes and relationships also close the movement. Further, shortly before, in mm. 84^6 and 85^6), both $c♯^1$ and d^1 are heard simultaneously over the closing tonic pedal.

Another pervasive idea is the falling fourth (4m), which appears in T, Sa, and 1N (in 1N inverted as a rising fourth, eventually a rising fifth). In Sa, the diminished fourth between the outer notes is also preserved. The descending fourth, starting on the sixth degree, appears twice, buried in the left hand above a D pedal near the end of the coda (mm. 84-86). Some analysts have linked this final descending fourth with the descending-fourth motive of the first movement. We will return to this question in the discussion of the sonata as a whole.

THE CODA

As in many of Beethoven's movements, the coda is the climax of the movement and here it contains some of Beethoven's most dramatic pages. Its great length has been noted above, since it is second in length only to the exposition.

---

[86] Note the typical enharmonic play on the exchange of g♭ and f♯ in the bass.

134

Example 2.7 The motives in P and their recurrence in the movement

The section divides into three parts: A, mm. 65-71, new climactic development of P1m; B, mm. 72-76, recall of 2N from the development section, mm. 37-38; C, mm. 76^4-87, final cadential phrases derived from P—2m and 3m, as the movement fades away to *pp*. The sectional lengths are: 7+4-1/2+11-1/2 mm.

Section A, as in so many of Beethoven's codas, is the section of harmonic tension (as in the first movement) as well as dynamic expansion, starting *pp* and ending *ff* (Ex. 2.8 on p. 136). The motive appears in the left hand while the right hand accompanies with offbeat broken chords at first in sextuplets, a purely pianistic setting. Starting on the low D, the motive descends to low B♭$_1$ and then low G♭$_1$, a half step above the lowest note of Beethoven's piano and the bass of the minor Neapolitan sixth on e♭, a most distant and black harmony. Each chord lasts a full measure. The dynamics change in each measure of mm. 65-68, progressing from *pp* to *cresc.* to *f* on the e♭ sixth chord. Thereafter, Beethoven speeds up the harmonic rhythm to two chords per measure, then three and four chords per measure before broadening out to two chords per measure, *ff*, in m. 71 (see Ex. 2.9 on p. 137). The bass notes rise partly chromatically to the dominant: G♭-A♮-B♭-B♮-c-c♯-d-e♭-e♮-f-g-g♯-a (m. 72), the rise intensified by increasing the upbeat broken-chord accompaniment to seven sixty-fourth notes after the sixty-fourth rest, at first in m. 69^6, then m. 70^{3,6}, and then on every eighth in m. 71 with the arrival of the *ff*, a good example of concinnity. For the chords, see the section on *Harmony*.

The basic intervallic movement in mm. 68-72 is in parallel sixths between the bass and soprano, the enharmonic equivalent of the diminished seventh. This is surely one of Beethoven's most striking passages regardless of period. The motivic content is less clear. All seems to derive from P1m, but the e♭ chord has only its rhythm, being a broken sixth chord, and the dissonant continuation features rising leaps of a major sixth, perhaps an extension of the key interval of a sixth from the e♭ sixth chord.

Section B culminates the long ascent of section A and opposes at its start the highest register of the early piano, again reaching f^3. Here, as in several Beethoven codas the composer recalls a new theme from the development, in this case 2N.[87] The citation of these phrases is a literal quotation of mm. 39-40. This time the theme does not disintegrate but repeats an octave lower, coming to an expected cadence on the low d and thus finds completion, denied in the development. The long bass rise is paralleled by the long soprano descent. All of B is set on a dominant pedal, alternating the tonic six-four and dominant chords, one chord per measure, intensified by the suspension of the fourth (d) over V. The simple and slow-moving chords create a welcome calm after the tensions of section A, a calm further supported by its soft *piano* dynamic after the first *fp*.

---

[87] See my article "Beethoven and the New Development Theme," Table 3, p. 335, listing 13 examples of this procedure in Beethoven, only three occurring in the early period. Besides this movement, they are in the Piano Sonata, Op. 2, No. 3/I and the String Quartet, Op. 18, No. 1/II.

Example 2.8 *The coda, section A (mm. 65-72¹)*

Example 2.9: The acceleration of harmonic rhythm in the coda (mm. 65-72)

Section C, the longest section, brings the movement to a close with the clearest derivations from P, here 2m and 3m. Phrase a (mm. 76^4-81^1: 5 mm.) develops 3m over harmonies related to the Neapolitan E♭ the second subphrase spinning out the motive on each larger beat in descending thirds: f-d-b♭-g-e♭-c♯. In moving from f^3 to $c\sharp^2$, a diminished twelfth, the sequence expands the diminished fourth of 3m. This unit, in octaves, moves from *pp* to the last *forte* of the movement on V. The final phrases, based on 2m and its inversion, have been discussed earlier. The movement fades away *pp* on a single note, the low D in the bass. Lack of accompaniment and rests in the final two measures recall the rhythmic vagueness and disintegration of the development, but with a regularity that controls the effect.

The entire coda section is built on a grand deceleration of surface rhythm, from the thirty-second and sixty-fourth notes in the accompaniment of P in section A, to upbeat thirty-seconds in section B, to movement in eighths, quarters, and dotted quarters in section C.

CONTINUITY

Unlike the *Presto*, the functions in the *Largo* are basically connected in various ways. The exposition contains only one apparent open articulation before S, the traditional place for this articulation in order to highlight the arrival of the second key and theme. In the *Presto*, Beethoven provides a dynamic setting for this articulation with a formal trill on V of the new key. Here, however, there is only a cadence on the wrong tonic, c^1, *piano*, and without a pause. S simply picks up the c^1 and makes it the upbeat to a new theme in another key, the dominant minor. The connection between the periods seems more important than the separation, a connection made also by retaining the same dynamic level.

The low dynamic level, in fact, not only links all the periods but it also links the main sections of the movement. In addition, the periods of P-T and S-K are joined by elisions plus anticipations, as the accompaniments of the followed period begin before the melodic line enters. A later Classic device, it remains a resource for Beethoven in his late works, as in the String Quartet Op. 132/I, S, and the *finale*. A surprising truncation occurs at the end of S^1 in the recapitulation as Beethoven cuts off the expected resolution of its closing dominant to start the coda. Tonic harmony follows that dominant, but without any feeling of connection. Other open cadences appear in this movement only at the end of the exposition, the end of section B, and within section C of the coda, as Beethoven gradually lessens the rhythmic flow toward the end of the movement.

Sound

Texture and Register

In creating the mood of sadness and melancholy, besides the use of the minor mode and traditional harmonic devices such as diminished sevenths, Beethoven resorts to the sound element as a powerful resource of color and expressive association. Beethoven's sensitivity to sonority has been remarked throughout the analyses in this volume and still awaits comprehensive study.

The first aspect of sound that immediately strikes the listener is the use of the low register of the piano contrasted with higher-register themes. The primary theme in the low range of the piano, starting around D and C♯ in the bass, contains thick chords of four-eight notes (even seven notes at the opening). Fuller chords of eight notes dominate Pb and its climax in m. 7^4. Throughout the movement, P remains associated with the darker register. Beethoven enlarges its return in m. 44 with an even fuller texture, especially in its first two measures, as indicated earlier. Pb's replacement by NPT retains the full chordal style of Pb. Though mounting into a much higher register it adds chordal fullness in each measure, starting with four voices and increasing to five and seven voices. P1m recurs at the start of the coda in its deepest register starting on D (two octaves below its original setting) and then falls on repetition to $B♭_1$ and, rhythmically outlined, to $G♭_1$, a half step above the lowest note of the early piano. These deep tones make an extraordinary impression even today on the modern piano. In the final presentation of P3m at the end of the coda, the motive remains locked in the same register as the movement's opening. Its low D, used for the final pedal, becomes the last note of the movement as well.

Two other themes related to P in sonority are S and 1N. Both contain full chords, especially S^1b^1, with its chords of 6-8 notes. Sa starts in a low-middle range and it is only in S^1 that the higher register is reached, in the counter-melody to S^1a^1 and extension of S^1b^1.

1N has a low placement throughout, situated between E and g^1. It sounds somewhat like a male chorus, its tenor melody doubled an octave below by what we could call the first bass. The melody and accompaniment make a general texture of 5-6 notes, rather like P and S. The mood, however, is totally different. These thick textures in P, S, and 1N differ markedly from the usual two- and three-voice piano textures of the eighteenth century.

Opposing the themes in lower registers are the much higher tessituras of T and 2N, and the start of section C of the coda. Both Tb and 2N reach the highest note generally available on Beethoven's piano, f^3, which is heard a remarkable eight times in the movement, starting with 2N, the highest range of the movement. This note, with its thin sound, is well suited to the poignancy of the passages where it is found.

Further contrast comes from the thinner textures in T, K, 2N, and the end of the coda as compared to the functions with full textures. T starts off in only two voices in typical melody-and-accompaniment texture, with a kind of Alberti bass. Only in Tb does Beethoven add two voices to strengthen the cadence. The first measure of K is in one-two voices, and then three voices, as the more linear bass builds up into a brief imitation by the tenor, so that the theme's last measures include four voices. 2N receives a simple repeated-note accompaniment in the left hand, dramatized by arpeggiated chords on the first eighth, the top note sustained on the dominant, a typical pianistic effect. Though in four voices, the texture seems much thinner because of the gap between the melody and the left hand. At the end, of course, only the melody continues, without any accompaniment at all, the extreme of the thin textures. Bare octaves (mm. 78^4-81^2) and monophony occur in the last portion of the coda and at the very end of the movement, linking the ending of the development with the dying away of the coda in texture as well as rhythmic effect.

We can see that low registers and thick textures are generally associated as are high registers and thin textures. These ideas generally alternate in the movement and thus have structural significance. However, as always, Beethoven is not absolutely schematic when it comes to expressive effects. Both light and shade are found in both groups.

Dynamics

The *Largo* contains the richest vocabulary of dynamic indications in the sonata, and most certainly in the early period—13 different markings. Two indications—*rinforzando* and *smorzando*— appear only in this movement of the sonata.

Rinforzando (abbreviated as *rinf.*) appears ten times (an eleventh is implied in a parallel passage, m. 57^4). The indication has two meanings, as Rosenblum points out:

> A short, sometimes forceful *crescendo* on a few notes, usually two to four . . . ; the other was additional emphasis or accentuation on a single note or chord, or on two or more notes.[88]

---

[88] Rosenblum, *Performance Practices*, 88-89. In the sonata's first edition, many *rinf.* marks fall within a group of notes rather than on its first note, as in S, m. 18^5, where it appears below notes 2-4 (see Plate 2.II). In addition, near the end of the coda, mm. 82^4 and 83^4, the *rinf.* appears below both notes of the sigh motives. In such cases, the *rinf.* would affect two or more notes. However, the best modern editions place the marking below only one note except in mm. 82-83.

In this movement, the term *"rinf.,"* appears on single notes, as in T, m. 9⁴, 11⁴, and 12⁴. It applies to high notes, as in T, or dissonant chords, as in S, m. 18⁴, or it occurs on an appoggiatura in a sigh motive, mm. 32¹, 82⁴, and 83⁴. The term here seems to mean "strengthened," since all appearances have a soft dynamic level. Of the three sigh motives near the end of the coda (mm. 81-83), the first is simply *pp*, while the next two are heightened by *rinf.*

The term *smorzando*, as Rosenblum indicates, is associated with such other gerund forms as *calando, mancando, morendo,* and *perdendo*. She states that

> According to Türk and others, they were originally synonymous with *decrescendo*. . . and diminishing, though Türk added (and Koch agreed) that *diluen*do, *moren*do, *perdendo,* and *smorzando* in particular signified a "complete disappearance" of the tone. Türk also remarked that *smorzando* and other such indications "may also be played with a little lingering" [i.e. a *ritard* in a passage] "toward the end of a composition (or section [of a composition])."[89]

The placement of this term exactly matches the contemporary definition. It appears three measures before the end of the development with 2N. In the first edition, the word is distributed over two measures, mm. 41-42. It comes after the start of the solo melodic line and therefore without a sounding beat. The marking suggests an even freer rhythmic effect, perhaps with a slight ritard. Preceded by a *piano* indication (*fp* in the left hand), a *pp* mark is added to the last note group of m. 42. This *pp* would seem to be a higher soft level after an even greater diminishing of sound.[90]

The remaining markings are as follows:

pp, p, f, ff, fp, ffp, sf, cresc., descresc. < > , >

We may start by observing where we find the lowest dynamic level of *pp*, which occurs eleven times. There are only four appearances, however, before the coda, where *pp* is marked most often. This softest level appears at the very start of the coda (m. 65) and in the final C section, which is basically *pp* except for a *cresc.* and *forte* to a half cadence in mm. 79⁴-81¹. It is expressively significant that nearly all the themes (except 1N and NPT) end softly, either *p* or *pp*.

Beethoven specifies the opposite extreme *ff* ten times: in the strengthened repetition of S¹a¹; near the cadence of K (a theme which is remarkably varied in dynamics); in the dialogue in the development between 1Nz and 2N, where *ff* is repeated on each main beat as a kind of dynamic accent (mm. 35, 37), in contrast to the *piano* of 2N; and at the peak of the chromatic passage in m. 71.

---

[89] Rosenblum, *Performance Practices*, 75-76. References are to Daniel Gottlob Türk, *Klavierschule* (Leipzig and Halle: Schwickert, 1789; facs. reprint Kassel: Bärenreither, 1962). This important treatise was translated and edited by Raymond Haggh as *School of Clavier Playing* (Lincoln: University of Nebraska Press, 1982).

[90] The Schenker edition does not space out the *smorzando* indication in m. 42 as in the first edition. The Wallner and Schmidt editions divide the word through m. 42, second eighth, since *pp* appears on the fourth eighth after the rests. Thus, the continuation of the indication through the fourth eighth is considered to be an error.

Three markings indicate sharp accents: *sf* on the offbeats in the countermelody of S¹a¹ and on weak beats (eighths 2 and 5) in the left hand for the chromatic coda passage, emphasizing the large leaps and diminished seventh chords; *ffp*, a very powerful accent, on the main beats in the repetition of S¹b¹, reinforcing the diminished seventh chords in this phrase; and *fp*, especially in the left hand in 2N, development section, for the long-held dominant preceded by an ornamental arpeggio.

Crescendos in this movement are short, no longer than a measure (i.e. six eighths) and have many different dynamic destinations: *f* (Tb, m. 15), or a sudden *pp* (P, mm. 7¹-8⁴), as well as *sf* (Pb, m. 7), *ff* (K, m. 28), or *fp* (m. 52¹). These markings lead to a climax note most often, as in Tb, or the start of a new dramatic unit (as in the development, mm. 34-35), or the arrival of a new thematic function (the *fp* for Tb in m. 52). The sudden *pp* in m. 8³ after the *crescendo* articulates the dominant chord ending P and elides with the start of T.[91] Briefer swells and diminishing of sound are indicated by < > or >. Short < > appear emphasizing the chromatic d♯ in Pb, for example. A *decresc.* occurs only twice, near the end of the development (m. 43⁴) and at the end of Pa¹ in the reprise leading to the unexpected NPT in *pp* (m. 48⁴).

The great range, number, and frequency of dynamic markings strengthen the dramatic character of this powerful movement. Beethoven's treatment of dynamics here goes far beyond the norm in his other early sonata slow movements, not to say Haydn and Mozart, and has more in common with his middle-period compositions.

Melody

Many melodic traits contribute to the unusual degree of affective tension in the movement. First, we should point to the unusually wide range of most themes as well as ranges that encompass dissonant intervals. While these have been mentioned in the discussion on Growth, it is useful to summarize and compare the ranges in a table (see Table 2.10 on p. 142). The only function with a narrow range, as we see, is 1N.

The widest range occurs in S¹ and 2N, both including the diminished fourth. The widest range of any section occurs in the coda, with its low $G\flat_1$, so that the section spans nearly the entire keyboard of the period.

Many dissonant intervals occur within themes, another distinctive feature of the music. These intervals include the diminished third (only in 2N), the diminished fourth, fifth, and seventh. The diminished fourth is the most important and frequent of these intervals and found twice in P (2m), where it is outlined as well in 3m. The diminished fifth appears in the second measure as an expansion of the diminished fourth. S includes the diminished fourth and seventh, and the initial melodic line in Sa is based on P4m, outlining the dimin-

---

[91] The Schenker edition's *dim.* in m. 83¹ is absent in the first edition of the sonata and was removed in the Schenker-Ratz revised edition

Table 2.10. Ranges of Thematic Functions in the Exposition, Development, and Coda

Function	Range	Interval
P	$c\sharp^1$-g^2	diminished twelfth
T	c^1-e^3	2 octaves and a major third
S	c^1-f^2	an eleventh
S^1	$G\sharp$-c^3	3 octaves and a diminished fourth
K	A-f^2	2 octaves and a minor sixth
1N	c^1-g^1	perfect fifth
2N	$c\sharp$-f^3	3 octaves and a diminished fourth
coda	$G\flat_1$-f^3	4 octaves and a major seventh

ished fourth. We should note too the large skips, often dissonant, in the bass of S^1b^1, with two diminished fifths, a minor sixth, major seventh, and descending minor seventh—all playing their role in the explosive effect of this phrase unit.

The minor second has long been associated with grief and tragedy, and it achieves great prominence in this movement. P starts with half steps (1m) and both Pa and b are saturated with them. After P, all functions except T, K, and 1N are stamped by this interval, which actually concludes the movement in the last measures. In the bass line, too, half steps and chromatic movement appear throughout the movement, most notably in the rising chromatic bass shaping the development and the long chromatic rise in the coda.

Irregularity of phrase and period length constitute a third source of melodic tension. Starting the movement with a five-measure phrase is surely unexpected, as is the consequent phrase of three measures eliding with T. And when Beethoven replaces Pb with a new transitional phrase, it retains the same odd length. Most irregular is the coda. In addition to the A section of seven measures, the C section contains progressively shorter units of 5+3+2+1-1/2 measures, as if the music gradually loses strength and purpose.

Harmony

The harmonic effect that stands out in the movement is the saturation with diminished seventh chords. Until the coda, these are the three basic diminished sevenths of the tonic, dominant, and subdominant.[92] Pa contains V^0_9 and Pb $\emptyset^0_9$/V. The three chords recur in the key of A minor in S and the development. It is S^1b^1 that contains all three in succession, organized as V^0_9, V^0_9/iv, V^0_9/V, V^0_9. The development, with 1Nz, presents V^0_9/iv, V^0_9/V, and at the end of the section, an implied V^0_9 of d, resolving to the tonic and the reprise.

[92] See Wintle, "Kontra-Schenker," 166-67, who calls the organization of the diminished seventh chords a "counter-structure" in the movement. Only in S^1b^1 do I consider the inversions of the chords. Wintle also reproduces and discusses Schenker's graph of the movement. He includes as well a detailed consideration of the analyses of the movement by Hugo Riemann, *L. van Beethovens sämtliche Klaviersonaten* (Berlin: Hesse, 1918-19), Diether De la Motte, *Musikalischer Analyse* (Kassel: Bärenreiter, 1968), 49-59, and Helmut Federhofer, "Zur Analyse des Zweiten Satzes von L. van Beethovens Klaviersonate Op. 10, No. 3," *Festkrift Jens Peter Larsen*, eds. Nils Schiørring, Henrik Glahn, and Carsten E. Hatting (Copenhagen: Hansen, 1972), 339-50.

In S¹b¹ the chords are treated freely in terms of resolution. Most are in the $^4_3$ position, with the seventh of the chord in the soprano, which skips or moves by step to the next seventh of the chord in an example of pure parallelism. The seventh is not resolved traditionally until the fourth chord resolves to i⁶ (see the theme on Plate 2.II).

The only major change with regard to this plan in the recapitulation concerns the new transition to Tb that replaces Pb and features V^0_9/iv rather than V^0_9/V as in Pb. This substitution occurs, according to Wintle, in order to preserve the V^0_9/V for the climax chord in S¹b¹.

Concentration on the diminished seventh chord reaches its apogee in the coda. The treatment of these chords in the A section, mm. 68-70, differs from the preceding examples (see Ex. 2.9). The first two chords resolve not as dominants but as diminished sevenths on the raised second degree to tonic $^6_4$ chords of E♭ and F, a favorite progression of the Romantics in the nineteenth century. After this sequence, Beethoven resorts to a purely chromatic succession of diminished sevenths on c♯, d, e♭, and e♮. All these can be heard as partly enharmonic equivalents of the three chords used in the body of the movement (the only enharmonic chord is the one on d spelled as V of c minor, equivalent in sound to V^0_9/V): V^0_9-V^0_9/V-V^0_9/iv-V^0_9. After this climactic use of the chord, it reappears after m. 70 only in the quiet closing section C. Two diminished sevenths occur on weak beats (84⁶, 85⁶), both of the tonic chord.[93]

Certainly, this treatment of the diminished seventh is radical in both its structural functions and voice leading. It links P, S, the development, the recapitulation, and the coda in one vast chain of dissonant harmony. In historical terms, the chord was associated with tragic and dramatic expression, and that is its overwhelming effect in this movement.

Another special chord in this movement is the Neapolitan sixth, a favorite chord and tonal relation of Beethoven, and significant in all the movements of this sonata except the Menuetto, as mentioned earlier. Here, the E♭ chords, first found at the start of NPT of the recapitulation, are in both major and the rare minor form (mm. 49-50). The next examples occur in section A of the coda, again as a minor ii⁶ in m. 67 and then major tonic in m. 68⁴. In section C, in the unharmonized spinning out of 3m in descending thirds, the note e♭² twice occurs unharmonized, followed by the leading tone, c♯², for the half cadence (m. 80³,⁴). All examples stand out as they are underscored by dynamics and other elements, the first by *pp*, the second by *f* after a *crescendo* and its very low register, and the last melodic examples by a *crescendo* to a *forte*, emphasizing the Neapolitan e♭ heard in three octaves as a quarter, not eighth note.

---

[93] The last two appearances occur over a tonic pedal combining c♯¹ and d¹ simultaneously as V^0_9 is combined with a d pedal heard on three levels. I have not stressed enough the dissonances produced by the appoggiaturas and non-harmonic tones added against the diminished seventh chords, as in P, Nz, and PT.

A third unusual harmonic effect is the use of the augmented sixth chord at the start of S, a chromatic off-tonic opening that creates suspense rather than clarity. Tonally, besides the harmonic indirection caused by the use of C major in Tb of the exposition and the harmonization of NPT, the inclusion of such keys as F and B♭ connect the movement with the first and last movements.

Rhythm

The movement contains the largest range of surface rhythmic values in the sonata, from dotted quarters to sixty-fourth notes. Dotted rhythms, syncopations, written-out ornaments (mm. 10^3, $13^{2\text{-}3}$) and ornamental repetitions (m. $18^{5\text{-}6}$) introduce further variety and contrast. As in the first movement, the primary theme displays the least rhythmic variety, moving for the most part in simple weighty eighth notes. 2N is also rhythmically repetitive, its sole pattern on the eighth-note level replicated throughout each measure except for the unique rhythmic effect of the last three measures of the development. The A section of the coda constitutes the rhythmic high point of the movement, produced by the rapid motion of the accompaniment. As noted in the discussion of the coda, the entire section is constructed as a large-scale deceleration of surface rhythm.

Though the meter is 6/8, it is often treated as 2x3/8 so that the larger second beat is equal in weight to the first beat. Thus, themes can begin and end on either larger beat as we find in this movement. I call this type of meter "combined meter" since it combines two shorter meters within a larger metrical unit. It is termed "compound measure" by Floyd Grave.[94] The most common type is the 4/4 measure operating as 2x2/4. Combined meter was in use from the late Baroque through Schubert. It was familiar to Beethoven from his study of Bach's *Well-Tempered Clavier* and his early fugal studies. Another relatively early movement using this type of meter is the 4/4 first movement of Beethoven's String Quintet, Op. 29 (1801). When Beethoven made a précis of the Kyrie fugue from Mozart's Requiem in c. 1819-c. 1820, he specifically identified the many shifts of the subject from beat one to beat three. Several late Beethoven works use this metrical format perhaps inspired by the Mozart fugue, including the Gloria from the *Missa solemnis* (1819-20), the Piano Sonata, Op. 111/I (1821-22), the overture to *Die Weihe des Hauses*, Op. 124 (1822), the String Quartet, Op. 132/III (See Ch. 4), the *Grosse Fuge*, Op. 133 (1825), and the fugue in the String Quartet, Op. 131/I (1826).

Here in the *Largo*, the melodic lines of T, S, K, and 1N all enter on the second main beat of the measure, T, K, and 1N preceded by their accompaniment that starts on beat one. This device of combined meter leads to extensions and compressions of half measures, thus increasing rhythmic flexibility and unpredictability. While P is eight measures long, its additional cadential half measure

---

[94] See the important article by Floyd Grave, "Metrical Displacement and the Compound Measure in Eighteenth-Century Theory and Practice," *Theoria* 1 (1985): 25-60. Grave identifies Beethoven's use of this meter in the Piano Sonata, Op. 111/I and fugue in the String Quartet, Op. 131/I. See also my article "Beethoven and Mozart's Requiem: A New Connection," 471-74, where I add other examples cited above. See Plate 1, p. 461, for the Beethoven leaf and 468-69 for the transcription.

elides with T. The T period itself, as well as S, are both eight and a half measures in length. In the coda B section, 2N finally comes to a normal cadence but it occurs in an additional half measure, so that all the following phrases in C start on the larger beat two. Indeed, the final cadence of the movement itself appears on the larger beat two of m. 87.

EXPRESSION

In the piano sonatas, this movement is the first of a handful of slow movements in the minor mode. It is the only such movement in the early sonatas. The next examples are the "Funeral March on the Death of a Hero" in a♭, Op. 26/III (1800-01), the first movement of the "Moonlight" Sonata in c♯, Op. 27, No. 2 (1801), and the *Andante*, also in d, of the "Pastoral" Sonata, Op. 28 (1801), a very different movement from Op. 10. Czerny described it as being "a simple narration—a ballad of former times."[95] The only other extensive, deeply expressive slow movement in minor in the piano sonatas is the much later 6/8 *Adagio* of the "Hammerklavier" Sonata, Op. 106 (1817-18).

The key of D minor itself is rather uncommon in Beethoven's music (the Ninth Symphony being the exception), and was used in other media for certain very dramatic slow movements. These include the *Adagio affettuoso ed appassionato* in 9/8 of the String Quartet, Op. 18, No. 1/II, the only other slow movement that can be compared to the *Largo* of Op. 10, No. 3 in the early period. As we know, this movement has a program, revealed in Beethoven's jottings in the sketches, which depicts the Tomb Scene from Shakespeare's *Romeo and Juliet*.[96] Other examples include the mysterious *Largo assai e espressivo* in the "Ghost" Piano Trio in D, Op. 70, No. 1 (1808) and the brief *Larghetto* marking Clärchen's death in the incidental music to Goethe's *Egmont*, Op. 84, No. 7 (1809-10), another connection with the theme of death. The music, in 9/8, also contains in measure 2 the same diminished fourth, f^2-$c\sharp^2$, so important in the Op. 10 *Largo*.

Many expressive associations were attached to the key of d minor as indicated by Steblin's survey of theorists from the late seventeenth to the early nineteenth centuries.[97] While Baroque theorists found the key to be associated with piety, gaiety, or as Rameau said, "sweet and tender" emotions, several later theorists related this key to the expression of melancholy. These theorists are Francesco Galeazzi (1796), A. E. M. Grétry (1797), Pietro Lichtenthal (1826), J. A. Schrader (1827), and Henri Weikert (1827). G. F. Ebhardt (1830) described the association as "gentle sorrow but also wildness."[98]

---

[95] Czerny, *On the Proper Performance*, 51.

[96] See Myron Schwager, "Beethoven's Programs: What Is Provable?," *The Beethoven Newsletter* 4 (1989): 49-55; and Hanna Weill, "The Two Versions of the *Adagio* of Beethoven's String Quartet, Op. 18, No. 1: Revisions in Dynamics, Harmony, and Rhythm," *The Beethoven Journal* 10 (1995): 60-65.

[97] See Rita Steblin, *A History of Key Characteristics in the Eighteenth and Early Nineteenth Centuries* (Ann Arbor: UMI Research Press, 1983), 242-44 and her list of sources.

[98] It may be that Mozart's use of the key of D minor in his operas, especially *Don Giovanni*, and the Requiem, inspired this association. J. A. Schrader (1827) and Ferdinand Hand (1837) make this specific connection with Mozart's music.

Another factor in the expressive associations of the *Largo* is the term "mesto" appended to the tempo designation. Theorists of the time, such as D. G. Türk (1789) and H. C. Koch (1802) define *mesto* as meaning "sad" (*Traurig*).[99] The term is also attached to the tempo heading of the moving, lament-like slow movement in f minor of the "Rasumovsky" String Quartet, Op. 59, No. 1/III, "Adagio molto e mesto" (1806). For Thomas Busby, the term is "signative of a pathetic and melancholy style of performance."[100] This style is described by Czerny as one where

> the hands and fingers must bear on the keys with a different, and heavier weight ... in order to produce that significant kind of tone, which may duly animate the slow course of an earnest Adagio.[101]

As Elaine Sisman has shown, the term was used by many composers in the eighteenth century. She notes eight examples in C.P.E. Bach keyboard works dated 1749-66, all in minor, plus other examples in Telemann, Quantz, and Haydn. The Haydn example is, surprisingly, the beautiful slow movement in F♯ major (not minor) of his String Quartet, Op. 76, No. 5 (1797), another *Largo*, this time *Largo ma non troppo, cantabile e mesto*.[102] Clementi too included the term in two piano sonatas, one again in major: Op. 7, No. 1/III (A♭ major), 1782; and Op. 40, No. 2/II (b minor),1802.

The association of the Op. 10 *Largo* with the expression of melancholy is undoubtedly due first of all to the remarks of Anton Schindler in his biography of Beethoven, the first edition of 1840, and then more fully in the third edition of 1860. The well-known statements run as follows:[103]

> [Beethoven] was more explicit when I asked him about the Largo in the D major sonata opus 10. He told me that at the time he had written it, audiences were more poetic (sensitive?) than now (1823), and that for this reason it had not been necessary to supply them with the idea. Everyone, he continued, had sensed in the Largo the spiritual condition of a person consumed by melancholy, and had felt the many nuances of light and shadow in this portrait of depression. ...
>
> Beethoven himself said that the pace of this rich movement must be changed fully ten times, though only so as to be perceptible to the most sensitive ear. The principal theme is always to be repeated in the tempo of its first statement; all the rest is subject to variation in the tempo, each phrase according to its own meaning.

---

[99] H.C. Koch, *Musikalisches Lexikon*, col. 952, Türk, 115. It should be noted that in his English translation of Türk (see above, n. 89), Haggh translates "Traurig" as "melancholy" in Ch. Six, par. 43 and 44.

[100] Thomas Busby, *A Complete Dictionary of Music*, 2nd ed. (London: Richard Phillips, 1806).

[101] Czerny, *On the Proper Performance*, 42.

[102] Sisman's examples were listed on a handout for her paper, "Paradoxical Emblems of Melancholy in the Age of Kant," in the Symposium at Princeton University, "Music and Melancholy," 2002.

[103] See *Beethoven As I Knew Him, A Biography by Anton Felix Schindler*, ed. Donald W. MacArdle, trans. Constance S. Jolly (Chapel Hill: University of North Carolina Press; London: Faber and Faber, 1966), 406 and 421. Only the first part of Schindler's remarks were published in 1840, without reference to tempo changes.

In 1977 it was revealed that Schindler had forged numerous entries in Beethoven's Conversation Books, so that one must be very careful if not skeptical concerning the veracity of his many statements about Beethoven and performance.[104] In the analytical portions of his book he shows preferences for considerable use of rubato and slow tempos, ascribing these to Beethoven. Yet, we know that Beethoven liked fast tempos and he strictly controlled variable tempo indications in his music, especially in his early works. Schindler states that audiences were more "poetic" when Beethoven wrote the *Largo* than in later years and therefore had no need of explanatory titles. However, no more than two years later Beethoven added the title "La Malinconia" [Melancholy] to the slow introduction of movement IV in his String Quartet, Op. 18, No. 6. Why one and not the other?

Schindler's first connection with Beethoven can be documented only from 4 November 1822 to May 1824. His presence is marked again in the Conversation Books from June 1825. From December 1826 Schindler attended to Beethoven's needs until the composer's death on 26 March 1827. It is difficult to believe that Beethoven would speak with Schindler about the *Largo* of a sonata composed twenty-five years earlier. Schindler's remarks to Lenz in 1856 seem very strange indeed (see above, p. 95). He asserted that, according to Beethoven, the *Largo* and finale had an "inner connection" and therefore the Menuetto was unnecessary. However, it is inconceivable musically to move directly from the slow movement to the humorous *finale*. This statement alone shows that Schindler had no real understanding of the *Largo*.

Czerny also remarked that "This *Adagio* [sic] is one of Beethoven's grandest but most melancholy, and must be played with the most attentive expression."[105] One wonders whether Czerny was influenced by Schindler's statement, also published in his 1840 biography. On the other hand, Schindler may well have been influenced by Czerny's suggestions for rubato in this movement.

Despite recent doubts about Schindler's veracity, however, musicians and scholars have accepted the association of melancholy with the *Largo* because several aspects of the movement support this association. Nevertheless, scholars and analysts have devoted their efforts to explaining the musical traits of melancholy in the string-quartet introduction rather than the untitled *Largo* of Op. 10, No. 3. The comprehensive study by Arno Forchert also presents a valuable perspective on the expressive associations with melancholy in the eighteenth century, after the long history of this "humor" going back to ancient Greece.[106] Forchert refers to the expression of melancholy in eighteenth-century

---

[104] See Lühning's article "Das Schindler-und das Beethoven-Bild." The forgeries were detailed by Dagmar Beck and Grita Herre, "Anton Schindlers fingerte Eintragungen in der Konversationsheften," in Harry Goldschmidt, ed., *Zu Beethoven* 1 (Berlin: Verlag neue Musik, 1979), 11-89.

[105] Czerny, *On the Proper Performance*, 42.

[106] See Arno Forchert, "Die Darstellung der Melancholie in Beethovens op. 18, 6," in *Ludwig van Beethoven*, ed. Ludwig Finscher, "Wege der Forschung," vol.428 (Darmstadt: Wissenschaftliche Buchgesellschaft, 1983): 212-39. This volume contains another essay on the same subject by Carl Dahlhaus, "La Malinconia," 200-11.

German poetry, which features "vacillation between joy and pain, between deep depression and overwhelming joy, and sudden unmotivated change of mood."[107]

Examining Beethoven's *Largo*, we find sharp mood shifts, between P and T, T and S, S and K and 1N, 1N and 2N. The low, thick texture of P corresponds to the association of melancholy with darkness of soul, grief, and depression. Still, Beethoven also reaches an opposing tranquil mood in the same register with 1N. Similarly, despite the high registers of T and 2N, the themes convey contrasting moods of warmth and joy on one hand, and sighs and sorrow on the other.

The unusual tensions in the movement, found especially in harmonic, sound, and melodic aspects, have been documented in the preceding discussion. Extensive use of diminished seventh chords corresponds to their importance in two of the chromatic passages in "La Malinconia." Further, chromatic eruption in the coda from the depths of the piano corresponds as well to the final steep chromatic rise ending "La Malinconia." However, while the introduction cadences suddenly and briefly in the minor (having started in the major), the *Largo*, in contrast, resolves harmonic tensions in both coda B and C sections, though with lessening energy to total exhaustion. As Maynard Solomon observes, the ending of this movement "foreshadows the disintegrating passage at the close of the *Eroica* Symphony's Funeral March."[108]

How much Beethoven himself suffered from melancholy we do not know. In his letters about the onset of his deafness (1801) and in the famous Heiligenstadt Testament (1802) the word is not found. In one of the first Beethoven letters that has survived, however, Beethoven speaks of this condition. The letter was sent to Dr. Joseph Wilhelm von Schaden, Augsburg, on 15 September 1787:

> For the whole time [since his return to Bonn] I have been plagued with asthma; and I am inclined to fear that this malady may even turn to consumption. Furthermore, I have been suffering from melancholia, which in my case is almost as great a torture as my illness.[109]

In his later letters and Testament cited above, Beethoven speaks rather of "resignation" and "patience," but in a second letter to his friend in Bonn, Franz Gerhard Wegeler (16 November 1801), exhibiting a complete change of mood,

---

[107] Forchert, 225. Of the large bibliography on the subject of melancholy see also Günter Bandmann, *Melancholie und Musik: ikonographische Studien* (Cologne: Westdeutscher Verlag, 1960) and Folke Nordström, *Goya, Saturn, and Melancholy* (Stockholm: Almqvist & Wiksell, 1962), a study of the work of Francisco de Goya (1746-1828), Beethoven's great artistic contemporary. Goya's famous set of *Caprichos* were produced in early 1799, shortly after the completion of Op. 10, No. 3. With regard to the *Capricho* 43, "The Sleep of Reason Produces Monsters," Nordström, 218, points out "how Goya represented melancholy by symbolical postures and nocturnal animals." See also his chapter on this *Capricho*, 116-32. I am grateful to Hannah Abrahamson for this reference.

[108] See Maynard Solomon, *Beethoven*, 2nd rev. ed. (New York: Schirmer Books, 1998), 138.

[109] Anderson, I, No. 1; *BGA*, 1, No. 3. Beethoven had returned from Vienna to witness the death of his mother from consumption on 17 July 1787. The references to "resignation" appear in Beethoven's letters to Wegeler on 29 June 1801 and Carl Amenda on 1 July 1801, as well as in the Heiligenstadt Testament, 6 and 10 October 1802, the last also referring to patience on Beethoven's part. See *BGA*, 1, Nos. 65, 67, and 106; Anderson, I, Nos. 51 and 54; III, Appendix A.

Beethoven asserts in a well-known statement: "I will seize Fate by the throat; it shall certainly not bend and crush me completely."[110]

Sketches for the Second Movement*

Sketches in the Fischhof Miscellany: f. 44v, sts. 11, 13-14; f. 45r, sts. 10-16; f. 44r, sts. 2-3, 6, 8-15 (see Plate 2.III). Transcriptions: Johnson, II, 39-41; N II, 38-39.

The sketches in the Fischhof Miscellany are clearly earlier than those in the Kafka Miscellany and the sketches that come closest to the f. v. are again the sketches for the coda, which will be discussed separately. Although six pages with sketches for the *Largo* have survived, there is no final version of a theme and certain themes are entirely absent: T, K, and 1N.

Earliest sketches for the movement appear on f. 44v and are transcribed in N II, p. 38, as well as Johnson, II, 41. Here we find the key, meter, and mm. 1-2 of Pa, starting in the original register. However, Beethoven extends the theme differently, using the half-step motive (P2m) plus a return to mm. 1-2 an octave higher. The implied length is the same—8-1/2 mm. and the same large range occurs, spanning the same notes, $c\sharp^1$-g^2. The move to the higher octave differs in the f. v., where only the first measure recurs a ninth higher. Following the theme is Beethoven's verbal indication that the section will close in A minor (*"hernach geschlossen in a moll"*). An attempt at the start of Part II (*"2ter Theil"*), the development, shows the use of P1m in the remote keys of b♭ and c, keys that Beethoven rejected later on. Nevertheless they show Beethoven trying out extreme harmonic effects, even at this early stage. After all, b♭ is the minor Neapolitan of a, and this relationship of e♭ to the tonic is a feature of the movement.

The first draft (f. 45r, Johnson, II, 39) remains bare. Again, only P, mm. 1-2, stay the same, followed here by the outer notes only of two unwritten measures, $c(\sharp)^1$-$b\flat^2$ and $e\flat^1$-$e\flat^3$, indicating very wide ranges. After a brief cadence formula in F, an idea derived from P starts in a but now modulates for a second time to F followed by a double bar. The modulation from a to F takes up only eight measures. Part II begins with two measures of left-hand accompaniment in b♭. A new lyrical idea in sixteenths then appears in b♭ and c, ending d:V with an etc. This passage links tonally with the first sketch for the same section.

A second draft (f. 44r, sts. 5-15; see Plate 2.III) is an attempt at outlining the entire movement, though most material differs from the f.v. The draft does not begin with P but with what seems to be the transition, which modulates from d to C, like the final T. Descending scale motives, more sixteenth-note motion, and a high register remind us of T, but as the phrases develop the key of C becomes the second key area, with a strong cadence there. After a double bar, new material appears, partly in broken chords, but not well defined, and it

---

[110] For the later letter to Wegeler and quotation, see Anderson, I, No. 54; BGA, 1, No. 70: "ich will dem schicksaal in den rachen greifen, ganz niederbeugen soll es mich gewiss nicht."

*See 118-20 for information about the sketch sources and abbreviations.

PLATE 2.III OP. 10, NO. 3/II: SKETCHES IN THE FISCHHOF MISCELLANY, MUS. AUTOGR. BEETHOVEN 28, F. 44R, WITH THE FIRST LONG CONTINUITY DRAFT FOR THE SECOND MOVEMENT, FROM THE TRANSITION THROUGH THE LONG CODA, STS. 5-15. *Statsbibliothek zu Berlin-Preussischer Kulturbesitz, Musikabteilung mit Mendelssohn-Archiv.*

passes through the keys of Bf, F, and d. After an indication "d. c." for P, a new T moves to g, and cadences there, followed by a bass line with repeated eighths indicated for eight measures, returning at the end to d: V.

Until this point, except for the choice of keys, none of the phrases belong to the f. v. Suddenly, however, the movement begins to take shape. S and S^1 appear in d (sts. 11-12) with some slight differences in the ornamental figure and some notes; the upbeat is lacking as well (addition of the upbeat occurs in a later stage in many of Beethoven's sketches; see the discussion of 1T's sketches for the first movement). S appears an octave higher than the f. v. The extension of S^1b^1, however, occurs in the bass, uses the inversion of the motive, and is a module of one measure rather than a half measure—it is not compressed. The entire theme is 9-1/2 measures, not 8-1/2 measures long, not a great difference. At last, Beethoven has found his secondary theme. Three brief sketches on sts. 2-3 contain what seems like another phrase for the development in bf; a phrase for T? in Bf, and another more active phrase in Bf falling more than two octaves. None of these ideas appear in the f. v

Sketches in the Kafka Miscellany: f. 156v, sts. 3-12; f. 157r, sts. 6-10; f. 157v, sts. 1-2. Transcriptions: Kerman, p. 21; N II, 38-39.

As in the sketches for the other movements, the Kafka leaves show an advance in the evolution of the movement as well as some experimentation later rejected. Sketches appear on three pages and each page will be considered separately.

A draft for P and T appears on f. 156v, sts. 5-7. It contains the f. v. of Pa except for the repeat of m.3. Here the cadence is on the subdominant for the first time. We see that Beethoven was concerned with giving Pa an impressive length, and through the repetition of m. 3 and extension to the cadence on iv, the opening phrase becomes 6 mm. long, an unconventional beginning. The continuation, however, was still a problem. Beethoven lengthens the theme with two substantial phrases, one a development of P1m in a sequence extending the subdominant and touching on the Neapolitan: g-E♭-d (4 mm.). The third phrase moves in dominant harmony of d, ending on V (5 mm.). Together, the three phrases make a very long P of 15 mm., later cut to 8 (-1/2) mm. and with minimal development.

A figured bass sketch for T starts on B♭ and leads to the dominant minor (also a Neapolitan relationship) and a phrase probably around V functioning as Tb. This unit is a breathless idea using upbeat repeated eighths with initial eighth rests, somewhat like 2N in larger values. The theme descends chromatically in a series of tritone leaps from f^2, e^2, $e♭^2$, d^2, $c♯^2$, c^2, and b^1. This chromatic sequence, however, anticipates the chromatic passage in the coda that had already been worked out (see below) and so it was eliminated. A notation follows on st. 7 regarding the second part of the movement. It refers to the recurrence of Pa, mm. 1-2, where it appears an octave higher on a V pedal as a kind of retransition. In the end, however, Beethoven discarded all these ideas except for Pa and the secondary key of a minor.

One other theme is notated on the Kafka sketches for the development (f. 157r, sts. 5-7). This is 2N, which has already appeared in the long coda sketch in Fischhof (see below). The theme is first harmonized on the diminished seventh chord of g, again indicating the importance of the key in this preliminary phrase, and then the melody repeats in the tonic d, functioning as the retransition, as in the f. v. In the first of the two measures in d, Beethoven already writes "ohne Bass," the presentation of the latter part of 2N being unaccompanied, an early conception that remained in the f. v. However, the theme moves in a steady rhythm without the disorienting rests of m. 42 in the f. v. Three eighths from the end of the theme Beethoven appends the term *calando*, a relatively rare kind of notation in the sketches.[111] Beethoven replaced it eventually with the more extreme *smorzando*, lasting much longer—a measure and a half. Melodically, 2N is less varied and extended in range than its final form. A fermata on the

---

[111] Rosenblum, *Performance Practices*, 80-82, list examples in early Beethoven where the term *calando* refers only to a *decrescendo* without a ritard, though there are also ambiguous passages, including this one. See her survey, 74-83.

last thirty-second note, not found later, invites a slight retard with the *calando*. After 2N, the reprise starts with mm. 1-4 of Pa placed an octave higher, a typical intensification at this point of the structure but not retained by Beethoven. What does remain is the imitation of 4m in mm. 3-4, a significant enrichment of the texture and expressive effect.

Despite the many sketches for exposition, development, and recapitulation few ideas remained: Pa, S, and 2N, the imitation in Pa¹. Beethoven tried out three keys for the second key area: a, C, and F, but returned to his first choice in the end. Still, the keys of C and F were to remain important in the final structure as well as B♭ and to a lesser degree the key of g.

Sketches for the Coda

Most interesting in these sketches for the *Largo* are the sketches for the coda, which come closer to the f. v. than any other section. As in the first movement sketches, they emerged at an early stage of composition when much of the thematic material of the other sections was still not worked out.

In the first fragmentary sketches for the movement in Fischhof, f. 44v, sts. 11-14, we find notated the low e♭-minor broken sixth chord resolving here to g-minor and d-minor harmony. This chord, starting on $G♭_1$ and found in the third measure of the coda's f. v. (m. 67) was one of Beethoven's first ideas for the movement, and it recurs in two drafts for the coda in both Fischhof and Kafka.

The first CD of the exposition and development in Fischhof f. 45r also contains a brief coda on sts. 14-15 of about 12 mm., including an "etc." in m. 5 after a cadence on V. Like all the coda sketches, the coda begins with P1m in the low register of the piano, here on D. Like the f. v. P1m is repeated sequentially in Bf_1 but then the sequence continues to G_1 followed by a move back to d:V. After this cadence, the concluding phrases appear in the treble using notes 1-4 of Pa. A few measures of tremolo in the bass precede a final $c♯^1$-d^1 ending, the repeated tonic concluding on the large beat two, as in the f. v.

The long CD 2 is followed by the longest continuity draft of the coda (f. 44r, sts. 12-15), a total of 27 mm., four measures longer than the f. v. if we include the revised ending. The draft follows S, as in the f. v., and contains all three sections of the coda. The A section starts as in the f. v. After three measures there appears a rising chromatic bass from G♭ to B♭, but then a cadence on V stops the rising motion and mm. 1-3 of the opening return, a surprising redundancy that was later eliminated. After the return of these measures, a longer five-measure rising chromatic bass occurs from A to g♯, with the same type of broken chords as before but here many of the chords replicate the choices of the f. v., and even an acceleration in the chromatic notes appears in the fourth measure. The B section follows with 2N in the tonic, the notes somewhat different from the f. v. Though only two and an eighth measures were written out, a repetition an octave lower, as in the f. v., is indicated by the word "ancora" after the start of the first measure an octave lower. Section C is not entirely written out since it has an "etc." after two measures. The section starts on beat two but an octave lower than the f. v. The Neapolitan major chord stands out even more predominantly, and the phrase ends on c♯^{1}, an octave below the f. v. A shorter, simpler conclusion follows in a revised ending of 4 mm., not 6-1/2 mm., without P2m and the final tonic pedal point. If we compare the lengths of each section we find that A is twice as long as the f. v. largely because of its redundant first six measures (14 mm. vs. 7 mm.). The implied length for section B is the same as the final f. v., 4-1/2 mm. Section C nearly matches the length of the f. v., 10 mm. vs. 11-1/2 mm. The coda CD is remarkable in its vision and completeness.

Still, as always with Beethoven, the coda sketches in Kafka show the composer exploring other possibilities and refinements for Section A, and coming much closer to the f. v. of section C. Two versions are drafted for section A. On f. 156v, after a two-measure harmonic transition, Beethoven begins the coda in e♭ minor; P1m appears on e♭ and then C♭, the same descent in thirds but to a very distant chord in the context of d minor. After a further descent by a diminished third to A♮ and an ascent an octave higher, the same chromatic rise occurs from A to a in the bass as in the f. v., with resolution as well to the tonic six-four and two further measures on the dominant (which may be intended for 2N, though the theme is absent).

A comparison of the broken chords and the intervals found here shows an even closer identity exists with the f. v. than in the long Fischhof coda draft, an identity of chords, top notes, and the important upward leap of a sixth. Even two *sf* marks are noted on two of the high notes of the skips, as in the f. v. The harmony accelerates as well, but is organized differently toward the end of the passage, so the chords move from one chord per measure to four per measure near the end of the passage. A slight broadening effect occurs at the end, too, which is much extended in the f. v. but found not at all in Fischhof.

On the top staves of fol. 157v, Beethoven experimented with yet a fourth beginning to the coda, here with P1m on I-V-I of the shockingly remote key of D♭ major. Then there continues a recall of 2N in D♭ (two beats only and an "etc."). An enharmonic modulation of d♭=c♯ precedes a return of 2N now in d minor, descending in groups of three eighths to C♯ and what may be supposed as a cadence in d followed by the C section. In this version, Beethoven omits entirely the rising chromatic passage in favor of an even more radical choice of key. Both Kafka versions of section A of the coda start in very remote keys, a half step above and a half step below the tonic, including the minor Neapolitan. The intention is clear—to introduce an extreme tonal deviation at the start of the coda. These sketches provide another illustration of the fact that the sketches may well be more radical than the f. v.[112]

On f. 156v, sts. 3, 8-9, and 11-12 Beethoven sketched the f. v. of almost all of section C, minus the last two measures. Two of these measures are worked

---

[112] Similarly, Beethoven's early tonal sketches for the development section of his Quintet, Op. 29/I were more remote from the f. v., featuring keys related to A major and third relationships rather than final choices emphasizing keys related to the closer C minor and fifth relationships. See my article, "Beethoven's Sketches for his String Quintet, Op. 29," 459-60.

out in two revisions of the low tonic pedal of mm. 84-86[1]. The distribution of notes still differs somewhat. The dissonant combination of d^1 and $c\sharp^1$ is still lacking, while the descending fourth is less perceptible in the second version, but found not at all in the first version.

From these extant sketches we can see that while Beethoven had built a magnificent coda, he had yet to discover and refine almost all his ideas for the body of the movement.

The Third Movement: Menuetto -Trio, *Allegro*

Few minuets appear in Beethoven's piano sonatas, as this eighteenth-century dance gives way to the scherzo in the sonatas and other genres. In the piano sonatas, only four such movements are entitled "Menuetto," those in Op. 2, No. 1, Op. 10, No. 3, Op. 22, and the middle period, Op. 31, No. 3, all four-movement sonatas. Tempos are not quick, the *Allegro* in Op. 10, No. 3 being the fastest speed, while others, which are marked, specify *Allegretto* (Op. 2, No. 1) or *Moderato e grazioso* (Op. 31, No. 3). Two movements are called *Tempo di Menuetto* and these appear in two-movement sonatas. The first is the finale of the early easy sonata, Op. 49, No. 1, a five-part rondo. Another example, the first movement of the middle sonata, Op. 54 (1804), "In Tempo d'un Menuetto," has a unique structure in a complex example of wit and humor.[113]

A fine detail of the Menuetto of Op. 10, No. 3 is the very start of the movement, coming as it does after the sorrowful ending of the *Largo*. Rather than opening immediately with a D-major chord, Beethoven presents a tied a^1 upbeat, unharmonized, so that the D-major chord is delayed a beat, making a small harmonic bridge between the movements and a less jarring change of mode.[114]

The brief Menuetto shares several features with Beethoven's minuet/scherzo-trio movements in the early piano sonatas. One is the two-reprise form of the Menuetto and its overall rounded binary form, A-B-A[1]. However, the first part of the Menuetto cadences in the tonic, not the dominant, resembling in this aspect only the Scherzo of the Piano Sonata, Op. 2, No. 2 (see Table 2.11).

The Trio is the only one of the early piano sonatas that is not organized in rounded binary form (see the discussion of the Trio below). We should take note of the choice of the subdominant key, G, while previous trios are set in the opposite mode, mainly tonic minor or relative minor (tonic major in the F-minor sonata, Op. 2, No. 1).[115] A typical feature is the rhythmic relationship of minuet/

---

[113] See Martha Frohlich's excellent analysis of this movement and the sonata as a whole in her article, "Beethoven's Piano Sonata in F Major, Op. 54, Second Movement: The Final Version and Sketches," *JM* 18 (2001): 98-128.

[114] Leonard G. Ratner points to a similar bridge provided by an unharmonized c^1 at the start of the *Adagio* in the Sring Quartet, Op.59, No.1. This note connects the previous *scherzando* movement in Bf to the key of F minor, though the uncertainty of the new key is prolonged until the entry of af in the second measure. See his valuable article, "Texture, A Rhetorical Element in Beethoven's Quartets," *Israel Studies in Musicology* 2 (1980): 56.

[115] While the modal relationship remains in most of the piano sonatas, it is found, for example, only in the symphonies in minor, not major.

Table 2.11. Timeline: Movement III

Menuetto

Key: D   Meter: 3/4

```
                    (a)
A      Pa     b           |a¹     b¹              ‖
       0³     4²    7-8   8³      12²     16
       D            D:V   (e)     D       D:I

B      ‖: c   (four imitative entries on F#- b-e²-a¹)
       16³    19    21    23
       b      E     A     D

                                              (b)
A¹     a²     b²          |a³x    x       x¹    d   |
       25     28³   31-32 32³     35      37    39
                    D:V   (e)     (G)     D

coda   ax-bx dialogue bx                  ‖
       43¹·³  47³   49    54              54 mm.
       D:I          d-D   D:I
```

Trio

Key: G

```
                    (a)
A      Sa     a¹    b     c       RT      |
       54³    58³   62³   66³     69
       G            e     D:V     D:I=G:V-V⁷

A¹     S¹a·¹  a¹·¹  b¹    b²              |
       70³    74³   78³   82³-86          32 mm.
       G            e     D:V     Menuetto Da Capo ma senza Replica.
```

scherzo and trio, the trio offering a much faster surface rhythm in triplets (as in this movement) or eighths in both hands.[116] Unlike previous piano sonatas, the *da capo* indication at the end of the trio is "senza replica," meaning that both parts of the Menuetto are not to be repeated when the movement returns. The indication next appears in the Piano Sonatas, Op. 22/III and Op. 26/II.[117]

THE MENUETTO

The Menuetto sustains the lyric intensity of the *Largo* though in a gentler and more limited manner. The relaxed lyrical minuet is also a Beethoven type, and in most examples, the lyricism represents a response to the previous movement.

---

[116] Faster surface rhythm occurs as well in the later trio movements discussed in this volume, in Op. 96/III and Op. 132/II (the Allemande).

[117] An early example of this indication appears in the Scherzo of the Piano Trio, Op. 1, No. 1 (c. 1794). See the article by Max Rudolf, "Inner Repeats in the *Da Capo* of Classical Minuets and

Though the melody in Part I is a parallel period of 8+8 measures, its second phrase intensifies by its start a step higher in E minor and the tonicization of the minor mode for three measures before the return to D for the tonic cadence. The gradual descent of each phrase after the initial leap—the Menuetto is the only movement in the sonata to start with a leap—is expressively inflected by a series of sigh motives in nearly half the measures. Indeed, the sigh is the emblem of most of the movement and source of its lyric character.

Part II of the Menuetto brings another eight-measure period with a surprising series of subject entries in learned style and mostly quick surface rhythm in eighth notes. The two-measure subject in bass, tenor, soprano, and alto entries, rises rapidly through the keys of b, E, A, and D, the entries briefly overlapping and then dropping out. *Sforzandos* placed on the long first note of each phrase emphasize the dominant on which the subject begins and also the intervals of imitation at the eleventh above and the fifth below at the end of the series. The bass opens with an ascending octave skip, rhyming with the start of Part I with its ascending sixth. The sharp contrast and forcefulness of Pc go beyond the contrasts introduced in other B sections of the preceding minuet/scherzos.

Like most earlier minuet/scherzos of the sonatas, however, and characteristic of Beethoven in general, the A^1 section returns in an enriched textural, melodic, and harmonic setting (see Ex. 2.10). The theme is placed in the alto at first (left hand), accompanied by a long trill above (mm. 25-28^1). Pa begins from m. 1^2 of the opening, without the rising skip and tied note, and ornaments the long note of m. 3. Starting in m. 28, Beethoven further enriches Pa by presenting the melody in octaves so that it is heard an octave higher. New harmonic ef-

Example 2.10 *Intensification of P in Part II (mm. 32^3-43)*

Scherzos," in *Max Rudolf, A Musical Life: Writings and Letters*, eds. Michael Stern and Hanny Bleeker-White (Hillsdale, NY: Pendragon, 2000), 123-34, with detailed references to the music of Mozart and Beethoven. For Beethoven, see 128-31. In the Op. 10, No. 3, Beethoven evidently preferred brevity after the very long slow movement, with greater weight transferred to the *finale*.

PIANO SONATA 157

fects include a chromatic passing tone on a♯ and secondary dominant of ii (mm. 28^2–29^1), leading into Pb. These enrichments serve as a prelude to the effective extension of Pa³–b from eight to ten measures, thereby breaking the march of eight-measure periods. A rising sequence of Pax tonicizes e and G, arriving with a *crescendo* to the melodic apex on d^3-e^3 in m. 38. This measure is further emphasized by the less frequent, augmented ii $^6_{4\ 3}$ chord and a *sforzando*, a typical example of concinnity, as melody, harmony, and dynamics coordinate to intensify the climax of the section. A new descending d phrase, with added chromaticism and an acceleration of harmonic rhythm, sustains the intensity despite the piano dynamic. Thus, the return of A is lengthened and deepened, and it becomes the highpoint of the Menuetto, indeed of the entire movement.

Following this climactic area, Beethoven introduces a quiet coda in the low register, which features a dialogue of motives from Pax and bx, with an inversion of the neighbor-note figure in mm. 5-6. Several fine details occur here: the tonic bass note on D of the cadence to P^1 anticipates the melody, a device prevalent in earlier movements; Pax appears not in the soprano but a low tenor register, and notes 1-2 are repeated, not held over (since the bass is tied); notes 5-6 are lengthened to dotted halves, emphasizing the sigh; in the repeat of Pax, note 4 is staccato, not legato; the motive from Pb appears in both original and inverted forms, shifting to the minor and a lower chromatic neighbor before the major returns; the bass notes alternate D and E, the very first bass notes of Pa; and an acceleration of harmonic and surface rhythm precedes the final appoggiatura cadence. All this takes place *pianissimo*. Despite so many transformations, alterations, and structural devices, the coda makes a warm and tranquil ending to the Menuetto, closing with a sigh.

Two further aspects of the Menuetto deserve comment: the full texture with often five-six voices;[118] and the syncopations created by tied quarters over the barline, which introduce rhythmic vitality in a movement with strong downbeat sigh figures. Two such syncopations in the left hand promote continuity at cadential gaps in the right hand (mm. 7^3, 31^3), and a tied note with a *sf* reinforcement strengthens the melodic climax in m. 37^3. The sophistication of the Menuetto reflects the care taken by Beethoven to maintain the high quality established by movements I and II.

The Trio

Even while the Trio seems utterly contrasted to the Menuetto, certain features link the two. The Trio also begins with an upbeat and an upward leap, here of a fourth. The upward leap is expanded to a seventh and octave in Sb, the octave also found in the Menuetto at the start of Part II. By concluding the Trio with three leaps of the octave on the dominant note of D, from A to a^2, Beethoven connects the end of the Trio with the start of the Menuetto via the same note,

---

[118] See Uhde, *Beethovens Klaviermusik*, vol.II, 196-99, for an unusual focus on the chordal texture of the Menuetto.

though not in the same register. Another common element is dialogue texture. The trio introduces a dialogue between bass and soprano, accomplished by the left hand crossing over into the soprano register, a texture that relates to the dialogue arrangement in the directly preceding coda of the Menuetto.

In all other aspects, however, the Trio makes an absolute contrast to the Menuetto. In terms of Growth, the Trio surprisingly lacks a second part, which Beethoven replaces by a varied repeat of Part I. The variation replaces the staccato upbeats with slurs connecting the two notes, though note 2 remains clipped by a staccato. This is a favorite type of slurring in Beethoven's music, and we find it again in the refrain of the Violin Concerto. Varying the articulation of a phrase or theme is also a frequent device in Beethoven's music (as in the Menuetto, m. 48).

Another change concerns the final cadence. At the end of section A, a brief modulation occurs to D major, the D chord becoming V^7 of G for the repeat. At the end of A^1, Beethoven remains on the dominant of D for four measures, including a sudden silence of four beats (another humorous touch). This dominant is then resolved by the return to the Menuetto and tonic of D major. The listener might well think that Part II was about to begin since there are examples in the minuets and scherzos of a varied Part I rather than an exact repetition, as in the Scherzo of the later Piano Sonata, Op. 26 (1800-01) and the Menuetto of the String Quartet, Op. 18, No. 5 (1798-1800). Part II, however, never arrives: the joke of the movement.

Unlike the Menuetto, the Trio is unified in rhythm, texture, and theme. Rhythmic integration derives from the nearly steady triplet accompaniment in the right hand to the broad melody in quarters. Triplet motion ceases only at the cadence of section A, as the rhythmic motion shifts to the soprano line in eighth notes. (We should note how Beethoven continues the triplet figure into the soprano in m. 67, beat one, avoiding a sharp rhythmic break between phrases.)

The melodic line of the Trio, as in the Menuetto, Part I, contains sixteen measures, divided into four defined phrases of four measures each. The first two, Sa and a^1, are arranged as a parallel period, 4+4 measures, moving harmonically I-V, V-I, a Classic formula found in 1P of the Violin Concerto/I. The third phrase, Sb, tonicizes the key of e, while the fourth phrase, Sc, cadences in D, or in A^1 ends on V of D. Phrases a and a^1 subdivide further as 2+2. Pax, on the tonic chord, is disjunct, staccato, and *forte*; Pay, on the dominant chord, is more conjunct, partly slurred, and *piano*. Such balanced phrases, subphrases, and contrasts, like the parallel period in the Menuetto in Part I, are Classic formulas especially popular in the later eighteenth century.[119]

Harmonically, we should note the same reference to E minor as in the start of Pa^1 (m. 9) in the Menuetto. Most interesting is the treatment of harmonic rhythm. In the Menuetto, the harmonic rhythm is fairly steady at one-two chords per measure, and often one chord per measure. In the Trio, by contrast,

---

[119] See Gjerdingen, *A Classic Turn of Phrase* and additional references in Ch. 1, n. 38.

PIANO SONATA

the harmonic rhythm is far slower, moving in blocks of two-four measures (see Ex. 2.11). A subtlety occurs here as the upbeats in S are first harmonized with the prevailing chord, but in Sb the upbeat is harmonized with its own chord, so that the chords change on beat three, not beat one. This syncopation of harmonic change continues into Sc, where V^7 of D occurs not on beat one of m. 67 but beat three of m. 66. Actually, the octave leap in m. 66^3 overlaps an ornamented octave leap in the right hand (g^1-g^2 in broken triads) on the seventh of V in m. 67, beats one-two. As we see, the manipulation of harmonic rhythm remains an important element throughout Beethoven's music, from early to late works.

Another striking contrast between the Menuetto and Trio concerns dynamics. The Menuetto's lyricism is complemented by its generally low dynamic level, with louder *sforzandos* occurring in its B section and climax in A^1. On the other hand, the boisterous Trio starts *forte*, balances *forte* and *piano* in Sa, but returns to *forte* in Sb, and reaches *fortissimo* in Scx before dropping down to *piano* in Scy. In A^1, all of Sc is *fortissimo*, making a strong dynamic articulation before the return of the Menuetto starting *piano dolce*, but only after four beats of rests, which soften the juxtaposition in addition to being a humorous touch.

Example 2.11 Harmonic rhythm in the Trio

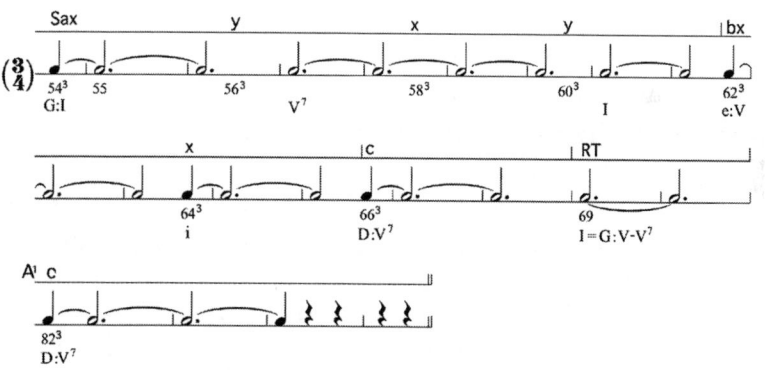

Note: The upper tie indicates sustained harmony, the lower tie ornamental change.

Sketches for the Third Movement*

Sketches in the Fischhof Miscellany: f. 44v, sts. 1-4. Transcriptions: Johnson, II, 42.

These staves contain sketches for both minuet and trio. The minuet sketch, with the heading "Min," consists of only eight measures, cadencing on the tonic, as in the f. v. Also like the f. v. is the upbeat start on the fifth, here a^2, as well as the descending melodic contour. Otherwise the theme differs entirely from the f.v.,

---

*See 118-20 for information about the sketch sources and abbreviations.

featuring as it does a long series in hemiola of descending thirds from a^2 to cs^1 in quarter notes, followed by a simple cadence with thirds at the start and end of the phrase. The theme is not lyrical but rhythmic and has the style of an orchestral dance rather than a keyboard piece.

It is the trio that comes close to the f. v. in key—G major—and thematic material. In contrast to the f. v. this trio has the expected two parts, organized in rounded binary form. Only the melodic line appears with rests for the reply in the second melodic voice. The melody here starts in the soprano, i.e. right hand, not in the bass as in the f. v. In Sb, rather than extended leaps, Beethoven has written a less dramatic continuation in rising thirds, repeated in a falling sequence on g^2, e^2, and $c\sharp^2$, recalling the skips of thirds in the minuet sketch. These thirds elide with a cadence in the dominant using an inversion of Say.

The big surprise comes in Part II with a sudden modulation to B♭ major. Repetitions of Say in B♭ are followed by modulations to c and g or d minor, with a cadence on g/d: V. The return to Sa in G major concludes with V^7/IV progressions and a dissonant cadence on $V^7/\flat VII$ and then V^6_5 of D, each chord with a fermata.[120] Ending on V resembles the f. v., the fermata replaced by four quarter rests. As Johnson observes, there is no hint of the triplet accompaniment.[121]

The turn to B♭ connects the trio to the surrounding movements, all of which touch on the chord or key, which form part of the larger D minor tonality so important in the sonata as a whole. Beethoven evidently decided to keep this tonal reference out of the third movement, which reestablishes D major after a long slow movement in D minor.

Sketches in the Kafka Miscellany: f. 156v, sts. 1-4; f. 157r, sts. 3, 4-7, 11-12; f. 59v, st. 1. Transcriptions: Kerman, p. 22; N II, 39-40.

While the Trio in Fischhof was close to the f. v., the Menuetto Part I is notated in almost final form in Kafka. The Kafka leaf also contains a long draft for the coda of the Menuetto, but of no other section of Part II except for a hint of the end of B and return of A^1. P appears on two staves, treble and bass only. Primarily, the sketch lacks the tied upbeats that lend such grace and rhythmic interest to the theme. Also absent are the appoggiatura and bass link in mm. 7-8. Here, P ends in m. 7^1 followed by four silent beats, an awkward and unmotivated break. Nevertheless, Beethoven does use the untied version at the start of the theme in the coda of the f. v.

On f. 157r, st. 3, a hold on g^1 and the start of Pa seem to indicate the end of the B section and return to A^1. This concept was not used in the f. v. that approaches A^1 continuously from the last entry of the subject in B. Most interesting on this page is a long sketch for the coda, on f. 157r, sts. 4-7, with Beethoven's inscription "in den tiefen 2ter thei[l] thema." Here is a decision to use the low register for the coda, in the f. v. for the entire coda.

---

[120] Note 3 from the top seems to be a^1, not g^1, on the final V^6_5 chord.
[121] Johnson, II, 338.

The coda here is 19 mm. long as against 11 mm. in the f. v. The first 8 mm. appear in the same low register as the f. v., using Pax. However, then Pa itself returns in its original register in a kind of resolved form, descending by step to a^1. This four-measure phrase repeats with an extension to five measures and ends with a descending D-major triad to the tonic d^1. The top note of the triad, a^1, has a tied upbeat, which may be the source of the use of ties in the f. v.

Looking at the first part of the coda, we find a similar dialogue texture to the f. v., but the response is a variation of Pax, not the quiescent motive from Pby. Both x motives have chordal outlines, I answered by V as in the f. v. Both motives are active, containing ascending skips of a sixth and seventh, and anticipating in this way the return of Pa. Another coda sketch on f. 157r, sts. 11-12, presents Pa in a higher register, starting on d^2. Harmonized on a four-measure tonic pedal, the melodic line emphasizes appoggiatura figures from Pa, m. 2, in a more expressive version of the theme. This version was not used by Beethoven, though he emphasized the appoggiatura in the coda dialogue. In general, the coda is too long in relation to the modest proportions of the Menuetto, longer even than all of Part I and half as long as Part II. Beethoven finally used only the dialogue portion of the coda, remaining in the low register as a response to the prominence of the high register in the climax of Part II.

On f. 59v, st. 1, one is surprised to find nearly the final version of the trio, mm. $1-8^1$ in A♭ major. Johnson suggests that the trio was first destined for the earlier Piano Sonata, Op. 7 (1796-97).[122] In this version the bass starts on beat one in mm. 1 and 5, and the bass reply in m. 3^3 comes on the first, not second degree. The sketch in Fischhof is a substantial advance on this version, and the trio itself more appropriate for Op. 10, No. 3 in light of its humorous finale.

The Fourth Movement: Rondo, *Allegro*

The rondo *finale* of Op. 10, No. 3, bears the title "Rondo" as do most of the rondo movements in the piano, violin, and cello sonatas in the period 1796-1804 (including the "Waldstein" Piano Sonata, Op. 53), and all the concertos.[123] In his "Anecdotes and Notes about Beethoven," Carl Czerny cited three types of Beethoven improvisations, which are listed here:[124]

> 1. In the form of a first movement or rondo *Finale* of a Sonata. He would play a normal first section [i.e.Part—"Theil" in the German original], introducing a second melody, etc., in a related key. In the second section, however, he gave full rein to his inspiration, while retaining the original motive, which he used in all possible ways. *Allegros* were enlivened by bravura passages, many of which were even more difficult than those found in his sonatas.

---

[122] Johnson, I, 337.

[123] For the background to the rondo, see the references to Cole, *NGD* and Ratner, *CM*, in Ch.1, n.67.

[124] Carl Czerny, "Anecdotes and Notes about Beethoven," included in Paul Badura-Skoda's edition of *On the Proper Performance*, 15.

Table 2.12 Timeline: Movement IV

Key: D   Meter: **c**

```
A (see below)        B                           A
(x,y)                (xm¹)              (xm²)
 P                    |T                 |1S            |P           |
 0⁴·⁵   4³⁻⁴   7     9¹·⁴        16     17      24      24⁴·⁵
 G-D    D:V   D:vi   D:I   mod. to A   A:v             D:V⁶₅   G-D

C
(x,y¹)    (y²,y³)              (y⁴,y⁴·¹)
 2So       2Sa                  b                              |Pa          |
 33        35      37     39    41     43    44       45    45⁴·⁵   48⁴
♭VI=B♭:I            g      E♭    E♭         mod. to F  F:vii⁶  F      d:vii⁶

                    A¹           D
(xm)                                        (x,x¹)    (x¹,x²)    (x¹)
 b¹                 |P¹          |T¹         |3Sa       b          c          |
 49⁴·⁵    55       55⁴·⁵    64¹·⁴   68       72         74         78
          d:V⁷     G-D      D:I    G, mod.b  b:V ped. . . . . .B♭,d

                    A²
(x¹·¹)
 d                  |P²                     |
 79⁴·⁵    83       83⁴·⁵          92¹
 around V  d:V     G-D            D:I=

coda                                                                 (x⁵)
Px+y⁴·²    seq.          y⁴·² ext. cadenza  |Px-y   Px³r  |1Sa+Px²+Tm  |K      |
 92²       93²       94²      95⁴    98-99    99⁴·⁵  101⁴·⁵  106         110-13
 G:V ped.  b:V ped.  D:V ped. . . .D:V⁷       G,g    E♭-D    D:I ped. . . . . . .
                                                                                113mn

Timeline of P
            (xm)
Pax,y    b              |a¹x seq.    c         |a¹x         c         |1T
 0⁴·⁵    2⁴·⁵   4³⁻⁴    4⁴·⁵    6²·⁵    7     7⁴·⁵    8²·⁵       9¹
 G-D            D:V                     D:vi                        D:I
```

2. In free variation forms somewhat like the Choral Fantasy, Op. 80, or the choral *Finale* of the Ninth Symphony; both those pieces give a true picture of his improvising in this manner.

3. In a mixed form, one idea following the other in a potpourri, like the Solo Fantasy, Op.77.

Often a few insignificant notes were all that were needed to improvise a whole piece, for example the *Finale* of Op.10, No.3 in D major.

PIANO SONATA 163

Czerny's reference to this movement suggests that it may embody an improvisatory style typical of the composer and, as we will see, several stylistic traits indicate this relationship. Czerny's remarks regarding the first type of improvisation can also be applied to this movement.

Like the first movement, this rondo is another example of a monothematic movement, quite unusual for the rondo style of the period, and not found in the other rondos of the piano sonatas and the rondos analyzed in this volume—in the Violin Concerto and String Quartet, Op. 132. As shown on Table 2.12, the movement is only one of two multicouplet rondos in the Viennese piano sonatas, containing three contrasting episodes— in Op. 10 without a complete sonata-form.[125] The form belongs to Beethoven's early style and this movement represents Beethoven's finest realization of this earlier rondo type (see the Timeline 2.12 on p. 162).

THE REFRAIN

The refrain of eight measures appears four times, the first two presentations being unchanged, and the last two with variations clarifying the rhythm and tonality of the theme. The essential length of the refrain does not change either, except for its final appearance which does not elide with the next period as earlier, and so is lengthened by a quarter note.

Unlike most rondos in the early piano sonatas, the refrain is not in the singing style but in a comic, capricious style, though its expression is transformed in episodes C and D (see Ex. 2.12 on p. 164). The theme begins ambiguously in rhythm and key. Does it start on the upbeat, as written, or on the downbeat? Since its three opening eighth notes are twice followed by rests of five eighths—the rests being longer than the motives—the meter is unclear. Regularity of motion takes place only in mm. 3-4 (Pb, with upbeat), where the left hand and harmony move in steady quarter notes, though they land on V with two fermatas in the melody at the half cadence. These fermatas on beats three and four again inhibit the rhythmic flow, especially the V cadence on the seventh eighth.

In the parallel four measures (mm.5-8, a^1) motives x and y develop sequentially but move to a deceptive cadence on vi followed by another long rest of five eighths before the final cadence elides with Episode 1 (m.9). The slurs of the three eighths, and the beaming of the notes in groups of three crossing the barline also suggest a downbeat performance (as we usually hear), not upbeat. Only with the start of the episode does a steady beat emerge.

Harmonic ambiguity relates to the opening chords. Are they in D: I-IV or in G: V-I? The sequence in phrase a^1 (mm. 5-6^1) implies G:V-I and thus an off-tonic start to the movement since the chords following the opening are V/vi-vi and V/V-V.[126] As the movement progresses, the varied returns of P, and motivic

---

[125] The multicouplet rondo *finale* of Op. 14, No.2 has no relation to the sonata-rondo.
[126] Off-tonic starts occur before Beethoven in, for example, Haydn's String Quartet, Op. 33, No. 1, and Mozart's "Prague" Symphony, No. 38, K. 504 (*Allegro*). For the broader aspect of this treat-

Example 2. 12 The refrain (P) (mm. 0$^{4.5}$-9.

development in episode D and the coda clarify the upbeat rhythm and V-I harmonic relationship of the opening.

The basic motives of P, identified here as x and y, consist of a melody and bass, a rising questioning line combined with a falling broken triad. This combination is an early example of Beethoven's use of a melody and its bass independently, which we know so well from the piano variations Op. 35 ("Prometheus," 1802) and the *finale* of the *Eroica* Symphony (1803).

The Varied Returns of the Refrain

Beethoven elaborates the refrain in its last two appearances in two different ways. In A^1 (mm. 55$^{4.5}$-64^1), the elaboration is contrapuntal—in learned style—and rhythmic. In Pa, the expected repetition of Px and y occurs only at the start. Then Beethoven omits y entirely and replaces it with a three-fold stretto of Px at the octave, thus also filling in four of the five eighth-note rests (Ex. 2.13). In Pa^1, the stretto at the octave of Px continues in the sequence of the motive so that motion is continuous until the deceptive cadence. Beethoven preserves, however, the long rests in m.7 of the refrain.

In A^2 (m.83$^{4.5}$-92^1) Beethoven also fills in most of the rests except those in m.7 and intensifies the surface rhythm even more. However, here he develops Py in essentially a dialogue texture (see Ex. 2.14). First, y does not combine with

---

ment of tonality, see Leonard G. Ratner, "Key Definition—A Structural Issue in Beethoven's Music," *JAMS* 23 (1970): 472-83.

PIANO SONATA

Example 2.13 Varied return of A^1 (mm. $55^{4.5}$- 64^1)

Example 2.14 Varied return of A^2 (mm.$83^{4.5}$-92^1)

x but answers x. The second reply is ornamented as the descending triad is filled in to make a descending scale of five sixteenth-notes. In Pb, the last three notes elaborate the left-hand harmony, making some strong dissonances. When Pa^1 returns, the scale motives of y^5 overlap x in the rising sequence, accelerating to thirty-seconds to preserve the outline of the descending fifth. Beethoven makes further changes in the cadence measure. He adds y^5 in stretto to the final appearance of x. The phrase ends an octave lower with a new turn at the final cadence (m. 91$^{3-4}$). Increase in sixteenth-note motion and stretto antcipate the start of the coda in m.92.

The Treatment of Motives x and y

Motive x (see Ex. 2.15, p. 167)

With regard to motive x, Beethoven changes the direction and size of the skip of notes 2-3 in Episode D and the coda. In episode D, notes 2-3 dramatically expand from a third to an octave, descending and ascending (x^1, x$^{1.1}$), and the rising third is inverted to a falling third in between the octave versions (x^2). It is this version that one hears at the very end of the movement until the last four appearances where the falling motive expands to a fourth (x$^{2.1}$) and alternates with a complete inversion (x^4). The motives x^2 and x$^{2.1}$ have an effect of a question (x) resolved by its answer (rising third answered by the falling third and fourth, and the final inverted form). The inverted form (x^4) is perhaps hardly noticed since it comes so late in the movement, *piano*, and deep in the bass. The main effect of an answer comes from the falling interval of a third, emphasized in the last passage of the coda (mm. 106-110). Perhaps unnoticed is another version of the motive, x^5. This version is outlined in the final right-hand rising passage of broken chords (mm. 110-12^1). It reverses the intervals to a rising third followed by a half step—a^1-c♯^{2}-d^2 (and an octave higher). Here, the half step resolves to the tonic note d, not the subdominant note g, in a final resolution of the motive. Most beautiful is the use of the rhythm of x (x^3) in the syncopated chordal passage of the coda (see Ex. 2.19).

Another version of the motive x is xm, that is, the fragmentation of the motive to its first two notes, the half step (see Ex. 2.15). This version, inverted, appears in Pb, the start of 1T, and the chromatic sequential extension in minor in Episode C (mm. 49$^{4.5}$-55). The half step in x becomes a series of chromatic scales, rising and falling in 1S, and is the source of all prominent half-step motion in the movement.

Motive y (see Ex. 2.16, p. 168)

Besides filling in and thus melodizing the triad in A^2 (y^5), Beethoven extends the triadic idea in Episode C, first rising in 2So (y^1) and then falling in 2S for more than two octaves in major and minor (y^2). The descending version is followed by rising eighths outlining the triad on the quarter-note level, as Beethoven uses the devices of inversion and augmentation (y^3). These passages (mm. 33-40) lead to a long unison of broken triads in sixteenths, a diminution of the original

Example 2.15 Development of Px

eighth-note rhythm (y^4). The triadic material contains some ornamental notes (passing and neighbor notes), the passing notes between the fifth and the third anticipating the filled-in y motive in A^2 (mm. 40-45). In the combination of motives x and y starting the coda, $y^{4.2}$ appears in eighths, as in the original y. The final appearance of y occurs in the coda in overlapping dialogue with x (x-y) in G major and G minor (mm. $99^{4.5}$-101). This version also recalls the overlapping-dialogue in 2So (start of Episode C).

The upbeat rhythm of Pa also clarifies at the start of Episode C in 2So, with the placement of Px as upbeat to beats three and one (mm. 34-35). In Epi-

Example 2.16 Development of Py

sode D, motive x is partly inverted so that notes 2-3 are descending in thirds and octaves and also rising in octaves. These versions have a natural accent on note 2, which appears on beats one and three, often with a change of harmony and emphasized with *sf* marks on beats one and three in mm. 77-78. In A^2, Beethoven also joins the inversion of the two-note upbeat motive (Pxm) in Pb with two-note beams and slurs, thus emphasizing the upbeat once again. However, at the start of the coda (mm. 92-95) a metrical displacement takes place. The first beat of m. 92 is like a fifth beat, ending the refrain. Beethoven then adds *sforzandos* on beats two and four, which function like beats one and three, as the barline shifts one beat to the right. While motive x still retains its ambiguous rhythmic placement, moving to beats two and four, the harmonization of its first note as a V^7 strengthens an upbeat effect. Motive y, with its *sforzandos* on the new beats one and three becomes purely down beat until mm. 96-97, with the shift back to the old meter, giving motive y also an upbeat effect.

In the last resolved presentation of Px notes, 2-3 always descend, and the motive regularly appears on the upbeats to beats three and one. The upper notes twice make a descending tetrachord on these beats: B-A-G-F♯ before the harmony alternates I and V (mm. 110-11) also on beats one and three until the final tonic.

THE CONTINUITY BETWEEN THE REFRAIN AND EPISODES

In connecting the refrain to the episodes, Beethoven exploits several devices for achieving continuity. One consists of presenting the accompaniment before the entrance of the theme, a Classic device prominent in the first and second movements. This occurs at the start of Episodes B and D with 1T (mm. 9, 64), within D (m. 72), and the end of the coda (m. 106). In each case, the accompaniment starts on beat one before the upbeat theme or motive enters as an upbeat to beat two or on beat four. Beethoven also connects the refrain to Episode C via a deceptive cadence on ♭VI. The chord then becomes the new tonic at the start of the episode. The very use of a deceptive cadence connects with the deceptive cadence in the refrain itself, heard four times in each appearance of the refrain. It also recalls the emphatic deceptive cadence in the first movement, connecting Pa in minor with the main part of the development. On the other hand, each episode ends with an open cadence on V and a fermata, firmly separating the episode from the refrain. A similar break, but with a cadenza on V^7, occurs in the coda, just before the false recapitulation of Pax and y (see mm. 98-101). These open cadences are more characteristic of the early than later styles. A similar cadence marks the end of the development in movement I as well.

THE EPISODES

The lengths of the episodes and coda are 16, 23, 20, and 22 measures. After the shorter first episode, the next episodes and coda are nearly equal in length, the longest section being the second, episode C.

Each episode differs in keys, material, and expression. The first episode, B, represents a kind of small continuation that could make an exposition with P appropriate for a brief sonata-rondo form. The episode introduces two new themes. A lyrical T makes the modulation from D to A with its thrice-heard subphrase Tx, which appears on three octave levels. The repetitions are modified by a chromatic note $a\sharp^1$ that is connected with the chromatic 1S. Against T, which is mainly in eighth notes, is the steadily moving bass in sixteenths, establishing a regular metrical pulse absent from the refrain. On the third presentation, Tx appears in the left hand as an alto part, starting on g^1, while the right hand varies the basic motive of the bass in a high register as a countermelody, the phrase making a quick modulation to A major and a cadence on A:V. The emphasis on G melodically and harmonically in most of T relates to the tonal ambiguity at the opening of the movement and apparent off-tonic start in G. A special feature of the bass is the repeated outline of a descending tetrachord (mm. 9^3-13^1), B-A-G-F♯, which will recur at the end of the movement.

1S seems most disappointing, 1Sa being essentially a chromatic scale mounting two octaves from e^1 to e^3, with some tied notes at the start that recur in the more varied 1Sb. After 1Sa recurs, 1Sb turns into a brief retransition to D major, ending on a V_5^6 chord and fermata. The theme, especially the chromatic scale, reminds one of an uninspired improvisor who, in desperation, resorts to a simplistic contrast to preceding ideas. On the other hand, it may be another humorous element in the movement. Yet, as we will see, Beethoven finds an honored place for this crude material. As mentioned above, both 1T and 1S are connected to the half step in Px (Pxm). The episode divides into two eight-measure periods, counting as the first measure the elided bass accompaniment.

In Czerny's description of Beethoven's improvisations of a first movement or a rondo *finale*, he remarks that Part II is the most developmental with relation to the "original motive" and also the most bravura in piano style. This is what we find in most of the remaining portions of the movement.

Episode C, the longest episode, is the most like a development section. The first main part develops Py and the second Pxm. First come two introductory measures (2So) on ♭VI (a B♭ major chord). Px is transferred to the bass and is repeated against overlapping, rising triadic forms of Py in the soprano. The first portion of the episode, 2Sa and b (11 mm.) develops Py (2Sa), which takes different rhythmic forms. First there appears a sequence of steeply descending broken chord ideas, starting with syncopation, answered by Py rising, augmented, and inverted, the motives divided in 5+3 beats. This melodic unit combines with an Alberti bass in sixteenths, another version of the triadic idea. The soprano overlaps the changing harmonies in the bass by one beat every two measures, creating a clash of I over V chords (Ex. 2.17 on p. 172).

After this exciting descending sequence in thirds, B♭-g-E♭ (six mm., 3x2), Beethoven lands on the Neapolitan chord in a five-measure unison passage rising two octaves still based on triads and triadic inversions derived from y, figures that are filled in with passing tones. The harmony at the end suddenly rises chromatically from $e♭^1$ to $e♮^1$ in the bass, moving surprisingly to F major vii^6 with a fermata. This eleven-measure section has the most active surface rhythm of the movement, the unison passage being most intense with sixteenths in both hands before the sudden slowdown in m. 45 and its nearly whole note and fermata.

The second section of ten measures emphasizes Pa and Pxm. The surprise is the false recapitulation of Pa, mm. 1-3, in F major, the relative major of D minor (♭III of D major), with a cadence that suddenly turns to d:vii^6. The motion starts and stops, with rests of five eighths in Pa and seven eighths following the fermata. Again, a passage, here in eighths, restores the momentum. The passage, once more in unison, mounts from the low register to g^2, using the half-step motive of Pxm, as found also in Pb. It then descends chromatically to a cadence on V^7 of d, partly with an implied two-voice melodic line. The blatant chromaticism in mm. 52-54 also recalls 1S. The episode has the most irregular phrase lengths: 2+6+5+4+6 mm., the larger subdivision being 2+11+10, as the two main sections are almost equally balanced. A larger pattern of rhythmic deceleration structures the episode as well. It is a motion-rest plan, with movement in sixteenths in most of the first section and in eights and long rests in the second section.

PIANO SONATA   171

Example 2.17 *Overlap of I and V in Episode C (mm. 35-36)*

Episode D combines the functions of recapitulation and a second development. After the first varied return of A^1, T^1 begins as before, but its repetition of Tx clearly modulates to G major (x^3, mm. 66^4), making explicit its subdominant tendency. A third appearance of x^3 in the tenor is harmonized in G, while a partial fourth recurrence in the alto modulates suddenly to B minor and a second development of Px but also Py (mm. 72-83). Thus, T does not lead to a reprise of 1S, as in a sonata-rondo, but to new development of P.

In this section notes 2-3 of Px are expanded to both falling and rising octaves (x^1, $x^{1.1}$) and the rising third is inverted to a falling third (x^2; see Ex. 2.15). The x motives are at first combined with another countermelody in sixteenths in the right hand, outlining triadic figures related to Py. In the next six measures, Beethoven introduces a typical and effective suspense passage with x^1 and x^2 descending on three octave levels in the left hand against high repeated eighth notes in the right hand, making an enharmonic modulation from B minor back to D minor in mm. 77-79. At the point of the modulation, Px^1 appears in a plunging chromatic series on e^2, f^1, g♭, and G, each motive starting on the last note of the previous motive until the note G♯ when $x^{1.1}$ takes over. The rising octave form elaborates the dominant pedal of d on A, together with a new brilliant passage in sixteenths falling to A. This is one of the most sophisticated harmonic passages in the sonata and will be discussed further in the section on Harmony.

Unlike Episode C, this episode returns to symmetry according to its main thematic and harmonic events, typical of the rondo style. The total number of 20 measures are subdivided into 8(T)+8 (Px, y modulation)+4 (V pedal of D minor). However, the surface rhythm highlights the passage of enharmonic modulation and makes an a-b-a subdivision of the measure groups: motion (sixteenths)-rest (eighths)-motion (sixteenths): 10+6+4 mm.

THE CODA

Each of the main movements of this sonata contains a long and significant coda, as in most larger movements of the works studied in this volume. Even in his early works, Beethoven assigns such structural significance to the conclusion of a movement that he often sketches this segment before the movement itself is fully blocked out, as we have seen in the sketches for the first and second movements in this sonata.

The rondo's coda (mm. 92-113) is slightly less than 20% of the total length of the movement and is the next to largest section of the movement, second only to the main development section in Episode C. The coda contains four units. As in the first and second movements it starts with a modulation, here a sequential canon between left and right hands in which Px and y are both melodically continuous and vertically combined:

$$x\text{-}y^{4..2}$$
$$y^{4.2}\text{-}x$$

This occurs in a mirror format (see Ex. 2.16, mm. 92-95). Thus, through variation, $Py^{4.2}$ becomes the inversion of Px—the two become one.

After rising in thirds on the dominants of G-b-D, with metrical displacement, the meter is restored in m. 96 on the dominant pedal of D. The sequential expansion of $y^{4.2}$ continues on the pedal in a second rising sequence. Starting in m. 95^4, the sequence presents V^6 of each degree from I to V, ending on V^7 with a fermata and d^3 in octaves as appoggiaturas. These notes resolve in a brief cadenza to the low $c\sharp^1$, again lengthened by a fermata, like the end of the episodes.

The implication is a return to P, and this occurs in the second event of the coda, a second false recapitulation of Px and y in an overlapping arrangement, with Px in the bass and Py in the treble, recalling 2So. The key is G major and then G minor, and each appearance ends with suspenseful rests of three eighths. The clear key of G confirms the subdominant implication of the rondo's opening.

Following this clarification is the most unexpected and magical portion of the coda, the syncopated chordal passage based on the rhythm of Pax (=Paxr), mm. $101^{4.5}$-105. This is the passage that was cited with enthusiasm in the AmZ 1799 review (starting with the preceding presentation of Px-y in G/g). The passage continues the previous *pp*, starting in the Neapolitan E♭ and ending in D (for the chordal progression, see the section on Harmony below).

The fourth and concluding segment in the coda first recalls the chromatic scales from Episode B (mm. 106-09), sweeping across the keyboard in three-octave spans, from d to d^3 and back. The scales, now ennobled, combine with a transformation of Pax^2 in the bass, first heard in Episode D, with notes 2-3 descending as if in reply to the original ascending question. Both elements appear over the final tonic pedal, the top notes of x^2 outlining the descending tetrachord from the left-hand accompaniment of T in Episode B. Px^2 appears here in resolved form, tonally and rhythmically clarified (see Ex. 2.15), just as Beethoven presented the resolved forms of his descending scale idea at the end of the coda of the first movement.[127]

Beethoven adds four more measures to this closing section in which $x^{2.1}$ and the final exact inversion of x, x^4, alternate in the bass while a new rising

---

[127] See also Kerman's remarks regarding such resolutions in Beethoven's codas, cited on 112.

countermelody in sixteenths outlines I and V chords. These broken chordal figures are associated with Py. Carefully varied as they rise and fall four octaves, the high notes of the rising subphrases are a^2-$c\sharp^3$-d^3, another varied and resolved form of Px, with the half step now moving to the tonic note of D major, not the third of G. Thus, both Px and y infuse the final right-hand passage of the movement, which further includes the last resolved forms of Px in the bass. The movement disappears with descending tonic chordal figures ending on a single low note, D, the same note that ended the *Largo*, but with a totally different effect.

The coda, like all sections except Episode C, also contains symmetrical subdivisions: 8+2+4+4+4 mm. The surface rhythm creates a different grouping, similar to Episode D: motion (sixteenths)-rest (eighths, syncopations)—motion (sixteenths): 8+6+8 mm.

Harmony

It was impossible to discuss the episodes and coda without references to modulation and special harmonic effects. This discussion focuses on a summary regarding tonal choices and a consideration of two harmonic passages not specifically analyzed in the preceding discussions.

The keys chosen in the movement are found in the preceding movements of the cycle as well (see Table 2.13). They will be discussed further in the concluding section on cyclic integration.

Table 2.13 Keys in the Episodes and Codas

Sections	Keys
B, Ep. 1	D-A-D:V
C, Ep. 2	B♭-g, E♭-F-d:V
D, Ep. 3	D-G-b-B♭-d:V
Coda	G-b-D-G/g-E♭-D

The first episode follows the traditional choice of the dominant key as the secondary key of the section. Episodes 2 and 3 are far more modulatory, however, the harmonic style supporting the motivic development. In Episode C, Beethoven emphasizes the flat keys, related to D major through D minor. Starting with the deceptive cadence on ♭VI, establishing the key of B♭ the keys move down rapidly by thirds, a frequent Beethoven sequence, and reach ♭II, the Neapolitan key of E♭, a favorite Beethoven destination. Here, as in the development of the first movement, the descending keys are tonicizations of the Neapolitan chord.[128] The E♭ chord receives further emphasis from the long unison that follows with the extension of Py, making a five-measure E♭ area before the

---

[128] See Thompson, "An Evolutionary View," 144-47, and the discussion on the development of the first movement, 108-09.

modulation to F. The surprising move to F, not a closely related key to E♭ though the relative major of d, occurs through the enharmonic reinterpretation of the diminished seventh: the V_9^0 of E♭:IV becomes the V_9^0 of F.

Beethoven couples the harmonic surprise with the surprising false recapitulation of Pa, which itself makes a sudden turn to d:vii^6, a dramatic shift underscored by a nearly full measure of rest that follows. The arrival in d, however, is strongly undermined by the chromatic passage in mm. 52-55, as Beethoven keeps the harmony in suspense.

While the second episode features key relationships of D minor, the third episode combines sharp and flat keys. The central harmonic event is the suspense passage that modulates from b to d via B♭, bringing another half-step relationship, b-B♭ (see Ex. 2.18). The harmony first hovers around b:V, the development of Px in the left hand and the accompaniment in repeated eighths in the right. The enharmonic modulation occurs as c♯^{3}-a♯^{2} in the accompaniment, m. 76, are repeated with a change of notation to d♭^{3}-b♭^{2} in m. 77. A rising chromatic melodic line carries the harmonic progression as follows:

$$b:V_{4\atop 3}^0 = B♭:V_9^0/V\text{-}I_4^6\text{-}iv_5^6\text{-}V_6^0/V = d:V_{4\atop 3}^0\text{-}V_9^0/V\text{-}V$$

One should note the remote iv^6 chord in the passing B♭ tonality, recalling the great emphasis on this E♭-minor chord in the *Largo*.

Like Episode D, the coda too passes through sharp and flat keys, and confirms, as stated earlier, the subdominant implications of Px-y. The subdominant plays a role in the harmonization of T in the first and third episodes, and it starts the opening sequence of the coda. These connections strengthen the role of the key in the movement as a whole.

Example 2.18 Suspense passage with enharmonic modulation in Episode D (mm. 74-80^1)

Example 2.19 Syncopated chordal passage in the coda (mm. 101⁴·⁵-105)

Most memorable in the coda is the chordal passage based on Paxr in mm. 101⁴·⁵-105 (see Ex. 2.19). Using the rhythm of a motive would seem to be the ultimate technique of motivic development. The turn to G minor in the reprise of Px-y becomes the springboard for modulating once again to the Neapolitan key of E♭ major. This beautiful passage exploits the old sequence of the circle of fifths, beginning not on the tonic but with the G minor chord functioning as iii: iii-vi⁷-ii⁷-V⁷. After V⁷ we would expect I⁷, but the tonic never appears—another remarkable stroke. Instead, in another surprise, e♮ is introduced into the chord following V⁷ of E♭ changing it into d:ii $^4_3$, which then resolves to V⁷-I $^6_4$ of D major, V⁹⁻⁷ (with suspended fourth), and V⁷, the following tonic an elision with the concluding tonic pedal of the coda. The resolution to the major I $^6_4$ has true magic as does the delay of V⁷ from the ninth and the suspension. Here Beethoven has sustained the harmonic tension with great skill and sensitivity. We should note too how the passage is given directionality by the descending melodic line: b♭¹-a♭¹-g¹-f♯¹-e¹-(d).

The start of the coda in G and return in the middle to G/g reminds us of the traditional role of the subdominant as a closing gesture, also found prominently in the coda of the first movement. The return to E♭ major at the end of the movement not only recalls its appearance in Episode C, but also in the closing portions of the codas in the first and second movements.

Sound

The dynamic range and types in the *finale* are almost identical to the first movement. While the first movement has nine dynamic marks, the Rondo has ten, spanning *pp* to *ff*. The usual loud level of *f* appears in the Rondo especially near or on the highest note of P, e³, which is tied over (mm. 3⁴-4¹).[129] Otherwise,

---

[129] In the first edition of the sonata, the placement of the *forte* differs from the Schenker and

the dynamic extremes *ff* and *pp* are not infrequent. For example, *pp* occurs with the start of Pa¹, the false recapitulation in Episode C in F major, the start of the suspense passage in B minor in Episode D (mm. 74-76), the second false recapitulation in G/g, and the first two measures of the syncopated passage in the coda starting in E♭ major. As Miriam Sheer observes, *pp* is a level often used for "tonal distancing," and most examples in this movement underscore remote keys as well as the first false recapitulation in a surprising key.[130]

Several appearance of *ff* indicate Beethoven's pleasure in loud extremes, occurring as a shock in Pa¹ (m. 7$^{4.5}$), at the climax in 1Sb¹ of Episode B on e³ (m. 23), the start of the big unison in E♭ in Episode C, and the end of the first part of the coda (m. 98).[131] Many *sforzando* marks, another Beethoven hallmark, emphasize metrical displacement (start of the coda, mm. 92-95), syncopated notes, and the dissonant chords with enharmonic modulation in Episode D (mm. 78-79). The *finale* closes *piano*, as in a few other early piano sonatas: Op. 2, No. 2, Op. 7, Op. 10, No. 1, and Op. 14, No. 2. Within the sonata itself, all movements end *p* or *pp* except the *Presto*.

The union of Px and y establishes the precedent for several settings in countermelody texture, which was so prominent in the first movement. Here we find examples combining a faster-moving line in sixteenths with a slower one in eighths, as in Ta¹, where the transitional phrase moves to the alto while the turn figure from the left-hand accompaniment is repeated in double counterpoint above in the treble (mm. 13³-15²). A similar effect occurs in Episode D, with the development of Px in the left hand against sixteenth-note figuration in the right (mm. 72-73, 80-82). The most striking example marks the end of the coda when Beethoven joins the chromatic scales of 1S in the right hand with the resolved forms of Px in the left (mm. 106-09), followed by broken-chordal figuration against the bass motives (mm. 110-12¹). We must not forget the descending tetrachord outlined by the resolved motives in the bass as well (mm. 106-110¹).

Beethoven also introduces learned counterpoint in the strettos of Px in A¹ and the canonic sequence with Px and y at the start of the coda, which thus begins and ends with contrapuntal textures. These examples relate to the imitative texture of the B section in the Menuetto, which therefore does not remain an isolated event. In A², the dialogue arrangement of Px-y, partly overlapping, recalls the overlapping of the motives in 2So and connects with the dialogue textures in the first and third movements. The motivic textures found in this movement remain characteristic of Beethoven's music throughout his life, greatly deepening in his late quartets (see Ch. 4).

Schenker-Ratz editions. In the first two appearances of Pa, the *f* occurs on a², the note before the climax on e³. In the next two appearances it is placed on e³ itself. The Schmidt edition in the *Werke* and Henle-Wallner edition follow the first edition.

[130] Sheer, "The Role of Dynamics in Beethoven's Instrumental Works," I, 187-88.

[131] The *ff* on the deceptive cadence on ♭VI in 2So does not appear in the first edition. It is found in both the Schenker and Schenker-Ratz editions, but placed in parenthesis in the Henle-Wallner edition and omitted entirely in the Schmidt edition.

Expression

Nineteenth-century references to this movement by Lenz, Marx, and Reinicke do not mention humor as a component of its expressive character. Carl Czerny, however, who knew Beethoven, characterizes the movement as "Humorous, like the Finale of the 5th Sonata, but more serene and capricious."[132] Most twentieth-century discussions of the sonata, however, describe the movement as humorous. Thus Denis Matthews points to "the Haydnish humour of the rondo-finale."[133] The question of what constitutes humor in instrumental music is a tricky one and has been dealt with extensively with relation to Haydn by Gretchen A. Wheelock.[134] There is no such comprehensive study on this subject with respect to Beethoven, however, and few good discussions exist comparable to those by Martha Frohlich and Janet Levy.[135]

In the summary that follows, it is helpful to keep in mind the remarks on humor in music by Christian Friedrich Michaelis (1770-1834), from his essay "Über das Humoristische oder Launige in der musikalischen Komposition:"[136]

> The humorous composer distinguishes himself through curious fancies that provoke smiles; he disregards the conventional, and without violating the rules of harmony—indeed often with the finest use of contrapuntal art—his imagination sets in motion such an amusing game with the melody and accompaniment that one is astonished at the newness, the uniqueness, the unexpected; and because all the bold modulation and lively variety combine in a beautiful, interesting whole, it is attractive and delightful.

In this movement, the refrain contains several humorous elements: first, the extreme brevity of the motives; second, both meter and key are unclear; third, in the first two measures, there are more rests than notes, the meter thus being further undefined; fourth, the extension of Px and y in mm. 7-8 is highlighted by a sudden *ff*, though framed by the same *piano* cadence, the first deceptive. The fourfold repetition of that deceptive cadence, found in all four presentations of the refrain, can also be considered a humorous aspect in its mechanical recurrence, and Beethoven picks it up for a fifth deceptive move—but one to B♭—for the start of Episode C.

---

[132] Czerny, *On the Proper Performance*, 42.

[133] Denis Matthews, *Beethoven Piano Sonatas*, BBCMusic Guides (London: BBC, 1967), 20.

[134] See her study, *Haydn's Ingenious Jesting with Art: Contexts of Musical Wit and Humor* (NY: Schirmer Books, 1992).

[135] See Frohlich, "Beethoven's Piano Sonata in F major Op. 54," 99-102; and Janet M. Levy, " 'Something Mechanical Encrusted on the Living': A Source of Musical Wit and Humor," in *Convention in Eighteenth- and Nineteenth-Century Music*," 225-56 (including examples in Haydn and Mozart in addition to Beethoven). References to humor and combining the serious and comic styles can also be found in my article, "The *Andante con moto* in Beethoven's String Quartet Op. 130," 229-34. Some points in my summary that follows are also made in William Kinderman, "Beethoven's High Comic Style in Piano Sonatas of the 1790s," *Beethoven Forum* 5 (1996): 133-35. For bibliographical references to studies on Beethoven's humor, see Frohlich, n. 9, and Kinderman, n. 3.

[136] *AmZ* 9, no. 46 (1807). The translation comes from Wheelock, *Haydn's Ingenious Jesting*, 196.

Another repetitive, mechanical effect is produced by the many cadences on V with fermatas: two such cadences occur unchanged in Pa in all appearances, making eight of them; one such cadence ends each episode, making three; two of them, not on V of D but vii⁶ of F and d, punctuate Episode C; and two end the first part of the coda, producing a grand total of fifteen such cadences in the movement, surely a huge exaggeration.[137]

Tonal surprises and evasions also have their humorous implications. In Episode C, after fiery sequences lead to the Neapolitan key of E♭, Beethoven quietly introduces a surprise modulation to the disrelated F major (that is, disrelated to E♭, and a false recapitulation of most of Pa, which itself suddenly cadences in d minor). The surprise is so great after this second quick modulation that it inspires an extended rest of seven eighths. Another seemingly humorous effect is the overlap of tonic and dominant harmonies in the opening sequences of Episode C (mm. 36, 38, and 40). The tonic chordal melody in the right hand extends too far down into the first beat of the next measure, thus clashing with the regular change of harmony to V in the accompaniment. The largely chromatic, simplistic 1S may also be humorous, and it ties in with other such chromatic movement closing Episode C.

These jokes well reflect what we know of Beethoven's humorous side, his ubiquitous puns in the letters and jocular canons (more in evidence in Beethoven's later years). The composer's greatest monument in the humorous style is surely movement II of the "Rasumowsky" String Quartet, Op. 59, No. 1 (1806), the *Allegretto vivace e sempre scherzando*.

Despite the obvious humor in the movement, there is also an impressive process of motivic development, clarification, and resolution. Both Episodes C and D contain stormy passages, and Episode D a mysterious passage of harmonic suspense. The syncopated chordal element in the coda suggests the sensibility mode. Brilliant style marks the first episode, the end of Episode D and the end of the coda. As in some other movements, Beethoven here combines the comic and serious styles with great success and originality.

As we see in this sonata, Beethoven has based both movements I and IV on minimal material. These movements exemplify some of the profound statements made by the theorist Francesco Galeazzi in his description of sonata form published in 1796, shortly before the composition of Op. 10, statements that particularly apply to Beethoven in so many of his works:

> This much is certainly true, that the best composers do not make any choice of motives [i.e. subjects]; to them they are all equally good.... The art, then, of the perfect composer does not consist in the discovery of galant motives, [or] of agreeable passages, but consists in the exact conduct of an entire piece of music. It is principally

---

[137] It may well be that in contemporary performance these fermatas were varied beyond Beethoven's ornaments. Malcolm Bilson plays one such elaboration for the last appearance of the refrain in his recording of the sonata.

here that one recognizes the ability and knowledge of a great master, since any most mediocre motive can, [if] well conducted, make an excellent composition.... Every good composition must always grow in effect from the beginning to the end.[138]

Sketches for the Fourth Movement*

Sketches in the Fischhof Miscellany: f. 30v, sts. 5-16. Transcriptions: Johnson, II, 43-44.

Fewer sketches survive for this movement than for the earlier movements and very little close to the f. v. The function for which most sketches appear is surprisingly 1S and most of these occur in Fischhof. A close approximation to the f. v. is in Fishhoff, f. 30v, sts. 14-15. The theme has seven measures, not eight. The few differences can be found in m. 4, which does not contain the tied note but sixteenth-note figures mostly based on beat two of the f. v. Beethoven probably found its sequential style too mechanical and so altered melody and rhythm in favor of greater variety. Measure 7 in the sketch is a condensed version of mm. 7-8, the f. v. filling in the skip in a quasi-cadenza from e^3 to g^1, not g^2 as in the sketch.

Six other sketches for 1S in A major can be found in the two sketch sources, four in Fischhof before or near the f. v. These appear on f. 30v, sts. 5-6, 7-8, 9-10, and 12-15. Only the first sketch in Fischhof is chromatic (another version appears on st. 16). All are seven measures long except the first, which is five measures; the fifth measure, with a fermata on g^2, appears in a revision on st. 6. All, however different, contain the same harmonic rhythm with one chord per measure, and the same pattern of chords alternating V and I. Most also include the framing notes of e^3 to g^1 or g^2,[139] and all, in Fischhof or Kafka, end with fermatas.

Sketches 2 and 4 have longer notes at the start of all or most measures, thus anticipating the tied quarters of the f. v. Of special interest is the melodic figure in sketch 3, which became the accompanimental motive of 1T in the f. v.

Sketches in the Kafka Miscellany: f. 155v, sts. 5-12; f. 156v, sts. 11,12; f. 157r; sts. 1-2, 9-12. Transcriptions: Kerman, 22-23.

The melodic figure that became the motive in the accompaniment of T recurs in Kafka twice, first as a one-measure notation on f. 155v, st. 5, and then in a different version on st. 6 marked "oder," of four measures that contain rising chromatic scales with the neighbor-note figure. It too has the framing notes of e^3 and g^2 ending with a fermata. A third version of Th as 1S appears on st. 8 with sequential repetition and a cadenza from e^3 to $c\sharp^2$ with fermata.

On f. 156v, st. 12, at the bottom of the page, we find the basic motive of the movement, Px. It appears with the opening pitches, the three notes connected with one beam and a slur as in the f. v., though without a barline. The

---

[138] See my article, "Francesco Galeazzi's Description (1796) of Sonata Form," 189-91.

[139] The revision of sketch 3 on f. 30v, st. 11, introduces e^3, which was lacking in the first version, whose highest note was d^3.

* See 118-20 for information about the sketch sources and abbreviations.

notation has the inscription above "zum Rondo." However, Py is absent here and in all the surviving sketches.

Of the remaining Kafka sketches, the closest to the final version are, once again, the coda sketches on f. 155v, sts. 7-9. On st. 7, there appears the broken chordal passage that ends the movement, mm. 110-112^3 and another shorter, slightly different notation of mm. 110-11. In both, only a few notes differ from the f. v. but these are crucial. The first version on st. 7 lacks the first high note on a^2 in the outlined variation of Px, a^2-$c\#^3$-d^3, but f♮ instead. In the improved second version, on st. 9, the Px motive is outlined starting from a^2 but the figuration omits the seventh of the dominant chord, g^2, found in the first and f.v. in m. 111^4. In the end, Beethoven combined these details in the two sketches for the f.v.

The second sketch is preceded by a descending largely chromatic scale from d^3, in three octaves and two measures in length. Here is the recall of the chromatic scale of 1S at the end of the coda. The more elaborate f. v., however, presents both rising and falling chromatic scales, each two measures long, that are fully chromatic.

For most of the remaining sketches, we can find resemblances to various passages in the movement, though they differ from the f. v. for the most part. For example, a contrapuntal sketch on f. 157r, sts. 11-12, contains a sequence of Px in the inner voice over a V pedal with sixteenth-note sequences above. Is this related to the dominant pedal in b of Episode D (mm. 72-74)? In two other brief sketches on f. 157r, sts. 1-2 and 9-10, the cadence of P resolves deceptively to V^7/b and V^7/C respectively. After both cadences, modulation follows. In the first example, Px appears in e, at the end of a sequence in b-a-G. In the second version, Px is found immediately on V^7 of C, and after the tonic of C there occur rising broken chords mostly in sixteenths suggesting a modulation to D minor or major. These passages are probably early ideas for the start of Episode C, with its deceptive cadence in B♭ and modulation to that key. But there, Beethoven features Py, not x. Still, the broken chords could be related to the sixteenth-note motion ending the first half of Episode C. The deceptive cadence to b relates to Episode D, but b there is a goal of the modulation, not a starting point. At the end of the sketch Px appears below repeated notes in the right hand, like the B-minor portion of Episode D, but in e. All the sketches with Px show only the original rising version, without change of size or direction, besides a change from the major to minor third.

In both Fischhof (f. 30v, sts. 12-13) and Kafka (f. 155v, st. 12) two-measure progressions contain modulation from G to b via an augmented sixth of b (with e♯). The example of Kafka in suspension style comes very close to the f. v. in Episode D, mm. 70^3-72^1, left hand, connecting T^1 to the central developmental area of the episode.

On the whole, the sketches for this movement represent an early stage of composition, and much material was never used.

Integration of the Cycle

The usual association with the concept of cyclic integration is thematic, as analysts search for thematic returns and connections among the movements. Beethoven did leave several examples in cyclic form, and these are listed and discussed in Chapter 4, since most examples appear in Beethoven's late works. Large-scale recurrence in the early period is rare and only two examples can be found: the Serenade for Violin, Viola, and Cello, Op. 8 (1796-97), and the Bonn cantata on the death of Joseph II, WoO 87 (1790).

In the early works as later, many other stylistic elements act to unify the sonata as a whole. Attempts have been made by Réti and Uhde to derive the primary themes of movements II-IV from the opening phrase of P in the first movement.[140] Such thinking is more in line with twentieth-century compositional practices than those of the eighteenth century. It is wiser to be circumspect with regard to such connections and to deal with more concrete relationships.[141]

Michael Tusa, in his key article "Some Factors for Cyclic Integration in Beethoven's Music," has provided logical criteria for investigating this aspect in all of Beethoven's music, and also the music of other composers.[142] The subheadings below derive from his study and have been used in Chapter 1 as well.

THEMATIC RELATIONSHIPS

Movements I, II, and IV start with a half step and the "opening gesture of the outer movements . . . outlines the interval of the fourth." The descending tetrachord of I/P, notes 1-4, recurs at the end of the codas of the first, second, and fourth movements, moving down from the sixth to the third degrees b (b♭)-a-g-f♯ (f♮)—and in movement I, followed by g-d (see Ex. 2.20 on p. 182). We may also add the thematic use of striking or recurring rests in each movement, each example with a different purpose and effect.

STRUCTURAL PARALLELISM

Tusa points out that such parallelism "is one of the most important means to cyclic coherence in Beethoven's early Viennese works." He emphasizes the presence in this work of long codas in movements I, II, and IV, all with a two-part structure, the first modulatory and the second confirming the tonic, though the confirmation can come late, as in the *finale*. Both codas of movements I and IV

---

[140] Rudolf Réti, *Thematic Patterns in Sonatas of Beethoven*, ed. Deryck Cooke (NY: Macmillan, 1967), 190-92; Uhde, *Beethovens Klaviermusik*, 176-77.

[141] With regard to thematic resemblance in Classic music the best guide is Jan LaRue, "Significant and Coincidental Resemblance between Classical Themes," *JAMS* 14 (1961): 224-34; reprint *JM* 18 (2001): 268-82.

[142] For Tusa's remarks and diagrams with relation to Op. 10, No. 3, see 159, 163, 166, 169-71, 174, 177. Other points quoted in my summary are made on 163 and 173.

Example 2.20 The descending tetrachord at the end of movements I, II, and IV

I/ mm.333³-37

II/ mm. 84³-86²

IV/ mm. 106³-108¹

contain resolutions of the main P ideas and both of these are placed in the bass voice. Further, Tusa shows that the two chordal passages in the codas have nearly identical soprano lines. Another structural parallel not mentioned by Tusa is the presence in movements I, II, and IV of lyrical transitions, the only lyrical element in each movement.

THE CYCLIC *FINALE* CODA

As Tusa points out, "In certain early works the coda of the last movement plays a special role in tying the movements of the cycle together." Such codas occur in all works in this volume, including those of the middle and late periods, with the exception of Op. 96. We have pointed out some connections of the *finale*'s coda with other movements. Another concerns the emphasis on the Neapolitan key and chord, which plays an important role in the development section of movement I and Episode C of the rondo, as well as the codas of movements I and II.

Tonal Cross-References

Tonal cross-references refer to keys "outside the traditional polarities of the Classical forms." Such cross-references are embodied in all works in this volume, and while they occur before Beethoven in the music of seceral composers, the most important models for Beethoven were probably the late works of Haydn.[143] This sonata is highly integrated by the recurrence of keys associated with both D major and D minor, the latter also the key of the *Largo*. Both episodes C and D in the rondo end in D minor. Both the development of the first movement and Episode C of the last exploit the same descending key sequence in thirds: B♭-g-E♭, initiated in both cases by the same deceptive cadence to B♭. The Neapolitan key and chord of E♭ seems to be ubiquitous in movements I, II, and IV as well as the codas of these movements. Very unusual is the use of the Neapolitan minor chord (which we associate with the development of the *Eroica* Symphony/I) in the *Largo*'s recapitulation and coda, and the chord makes a brief appearance again in Episode D in the enharmonic modulation from b to B♭ and d.

Tusa, on the other hand, stresses the key of G major and minor as a unifying key in all movements. In the first movement, the reprise ends in G major, which is then the springboard for the modulation in the coda to G minor and E♭ major. In the *Largo*, he cites the move to iv in the first cadence of Pa, and we can add the first appearance of 2N in the development in the passing key of G minor. Of course, G is the key of the Trio in movement III, and the key too of the off-tonic start of Px-y of the rondo, including the second false recapitulation in the coda in G/g.

Other keys also recur, such as A minor, the key of $1S^1$ in the *Presto* and S in the *Largo*; and B minor, the key of 1T in the exposition of the first movement, the start of Part II in the Menuetto, and the central key of Episode D in the Rondo. Even the key of F in 1N in the *Largo* returns in the first recapitulation in the rondo's Episode C.

As mentioned much earlier, unity derives as well from the intensive motivic development in the flanking monothematic movements I and IV. Tusa rightly states that the sonata "is arguably the most integrated of any of Beethoven's early works, this despite the widely diverging 'characters' of the individual movements."

List of Editions

The best modern editions of the Vienna sonatas are by Heinrich Schenker and Erwin Ratz, eds. (Vienna: Universal Edition, 1946); B. A. Wallner, ed. (Munich: G. Henle, rev. ed., 1975/76); and Hans Schmidt, ed., *NGA,*, Abt. VII, Bd. II, *Klaviersonaten*, I (1971). The Schmidt edition is the most reliable. Of great value has been the publication in facsimile of all the first editions of the piano

---

[143] See Ethan Haimo, "Remote Keys and Multi-movement Unity: Haydn in the 1790s," *MQ* 74 (1990): 242-68; and Johnson, "1794-1795: Decisive Years in Beethoven's Early Development," 1-28.

sonatas by Tecla Edition (London, 1989), with prefaces by Brian Jeffry. The original Schenker edition (c. 1923), with corrections, English translation, and introduction by Carl Schachter has been published in two vols. (New York: Dover, 1975).

Two other editions of the piano sonatas deserve mention for their commentary, though not textural accuracy. These are the editions edited by Donald Francis Tovey and Harold Craxton (London: Associated Board of the Royal Schools of Music, 1931); and by the great Beethoven pianist Arthur Schnabel (New York: Simon and Schuster, 1935). See also William S. Newman, *Beethoven on Beethoven*, "Source Manuscripts and Editions," 31-44. The most recent editions are by Barry Cooper (2007), replacing the Tovey edition; and by Norbert Gertsch (in progress, Henle), replacing the Wallner edition.

CHAPTER 3
Violin Sonata in G major, Op. 96

Background

Beethoven composed ten violin sonatas which, as a group, perhaps constitute the richest collection of violin sonatas by any composer. It is rivaled only by Mozart's fifteen mature works in the genre. Beethoven knew some of Mozart's violin sonatas. He modeled his own early piano quartets (WoO 36, 1785) on sonatas K. 379 (1778), K. 380 (1781), and K. 296 (1781). As Brandenburg observes, without the example of Mozart's last violin sonatas, such as K. 454 (1784) and K. 526 (1787), Beethoven's first published set, Op. 12, "would be inconceivable."[1]

We should note the musical context for the Op. 96. The list of major works dating from 1810 to 1812 includes the String Quartet in F minor, Op. 95 (1810-11), the Piano Trio, Op. 97, "Archduke" (1810-11), and the Symphonies No. 7, Op. 92 (1811-12) and No. 8 (1812). All these works were published much later than these dates, Opp. 92, 95, and 97 in 1816 (like Op. 96), and Symphony No. 8 in 1817. The late dates of publication of the chamber works have given rise to speculation that Beethoven delayed publication in order to perfect the compositions.

Neither of the chamber works resembles Op. 96 in mood and intimacy, though certain traits are held in common, such as the distant third relations of the second movements (Op. 95, f-D; Op. 96, G-Ef; Op. 97, Bf-D), though these are also found earlier, and the use of connected movements: in Op. 95, movements II-III, and in Op. 97, movements III-IV. Actually Op. 95 comes closest to Op. 96. Both works link the slow movement and scherzo, not *finale*, as in Op. 97 and many other of Beethoven's works, and they make the connection in a similar manner (see the discussion on 231-32). In addition, the *finale* of Op. 96 reflects the strong influence of the *finale* in the earlier String Quartet in Ef, Op. 74 (1809).

After the composition of Op. 96, there ensues a relatively fallow period of three years before works of the late style emerge, such as the two cello sonatas, Op. 102 (1815), the song cycle "An die ferne Geliebte,", Op.

---

[1] See Sieghard Brandenburg's valuable article, "Beethoven's Opus 12 Violin Sonatas: On the Path To His Personal Style," in *The Beethoven Violin Sonatas, History, Criticism, Performance,* eds. Lewis Lockwood and Mark Kroll (Urbana and Chicago: University of Illinois Press, 2004), 5-23.

98 (1816), and the Piano Sonata, Op. 101 (1816). As we shall see in the following consideration of the sonata, many important traits of the late style already mark this very special work.

In his article on the Op. 12 sonatas, Brandenburg points to the Cello Sonatas, Op. 5 (1796/97) as the works in which Beethoven worked out the role of the independent string part combined with piano. In Beethoven's earliest attempts at the violin-piano duo, the violin part is still very subordinate, reflecting the style of the accompanied sonata, though the violin is still essential to the texture. These earliest compositions comprise fragments of a slow movement and a rondo finale in A major, Hess-Green 45 (1790-91), a rondo in G, WoO 41 (1792), and the twelve variations on Mozart's aria "Se vuol ballare" from *Le Nozze di Figaro*, WoO 40 (1793).[2] The Violin Sonatas Op. 12 (1797-98) are completely different from these works. In these long, brilliant sonatas Beethoven makes the violin an equal partner to the piano. The sonatas can be compared in their seriousness and scope with Beethoven's piano sonatas Op. 2 (1793-95) and Op. 7 (1796-97).

Nine of Beethoven's violin sonatas were written in the short span of six years (1797-1803), while the last sonata, the work with which we are concerned, came into being nine years later in 1812 and was published as late as 1816 (see Table 3. 1). Only two sonatas are known to have been written for specific performers: the "Kreutzer" Sonata, Op. 47, for George Polgreen Bridgetower (1779-1860), a brilliant mulatto virtuoso; and Op. 96 for Pierre Rode (1774-1830), a famous French violinist. Both performers visited Vienna, their presence inspiring Beethoven to compose his two greatest sonatas.[3]

---

[2] For the early fragments, see Beethoven, *Supplemente zur Gesamtausgabe*, ed. Willy Hess, 9 (Wiesbaden: Breitkopf & Härtel, 1965), 115-118. Though Hess includes the fragments in a section for works of uncertain authenticity, Brandenburg points out that these fragments are in autograph. The rondo in G and variations are included in the Beethoven *Werke*, Abt. V, in II of the *Werke für Klavier und Violine*, ed. Sieghard Brandenburg (Munich: G. Henle, 1974). The volume also contains *Sechs deutsche Tänze*, WoO 42 (1796) for piano and violin, very simple and modest pieces. The edition in this volume of the Sonata Op. 96 is the best one available and was consulted for this study. The Sonatas Opp. 12, 23, and 24 comprise volume I of this edition, and the remaining sonatas volume II. All the sonatas were first published as piano-violin sonatas, placing the piano first in the title.

[3] For the dates of the Violin Sonatas see the Work-list by Douglas Johnson and Scott G. Burnham in the article, "Beethoven," *NGD*, 2nd ed., 3: 118-19. For Op. 47, Beethoven had already composed the *finale* in 1802 as the third movement of the Violin Sonata, Op., 30 No. 1, a movement whose length, complexity, and energy were inappropriate for that lyrical work but most suitable for the brilliant sonata intended for Bridgetower. For a study of this sonata, see Suhnne Ahn, "*Quasi come d'un concerto*: Genre, Style, and Compositional Procedures in Beethoven's *Kreutzer Sonata*" (Ph.D. diss., Harvard University, 1997); UM-9721651. There are two books on the performance of the Beethoven Violin Sonatas by eminent violinists: Joseph Szigeti, *The Ten Beethoven Sonatas for Piano and Violin*, ed. Paul Rolland (Urbana: American String Teachers Association, 1965); and Max Rostal, *Beethoven, The Sonatas for Piano and Violin: Thoughts on their Interpretation*, trans. Horace and Anna Rosenberg (Toccata Press, 1985). A German edition was published earlier (Munich: R.Piper, 1981). Rostal devotes a full chapter to each of the ten sonatas, but with remarks mostly on performance aspects. This volume has a chapter by Günter Ludwig, "Postscript from the Pianist's Point of View," with a useful survey of pedal markings, 189-202.

Table 3.1 Overview of Beethoven's Violin Sonatas

Opus Number	Keys	Dates of Composition
Op. 12, Nos.1-3	D, A, E♭	1797-98
Op. 23, Op. 24	a, F	1800-01
Op. 30, Nos. 1-3	A, c, G	1801-02
Op. 47	a	1802-03
Op. 96	G	1812

Pierre Rode, a student of G. B. Viotti, was coauthor of a treatise on violin playing (1803) with two of France's leading violinists, Pierre Baillot and Rodolphe Kreutzer. It was Kreutzer, in fact, who received the dedication of the Sonata Op. 47. Rode's thirteen violin concertos "represent . . . the model of the French violin concerto, accepted as such by the entire generation and respected even by Beethoven."[4] His *24 Caprices* (1815) are still studied by budding violinists. From 1799 to 1814 Rode toured Europe, arriving in Vienna in December 1812. He gave two concerts in the large and small Redoutensaal on 6 and 31 January 1813, and the first two performances of Beethoven's new violin sonata on 29 December 1812 and 7 January 1813. The sonata performances took place in the palace of Prince Lobkowitz,[5] the piano part played by Archduke Rudolph (1788-1831), Beethoven's only composition student and devoted patron.[6]

---

[4] Boris Schwarz/Clive Brown (work-list), "Rode, (Jacques) Pierre, (Joseph), *NGD*, 2nd ed., 21: 492.

[5] Prince Lobkowitz (1772-1816) was one of Beethoven's most important patrons, the dedicatee of such major works as the Op. 18 and Op. 74 string quartets, Symphonies Nos. 3, 5, and 6 (the last two with Count Rasumovsky); and the song cycle "An die ferne Geliebte," Op. 98. For a biographical study of this passionate music lover, see Jaroslav Macek, "Franz Joseph Maximilian Lobkowitz, Musikfreund und Kunstmäzen," in *Beethoven und Böhmen*, eds. Sieghard Brandenburg and Martella Gutiérrez-Denhoff (Bonn: Beethoven-Haus, 1988), 147-202. See also Tomislav Volek and Jaroslav Macek, "Beethoven und Fürst Lobkowitz," *ibid.,* . 203-17. An earlier article in English that covers some of the same ground with relation to the early rehearsals of the "*Eroica*" is "Beethoven's Rehearsals at the Lobkowitz's," *Musical Times* 127 (1986): 75-80.

[6] The Archduke Rudolph (1788-1831) was the youngest son of the Emperor Leopold II and brother of Emperor Franz I. Beethoven dedicated many of his greatest works to the Archduke, including the Triple Concerto, the Fourth and Fifth Piano Concertos, the Piano Sonatas "Das Lebewohl," Op. 81a. the "Hammerklavier," Op. 106, and his last piano sonata Op. 111, as well as the Op. 96 Violin Sonata, the "Archduke" Piano Trio, Op. 97, and the four-hand piano arrangement of the *Grosse Fuge*, Op. 134. The Archduke was a gifted composer and pianist. Beethoven's *Missa solemnis*, Op. 123, originally intended for the installation of the Archduke as Archbishop and Cardinal of Olmütz on 9 March 1820, is dedicated to him. For an excellent study of this remarkable figure, see Susan Kagan, *Archduke Rudolph, Beethoven's Patron, Pupil, and Friend, His Life and Music* (Stuyvesant, NY: Pendragon, 1988). Some of his music has recently been published and recorded.

Much has been made of Spohr's scathing remarks in his autobiography about Rode's solo concert on 6 January 1813. He noted that Rode's playing "had deteriorated. I now found his playing cold and mannered, missed his former audacity in overcoming great difficulties, and felt particularly dissatisfied by his cantabile playing." He also remarked that Rode had "lost a great deal of technical assurance" in the playing of his E major variations, which Spohr had heard Rode play superbly ten years earlier. He noticed that Rode had simplified several passages in the variations and "even played these simplified passages hesitantly and uncertainly."[7]

It is hard to believe that Rode played so poorly—he was only 38 years old. Spohr may have had ulterior motives in criticizing Rode so severely, either personal, as a younger rival of Rode's, or national. The report of the concert in the *AmZ* both contradicts and confirms Spohr's criticisms.[8] The reviewer notes some disappointment on the part of the audience, and especially Rode's cutting tone in the *Adagio* of his concerto, which therefore "left one cold." The harsh tone was less in evidence in Rode's next solo recital in the smaller concert hall on 31 January, but this concert was also not completely successful according to *AmZ* reviewer, who criticized Rode for lacking fire, and what we would call charisma, "that magic that charms and inspires all."[9] On the other hand, the reviewer did not note any lack of technical facility. He wrote that Rode's "bow stroke is large, long, and powerful . . . ; he has a correct, pure intonation, and is secure in leaps to the farthest height; his double stops, though there were few, are good, and he overcame great difficulties in the *Allegro* with lightness."[10] However, there had already been an unsuccessful concert in Paris on 22 December 1808 where his newest concerto was criticized for "suffering from Russia's cold" (Rode had just returned from a stay in Russia).[11] Rode's new concerto played in the first Viennese concert was also criticized as being "too affected and mannered" (zu gesucht und manierirt)."

---

[7] The English translation comes from the chapter by Sieghard Brandenburg, "Violin Sonatas, Cello Sonatas and Variations," in *Ludwig van Beethoven*, eds. Joseph Schmidt-Görg and Hans Schmidt (Bonn: Beethoven-Archiv and Hamburg: Deutsche Grammophon Gesellschaft MBH, 1969), 144. For the German text see Louis Spohr, *Lebenserinnerungen*, ed. Folker Göthel, vol. I (Tutzing: Schneider, 1968), 159. Since Spohr's autobiography was written late in life—it was published posthumously—his remarks about Rode may well be inaccurate and self-serving.

[8] 17 February No. 7 (1813), col. 114.

[9] "jene Zauber, der Alles entzückt und begeistert."

[10] "Sein Bogenstrich ist gross, lang und kräftig, sein Ton voll und stark—ja fast zu stark, schneidend; er hat eine richtige, reine Intonation, und ist in Sprüngen bis in die entfernteste Höhe sicher; seine Doppelgriffe, obgleich dieselben nur sparsam vorkamen, sind gut, und er überwindet im Allegro mit Leichtigkeit grosse Schwierigkeiten. . . ."

[11] Schwarz/Brown, "Rode," 491.

One can imagine Rode's shock when sight-reading Beethoven's lyrical, intimate, and subtle work. Unlike Op. 47, Op. 96 is not virtuosic. Not only that, but the violin part is technically easy, most of it in the first three violin positions. Could it be that Beethoven had heard that Rode's technique was limited and had composed the part accordingly?

A few Beethoven letters refer to the sonata. In the first, dated shortly before the first performance on Thursday, December 29, Beethoven wrote to the Archduke that the copyist will start work on the last movement early the next day. Beethoven remarked that he had not "hurried unduly to compose the last movement merely for the sake of being punctual. The more so as in view of Rode's playing. I have had to give more thought to the composition of this movement. In our Finales we like to have fairly noisy passages but Rode does not care for them—and so I have been rather hampered."[12] It may be that Rode's dislike of "noisy passages" also applied to the other fast movements of the sonata and this accounts for its lyrical style. Despite Beethoven's remark, the *finale* contains many brilliant passages as well as lyrical moments. Beethoven, however, believed the performance should go well. The letter suggests that the sonata was composed specifically for Rode and that it was written hurriedly, being finished at the last moment. It may well be that the haste in which the sonata was completed prompted Beethoven to use the *finale* variations of his String Quartet, Op. 74 (1809) as a model for the variations of Op. 96 (see 265-66).

Nothing is known of Beethoven's earlier contact with Rode when Rode indicated his preferred style for the *finale*. Rode performed the sonata at sight, as suggested by a letter from the Archduke to Beethoven dated 5 January 1813, in which Rudolph stated that he could send the violin part to Rode so he could play it over before the second performance on 7 January. Rudolph also asked Beethoven to come hear him play the piano part.[13] Beethoven responded the next day that it would be best if he, not Rudolph, send the part with a "Billet doux" so that Rode would not be insulted by the request to look over the music.[14] Beethoven added that he would come to Rudolph at his usual time to hear him perform the sonata. In this letter and another, addressed to the Countess Maria Eleonora Fuchs, shortly after 6 January 1813, Beethoven alluded to his bad state of mind. To the Countess, whose invitation he rejected, he referred to his "tattered heart"

---

[12] Anderson, I, No. 392; BGA, 2, No. 606: "so habe i(c)h um die blosen Pünktlichkeit willen mich nicht so sehr mit dem lezten Stücke beeilt, um so mehr, da ich dieses mit mehr Überlegung in Hinsicht des spiels von *Rode* schreiben muste, wir haben in unsern *Finales* gern rauschendere Passagen, doch sagte dieses *R* nich zu und—schenirte mich doch etwas—übrigens wird Dienstags alles gut gehn können."

[13] BGA, 2, No. 614.

[14] Anderson, I., No. 402; BGA, 2, No. 615.

("Mit einem überall zerissenen Herzen") and having to work in order not to go hungry. He also wrote that he was disappointed that Rode had not requested a new or unknown work by him for the concert on 6 January in the large Redoutensaal "because for him most of all I would have made an exception in that."[15] At his big solo concert Rode included only the first movement of Beethoven's Fourth Symphony. The references to Rode in these three letters are cordial and respectful.

SOME CONTEMPORARY REVIEWS

Three favorable reviews of the sonata were published. One appeared shortly after the first performance on 4 January 1813 in Glöggl's Linz *Musikalische Zeitung*. The reviewer refers to a "good" performance, though the Archduke Rudolph played the piano part "far better, more in accordance with the spirit of the piece, and with more feeling than that of the violin. Herr Rode's greatness seems to lie not in his playing of this kind of music but in his concerto performances. . . . " As for the music itself, the reviewer wrote that it "surpasses" almost all of Beethoven's violin sonatas "in popularity, wit, and spirit."[16]

Two reviews were published of the first edition in 1817 and 1819.[17] Both praise the close relation of the instruments. The reviewer in the *AmZ* remarked that "the violin is obbligato throughout;" that "the two parts [are] consummately partnered," and that the work is not difficult to perform, the reviewer comparing it in this regard to Beethoven's Op. 1 piano trios! Earlier the same reviewer commented: "It seems almost as if this great composer is coming back to melody in his latest works and that, on the whole, he has become more or less good-humored." Here "the master is in earnest . . . although the earnestness is of a comfortable kind, and he does not at all shun what is agreeable."[18] The third review appeared in the *AmZÖ*. These effusive remarks indoubtedly reflect the great enthusiasm of S. A. Steiner, the publisher of both the sonata and the journal, and they also partly draw on the *AmZ* review. The reviewer states, "In this work by the great genius . . . a great wealth of pure artistic feeling may be discerned, a richly imaginative surge of ideas, and that originality which chiefly characterizes his work. . . . " The sonata is called "excellent."[19]

---

[15] BGA, 2, No. 616: "denn *bey ihm* hätte ich hierin vor allen andern eine Ausnahme gemacht."
[16] "Popularität, Witz, und Laune." The English translation is from Brandenburg, "The Violin Sonatas," 143-44. For the German text, see *TDR* III, 351.
[17] See Kunze, ed., *Die Werke im Spiegel seiner Zeit*, 323-25.
[18] English translation from Brandenburg, "Violin Sonatas," 145-46.
[19] Ibid., 146. The journal is the *Allgemeine Musikalische Zeitung mit besondere Rücksicht auf den österreichischen Kaiserstaat*. Further comments on the single movements will be incorporated in the discussion of the movements.

CHRONOLOGY OF THE SONATA[20]

All the sketches but one for the sonata appear on the last pages of the Petter sketchbook, fol. 72^v-73^v, after the sketches for the Eighth Symphony, whose autograph score is dated October 1812. The sketches for Op. 96 were apparently made in December 1812 in preparation for the first performance on December 29. This dating is supported by Spohr, who was in Vienna in December 1812 and remarked that the impending arrival of Rode was known from the beginning of that month.[21] It is thus probable, as Brandenburg suggests, that some private concerts were arranged in the palace of Prince Lobkowitz involving the Archduke Rudolph, and it was for these concerts that Beethoven decided, or was asked to compose a violin sonata for Rode and the Archduke.

Though Nottebohm stated that only sketches for movements II-IV appear in the sketchbook,[22] (a statement reiterated in JTW, p. 214, and corrected on p. 215), Brandenburg did find some sketches in pencil for the first movement on fol. 72^v.[23] The advanced draft for the Scherzo on fol. 73 suggests that further sketches for the other movements were probably notated on four missing leaves between fol. 72 and fol. 73 and two leaves between fol. 73 and fol. 74, as shown by Brandenburg and JTW.[24] Several sketch transcriptions are given in N I for movements II and III, plus a sketch for the theme of the finale.[25]

As shown by Obelkevich, a draft for the theme of the *finale* appears as early as 1807/08 on a sketchleaf in the Gesellschaft der Musikfreunde, Vienna, Beethoven Autographe, Ms. 41. The theme appears in A major and may have been intended for the cello sonata in A, Op. 69.[26]

The original autograph and parts are lost. What exists today is an autograph score that still contains several large and small changes. The autograph, which is housed in the Pierpont Morgan Library, New York City, with the library number MA 16, is inscribed "Sonate. im Februar 1812 oder 13"; Beethoven apparently could not remember the date of the original

---

[20] This section draws on Sieghard Brandenburg, "Bemerkungen zu Beethovens Op. 96," *B-J* 9 (1973-77) 11-25; JTW, 307-19 (on the Petter Sketchbook); and Mary Rowan Obelkevich, "The Growth of a Musical Idea—Beethoven's Opus 96," *Current Musicology* 11 (1970): 91-114. This pioneering article presents a detailed discussion of the autograph sources and the most extensive consideration of changes on the autograph score. It contains several facsimiles and transcriptions, some of which of necessity are duplicated in this chapter. The Petter Sketchbook is housed in Bonn, Beethoven-Haus, Mh 59, SBH 639.

[21] See Brandenburg, "Bemerkungen," 15.

[22] N I, 28.

[23] See Brandenburg, "Bemerkungen," 20.

[24] See Brandenburg's diagram in ibid., 22.

[25] N I, 26-28.

[26] See Obelkevich, "Growth of a Musical Idea," 91, and Brandenburg, "Bemerkungen,", 22-23. The date comes from Brandenburg.

score. Brandenburg suggested that this autograph dates from early 1815 on the basis of the rare Italian paper used, which was available only from 1814 on. However, more study of the paper and its dating is needed. Two drafts on the same paper for the finale theme in one draft and the theme plus the first variation in another draft represent early compositional stages surely in December 1812.[27] However, the fact that Beethoven waited so long to publish the sonata and the only extant autograph contains so many revisions shows that Beethoven was dissatisfied with the original version of the music.

A letter from Beethoven to the Archduke in early 1815 asks for the scores of Op. 96 and Op. 97, the "Archduke" Piano Trio, which Beethoven could not find. He promised to have the music copied quickly and returned in three or four days.[28] He probably needed these scores with respect to the sale of these and other works to S. A. Steiner on 29 April 1815. Some corrections could still have been entered after that date. The sonata is described as "Grand" on the list for Steiner's contract.[29] An announcement of the publication of the sonata in parts, with a dedication to the Archduke Rudolph, appeared in the *Wiener Zeitung* on 29 July 1816, together with editions of the Piano Trio Op. 97 and the song cycle "An die ferne Geliebte," Op. 98. The first score edition appeared in London in an edition by Robert Birchall on 29 October 1816. The extant autograph was not used as the *Stichvorlage* (printer's copy) for the first edition although it contains some instructions for the copyist. That copy was probably made by Anton Diabelli for Steiner since the autograph contains a few additions in his hand.[30] Another, lost copy was made for Birchall.

Some Remarks on the Autograph

The autograph has been made available in an excellent facsimile edition that was published in 1977 in commemoration of the 150th anniversary of Beethoven's death.[31] This manuscript has many small changes and some larger ones; the latter will be discussed in the analysis of each movement.

---

[27] See my analysis of these drafts in the section on the last movement. That the dating of the final version needs further investigation was indicated to the writer by Brandenburg in a discussion of this problem.

[28] Anderson, II, No. 592; BGA, 3, No. 801.

[29] Anderson, III, Appendix F, No.6.

[30] Anton Diabelli (1781-1851), composer and later publisher, was an assistant to S. A. Steiner in 1815-17. He is, of course, the composer of the famous waltz on which Beethoven wrote thirty-three variations, Op. 120 (1819, 1823). The reference to Diabelli's hand is in Brandenburg, "Bemerkungen," 24-25.

[31] Ludwig van Beethoven, *Sonate für Klavier und Violine, G-dur Opus 96*. Facsimile nach dem in Eigentum des Pierpont Morgan Library New York befindlichen Autograph (Munich: G Henle, 1977), with a "Geleitwort" by Martin Staehelin. The two forms of the watermark are reproduced in the postscript.

Of the smaller changes, refinements are made in the accompaniment in cadences and leadbacks, and also in some notes (as in the bassline of movement IV/Variation 3). Later penciled additions include the *attacca* indication after the second movement and several indications in the *finale*, Variation 3: fingerings for the piano left hand, the notation of "espressivo" at the start of Part II, and "a tempo" after four measures of the "espressivo." Most changes occur in the slow Variation 5 of the finale and its remarkable cadenzas. Clearly, the version performed by the Archduke and Rode was inferior to the version known today, perhaps something like the differences between the two versions of the String Quartet, Op. 18, No. 1.

Table 3.2 Violin Sonata, Op. 96: Gross Form

Movement	Key	Tempo	Meter	Length in mm.	Form
I	G	Allegro moderato	3/4	282	Sonata form, exposition repeated (2 endings) 95+187 (46-2/4/92-1/4/47-2/4)
II	E♭	Adagio espressivo	2/4	67	Ternary: A (10-5/16)-B (26-3/16)-A¹ (10-5/16), B¹ (5-3/16), coda (14), ends g: aug. 6th
III	g-G	Scherzo. *Allegro*	3/4	129	Large ternary: Scherzo-Trio-Scherzo-Coda
	g	Scherzo		32	Binary, with varied repeats: A-A¹, B-B¹⁻ (2x8+2x8)
	E♭	Trio		51	Rounded binary: A (16, varied rep. 2x8)-B (4)-A¹ (31, with varied rep. 2x12+7)
	g	Scherzo *da capo*		32	Written out
	G	Coda (original title)		14	
IV	G	Poco Allegretto (+ 3 tempo changes, ending *Presto*)	2/4	295	Theme (32 mm.) with varied rep. (2x8+2x8), 7 var., coda (51 mm.)

This sonata is the last of three violin sonatas in four movements, the others being the sonatas in F ("Spring"), Op. 24 (1800-01) and in C minor, Op. 30 No. 2 (1801-02). For a list of Beethoven's four-movement chamber works, see Chapter 2, Table 1, and the ensuing discussion.

The connection of the slow movement to the Scherzo is the sole example of connected movements in the violin sonatas, though many examples can be found in other genres by Beethoven from the middle period onward. What is unexpected here, as mentioned earlier, is the connection of the *Adagio* to the Scherzo, since in most examples the slow movement connects to a fast *finale*, as we have seen in the Violin Concerto (see the discussion of the second movement).

Beethoven introduces an overall pattern of rising peaks in the violin part: e^2 in the first movement; a slight fall to $e\flat^2$ in the second movement, coda; $b\flat^3$ in Part II of the trio of the Scherzo; and d^4 at the end of the cadenza shortly before the close of the sonata. As we see, the high notes are placed near the end of a section or movement except for the first movement.

The sonata is imbued with features of the late style. Its pervasive lyricism (except for the Scherzo) reflects the turn to a more songful and intimate expression in several late works, as in the first movements of the piano sonatas Opp. 101 (1816), 109 (1820), 110 (1821-22), and the String Quartet Op. 127 (1824-25). Connected movements appear even more frequently and extensively in the late period than previously, as in the String Quartet Op. 132 where movements IV-VI are linked together.

Beethoven here gives special weight to the lowered submediant ($\flat$VI) relationship throughout the sonata. Lenz described it, metaphorically, as the love of G major for E$\flat$ major.[32] The third relationship does not appear as the second key area in this sonata-form movement, although it was introduced in Beethoven's String Quintet Op. 29 (1801) and found in many Beethoven works thereafter (and also in the first movement of Op. 132). Instead, the key of E$\flat$ figures in each movement of Op. 96 in a different way. It appears as the tonic key of the *Adagio* and Trio section of movement III. In the opening movement it is first heard in the recapitulation as a large area reharmonizing P^1 and 1T, and then in 2S (which had appeared in B$\flat$, a fifth above, in the exposition). In the *finale*, the key recurs most briefly, first with the recall of the theme after the slow variation 5 (a double return here of theme and key); and then in the concluding imitative entry in Variation 7.

The chromatic relation of G and E$\flat$ irst appears in Beethoven's earlier Violin Sonata, Op. 30, No. 3 (1802), where the slow movement is in E$\flat$ a key that also returns briefly near the end of the finale. E$\flat$ mediates in Op. 96 between the more distant and coloristic key of G major and the closer

---

[32] Lenz, *Kritischer Katalog*, Dritter Theil. II Period op. 21 bis op. 100, 274.

habitat of G minor, where it is the diatonic submediant. G minor appears as a rare choice in the sonata in variation 7 of the *finale*, where it functions as the traditional variation in the opposite mode. Indeed, Eb was often the preferred slow-movement key of symphonies in G minor in the Classic period, such as the two examples by Mozart, K. 183 and K. 550, as well as two early examples by Sammartini in the 1740s, J-C 57-58. The recurrence of large blocks of a secondary key can be found in some other works by Beethoven. In the Violin Concerto, it is the subdominant major and minor; in the Ninth Symphony it is the submediant Bb found as the secondary key of the first movement in D minor, the tonic of the *Adagio*, and the key of the Turkish variation in the *finale*, whose tonic is D major.

Another late feature is the chorale-like primary theme of the *Adagio*, and its association with prayer. Several examples appear in Beethoven's late works, such as the *Adagios* of the Cello Sonata, Op. 102, No. 2/II (the only example in minor), the Ninth Symphony/III, and the String Quartet Op. 132/III (see also 234-36).

The cycle as a whole makes a unique expressive sequence. The first movement seems dreamlike, expressing a world of perfect happiness, joy, and intimacy. However, the *Adagio* turns inward in prayer and pain, not unlike the famous Cavatina in the late String Quartet Op. 130/V (1825). From this abyss the music gradually returns to an energetic, optimistic world in the Scherzo and waltz-like Trio. The variation *finale*, as in so many Beethoven works, achieves a resolution of past tensions. Its theme is in a popular, even Haydnesque vein and the series of wide-ranging variations includes a slow variation that recaptures the mood of the *Adagio*. The variations have another function: to conclude the cycle with a thematically unified movement as opposed to the considerable contrast in the preceding movements. These variations resemble Beethoven's late variation sets in their continuity and use of double variation.[33]

In a recent eloquent study of Op. 96, Maynard Solomon views the entire sonata as a work in the pastoral style, and indeed there are several concrete features one can link to pastoral associations.[34] In the first movement, which has a typical moderate tempo, Beethoven avoids the dramatic

---

[33] For discussion of double variation and continuity in the variations of the *finale*, see 264-68.
[34] See his near-programmatic description of the sonata in "Pastoral, Rhetoric, Structure: The Violin Sonata in G, Op. 96," in: *Late Beethoven: Music, Thought, Imagination* (Berkeley, Los Angeles, London: University of California Press, 2003), Ch. 4, 71-91. Solomon's attitude is indicated by the following: "From the start, pastoral style has been a global metaphor for an extensive range of affects and images, including burdensome issues and unsettling states of being" (71). There is a vast literature on the pastoral style, going back to the ancient Greeks. For summaries relating to music, see the article by Geoffrey Chew and Owen Jander, "Pastoral," *NGD*, 2nd ed. 19: 217-25; the entries on "Pastorale" in the *Handwörterbuch der musikalischen Terminologie*, ed. Hans Heinrich Eggebrecht, Ordner III: M-R (Stuttgart: F. Steiner, 1996), especially 11-14; Ratner, *CM*, 16, 21; and the article "Pastorale" by Hermann Jung [Hans Engel] in *MGG*, 2nd ed., Sachteil, vol. 7 (1997), col. 1499-1509 (with a long bibliography).

and disruptive. The minor mode as chord and key is little in evidence except for the minor-second sigh motives of the final K theme which dominate half the development. The opening trill is described as birdsong by Lenz[35] and Solomon, and the movement features sonorities of parallel sixth chords and thirds, also associated with the pastoral style. A simple waltz theme of the Trio, with its drones and round-like canon, similarly evokes pastoral associations as does the folk-like theme of the finale.

Two of the early commentators on the sonata use pastoral imagery. The reviewer in 1819 remarks:

> The Adagio espressivo (E flat major, 2/4) might be called an eclogue, so tenderly does the Arcadian shepherd make complaint of his unhappy love to the hills, trees, bushes, fountains, and flowers, so tenderly unburdens his feeling in song that Chloe cannot remain impervious. How satyr-like, by contrast, are the droll capers of the Scherzo. . . .[36]

A comparison of the sonata to pastoral style is most developed by Lenz. His general statement, given below, is later elucidated in detail:

> According to our feeling, Op. 96 follows a life in nature that is ignited by a bird trill, then spread in Beethoven's pantheistic point of view, meditatively, pensively in the Allegro, elegiacally inspired in the Adagio, humorous throughout in the Scherzo, dithyrambically inspired in the Finale, in the middle of the delight in dance and song of a poetic people.[37]

Still, the sonata is somewhat distant from the literal pastoral style described by the music theorists and illustrated in two works by Beethoven which he called pastoral: the "Pastorale" in his ballet *Die Geschöpfe des Prometheus* (No. 10), Op. 43 (1800-01) and the Pastoral Symphony, Op. 68 (1807-08).[38] The little-known "Pastorale" of the ballet exemplifies many of the clichés, some mentioned by the theorists, associated with the pastoral instrumental style: the major mode, 6/8 meter, drones, simple harmony, parallel-third textures, frequent melodic repetitions, four-measure phrases, and wind melodies.[39] The 6/8 meter, linked with the Siciliano, and the drones,

---

[35] Lenz, *Kritischer Katalog*, 275.

[36] The English translation comes from Brandenburg, "Violin Sonatas," 146. For the original German text, see Kunze, ed.,*Die Werke im Spiegel seiner Zeit*, 325. The imagery regarding the *Adagio* seems to be influenced by the text of "An die ferne Geliebte," published at the same time as the sonata.

[37] Lenz, *Kritischer Katalog*, 269-70: "Unserem Gefühl nach vertritt op. 96 ein Naturleben, das sich an einem Vogeltriller entzündet, dann in Beethovens panteistischer Naturanschauungsweise verbreitet, beschaulich sinnend im Allegro, elegisch durchglüht im Adagio, humoristisch durchdrungen im Scherzo, dithyrambisch begeistert im Finale, in Mitten der Tanz- und Sangeslust eines poetischen Volks."

[38] For the Pastoral Symphony, see F. E. Kirby, "Beethoven's Pastoral Symphony as a *Sinfonia caracteristica*," MQ 56 (1970): 605-23, reprinted in *The Creative World of Beethoven*, ed. Paul Henry Lang (New York: Norton, 1971), 103-21; and David Wyn Jones, *Beethoven: Pastoral Symphony* (Cambridge: Cambridge University Press, 1995), especially 12-18.

[39] For quotations from the theorists, see the entries in Eggebrecht, *Handwörterbuch*.

linked with the Musette, are especially emphasized by the theorists, and occur also in the finale of the Pastoral Symphony. The long drones of the A section in the Trio of Op. 132, second movement, are another typical example of the pastoral topic.

Tempo: Early Metronome Marks for the Sonata

Three sets of nearly contemporary metronome marks for the sonata have come down to us. One set is provided by Carl Czerny[40] Another set was sent in a communication of 1857 from Karl Holz (1799-1858) to Lenz.[41] Holz played second violin in the Schuppanzigh quartet from 1823 and probably met Beethoven in 1824. In 1825, he became Beethoven's close friend and secretary.[42] Holz states he had played the Op. 96 sonata with Beethoven, a dubious claim since Beethoven was very deaf in the last years of his life.

Holz also compares his set to the metronome marks given for the sonata in the collected Beethoven edition published by Tobias Haslinger. Haslinger's edition was announced in December 1828. According to O. E. Deutsch, most scores of the Haslinger edition, except for the concertos and some piano sonatas, appeared between 1833 and 1835.[43] The 1828 announcement states that Czerny, Holz, and Ignaz Schuppanzigh had undertaken to correct the musical text and to add metronome marks to Beethoven's works.[44] Since Holz did not add such marks to Op. 96, those indications must stem either from Czerny or Schuppanzigh, both closely associated with Beethoven performance. Schuppanzigh (1776-1830) was the first violin of the quartet that premiered many of Beethoven's string quartets, including probably the "Rasumovsky" quartets, Op. 59, and most of the last quartets. He led many orchestral performances of Beethoven's music and was the concertmaster for the performance of the Ninth Symphony.[45]

The three sets of metronome marks are given in the table on p.198. All three indicate faster tempos than we find in the superb performance

---

[40] Czerny, *On the Proper Performance,*, Ch III, 86.

[41] Lenz, *Kritischer Katalog*, 280-81. Holz also included in his communication metronome markings and comments on the performance and musical text for Beethoven's last five quartets. These markings and comments are presented and discussed in Emil Platen, "Zeitgenössische Hinweise zur Aufführungspraxis der letzten Streichquartette Beethovens," in *Beiträge '76-78, Beethoven-Kolloquium 1977*, ed. Rudolf Klein (Kassel: Bärenreiter, 1978), 100-07.

[42] For Holz, see the article by Donald W. MacArdle, "Beethoven and Karl Holz," *Die Musikforschung* 20 (1967): 19-29.

[43] See the corrected portion of his article "Übersicht der Gesammeltes Werke Beethovens im Verlag Haslinger," reprinted with the article by Alexander Weinmann in Kurt Dorfmüller, ed., *Beiträge zu Beethoven-Bibliographie* (Munich: G. Henle, 1978), 279.

[44] See Otto Erich Deutsch, "Beethovens gesammelte Werke, Die Meisters Plan und Haslingers Ausgabe," *Zeitschrift für Musikwissenschaft* 13 (1930-31): 66-67.

[45] For Schuppanzigh, see Donald W. MacArdle, "Beethoven and Schuppanzigh," *Music Review* 26 (1965): 3-14.

of the sonata by Joseph Szigeti and Artur Schnabel, recorded in a live performance on 4 April 1948 (Pearl, GEMM, CD 9026). While Holz's tempos are not too different from Czerny's, excluding a faster *Adagio* tempo, the Haslinger tempos are substantially faster except for the *Adagio*, whose tempo is slightly slower than Czerny's.[46] Holz additionally provides five metronome marks for the fourth movement, two of which are given in Haslinger's edition, and he also includes remarks on the performance of the Trio and Variation 7. (The basic value for the *Adagio* is mistakenly given by Holz as a sixteenth and by Haslinger as a quarter, and is corrected here to an eighth.)

Table 3.3 Three Sets of Metronome Marks for Op. 96

Movement			Czerny	Holz	Haslinger
I	Allegro moderato	♩ =	132	126	138
II	Adagio espressivo	♪ =	58	69	56
III	Scherzo. Allegro	𝅗𝅥 =	80	*80	96
IV	Poco Allegretto	♩ =	100	104	120
	Adagio espressivo, Var. 5	♪ =		69	72
	Allegro, Var. 6	♩ =		132	152
	Var. 7	♩ =		**116	
	poco adagio	♩ =		69	
	Presto	𝅗𝅥 =		132	

* Holz: "In the Trio the same tempo and the last 7 measures very ritardirt (retarded)"
** Holz: last 2 measures *ritardando*

[46] Sandra P. Rosenblum, "Two Sets of Unexplored Metronome Marks for Beethoven's Piano Sonatas," *Early Music* 16 (1988): 58-71, deals with two sets of Czerny's metronome marks in the Haslinger edition which she compares to two other sets in Czerny's Op. 500 and his later Simrock edition (1858-68). Czerny's markings in Op. 500 are generally the slowest. See also the discussion of the markings by Czerny and Moscheles in Ch. 2, 98-99). Holz's specifications of retards in the Trio and Variation 7 are suspect since Beethoven usually indicated major effects of that kind.
[47] In a letter to William Newman dated 13 November 1978, the conductor Max Rudolf

The First Movement: *Allegro moderato*

Expression

The gentle, intimate, lyrical character of the first movement has been widely recognized. As Czerny remarked in his Op. 500, "This piece, which is written in a calm, noble, melodious, but also witty character, must be played with tenderness and feeling."[47] He pointed out that the tempo, *Allegro moderato*, is "almost *Tempo di Menuetto*" and that the movement "is neither in a brilliant, nor at all in a bravura style." Peter Cahn[48] has remarked that very few of Beethoven's first movements have such a moderate tempo, another example being the first movement of the Piano Trio, Op. 97 (also *Allegro moderato*, as is the *finale*), a work written shortly before Op. 96 and published many years later together with Op. 96 in 1816.

Another meaningful description of this movement appears in the 1819 review of the sonata, which stated:

> This movement is distinguished by a particular serenity, a general appealing accessibility, honest solidity, and consistent organization. It has an innocent ease; without exposure to burning sunbeams, without coming to grips with storm and tempest, and without having to combat giants or slay dragons, we tread the thornless path unmolested.[49]

Growth

This movement is a rich multithematic structure, with eleven functions, strong contrast between 1P and 1S, and several derivations (see the timeline on p. 200).

The opening theme in the solo violin furnishes the basic motives for the movement: the trill, extended in ST and the coda (mm.262-67); the appoggiatura or sigh motive, heard in m.1, beat 1, and m.3, beat 3, that recurs in 1T, 1S, 2S, 2K, and KT; and the broken chord material in Pay, extended in 2P and found in 1K (see Ex. 3.1 on p. 201). The sixth-chord sonority in 2P also becomes a significant element in the movement (see the remarks on Sound).

---

states that the correct translation of Czerny's adjective "humoristischen" is "witty," not "humorous," as given in the later nineteenth-century translation of Czerny's remarks on Beethoven's works with piano. He asserts that " 'Humoristisch' at that time [i.e., for Beethoven and Czerny] meant 'launig, geistreich.' . . . The term signifies 'witty' with all its ramifications, from 'charming' to 'ironical.' . . . How do we then explain that the first movement of Op. 96 should be performed 'aber auch (mit) humoristischen Character'? I have observed that the word often applies to movements notable for relatively brief phrases interrupted by rests or by pronounced phrasing, serving a lively interplay of a musical idea, in *pp* contrast to the uninterrupted flow of the line. Moreover, "humoristisch" usually refers to subtle dynamic inflections not indicated in writing, and to flexibility in pacing." The writer goes on to analyze these qualities in the primary theme.

Table 3.4 Timeline: Movement I

Key: G   Meter: 3/4

		(om)			(1Py)	(1Pxm)		(1Pom,2T)	
exp.	1P	:o x y	o¹ x¹		2P		1T	2T		1S	1S¹
	0³	1³ 2³ 4³	6³ 8³		10 10³	20	33	41	49	59
	G		V⁷/IV IV				D:V ped.	I		V-fVI

	(1Pom)	(2T,2S)	(2Pm)	(2Tb)	(1Pom	(3K)			
	2S	2S¹ ST	|1K	2K	3K	KT	|1.	|1Po :|| (the repeat
	59²	63² 66	72	77	84³	91³	95a	a³-96a	goes back
	(B♭-D)	B♭D			V ped ....G				to m.1³)

		2.		(1Pom)		(+Ny)			
dev.	KT	|3K	KT	|3Km		|2K¹	seq.	seq.
	95b	98	102³	105³	109³	111	116²	120²	124²
	G,c,B♭	B♭V ped...........		(c)	a:V ped...	E	a	d

		(2KNy)	
	Ny ext.	|RT	|1Pom. anticip.
	127-130	131	139³
	d-e-D	G:V	I

	1Po¹	1P¹	1Po²	o³	x²	2P¹	|1T	2T	|1S	|1S¹	2S
rec.	141³	143³	147³	148³	149³	151³	159	172	180	188	198²
				E♭		G:V		V♭VI (E♭-G			

	2S¹	ST	|1K	2K	3K	KT
	202²	205	211	218	223³	230³
	E♭)	G			V: ped.	

	KT	|1Po x	|2Pm¹+inv.		|1Po dialogue canon
coda	234²	238³ 240³	242	243	247³ 250³	254³
			C	F:V⁶₅	V⁰₉ chords G:V⁰₉- V/V	I⁶₄

	(Pom)				(2K)	
	|cadenza	|2Pm+inv.	|1Po+2Pm	1Px³	|NK ||
	260	261³ 268	271	275³	277³ 279	281 mm.
		V⁷	V⁷	I: ped.....	..............IV-V-I	

VIOLIN SONATA   201

Example 3.1   1P and 2P (mm. 1-19)

The sigh in 3K and its extension in KT receive extensive emphasis in the development (21 mm.), while the broken-chord idea has its apotheosis in the coda. Po or Pax and its trill (plus its extension) are heard over twenty times in the movement. There is, however, no literal recurrence of material from 1P in later functions of the exposition, excepting the chordal motive that flows from 1P into 2P. Rather, Beethoven proceeds via similarities, not exact duplications. Within the overall lyrical and tranquil mood, all the thematic functions have distinctive profiles and provide considerable contrast in all musical elements. The most individual ideas are 1P, 2P, 1S, and 3K (see the music examples in this discussion).

The proportions of the movement show an emphasis on the exposition and recapitulation, which are nearly equal in length—94-1/4 vs. 92-1/4 mm.[50] The development and coda too are close to the same length—46-2/4 vs. 47-1/4 mm.; both are almost half the length of the exposition. The fairly brief development reflects the lyrical orientation of the movement and occurs in some other late lyrical movements in the Piano Sonatas Opp. 101/I and 110/I. These proportions undoubtedly help produce the feeling of balance and calm that pervades the movement.

CONTINUITY

As he does in many middle and late works, Beethoven achieves a remarkable continuity in the movement by avoiding open cadences and using various methods for weakening and bridging articulations. The entire movment contains only one open cadence. This is the cadence ending the first statement of 1P in m.6, beat 2, and even there the root-position tonic chord occurs on the weak beat of the measure. A deceptive cadence to ♭VI links 1S to 2S (see Ex. 3.8). Here the melodic line is separated from 1S, an open effect, but the cadence joins the themes and is indeed highlighted by the preceding *ritard*.

Beethoven uses five types of articulations when creating the beautiful flow of the movement: elision, truncation, extension, overlap, and anticipation. Five functions connect via elisions, the most common type of continuous connection: 2P-1T, 1T-2T, 1S-1S^1, ST-1K, and 1K-2K. More unusual are the examples of truncation. The first occurs between 2S and ST, where the last cadential measure of the repeated phrase of 2S is cut off by the chromatic movement of the trill and modulation back to the main key at the start of ST. Another example of this dramatic device then occurs between 2K and 3K. The three-measure phrase of 2K ends on a half cadence: vii^6/V-V, but upon the phrase's repetition the V chord becomes the V^7 upbeat to 3K (Ex. 3.2).

The extension of 3K^1 leads into the repeat of the exposition (first ending) or the modulatory start of the development (second ending), creating an unbreakable continuity between exposition and development. The connection of the recapitulation to the coda parallels the connection of the expostion to the development by extending 3K. Here, however, the phrase moves to the subdominant and 1Po on beat 3 overlaps the ending of the accompaniment on beat 1 of the next measure (mm. 238-39). Early examples of such continuations occur in the Piano Sonata, Op. 10, no. 3/I.

Most charming is the anticipation of the trilled start of the recapitulation by the piano at the end of the retransition (Ex. 3.3). An octave higher

---

[50] Only two measures are omitted in 2P in the recapitulation (equivalent to mm. 15-16). Two beats of the first ending of the exposition are not included in the length of the exposition since they modulate back to the tonic.

VIOLIN SONATA

Example 3.2 Truncation of 2K and start of 3K (mm. 79-80)

Example 3.3 Anticipation of the trill starting the recapitulation (mm. 139³-43³)

than the violin, the piano trill twice starts on beat 3, with the accompaniment of the violin on a plucked open G string, the violin then echoing the trill at its original pitch. The passage sounds like a pair of birds in dialogue. Perhaps this is what Czerny referred to when he mentioned the wit in this movement. The start on beat 3 shifts the barline one beat to the left as well (see the discussion of rhythm below).

THE CODA

As always in the later Beethoven works, the coda contains many remarkable expressive effects and intensifications. As indicated earlier, the coda is nearly the same length as the development. Typically, the transition to the coda parallels the transition to the development, with the extension of 3K bridging the sections. 1Po-ax frames the coda, appearing at the start in the subdominant, C, and ending in the tonic. As is often the case, the coda is marked by harmonic tension before the final confirmation in the tonic. In between the framing appearances of 1Po-ax, Beethoven develops 2P, continues it in dialogue with 1Po, and introduces a cadenza-like passage in the piano and violin. The music then gently settles largely on the tonic with 2P until 1P returns in combination with 2Pm, the movement ending with rising scales to a *forte* on V-I. The entire section is thus based on the two primary themes plus the cadenza.

This brief summary cannot begin to convey the magical effects in this section. The development of 2P occurs within a series of chromatic diminished sevenths sliding down by step—not distant chords but as always vague, implying the minor mode, and set in mirror relationship (Ex. 3.4). The soprano alternates the rising and falling forms of the broken-chord motive until the rising, original form in the movement remains as a dialogue that begins on 1Po in the deep bass register with the violin two octaves above. The first presentation, with the cross relation of $f_\natural$ in 1Po versus $f_\sharp$ in the V_9^0 chord above, sustains the harmonic tension. After the diminished-seventh chord, the violin takes the lead. The sustained chords lengthen progressively: 3-2/4 mm. (V_9^0), 4 mm. (V_5^6/V)-5-1/4 mm. (I_4^6). The hushed passage finally erupts into a *crescendo* with the I_4^6 chord and fragmentation of 1Po to notes 2-4, set in canon (mm. 256-59). The canon mounts to a *fp* and the cadenza that culminates the passage.

We know of a few cadenzas in Beethoven's piano sonatas, as in the first movement of the Sonata, Op. 2, No. 3 (1794-95) and the first and final movements of the "Waldstein" Sonata, Op. 53 (1803-04). But one does not expect to find a cadenza in such a lyrical work; perhaps it is a nod to Rode. Unlike the brilliant cadenza near the end of the fourth movement, this cadenza has many special features. The sixteenth-notes of the cadenza introduce the first sustained sixteenth-note motion in the movement, which culminate the previous *crescendo* and rising canon. The fast surface rhythm, however, is countered by an immediate drop to *piano* until

VIOLIN SONATA 205

Example 3.4 *The coda: chromatic development of 2P, dialogue of 1Po, and cadenza (mm. 242-67)*

another *crescendo* starts with the third entry in the piano's left hand. The *crescendo*, however, reaches no specified peak and then fades away with a triple trill in the violin and both hands of the piano to a *sempre piano* for the next passage. Here, unlike other passages, the two instruments play the trill together.[51]

The melodic line of the cadenza is written out in normal values, not in small notes and unbarred figuration as in the Piano Sonata, Op. 2, No. 3/I, which is actually more characteristic of Beethoven's cadenza-like passages near the ends of non-concerto movements. What is unlike most of Beethoven's written-out sonata cadenzas, however, is the chromatic melody found here, which picks up the idea of chromatic contrast from the previous diminished-seventh passage (see Ex. 3.4 on p. 205). The melodic line is presented imitatively in three entries and differs in each. The first entry, in the piano's right hand, is the most chromatic and longest—2 mm.; the violin entry, a fourth below, is less chromatic and shorter, 1-2/4 mm.; the third entry, in the piano's left hand, occurs at the unison with the violin entry, and is the least chromatic and shortest—1-1/4 mm. The chromatic notes themselves are most peculiar, as often in late Beethoven, surrounding the basic notes of the harmony with double neighbors combined with chromatic appoggiaturas. They introduce over the I_4^6 chord the sharp second and fourth degrees as well as the flat sixth and seventh degrees, while the following entries over V^7 introduce the sharp sixth, first, and fourth degrees—all lines though easily playable. Actually, in the first entry the flat sixth degree acts as a raised fifth degree and flat seventh as a raised sixth degree (it would be illuminating to see the sketches for this remarkable passage).

After this tense, contrasting section comes the coda to the coda, with 2Pm in original and inverted forms, a diatonic resolution of the earlier passage of diminished sevenths. First the inversion in the soprano is answered by the original form in the bass, and this form finally prevails in the passage near the end of the movement (mm. 275-77). Colored by the sustaining pedal of the piano, the passage is a kind of gentle, concluding sing-song placed in the deep range of the piano.

Harmony

Several more features of the harmonic aspect require comment. One relates to harmonic rhythm and the sustaining of chords over the barline. We see this happening at the very opening of the movement with 1Po and the start of 1Pa (mm. 2-3¹; see Ex. 3.1). This device is also found in the large-scale harmonic deceleration in most of the coda, mm. 243-78¹, from the series of diminished seventh chords to the final four-measure phrase ending the movement, a total of 35-1/4 measures. The deceleration brings

---

[51] Johansen, "Beethoven's Sonatas for Piano and Violin," 85.

the movement to a close with a large-dimension motion-rest plan, a long, written-out harmonic ritard (see Ex. 3.4).[52] The long passage from m. 247 to m. 278¹ makes one grand cadential progression for about two-thirds of the coda (Fig. 3.1).

Figure 3.1 Harmonic Deceleration in the Coda, mm. 243-78¹

no. of mm.:   1-1-1-1-3-2/4—4--   7—9-1/4—7-1/4

chords: V_9^0 seq. G:V_9^0 V_5^6/V I_4^6 V^7 I

In the deceleration the harmony changes on beat 3 in mm. 250 (to V_5^6/V), 254 (to I_4^6) and m. 261 (to V). In addition, there are long overlaps between the melodic and harmonic sections. Thus, the V_9^0 ending the sequence of diminished seventh chords holds over for the first 2-1/4 mm. of the dialogue section (mm. 247-50²), the I_4^6 chord concluding the dialogue section continues into the cadenza (mm. 254³-261²), and the V^7 ending the cadenza is prolonged into the final dialogue section, mm. 261²-270, the tonic arriving in the middle of the dialogue in m. 271. Such syncopation, delay, and overlap of harmonic change profoundly enhance the musical flow, as in so many late works as well.

Like many later Beethoven works, the harmony is colored by third relationships as cited above: D-B♭ in 2S, exposition (Ex. 3.2), and G-E♭ in 2S, recapitulation, as well as 2P and 1T in that section. In 2S, the new key acts as a tonicization since 2Sa cadences with beautiful effect in D. On repetition, 2Sa¹ starts again in B♭ but its cadence is cut off by ST, where the modulation back to D takes place. The same effects occur in the recapitulation with regard to the keys of E♭-G. Other third relationships appear in the development, as we shall see. A very unusual setting is the placement of 3K on a long V pedal rather than the traditional tonic pedal, thus keeping the end of the exposition and recapitulation in harmonic suspense until eventual resolution (Ex. 3.5). That resolution is long postponed in the development; V of D modulates eventually to B♭, the same third relation as in the exposition. After a transposition of 3K on B♭V, further modulation takes place to A minor, B♭ being its Neapolitan, another distant and favorite key relationship. Thus nearly half of the development rests on dominant

---

[52] For Beethoven's organization of harmonic rhythm, see the classic article by LaRue, "Harmonic Rhythm in the Beethoven Symphonies," 8-20; reprint *JM* 18 (2001): 221-48. LaRue points out motion-rest patterns of harmonic rhythm in a smaller dimension that stabilize ends of sections before double bars, as the end of Part I in Symphony No. 4/III and the end of the exposition in Symphony No. 2/I. See 12-13 (229-30).

Example 3.5 3K, exposition, harmonization on a V pedal (mm.84³-95²)

harmony, with all the tension associated with that harmony. The tension resolves in the second half of the development beginning with 2K¹ (and its new extension Ny). The basic keys descend traditionally in fifths: E-a-d-G, and the first three keys sit squarely on the tonic before modulating. E major sounds exotic in the center of the development (m. 116), making another third relation with G on the sharp side.

We notice as we consider the larger tonal scheme, the deemphasis on minor keys besides the relatively limited points of rest in the development on A minor (8 mm.) and D minor (4 mm.), recalling the general avoidance of minor keys in the "Pastoral" Symphony/I. Nuances of the minor derive from sources other than modulation: the lowered sixth degree in 3K, the harmonization at the end of the retransition with a minor iv^6 alternating with V before the anticipation of the recapitulation on tonic G-major chords, and the exquisite diminished seventh chords of the coda.

Another late feature is the emphasis on the subdominant chord and key. This occurs with the tonicization of C at the end of the repeat of 1Po-x at the opening of the movement, so that 2P (based on 1Py) actually starts on a C-major chord (Ex. 3.1). Another theme starting on IV is 1K. In the coda, the subdominant nuance returns, with the recall of 1Po and x in C-major after the transition to the coda, and the subdominant chord is held for five beats in the final cadence of the movement (replete with f♮ in the scale e^1-e^3 above the C-chord).

Sound

A recurring idea that functions as a motive is that of sonority: of parallel sixth chords (in 2P) and parallel thirds in several ideas, especially 1S and 2K in melodic doubling. It is 2K that dominates the second part of the development (starting in m. 116). In that section, Beethoven gives the theme a new y subphrase extension also in parallel thirds (mm. 119-20), and extends it with a long *crescendo* leading to a recall of the parallel sixth-chord sonority shortly before the recapitulation (Ex. 3.6d and e).

Another special feature of the sonority is the delicate high register of 2P, 1K, the last seven measures of the retransition, and the piano's transposed 1S in the recapitulation, reaching a^3. These ethereal sounds have a spiritual resonance felt by every performer and listener. Appearing in several late works, particularly the piano sonata Op. 110, such sonorities again link the sonata to the late style.

The treatment of dynamics also connects the sonata with the late works. As Miriam Sheer has pointed out, many late works are subdued in dynamics.[53] The range of dynamics in the entire sonata is ***pp-f***; no *ff* appears at all. In this movement, every function starts *piano* or *cresc*. Long stretches of *piano* produce a gentle, meditative aura. The loudest area in the movement is ST, with a two-measure *crescendo* to a *forte*, and a series of

---

[53] See her doctoral dissertation, "The Role of Dynamics in Beethoven's Instrumental Works," and her article "Dynamics in Beethoven's Late Instrumental Works," 358-78.

Example 3.6 Examples of parallel third- and sixth-chord sonorities in various functions:

a. 2P (see Ex. 3.1)　　　b. 1S (See Ex. 3.8)　　　c. 2K (see Ex. 3.2)

d. 2K¹ *in the development (mm. 116-20)*

e. RT *(mm. 131-37, and Ex. 3.3)*

f. 2Pm coda (mm. 268-75²)

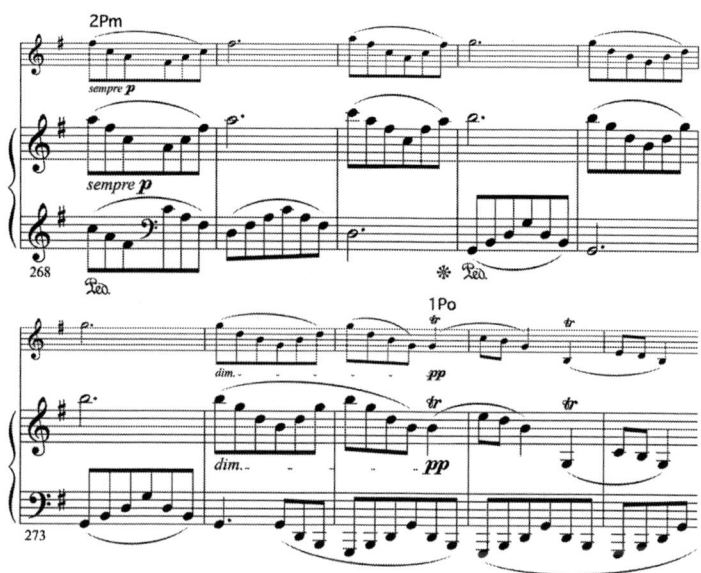

sforzandos on eight quarters; a second, measure-long *crescendo* ends *piano* at the start of 1K. Next to ST in loudness is 1T, another transition, which includes a *crescendo*, *f-p* contrasts, and *sf*.

A distinctive feature of the movement, if not of the entire sonata, are the many *crescendo-piano* effects. There are four such examples here, heard seven times in the exposition and development, and three times in the recapitulation:

1. 1Ta and a¹: in each phrase, two measures of *crescendo* to one of *piano*.
2. From the end of ST to 1K.
3. From 3Ka to its cadence: three measures to three beats heard twice and a third time in the development (see Ex. 3.5).
4. From the second ending of KT modulating to B♭:V, with *p* on V.

Various effects are produced by these examples. The obvious and older type is a more continuous linking of phrases, postponing a sense of arrival. This occurs in examples 2 and 4. However, in examples 1 and 3 the sudden dip to *piano* highlights a brief expressive lyrical figure (in minor in example 3), as a response to a more vigorous statement. There is a certain poignancy in these passages that helps create a profound effect of inwardness in the movement.

The longest *crescendo*, mm. 128-32, spans five measures and drives from the end of the development into the retransition, coinciding with the modulation back to the tonic key. It is one of the few *crescendos* here that ends in a *forte* and a dramatic climax, a climax, however, that dissipates almost immediately (see Ex. 3.6e).

Beethoven reserves a *pianissimo* marking for certain special places. The first, m. 94, appears after a two-measure *diminuendo* from *piano*, ending the exposition on the lowest dynamic level, a rare effect (see Ex. 3.5). The same pattern repeats at the start of the development (mm. 98-102^2), thus linking the exposition and development. No *pp* recurs in the recapitulation until the same passage in KT in m. 223, and it not only bridges the coda but continues for a total of 22-1/4 mm. until the *crescendo* leading to the cadenza in m. 255—a remarkably long, hushed passage on this lowest dynamic level of the sonata (Ex. 3.4). The *pianissimo* returns one last time for the penultimate phrase of the movement, thereby bringing the return of Po-x in mm. 275^3-78. Once again the *pp* is reached via a preceding *piano* and *diminuendo* and followed here by a *crescendo* to a *forte*, ending the movement.

In considering the relationship of the two instruments one to the other, we notice that here, as in the following movements, the piano generally leads and the violin follows, unlike the "Spring" and "Kreutzer" sonatas. The one solo for the violin is at the very start of the movement, the opening unique in Beethoven's violin sonatas in the presentation of the basic motive by the unaccompanied violin. After the violin plays 1P, it is the piano that introduces the material first. Beethoven varies the texture in many ways, as in the canonic dialogue in 2T, hocket in the development of 3K (mm. 102^3-05^2 and 109^3-116^1; see Ex. 3.7), and most strikingly, the dialogue, later canonic, on 1Po in the coda (mm. 247^3-59) (Ex. 3.4).

The recapitulation of 1P, however, reverts to the piano. The piano part has a large range of sound of over five octaves (G_1-a^3), going beyond the normal top note of f^3 or g^3 of the 18th-century fortepiano. This indicates that Beethoven had a larger piano in mind, with an extended keyboard and richer sonority. The violin, in contrast, reaches only e^3, with a total range of only two octaves and a sixth (from g), and it is often subdued, playing on its lowest three strings.

Starting in the early 1790s, Beethoven began to indicate the use of the pedal in his piano music, a subject about which much has been written.[54] Newman cites an early sketch dated 1790-92 in the Kafka Miscellany showing a repeated B♭ major chord with < > signs and the words "mit dem knie" [with the knee pedal].[55] The first published pedal indications in Beethoven's piano music appeared in 1801, for the first two

---

[54] At first the references were to the knee lever on German and Austrian pianos, and Beethoven used the indications "con sordino" and "senza sordino" through the Third Piano Concerto, performed in 1803. Thereafter, Beethoven employed the common signs "ped." and "0," found also on the autograph of Op. 96. For valuable information on this subject, see Newman, *Beethoven on Beethoven*, "Beethoven's Use of the Pedals," 231-52; and Rosenblum, *Performance Practices*, Ch. IV: "The Use of the Pedals," 102-43.

[55] Newman, *Beethoven on Beethoven*, 233.

Example 3.7 Hocket of 3K in the development (mm. 109^3-116^1)

piano concertos, Opp. 15 and 19, and the piano quintet Op. 16, works which were composed by or in the mid 1790s (Op. 16 in 1796), though the concertos were revised after their early performances in 1795.[56] Newman found nearly 800 original pedaling indications in Beethoven's piano music, but only about 15% appear in his chamber music.[57] Newman mentions seven uses of the damper pedal in Beethoven, the one found in Op. 96 being for the purpose of creating "a collective, composite sound."[58]

In this movement, the indications for use of the sustaining pedal appear only in the remarkable coda section, where they are associated almost entirely with the low *pp* and *p* dynamics, though also with 6-2/4 measures of *crescendo* (mm. 255-59 and 279-80²). In mm. 243-46, they are marked for each measure of the series of diminished-seventh chords, thus blending the notes of each chord in this coloristic passage. Then follow indications of the sustaining pedal within the next 33 measures (mm. 247-80) as shown in the table below (see also Exx. 3.4, 3.6f).

---

[56] Rosenblum, *Performance Practices*, 121.
[57] Newman, *Beethoven on Beethoven*, 232.
[58] Newman, ibid., 240-43.

The length of each sustaining pedal supports in general the long harmonic deceleration of the cadential progression, giving greater resonance to each chord, especially within the low dynamic range. The longest sustaining pedal underlines the final tonic pedal point. In its cadential and harmonic functions the sustaining pedal is structural, not coloristic.

Table 3.5 The Use of the Sustaining Pedal within mm. 247-80

Measures	Number of measures	Chord
247-50^2	3-2/4	V^0_9
251-54^2	3-2/4	V^6_5 of V
255-59	5	I
268-70	3	V
271-77	7	I
279-80^2	1-2/4	IV

Rhythm

The calm expression of the movement derives in part from the restraint in surface rhythm. At first, the music moves only in larger values of quarters and eighths (P area), 1T adding the dotted quarter. Starting with 2T, Beethoven introduces triplets, and these remain the fasted notated unit of the surface rhythm until the coda, with two exceptions. In 1S, a new distinctive and repeated rhythmic figure appears, the "dotted" rhythm bringing the first sixteenth notes of the movement. In 2S^1 and ST, Beethoven picks up the trill motive in a nine-measure section of trills that heighten the rhythmic activity enormously.

Triplet rhythm dominates the development, which forms the rhythmic climax of the movement. There are three stages of rhythmic intensification. First, unbroken triplet motion occurs in the left hand in mm. 95-116, carried over from 3K in the exposition from m. 84^3. The triplets also briefly appear in the right hand as well as in the violin together with the left hand. An Alberti bass in the left hand accompanies the presentation and expansion of the expressive 3K theme in large rhythmic values for a total of 31-2/4 mm. In the second stage, both hands contain triplet motion (twice with the violin) starting in m. 116^2, with the sequential development of 2K. However, quarter notes articulate beat 1 of mm. 1-3 of the four-measure phrase treated in a modulating sequence (mm. 116^2-26). Finally, incessant triplet motion returns intensified by steady triplets in both hands in mm. 127-39^2. The rhythmic drive is strengthened by the five-measure *crescendo*

VIOLIN SONATA

to a *forte* (mm. 128-33) and the participation of the violin in triplet motion at the start of the retransition on the dominant preparation (mm. 131-33). This passage, from mm. 128-33, is a good example of concinnity: all elements working together to make the climax of the entire development section (see Ex. 3.6e). The passage ends with the trilled anticipation of the tonic chord and 1Po in quarter notes and a quarter rest, a sudden near cessation of rhythmic motion as the surface rhythm resumes its slower motion for the start of the recapitulation. This conclusion of the development constitutes one of the great surprises of the movement (see Ex. 3.3).

The only steady sixteenth-note motion appears in the coda's cadenza and final cadence, as noted earlier. Otherwise, the coda's more restful effect is due to the prevailing larger rhythmic values, excluding the triplet entirely.

Let us return to the opening of the movement, to 1Po and its continuation, mm. 1-10 (Ex. 3.1). It is clear that the very opening and even the continuation of the theme do not have a defined metrical character. Since the theme starts on an upbeat and is unharmonized at first, its metrical position is uncertain; the upbeat could easily be heard as a downbeat. This possibility is reinforced by the unchanging tonic chord repeated over the barline in mm. 1-2, 2-3, 7-8, and 8-9. Johansen suggests the following scansion of these measures that indicates their metrical ambiguity (Fig. 3.2).[59] The light cadence in m. 6 on the weak second beat adds to the lack of metrical definition.

Figure 3.2 Scansion of 1P, mm. 1-10

1/ 2 3 <u>1</u> / 2 3 <u>1</u> / 2 3 4 / <u>1</u> 2 3 / 4 5 6 / 7 <u>1</u> <u>1</u> / 2 3 <u>1</u> / 2 3 <u>1</u> / 2 3 4 / <u>1</u>
          V I   V I

As Johansen observes: ". . .the accent does not coincide with the barline, and the harmonies all resolve in the middle of the measure, as though the entire opening phrase to measure 10 were unfolding and awakening."[60] Metrical clarity and stability come first with 2P and the transition ideas. At the end of the retransition, the two-measure anticipation of 1Po's trill starts on beat 3 as well, moving the barline one beat to the left and pushing back the metrical shift two additional measures (Ex. 3.3).

Hemiola is another, though less outstanding feature of rhythmic dissonance in the movement, the 3/4 meter inviting this traditional device. It occurs twice in the movement, with triplet groupings. First, it appears in 2K, the only brilliant theme in the closing section, which has the following scansion in mm. 79-81, 82-84² (see also Ex. 3.2).

---

[59] Johansen, "Beethoven's Sonatas for Piano and Violin," 71. See Ratner, *CM*, pp. 71-80 on "Scansion," especially pp. 73-80.
[60] Johansen, loc. cit.

Figure 3.3 Hemiola in 2K

1 2 <u>1</u> / 2 1 <u>2</u> / 3 <u>1</u>   2 /
$\qquad\qquad\qquad$ vii⁶/V V

Here too Beethoven ends the phrase with a cadence on a weak beat, in this case beat 3. On the repeat, the resolution is truncated and 3K starts in its place.[61]

A second example of hemiola on a smaller level within triplet groups occurs near the end of the retransition, just before the anticipation of 1Po, mm. 138-39^1 (Ex. 3. 3). The 12 eighth notes are grouped 6 x 2 rather than 4 x 3. The hemiola acts as a rhythmic modulation back to the duple meter of the opening. In this most delicate passage, V is preceded by a minor iv⁶. The cadence to G occurs in m. 139, beats 2-3, as beat 2 reverts to the triplet grouping and elides on beat three with the G chord. The hemiola thus extends the rhythmic dissonance back five beats from the anticipation of 1Po in m. 139^3.

Melody

With regard to phrase structure in this movement, Beethoven departs from regular four- and eight-measure phrase organization in most functions, both innately and via elisions, truncations, and extensions. The table below gives the total number of measures in each function (see Table 3.6).

Table 3.6 Lengths of the Thematic Functions

Function	1P	2P	1T	2T	1S	2S	ST	1K	2K	3K
No. of measures (excluding elisions)	10	9	13	8	18	7	6	7	5-2/4	11 (with first ending)

Only 2T has a regular structure of eight measures subdivided 4 + 4. The 1S theme (mm. 41-58/59) constitutes the longest single function and it stands out for its beauty and individuality (Ex. 3.8). Like many later Classic S themes, especially in Mozart, 1S is essentially a double period, where the first period ends on V and the second period, parallel to the first, is expected to end on the tonic. Here the theme starts as a regular parallel period featuring a new dotted rhythm and syncopation, with x and y contrast within each phrase. However, a few irregularities remove it from the traditional format. 1Sby does not parallel 1Say, but unexpectedly introduces a new ending and intensification with a long descending scale in triplet rhythm and a ritard for the last two beats, the dominant harmony prolonged from measure 6 of the period. The theme then repeats in the

---

[61] Johansen, ibid., 76.

VIOLIN SONATA

Example 3.8 1S and the start of 2S, exposition (mm. 41-59)

violin and additional irregularities occur, with a two-measure extension of 1Sb, also lengthening the ritard before the *a tempo* in 2S, and a deceptive cadence to ♭VI. Thus, the theme never cadences in the tonic and the digression to ♭VI is not resolved until the strong tonic cadence at the start of 2K.

Many subtleties mark the treatment of phrase structure throughout the movement. Peter Cahn points out the three-measure phrases in mm. 17-25 (end of 2P-1Ta) and the three-measure slur bridging the subphrases 1Px and y (mm. 4-6) reflecting "the rhythmic-metric variety" in the movement.[62] We can add the three-measure slur in mm. 10-12, bridging 1P and 2P, and several later examples such as 2K, in addition to its hemiolas. The elision of phrases also contracts some four-measure phrases into three measures, as 1Tb^1 elides with 2T (mm. 30-32) and 1Ka^1 elides with 2K (mm. 76-81), itself composed of three-measure phrases. Other irregular lengths come from extensions, particularly of 3K (4+7 mm. into the first ending and 4+9-2/4 mm. into the second ending). Additional long extensions in the development add breadth and drive to the section.

The longest phrase appears in the coda—the dialogue of 12-1/4 mm. between the piano and violin (mm. 247^3-59; Ex. 3. 4). The following cadenza section has its irregularities too because of the contracted entries so that the final trill is heard in all three parts only in the last 2-2/4 measures of the eight-measure unit (mm. 265^2-67). Thus the flow of the music is fundamentally enhanced by the flexible and unpredictable phrase groups, as it is by the elisions and overlaps of functions and harmonies.

Two Major Revisions in the First-Movement Autograph

Two of the three most memorable features of the coda underwent final revisions at the autograph stage.[63] Page 5 of the autograph contains mm. 101-21 of the development section on staves 8-20. Above this material on staves 1-3 and 5-7 is a sketch for what became the dialogue section on 1Po in the coda (Plate 3.I). There is no thematic connection with the music of the development and this sketch. Beethoven probably sketched the passage on the first page of an empty bifolio, crossed it out, and then used the rest of the page for writing out the autograph. The harmonic implication—most of the sketch is in B♭ major—suggests that he intended the sketch for the development section since that key is the first important key of the development, established by the continuation of 3K (mm. 97-108).[64] Thus Beethoven probably thought of developing 1Po near the start of the development. However, the final version of the development excludes any reference to 1P until the anticipation of the recapitulation. The melodic mate-

---

[62] Cahn, "Violinsonate G-dur," 89.

[63] Transcriptions of these passages are given in Obelkevich, "The Growth of a Musical Idea," 105.

[64] The first note of the sketch is a strange f♭ implying A♭, a key not used in the movement. Perhaps f♯ was intended, with a suggestion of C minor, a key found as a passing modulation to B♭ in mm. 95^3-96^2.

VIOLIN SONATA

PLATE 3.I *Op. 96/1 A sketch of the coda dialogue passage found in the development.* Autograph, Pierpont Morgan Library, N.Y. City, MA 16, p.5

rial of the sketch presents 1Po first in the piano right hand, then in the left hand, and finally in the violin, and Beethoven extends notes 2-4 down to the B♭ chord. The extension appears in a canonic setting in the final version, but no overlapping is found in the sketch. Obelkevich suggests that the sketch ends in G minor but it could well be on V of B♭.

In the autograph of the coda, the final version of the dialogue is written out on p. 13 as an insert for p. 12, placed after the series of diminished seventh chords. The second major revision of the movement concerns this harmonic passage, utilizing the arpeggio motive from 2P. The passage originally had a different continuation, which moved directly into the cadenza (Plate 3.II). Thus the insertion of the dialogue was a late decision on Beethoven's part. The diminished-sevenths originally continued the sequence in m. 247. Then Beethoven extended the inverted form on a V^4_3 chord and the two G-major root position chords (root position is implied but not written out for the second chord), which connect to the I^6_4 of the cadenza. This approach to the cadenza is short and much less dramatic than the approach via the dialogue section. In the final version, the dia-

PLATE 3.II OP. 96/I A DELETED CONTINUATION OF THE CODA DIALOGUE PASSAGE FOUND IN THE DEVELOPMENT. *Autograph, Pierpont Morgan Library, N . Y. City, MA 16, p.12.*

logue ends with a G chord but it is I^6_4 and thus overlaps with the harmony of the cadenza (mm. 255-59). Beethoven dramatizes the approach to the cadenza by the rising canon between the violin and piano left hand, and the crescendo to a *fp* at the start of the cadenza. In place of a four-measure extension of the arpeggio passage leading to the cadenza, Beethoven adds no fewer than 13 measures in one of the most impressive passages of the entire sonata. Transferring the dialogue from the development to the coda also provides another striking illustration of Beethoven's search for the right and most effective place for his ideas.[65]

---

[65] There are many examples of such transfer of ideas in Beethoven's sketches and drafts. One important example occurs in the first movement of the *Eroica* symphony, where the initial part of the extended and climactic transition in the recapitulation (mm. 430-440) was first placed in the exposition. See Gustav Nottebohm, *Ein Skizzenbuch von Beethoven aus dem Jahre 1803* (Leipzig, 1880; reprint New York and London: Johnson Reprint Corp., 1970), 11.

VIOLIN SONATA

Performance and Textual Problems

The first problem concerns the opening trill and its recurrences: should the trill start on the main or upper note and should it include a suffix (Nachschlag)? William Newman has considered the problems most carefully, as he has the whole category of Beethoven trills. Regarding this trill, he states that all factors "point persuasively, though not conclusively, to a start on its main note and the omission of the suffix."[66] He remarks that all available recorded performances since World War II that he examined contain main-note starts without a suffix, while editorial additions to the sonata up to about World War I also indicate main-note starts but add a suffix. Both Newman and Max Rudolf examine key passages in the movement where a start on the main note seems highly preferable if not utterly necessary. The passages include mm. 62-63, the first ending, m. 95, and the retransition, 139-41. In each case, the trill is approached by a step down (cases 1 and 3) or by half-step motion down and then up to a repeat of P (case 2). With regard to the suffix, Rudolf's remarks are telling: "To me . . . a Nachschlag would make the delicate interplay of an idea too heavy and would destroy the Zartheit [tenderness] considered essential by Czerny."[67]

Example 3.9 Textual problem m. 158, recapitulation

[66] Newman, *Beethoven on Beethoven*, 217. For a detailed analysis of this trill, see also Newman, "The Opening Trill in Beeethoven's Sonata for Piano and Violin Op. 96," in: Martin Bente, ed., *Musik-Edition, Interpretation, Gedenkschrift Günter Henle* (Munich: G. Henle, 1980), 384-93. For the same conclusions, see Rudolf, *A Musical Life*, 329-32.

[67] Rudolf, ibid., 331.

A small textual problem occurs in m. 158 regarding note 5 in the violin (Ex. 3.9). Though the entire passage is in E♭ major, the note lacks a flat sign in the autograph and first edition.[68] Some editors and performers prefer a♮ here, but Sieghard Brandenburg in his edition of the sonata rightly adds a flat in parentheses next to the note. This solution follows the parallel passage in the exposition, m. 19 (piano, right hand), and avoids anticipation of the $a_\natural^1$ in the V$^6_5$ of V chord that follows in the next measure.[69]

The Second Movement: *Adagio espressivo*

The *Adagio espressivo* is both the shortest and greatest slow movement of the violin sonatas. Despite its unique power, however, it still shares several traits with earlier slow movements in the violin sonatas, revealing certain recurring preferences. Thus, in addition to Op. 96, five movements are in 2/4 meter, four are *adagios*, three contain "espressivo" in their tempo headings (Op. 12, No. 3, Op. 24, and Op. 30, No. 1), and four place the slow movement in the submediant key (Op. 12, No. 3, E♭-C; Op. 30, No. 2, c-A♭; Op. 30, No. 3, G-E♭, ♭VI, as in Op. 96; and Op. 47, a-F). The length of the slow movements varies greatly, the longest movements being the variation set of Op. 47 (235 mm.) and the sonata-form layout in Op. 23 (207 mm.).

Another earlier preference reflected in this *Adagio* is the form, which is essentially ternary. Five slow movements display this structural plan (found also in Op. 12, Nos. 2 and 3; and Op. 30, Nos. 1 and 2), a plan less frequent in Beethoven's music in other instrumental genres (see the timeline on the facing page, Table 3.7).

As we see from the timeline, Beethoven modifies the A-B-A¹- coda design with a brief and varied recall of the opening of B (1S), but in a cadential setting and small, closed parallel period. The inner proportions of the movement differ markedly from the other ternary movements in the great length of the B section, more than twice the length of A, and the span of the coda, three measures longer than A:

A:	11 mm. (omitting the upbeat of B)
B:	26 mm.
A¹:	11 mm.
B¹:	5 mm.
coda:	14 mm.

---

[68] The problem was first raised by Günter Henle "Ein Fehler in Beethovens Violinsonate?", *Die Musikforschung* 5 (1952): 53-54.

[69] It should be noted that in the Brandenburg edition of Op. 96, piano part, m. 254, the indication for lifting the damper pedal is placed too late. The sign should be below beat 3, as indicated in the autograph, not slightly later.

VIOLIN SONATA

Table 3.7 Timeline: Movement II

Key: E♭ Meter: 2/4

```
            (ar)    (ar) (ar)
A     Pa   b    |  c    d    dy ext.        |
1-11²  1   3      4    5    7    8²         11²
      E        V                             I


            (ah)              (a)        (1Sbm)
B     1Sa   ax¹  b    |  2Sa   b   | RTa        b        |
11²-37 11²  14²  17     21     21    26   32        36
       E♭               A♭ :I  (f)        E♭ :V ped. (chromatic harm.)


      (Nh)
A¹    P¹          |
38-48² 38         48²
      E♭          I


      (Nh)
B¹    1Sax²    x³
48^{2.5}-53  48^{2.5}   51²


      (2S,1Sh)   (1Sbm)    (y²m)  (Ny1m)
coda  N (canon) x   y     x¹   z  | K      KT       ||    67 mm.
54-67  54           56    58  60   62     66       67

      E♭ ped. to the end             E♭: I   g: iv³^{6♯}
```

Starting with section B, all themes and sections elide, excepting A¹-B¹, nearly achieving an unbreakable musical flow, as in the first movement. Here, 1S elides with 2S, 2S with RT, RT with P¹, and the end of B¹ with the coda.

SECTION A

The memorable opening theme presented by the piano alone may truly be termed a chorale melody, with a three-measure extension of its final "Lebewohl" cadence in the violin and then the piano (Ex. 3. 10 on p. 225).[70] Like the chorale in Beethoven's time, the melody is in duple meter and consists of a series of four two-measure phrases. Each phrase has the same or nearly the same rhythm, mainly in eighths, and each note is harmonized separately.[71] The melody is combined with a flowing semi-contrapuntal inner voice

---

[70] For Beethoven's use of the chorale, see below.
[71] For references to the theoretical specifications for the organ chorale of the late eighteenth century, see the summary concerning the chorale melody of the "Heilige Dankgesang" in the String Quartet Op. 132/III (Ch. 4). However, the chromaticism and dissonances in m. 7 are not "in style."

in steady sixteenth notes, an accompaniment that helps give the melody its beautiful *cantabile* quality. The sixteenth notes persist to the very end of the theme, as accompaniment to the "Lebewohl" extended cadence.

In m. 7, Beethoven intensifies the final cadence with a series of six, partly chromatic chords mainly on the sixteenth-note level that remind us of J. S. Bach's chromatic harmonizations in some of his chorale settings, as in the chorale "Es ist genug." This measure contains two irregular resolutions of V^7/IV: to V^0_9 of ii and to ii^6. The V^0_9 of ii seems to have an irregular resolution to V^4_3, but its $d\flat^1$ is really $c\sharp^1$ and the chord is really a diminished-seventh chord on the raised sixth degree, a favorite Romantic chromaticism, that acts as an appoggiatura to the dominant-seventh chord.[72] Such chromatic details remind us of Beethoven's late style. These chords introduce a harmonic tension that clouds over the serene effect of the melody, anticipating the painful expression that finds its fullest elaboration in the B section.

Besides this cadential measure, the theme is set with a straightforward harmonic vocabulary. However, before the final tonic cadence, each phrase ends on V-B♭. The strongest intermediate cadence in m. 4 contains a tonicization of V with the diminished seventh chord—V^0_9. By ending each phrase but the last on V, Beethoven keeps the harmony in suspense and thus achieves a strong continuity, so important in the sonata as a whole. This continuity is strengthened by placing each cadence on the weak second beat of the measure, including the final cadences in mm. 8-11.

As preferred in late eighteenth-century chorale style, the melody has a limited range. It spans only a minor seventh, d^1-c^2 and reaches its highest notes early, in m. 2. Also typical is its conjunct melodic motion, varied by only four skips, all being thirds except for the descending fifth in m. 2. If we look more closely at the melodic contour, we find an overall descending melodic line in the high notes of each phrase, from c^2 (m. 2) to $b\flat^1$ (m. 4), g^1 (m. 5), $a\flat^1$ (m. 7), g^1-f^1-$e\flat^1$ (m. 8), having perhaps a connection with the descending melodic line in the B section, 2S.

The low range of the melody with its deep bass line also makes its effect, especially in contrast to the higher violin solo in section B. The *cantabile* style is indicated by the slurs Beethoven applied to both right and left hands. However, they do not always coordinate, as in many Beethoven works, including the symphonies. Thus, in mm. 1-2, a two-measure slur

---

[72] The diminished-seventh chord on e♮ first presented in m. 3 (last eighth) as V^0_9/V of B♭, to which it resolves. This normal treatment serves as the backdrop for the enharmonic resolution of the chord in m. 7. Beethoven may well have known Bach's chorale harmonizations. Martin Zenck has shown that much of Bach's music, including the chorales, was published in Vienna and available to Beethoven. In fact, the Archduke Rudolf's library also contained rare editions of the chorales published in 1765 and 1769 as well as their corrected versions of 1784-87. See Martin Zenck, *Die Bach Rezeption des späten Beethoven* (Wiesbaden: Steiner, 1986), Ch. 3, "Das Wiener Bach-Repertoire des Beethovenzeit," 36-107.

VIOLIN SONATA   225

Example 3. 10 The opening chorale melody, P, and start of 1S (mm. 1-15)

in the right hand contrasts with one-measure slurs in the two lower parts. Measure 4, beat 2 of the melody is slurred over the barline with mm. 5-6, thus bridging the cadence.[73] In the recapitulation Beethoven apparently simplified the slurring of the melody, there in the violin, by indicating slurs for mm. 38-39, 40-43, and 44-46.[74] Slurs in the bass appear only for mm. 1-3 in one-measure groups. The inner voice, now in the piano right hand as its top part, receives the most varied slurring in mm. 38-43^1 of the theme. The slurs include two-beat and measure slurs as well as slurs from the last repeated note into the following group and across the barline (mm. 42-43^1).

One of the sketches for the theme in the Petter Sketchbook contains some earlier details revised later by Beethoven (Ex. 3. 11).[75] Thus the melody in m. 3 originally had an a♮^{1}, which weakened the effect of the a♮^{1} in m. 4 and extended back the tonicization of V. Similarly, the E♮ in the bass in m. 3 originally appeared in m. 4, first eighth. The placement in m. 3 allows a full beat for V/V in m. 4 and a slower harmonic rhythm to emphasize this important cadence.

Also weaker in the early version was the anticipation of the tonic cadence in m. 6 with the repeat of mm. 5-6 in mm. 7-8 rather than the intensification of the final measures and the "Lebewohl" ending. Here we see too that the series of dominant cadences was a later feature of the theme. For the second half of P Beethoven originally introduced dotted rhythm, which survived only in m. 4^2 of the final version. The decision favoring rhythmic simplicity in the theme sets it apart from the B section, with its complex and active rhythm in the piano part.

Example 3.11 Sketch of P and start of S in the Petter Sketchbook

---

[73] Similar cross- phrasing occurs in mm. 4-5^1 of the *Adagio* in the "Pathétique" Piano Sonata, Op. 13 (1797-98), though the slur follows only the first edition since the autograph is lost.

[74] The long slur given in the Brandenburg edition is a phrase slur, being impractical as a performance slur. However, considering Beethoven's often overly long slur markings, it is possible that he intended single slurs in mm. 40 and 41, and a two-measure slur in mm. 42-43; but this would exclude the bridging slur between phrases b and c. While the edition has only one long slur in mm. 44-46, the autograph presents two slurs: a slur from m. 44 to m. 45^1, and another slur across the barline from m. 45^2 to m. 46.

Section B

In this long modulating section, the solo violin carries all the new thematic material (1S, 2S, RT), as in the early ternary movement of Op. 12 No. 3, but on a vaster, more complex canvas. Here, the solo violin represents the more personal inward expression as opposed to the congregational chorale, and 2S is one of Beethoven's most tragic passages.

The harmony moves far afield, starting in E♭ and modulating to A♭ at the end of 1S, with a tonicization of D♭ (IV/IV). A more unstable 2S goes from A♭ to the dark key of E♭ minor via F minor, and touching on the remote G♭ major (♭III) before returning to E♭ minor and then E♭ major for the retransition (Ex. 3.12 on p. 228).[76] Only one formal cadence occurs before the retransition, ending 1S on the tonic of A♭.

The melodic style differs entirely from the chorale. It is more like an arioso, being irregular in phrase structure and rhythm. Located generally in the upper register, the line's total range spans over two octaves, b♭ to c♭^{3}, found in 2S. Both S themes have irregular lengths, nine and eleven measures. Both themes are far more disjunct than P, especially 2S, with large leaps of octaves as well as a minor seventh and major sixth. The two S themes also contrast in rhythm. 1S offers much rhythmic variety in harmony and surface rhythm, the latter ranging from dotted quarters to sixty-fourth notes in the ornamental cadence *molto dolce*. On the other hand, 2S features larger values in the surface rhythm of halves and quarters combined with the slowest harmonic rhythm of the B section. In 2Sa and the start of 2Sb, the harmonic rhythm moves in half notes (mm. 22-26) and thereafter in quarter notes, coordinating with the rare melodic movement in simple quarters in 2Sb (mm. 26-30).

Dynamics and expressive indications play an important role in delineating these ideas. 1S starts *espressivo*, suggesting some tempo flexibility; 1Sb contains < > marks in m. 17 and m. 18 for the entire measure. The more dramatic and strange 2S features three *crescendo-piano* effects in mm. 21-22, 23-24, and 25-30, the final *crescendo* being the longest of all—5 measures versus 1-1/2 measures earlier. These effects engender a powerful expression of denial rather than fulfillment. The longest *crescendo* in 2Sb has the longest slur of the movement, 6 mm. (mm. 26-31), which indicates the unbreakable unity of these measures as well as a legato performance.

Most unusual in this remarkable section is the piano accompaniment. 1S is supported by tense offbeat syncopated figures, making four impacts a measure, and having a tricky coordination, frequently offbeat, with the violin part. In 2S, the surface rhythm of the accompaniment ac-

---

[75] N I, 26.

[76] Johansen, "Beethoven's Sonatas for Piano and Violin," 89, describes 2S as being in fantasia style and points out that the harmony moves essentially from IV (A♭) to V.

Example 3.12 2S complete (mm. 21-32[1])

celerates to steady thirty-second notes combined with pulsing eighth notes exchanged between the hands, at first in dialogue (mm. 21-25), the thirty-seconds then remaining in the right-hand. The accompaniment provides an urgent background to the slow-moving, solemn melody above. Further, the first note of each thirty-second note group is almost always a dissonant appoggiatura, often chromatic, a half-step below the harmony note. Most of 2S is in minor, the harmony intensified with two strategic diminished sevenths—of iv (m. 29^1) and V (m. 30^2), the latter sustaining the minor color to the end. The cumulative tension of this section is enormous, almost unbearable. Then, within two measures, this unique vision in Beethoven's music fades away into the retransition.

As so often in Beethoven, the retransition has dramatic aspects (Ex. 3.13). The key of E♭ major is immediately reestablished on the second beat of the initial measure with c♮^{1} not c♭ in the melodic line. The six measures of the retransition divide into 4 + 2 measures, RTa and b. Phrase a rests on V and recalls the ornamental cadence of 1S also in its first figure (notes 1-4). Entirely in the violin and cadenza-like, phrase a has a sparse accompaniment as it mounts nearly two octaves. Anchored around the

Example 3.13 The retransition and return of P (mm. 32-39)

notes of the dominant chord, it speeds up to its climax on $a^\flat$ from thirty-second to sixty-fourth notes. Beethoven resolves the long dominant pedal essentially only at the start of P.[77]

Though the long rise seems to call for a *crescendo*, the cadenza is *piano*, as the *crescendo* is withheld until phrase b, which leads back to the chorale with a new kind of intensity. A complete contrast follows the cadenza as phrase b starts with a slow chromatic descent in the violin in eighth notes (mm. 36-37, first eighth) and a series of diminished-seventh chords in the piano (mm. 36^2-37^1) finally cadencing in E♭ with the return of P. These dissonances recall the dissonant harmonization of m. 7 of the chorale; the sudden rhythmic slowdown prepares the return of P as well. A concinnity here of sound, harmony, and rhythm produces a highpoint of tension just before the recapitulation. The long phrase slur from the big rise of the cadenza (m. 34^2) through phrase b indicates an unbroken continuity between the phrases despite the contrast·

Section A[1]

The changes here are few though telling. P now recurs in the violin, not the piano, though at the same register. The violin sings the chorale as if it too has received consolation and hope from this noble prayer. While the dynamic level in the keyboard part is piano as before, in the violin it is *mezza voce* (meaning *mezzo forte*).[78] While the louder dynamic may have been introduced because the melody is placed mainly on the fairly weak D-string of the violin, Beethoven often heightens the dynamic level at the start of the recapitulation, as in the Violin Concerto and Quartet Op. 132, first movements. This frequent device must be considered within the context of each movement, but in all cases the intensification highlights the start of the reprise.

The piano part is essentially the same. As mentioned earlier, Beethoven places the middle voice in the piano right hand with new slurring. At the end of the "Lebewohl" cadence, the original violin part appears in the piano an octave higher, enriched with third and octave doubling.

A cadential transformation of 1Sa with an ornamented repeat appears now in the piano, while the violin carries the syncopated accompaniment. This accompaniment continues into the coda, linking the sections in addition to the elision.

The Coda

The fourteen-measure coda can be divided into three parts: basically 8 + 4

---

[77] The implied tonic in the piano, m. 36, third eighth, is too weak (with only the interval of a third, $e\flat^1$-g^1) to function as the resolution of the four-measure dominant pedal.

[78] In Koch, *Musikalisches Lexikon*, article "Mezza," the term "mezza voce" is defined as

+ 2 mm. The last two measures make the connection to the Scherzo with a tremolo on the E♭ chord (m. 66) to a simple quarter with fermata in the final measure. Beethoven adds a c♯¹ there in the violin making an augmented- sixth chord in g. As often in Beethoven the harmonic suspense is underscored by *pp*, the lowest level in the movement. The final chord is heard at first as V⁷/IV in A♭. Since this chord had appeared several times in the coda, its enharmonic resolution in the Scherzo comes as a surprise if not a shock (Ex. 3.14).

Example 3.14 End of the coda and connection to the Scherzo (mm. 65-67)

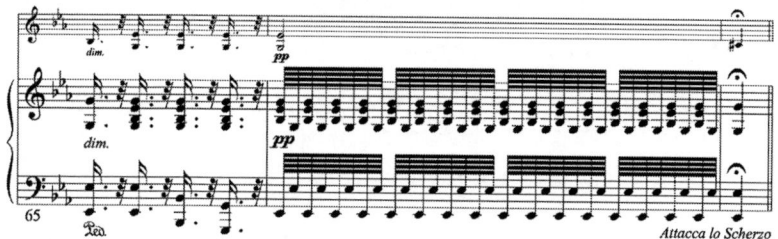

An earlier model for such a connection to the Scherzo appears in the String Quartet Op. 95 (1810-11) at the end of the coda in the D-major second movement. The movement has a ternary form as well, though much longer and more complex than the one in Op. 96, albeit with similar proportions. Several features of the conclusion are extremely similar. The movement closes on a reiterated tonic chord in the last three of four measures, also reaching *pianissimo* in the third measure from the end. The penultimate measure presents a thin octave on the tonic note d² which is reharmonized in the last measure as a diminished-seventh chord on b. This chord can be heard as the diminished-seventh of V of D, a chord implied close to the end of the coda (mm. 184 and 186), just as the augmented-sixth chord in Op. 96 is prepared earlier as V⁷/IV. The chord resolves as the diminished-seventh in C minor at the start of the Scherzo, the tonic key of F minor reached only later in m. 9 (this off-tonic start does not occur in Op. 96, however). The pivot chord in the last measure also has a fermata and the two movements connect with an "attacca subito," as in Op. 96 with its "Attacca lo Scherzo." In a final identical detail, Beethoven reiterates the chord at the start of the Scherzo, with the same soprano note as he does in Op. 96, thus

---

meaning "with half voice, with half strength of the tones" (mit halber Stimme, das ist, mit halber Stärke des Tones). In his definition of *mezzo forte*, he also gives the meaning as "half strong" (halb Stark) but also "the mean between strong and weak tone" (oder das Mittel zwischen starkem und schwachem Tone). Sheer, "The Role of Dynamics in Beethoven's Instrumental Works," Vol. I, 450-51, asserts that Beethoven used *mf* as an independent level only in his early works. In the middle period, Beethoven prefers the term *mezza voce*. Both *mezza voce* and *mezzo forte* were applied "almost always as a reinforcement of the main melodic line within a *p* context and . . . . not [as] an independent level." Several examples occur in late works as well.

linking the movements both harmonically and melodically (see Ex. 3.15).

The coda combines the stability of section A with the tension and sorrowful expression of section B (Ex. 3.16 below). Providing stability is the long tonic pedal throughout the coda as well as the repeated harmon-

Example 3.15 End of the coda and connection to the Scherzo of the String Quartet, Op. 95/II (mm. 184-92) with the first eight measures of the Scherzo

ic progressions (see below). As in many Beethoven codas, the composer introduces a new theme, N (mm. 54-62^1), which also incorporates some earlier ideas in an example of the old device of thematic recombination.[79] Beethoven recalls section B with the syncopated piano accompaniment of 1S in the first eight measures (mm. 54-61),[80] the turn figure and sixty-fourth note arabesques from 1S and the retransition, a hint of 2S (mm. 54-55), and the disjunct melodic style associated with 2S. The total melodic range is the widest in the movement, $b\flat$-$e\flat^3$, and $e\flat^3$ is the highest note of the movement, placed in the violin (m. 60).

Example 3. 16 Start of the coda, with long tonic pedal and canon between the violin and piano (mm. 54-59)

[79] For another example of new themes in the coda, see the String Quartet, Op. 132, finale.
[80] A somewhat similar effect occurs in the coda of the *Adagio* in the Violin Sonata, Op. 30, No. 1, which incorporates the dotted rhythm of P in the accompaniment of new themes.

Beethoven treats N canonically, its four-measure phrase in the violin iniated at the unison somewhat inexactly by the piano two measures later. As the violin descends to a cadence on its lowest note, the accompaniment partly descends with it, drawing out the arabesque figure from m. 57. The canonic texture anticipates the stricter canon in the Trio of the Scherzo, and both are linked with the fugato in variation 7 of the *finale*, as Beethoven integrates imitative texure in the sonata as a whole.

Further harmonic stabilization comes the nearly four-fold repetition of the two-measure harmonic progression in mm. 54-55: (I)-V^7/IV-V^0_9. These chords underpin the melodic repetitions produced by the canon. The only changes are the longer quarter-note tonic chords in repetitions 2-4, and the dark nuance of the minor subdominant preceding the diminished-seventh chord in the last repeat. This is the only time the V^7/IV resolves to the subdominant. In the first three presentations, the diminished seventh takes up all of the second measure, increasing the tension with stressed dissonance and the inflection of the minor mode via the lowered sixth degree in the chord—C♭. The harmonic tension relaxes to simple V^7-I chords in the next four measures, while the final extended tonic chord starts in m. 63^2.

The closing K unit utilizes a variant of the arabesque figure of N. This phrase starts on the tonic on beat 2, not the V on beat 1 that is held over from section 1, connecting the sections harmonically. The barline here shifts back a beat so that K's beginning sounds like a downbeat. Johansen shows the larger scansion of mm. 62^2-67 as follows:[81]

```
1 | 2 1 | 2 3 | 1 2 3 4 | 1 | 2 |
I    V I      (8ths)       aug. 6th
```

Three *crescendo-piano* indications occur in the coda, mm. 55-61, as in section B, 2S, though all the *crescendos* are shorter. Like 2S, the first two *crescendos* are brief, lasting here for only one measure (mm. 55, 57). The sudden *pianos* highlight the imitation in the piano and violin respectively. The third, longer *crescendo* (mm. 59-61, third eighth) leads to the close of the largest portion of the coda. Like the longer *crescendos* near the end of 2S and the retransition, it is attached to a descending rather than ascending melodic line, a more intense effect. All the long *crescendos* occur at the ends of sections, another unifying element in the movement.

BEETHOVEN AND THE CHORALE

The chorale melody in the *Adagio* is not unique in Beethoven's late instrumental works. The most famous example is the chorale melody in the Lydian mode of the "Heiliger Dankgesang" in the Quartet Op. 132/III (see Ch. 4). At least two additional prominent examples can be found. One occurs in the "Adagio con molto sentimento d'affetto" of the Cello Sonata, Op.

---

[81] Johansen, 94.

VIOLIN SONATA

102, No. 2 (1815), written fairly close in time to Op. 96. This movement, also an A-B-A¹ form, has a brief coda and a longer transition to the fugue *finale*, anticipating the fugue subject. It contains a chorale melody at the start of the A section that shares certain features with the chorale in Op. 96, though it is the only example in minor (D minor) rather than major. This is a stark theme in the tragic mode (see Ex. 3. 17).

Eight measures long, the chorale divides into four two-measure phrases as in Op. 96; each phrase has exactly the same rhythm, ending with an eighth rest. Unlike Op. 96, each note of the melody is harmonized separately in chordal texture, without a flowing inner part. Further, each phrase ends on a different degree with local tonicization. The cadences rise and fall in thirds: F-I, d-V, C-I, and a-I (on the notes F-A-C-A). The return to the tonic is effected by the next period, 2P. Also unlike Op. 96, the B section, in D major, is a relaxation rather than an intensification.

A third slow example is the first theme of the *Adagio* in the Ninth Symphony, the movement in B♭ organized as an alternating variation form like the "Heiliger Dankgesang." Beethoven presents the melody (mm. 1-24) far more complexly, with an introduction, wind echoes of phrase endings, and partial phrase repetitions, the last two creating irregular phrase lengths of 5, 3, and 6 measures.[82] The theme modulates at the very end to a key a third away in which S appears (in D and G). The chorale melody cadences only once on the tonic. This occurs after its second variation—

Example 3. 17 Chorale-like 1P in Beethoven's Cello Sonata, Op. 102, No. 2, Adagio

[82] Two analyses of the beautiful theme are especially valuable. See Heinrich Schenker,

its last appearance as a complete theme—on the weak fourth beat of m. 119, another remarkable example of Beethoven's desire to de-emphasize cadences and maintain an intensive musical flow. Use of an introduction and interludes between phrases relates the theme to the chorale of Op. 132 and the standard procedures of organ chorales of the late eighteenth century. As always in Beethoven, each chorale example differs in treatment and structure. Beethoven's expressive melodies in chorale style call to mind the occasional prayers that the composer noted down in his diary (*Tagebuch*) of 1812-18 and even in his sketches.[83]

The Third Movement: Scherzo, Allegro

The Scherzo in Op. 96 is the only such movement in the Beethoven works discussed in this volume. Meaning "joke" in Italian, the term has a long musical history. Dating from the early seventeenth century, the term was first associated with vocal music, such as Monteverdi's *Scherzi musicali* of 1607 and 1632. Already in 1614, however, the term appears in a collection of pieces for instruments, the Op. 8 by G. A. Cagiasi.[84] During the later Baroque and early Classic periods some instrumental pieces carried this title, one even by J. S. Bach (in the A-minor keyboard partita). Haydn's String Quartets, Op. 33 (1781), with six Scherzos rather than minuets, made the term current, though the movements had moderate tempos. It is with Beethoven, however, that the modern scherzo is justly associated, since such movements appear in his works from the Bonn period, in the Piano Trio in E♭, WoO 38 (?1791), to his last completed work, the String Quartet, Op. 135 (1826).[85]

The scherzo replaced the minuet in many of Beethoven's multimovement cycles, but the minuet remained an alternative for Beethoven through

---

Beethoven's Ninth Symphony (Vienna, 1912), trans. and ed. John Rothgeb (New Haven and London: Yale University Press, 1992), 185-92; and the study of the Ninth Symphony by Donald Francis Tovey, in *Essays in Musical Analysis*, vol. II (London: Oxford University Press, 1935), 331-32.

[83] For a revised translation of the *Tagebuch*, see Maynard Solomon, *Beethoven Essays* (Cambridge, MA: Harvard University Press, 1988), 233-95. For the German text, see Solomon, *Beethovens Tagebuch*, ed. Sieghard Brandenburg (Mainz: Hase & Koehler, 1990). See also Solomon's important survey "The Quest for Faith," in *Beethoven Essays*, 216-29.

[84] Tilden A. Russell and Hugh MacDonald, article "Scherzo," NGD, 2nd ed., 22: 486.

[85] For surveys of the scherzo see the articles by Eugene K. Wolf, *The New Harvard Dictionary of Music*, ed. Don Michael Randel (Cambridge, MA: The Belknap Press of Harvard University Press, 1986), 732-33, and Russell and MacDonald, 486-89. See also Gustav Becking, *Studien zu Beethovens Personalstil: Das Scherzothema* (Leipzig: Breitkopf & Härtel, 1921); Michael Luxner, "The Evolution of the Minuet/Scherzo in the Music of Beethoven" (Ph. D. diss., Eastman School of Music, 1978); Joseph Gemeiner, *Menuett und Scherzo: Ein Beitrag zur Entwicklungsgeschichte und Soziologie des Tanzsatzes in der Wiener Klassik* (Tutzing: Schneider, 1979); Wolfram Steinbeck, " 'Ein wahres Spiel mit musikalischen Formen': Zum Scherzo Ludwig van Beethovens," *Archiv für Musikwissenschaft* 38 (1981): 194-226; and Tilden A. Russell, "Minuet, Scherzando, and Scherzo: The Dance Movement in Transition" (Ph. D. diss., University of North Carolina, Chapel Hill, 1983).

the Eighth Symphony (1812). A unique late appearance of the dance gently ends the "Diabelli" Variations as Variation 33, Tempo di Menuetto (1823). Beethoven's early and middle scherzos in the minuet position normally follow the minuet in its bipartite form, the inclusion of a bipartite trio, and the *da capo* of the scherzo. Max Rudolf has shown that the two reprises of a minuet or scherzo were repeated in the *da capo* unless the indication for the *da capo* contained the words "senza replica," "senza repetizione," "senza ritornelli," or some such term.[86] In the scherzos of the Fourth Symphony and String Quartet, Op. 59, No. 2 (both 1806), Beethoven lengthened the scherzo movement by introducing a double-trio form, A-B(trio)-A-B-A, with changes in the type of scherzo return (without repeats, altered in dynamics, shortened). None of these examples, however, are labeled "Scherzo" despite the scherzo style. In *allegro* movements, the measure serves as the beat, with a predominance of quarter-note motion within the measure.

Only thirty movements by Beethoven bear the title "Scherzo" and most were written before 1803, including the famous and quintessential scherzo of the *Eroica* Symphony, Op. 55. Thereafter, only four movements are marked "Scherzo:" in the Cello Sonata, Op. 69 (1807-08); the Piano Trio, Op. 97 (1810-11); Op. 96; and the Piano Sonata, Op. 106 (1817-18). However, many movements embody the style without the title. Becking lists 27 but I would delete several of them as not being in the scherzo style (movements such as those in the Piano Sonatas, Op. 14, No. 1/II and Op. 27, No. 2/II, and the Quartet, Op. 132/III (a waltz-like movement; see below).[87]

In addition, Beethoven uses such terms as *scherzando* or *scherzoso* to designate movements with humorous elements. These are mostly *Allegrettos* or fast *Andantes* replacing the usual slow movement. Examples can be found in the Violin Sonata, Op. 23/II, Symphony No. 8/II, and the String Quartet, Op. 130/III. Functioning as the scherzo is the extraordinary second movement *Allegretto vivace* for the String Quartet, Op. 59, No. 1, inscribed "sempre scherzando." Though most typical scherzos have rapid tempos, some are more moderate allegros, as in Op. 96 (Ex. 3.18).

Most scherzos are in 3/4 but some Beethoven scherzos appear in such meters as 3/8, 6/8, 2/4, and ¢. Few scherzos are in minor, however, as in Op. 96. In scherzos and scherzo-like movements one is justified in searching for some humorous effects, which usually occur in such movements.[88] This holds true for the scherzo in Op. 96 as well.

---

[86] Max Rudolf, "Inner Repeats in the Da Capo of Classical Minuets and Scherzos," in *A Musical Life*, 123-33. See the Menuetto in the Piano Sonata Op. 10, No. 3 (Ch. 2).

[87] See Becking, *Studien zu Beethovens Personalstil*, 12-13. See 138-39, for a discussion of this Scherzo.

[88] See this writer's article, "The *Andante con moto* in Beethoven's String Quartet Op. 130," 227-34.

Example 3.18 Scherzo, Part I, with varied repeats(mm. 1-16)

THE SCHERZO IN OP. 96

The strong contrast between movements II and III in Op. 96 was remarked by Riezler.[89] Yet, Beethoven maintains a degree of tension and serious expression that help make this movement a bridge between the deeply expressive *Adagio* and the vigorous *finale* with its folk-like theme. In fact, the movement shares features with both movements II and IV, like the minuet-trio of Op. 10, No. 3 (see Ch.2).

The Scherzo is a short movement, unified in idea, articulation, and dynamics (see the timeline on p. 239 and Ex. 3.18). A source of the more serious mood is the rare use of the tonic minor. There are only three scherzos in the tonic minor that are entitled scherzo: in the String Trio in C minor, Op. 9, No. 3/III, the Cello Sonata in A major, Op. 69/II, and Op. 96. The minor mode is sustained by the modulation to the dominant minor, D minor, at the end of Part I in the simple binary form. Another source of the serious

---

[89] Walther Riezler, *Beethoven*, trans. G. D. H. Pidcock (New York, 1938; reprint New York: Vienna House, 1972), 177.

VIOLIN SONATA   239

mood is the moderate tempo, and the persistent harsh *sfp* accents on the weak third beat, first on the two-measure level and then every measure to the cadence of Part I. The one-measure level continues as an intensification of Part II.

Table 3.8. Timeline, Movement III

Key: g   Meter: 3/4

		(a)				(a)				
Scherzo:	Pa	b	|a¹	b¹	|c		|c¹		|
	0³	4³	8¹	8³	12³	16¹	16³	24¹	24³	32¹
	g	g-d	d:i	g	g-d	d:i	d-g	g:i	g-d	g:i

					(Sam)		vn. line of canon		
Trio:	Sa		|a¹		|b		|a	Nb	Nc
	32³	40¹	40³	48¹	48³	52¹	52³	56	60³
	E♭ ped. B♭:I		E♭ -B♭	B♭ :I		E♭:V ped. I from 49		E♭ :I ped.____| until 60²	

	a	Nb	Nc	Nb¹	K		| written-out *da*
	64³	68	72³	76³	80 I	80³ piano, vn.+ piano l.h. r.h.	83 E♭:I	*capo* of Scherzo follows

				(b²)		
Coda:	Pa²	b²		|b³	K	|
	115³	119³	123¹	123³	127-29	129 mm.
	G		G:I		G:I ped.	

A connection with the second movement is the use of the same key–E♭–for the much longer trio. On the other hand, the relaxed mood of the Trio's Part I, produced by a simple waltz melody on a drone bass with its folk-music associations, anticipates traits of the *finale* theme (Ex. 3.20). The three-part canon in Part II of the Trio seems to revert to the serious style that relates to the fugato in Variation 7 of the *finale*. However, its round-like character also fits the popular tone of the *finale*'s theme.

Example 3. 19 *Scherzo, Part II, melodic line (mm. 16³-24²)*

Two other features connect the movement to the variation *finale*. One is the use of varied repeats of both parts of the Scherzo and Trio (excluding phrase b), and even the second phrase of the return of the Scherzo's Part I in the coda. Another feature is the shift to G major in the coda, anticipating, indeed overlapping with the return to G major in the *finale*.

Despite the serious aspects of the movement, a few humorous effects make their appearance. Most obvious is the Scherzo is the unexpected treatment of Part II, which is nothing but an extension of Part I, mm. 5-6 of the cadential phrase. This is a complete surprise and melds the parts rather than keeping them distinct. Beethoven avoids here the usual structure of Part II as parallel to Part I or a contrast-return arrangement (that is, rounded binary form), as we see in another brief Scherzo in the "Spring" Sonata. The two parts do have rhyming cadences in the final two measures, however (Ex. 3. 19).

A second possibly humorous effect may be the treatment of the Trio's waltz theme. A charming beginning and contrasting phrase are entirely *piano*, homophonic, and sectional, the repeated Part I solely in the piano. Then, at the return to section A in this rounded binary form, Beethoven introduces an unexpected three-part round, shaped by long *crescendos* and *diminuendos* and exploiting both high and low ranges. What an unexpected transformation this is! The theme itself can be viewed humorously too since it is nothing but an elongated and varied E-flat major scale. Starting not on $e\flat^2$ but g^2, it soars into the stratosphere to the highest violin notes of the sonata thus far. Even the new phrases functioning as countersubjects in the canon are basically scalewise melodies, descending rather than ascending. Such stepwise melodies engender a more relaxed, tranquil mood as we have seen in the first movement of the Violin Concerto (1P, 1S).

The short type of scherzo is called "epigrammatic" by Luxner. He describes it as having a first part up to 8 mm. long and a second part up to 32 mm. long. Most examples contain limited modulation to the dominant or relative major. This group includes the scherzos in the Violin Sonata, Op. 24/III (1800-01), Piano Sonatas Op. 106/II (1817-18) and Op. 110/II (1821-22), and the String Quartet, Op. 130/II (1825).[90] Indeed, most examples are late, thus once again linking Op. 96 with the late period.

In Op. 96, each part of the Scherzo is only 8 mm. long but the repeats are written out and varied in two ways: the melodic line passes from the piano to the violin; and the piano accompaniment changes from chordal style on the quarter notes to an oom-pah setting with the right hand on

---

[90] Luxner, "The Evolution of the Minuet/Scherzo," 106. Luxner also includes the parallel movements in Op. 27, No.2 and Op. 130/IV, which I do not believe are scherzos. As in Op. 96, the Scherzo in Op. 106 has varied repeats (each part is repeated an octave higher), and the Scherzo with repeats returns in the *da capo*.

VIOLIN SONATA 241

the offbeat producing a steady eighth-note surface rhythm. Both hands play in octaves for phrase one, while the right hand has chords for phrase two. The variation causes an unexpected intensification in surface rhythm, sonority, and range. For Part I, the variation also stabilizes the harmony of Pa, which at first sits on the dominant in mm. 1-3 as Beethoven postpones the first tonic in root position until m. 4. In the variation, the harmony strikes root-position tonics in measures 1 and 3 as well. The bass line becomes more contrapuntal and motivically worked out, including imitation of the opening in mm. 10^3-12^1. Small harmonic changes also occur in the variation of Part II, which similarly contains a new motivic bass. Both variation basses feature motives with falling (Part II) and rising thirds.

In addition to the variations we find several other sources of intensification in the scherzo, some already mentioned. These include the sharp sfp accents, and the rising chromatic line in Part II, mm. 27-30, beat 3—a^2-$b\flat^2$-$b\natural^2$-c^3—to the highest note of the scherzo, c^3. This chromatic rise overlaps with a preceding chromatic melodic rise on beat 2 of mm. 17-20: $e\natural^2$-f^2-$f\sharp^2$-g^2. This part as well contains one-measure modules, a larger range, and a more disjunct melodic style (note also the augmented fifth in mm. 29-30). While Part I contains balanced phrases and subphrases (mm. 1-4), Part II is continuous and developmental, and drives in a straight line to its cadence.

The Trio

In five epigrammatic Scherzos the Trio is longer than the Scherzo.[91] In Op. 96 the Trio is 51 mm. long and unlike the Scherzo is in rounded binary form. Also unlike the Scherzo is the contrapuntal texture in most of Part II, a feature as well of the Trios in the violin sonatas Op. 24 and Op. 30, No. 2 (see the timeline). The strong contrast provided by the trio, especially its lyrical style, has a long history. Here, the popular, pastoral waltz style recalls the many Ländler trios in the later symphonies of Haydn, Mozart, and even Boccherini (see his Symphony in C minor, Op. 41, 1788, Mozart's Symphony No. 39 of the same year, and Haydn's Symphony No. 97, 1792). Despite the relaxed beginning, there are many sources of intensification:

 1. The Trio encompasses a much larger and higher melodic range than the Scherzo. The opening violin melody spans two octaves, g^1-g^3, and in Part II, the violin ascends to $b\flat^3$ as does the piano right-hand (see Ex. 3. 20).

 2. Beethoven varies the return of A by introducing a three-part canon or round based on Pa, mm. 1-4. The canon is at the unison and two octaves below (see Ex. 3.21). The line in each part continues with two new four-measure phrases we can identify as Nb and

---

[91] Luxner, loc.cit. Luxner's reference to the Trio in Op. 24 in this regard is incorrect. Op. 106 has two trios.

242   TRANSCENDENT MASTERY

Example 3.20 Trio, Part I, opening (mm. 32^3-40^2)

Nc, the last paired in tenths and sixths. Phrases b and c are interrelated as c reverses the basic subphrases of b (x-y, y-x). Section A lengthens to 12 measures and the round continues for another 16 measures in a written-out repeat, extended and varied at the end as Nb and Nc conclude with a two-beat overlap of the final K phrase on the tonic in m. 80, starting in the piano's left hand (see the diagram below).

Figure 3.4. Outline of the Canon, mm. 52^3-83

	A^1			A^2					
vn.	a	b	c	a	b	c	b^1		K
piano, r. h.		a	b	c	a	b	c		K
piano, l. h.			a	b	c	a	ay-y^1	K	
measure	52^3			64^3			76^3	80^1	80^3

    3.   Underlying the canon is another source of intensification, two long *crescendos* and *diminuendos*. A^1 has a *crescendo* for all 12 measures, though the peak is not specified. A^2 has a *diminuendo* starting in m. 64^3 to *p dim.* (m. 76) for 15 and 1/4 measures and *pp* marked for the last four measures (from m. 80).

VIOLIN SONATA 243

Example 3.21 Trio, Part II, start of A^1 with three-part canon (mm. 52^3-64)

4. A fourth source of heightened tension is rhythmic. The trio introduces eighth-note melodic motion, especially in Pay and Pb, and eighth-note motion increases in the bass toward the end of the canon. Further, the new phrases in the canon are syncopated, as beat three is tied over to beat 1 of the next measure in each measure. The emphasis on beat three connects with the accented third beat in the scherzo as well.

Despite these sophisticated devices, the popular aspect is reflected in the simple harmony underpinning the canon. Beethoven alternates V^7 and I chords every measure after the first two measures on the tonic. He places the first eight measures on a tonic pedal thus recalling the drone effect of Part I. The alternation overlaps Sa and Nb, starting in mm. 3-4 of Sa. The final four-measure tonic is a natural outcome of the chordal alternation, which lands on I for the ending of the canon.

It is well known that Beethoven wrote many canons in his later years which he dedicated to his friends and visitors. This canon, though without a text, seems to belong to the same genre and appears at the start of Beethoven's more intensive production of such pieces. It also reflects his deepened interest in contrapuntal techniques in the late period.[92]

THE CODA

After the written-out *da capo* Beethoven adds a fourteen-measure Coda, Beethoven's own designation. The Coda, with a surprising change of

---

[92] Another, more complex canon in two voices appears in the trio of the late Piano Sonata, Op. 101/II (1816).

mode to G major, draws entirely on the Scherzo, Part I. It presents Part I, mm. 1-8, now starting on a vii^6/V rather than an augmented sixth chord, and then Pb in the violin. This phrase has the oom-pah accompaniment of the varied repeat that continues to the penultimate measure. A concluding three-measure tonic pedal is enlivened by a high violin trill on b^2 plus a *crescendo* to *forte* on the final chord, an exciting ending. The violin and piano end high, on the fifth of the chord, which by this time had less finality (Ex. 3.22).

Luxner points out that codas appear mainly in Beethoven's scherzos and minuets with trios in a different key, thus, we may add, strengthening the tonic key at the end. Luxner makes two further valuable observations. He notes that when the trio is longer than the scherzo/minuet, the coda based on the scherzo (or minuet) can thus lengthen the *da capo* and help balance the movement. Additionally, in binary scherzos, such as Op. 96, the coda based on the opening can function as a thematic return, "compensating for its omission in the second reprise."[93]

Early reviewers of the sonata allude to various expressive associations, but none recognized the bridging function of the movement. The *AmZ* review of the first edition in 1817 refers to the "expressive [affectvolles] *Scherzando* in G minor, with pleasant *Trio* [in] E♭."[94] On the other hand, the 1819 review of the first edition in the Viennese *AmZ* asserts that the movement "is dominated by humor, merriment, and waggishness, with a generous dose of malice thrown in, for if, as in the trio, some caution and moderation seem to be introduced, the return of the minuet puts us back where we were, the frivolous old dance gets under way again and ends up in an atmosphere of pert exuberance."[95] Czerny, however, described the movement as "Also earnest [as the second movement], but lively and very wittily marked, as the capricious effect lies particularly in the *sfp* of the 3rd quarter of the bar."

Example 3.22 Coda, ending (mm. 123^3-29)

[93] Luxner, "The Evolution of the Minuet/Scherzo," 41.
[94] Kunze, ed., *Die Werke im Spiegel seiner Zeit*, 334.
[95] Kunze, ed., ibid., 325. For the English translation, see Brandenburg, "Violin Sonatas,"

Differences in the Draft and Autograph

The most advanced draft that has survived for the sonata is the complete draft of the third movement in the Petter Sketchbook. The draft has been transcribed by Brandenburg and, as he states, "[it] represents the last step before the working out of the score."[96] Some important differences, however, still remain (see Ex. 3.23).

1. There is no indication of the varied repeats in the Scherzo and Trio, evidently very late additions. Beethoven only notated repeat marks for the Scherzo, Part I.

2. The *sfp* in the Scherzo appears as *sf*, indicating a louder dynamic level, while the Trio has no dynamic marks at all. As we know, Beethoven often left the addition of dynamics for the score at a late stage of a work. While the draft includes most of the slurs over the barline in the Scherzo, no slurs or ties are found in the Trio.

3. Measure 7 of the Scherzo differs in its tied note and climax on a^2. Beethoven later reserved tied notes for the Trio and a^2 for the start of Part II of the Scherzo.

4. Part II of the Scherzo rises into a much higher register, reaching g^3. In the end, Beethoven transferred the high register to the Trio as one of its special features.

5. The Trio is still not fully realized and the canon needed more work.

   a. In Part I, mm. 4-6 are missing and the ornamentation in eighth notes of m. 4 first appears in the canonic entry in the piano's left hand. We find no indication of the drone accompaniment.

   b. The Trio's Sb phrase doubles in length as Beethoven repeats the phrase an octave higher. In the final version, Beethoven rejected the repetition probably because of the effect of excessive repetition and anticipation of the upbeat motive of Sa. The repeat at the higher octave leads to a descent of a seventh to the beginning of the canon rather than a simple continuation on the same note.

   c. Beethoven has not fixed the canon's melodic line, which lacks Nc and locates Nb an octave below the final version, without a cli-

---

148. Scherzos are often called minuets by reviewers in the early nineteenth century. Max Rostal, in his book *Beethoven, The Sonatas for Piano and Violin*, 178, agrees with the *AmZ* reviewer regarding the Scherzo: "This movement is usually regarded as being 'playful,' a view I do not share at all, despite its marking 'Scherzo.' Its mode of expression—with the exception of the Trio—is rather uncanny, shadowy, tense, even alarming or, to quote Beethoven himself (although in another connection) *beklemmt*...." In a footnote the translator of this book gives the following words as equivalent to the German word: "uneasy, anxious, or oppressed." This word appears in the middle section of the Cavatina in Beethoven's late String Quartet, Op. 130.

96 Brandenburg, "Bemerkungen," 21. The transcription is found on the same page.

Example 3.23 Draft of the third movement, Petter Sketchbook: fol. 73ʳ, staff 14, 73ᵛ, staves 2-4., 6-8, 10 (transcribed by Sieghard Brandenburg)

mactic melodic effect. The second entrance in the left hand shows that Nc evolved from a repeat of Nb an octave lower. Beethoven later corrected the static bass at the end by moving the second bass entry an octave higher so the bass line could rise to e♭² in order to descend gradually to the final low E♭.

6. The coda is shorter by 4 measures and does not include Pb and its variation. In place of Pb, Beethoven repeats the initial motive of Pa in a¹ and b¹ four times in two-measure modules. In a second version, the composer worked out a less repetitive phrase. The draft also lacks the more effective steady melodic rise to the cadence in the final version where the ending on the fifth of the chord is also not anticipated. We should note the use of the term "Coda," even in a draft.

The Autograph

Only one major change occurs on the autograph (p. 18). The Trio theme, Part I, was first placed in the piano and then repeated in the violin. Just the leading parts were written down and then crossed out. On the next page, the Trio contains the final version with the violin first presenting the theme, unlike the Scherzo where the piano leads. On p. 18, we find the non-ornamental version of the melody in m. 4. On p. 19, m. 4, Beethoven added the ornamental notes over the first version, with the note names written above the staff. He also corrected the final notes of the subphrases of Sb, which he had copied from the draft. Rather than skipping down a sixth to f^1 and $e\flat^1$, he altered the notes to be a third higher, $a\flat^1$ and g^1, so the skip down was only a fourth and thus maintained the smooth melodic effect. The skip down to g^1 had already occurred in the draft, however, when Sb was repeated an octave higher, probably in order to make a connection to the upbeat of the canonic melody.

The Fourth Movement: *Poco Allegretto*

Background

It is well known that Beethoven is a great master of variation form, indeed, perhaps the greatest. Besides Beethoven's use of varied thematic returns in such movements as rondos, there exist some 76 variation movements or independent variation sets by the composer.[97] These date from his earliest set of Nine Variations on a March by Dressler, WoO 63 (1782) to the variation movement in his last string quartet, Op. 135 (1826). Beethoven wrote many early independent variation sets on popular melodies for the piano when he was active as a virtuoso pianist. However, his greatest variations were composed in the middle and late periods.

Beethoven included variations in almost all the genres except, strangely enough, the cello sonata. His slow-movement symphonic variations, and the slow variations in the Piano Trio, Op. 70, No. 2 and String Quartet, Op. 132 were influenced by Haydn's alternating variation form (see the discussion on p. 336). Beethoven's most famous variation sets contain many innovations and departures from Classic "decorum."[98] Even when following the theme's structure—its melodic and harmonic outline—Beethoven is able to transform the character and texture of his model in many remarkable ways. Beethoven also invented many new methods of organizing a variation set, as we will see here in the *finale* of Op. 96. Besides the monumental set of variations concluding the *Eroica* symphony, many musicians feel that Beethoven reached the peak of variation writing

---

[97] See the list of Beethoven's variation sets in Sisman, *Haydn*, Table A.3, 272-75.
[98] See the chapter: "Conclusion: Beethoven and the Transformation of the Classical Variation" in Sisman, ibid., 235-62.

in his late period, after 1815. These great sets are the "Diabelli" variations, Op. 120 (1819, 1823), the slow variation movements ending the late piano sonatas in Op. 109/III (1820) and Op. 111/II (1821-22), the slow-movement variations in four of the last string quartets, Op. 127/II (1824-25), Op. 132/III (1825), Op. 131/IV (1825-26), and Op. 135/III (1826), and both the slow and fast variations in the third and fourth movements of the Ninth Symphony, Op. 125 (1822-24). Though the variations in Op. 96 fall toward the end of the middle period and have much in common with the style of middle variation sets, some features relate to the later achievements in the form as well, despite the constraint Beethoven felt in writing the movement to suit Rode's personal preferences.

The use of the theme and variation form in the *finale* of a multi-movement cycle is uncommon in Beethoven, who prefers to compose slow-movement variations (as we have seen in this volume with respect to the Violin Concerto and Quartet, Op. 132). Only six fast *finale* variations can be found in Beethoven's mature works: two in the Violin Sonatas, Op. 30, No. 1 (1801-02) and Op. 96, the Piano Trio with clarinet, Op. 11 (1797), *Eroica* Symphony (1803), String Quartet, Op. 74 (1809), and Ninth Symphony (1822-24).[99] The variation *finale* of Op. 96 is thus the last and certainly the best example of this type in the chamber works. Otherwise, the slow variation set prevails. Slow-movement variations also appear in two Violin Sonatas, Op. 12, No. 1 (1797-98) and Op. 47 (1802-03).

Sisman has pointed out that in the early Classic period and early Haydn, the first and final movements were preferred locations for the theme and variations.[100] Nevertheless, important sets of *finale* variations were still composed by Mozart in his Piano Concertos, K. 453 (1784) and K.491 (1786), String Quartet, K. 421 (1783), and Clarinet Quintet, K. 581 (1789), as well as in his mature piano and violin sonatas. Perhaps these served as precedents for Beethoven. As a young composer of fourteen, in fact, Beethoven used as a model Mozart's Violin Sonata, K. 379 for his first Piano Quartet, WoO 36 (1785), and this sonata concluded with a theme and variation movement, though in a moderate tempo, *Andantino cantabile*, ending *Allegretto*.

In the variation *finale* of Op. 11, Beethoven used as the theme a popular melody by another composer, Joseph Weigl, the terzett (No. 12), "Pria ch'io l'impegno" from Weigl's comic opera *L'amor marinaro* (1797).[101]

---

[99] The form of the Ninth Symphony *finale* has been variously interpreted. See, for example, James Webster, "The Form of the Finale of Beethoven's Ninth Symphony," *Beethoven Forum* 1 (1992): 25-62. I prefer to consider this movement as a synthesis of the theme and variation form with the rondo.

[100] Sisman, *Haydn*, 109-11.

[101] See K-H, 25. Several other composers used this theme for variation sets, including Paganini (1828).

Usually, such variation sets on popular, commonly operatic melodies were composed as independent sets for piano, and sometimes for piano with violin, cello, or another instrument, as we also find in Beethoven's works, and were not used within a larger, multimovement cycle.[102]

Nottebohm pointed out a resemblance of the start of the Op. 96 variation theme to a song by J. A. Hiller, "Der Knieriem bleibet," from Hiller's Singspiel *Der lustige Schuster* (1771), based on Part II of the comic opera *Der Teufel ist los* by J. C. Standfuss that survives only in Hiller's expanded version.[103] However, only the first two measures are the same (though Hiller's melody begins with an upbeat) and one wonders if the resemblance is simply coincidental, as are so many other thematic resemblances.[104] The resemblance has some value, nevertheless, in pointing up the popular character of Beethoven's melody.

A much earlier sketch of the theme has been found on a page of sketches that Brandenburg dates 1807/08 (Vienna, Gesellschaft der Musikfreunde, Beethoven autograph, Ms. A 41), and it provides another example of Beethoven using material drafted earlier for a later work (as the Allemande in Op. 132/II).[105] As Brandenburg remarks, the theme was probably intended for the Cello Sonata in A, Op. 69, and it occurs with sketches for the *Choral Fantasy*, Op. 80 and the Lied, "Mignon," Op. 75 No. 1. A transcription of the entire theme is given in Obelkevich (see Ex. 3. 24 and Plate 3.III).[106]

The theme appears on three staves: the melody for the cello on the top (surely meant to be played an octave lower), right-hand figuration in the middle only in m. 1, and a simple bass line below. Like the final version, the theme has two parts, each eight measures long, and repeat marks for both parts given at the end of Part I. The basic motives are the same as in Op. 96 and the first five measures are exactly the same, as are the move to IV in m. 6, the close of Part I on the tonic, with the third in the melody, and the bass line of Part I. Part II develops the motives of Part I, as in the final version, but without a dramatic modulation, keeping the inflection of the subdominant and extending the motive in m. 2, found only at the cadences

---

[102] There are eight such variation sets for chamber groups, four based on themes from Mozart's operas (*The Marriage of Figaro*, *Don Giovanni*, and *The Magic Flute*). These are, in chronological order, WoO 40, 28, 45, Op. 66, WoO 46, Opp. 121a, 105, and 107 (the first five are dated 1792/93-1801).

[103] See N I, p. 30. For the entire melody, see Obelkevich, "The Growth of a Musical Idea," 92. See also 93 and 113, n. 3 for further information.

[104] For example, a late Sammartini string quartet in D (c. 1771) has a slow movement starting almost exactly like the slow movement of Beethoven's Cello Sonata Op. 69. The most famous of such similarities is the resemblance of the opening of the young Mozart's overture to *Bastien und Bastienne*, K. 50 (1768) to the prmary theme of Beethoven's *Eroica* Symphony, first movement.

[105] Obelkevich, "The Growth of a Musical Idea," 92, dates the sketch 1809. See Brandenburg, "Bemerkungen," 22-23.

[106] See Obelkevich, 91. The transcription was made by Erich Hertzmann.

Example 3.24 The earliest sketch of P in A major, made in 1807/08 for another work (Op. 69?). Vienna, Gesellschaft der Musikfreunde, A 41 (see also Plate 3.III). Transcribed by Sieghard Brandenburg

of both parts in the final version. Clearly, Beethoven, being fairly pressed to compose the finale, had found an appropriate theme that required only a final stage of polishing.

The Theme: Final Version

This lilting theme, with its catchy tune, is one of Beethoven's most ingratiating melodies. Czerny pointed out that the theme, "which is in a very moderate tempo," should be performed "with extreme delicacy and taste." Its basic form is simple and symmetrical. There are two periods, each eight measures long, and each period is repeated. This form is traditional, unlike the themes for variations in Op. 61 and Op. 132 (see Ex. 3.25a on p. 253).

First, the piano presents the melody, with violin accompaniment; then the violin joins the piano on the melody an octave below. This alternation sets the pattern for most of the variations, where the varied line first appears in the piano and then shifts to the violin in the repeat, as in variations 2, 3, 4, and 6, while in the slow variation 5, Beethoven alternates piano

VIOLIN SONATA   251

PLATE 3. III *Sketches for Op.96, A 41, p.1. Archiv der Gesellschaft der Musikfreunde in Wien.*

and violin with the phrases of each Part. This double presentation of the theme also occurs in the variation movements of the Violin Sonatas, Op. 30, No. 1 and Op. 47. As always, in Beethoven, there are special features, as we can see in the timeline on p. 252 (Table 3.9).

HARMONY

We notice first of all that Beethoven has used a simple two-reprise form in which each part ends on the tonic. The tonic ending of Part I is rare in Beethoven's original variation themes in two-reprise form, though it is common in Mozart.[107] Within each period, the harmony moves differently. In Part I, mm. 1, 3, 5, and 8 have tonic chords in root position alternating with dominants in mm. 2 and 4; then a longer, tenser progression away from I occurs in mm. 6 and 7: ii$^6_5$, V$^6_5$/V-V. In the repeat, Beethoven varies and enriches the harmonic effect. He places all of mm. 1-4 on a V pedal, avoiding the simple root positions of the initial presentation, a refinement absent from the variations. He adds sevenths to most of the dominants, a vi chord in m. 5, last 8th, and lengthens the ii$^6_5$ of m. 7 by an 8th, all typical touches of the late style in the concern for small details.

---

[107] Sisman, *Haydn*, 198, states that 31% of Mozart's themes in variation sets contain first parts ending in the tonic. A familiar example is the theme for the first-movement varia-

Table 3.9 Timeline of P: Movement IV

Part I

	ax	x^1	a^1	x^2	(x) ext.		rep. 9-16
	1	3	4	5	7	8	
G:	I		V			I	
rep:	V ped . . .					I-iii (b)	

Part II

	(a)			(bx⁴)	(x)		
	b	x^3	x^4	cx^5	ext.		rep. 25-32
	17	19	20	21	23	24	
B:	V ped . . . . B-b			(C)	G:V	I-iii (b)	
						rep.: I	

By simplifying the harmony in Part I, Beethoven highlights the brilliant color in Part II. Once again, Beethoven turns to a chromatic third relationship, here a third higher than the tonic, as he sets most of the third phrase (Pc) in B major. The pivot is the G-major tonic in m. 16 that becomes VI in b minor, as suggested by the link in the bass that moves to V^0_9/V of b before m. 17. The return to G is craftily managed in quick changes by "turning on a note" (to quote Leonard Ratner), as the note b is reharmonized with a b minor tonic 6/4 and then as the third in V^7/IV, resolving to IV (C major); the half-step move from B/b to C exploits Beethoven's favorite half-step Neapolitan relationship (see Ex. 25a).[108] B minor also both precedes and follows the modulation to B major, in a good example of achieving a distant modulation through modal interchange.

All of phrase 3 is set on a V pedal, following the model in the repeat of phrase 1, but the progressions are reversed, as V and I chords alternate rather than I and V, thus keeping the harmony in greater suspense. The fourth, final phrase moves with a single, four-measure progression: V^7/IV-IV-V^7-I, each measure featuring one chord. In the repeat, the main change is the addition of the seventh to V, in phrase 3, confirming the key of B more strongly than the simple V-I progression, which could also be heard as I-V, in analogy with phrase 1 (Pa). Certainly the remote remodulation and chromatic return to the tonic provide harmonic tension and color throughout the movement, as do the chromatic harmonies in the Larghetto of Beethoven's Violin Concerto. Not many themes in Beethoven's variation sets contain such harmonic effects.

---

tions of the Piano Sonata in A, K. 331. The percentage in independent variation sets is much higher—65%. A special example in Beethoven is the theme of the second-movement variations in the "Appassionata" Piano Sonata, Op. 57 (1804-06). Here the static harmonic effect helps achieve a mood of utter calm between two stormy movements.

[108] This is one of many examples of Beethoven's freer treatment of the $^6_4$ chord. Another well-known example is the move from i^6_4 to i in mm. 33^2-35 in Beethoven's Ninth Symphony/I.

VIOLIN SONATA

Example 3.25

    a. The P theme, final version (mm. 1-32)

b. The later appearance of P, Part I, in E♭ (mm. 164-70)

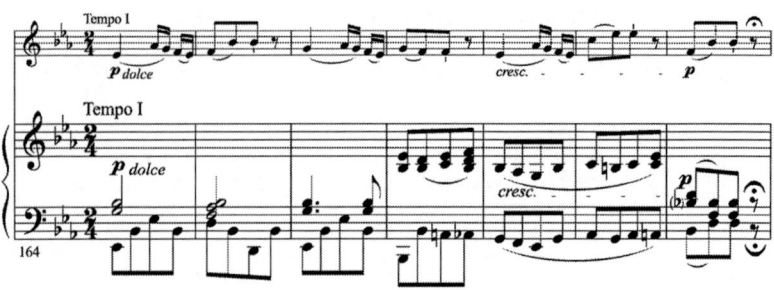

c. The last appearance of P in the coda (mm. 245-48)

Melody

As simple and artless as the melody sounds, it is anything but that. An aspect of that simplicity is the restricted melodic range. While Part I has an octave range, g^2-g^3, Part II extends only to a minor seventh, $f\sharp^2$-e^3.

In each part, the first phrase has two subphrases of two measures each, while the second phrase is a long four-measure unit because of the extension of its second measure plus cadence. The pattern becomes:

$$2+2+4\ (1+2\times1+1)$$

Each two-measure subphrase is articulated by an 8th rest at the end of the measure, as is the extended measure.

The repetition of each part contains a melodic link for the repetition of each period and the connection to Part II and Variation 1. This upbeat scale motive of three 8ths is used in variations 1-3, while the later variations have other linking ideas. The motives in mm. 1-2 and the linking motive constitute all the thematic material, but it is heard in almost constant melodic variation (see Ex. 3. 26). In Part I, only measures 1 and 5 are the same, arranged in a parallel period. In Part II, only measures 18 and 20 are the same. Further, Beethoven makes the notes of the last two measures of each part identical in a traditional rhyming device. Otherwise melodic intervals are expanded and contracted, and there are six versions of the subphrase. Part II introduces ornamentation of m. 17 in m. 19, and this ornamentation continues in m. 21, linking the end of phrase 3 and the start of phrase 4. The ornamentation also increases melodic motion toward the end of the theme.

VIOLIN SONATA

As Ex. 3. 26 shows, the opening skip of a 4th is altered to a 2nd in m. 3, which is picked up for the start of Part II in m. 17. Beethoven strikingly varies the skip between the two measures of the subphrase, which expand from a 2nd to a 3rd to a 6th, and is then flattened to a unison before rising to a 4th. The interval of the sigh motive in m. 2 is altered as well, rising mostly a 4th, but also a 3rd, and falling (in reply) a 2nd. A rise of the 6th, the largest melodic skip, continues via a skip of the 3rd to the climax note of the melody on g^3 in m. 6 (and its repeat in m. 14). The lower climax in Part II, e^2, appears in a parallel position in mm. 22 and 30, but is approached less dramatically by a rising 4th. This lower tessitura and climax of Part II become aspects of the theme that are both maintained and altered in the variations to come.

A subtle change occurs in the slurring of m. 1, beat 2 in the repeat of each part. Usually the 16ths are grouped 2 + 2, but toward the end of the repeats, a contrasting larger module is created by a longer slur going across the beat and affecting notes 1-3 or 1-5 (Part II) of the measure (see Ex. 25a). Such subtle alterations are typical of Beethoven.[109]

Example 3. 26   Px changes in interval and direction

[109] See the examples in the *Eroica* Symphony in my article "Exploring the *Eroica*: Aspects of the New Critical Edition," in *Haydn, Mozart, and Beethoven: Studies in the Music of the Classical Period, Essays in Honour of Alan Tyson*, ed. Sieghard Brandenburg (Oxford: Clarendon Press, 1998) 200-06.

Sound

The piano introduces the theme in the high soprano register, unusual for a theme in a variation set. It has a pipe-like or flute-like sound, enhancing a pastoral association. When the violin has the theme, it simply doubles the piano an octave lower on its gentle D and A strings.

The piano's left hand moves in steady eighth notes except for the syncopation in m. 8, being at first linear and in the repeat with harmony notes added, usually on the first and third 8ths. The rhythmic motion and character of the left hand was a problem for Beethoven and the two early versions of the setting of the theme show different solutions (see below).

In between the high soprano and bass, the violin plays double stops on its lower strings, filling in the harmony of the bare two-voice texture in the first presentation of each part. More interestingly, the violin part is written in larger and more varied rhythmic values than the theme or the bass. The violin also holds or slurs notes over the barline, sustaining the sound and harmony across the eighth-note rests in the melody.

While the theme is generally *piano*, Beethoven supports the four-measure phrases with a three-measure *crescendo* to a *piano* on the cadence. The device here is one of intensification as it coordinates with the longer phrase and melodic climax of each part. It recurs only in the slow variation 5 because of the overall dynamic plan of the movement.

Three Earlier Versions of the Theme

A. The version in the Petter Sketchbook. fol. 73v, staves 13-16[110]

This earliest sketch for the sonata itself is mostly melodic (Ex. 3.27). No repetitions of the periods occur but the theme is close to the final version and the Cambridge draft, and it contains the modulation to B major. The shortened beat 2 appears only in phrases a^1 and c. Like the two later drafts, phrase b starts with a rising fourth on f♮ and not on a♮. Unlike these drafts ornamentation is not yet present in phrases b and c, nor the climax note on e^3 in phrase c. The few quarter-note harmonizations relate to the quarter-note accompaniment in the later drafts. The *crescendo-piano* dynamics, already present in this early stage in phrase c, are actually absent in the Cambridge draft, reappearing in the Paris draft only in mm.5-8 and at the end. Beethoven places the first period in the middle range starting on g^1 and the second period in the higher octave starting on f♯². This indecision regarding the octave location of the theme is resolved only in the final version.

---

[110] See N I, 27-28, and Obelkevich, "The Growth of a Musical Idea," 96, with some differences and a facsimile of the sketch. The example given comes from Nottebohm with a few details from Obelkevich.

VIOLIN SONATA

B. The second of these three versions appears in the autograph of Beethoven's song "An die Hoffnung," Op. 94, and is a discarded attempt at a clean copy of the *finale*. It is crossed out with a large X (see Plate 3.IV). The paper on which the song and draft are written is identical to the paper used for the autograph of Op. 96.[111] Only mm. 1-23 appear; the last measure of Part II and the repeat of this part are omitted. Of these measures only mm. 1-8 are written out completely, the piano part lacking the octave sign for mm. 2-7. Measures 8-23 contain only the melodic line in violin I and then the piano. Several differences from the final version can be observed. Structurally, the linking motive is still absent; it is omitted in m. 8 while m. 16 is empty. Some further differences from the final version include the following:

Example 3.27 The earliest sketch of P for Op. 96 in the Petter Sketchbook (N I)

[111] See Brandenburg, "Bemerkungen," 19, where Brandenburg gives reasons for dating the song in early 1815 with relation to early datable sketches. The MS is listed in Barbara Marenholz Wolff, *Music Manuscripts at Harvard* (Cambridge, MA: Harvard University Library, 1992), No. 53, "An die Hoffnung." The reference mistakenly identifies the draft as belonging to the third movement. A reproduction of this page is given in Oswald Jonas, "Bemerkungen zu Beethoven's Op. 96," *Acta musicologica* 37 (1965), Faks. I facing p. 88. In this article, 87-89, Jonas discusses for the first time some differences from the final version found in the drafts in Cambridge and Paris as well as changes on the autograph. He also refers to textual problems in the autograph and first plus later editions.

m. 1: The use of an arpeggio at the start of the melody later disappears, probably because it weakens the naïve character of the theme. In this and parallel measures the slur appears over the entire measure instead of two paired slurs on beat 2. The composer reserved this broader effect for the ends of both parts and even there does not include the entire measure. The long slurs produce a lessened rhythmic vitality on beat 2.

m. 5-6: In m. 5 we find a vi chord rather than the tonic, and in m. 6 the sustaining of V^6_5/V for two beats rather than just beat 2. These chords strengthen a sense of modulation to the dominant, a modulation Beethoven later decided to avoid.

m. 17: The rising fourth from $f\sharp^2$ rhymes with the start of Part I, but the $f\sharp$ is overemphasized as it recurs at the start of three of the four measures in the phrase. The leading tone, $a\sharp^2$, thus varies the melodic line, and it defines the new key more immediately as well. This half-step motion also connects with the melodic half steps in m. 3 of the theme.[112] Interestingly, the early jotting of the theme in

m. 19: Phrase 3 opens with a different ornamentation of beat 1 that overemphasizes the note b^2, heard twice before and twice after this measure (in mm. 18 and 20). The skip down from the leading tone also has some awkwardness. However, the paired slurs were eventually transferred to the sixteenths in m. 1 and its recurrences.

m. 21: The final phrase again begins with a rising fourth, here in C, rather than the half-step b^2-c^3. The three-fold repeat of the rising fourth becomes monotonous, while the half-step b-c makes a strong melodic and harmonic effect in the move to the subdominant. In the final version, the ornamented beat 1 adds rhythmic continuity and drive.

Beethoven also did not fix the accompaniment. This was a major problem, as we will see with respect to a second version of the theme. Here, the piano left hand has quarter-note motion (in eighths and eighth-rests) rather than a flowing eighth-note line. The violin accompaniment comes closer to the final version but lacks its rhythmic variety—the many syncopations and ties—as well as the 4-3 suspension in m. 7.[113] Measure 8 contains a relaxed broken chord rather than the more tense syncopation of the final version. The combination of the slow-moving bass and accompaniment makes a stodgy background to the active theme that required correction.

---

[112] See Obelkevich, "The Growth of a Musical Idea," on this point, 93-97.
[113] A somewhat unclear facsimile is included in Obelkevich, ibid, 98-99, and the first page in Jonas, "Bemerkungen," Faks. II, between 88 and 89.

VIOLIN SONATA   259

PLATE 3.IV: *A SECOND EARLY VERSION OF P FOR OP. 96, FOUND WITH THE AUTOGRAPH OF THE SONG, "AN DIE HOFFNUNG," OP. 94. Reprinted by permission of the Houghton Library, Harvard University, fMs Lowell 12, fol. 1r.*

C. Another attempt at these measures with a different variation 1 occurs on two manuscript pages in Paris (see Plate 3.V).[114] The paper again is the same as that used for the autograph,[115] but the

---

[114] Brandenburg, "Bemerkungen," 12.
[115] This writer examined the draft in Paris. Obelkevitch, 99, incorrectly states that the second sheet in oblong.

second page has been pasted on an oblong sheet of paper and cut after the end of the variation. The MS approaches a fair copy since several slurs and dynamics are included, and the writing is careful and clear. However, on page two after the conclusion of the theme, a sketch appears for the first variation that Beethoven decided not to include in the final version (the sketch is discussed below, 269-70). This draft constitutes a later version of the theme based on the Harvard version, but with certain differences, and strong differences still remain from the final version, as indicated below.

1. The bass is written out as simple quarter notes when the piano has the theme.

2. Beethoven has changed the violin accompaniment entirely to broken chords in upbeat sixteenths which move to the right hand of the piano when the violin takes the theme. Thus a far more active accompaniment supports the theme in comparison to the Harvard draft. In the final version Beethoven returned to the slow-moving accompaniment in the violin but combined it with a more flowing bass line in eighths. The tessitura of the entire setting is much lower than the final version as well.

3. In the repeats of the theme, the violin plays the melody alone rather than doubling the melody in the piano an octave below, as in the final version.

4. The draft contains the harmonic differences found earlier in mm. 5 and 6. In addition, unlike the final version, m. 21 has a V^2/IV instead of V^7/IV and m. 22 a IV^6-IV and not a simple IV chord. Thus the final version has simpler root-position chords allowing for changes in the variations.

5. The linking motive is still absent but the harmony in both mm. 16 and 24 approaches the final version with I-vi chords, the more intense V^0_9/V of B major still lacking.

6. While the last measure sustains the melodic ending and tonic chord for both beats, a connection to the first variation is made in the right-hand accompaniment. The final version has a briefer tonic ending and upbeat motion into the first variation.

7. The melodic line in Part II follows the earlier version but the ornamentation in m. 19 is duplicated in m. 21, connecting the phrases as in the final version, though the ornamentation itself differs.

8. The longer slur for m. 1 and some parallel measures remains, though often omitted. In one case, mm. 11-12, one long slur affects both measures.

9. Most of the final dynamics are noted down: *dolce* at the start and the *crescendo* for the second phrases of each part, though the *piano* appears only in mm. 8 and 32.

VIOLIN SONATA

As so often in Beethoven's sketches and drafts, certain rejected features are incorporated later in the movement as the composer finds the right place for the right idea. In this case, a steady accompaniment in broken-chord sixteenths underpins the return of the theme in the coda (mm. 245-60), and the left-hand accompaniment in quarter notes makes its appearance there as well (mm. 253-60) and in the last 20 measures of the movement (see the discussion of the coda, below).

THE VARIATIONS

In the *AmZ* review of 1817, the variations are described as being developed in an "abundant, often surprising and always interesting manner."[116] The reviewer also emphasizes the "quick exchange of keys" in the theme that always occurs in the variations.

The seven variations and coda have both traditional and novel features, and each category will be discussed separately below.

TRADITIONAL FEATURES OF THE VARIATIONS

The variations contain three traditional types: the slow variation within a fast variation set (No. 5), contrapuntal variations, and a variation in the opposite mode (here a *minore*), the last two combined in Variation 7 in G minor (though Variation 3 is contrapuntal as well). All the three other variation sets in the violin sonatas contain a variation in the tonic minor. In each case it comes just before the last variation, a late position as in Op. 96. The only contrapuntal variations appear in the fast *finale* variation set of Op. 30, No. 1, where the second such variation (No. 5) is also a *minore*. Slow variations are reserved by Beethoven almost exclusively for long variation sets, such as the "Righini" (WoO 65), "Prometheus" (Op. 35), and "Diabelli" (Op. 120) variations for piano, as well as the variation *finale* of the *Eroica* Symphony.

Also traditional is the partial organization of the variations by acceleration of the surface rhythm, variously called "division variations" (Ratner) or "progressive diminution" (Sisman).[117] This method harks back to the Renaissance, as we can see in the variation set "Loth to Depart" by Giles Farnaby in the Fitzwillian Virginal Book. The increase of surface rhythm creates drive, directionality, and intensification despite the underlying thematic repetitions. A similar approach is found in other variation movements discussed in this volume—in the Violin Concerto and String Quartet, Op. 132. Table 3.10 summarizes the basic rhythmic patterns of the variations and coda (see also Ex. 3.28).

---

[116] Kunze, ed., *Die Werke im Spiegel seiner Zeit*, 324: "auf vielfältige, oft überraschende, und stets interessante Weise."

[117] See Ratner, *CM*, 256; Sisman, *Haydn*, 242.

PLATE 3.V *A more advanced draft of P, with a different Variation 1. Cliché*, Bibliothèque Nationale de France, Paris Département de la musique, Conservatoire collection, Beethoven Ms. 60(1).

VIOLIN SONATA

PLATE 3.V PAGE 2

Table 3.10 Surface Rhythm in the Variations

Var. 1: entirely in 8ths (*Poco Allegretto*)

Var. 2: entirely in triplet 8ths

Var. 3: bass line in 16ths plus a syncopated treble in quarters and some 8ths

Var. 4: mainly 8ths and 16ths.

Var. 5: This slow variation contains the largest range of rhythmic values from quarters to many triplet 32nds and some 64th notes (*Adagio espressivo*)

Var. 6: entirely in 16ths (*Allegro*); transition mostly in 16ths

Var. 7: basic movement in 8ths; counterpoint in quarters

Coda: theme accompanied in 16ths; cadenza mainly in 16ths *poco adagio*: theme, Part II, accompaniment in quarters
Presto: 8ths, accompaniment in quarters

Analyzing these rhythmic patterns we discover that there is no straight line in the acceleration, as one should expect in a fairly long movement with seven variations and an extensive coda. What we find are areas of acceleration, mixed effects (as in Variation 4), and slowdowns (Variation 7) that offer both intensifications and contrast.

All the variations are double variations with varied repeats, except for Variation 1 and 5. We associate the double variation with the late quartet variations in Opp. 127 and 131 (such variations are absent from the earlier quartet variations). However, a few examples occur in earlier violin sonatas, in each case near the end of the set: Variations 3 and 4 in Op. 12, No. 1; Variations 5 and 6 in Op. 30, No,1; and Variation 4 in Op. 47. None use the double variation as extensively as Op. 96. Looking at the piano sonatas, only the variations in Op. 109, with four of six such variations, resembles Op. 96, though the variations are more complex. Thus, in this aspect too, Op. 96 anticipates the late style.

All double variations follow the same format, with the piano first presenting the variation and then the violin on the repeat, the piano right hand taking over the violin accompaniment. Beethoven here is careful to give each instrument a chance to shine, particularly the violin, undoubtedly a nod to Rode. A similar consideration holds true for Variation 1, with repeat marks, that is organized as a dialogue between the instruments, and Variation 5, without repeat marks and double variations, where the main phrases alternate in the piano and violin. In the examples of double variation the harmony is repeated exactly or nearly so and only the harmony of the first presentation of Part I is followed.

All the variations are unified in motive and texture. They embody the traditional melodic-outline and constant-harmony types, with some departures.[118] Czerny remarks that the tempo of the variations following the theme should be "rather more animated and marked. The *Adagio* very slow ... and the succeeding Variation, together with the conclusion, lively and powerful." Czerny often favors a variable tempo for a variation set, as one can see from his comments about other variations by Beethoven (as those in the Violin Sonata, Op. 47/II).

NOVEL FEATURES OF THE VARIATIONS

One uncommon aspect is the rondo-like return of P, Part I, in E♭ major after the slow Variation (mm. 164-73, Ex. 3. 25b). Beethoven highlights the thematic return, with a tonal return, the first, longer occurrence in the *finale* of this important secondary key of the sonata (a second recurrence appears in Variation 7). Another function of this return is transitional—the quicker tempo makes a bridge from the slow Variation 5 to the faster Variation 6, supported by the modulation back to G major. Following this unusual return, a more traditional recall of the theme occurs in the tonic at the start of the coda in a new setting.

Even more novel is the relation between dynamics and structure. Beethoven has organized the variations and coda by alternating *piano* and *forte* dynamic levels. A similar type of organization appears in the *finale* variations of the String Quartet, Op. 74. Composed in 1809, only three years before Op. 96, it was undoubtedly a model for the later work. The movement in Op. 74 even has a similar tempo—*Allegretto*—and the same 2/4 meter. The variations in Op. 96, however, carry out the pattern more systematically and on a larger scale (see Table 3.11 and Ex. 3.28).[119]

The most nuanced variation of all is the extraordinary Variation 5, containing 26 markings within a basic soft dynamic level. Nothing like it occurs in Op. 74. Beethoven also reverses the pattern of alternation in Op. 96. While the themes of both sets are basically soft, Beethoven initiates the chain of dynamic shifts with a *forte* variation in Op. 74 but a *piano* variation in Op. 96.

If we compare the organization of tempos in both sets we also discover similarities. Both movements accelerate the tempo, reaching the fastest tempo at the end of the movement, though the tempo is faster in Op. 96—*Presto*, while it is *Allegro* in Op. 74. In both movements the tempo acceleration starts with Variation 6: *Allegro* in Op. 96 versus "un poco più

---

[118] For an explanation of these types, see Elaine Sisman, article "Variation," in *The New Harvard Dictionary of Music*, 903-04. The meaning of these terms will become clear with the analysis of the variations.

[119] For a discussion of the organization in Op. 74, see Sisman, *Haydn*, 242-43. The theme is not entirely soft but contains *forte* cadences. The first period of the coda also includes a varied spectrum of dynamics.

vivace" in Op. 74. A typical feature in Op. 96, not found in Op. 74, is the slowdown shortly before the end with "poco adagio" followed by the *Presto* rush to the final cadence. This kind of slowdown near the end of the final movement occurs in many Beethoven works, such as the Fourth Symphony/IV, Op. 60 (1806), Fifth Piano Concerto/III, Op. 73 (1809), and even the Ninth Symphony/IV, Op. 125 (1822-24). A Haydnesque technique of surprise (see his Symphony No. 97/IV, 1792), it was taken over by Beethoven with many different twists. Here in Op. 96, the *poco adagio* (mm. 275^2-87) brings a mood of tender recall with Part II of the theme in B and G, while in the Ninth Symphony/IV (mm. 916-19), the *Maestoso* is the last assertion of grandeur. The tempo acceleration is another aspect of the overall organization of the variations since it intensifies the latter portion of the set by producing a more powerful drive to the conclusion.

Another less common and late feature is the continuous connection of the variations and coda. Unlike the theme, all the variations except 5 start with an upbeat. This may actually function as the beginning

Table 3.11. Organization of Dynamics in the Variations

Tempo:	*Poco Allegretto*
Theme:	*dolce, cresc.-p* four times (with repeats)
Var. 1:	*p*, < > in each measure except at the final cadence
Var. 2:	*f, sempre f*
Var. 3:	*p dolce, sempre p; p cresc.* >, m. 97^1 (left hand)
Var. 4:	*f* and *p dolce* alternate every 2 mm.; ends *p* (connecting dynamically to Var. 5)
Var. 5:	*Adagio espressivo* basically *p*, with the most varied nuances, including < >, *cresc.-p* (three times), *dolce, dim.*, ***pp***, a total of 26 markings
Tempo I (P)	*p dolce, cresc.- p,* < >
Var. 6:	*Allegro f, sf* every measure or two measures, trans. *sf*
Var. 7:	***pp***; at end, *cresc.-f*
Coda: (P)	*p, cresc.-p, cresc.* (cadenza): *f* *poco adagio*: (P, Part II): *p* *Presto*: *f*

VIOLIN SONATA

Example 3.28 *The first few measures of Variations 1-7*

of the variation, as in Variations 1 and 2, or may be a link that anticipates the rhythmic pattern of the variation, as in Variation 3, or may simply maintain the momentum, as in Variation 4. Elisions connect Variation 4 with Variation 5, the extension-transition of Variation 5 with the return of P, and Variation 7 with the coda. A seemingly open articulation on V ends the recall of P in E♭ after its modulatory extension back to G. Though a fermata separates the recall from Variation 6, the dominant harmony holds over for the upbeat to Variation 6. A separate, brilliant transition based on the half-step motive in Variation 6 connects the ebullient Variation 6 to the mysterious Variation 7. The transition ends abruptly on V^7, a chord falling on the last eighth of the measure that resolves after an eighth rest to the initial tonic note of the subject, *pp*. We thus see that Variations 5-7 are all joined via extensions or a formal transition. Further, Beethoven binds the four sections of the coda through sustained harmony, harmonic digression, and elision (see below).

As the following discussion of the individual variations shows, yet another important grouping of the variations consists of the alternation of more complex and expressive variations with simpler ones. The more complex variations are those marked *piano*—Nos. 1, 3, 5, and 7; and the simpler types are those marked *forte*—Nos. 2, 4, and 6. The simpler types are also in the brilliant style, demanding increasing virtuosity until the final cadenza section. Most of the complex types are contrapuntal—Nos. 1, 3, and 7.

A further means of grouping, as Johansen points out, is the alternation of variations with accentuations on weak and strong beats.[120] These rhythmic features coordinate with dynamics and complexity, the weak-beat types being Nos. 1, 3, 5 (partly), and 7.

The foregoing analysis shows that Beethoven has used multiple means of organization for the variations, going far beyond traditional approaches. They include devices that produce both sharp contrasts between variations, and an overall integration and momentum.

Variations 1-4 and 6

These are the most straightforward variations, accelerating from eighths to triplet eighths to sixteenths. No. 6 has the fastest surface rhythm, the melody moving entirely in sixteenths in *Allegro* tempo.

Variation 1

This variation groups with the delicate and expressive character of Variation 5. It immediately transforms the theme from the folk-like to a lyrical and reflective world. As mentioned above, this is the only variation with repeat marks for both parts. It uses the upbeat linking motive and even more a neighbor-note motive (with its inversion), both derived from the theme, the latter derived from m. 3, notes 1-3 (b^2-c^3-b^2). Slurs group eighths

---

[120] Johansen, "Beethoven's Sonatas for Piano and Violin," 101.

VIOLIN SONATA   269

2-4 of the steady eighth-note motion with only two exceptions, where the slurs cross the barline (the upbeats to Parts I and II and Pa¹). Thus the variation has a strong upbeat emphasis.

Beethoven organizes the four- and five-part texture as a dialogue between the violin, which leads, and the piano. The instruments alternate mainly every two measures, the violin playing with the piano, while the piano responds alone. The violin is associated with a low register and the piano response with a high register. The note-against-note texture is basically contrapuntal though the chordal effect obscures this aspect. Most important are the mirror relationships of the neighbor-note motive (as in m. 33) and the occasional motivic combinations (mm. 34-35).

Each group of eighths 2-4 receives a < > sign, which lends an expressive nuance to each measure, especially the weak second beat (third eighth). The nuance coordinates with the melodic outline moving by step and often half-step. Beethoven touches on some notes of the theme in each measure and retains the climax notes at pitch in each Part.

An enriched harmony supplies further nuances to the theme. While adhering to the basic harmonic framework, Beethoven adds a few diminished-seventh chords with their minor-mode flavor (mm. 33, 46), and several neighbor-note and passing chords. The result is a fast harmonic rhythm with three chord changes in most measures. Consider, for example, m. 35, originally only a tonic chord, but here with four harmonic changes: I-vi-ii^6-V$^0_9$/V. On the other hand, m. 6 drops V$^6_5$/V and emphasizes IV with a neighbor-note #II² instead. Part II is approached not by a diminished-seventh chord but an augmented-sixth chord.

Example 3.29 The sketch for Variation 1 in the Paris draft

The Sketch for Variation 1 in the Paris Draft

An earlier attempt at Variation 1, Part I, appears on the Paris draft discussed above. It is found on the second leaf after the end of the theme (see Plate 3.V, p. 261 and Ex. 3. 29). After the tonic cadence Variation 1 begins on the down beat in the next measure, connected by the rising arpeggio in the right hand. The variation has no double bars, and the last measure contains the beginning of a varied repeat of Part I. Thus both the concepts of continuous connection and double variation are already present.

Only the piano part is written out. While the bass and inner parts create a composite rhythm of steady eighths, resembling the final Variation 1, the treble has a mixed rhythm of eighths and quarters. A *piano* dynamic is implied, as in the final version. Most striking is the freely imitative texture in four parts (with added doublings). Contrapuntal variations of this type normally come later in the set, in the final version as Variation 7. Thus, this conception is more radical than the dialogue texture of the final version, though it too has contrapuntal aspects.

The fast harmonic rhythm parallels the final version. However, the chords in mm. 4-5 are far more distant from the theme, with tonicizations of V and vi, and a minor V^9 in m. 6. These chords elaborate the different harmonization of P for these measures in the Paris draft.

Variation 2

The melodic variation moves throughout in steady triplets as if the meter were 6/8. The rhythm suggests a gigue topic.[121] Because slurs connect eighths 2-3 and 5-6, the staccato eighths 1 and 4 on the beat receive the strongest emphasis. Most of the first eighths and some of the slurred notes 5-6 outline the main notes of the theme. Beethoven also sets the melodic line against a highly rhythmic accompaniment with a different pattern: ♩ , ♫ , which also emphasizes the down beat.

The melodic line incorporates the lower neighbor-note figure, thus connecting Variations 1 and 2 thematically. A special feature here is the mordant on the second eighth, giving an additional accent to the weak part of the beat, and also strengthening the neighbor-note figure with the upper neighbor, its inversion. Unlike Variation 1, the melodic line is placed in the middle register, reaching its high climax only at the end of Part II (d^3) rather than in Part I. In contrast, the piano accompaniment of the violin solo has a large range reaching up to g^3 near the end of both Parts, with full five-six note chords. The variation follows the harmonic setting of the theme almost exactly.

Variation 3

In this *piano* variation the motion is transferred to the bass, which moves in steady sixteenths. In the double variation the bass remains the same; only

---

[121] For further references to the topics in the variations see Johansen, ibid., 103-10.

the treble lines in the piano and violin are exchanged at pitch. The piano right-hand and the violin contain syncopated melodic lines moving mostly in quarters and tied eighths. They proceed largely at the same time in thirds and sixths, with occasional suspension harmonies. Thus, two rhythmic styles mark this variation, steady, undifferentiated movement in the bass versus nearly unbroken rhythmic dissonance in the upper parts. The P theme is much less perceptible in this variation. Normally only one or two notes of the theme appear in either the bass or treble in each measure, though the climax in Part II on c^2-e^2 is included.

The bass line incorporates several figures but two predominate: a rising three-note pattern, often with a pickup from the previous beat making a rising four-note pattern (see mm. 81, 85-86). The rising fourth is conspicuous in the theme and the rising four-note idea reproduces the melodic linking motive in Variation 1 in diminution. The origin of the three-note figure is not clear, but perhaps the figure fills in the rising third on the two climaxes of P. It is especially prominent in Pb. The bass melody has a large range of two octaves, D-d^1 and a varied melodic curve. It descends nearly two octaves in Pa before rising for a varied repeat in Pa^1. While Pb is static around the dominant pedal of B major, for the closing phrase the bass again plunges two octaves before a slight rise to the tonic G cadence. The two treble lines, on the other hand, move within a much narrower range, the higher line from e^1 to g^2, slightly more than an octave. Both lines are subordinate to the bass line and in Pb sink to a much lower range, highlighting the piano left hand and rising three-note motive. The musical space here has been collapsed.

Unlike Variation 2, Beethoven makes several harmonic changes in Part I, enriching mm. 1-6. These are substitutions and changes of inversion, both producing a faster harmonic rhythm, also found in Variation 1 (see Table 3.12). As in Variation 1, m. 3 introduces vi (here with its leading

Table 3.12. Harmonic Alterations in Variation 3, Part I

measure	1	2	3	4
P	I	V^6	I	I -V^7
Variation 3	I^6-I	V^7/V-ii-V$^6_5$	I-vi-ii$^{5\flat}$/V	V$^6_5$/V-V-V^2

measure	5	6	7	8
P	I	ii$^6_5$-V$^6_5$/V	V (4-3 susp.)	I-I^6-vii^6
Variation 3	I^6-I-V$^4_3$/IV	IV^6-IV	V$^6_5$-V^7	I

tone d♯ heard twice), m.6 emphasizes IV, newly preceded by its dominant, and Part II is approached by an augmented sixth chord. Unusual progressions occur in m.2, where the V^7/V moves to a minor ii before resolving to V; and in m.3, where vi is changed to a diminished chord on ii of the dominant, to which it resolves (the note b goes to b♭). This also strengthens

A special marking at the start of Part II (m. 97) is *espressivo*, with *p cresc.* > in the bass all on the first beat. The marking "*a tempo*" appears in m. 101, implying some *ritard* in the first four measures in B major (Pb). These indications, however, do not recur in the repeat. According to Czerny, a *ritard* is "almost always" introduced with the indication *espressivo*.[122]

The indications in m. 97 emphasize the three-note figure, which should surely be underscored in all four measures of the *espressivo* and probably their repetition.

Several slurs in the bass part (mm. 80-83, 88-91, 97^1) indicate a legato performance, the slurs varying from one or two measures to slurs for each beat (the last most common). A two-measure slur (mm. 88-89) overlaps the start of the repeat of Part I thus avoiding a strong articulation.

Variation 4

Unlike the preceding variations, this variation exploits extensive contrasts in two-measure modules, creating an almost orchestral tutti-solo effect. *Forte*, in the first subphrase, is associated with powerful rising chords, in the piano of 5-9 notes. The chords occur both on and off the beat in a series of eighth notes. *Piano, dolce* in the second subphrase,[123] combines with a thin texture of two or three slurred lines arranged in parallel thirds, sixths, sixth chords, or contrary motion. The main melodic line descends largely scalewise in sixteenth notes, starting with a slower dotted eighth and sixteenth. All in all, Beethoven opposes three elements in the subphrases in an example of Classic balanced contrast: Sound (*forte* vs. *piano*, thick vs. thin, texture), Melody (rising vs. falling contours), and Rhythm (slower vs. faster movement).

The melodic range of both violin and piano is wide: two octaves and a sixth in the violin (g-e^3), and three octaves in the piano (g-g^3). In this variation, the melodic line adheres more closely to the outline of P. It contains many notes of the theme and the climax notes recur at pitch in each Part.

Harmonically, the variation also follows the theme closely, but with one striking exception. In Part II, Pb, the dominant pedal is replaced by chords in root position on V and I, and second inversions by first inver-

---

[122] Czerny, *Pianoforte School*, III: 34.
[123] Though the *dolce* marking appears only once in the variation, it undoubtedly should be assocated with all the *piano* indications.

sions in the tricky shift from B major to B minor. Some delicate harmonic nuances occur in Pa¹y (contrapuntal dissonances in the contrary motion of the scale lines), Pby (brief appoggiaturas), and Pc (the appoggiaturas become the diminished-seventh of B/b—m. 140). The y subphrase, in fact, has more variety in texture, harmony, and rhythm than the x unit.

The massive chords connect the variation with Variation 2, while the descending scale lines recall the descending scale motive in P. Variation 4 ends *piano*, with a *ritardando* for a smooth approach to the slow Variation 5.

Variation 6

The powerful impact of this variation stems from the influence of several aspects. First, there is the contrast to preceding musical events: the slow, expressive Variation 5, with its elaborate ornamentation and chromatic cadenzas; then, the unexpected recall of P in E♭ major in the original tempo with the modulation back to G; the tempo acceleration from *Adagio* to *Allegretto* to *Allegro*, together with an accelerated surface rhythm to steady sixteenths in the treble. All these combine to produce a feeling of both recapitulation and heightened expectation for the conclusion of the movement.

This variation seems like a triumphant climax. The *forte* dynamic is reinforced by the rhythmic intensity, together with the stomping effect of the *sf* accents on every first beat except at cadences. The beat rhythm of the bass line moving in eighths resembles the first presentation of the theme. Here, however, the notes are staccato, not suavely legato, and they pair with the accompaniment also moving in staccato eighths. Johansen calls this variation a kind of contredanse.

Sforzandos accent most of the basic notes of the theme, and other notes as well appear within the measure. Many allusions to the theme include the climax notes of Part II, though not Part I, which reaches the top note of e^3, as in Part II. The fairly wide melodic range is nearly the same in both reprises: $f\#^1$-e^3, $g\#^1$ (g)-e^3, though the tessitura in Part I is higher and the effect more brilliant. A lower tessitura in part II contrasts with the high range of the following transition to Variation 7. The melodic lines exploit several motives, some familiar, like the lower neighbor, relating the variation to Variations 1 and 2, the rising three-note motive in Pb, found in Variation 3, and descending seconds exploiting échappées and appoggiaturas (mm. 174^2, 176^2, 178^2, etc.). Slurs in the violin part suggest a legato style for the piano as well, which has only two slurs, in mm. 177 and 189. A long, five-measure slur at the start of the violin repeat of the theme (mm. 182-86) needs to be broken up in performance.

The variation follows the original harmonic progressions almost exactly. It even includes the 4-3 suspension in the penultimate measure of Pa¹.

Variation 5

This traditional slow variation, labeled *Adagio espressivo*, has a change of meter to 6/8, another common device. Because of the slow tempo, there are no repeats. Instead, the piano and violin alternate playing the phrases of the theme, Pa and b by the piano, Pa^1 and c by the violin. The variation also does not end on the tonic. Beethoven prolongs the penultimate measure on the dominant, seamlessly connecting the end of the theme with a four-measure modulatory passage that gradually moves to E♭ major, and the return of P and Tempo I in this key (mm. 159, last eighth-163).

The variation is the expressive heart and climax of the variation set. It returns to the deeply moving world of the second movement, also an *Adagio espressivo*. The simple texture is melody and accompaniment. Repeated chords in the accompaniment support an elaborate and deeply expressive melodic line, resembling an operatic aria. Such an accompaniment also allows some tempo fluctuation (*rubato*) in order to emphasize certain notes and climaxes (as the syncopations in m. 150^2).

The richly decorated melody outlines the theme and is heightened by syncopated sigh motives, which are often thematic notes and sometimes chromatic, on beat 1 of several passages (mm. 146, 147, 148, 150, 151, 158, 159). These include the two climaxes in the violin. The ornamental passages occur rather in the second half of the measure.

Part II is more motivic, featuring the three-note stepwise figure recalling Variation 3. It is in Pc that the great climax of the variation occurs in the violin, mm. 158-59^1. Together with a *crescendo* the line presents the notes of the original climax c^1-e^2 an octave lower, and then their reverse, e^2-c^3. The higher c^3 holds over the barline (it is heard for three eighth notes) before falling an octave and diminished fifth to f♯^{1} with a *decrescendo* sign to *piano*. The effect is one of a huge, poignant, unforgettable sigh. The c^3 is usually performed high on the A-string so that the slur to f♯^{1} can be made on adjacent strings. The thinner, tense sound heightens the effect of the climax (Ex. 3. 30a).

A special device in the variation, probably responsible for Czerny describing this variation as "fantasy-like," is the addition of two cadenzas in the piano. The first appears at the end of Pa on a V^7 chord and the second occurs a fifth below at the end of Pb on V^7/IV, just after the modulation to B major. Both are unique effects in Beethoven's music (Ex. 3. 30b). Each cadenza contains four descending chromatic scales, written as thirty-second notes (the last note of cadenza 1 is a sixteenth). The first three scales have seven notes and span a diminished fifth; the first scale is marked *pp crescendo*. The last scale has 19 notes and descends an octave and diminished fifth; it is marked *diminuendo*. In each cadenza the final note of the fourth scale has a fermata. A gradual *crescendo* to an unspecified peak occurs in the first three scales, while the fourth scale fades away. The scales

VIOLIN SONATA

Example 3. 30 Variation 5

a. Pc, violin part with large leaps (mm. 158⁴-159²)

b. Pa, first cadenza for the piano (m. 148)

are to be played slowly ("langsam")[124] and their effect is one of inexpressible pain, a not unlikely association for the tense tritone and chromaticism, both so often associated with tragic expression.

Beethoven integrates the chromaticism in the decorated rising scale on the tonic in the piano just before the cadence on V in m. 147, the violin's response with its own slightly shorter version on V^7 (m. 151), and chromatic melodic figures in the extension that leads to the return of P. The tritone recurs significantly once more in the great violin sigh of m. 159, with the same notes as the outer notes of the long descending chromatic scale of the first cadenza.

The chord progressions in the variation again follow the theme rather faithfully, but there are some striking exceptions. In m. 147, the V^6 chord holds over the barline for an eighth note with a chromatic sigh in the melody on a♯¹, making a dominant with an augmented fifth, the note a♯ associated with the B-major phrase. The syncopation of the harmony over the barline here and later in the variation is a favorite device of the late style to achieve a greater continuity and rhythmic flexibility (see the discussion of Op. 132). In the modulation back to the tonic in Pc, the V^7 of IV comes a half measure early to underlie the second cadenza, and then remains throughout the next measure (m. 157), thus receiving considerable emphasis. Beethoven alters the harmony once again in mm. 158-59, which form the background to the melodic climax in these measures. In place of IV for the entire measure in m. 158 we find IV^6-IV-ii. It is this A-minor ii chord that colors the climax note c^3 in these measures, holding over the barline for an eighth in m. 159, the minor mode intensifying the tragic expression (see Ex. 3. 30a).

No segment in the entire movement receives so many dynamic shadings and careful slurring as this variation. Several *crescendos* appear, including three *crescendos* to a *piano*, recalling the two in P, an effect otherwise absent in the variations because of the rigid dynamic plan. All three effects are shorter than the original, which extended through an entire phrase. All three coordinate important points in the structure: the first and longest pattern (m. 150-51) highlights the first melodic climax in m. 150; the second and third brief occurrences underscore modulations to and from B major (mm. 152-53, m. 156).

The artfully conceived transition to the return of P in E♭ is one of the most beautiful passages in the sonata. Beethoven unifies the transition with the thirty-second note sextolet introduced at the end of the third measure of Pc (Ex. 3. 31). This partly chromatic motive, almost always

---

[123] The indication "langsam" appears only in the first edition of Op. 96 and only for the first cadenza. The Henle edition of the violin sonatas, eds. Walther Lampe and Kurt Schäffer (rev. ed.: Munch-Duisverg, 1955) includes a *crescendo* hairpin sign under the third scale of the cadenza. This is an error

Example 3. 31 Transition from Variation 5 to the return of P in E♭ (mm. 160-63¹)

found on the weak third and sixth eighths, initiates a dialogue between the violin and piano of some four measures. After the first echo, each appearance of the motive in the piano is slightly altered as the harmony sinks down to E♭ through G minor, the D pedal in the bass becoming the leading tone of E♭. The larger melodic line descends with a long *diminuendo* to a *pianissimo*. Reaching V⁷ of E♭ (m. 163), the violin extends the motive with a *crescendo* in a sweeping, rising passage that falls at the end with a *ritard* to the return of P, *piano*, in a fourth example of a *crescendo-piano* effect.

The mode of passionate inward reflection heightened by intricate ornamentation recalls episodes one and two of the Violin Concerto, also in G major, though without any sorrowful implication. A climatic leap like that in m. 159 also occurs in the deeply reflective Variation 3 of the String Quartet, Op. 127 (1824-25). There, the end of the varied repeat of Part I contains an even wider descent in the first violin of two octaves and a diminished-seventh (g³-a♯), harmonized more richly by an augmented sixth chord, *forte*, > (see m. 66).

---

due to a misreading of the autograph by conflating the beam for the thirty-second notes and the horizontal line indicating the continuation of the *crescendo* (these lines are given by Brandenburg). The *decrescendo* sign for the fourth scale of this cadenza should affect notes 1-11, not 1-10 as in the practical Henle edition.

Variation 7

This variation is the second big surprise in the set in addition to the return of P in E♭. After the ebullient Variation 6, the ensuing brilliant transition would seem to be leading back to a full return of P in the tonic. However, it ends on a VI chord; its final cadence on I is truncated by a sudden eighth rest and the entrance of Variation 7 in the tonic minor and *pianissimo*. An entirely new mood makes its appearance, which we might label *ombra*.[125] It is established by the low dynamic, low tessitura in the opening, chromaticism, and syncopation, the last reminding us of Variation 3, which is also *sempre piano*. Unlike Variation 3, however, no other dynamics appear in this variation until the last two measures.

Variation 7 is the most radical in the treatment of the theme and harmony, in learned style, Beethoven works out the texture of a four-voice fugato with relation to the structure and harmony of the theme.[126] Part I retains the structure of the double variation: the piano alone plays the first presentation (mm. 117-24), the violin added for the varied repeat. Part II, however, has no repetition and both instruments develop the contrapuntal fabric for eight measures (mm. 233-40). An added four-measure phrase on the dominant (mm. 241-44) acts as a transition to the coda. The phrase makes the shift to G major with a *crescendo-forte* resolving into the full return of P in the tonic.

The Subject and real Answer consist of the first twelve notes or fewer (eight to ten) of P (mm. 1-3 or 1-2) in minor. Presented in equal eighth notes with a tie for the repeated notes 7-8, both the Subject and the Answer also start on the upbeat, the second eighth of the measure. It is a remarkable transformation of this popular melody (see Ex. 3. 32).[127] In another example of Beethoven's modernisms, the melodic line of P is treated like a twelve-tone row that is given a new rhythmic shape. The same kind of treatment on a grand scale can be found years later in the Grosse Fuge, Op. 133 (1825). However, rhythm is not the only altered element. Several chro-

---

[125] For a study of the *ombra* style, see Birgitte Moyer, "*Ombra* and Fantasia in Late-Eighteenth-Century Theory and Practice," in *Convention in Eighteenth- and Nineteenth-Century Music, Essays in Honor of Leonard G. Ratner*, 283-303.

[126] There is a question whether this variation should be called a fugue or a fugato. Warren Kirkendale considers it to be a fugato in *Fugue and Fugato in Rococo and Classical Chamber Music*, trans. Margaret Bent and the Author, 2nd ed., rev. and exp. (Durham, NC: Duke University Press, 1979), 242. Ludwig Misch also identifies the variation as a fugato and describes the structure in "Fugue and Fugato in Beethoven's Variation Form," *MQ* 42 (1956): 21-22. See also Imogene Horsley, *Fugue, History and Practice* (New York: The Free Press, 1966), 297-98. According to Horsley, 298, German theorists of the nineteenth century used the term fugato for "a short fugue or fugue exposition inserted in some other form." I believe the term fugato here would be the more accurate designation.

[127] Kirkendale, *Fugue and Fugato*, 242-43, also points out the derivation of the Subject from P. On 241, Kirkendale discusses the rondo-like returns of P.

VIOLIN SONATA

Example 3. 32 Variation 7: Transformation of Pa (mm. 1-3) in the Subject and Answer of the fugato

matic notes inflect the line, especially the raised tonic degree of note five in most appearances, and the raised third degree, with its subdominant implication as V of C minor or C major. Neither the Subject nor the Answer have clear tonal outlines, and the harmony is further affected by chromatic counterpoint (see below).

The entire fugato consists of a four-voice exposition and four-voice stretto. Part I contains the exposition. Entries of the Subject and Answer occur every four measures, first in the piano as bass-tenor entries, and then in the varied repeat in the violin and piano treble. Though the texture is ostensibly in three voices, both the exposition and the stretto contain a fourth entry in the piano treble, so that the violin functions as the alto voice in the imitations. A true four-part texture thickens the concluding transitional phrase, a texture anticipated at the end of the sixth measure of the stretto (m. 238, last eighth), in a typical late-style overlap, here of texture. The transition too has a contrapuntal element in Beethoven's favorite use of mirror writing.

Unlike Part II of P, the modulation is not to a distant key but to the subdominant, C minor, in which Part II begins. The impact of the key is weakened, however, since this modulation had been anticipated by the frequent subdominant harmony in the exposition and an actual modulation to C minor near the end of Part I (from m. 232, last eighth). We should also note how Beethoven obscures the beginning of Part II by the violin counterpoint, descending with syncopations from its highest note, g^2, two measures earlier. Besides the introduction of four-part texture near the end, Beethoven intensifies this Part in two additional ways. A stretto of the Subject occurs with four entries only two measures apart, on C, g, d^1 (violin), and f^2 (piano treble). Though not a true Countersubject, a new motive in quarter notes with various large skips is added to the entries in the stretto. In addition, entries 2-4 briefly modulate: c-g, g-E♭-E♭-g. Once again, and for the last time, the key of E♭ major is heard (mm. 239-40¹), most briefly of all but one must say still significantly. E♭, too, matches the expected distant key in Part II (although in the wrong place), since it embodies the idea of the third-relationship, here submediant rather than mediant.

An outstanding figure of the fugato is the use of chromatic motion, largely in the bass, recalling the old tradition of the chromatic variation. Thus, underlying the tenor entry in the exposition is a chromatic bass rising up an octave from G to g in a free pattern of rhythmic acceleration, moving from half notes to quarters and eighths. In the repeat, the bass moves down from g-d in a chromatic descending tetrachord against the violin's Subject entry (mm. 225-28).

The violin also moves up chromatically from b^1 to d^2 in mm. 229-31 against the Answer in the piano treble. The chromatic element in Part II, however, appears only in the bass counterpoint to the tenor entry in the stretto (mm. 235-37), the motion being E♮-F-F♯-G, leading back to G minor. Though each chromatic line differs in rhythm and length, it may be thought of, perhaps, as a free countersubject, largely replaced in the stretto by a second free countersubject, as mentioned earlier.

Despite the minor mode and chromaticism, Part I generally follows the harmonic outline of the theme, though the final measure of the first presentation originally on the tonic is replaced by chromatic movement from the sixth degree to the tonic that starts the varied repeat. This repeat ends with an anticipation of the modulation to the subdominant in its penultimate measure, as cited above.

Part II treats the harmonic plan with the greatest freedom in the variation set, the tonic key reached only in the transitional phrase and there on a dominant pedal. The tonic chord in root position is achieved only by elision with the return of P at the start of the coda.

CODA: MM. 245-95 (51 MM: 16+15+20 MM.)

Beethoven's variation sets contain many types of codas, and all exploit, as one would expect, various types of references to the theme. There is both an effect of reprise and rounding off of the variation set. Even an exact return of the theme, a *da capo*, may occur, as in the slow *finale* of the Piano Sonata Op. 109 (resembling Bach's "Goldberg" variations). The coda may be developmental, as in the *finale* variations of Beethoven's Violin Sonata, Op. 30, No. 1/III; or it may be in fantasy style, as in the slow variations in the Violin Sonata, Op. 47/II, with fragments and new forms of the theme, tempo changes, cadenzas, recall of earlier variations, and new mysterious harmonic effects. Indeed, we need a detailed study of the myriad ways Beethoven found to make a memorable ending to a set of variations.

The coda in Op. 96 is one of Beethoven's most straightforward. Organized in a ternary form, A-B-A¹, Beethoven begins and ends with different citations of P, separated by a brilliant cadenza section. It is the climax area of the *finale*.

SECTION A: THE RETURN OF P (MM. 245-60)

The coda starts with a full return of the theme without repeats, but still *piano* until the last phrase. Though it has the effect of a *da capo*, several details are somewhat altered to add greater intensity to the theme in addition to the faster *Allegro* tempo. While the theme remains in the piano in Part I, it moves to the violin alone in Part II, an octave higher than in its original appearance. The violin continues in this high range and does not therefore play in octaves with the piano as before, a more climactic effect. Beethoven restores the momentum deflected by the fugato variation with a sixteenth-note accompaniment in broken chords, first in the piano's left hand and then in the right hand for the violin entry, while the left hand supports the whole with block chords in quarter notes (see Ex. 3. 25c). In this exciting presentation, Beethoven emphasizes both the higher register and an intensified surface rhythm. As noted above, both types of accompaniment appear in the two early drafts of the theme.

Some small differences do not affect the theme essentially. These include an extension of the penultimate measure of the theme to connect to the cadenza (m. 260), and several small changes in the violin accompaniment, adjusting it to a slightly higher register. Some modification in the slurring is typical. The piano solo now incorporates the longer slur over notes 1-3 in m. 13 of the theme in all parallel measures. Most important, the *crescendo* that appeared in P m. 29, ending in *piano* in m. 32, finally resolves into a *forte* that starts in the cadenza section (mm. 257-61), a good example of Beethoven's long-range resolution of tension. Beethoven's music contains many instances of long-range resolutions in the coda of instability to stability and irregularity to regularity. In the works analyzed in this volume, we can point to the Violin Concerto/I, where the solo violin finally plays all of the 1S theme rather than just the second phrase only in the coda. In Op. 132/VI, the half-step motive e-f (also found as f-e in the first movement) appears as a major second e-f♯ only in the coda at the end of the quartet. In a famous example in the *Eroica* Symphony/I, the irregular 1P undergoes a process of transformation throughout the movement until it appears triumphantly in the coda in balanced phrases on I and V.[128]

---

[128] For a small but characteristic detail, Lewis Lockwood points to the treatment of the cadence of what I call 2S in the *Eroica* Symphony/I. This period cadences deceptively

Section B: The Cadenza (mm. 261-75)

Beethoven links sections A and B by holding over the G chord, which becomes V^7 of IV, an harmonic overlap. This brilliant section is almost entirely in sixteenths, sustaining the fast surface rhythm introduced in the accompaniment of P now in all parts. Like the variations, Beethoven takes care to feature both instruments, but here the violin leads. In the first part, sweeping scales in contrary motion with the bass (again mirror writing) are first set with the violin on top in parallel thirds with the piano right-hand. The violin moves from f♯^{3} down to e^1 and back up to g^3. In the repeat, the piano right hand and violin exchange parts, as in most of the variations (mm. 261-68^1). The scales are first harmonized with V^7 of IV to IV, before V-I chords, a subdominant emphasis that is a traditional closing effect.

Following the tonic cadence in m. 268 the violin has a solo cadenza outlining the tonic chord from b^1 and rising to the highest note of the sonata, d^4 (Ex. 3. 33).[129] After a V^7-I cadence, the piano plays the same solo cadenza (which is much easier on the piano). This portion of the *finale* is certainly the most difficult for the violinist and a challenge to Rode to demonstrate his virtuosity.

SECTION A^1: THE RETURN OF THE THEME PART II AND FINAL CADENCE (MM. 275^2-87; 288-95)

Another surprise comes at the end of the piano cadenza. Instead of the expected firm cadence V^7-I as in the violin cadenza, Beethoven changes the tempo to *poco adagio* with a deceptive cadence: the tonic moves to the augmented sixth of B major and to V of B, harmonizing the start of Part II of the theme, and thus eliding the sections. A hint of this surprising modulation to come appears in the solo piano cadenza, that changes a^2 to a♭, a chromatic note not found in the solo violin cadenza. The dynamic level shifts to *piano*. The return of Part II highlights the chromatic portion of the theme, recalling the modulation to B major. Such modulatory passages are characteristic of Beethoven's codas. Modulation often occurs at the start of the coda. Here it appears near the end, to postpone final confirmation by a last departure from the tonic key which has saturated most of the coda.

---

on V^0_9/vi (mm. 64-65, 471-72), connecting the first of two transitional units. The period returns near the conclusion of the gigantic coda, where the end of the theme remains on its dominant harmony rather than moving away toward other keys. The V^7 soon goes to the final tonic chords of the movement, resolving the theme harmonically as well as the entire movement. See Lewis Lockwood, " 'Eroica' Perspectives: Strategy and Design in the First Movement,"in *Beethoven: Studies in the Creative Process* (Cambridge, MA and London: Harvard University Press,1 1991), 126-28.

[129] In the autograph, the last three eighth notes of the cadenza in the highest register are fingered 4-4-4, a strange fingering that would never be used today. In the first edition, only the first indication was kept. One wonders if the odd fingering could have stemmed from Rode. Oswald Jonas, "Bemerkungen," 89, discusses the fingering and suggests that it may have been intended for the piano. It is hard to accept this explanation since the piano cadenza is written six staves below the violin part, though the measures in question are below one another.

Example 3.33 Coda: end of cadenza 1, the solo cadenza 2, and start of Part II (mm. 256-76)

The presentation of Part II of the theme is not a simple repetition, however, but an arrangement in hocket, the phrases divided between the violin and piano (mm. 275²-87). This old Medieval device intrigued Beethoven and he applied it to melodies, chords, broken chords, and cadential figures. An extreme example occurs in the String Quartet Op. 132/I where at the start of the coda the four notes of 1P are divided in succession among the three lowest instruments. Several examples appear in the first two movements of the String Quartet Op. 59 No. 1 (as in I, mm. 85-88, 144-49; and II, mm. 35-38, 72-77, 112-13) and the famous conclusion of the *Alla danza tedesca* in Op. 130/IV (mm. 129-36).

In Op. 96 the melody divides between the instruments in progressively shorter distances: 3 x 2 measures, 4 x 1 measure, 4 x 1/2 measure, as the penultimate measure is extended on the tonic. Beethoven sets the last six measures on a dominant pedal point alternating V-I$^6_4$, keeping the harmony in suspense. The Presto conclusion starts on V, not I, as the harmony of the theme again overlaps the Presto beginning. Here, it is the piano that carries the melodic line *forte*. Alternating broken V and I chords, derived from the penultimate measure of P, the piano rises for nearly two octaves from a^1 to g^3 in an exciting, climactic conclusion. Not many of Beethoven's codas end this way. A similar rise, however, occurs at the end of the Violin Concerto and first movement of the Piano Sonata, Op. 10, No. 3. As mentioned earlier, the ultimate example of this effect is the ecstatic rise to the climax ending the Piano Sonata, Op. 110.

Though the variations themselves do not reflect the popular style of the theme, Beethoven sustains the popular element through the rondo-like recurrence of P: most of Part I in E♭-G that connects Variations 5 and 6; the entire theme at the start of the coda; and Part II at the end of the coda. In this way, the attractive, catchy theme, always so pleasing for the audience, is not obliterated by the composer's artful chain of variations.

Max Rostal's remarks from a performer's point of view make a worthy coda to this analysis of Op. 96:[130]

> I most warmly recommend that all interpreters take this unique and superb Sonata, Op. 96, to their hearts, even more than the works of this series which preceded it. Beside all the other splendid [Violin] Sonatas of Beethoven I hold this last in particular as the crown of the genre. My wish is that all its interpreters should attempt to discover the deeper meaning of this work; its interpretation is not easy, but a profound musical and spiritual experience will be theirs.

---

[130] Rostal, *Beethoven, The Sonatas for Piano and Violin*, 187.

CHAPTER 4
String Quartet in A minor, Op. 132

Background

Beethoven's sixteen string quartets have long been considered among the greatest works in the genre. They were written after a rich history of quartet composition in the second half of the eighteenth century, especially by Austrian, Italian, and French composers. For Beethoven, most important were the series of quartets by Haydn and Mozart, the last two complete quartets by Haydn, Op. 77 (1799) overlapping the period of composition for Beethoven's first set of quartets, Op. 18. Beethoven's quartets were produced in spans of one-three years from the early to the late style periods, as shown by the table below.

TABLE 4.1 OVERVIEW OF BEETHOVEN'S STRING QUARTETS

Period	*Opus Number*	*Dates*
Early	Op. 18, Nos.1-6	1798-1800
Middle	Op. 59, Nos.1-3 ("Razumovsky")	1806
	Op. 74 ("Harp")	1809
	Op. 95 ("Serioso")	1810-11
Late	Opp. 127, 132, 130 ("Galitzin")	1824-25
	Opp. 131, 135	1825-26
	second finale to Op. 130	1826

A seventeenth quartet, rarely performed, is Beethoven's arrangement for string quartet of the Piano Sonata, Op. 14, No. 1 (1798), the key changed from E to F, Hess-Green 34 (1801-02).

Quartet composition in Beethoven's last years was launched by the commission of Prince Nikolaus Galitzin (1794-1860). A great admirer of Beethoven's music, Galitzin organized the only complete performance of the *Missa solemnis* given during Beethoven's lifetime (St. Petersburg, 7 April 1824, a month before the Viennese performance of three movements of the Mass). In Galitzin's letter, dated 9 November 1822, the Prince asked Beethoven if he would "compose one, two, or three new quartets" for a fee of his own choosing.[1] Beethoven accepted the commission on 25 January 1823, specifying an honorarium of 50 ducats a quartet. He added that "since I see you are cultivating the violoncello, I will take care to give you satisfaction in this regard," a promise well kept.[2]

---

[1] BGA, 4, No. 1508.
[2] BGA, 5, No. 1535; Maynard Solomon, Beethoven, 2nd rev. ed., 412. The translation is Solomon's. Beethoven had already offered a string quartet to C. F. Peters in a letter of 5 June 1822. No quartet sketches, however, are known for that year according to Sieghard Brandenburg, "Die Quellen zu

Beethoven had to wait until he completed the *Missa solemnis*, "Diabelli" Variations, Ninth Symphony, and the last set of Bagatelles, Op. 126, before embarking on his final group of five string quartets. In his last years, Beethoven concentrated almost exclusively on composing quartets, except for occasional canons, brief piano pieces, and the four-hand arrangement of the *Grosse Fuge*, Op. 134 (1826). The dates of the three Galitzin quartets are listed below:

Op. 127 in E♭   May/June 1824-February/March 1825

Op. 132 in a: February-July 1825

Op. 130 in B♭: May-November/December 1825

The lower opus number for Op. 130 was given by the publisher Artaria, whose edition is dated May 1827, while Op. 132 was published by Schlesinger in Paris and Berlin in August-September 1827, both editions appearing posthumously.[3]

The chronology of Op. 132 has been spelled out by Sieghard Brandenburg.[4] Many sketch sources were used: sketchbooks like the de Roda Sketchbook, two pocket sketchbooks, one being the Moscow Sketchbook, conversation books, separate leaves, score sketches, etc.[5] The score sketches were used as the basis for the autograph. As Brandenburg states (p. 280): "We may assume that the autograph was written out movement for movement in a close chronological connection to the score sketches." He suggests the following completion dates of the movements: movement I, April; movement II, probably not until

---

Entstehungsgeschichte zur Beethovens Streichquartett Es-Dur Op. 127," B-J 10 (1978-81): 233. For the dates of all the string quartets see the Work-list by Douglas Johnson and Scott G. Burnham in the article "Beethoven," NGD, 2nd ed., 3: 117.

[3] For information about Op. 132, see the entry in KH, 400-03. While the date of publication is given there as September 1827, an independent Paris edition in parts was announced on 22 August 1827 in the *Bibliographie de la France*. See Alan Tyson, "Maurice Schlesinger as a Publisher of Beethoven," *Acta musicologica* 35 (1963): 182-91, and Kurt Dorfmüller, ed., *Beiträge*, 352.

[4] See his article, "The Autograph of Beethoven's String Quartet in A Minor, Opus 132: The Structure of the Manuscript and its Relevance for the Study of the Genesis of the Work," in *The String Quartets of Haydn, Mozart, and Beethoven: Studies of the Autograph Manuscripts*, ed. Christoph Wolff (Cambridge, MA: Harvard University Dept. of Music, 1980), 278-300 (discussion on 301). The information that follows is drawn from this important study. A new critical edition of Op. 132 had been made for the *Beethoven Werke* by Emil Platen, and a study score of this edition is available (Munich: G. Henle, 2002). This score is the most accurate we have and includes the differentiation of staccato marks as discussed in Ch. 2. Platen includes a summary of sources and a brief list of textual problems. The score will eventually be published in the complete works, Abt. VI, Bd. 5, Streichquartette III.

[5] See Ludwig van Beethoven, *Moscow Sketchbook from 1825*, Facsimile, Study, Transcription, and Commentaries by Elena Vjaskova (Moscow: The Gnesins Musical Academy of Russia, 1995). The text is in Russian, German, and English. The sketchbook was first published in facsimile with commentary by M. Iwanow-Boretzky, "Ein Moskower Skizzenbuch von Beethoven," *Musikalische Bildung* No. 1- 2 (Moscow), (Jan.-March, 1927), 9-91. The commentary is in Russian and German (see JTW, pp. 419-23). This sketchbook contains sketches for movements III-VI, as well as sketches for the Quartet, Op. 130/I. Sketches, some very early, for movements III-VI, with a page of sketches for movement II, appear in the de Roda Sketchbook (now in Bonn; see JTW, pp. 306-12). Transcriptions of the sketches were first published by the Spanish collector Cecilio de Roda, "Un quaderno di autografi di Beethoven del 1825," *Rivista Musicale Italiana* 12 (1905): 63-108. Later articles give transcriptions of sketches for Op. 130 and the *Grosse Fuge*, Op. 133. Some transcriptions of the Op. 132 sketches are also included by Brandenburg in his article, "The Historical Background to the 'Heiliger Dankgesang'" (see 290-91)

May; movement III, June; and the rest of the quartet by the end of July. Several corrections and additions probably continued into the fall. However, as is well known, at least three early versions of the rondo refrain of the *finale* appear among sketches for the Ninth Symphony in 1823. Beethoven had considered the theme for use in an instrumental *finale* for the symphony (see below, 373-75).

The first copy of the parts was made by Joseph Linke (1783-1837), cellist of the Schuppanzigh quartet, which gave the first performance of the work. However, Linke copied only movements I-IV; the remaining portion was copied by 13 August by Karl Holz (1799-1858), Beethoven's close friend in his late years and second violin in the Schuppanzigh quartet. Beethoven then corrected this copy, also making "smaller corrections and additions in the autograph" as well as the parts.[6] The complete autograph of the quartet is housed in the Deutsche Staatsbibliothek zu Berlin-Preussischer Kulturbesitz, and has been given a detailed description by Brandenburg. Some major revisions are revealed in Brandenburg's study, which will be cited later on. This is the only autograph of a late quartet that has remained intact. Movements of the other quartet autographs have been dispersed in several libraries and even continents.

Several letters survive concerning the quartet. In three, dated 11 and 24 August, to Beethoven's nephew Karl and his friend Holz, Beethoven refers to the quartet as having six movements, not five, as usually stipulated in modern references.[7] The recitative section before the *finale* was evidently considered a fifth movement. In the letter of 11 August to Karl, Beethoven also expressed his "mortal fright" (Todesangst) about the possible loss of the autograph when it was taken away for copying. He wrote: "The ideas for it are only jotted down on small scraps of paper and I shall never be able to compose the whole quartet again in the same way."[8]

A third letter probably written on 15 August to Holz has always been cited for its valuable and rare remarks regarding performance practice. It is here that Beethoven requires Holz and the copyist Rampl to differentiate clearly between staccato lines and dots, and to place accurately dynamics, slurs, and other such marks (called by Beethoven "Espressionen"). Holz was admonished to maintain accurately the placement of < > signs, and the differentiation between < on or after the beat.[9]

---

[6] Brandenburg, "Autograph," 281. Actually, three copies were made of the parts, the first set, written by Linke and Holz, sold to Maurice Schlesinger in September 1825. These parts became the *Stichvorlage* for the Paris edition. According to Brandenburg, n. 18, and Platen's critical edition, these parts, Platen's Source B, were in private possession in Paris. They were sold in auction to a private collector in 2006. Another set of corrected parts, Source C, was copied by Wenzel Rampl and sent to Prince Galitzin, the parts presently located in the Beethoven-Archiv, Bonn. A third set of parts, now lost, was made for the first public performance of the quartet on 6 November 1825.

[7] See BGA, 6, Nos. 2029, 2042-43; Anderson, III, Nos. 1410, 1415-16.

[8] BGA, 6, No. 2029; Anderson, III, No. 1410

[9] BGA, 6, No. 2032; Anderson, III, No. 1421. See the reproduction of the first violin part of the end of movement III and movement IV copied by Linke in BGA, 6, 139; and the recitative and start of the finale copied by Holz in BGA, 6, 140, with Beethoven's correction of a staccato mark written as a dot instead of a stroke at the end of a slur in the *finale*, mm. 6 and 14.

Several rehearsals and early performances of the quartet are known.[10] The first rehearsal with the Schuppanzigh quartet took place on 7 September 1825 in the rooms of Maurice Schlesinger at the inn "Zum Wilden Mann." Schlesinger, a leading Parisian publisher, had acquired the quartet and wished to hear it. Beethoven's good friend Johann Wolfmayer was there and so moved by the "Heiliger Dankgesang" that he wept when hearing it. In the next rehearsal on 9 September the quartet was played twice, each playing taking a reported three-quarters of an hour, and a larger group of fourteen listeners was present. An even larger audience attended the rehearsal on 11 September, including Carl Czerny and the Abbé Stadler. Beethoven sat near the piano beating time.[11] A fifth presentation of both Opp. 127 and 132 occurred on 26 September with Holz as first violin. Thus, within twenty days, the quartet had been heard five times. At the second rehearsal, attended also by the English conductor Sir George Smart, Beethoven, according to Smart, directed the performers and at one point played a staccato passage on the violin a quarter-tone flat.[12] This intensive period of semi-private rehearsals and performances reminds one of the approach to twentieth-century works, representing the belief that frequent hearings are needed to make a work with novel features intelligible to an audience. The first public performance was given on 6 November at a benefit concert for Joseph Linke, together with a piano trio from Op. 70 and Piano Trio, Op. 97. The quartet gained great success, according to Beethoven's nephew, but not the reviewer (see below). Finally, on 20 November, Schuppanzigh himself was permitted to play the quartet at one of his public quartet concerts. Thus, this long and complex quartet received seven presentations within two and a half months.

---

[10] See Thayer-Forbes, 958-68. Extremely important are the descriptions of the rehearsals by the English conductor Sir George Smart. For later performances of the quartet until 1875, see Ivan Mahaim, *Beethoven, La Terre Natale et la Trilogie*, vol. 2 (Paris: Brouwer, 1964), 443-71. The double performance of Op. 132 noted below was preceded by four double performances of the string quartet Op. 127, two each by the Böhm and Mayseder quartets. These took place between 23 March and 29? April 1825. See the important article by Robert Adelson, "Beethoven's String Quartet in E Flat Major, Op. 127: A Study of the First Performances," *Music & Letters* 79 (1998), 219-43. For further information on the double performances of Op. 127, due to a suggestion of Karl Holz, see. 234-37. No other double performances of Beethoven's quartets appear on Adelson's chronological list of quartet performances in Vienna, 1823-28, 241-43. The conversation book for the discussion that took place just after the performance on 9 September has been published and includes an English translation. See *Beethoven im Gespräch*. Ein Konversationsheft vom. 9. September 1825, Faksimile, Übertragung, und Kommentar vom Grita Herre, Übersetzung ins Englische von Theodore Albrecht (Bonn: Beethoven-Haus, 2002). For the remarks in all the extant conversation books regarding the early performances of Op. 132, see *Ludwig van Beethovens Konversationshefte*, Bd. 8 (mid-July 1825-12 February 1826), eds. Karl-Heinz Köhler and Grita Herre, with the assistance of Günter Brosche (Leipzig: VEB Deutscher Verlag für Musik, 1981).

[11] Also among the listeners were two excellent women pianists: Mademoiselle Eskeles, perhaps Marie Eskeles, daughter of Beethoven's banker and a pupil of Moscheles, and probably Antonia Cibbini, née Koželuch (called "Cimia" by Smart).

[12] The passage may have been one of the fast staccato passages in the *Andante* of the slow movement (mm. 36, 120, 123, 125).

Table 4.2 The String Quartet, Op. 132: Gross Form

Movement	Key	Tempo	Meter	Length in mm.	Form
I	a	*Assai sostenuto-Allegro*	¢, c	264	unique; synthesis of sonata form, variation, rondo 74-28-90-39-33
II	A	*Allegro ma non tanto*	3/4	119-119	large A-B-A *da capo* *Allegro*: rounded binary 22+97(48/29/20) trio: A-B-C-A^1 A(22)-B(64)-C(16)-A^1(17)
III	F Lydian-D	*Molto adagio-Andante*	c-3/8	211	alternating variations A(30-1/2)-B(53-1/2)-A^1(30-1/2)-B^1(53-1/2)-A^2(43)
IV	A	*Alla marcia, assai vivace*	c	24	rounded binary 8+16(6/10)
V	(a)-F-d-a	*più allegro-Presto-poco adagio*	c, ¢	22	recitative: A-A^1-B A(7)-A^1(8)-B(7)
VI	a-A	*Allegro appassionato*	3/4	404	sonata-rondo A(33)-B(56)-A(34)-C(52)-A^1(15)-B^1(53)-D(36)-A^2(15)-coda: E(57)-E^1(53)

Title of movement III: "Heiliger Dankgesang eines Genesenen an die Gottheit, in der lidischen Tonart "*Andante*: "Neue Kraft fühlend"

This is the first of Beethoven's multimovement quartet cycles, to be followed by the six-movement Op. 130 and the seven-movement Op. 131 (1826).[13] In the Classic period, multimovement cycles were typical of serenades and some divertimentos, and the early Classic suite-symphony by such composers as J. J. Agrell, Fortunato Chelleri, and J. S. Endler. In the symphonic genre such cycles are occasionally found as well, especially in such programmatic works as Haydn's Symphony No. 45 ("Farewell"), 1772, and Dittersdorf's "The Rescue of Andromeda by Perseus," 1786, both works of five movements. Another program symphony by Haydn, No. 60 ("Il distratto"), c. 1774, contains six move-

---

[13] Brandenburg, "Die Quellen," shows that Beethoven considered expanding the cycle in Op. 127 as well, though he ultimately rejected the idea.

ments and derives from incidental music to a play by the same name (*Der Zerstreute*). Interestingly, Beethoven composed three early multimovement cycles in the divertimento-serenade tradition. These are the String Trio, Op. 3, before 1794 (six movements), the Serenade for String Trio, Op. 8, 1796-97 (eight movements), and the famous Septet, Op. 20, 1799-1800 (six movements). Beethoven's only earlier multimovement cycle in the "serious" genres is the five-movement Symphony No. 6 ("Pastoral"), 1808, also a program symphony.

The basic plan of a cycle with a central slow movement flanked by dance movements and two substantial outer movements reminds us of Berlioz's *Symphonie fantastique* (1830), and may have influenced Bartók's Fourth String Quartet (1928); the reverse layout, with a central scherzo flanked by two slow movements, appears in Bartók's Fifth Quartet (1934).

Besides the greater number of movements and incorporation of a brief recitative movement, this is the only late quartet without a scherzo. In its place is the waltz-like second movement in the traditional binary form but on a much larger scale and far more contrapuntal. Also on a much larger scale is the trio (which lacks a title). The folk style of the trio has connections with the trios of the quartets Opp. 131 and 135, as does the absence of the usual repeat marks and binary form.

Strong evidence exists that Beethoven at first intended to incorporate as movement four the *Alla danza tedesca* of the Op. 130 quartet. A much shorter version of the 3/8 movement exists in A major in both sketches for the quartet and in score with just the first violin part.[14] The original version was only 88 mm. (92 mm. with the second ending) as against 150 mm. in the final version. The structure of the autograph indicates the omission of nine pages where the Tedesca had been located. Why was this movement replaced by the march? Marius Flothuis pointed out that the triple meter would have been overemphasized since it already occurs in the second, third (*Andante* theme), and last movements.[15] We can add that Ländler would duplicate too closely the Allemande in the trio of the second movement. Instead, Beethoven selected the forceful march in 4/4. As Brandenburg pointed out, "it was only at a very late stage of composition that Beethoven became aware of the whole quartet and noticed the weight of single movements and the continuity between all these movements.[16]

The quartet is famous for its programmatic third movement, reflecting Beethoven's serious illness in mid-April to mid-May, 1825. The movement, inscribed "Sacred Song of Thanksgiving of a Convalescent to the Diety, in the Lydian Mode," contains a contrasting thematic section entitled "Feeling New Strength." It is arguably the most personal programmatic movement written

---

[14] Brandenburg, "Autograph," 283-85. For the early sketches and score of this movement, see 292-93. The dance was called "Alla Allem[anda]."

[15] Ibid., 301.

[16] Loc. cit.

by the composer. These inscriptions have led some analysts to believe that the quartet embodies a broader program. For the nineteenth-century theorist A. B. Marx, the quartet delineates the progression from sickness to health, the first movement describing the experience of illness itself.[17] Riemann, however, rightly pointed out a long time ago that the sketches for the quartet were begun before Beethoven's illness of mid-April, 1825, and Brandenburg states that the first movement was finished in April, certainly before Beethoven's illness.[18] Many of Marx's descriptive comments for the entire quartet are cited in Theodor Helm's long study of the quartet, published in 1885, and both early considerations of this work can be followed as well in the English translation of Helm's analysis by Ian Bent. These remarks also influenced Joseph Kerman in his observations on the quartet.[19]

Brandenburg, however, points out that the sketches do not reveal any "preconceived extra-musical program" for the quartet. On the contrary, there are drafts for movements of a very different character—an "Andante scherzoso," a "Romanza erzählend," and even a musical description of laughing.[20] Certainly, none of the early reviewers perceived the kinds of expression mentioned by Marx and Helm.

Tempo: Metronome Marks from Karl Holz

Emil Platten has published metronome marks for the last string quartets, which were sent to Lenz in 1857 by Karl Holz in a memoir about Beethoven and the last quartets.[21] Together with the metronome marks, Holz also sent several important corrections for the musical text of Op. 132 and Op. 131. However, as Platen points out, the metronome marks are often unconvincing, indicating slowish tempos for many fast movements, despite Beethoven's frequent preference for fast tempos in such movements, as shown by his own metronome marks (see Table 4.3 on p. 292).

As Platen indicates, Holz has a tendency to use a small group of metronome marks and to reuse the same numbers for larger and smaller values. Here, 92 applies to both the quarter and eighth in the first movement, and 58 applies to the quarter in the introduction to the first movement, the entire measure of the second movement, and the eighth in the third movement.

---

[17] A. B. Marx, *Ludwig van Beethoven: Leben und Schaffen* (1859), 303-12.

[18] TDR, V, 262.

[19] Theodor Helm, *Beethoven's Streichquartette* (Leipzig: E. W. Fritzsch, 1885), pp. 267-95, translated, with introductory remarks by Ian Bent, in *Music Analysis in the Nineteenth Century*, vol.II: *Hermeneutic Approaches* (Cambridge: Cambridge University Press, 1994), 238-66; and Joseph Kerman, *The Beethoven Quartets* (New York: Norton, 1966), 243. The best modern studies of the quartet are those by Kerman and Ratner.

[20] Sieghard Brandenburg, "The Historical Background to the 'Heiliger Dankgesang' in Beethoven's A-minor Quartet Op. 132," in *Beethoven Studies*, 3, ed. Alan Tyson, 164, 166, alludes to sketches for a finale in A major rather than minor, another point against Marx's interpretation.

[21] See Emil Platen, "Zeitgenössische Hinweise für Afführungspraxis der letzten Streichquartette Beethovens," 100-07. The memoir was published in Lenz, *Kritischer Katalog*, Vierter Theil (vol.5), (1860), 216-19, 224-28.

Table 4.3 Metronome Marks from Karl Holz for Op. 132

Movement	Tempo	Meter	Metronome Mark
I	*Assai sostenuto*	c	♩ = 58
	Allegro	¢	♩ = 92
	Adagio	c	♪ = 92
II	*Allegro ma non tanto*	3/4	♩. = 58
	L'istesso tempo	¢	o = 58
III	*Molto adagio*	c	♪ = 58
	Andante	3/8	♪ = 69
IV	*Alla Marcia, assai vivace*	c	♩ = 108
VI	*Allegro appassionato*	3/4	♩ = 132
	Presto	3/4	♩ = 160

Such manipulations are not found in Beethoven's metronome marks. Except for the marks for the first-movement introduction and the second movement, the marks indicate tempos that seem too slow. This is especially true for the "Heilige Dankgesang," unless Holz meant that a quarter rather than an eighth receives one beat, and this is also true for the *finale*. If we compare the tempos Holz indicates with the highly regarded performance of the Budapest String Quartet, most of the Budapest tempos are considerably faster.[22] The only tempos that resemble Holz's are those for the first-movement introduction and the second movement. The total time for the Budapest performance is 42'29", similar to the three-quarters of an hour noted by Sir George Smart, who heard two performances of the quartet on 9 September 1825.[23]

Rather than giving metronome marks for the recitative, Holz describes how it should be performed, emphasizing a variable tempo (partly indicated by Beethoven as well):

> The first few measures *poco a poco stringendo*. The first violin that enters is tied to no tempo and performs according to its own taste and feeling. The indication that appears in m. 7 *in tempo* holds only for this measure and should really be called *in tempo stringendo*. The F of the first violin before the *Presto* has to be held very long. Thereupon the passage falls rapidly until the measure before *poco Adagio*, which must already be retarded.[24]

---

[22] The recording was made during a performance at the Library of Congress on 20 December 1945. With the remaining late quartets, it is available on the label Bridge Records, GPO Box 1864. For Holz, see Ch. 3, 197.

[23] See above, 288.

[24] "Bei dem darauf folgenden Rezitativ sind die ersten Takte *poco a poco stringendo*, die hierauf eintretende 1. Violine, bindet sich an kein Tempo mehr und trägt vor nach eigenem Geschmack und Gefühl. Die im. 7. Takt erscheinende Ueberschrift: *in Tempo*, gilt nur für d i e s e n Takt, und sollte eigentlich heissen: *in tempo stringendo*. Das F der ersten Violine vor dem Presto m u s s s e h r l a n g e getragen [*gehalten*] werden, hierauf

STRING QUARTET

Holz, in his textual remarks, points out an error in the coda of Op. 132/I that has been corrected only in the new critical edition of Platen.[25] In m. 246³ the note in violin I should be e³ not g³, a significant difference. Beethoven changed the note on the autograph, where he had originally written the notes on beats 3-4 as g³-a³, two notes too high (i.e., with too many leger lines). The composer caught the error at a late stage but made the correction clearly to e³-f³. However, the correction was misunderstood by the printer of the first edition, who printed the notes as g³-f³, and these notes have been performed ever since. The choice of e³-f³ emphasizes the basic motive of the quartet and makes f³ the climax note of the coda rather than the structurally meaningless g³ (Ex. 4.1).

Example 4.1 Textual error in m. 246³ of the coda

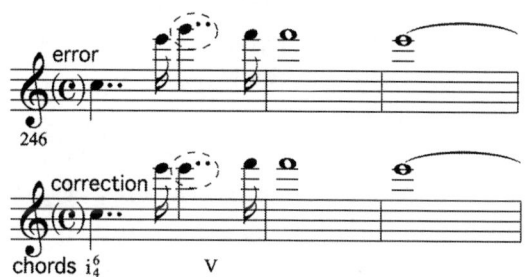

The First Movement: *Assai sostenuto-Allegro*

Growth

Of all the first movements in Beethoven's quartets, this is the only one in a unique form, one that synthesizes procedures related to sonata form, variation, and rondo. The first 74 measures consist of an introduction and sonata-form layout that incorporates the introduction both as a theme and a section. In fact, each of the "Galitzin" quartets opens with a slow introduction that recurs in various ways within the *allegro* movement that follows. A fourth example is the third movement in Op. 130 (*Andante con moto*), where the slow tempo of the recurring introduction is simply achieved by long notes. In Op. 132/I, the slow introduction recurs in the allegro in the same tempo, the note values augmented from half to whole notes. Of all the late examples, this introduction participates most fully in the structure (see the timeline on p. 298).

Harmonically and functionally, the exposition is clear. The second key area is not in the traditional relative major but a fifth below that key, the submediant F, a characteristic choice in the late period and in the "Galitzin" quartets, which feature more distant second key areas, a third above or below the tonic. The move to F is made immediately in 1T, but at first to F minor, a rather typical turn to the minor in T. The parenthetical key of D minor in 2Ta offers some needed tonal contrast and touches on a key significant later in the quartet.

---

stürzt der Lauf *rapid* bis zum Takte vor dem *poco Adagio,* der s c h o n retardirt werden muss (225)." See also Platen, "Zeitgenössische Hinweise," 101.

[25] See Platen's article. 102-03 and the "Comments" in his critical edition, 48.

Even the brief development of 28 mm. that ensues follows the traditional plan of sonata form. The keys of g-c/C-e support material from O and P as well as a recitative-like new idea, and each part of the development (17+11 mm.) ends with the same chordal motive from Pby (m. 20).

The rest of the movement, however, does not fulfill our expectation for sonata-form procedures. We hear the following:

    mm. 103-92 (90 mm.): an intensified and expanded repeat of mm. 1-74 in E minor and C major (the material largely a fifth higher)

    mm. 193-231 (39 mm.): a third, varied and condensed presentation of the exposition in a-A-a, including only O, P, 2T, and S

    mm. 232-64 (33 mm.): an area based on O and P entirely in A minor.

For modern analysts, the main problem is how to designate and understand the large section in e-C. The succeeding section in A minor clearly represents an abbreviated recapitulation in the tonic. The final section, a long and powerful coda also entirely in the tonic, expands the area of tonic stabilization together with the preceding section to 72 mm., nearly the length of the exposition.

Table 4.4 Analyses of the Overall Structure of Op. 132/I

Critic	1-74	75-102	103-92	193-231	232-64
1. A. B. Marx (1859)	Introd. Part I [Exp.]		Part II: Dev.?	Part III: Rec.	
2. Helm (1885)	Part I 9-72 73-74=T	Part II: Dev.	Part III: Reprise 119-87	Coda	
3. Mason (1947)	Exp.	Dev.	Rec. I	Rec. II	Coda
4. Kerman (1966)	Introd.-Exp.	Dev.	Rec. I	Rec. II	Coda not mentioned as a separate section
5. Rosen (1980)	Exp.	Dev.	Dev.-Rec. I	Rec. II	not mentioned
6. Agawu (1991)	"Statement of contrasting premises" (a-F)	"A prolongation of resulting conflict" (e, C, other keys)		"Resolution" (a/A/a)	
7. Ratner (1995)	Exp. I	Dev.(X)	Exp. II (103-88)	Rec.	Coda
8. Kinderman (1995)	Exp.	Dev. Pt. I	Dev. Pt. II	Rec.	not mentioned
9. Chua (1995)	Exp.	Dev.	Rec. I	Rec. II	Coda, mm. 254-258
10. Churgin	I (A1) Introd.-Exp.	Dev.	V (A2) Recurrence + Introd.	I (A3) Rec. + Introd.	Coda + Introd.

SOURCES

1. Marx, *Ludwig van Beethoven*, 325-27.
2. Helm/Bent (see n. 19), 243-51.
3. Daniel Gregory Mason, *The Quartets of Beethoven* (New York: Oxford University Press, 1947),189 (without measure numbers except for 2K).
4. Joseph Kerman, *The Beethoven Quartets*, 245-48.
5. Charles Rosen, *Sonata Forms*, rev. ed. (New York: Norton, 1988), 355.
6. V. Kofi Agawu, *Playing with Signs: A Semiotic Interpretation of Classic Music* (Princeton: Princeton University Press, 1991), 118.
7. Leonard G. Ratner, *The Beethoven String Quartets: Compositional Strategies and Rhetoric* (Stanford: The Stanford Bookstore, 1995), 263, 266
8. William Kinderman, *Beethoven* (Berkeley and Los Angeles: University of California Press, 1995), 299.
9. Daniel K. L. Chua, *The "Galitzin" Quartets of Beethoven* (Princeton: Princeton University Press, 1995), 67.

There is a long analytical history for this movement, and some of the analyses are summarized in the table above

Neither Marx nor Helm uses the term "exposition." They consider the exposition and E-minor-C-major section to start with P, while Ratner specifically and presumably the other writers mentioned in the table rightly begin these sections with the introduction, since it recurs at the start of all sections, though not separately for the coda. A major difference between Marx and Helm concerns the interpretation of mm. 103-92. While Marx describes it as Part II, which may indicate that it is a development section, Helm calls it Part III, the "Reprise," emphasizing the thematic parallelism rather than tonic resolution, which he transfers to his coda.[26]

In contrast, Marx designates Part III as the section in the tonic, though he delineates these sections mainly in terms of the key of the secondary theme. He does not mention the existence of a coda.

Kinderman considers mm. 103-92 as part of the development section, "treated as a recapitulation in the dominant preceding the 'true recapitulation'." Kinderman appears to be influenced by Rosen's brief remarks that "the middle section acts harmonically as a development and thematically as a recapitulation." Though Kerman calls the section in A minor a second recapitulation, he states that "to refer to the 'E-minor recapitulation' is to stretch terminology hard," because the section does not return in the tonic.

Ratner is the only analyst who has suggested that mm. 103-92 (he ends the section at m. 188, however) constitute a second exposition. He well pinpoints the ambiguity of this section by stating that "its harmonic layout is based on premises of exposition, while its melodic recall and rhyme perform the func-

---

[26] The designation of mm. 193-264 as one long coda is also made by Philip Radcliffe, *Beethoven's String Quartets* (New York: Dutton, 1968), 111-12.

tion of recapitulation." Chua summarizes the overall harmonic pattern as a gigantic I-V-I layout (omitting reference to the small development section and its modulations). Otherwise he follows Kerman. Agawu's analysis applies to the harmonic, not the melodic aspect, except for the development section. Much earlier than all the recent writers on this movement, Mason, in his rather generalized remarks, called mm. 103-92 a first recapitulation, the following section in A minor a second recapitulation, and the last 33 measures the coda.

Basically, Mason's interpretation seems to this writer the most convincing, though the terminology could be altered. Certainly, in mm. 103-92, the climactic presentation of O, and the intensified, expanded, and rescored presentation of material has most in common with a recapitulation. The identification of the section as a development is least convincing because of the melodic alignment with the exposition and the harmonic stability. Still, it is misleading to denote this section as a first recapitulation because it is placed a fifth higher than the exposition. One could make a compromise with sonata-form terminology by calling the section a *recurrence*, indicating the return of the material without the association of tonic resolution with the term "recapitulation."

The sections of the movement are: exposition-development-recurrence-recapitulation-coda. The recurrence recalls the circular effect of rondo returns, the "refrain" here being the entire exposition section. The recurrence and coda stand out as the sections of highest intensity in the movement, the coda functioning as the climax area of the movement, as in so many of Beethoven's works.

Some Precedents for a Double Recapitulation

There are a few precedents for the effect of a double recapitulation, though in the three examples discussed here the first recapitulation always starts in the tonic key. An example in the Haydn quartets occurs in the "Lark" quartet, Op. 64/6, first movement (new numbering). Here, recapitulation I (m. 105) contains P and a new development of 1K, partly in the tonic minor. In recapitulation II (m. 142), all the functions return except T.[27] At least two other examples can be found in Beethoven's music, both in sonata-rondo *finales*, reinforcing the rondo connection with Op. 132. In the Fourth Piano Concerto, Op. 58 (1805-06), the first recapitulation (m. 299) presents only second-key area material in the tonic (S-K). In the second, nearly complete recapitulation (m. 416), a varied P returns in the tonic followed by T but only Sa in the keys of F♯-C-G, the tonic presentation extended and climactic, omitting K and leading directly to the cadenza. More like Op. 132 is the layout of the *finale* of the Eighth Symphony, Op. 93 (1812), another unique form, though clearly related to the tradition of the sonata-rondo, as well as a five-part rondo on a grand scale. Ratner's outline of the form is most convincing (see Table 4.5).[28]

---

[27] See Floyd Grave, "Concerto Style in Haydn's String Quartets," *JM* 18 (2001): 93-95, and Figure 8, where Grave interprets the four-fold recurrence of P as a Ritornello, with two appearances in the long section he designates as the recapitulation.

[28] Ratner, *CM*, 254, with slight differences.

Table 4.5 Outline of the *Finale*, Symphony No. 8

A (m. 1),	exposition: F-A/C-C
B (m. 109²),	development 1
A (m. 161),	recapitulation 1: F-D♭/F-F
C (m. 282²),	development 2
A (m. 355²),	recapitulation 2: F-F
Coda (m. 438)	

Here, though P always recurs in the tonic key, S, in two keys a third apart, returns in the first recapitulation a fifth below the exposition, A♭/C vs. D♭/F, while in Op. 132, S returns a fifth higher. In recapitulation 2, S is heard completely in the tonic and the recapitulation is considerably condensed. In the second recapitulation of both the Fourth Piano Concerto and the Eighth Symphony, Beethoven omits K, as in Op. 132. The entire exposition serves as the refrain in the Eighth Symphony, somewhat like Op. 132.

In the following discussion of musical functions and elements, it should become clear that this remarkable movement, despite its strong contrasts, is one of Beethoven's most unified achievements. The high integration stems from the many derivations, developments, transformations, and variations of material within and between functions, and in the relation of the main sectional divisions (see Table 4.6, timeline, on p. 298).

THE INTRODUCTION

The brief subject of two measures is presented in half notes in the style of a cantus firmus (Ex. 4.2 on p. 299). It alternates four times in original and inverted forms on tonic and dominant, giving the section something of the character of a fugal exposition. The inverted form is further presented in a mirror between the outer voices (mm. 3-4, 7-8). Registral and textural expansion is paralleled in the recurrence and recapitulation sections. Here, while the theme in the cello remains in the lower register, the answer in violin I is an octave and a fifth higher, and the inversion in violin I starts nearly two octaves above its initial entry. Additionally, notes 3-4 are an inversion of notes 1-2, thus emphasizing the basic interval of the half-step that pervades the movement and indeed unifies the entire cycle, especially dominating the *finale*.

The subject represents a permutation of the "pathotype" fugue subject known to Beethoven through fugues by Bach, Handel, and Mozart.[29] It draws on notes 5-6-7-8 (1) of the harmonic minor scale, here in the order 7-8-6-5, and

---

[29] See Warren Kirkendale, *Fugue and Fugato*, 91; this writer's "Beethoven and Mozart's Requiem: A New Connection," 467-70; Ratner, *CM*, 269. There is a long history of Beethoven's involvement with this subject type. Beethoven introduced it as a new theme as early as his Piano Trio, Op. 1, No. 2/I (1794-95), where it appears in a contrapuntal passage in the development section. He also copied fugues by Handel and Mozart based on this subject: Handel's choral fugue "And With His Stripes" from the *Messiah*, and Mozart's C-minor fugue for two pianos, K. 426. Further, c. 1819-20 Beethoven made a précis of Mozart's Kyrie fugue from the Requiem, K. 626, another fugue using a pathotype subject. A similar imitative motive, beginning with a rising half step and followed by a skip of a sixth (major, not minor), received many sketches and was finally rejected for the first movement of the "Appassionata" Piano Sonata (1804-06). See Frohlich, *Beethoven's "Appassionata" Sonata*, 109-15, especially 115, with comparisons to the pathotype subjects in the late quartets and Op. 111/I.

Table 4.6 Timeline: Movement I

Key: a   Meter: **c**

Assai sostenuto   *Allegro*   *Adagio*   *Allegro*

exp.

					(+0I)						
0		0I	|Po	ax	ax	y	y ext.	bx	y	z	|P¹o¹
1		5	9	11²	13	14⁴	16²	18³	20	21	22

a: 1-V altern

			(0m,Pax)	(a)		(Pbr)	(0m, Pax)		
a¹	y ext.¹	bx¹	|1Ta	b		2Ta	b	|Sa	a¹
23	26⁴	28³	30	34	40²	40³	44	48¹,³	53
			f	F	d:V	d	F		

	(0m)		(0m, Pbx)	(0m)	(Pby)
1Ka	b	c	2Ka	b	KT
57	59	62³	67	70	73

dev.

	(+0I)	(+ax)	(+ym)		(ax)	(ax)			
0¹	|Pa²x	y²	a³x dev.	by¹	|1Na	b	|Pax dev.	by²	
75	79²	82⁴	85²	91	92³	97	99	102	
		g	c		C			e	

Adagio

recur.

0²	0+Pa⁴	0+Pa³	ax ext.	by³	|Po²	ax	a⁵	y ext.²	b¹x	y⁴	z¹
103	107	111	113²	118	119	121²	123	126²	128³	130	131
e											

Allegro

	(Pax)	(Pay)							
z¹ext.	|NTa	b	|1T¹	2T¹	|S¹	|1K¹	2K.¹	KT¹	ext.
132	134	137⁴	141	151²	151³	159¹,³	168	182	188
		d		c-C	a:V	a-C	C		C-a

rec.

	(0I)	(0I)					
0³+Pax	0+a³	0+a³	|Pay ext.+by⁵		|2T²	|S²	
193	199	203	206⁴	212	214¹	214²	223, 224
					a:V	A	a

coda

	(0I)		(Sr)			(Pax¹⁰+by⁶)			
0⁴+Pa⁶	a⁷		|N3K	|0Ix+ax⁸ +x⁹	ext.	|0m	|2Nx	x¹	y ||
232	236		241	247	249	254	258	260	262 264mm.
a						V: ped. i			

N. B. I stands for inversion.

STRING QUARTET

Example 4.2 Functions O, P, P¹, start of 1T (mm. 1-30)

Beethoven retains the skip of a minor sixth between notes two and three (as in the Kyrie fugue from Mozart's Requiem). As Kirkendale remarks, the subject is associated with "deep grief." Similar subjects appear in Beethoven's *Grosse Fuge*, Op. 133 (the original finale of Op. 130), and the opening fugue of the quartet Op. 131, a resemblance that has led some analysts to view these quartets as a larger unified cycle. This interpretation, however, seems doubtful, since other groups of works by Beethoven also contain certain similar motives, such as the tapping motive in works dating 1805-08: the Fourth Piano Concerto/I, Op. 59, No. 1/II, the Violin Concerto/I, and the Fifth Symphony.[30]

The introductory idea of Op. 132 may well have been influenced by Beethoven's work on an overture based on the name of Bach, sketches for which are found in late sketchbooks dating from the fall of 1821 to October 1825. They also appear in the sketchbook Aut. 11/2, dating from the fall of 1824 to January 1825, where they actually precede sketches for Op. 132. This well known theme on Bach's name, b♭-a-c-b♮, contains half-step motion around a central skip (here a minor third), which basically resembles the O subject in Op. 132 and the subject of the *Grosse Fuge*, Op. 133. The sketches for Op. 133 are also found in Aut. 11/2 as well as other sketchbooks for the Bach overture.[31]

Reappearances of O

The introduction functions in both the large and small dimensions. In the large dimension, it returns in new settings at the start of the recurrence and recapitulation, as indicated in Table 4.7 below.

Table 4.7 Varied Presentations of O in Subject (S), Answer (A), and Inverted (I) Forms

		S	A	SI	AI+mirror
Exp.:	key a:	i	V	I	V
	dyn.	*pp*	<>*pp*		<>*pp cresc.*
Recur.:		S	S		S (emphasizes S)
	key e:	i	i		i
	dyn.	*ff*	*p*	*cresc.*	*f*
Rec.:		S	A¹ +	SI (free mirror)	SI (emphasizes SI)
	key a:	i	(V)	i	i
	dyn.	*p*		*cresc.*	*f*

---

[30] See Solomon, *Beethoven*, 420, and Deryck Cooke, "The Unity of Beethoven's Late String Quartets," *The Music Review* 24 (1963): 30-49.

[31] See the transcriptions of the sketches for this overture, which was never completed, in N II, and the identification of the sources for the sketches in JTW. The transcriptions show considerable rhythmic variation of the theme, similar to the procedures used in the *Grosse Fuge*. The relation of the Bach theme to Op. 133 is discussed in Mahaim, 358-65.

In each case, the cello first presents the subject, and the register rises dramatically, the highest octave occurring in the recapitulation, as the second inversion of S starts on f^3. Dynamics alter as well, starting and ending on the *ff-f* level in the recurrence while in the exposition nearly the entire introduction is *pp*; both the soft and loud levels combine in the final presentation as in the recurrence, but with an emphasis on the soft level, recalling the exposition. While the recapitulation emphasizes the tonic, it also contains the alternation of S and A (Ax or AI), as in the exposition, and that section's emphasis on inversion.[32] In the recurrence, however, the new, unexpected tonic of E minor is nailed down by a three-fold reiteration of S. In the later appearances, most (recurrence) or all (recapitulation) entries combine with Px or Pa (recapitulation). All in all, the return in the tonic shares most features with the exposition, underscoring its function as *the* recapitulation.

In the small dimension O appears in its inverted form as a cantus firmus to Pa. Placed either below or above this basic phrase, it is usually divided hocket-like between two instruments. See Ex. 4.2, where, in the first presentation, the CF divides between the viola and cello. In the following examples it divides between violins I and II (mm. 23-26), and violin II and the viola (mm. 123-26). The most extreme hocket arrangement occurs at the start of the coda (mm. 232-35), where each note of the CF appears in a different instrument and different octave. Destroying any connection between the notes, this is a pointillistic setting that anticipates 20th-century techniques (Ex. 4.3 on p. 302). In the later appearances of O, most or all entries combine with Px or Pa (see below).

The Half-step Motive

The half-step motive in O is pervasive in the movement in both melody and bass. Each function in the exposition embodies this interval in different ways. Most saturated is Pa, which contains the notes of the CF as a descending tetrachord: a^1-$g^{1\sharp}$-f^1-e^1 (mm. 13-15^3), emphasizing f^1-e^1, in Pay, notes also highlighted in Po (Ex. 4.2). Another saturated function is 1T, both in melody and the half-step motion in the bass, while the imitation in 2T occurs at the half-step; e^1-a^1 vs. f^1-$b\flat^1$. Even the lyrical, consoling S places this interval in accented positions, $b\flat^1$-a^1 (mm. 49-50), $e\flat^3$-d^3 (mm. 53-54). Its bass line opens with the emblematic F-E (mm. 48-49) and ends with the briefer inversion, E-F (mm. 56-57). The active K section emphasizes half-steps in 1Kc (mm. 63-66) and 2K, where each phrase starts with a half-step.

The half-step motive f-e, notes 1-2 of the inverted O phrase, reaches its apogee in the climactic coda section after the pointillistic appearance of OI at the start of the section. The deceptive progression, beginning on VI, is inherent in OI and harks back to the first presentation of OI with Pa. It is the most important device for postponing the cadence in the coda until the march conclusion.

---

[32] The answer form, however, is harmonized within A minor, using the augmented $iv_5^{6\sharp}$ with the d♯ and its root-position diminished third, d♯-f. We should note the small < > in O, mm. 4 and 7, and some other dynamic shading in later appearances of O.

Example 4.3 Varied scoring of O combined with Pa (mm. 123-26, 232-35)

It appears with the entrance of the entire OI phrase at the outset of the coda in m. 232, and in a series of deceptive progressions allied with new forms of Pa or Pax in mm. 236 (cello), 247 (the violins), 249 (cello), and 254 (viola). The half step also saturates the wide-spanned eighth-note bass part in mm. 236-46 and the four-measure mirror tremolo of mm. 254-57. The tremolo combines f-e with d♯-e, creating mystery and dissonance in the buildup to the march (Ex. 4.4).

The diminished third between d♯ and f in this passage represents an extension of the half-step motive, containing as it does two half-steps. It is another prominent interval, found in Pb (mm. 16, 17—vn. II), 2Tb (m. 44), in outline in Sa¹ (m. 53—e♭-c♯, and in the ornamentation of Pa in the recurrence (mm. 127-28) and the coda (mm. 237-38).

An obvious extension of the half-step idea consists of prominent chromatic passages in the T section and, most important structurally, in the quarter-note bass motive in Pby (m. 20). This motive returns as a nearly full-blown descending chromatic tetrachord from i-V in the concluding march (mm. 258-61), a variant of its first thoroughly chromatic outline in m. 19, last note, to m. 21. In between these appearances, the motive marks off the two sections of the development and returns twice in the recurrence section, each time with a somewhat different melodic outline and harmonization, though retaining prominent half-step motion usually moving to V, a good example of the variation process in the movement (Ex. 4.5 on p. 304)

STRING QUARTET

Example 4.4 The half-step motive (Om) in the coda, in the cello (mm. 236-40), and in mirror format on V (mm. 254-57)

THE PRIMARY THEME

The setting of P consists of an overall statement-counterstatement arrangement, 13+8 mm., a later Classic layout not infrequently used by Beethoven. The condensed counterstatement omits the anticipation of Pa and the final components of Pb while varying the texture of the ideas as well (see Ex. 4.2).

No other P theme in the quartets embodies so much contrast in idea, texture, and expression. It reminds us of P in the first movement of the Ninth Symphony, where Beethoven expands the theme with a series of five contrasting phrases prefaced by the long introduction of sixteen measures (Po) that anticipates the opening motive of P. Only Po and Pa-b (mm. 1-4) are vital to

Example 4.5 Changes in the bass line and harmonization of Pby (Vc)

the structure, however. There too the theme is extended by counterstatement, though anticipating at first the second key of the submediant.

The tension of the P area is signaled by the cadenza-like Po in violin I, breaking the even rhythmic motion of O with a falling, then rising sixteenth-note passage around the diminished-seventh of A minor. The preceding short *crescendo* and increased quarter-note motion provide a link to the violent *forte* interruption, which begins and ends with the same basic half-step f^2-e^2, the harmony resolving weakly on beat four to i^6. A further delay of Pa comes from the anticipation of Pax at pitch in the high cello, making an altogether four-measure preface to the theme proper.

The theme itself has six components, though Pa is the most important thematic unit (see Ex. 4.2). Pa is constructed as a small period, x+y, the subphrases traditionally ending on V and i. However, the phrase starts on a deceptive cadence produced by the entrance of the inverted OI on the note f. The very start of Pa, however, is ambiguous. Does it begin on beat one or two? Here the version starting on beat two is clear since beat one is an appoggiatura. The composer emphasizes beat one as the start of the theme, however, in several places thereafter, as Ta (mm. 30-33), the development (m. 81), the recurrence (mm. 109, 123, 136), the recapitulation (m. 201), and the coda (mm. 232, 235, 236) (see Ex. 4.6 on p. 306).[33]

In Py, emphasis falls on the basic half-step f-e, and both subphrases end with sigh motives, strengthening the lyrical-tragic expression of this memorable phrase. The prominent dotted rhythm has a march-like association that becomes explicit at the end of the movement. Extension of Pay intensifies the dissonance and sighs, and leads into Pb. This most contrasting unit of the movement contains three different ideas and topics: the Neapolitan fanfare in dotted rhythm (bx), the quarter-note chordal motive harmonized by a descending chromatic bass (by), and the arioso-like broken chord in *Adagio* tempo resting on an unstable i_4^6, resolving to V with the return of the *Allegro* and Po (bz). Despite the strong contrasts within P, there are certain linking elements that keep these ideas together: the fanfare of bx includes the dotted rhythm of Pa; the by idea features half-step motion in the bass also prominent in Pa; and bz starts with the very same notes as Pa, a-b-c.

All of P, starting with Pa, is built on a plan of surface rhythmic acceleration and deceleration, the high point being Pbx, decelerating in Pby-z. While Pa is contrapuntal in its combination with O and local imitation in y, Pb is strictly homophonic, with unison, chordal, and melody + accompaniment as its three successive textures.

The Later Treatment of P

P elements return in 1T, 2T, S, and 2Ka to integrate the movement beyond the half-step motive. Besides Pax, found in most of 1T (a traditional linkage), it is the dotted rhythm in P that connects it to most of the following functions. Another connection with S is the melodic outline in m. 50, from beat two, which is an inversion of the first measure of Pax from its second beat.

Pa takes on new shapes and expression as the movement progresses and is never heard again as in the exposition (see Ex.4.6). In the development (m. 79), Px, starting on the leading tone of G minor, is extended to four measures as a small parallel period (see Pa^2). Fragmentation of Px occurs in this section as well as an N-like theme in C major (mm. 92-98) that stresses the sighs and dotted rhythm of P, as well as the upward motion of the preceding small period form of Px.

In the recurrence, another new variant of Pax as a small period, now descending (Pa^4), combines with the second entry of O (m. 107) and a free mirror of Px with the third O entry (Pa^3, m. 111). When the full theme returns, Pay is ornamented and thus intensified melodically as well as registrally, since the entire theme appears a fifth higher (m. 123, Pa^5). Furthermore, Pay picks up

---

[33] Some of the earliest sketches for Pax are also indecisive on this point. Those given in N II, 547, begin with the notes a-b on beat four or beat one. These versions are found in Aut. 11, Bundle 2, and one, appearing on. p. 47 of this source, was used for the start of the coda. The final march transformation has the a-b on beat one, like the earliest sketches.

Example 4.6 Different forms of Pa

the ♫ rhythm of 2T (and its reverse, ♫). Most striking is the poignant transformation of the arioso. The broken chord now rises to the highest note of the movement, b^3, followed by an extension with new, long sighs in *Allegro* tempo. Beethoven replaces the counterstatement by a seven-measure development of Pax-y in D minor (=NT), with new imitations, especially of Pay.

The composer reworks P completely in the recapitulation. Rather than presenting separate statements of O and P, as in the exposition and recurrence, both ideas combine in a brilliant condensation of the action. The total length of the section nearly equals the exposition's P area (with Po): 21-1/2 mm. vs. 20 mm.

Omitted are Po, Pb, and the counterstatement. However, Pbx is hinted at by the b-flats in mm. 207-10 that recall its Neapolitan harmony. Pby's bass makes a forceful appearance as it extends for an extra measure in *crescendo, forte,* and unison in the lower strings. Together with the trill figure in violin I, they stride to the V cadence, previewing the heroic stance of the coda.

Pa has no independent existence without O in the most intensive combination of these two ideas in the movement. Pax appears in every measure after the first two measures of O. The greatest tension occurs here in the harmonization of the ideas with the augmented sixth chord and its mirror half-step motion, including the root position featuring the diminished third, so important melodically, a recall as well of that augmented sixth in the recurrence (m. 105).

In this area, Beethoven includes four mirrors of Pax (especially beats two-four), two in the climactic phrase, a version, as noted above, that relates to S. The ending trill figure is a dramatic transformation of the sigh motive in the transformed extension of Pay.

Pax and O are the main protagonists in the coda, as O is fragmented while Pax dominates and becomes an assertive, powerful idea, transformed into an heroic march at the end. Five versions of Pa appear, three with accompaniment in sixteenths (Pa^{6-10}) as the entire coda is intensified by a faster surface rhythm. The units with P lengthen in groups of 4-5-6-7 measures. All versions of Pa start in the tonic as they reinforce, reiterate, and stabilize the tonic key. Pa^6 recalls the periodic form based on x in the development. Pa^7 serves in many ways as the assertive, powerful reprise of Pa, since the return of this phrase in the recapitulation is obscured by its combination with the inversion of O in the highest violin range (see mm. 203-06). This is the final appearance of both Pax-y. Both are ornamented by sixteenth-note figures on beats two and four, and the ending of y repeats rather than going off into a chromatic extension as earlier, another stabilizing gesture. The appoggiaturas in Pay receive double emphasis through *sf* accents intensifying the expressive effect of the phrase.

A new continuation takes off from the appoggiaturas of Pay in a series of delayed cadences, picking up the double-dotted rhythm of S and the ending of P in the recapitulation, also associated there with the appoggiatura motive. This passage also recalls the descending thirds in S. It leads with great leaps to the climax of the section with the only *ff* in the entire coda.³⁴ Here, the f-e motive emerges prominently for the last time, high in the violins (f^3-e^3) against another, even briefer periodic arrangement of Pax in descending sequence (Pa^8, only 2 mm.). Once again the idea is buried in the cello, here below the paired viola. Then Pa^9 returns to the first violin in a last, gentle triplet ornamentation of Pax, but most richly harmonized with the major seventh and augmented sixth above another repeat of the f-e motive in the cello. A second extension, here of Pax's sigh motive, continues the colorful harmonization in a chromatic progression of syncopated chords moving slowly downward in essentially half-note motion. These five measures constitute the rhythmic subclimax of the section. Thereafter, the sixteenth-note motion returns in the mirror phrase of the half-step motive, leading to the final transformation of Pax as an heroic march (Pa^{10}=2N). The theme is a repeated two-measure phrase, based on notes 1-5 of Pax, the tonic repeated in quarter notes in the first measure of the phrase, combined with the quarter-note descending tetrachord of the bass from Pby. While the theme appears in violin II, violin I continues with a sixteenth-note dissonant counterpoint against the march, creating strong dissonances on each beat. The sixteenth-note motion continues in the first violin to the final chord, using the technique of bariolage, featuring the open E-string to make a sonorous ending. More than half the section consists of *f-ff* levels, the soft passages offering contrast at the start of the coda (Pa^6, *pp*) and near the end with Pa^9 and its descent *morendo* to *pp* for three measures and another three measures in the mirror phrase before the short *crescendo* to the *forte* of the march. This descent to a mysterious *p* or *pp* is an old Beethovenian device to highlight a strong, decisive ending (see the endings of the Violin Concerto/I, Op. 10, No. 3/I, and Op. 96/I).

THE SECONDARY THEME

In contrast to P, S is a unified lyrical theme in the Classic format of the parallel period, which supports its stable character (mm. 48-57¹; Ex. 4.7). Phrase a (mm. 48-52) moves from the tonic to a half cadence on V (preceded by its I_4^6 and V); phrase a¹ (mm. 53-57¹) reasserts the tonic with a strong V⁷/IV-IV moving to a I_4^6-V-(I) cadence. As we have seen in many examples in this volume, the preliminary appearance of the accompaniment (Sh, m. 48) often occurs in the late eighteenth and early nineteenth centuries and is the setting for the three-note upbeat to Sa that Beethoven extends to nearly an entire measure as the upbeat to Sa^1.³⁵ As in so many late eighteenthth-century themes, the preliminary ap-

---

³⁴ There are only four *ff* in the movement, all only 1/2 m. or 1 m. long (mm. 62³, recurring in m. 177³, m. 103, m. 243). Reserving the only *ff* in the movement for the coda occurs in the *Adagio* of the quartet, Op. 18, No. 1 (1799-1800). See Weill, "The Two Versions of the *Adagio* of Beethoven's String Quartet, Op. 18, No. 1," 61. There, *ff* appears in m. 105, beat one, at the point where the words "se tue" are written in the sketches, words relating to the last events of the tomb scene in Shakespeare's *Romeo and Juliet*.

³⁵ Other examples of this device of anticipation occur at the start of the *finales* of both Op. 132 and Op. 130 (second *finale*), and especially in Op. 61/I and Op. 10, No. 3/I and II. See Roger Kamien, "Conflicting Metrical Patterns in Accompaniment and Melody in Works by Mozart and Beethoven: A Preliminary Study," *Journal of Music Theory* 37 (1993): 311-48.

STRING QUARTET

Example 4.7 The S theme in mm. 48-56 and the first measure of 1K (m. 57)

pearance of the accompaniment adds an element of asymmetry at the start of the theme, complemented by the extension of the last measure at the end (m. 56), making a theme of nine measures cadencing in the tenth measure. The last measure contains an expansion of the new sixteenth-note figure in m. 55 into a countermelody against the melodic line transferred to the cello. Only a light cadence resolves to the tonic in elision with 1K in m. 57. The extension of the second phrase of a melodic or parallel period is an old Classic device, as in the 1S theme in Mozart's "Jupiter" Symphony, K. 551/I (1788).

Besides the half steps in the melodic line, the dissonant harmonization of beat one in mm. 2 and 3 of Sa helps create the special expressivity of these measures. The dissonance increases in m. 6 of the theme—the start of Sa^1—with both the seventh and augmented fifth of the V^7/IV in the melody, outlining and then skipping a diminished third—an especially poignant effect; this interval recurs throughout the quartet in P and elsewhere (see above).

Sa^1 is not only intensified chromatically but also with a much more nuanced dynamic shading, ending "teneramente." Beethoven reorchestrates the textural setting of the theme in each appearance, exploiting the high cello and viola A-string (see Table 4.8).

Table 4.8 Reorchestration of S Melody

measure	Sa	Sa^1
48	vn. II	vn. I
159	vc., vc.+vn.I partly in octaves	vn. I + vc. in octaves
224	va., va.+vn.I in octaves vn. I partly below the va.	vn. I + vc. in octaves

As in some other late quartets (such as Op. 130/III/69-70 and Op. 131/V/Trio 1), the triplet accompaniment is organized in hocket between the pair of supporting voices in the theme's first two appearances and Sa^1 in the last appearance: va. and vc., vn. II and va. Note 2 of each triplet is an appoggiatura.

The main change in the three presentations of S, besides its textural setting and the new elaboration of its last measure in the C-major presentation, occurs in its third appearance in A major. Its first measure becomes entirely introductory as the three-note upbeat is dropped. While eliminating the upbeat is a typical Beethoven variation going back to his earliest Piano Sonata, Op. 2, No. 1/I, recapitulation, the effect here is extraordinary. The first eighth of the triplet on beat one does not sound; without the downbeat we are left with a startling void gradually filled in with the triplet background to S, first by vn. II and then together with vn. I, whose line outlines the missing upbeat but postpones the crucial appearance of c-sharp, establishing A major, until the very last beat. This is surely one of the remarkable passages in the quartet, as if its heartbeat had suddenly stopped and then gradually begun again (Ex. 4. 8). In Sa, only vn. II carries the triplet upbeat figure, while the cello fills in with larger values, a *sostenuto* setting allied with the theme. The extension here is altered to a varied repeat in minor, the return to the tragic world of the minor eliding with the start of the coda.

Some melodic intervals in Sh and aspects of the harmony—inversions, root positions, even a chord (vi in m. 225^3)—are slightly altered in each presentation of S, another aspect of the variation process in the movement. The extended upbeat in m. 5 of the theme also differs slightly in each thematic statement.

A final reference to S takes place in the coda after the last full appearance of Pa. This extended passage of postponed cadences (mm. 241-46) uses the double dotted rhythm of S, m. 1, which had reappeared at the end of P in the recapitulation. Also stemming from S is the descending four-note scale line (from

STRING QUARTET   311

Example 4.8 The approach to S (mm. 221-22) and S in A major (mm. 223-29)

m. 2) and descending skips of a third (from m. 3), the skips vastly expanded to a rising third, fourth, major sixth, and major tenths as the line builds to the *fortissimo* in m. 247.

The return of S in the tonic major occurs often in Beethoven's movements in minor, though sometimes with nuances, as in the Ninth Symphony, first and second movements, where the S and K areas contain a mixture of major and minor with concomitant expressive results—joy and sorrow intermingled. The preservation of the major in S and K in recapitulations in minor was an innovation of Haydn's in the 1780s. It was selectively continued by Beethoven though rejected by Mozart.[36]

---

[36] See Gregory John Vitercik, "Structure and Expression in Beethoven's Op. 132," *The Journal of Musicological Research* 13 (1993): 236-37.

CONTINUITY

From the middle period onward, Beethoven was concerned with establishing an unusually tight musical flow in sonata-form movements. He generally avoided the conventional formal cadences before T, S, and K.[37] The first movement of the quartet Op. 59 No. 1 brilliantly exemplifies such a flow: the only typical cadence occurs at the end of P; another open cadence appears atypically in the middle of T. Otherwise cadences are weak, elided, or avoided throughout the movement.[38]

In Beethoven's late works, the goal of achieving an intensive continuity is fully realized. Even in the exposition of the Ninth Symphony, first movement, the first perfect authentic cadence (V-I in the bass, 7-8 in the soprano) occurs only before the final K unit (mm. 149-50).

The late string quartets are marked by an intensive continuity between larger divisions as well as smaller units. Many of the devices for maintaining continuity are traditional while others are more personal (see also the discussion for movement VI). In Op. 132/I all larger sections connect by sustaining the same basic harmony. This occurs with all sections except the coda (Ex. 4.9).

Example 4.9 The same bass or harmonic root connecting three major formal divisions:

a. KT-development

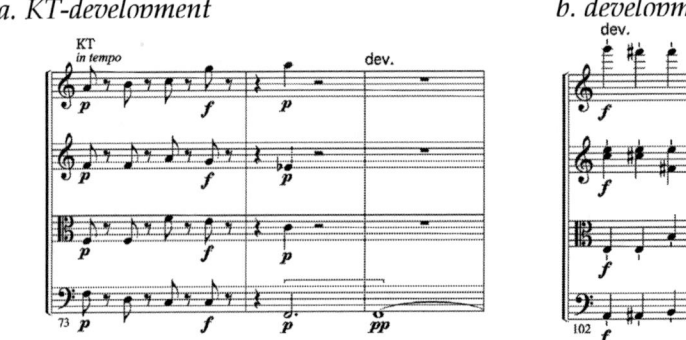

b. development-recurrence

c. KT¹ - recapitulation

---

[37] It is in the symphonies where such cadences remain prominent.

[38] See the analysis of the cadential structure in Ratner, *CM*, 423.

KT-dev. (mm. 74-75, open cadence otherwise and same bass note)

dev.-recurrence, 0 (mm. 102^{3-4}-103)

KT^1-rec. (mm. 192^4-193)

The device of linking themes and sections by the same harmony is especially characteristic of Beethoven and his late works. Here it also occurs in the linking of O-Po (mm. 8-9), P^1 to 1T (mm. 29^4-30), and 1T-2T (m. 40^2; see Ex. 4. 10). These examples as well as others below show connections often from weak beats or weak parts of beats, thus deemphasizing articulations and cadences, perhaps Beethoven's most pervasive means of achieving a nearly unbroken flow in the late quartets.

The end of the recapitulation joins with the coda (mm. 231-32) via a deceptive cadence (V-VI) created by the return of Pa combined with OI, which always begins on the sixth degree. In fact, this combination, when OI is the bass or soprano to Pa, creates an inherent delay of the tonic chord to the fourth measure (see mm. 13-16 and 23-26 as well as 232-35).

Delay of tonic resolution is another device enhancing continuity, with such resolution often appearing on weak beats or weak parts of beats. The delay can occur locally, as the dominant harmony ending O and starting Po (mm. 8^3-10^3) resolves to the tonic only on the weak beat four of m. 10, which is then prolonged for six beats in a stabilizing effect. The strongest postponement of tonic resolution occurs in the coda where Beethoven delays a typical I_4^6-V progression four times between m. 242 and m. 258 (the progression appears in mm. 242, 244, 246, and 253). Thus, the final resolution in m. 258 comes with enormous force. This cadence, preceded by a four-measure ornamented dominant pedal and ending with 7-8 in the melody in violin II, is the only strong perfect authentic cadence of the movement besides the very final cadence measures. Yet, even here, a dissonant appoggiatura on b^1 weakens the effect of tonic arrival on beat one, despite the tonic note sounding on four octaves at that point.

A more traditional method for achieving continuity is the elision of functions (see the discussion of the Violin Concerto). This device is also newly treated, as indicated below:

Pbz-P^1 (mm. 21-22): resolution of I_4^6 to V (only in the exposition; see Ex. 4.2)

S-1K (mm. $56^{4.5}$-57): imperfect cadence from last eighth of m. 56 (see Ex. 4.7)

1K-2K (mm. 66^4-67): weak perfect authentic cadence from the last sixteenth of m. 66

2K-KT (mm. 72-73): imperfect cadence, *cresc.-p*

The link between P^1 and T (mm. 29^4-30) takes place via a brief anticipation of the melodic note and harmony of the next measure from the last sixteenth of m. 29.

Example 4.10   Cadence before 2T in the exposition, m. 40, beat two

Even more extreme than the exposition of Op. 59, No. 1/I are the two formal cadences in the exposition. One is the open half cadence ending 1T—in d, a, a—in the three main sections of the movement and the strongest cadence in these sections, though on the weak second beat of the measure (see Ex. 4.10). The other formal cadence is the weak, elided perfect cadence to 2K, as indicated above, delayed until the last moment (though in the recurrence, mm. 181-82, the cadence is normalized by a two-beat dominant in root position preceding the tonic chord).

Such an extreme delay also marks the cadence before S. Traditionally this cadence rests on a strong beat on V, but Beethoven delays the I_4^6-V progression to the last two beats or less before the entrance of the theme. Thus, the dominant-seventh chord appears on beat four (m. 47) or the last sixteenth of the measure (mm. 158, 222). The third appearance is the most extraordinary. 2T reaches its highest note, a^3, near the cadence and the richest harmony (V_9^0/V-VI) precedes I_4^6-V. However, the cadence is followed by a dramatic silence on the first part of the first beat of the next measure and the tonic chord only gradually emerges (see above, p. 310 and Ex. 4.7).

Within themes and phrases, melodic decorations, developmental extensions in Pa and S, and the emphasis on non-tonic chords, especially the dominant, enhance the flow of ideas and lines. Ratner well summarizes the treatment of cadences in the movement as follows:

> Throughout the movement, Beethoven repeatedly approaches the authentic cadences only to avert them by textural, melodic, or rhythmic blurrings, as in mm. 22-23, 47-48, 55-56, 73-74, etc. We must reach the very end of the movement before we hear straightforward, solid V-I cadences in A minor. Thus, the assignment of cadential action to melodic line rather than to firm bass support, together with the compromising of strong cadential action to articulate phrases and periods, creates both focus and flow to the harmonic continuity, a play of centripetal and centrifugal forces at close quarters.[39]

Sound

From the start, Beethoven's quartets exploited a considerable variety of texture, all parts participating in thematic presentations well beyond what is found in

---

[39] Ratner, *String Quartets*, 267.

the mature quartets of Haydn and Mozart. That independence and variety deepened in the Razumovsky, Op. 74, and Op. 95 quartets. Yet, nothing could prepare us for the textures, new sonorities, and equality of parts marking the late quartets composed nearly fourteen years later. Op. 132 fully represents that aspect of the style, which was especially emphasized in the early reviews of the quartets (see below).

In the striving for what Beethoven described as "a new manner of voice treatment,"[40] there is the well-known resort to contrapuntal textures and devices as well as linear freedom in the part writing, where themes move throughout the texture at various ranges, and even accompanimental parts are more highly individualized. The resulting equality of parts is not a true equality, of course, except in contrapuntal passages—Violin I still leads. However, the combination of contrapuntal arrangements and thematic-motivic dialogue creates a thematization of texture that is perhaps the most signal achievement in these quartets.

Contrapuntally, the first movement is notable for its many combinations of O and Pa, and the use of both melodic inversion and mirror writing as well as invertible counterpoint. The fugal imitation in O recurs twice more in totally different arrangements, typical of the reorchestration of material found throughout the movement, including homophonic textures, here especially in S. In addition, 2T picks up the imitative presentation of O with four overlapping entries (the fourth entry being partial and a closer stretto). Local imitation also occurs in the extension of Pay (mm. 15^{4}-18). The free contrapuntal writing in the active 1K exploits double counterpoint (mm. 57-58, exchange of violin I and cello parts), imitative dialogue, and mirror writing.

The lower parts frequently contain thematic material and they often exchange their location so that the viola can be a light bass or even soprano voice (m. 154^{1-2}). If we compare the first part of the setting of P and P^1 in the exposition, we have a typical example of the remarkable variety Beethoven was able to achieve (see Ex. 4.2 and Table 4.9 on p. 316).

Another favorite device, hocket, is not only used for the accompaniment to S but also for varying 1Tb in the recurrence. The theme divides between the violins, vn. I an octave above vn. II, though vn. II starts the phrase (mm. 145^{2}-47). The hocket of OI at the start of the coda is the extreme example in all of Beethoven's music of the composer's use of this favorite device, which embodies the concept of sharing material among the voices (see p. 301 and Ex. 4.3).

---

[40] See Thayer-Forbes, 982. The original German text is given in Wilhelm von Lenz, *Kritischer Katalog*, Vierter Theil (vol.5), (1860),[cited in chapters 2,3],217. Beethoven made the reference in a conversation with Karl Holz, which Holz sent in a communication to Lenz shortly before he died. Beethoven remarked "Sie werden eine neue Art der Stimmführung bemerken." Holz explains the meaning of "Stimmführung" as referring to the "instrumentation, the distribution of roles" ("hiemit ist die Instrumentirung, die Vertheilung der Rollen gemeint").

Table 4.9 Reorchestration of P (Exposition)

P (mm. 11-18) P¹ (mm. 23-28²)

o vc., high omitted

a vn. I; O, va., vc. vn. II, vc. in octaves; ay –va.; O, vn. I, II

ay ext. imit.: va., vn. I, imit: vc., vn. II, vn. I, vc.
vn. II, vn. I, vn. II

EXPRESSION

The movement exploits many Classic topics, though some appear in the "wrong" place. Ratner points out the broad contrasts of "*alla breve* action," associated with O, and "legato performance," found in much of P, T, S, and K.[41] "Cuts" in the flow stem especially from the chordal ideas of Pby and KT.[42] The thoroughgoing learned style of the movement, associated with O and the combination of O and Pa, also recurs in several imitative passages in 1T, 2T, NT, and 1K as well as the use of suspensions and the final counterpoint to 2N in the coda.

The four-note O idea relates, as indicated above, to the pathotype fugue subject, associated with "deep grief." Ratner describes the O section as a "quasi-ecclesiastical opening with its color of pathos, a requiem song."[43] Another figure often associated with the lament and death is the descending tetrachord in minor, moving from i to V. Outlined in Pa, it emerges most prominently in the final clarified form of the bass motive of Pby in the concluding measures of the coda (mm. 258-61; see Ex. 4.5). In fact, the half-step (minor second) motive that pervades the movement and quartet as a whole was associated with tragic expression from the Renaissance on, reinforced here by the many sigh motives.

Marx and Helm aptly described the P theme as a lament, but the dotted rhythm also suggests the march, which emerges in the dramatic transformation of Pax as 2N in the final measures. The general style of Pa, as Ratner remarks, is "a hesitant *empfindsamer* song,"[44] while the broken chord of Pbx suggests a fanfare and the *Adagio* an arioso. Po has a cadenza-like brilliance, and brilliant style returns in 1K especially. While a suggestion of gavotte rhythm marks 2Ta's point of imitation, a relaxed singing style in S conveys a mood of consolation, as observed by Marx and Helm.[45]

Agawu points to a lack of coordination between the harmonic background and some topics.[46] The cadenza-like Po resolves its harmony not on

---

[41] Ratner, *String Quartets*, 264.

[42] Loc. cit.

[43] *Ratner,* String Quartets, 265. For the expressive association of the descending tetrachord mentioned below, see Ellen Rosand, "The Descending Tetrachord: An Emblem of Lament," *MQ* 55 (1979): 346-59.

[44] Ratner, loc.cit.

[45] Helm, *Beethoven's Streichquartette*, trans. Bent, 246.

[46] See Agawu, *Playing with Signs*, 121-26.

beat one but beat four of m. 10, a weak articulation that weakens the introduction of the march topic in P. Pb's fanfare is attached to a remote chord—the Neapolitan—not the usual tonic or dominant, while the gavotte reference appears uncharacteristically in the middle of T and in a "parenthetical harmony" rather than at the start or end of a section. These disjunctions increase the expressive tension of the movement, which is the most tragic of the cycle.

The Second Movement: *Allegro ma non tanto*

After the intensity, contrasts, and complexity of the first movement, Beethoven obviously felt it would be impossible to present another movement with similar effects and demands on the listener. High contrasts and nervous intensity are followed here by a wonderful calm produced by the tonic major key, A major, a greater degree of regularity, and various types of simplicity.

The movement is in the traditional A-B-A da capo form associated with the minuet-trio prototype and in the traditional 3/4 meter. It has only one tempo mark, *Allegro ma non tanto*, and no designation for the trio, which opens and closes in A major as well. The large contrast here occurs between the A and B sections. A is contrapuntal—learned—and monothematic. B, with its own A-B-C-A^1 form, is homophonic in a relaxed popular style, juxtaposing as it does a musette and Allemande, a kind of Ländler.[47] The large contrasts here, in fact, point ahead to the contrasts between the A and B sections of the *Adagio's* "Heiliger Dankegesang", though the B section there is far more intricate. The A section of this movement, with its smooth and steady counterpoint, again represents Beethoven's profound involvement with contrapuntal textures in his last works, including the first and third movements of this quartet.[48] The musette and Allemande, on the other hand, represent Beethoven's turn to a more popular and lyrical mode in his late quartets.[49]

Ratner has rightly called the A section of this movement a waltz, while Helm describes it as "a sort of intermezzo," perhaps because of its lyrical character.[50] Ratner has reduced mm. 1-70 to their basic melodic-harmonic outline generally moving on the measure level.[51] These regular metrical units provide a relaxed background for the contrapuntal and motivic developments in the movement.

---

[47] According to H. C. Koch, an Allemande was faster than a Ländler. See the articles "Allemande" and "Ländler" in his *Musikalisches Lexikon,*, cols. 132, 889.

[48] Precedents for the intensive counterpoint of the waltz can be found in the tradition of the contrapuntal minuet in Vienna, as, for example, in the canonic minuets in Haydn's Symphony No. 44 and String Quartet Op. 76, No. 2, and Mozart's Symphony No. 40, K. 550. Trios in Ländler style appear in many later works by Haydn (Symphony No. 97) and Mozart (Symphony No. 39, K. 543). Kerman, *The Beethoven Quartets*, 253, cites the contrapuntal minuet in Mozart's String Quartet K. 464/II (72 mm.), a work that Beethoven copied, as a model for the waltz. There, too, the minuet develops and combines two contrasted ideas, each two measures long.

[49] Kerman, ibid., 200-04.

[50] Ratner, *String Quartets*, 268; Helm, *Beethoven's Streichquartette*, trans. Bent, 251. The large A section is not a minuet as asserted by Daniel K. L. Chua, *The Galitzin Quartets by Beethoven* (Princeton: Princeton University Press, 1995), 108-09.

[51] Ratner, *String Quartets*, 270.

The A section is in a traditional rounded binary form, with an enhanced return of the opening contrapuntal unit (P), rhyming cadences, and near-rhyming starts to Parts I and II. Quite unusual for such a form is the long development section in Part II, more than twice the length of Part I. The long coda nearly matches the length of Part I as well (see Table 4. 10).

The waltz is a striking examples of complete monothematicism, every measure derived from the material in mm. 5-6. As Kerman observes, "only minute scrutiny will reveal all the facets of this superbly polished piece of musical jewelry."[52] Five elements, the complete a and b ideas plus three b motives, comprise the musical material for the waltz. Of later motivic variants, by^1 is the most important (see Ex. 4.11).[53] Measures 1-4 function as a unison introduction (Po), presenting Pa in a rising sequence (Pa contains sequential repetition of its basic motive as well). Measures 5-6 introduce the material of the A section in a two-measure phrase, Pa in equal quarters combined with a distinct melody, Pb. The subject-countersubject relationship recalls the combination of O and Pa in the first movement. Beethoven contrasts the lyricism of Pbx with the humor of bz, when extended (as in mm. 11-12) and especially when in canon.

The rest of the waltz section develops the material in mm. 5-6. This occurs melodically with fragmentations, extensions, and variants; and contrapuntally, with examples of canons of a and bz (as in mm. 27-30), motivic combinations (of bx+z, mm. 37-38, 45-50), double counterpoint (as in mm. 49-50 of mm. 47-48), and mirror writing, especially important in the coda using by^1 (mm. 103^3-107^2). As in relief from the steady counterpoint, Beethoven often treats by^1 in dialogue (mm. 63^3-68, 99^3-103^2, second ending).

Table 4.10 Tonal Outline of the Waltz

A						
	1	13	22^2			
	A	E	E:I			22 mm.
B	|2.					
	22^2 22^3	31	43^3	56^3	67^3	48-1/3mm. (50-1/3 mm.)
	E:I C	F	C	a	A	
A^1						
	71	99^2	100	102	103	28-2/3 mm.
	A	A:I	a	C		
coda	|2.					
	99^2	119		19-1/3 mm.	total: 119 mm.	
	A:I					

N.B. The B section starts in mm. 22^3 and is two mm. longer when repeated because the second ending of A^1 contains two additional measures for Po. The coda starts in mm. 99^3.

[52] Kerman, *The Beethoven Quartets*, 251.

[53] For other motivic variants, see the article devoted to this movement by Nicole Schwindt-Gross, "Zwischen Kontrapunkt und Divertimento," in *Studien zur Musikgeschichte. Eine Festschrift für Ludwig Finscher*, eds. Annegrit Laubenthal and Kara Kusan-Windweh (Kassel: Bärenreiter, 1995), 455.

Example 4.11 Five basic elements of the waltz

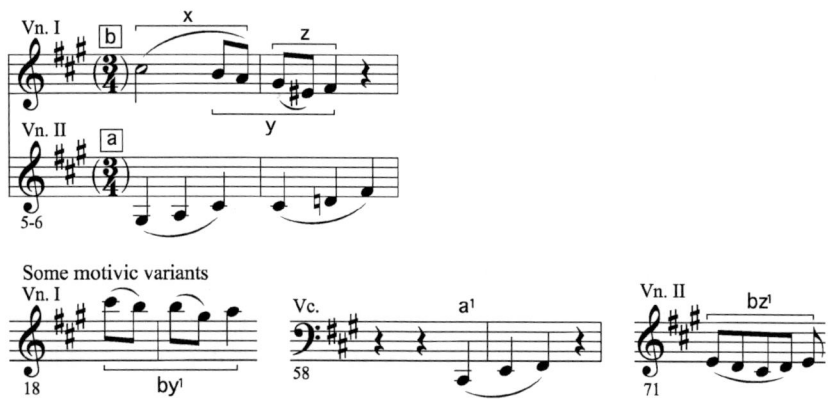

The composer intensifies the development with an accumulation of contrapuntal devices, especially canon and motivic combination. The concluding portion of the development is heightened by the repetition in the last 16-1/3 measures (mm. 54³-70) of Pby and y¹ in every measure.[54] Beethoven enhances the recapitulation not only by adding a motive to the Pa+b combination (the new motive perhaps derived from bz is anticipated in m. 70), but also by introducing three canons of bz (mm. 76-78, 80-82, 84-86). The coda in general recalls several elements of the movement, concentrating on Pb to the near-exclusion of Pa: the dialogue of Pby¹, the one-measure textural changes, the alteration of Pa, the canonic duet of Pb, the extension in canon of Pbz, and the combination of Pbx and z.

Ratner points out two rhythmic ambiguities in the waltz section: note one sounds like an upbeat rather than a downbeat, undoubtedly because of the leading-tone-tonic implication of the half-step motion of notes 1-2. Phrase b can also be heard in a larger 3/2 measure in hemiola, as the melody can be grouped in two-beat units over two measures.[55] Surely the performance of the movement should convey these rhythmic nuances.

Furthermore, in the development and coda, variants of Pa—retrograde inversion, and triadic and seventh-chord forms—shift from beat one to beat three (mm. 57³-63², 107³-109). The motive Pbz, as Kerman indicates, moves from the first to the second, weak beat, in the canons of the recapitulation.[56] Other hemiolas appear at the cadences of Part I (mm. 18-20)—see Ratner's outline—within the development (mm. 41-44), and before the recapitulation (mm. 69-70). Another typical effect is the weak second-beat cadences of Parts I and II, and the coda. Such rhythmic manipulation is typical of Beethoven, especially in the late period, while the implied shift of the barline one beat to the right links the waltz with the Allemande, where complete metrical displacement occurs.

---

[54] See also Chua, *The Galitzin Quartets*, 114.

[55] Ratner, *String Quartets*, 269. Chua, *The Galitzin Quartets*, 112-21, deals extensively with these metrical ambiguities.

[56] Kerman, *The Beethoven Quartets*, 251.

While Beethoven moves to the traditional dominant key of E at the end of Part I, he emphasizes the third-relationships of C and F in the development, both keys being important in other movements in the cycle, particularly the tonic F in movements I and III. Both are linked to A major through A minor, a key that appears near the end of the development. The A minor-major juxtaposition relates to other such appearances in the first movement and especially the finale, with its long A-major coda. The return to A major at the end of the development (mm. 67^3-70) precedes and thus overlaps with the recapitulation. Beethoven changes the key signature, dropping the sharps for the entire development, since the main keys are connected with A minor. This is an old device, found in a few early sonatas and the development of Op. 10, No. 3/I (see Ch. 2). The modulations are not dramatized but appear as smoothly as all other aspects of this section.

Another important feature is the frequent dissonant harmony on beat one of the waltz, as the first note is treated as a non-harmonic tone, usually as an appoggiatura-leading tone to note two (see mm. 5, 7, 9, 13, etc.). The canon of Pb also creates strong dissonances (mm. 28-30), as can the changing tones of bz (mm. 37-40, 45-50).

One of the main sources of variety in the waltz is the remarkable variation of texture throughout the movement. Beethoven combines the voices in unison, duet, trio, and tutti groupings of many different kinds. The speed of change (textural rhythm) also plays its part in the texture and structure.[57] Thus Part I has the simplest and most regular groupings: unison (mm. 1-4), violin duet (mm. 5-6), viola-cello duet (mm. 7-8), violin duet (mm. 9-10), upper trio (m. 11), mixed trio (vn. I, two lower parts, m. 12), lower trio (mm. 13-14), upper trio (mm. 15-20^2), tutti (mm. 20^3-22). The one-measure changes here occur with the cadence in E. The development, recapitulation, and coda contain more four-part writing, and more varied and contrapuntal combinations as well as more one-measure contrasts, which occur near the end of the development and coda especially. Thus, in mm. 56-68, the texture changes quickly on the one-measure level, together with the emphasis on by and by^1: mixed trio, upper trio, mixed trio, upper trio, lower trio, tutti, upper trio, dialogue between low and high duets in octaves. These changes produce considerable drive to the recapitulation. Four-part texture heralds the end of Part I, the development, Part II, and the coda. Richness of sonority especially marks the coda's use of four-part mirror writing with by^1 in one-measure modules to the beautiful cadence on the leading-tone seventh chord.

Critics have pointed out the initial half-step motive in Po that opens the movement, relating this idea to the opening of movement I and the basic half-step motive in the quartet as a whole. However, the half-step interval does not stop with the opening measure but saturates the waltz through the frequent appearance of Pa and notes 2-3 of bz. It saturates the Allemande as well (see below).

---

[57] See Schwindt-Gross,"Zwischen Kontrapunkt und Divertimento," 451-52 and a facsimile of the earliest score-sketch for the movement, Anhang 2, 456. For textural rhythm, see LaRue, *GSA*, 91-92.

STRING QUARTET

The Trio, Section A: The Musette

The trio (Ex. 4.12) transports us to another world of seeming simplicity and a different type of tranquility, one associated with the countryside and country folk. This portion of the movement does not have a rounded binary form like the waltz but a kind of ternary structure, since all sections are discrete and contrasting. In general, Beethoven treats the trio of a minuet or scherzo with greater freedom than the main part of the movement. In five of the last string quartets, excluding Op. 130, as well as the trio of the Piano Sonata Op. 110, he abandons binary form entirely.

Section A is a musette, or rather, in musette style. It is based on a long pedal point on the tonic A of 22 measures. In section A^1, the return of the musette at the end of the trio, the same pedal lasts 17 measures. The sections have the phrase structure as shown in Table 4.11.[58]

Table 4.11 Timeline of the Musette

					(a)	(a^1)
A	Po	a	a^1	o^1	a^2	a^3
	119^3	122^3	126^3	130^3	133^3	137^3-41^2
	A major, I ped.					

		(a^2)	(a^3)	(ay^1,o^3)
A^1	Po^2	a^4	a^5	ext.
	221^3	224^3	228^3	232^3-38
	I ped.			

The phrase lengths include odd and even phrases, in A: 3+4+4 measures, and in A^1: 3+4++4+6 measures, with a typical phrase extension of six measures before an important cadence, here at the end of the trio. The three-measure and six-measure phrases are the only irregular phrases in the entire trio. Section A has an internal repeat, which is enriched by a tutti sonority versus the violin duo in the first presentation. In the return of A, the texture is further elaborated and expanded. We might call this procedure a theme and two variations, but the variations affect mainly the sound element, the texture, which becomes richer and more complex.

What strikes the listener most of all is the enchanting sonority, one of many such remarkable creations in late Beethoven. The first violin, high on the E-string, touches on the highest note of the movement, a^3, and plays the open A-string as a drone as well. Violin II, in eighth notes, doubles the melody a tenth below with an upper pedal on a^2. The first violin starts slowly, with a series of upbeats outlining the tonic sixth chord while alternating with the open A-string—this I call Po, an introductory phrase. The second violin enters at the first violin climax with a rising eighth-note arpeggio on the tonic (rising a

---

[58] I call the musette theme P in contrast to the dance that follows, which I designate as S.

Example 4.12 Second movement, trio (mm.119³-283) (c by G. Henle Verlag, Munich, used by permission)

twelfth, a-e²)—a free diminution. At the start of the repeat of the period, the arpeggio motive enters in all three lower voices one by one in imitation at the lower octave. The tutti drones that follow spread over four octaves, giving an extraordinary fullness of sound. This setting makes a brilliant contrast to the contrapuntal waltz.

A¹ returns with an even richer resonance since the viola doubles the violin II melody an octave below. This recall ends with the arpeggio motive in a closing function. It is heard three times, descending three octaves in the second violin and cello. Beethoven enhances the sound with a new gradual *crescendo* of 9-1/3 measures (m. 224³-33), starting with Pa, and then decreasing the dynamic level to *pp* for the last four beats, a totally new effect.

Several other long drones also appear in late Beethoven trio sections: the trio in the Ninth Symphony/II, Part II and coda; the first and third themes in the trio of the quartet Op. 131/V; and the spectacular central ostinato-drone in the trio of the last quartet Op. 135/II. A notable predecessor is the drone in the trio of the Seventh Symphony/III (1811-12). All produce strong contrast by evoking the folk style and are combined with simple, repetitive melodies. Beethoven's obvious models for such drone effects and folk-like melodies are the symphonies and quartets of Haydn, like the trio in Haydn's Symphony No. 88/III (?1787) and String Quartet Op. 76 No. 4/III (1797).

All is *legato* or sustained in this section. The melodic line of P, in quarters and eighths, hovers almost entirely around only four notes in the span $c\#^3$-$f\#^3$, the small range another folk-like trait, as is the omission of the leading tone in the entire section.[59] Three measures from the very end of A¹ Beethoven shifts the barline in a written-out *ritard*, achieved by grouping the beats 2+3+4 on the final sustained A-major chord. As so often in the quartet, the only moving line, here in the cello, ends on the last beat of the measure.

The musette also bears some resemblance (though not literal) to the first four measures of an early *Deutsche Tanz* for orchestra, WoO 8, No. 8 (1795) (see Ex. 4.13),[60] while the Ländler-like B section that follows is a literal borrowing (see below).

Sections B and C: the Allemande and Grotesque Dance

The static musette is followed by the active Allemande, moving in steady eighths in perpetual motion. This deceptively simple Austrian dance type consists of 64 measures organized in a strict succession of sixteen four-measure phrases. The pattern continues for another sixteen measures with a brusque new theme in C-sharp minor and unison texture (called a bear dance by Kerman)[61] which carries the action back to the musette.

---

[59] Basil Lam, *Beethoven, String Quartets 2*, BBC Guides (London: BBC, 1975): 25.

[60] However, the first four measures reproduced in Chua,*The Galitzin Quartets*, 121, contain several errors, including the highest notes, which do not duplicate the musette in the original dance. The upbeat is missing and the *sforzandos* appear on beat one instead of beat 2. The WoO number is not WoO 13 but WoO 8. A more correct version appears on 133 but still with the incorrect placement of the *sforzandos*. See the edition by Shin Augustinus Kojima, *Beethoven, Gratulationsmenuett und Tänze für Orchester, Beethoven Werke*, Abt. II, Bd. 3 (Munich: G. Henle, 1990).

[61] Kerman, *The Beethoven Quartets*, 252.

Example 4.13 Deutsche Tanz, WoO 8, No. 8 (1795) (mm.1-4)

All the phrases in the Allemande come from an early dance in A major and 3/8 meter. It appears on a Beethoven sketchleaf dated by Douglas Johnson c. 1793-early 1794, a dance that Beethoven never published. There are two version of the melody; the trio in A minor that follows the melody was not revised or re-used by Beethoven (see Plate 4.I). The original version of the melody on staves 1-4 is fairly clear except for phrase b beginning Part II (mm. 9-12). This phrase, as Sieghard Brandenburg observed in a letter to the writer, is repeatedly worked over in pencil and ink. In much later revisions, Beethoven added the title "Allemande" and also an indication "allemandenmässig," as well as the performance instruction "leggiermente." He also added harmonic fillers in the left hand, and first and second endings for each reprise of the dance (see Exx. 4.14 and 4.15).[62]

Gustav Nottebohm, the 19th-century expert on Beethoven's sketches, transcribed the revised version, which was then published in the Supplement of the old Beethoven *Gesamtausgabe*. It is identified as WoO 81 in the Kinsky-Halm Beethoven catalogue. Arnold Schmitz, who published the facsimile, transcribed the original version but included some features of the revision, such as the filler notes in Reprise I, as well as the title and performance indication.

Brandenburg believes the reworking originated in the winter of 1822/23 with relation to compiling Bagatelles 1-6 for the Op. 119 set after Nos. 7-11 had been published in Vienna in 1821. For these six new additions, which were published in London toward the end of 1823, Beethoven looked through several old sketches, that Barry Cooper calls his "Portfolio of Bagatelles." Nos. 1-5 were chosen from these early sketches dating c. 1794-1802, but they did not include WoO 81.[63]

This project explains why Beethoven could have had in hand such an early piece, written over thirty years before, for use in Op. 132. Actually, in Beethoven's late period he occasionally drew on earlier material, as is well known. Besides the use of early pieces in Op. 119 and the Allemande in Op. 132,

---

[62] I am very grateful to Sieghard Brandenburg for examining the leaf with the Allemande, in the Beethoven-Archiv in Bonn, BH 114, and for transcribing the original version of the dance. In his letter to the writer, Brandenburg suggested the late date for the revised version (see the discussion that follows). A facsimile of the leaf with the Allemande was published by Arnold Schmitz, *Beethoven: Unbekannte Skizzen und Entwürfe. Untersuchung, Übertragung, Faksimile*, Veröffentlichungen des Beethovenhauses in Bonn III (Bonn: Kurt Schroeder, 1924). The date for the leaf is given by Douglas Johnson, *Beethoven's Early Sketches*, I,45, where the leaf has the number SBH 631 (Schmitz mistakenly dates the sketches c. 1800). Beethoven wrote 37 dances called "ländlerische" or "deutsche" Tänze in the period c,1792-1802. All are in 3/4. The Allemande's revised version was also edited by Willy Hess, *Beethoven: Leichte Klavierkompositionen* (Zurich: Pelikan, 1946), and more accurately by Robert Forster, Beethoven, *Tänze für Klavier* (Munich: G. Henle, 1990).

[63] See Barry Cooper, "Beethoven's Portfolio of Bagatelles," *Journal of the Royal Musical Association* 112 (1987a): 208-28.

Plate 4.1 BEETHOVEN SKETCHLEAF, BH 114, Beethoven-Haus, Bonn. THE ALLEMANDE WoO 81 APPEARS ON STAVES 1-4, AND A FURTHER REWORKING OF PHRASE B ON STAVES 15-16. A DIFFERENT TRIO IS FOUND ON STAVES 3-6.

he took a sketch for the slow movement of the Violin Sonata Op. 30, No. 1, found in the Kessler Sketchbook of 1801-02 and turned it into the primary theme of the Op. 111 Piano Sonata, first movement, dated 1821-22. And, as Beethoven himself wrote in a few letters, he modeled the *finale* of the Ninth Symphony on the Choral Fantasy of 1808. Further, as mentioned earlier, the primary theme of the *finale* of Op. 132 was first intended for an instrumental *finale* of the Ninth Symphony and is found in at least three early versions among the sketches for the symphony dated 1823/24. As we learn from studying Beethoven's sketches, Beethoven did not like to waste his ideas.

The original version of the Allemande WoO 81, without its trio, was reused by Beethoven three times, in one of many examples of Beethoven's reuse of themes and pieces, a process that has been the subject of several studies.[64] The Allemande found its way first into the Piano Trio Op.1, No.2, slow move-

---

[64] A full discussion of the reuse of the Allemande is given in Leilani K. Lutes, "Beethoven's Re-uses of His Own Compositions, 1782-1826" (Ph.D. dissertation, University of Southern California, 1975), 231-47. The reuse in the piano trio and orchestral dance is also discussed in Ludwig Misch, *Neue Beethoven-Studien und anderen Themen*, Beethovenhaus, Bonn (Munich: G. Henle, 1967), 96-99.

ment, composed in 1794-95, where the original b phrase is the start of the primary theme's b phrase and the first portion of the transition—the meter is 6/8. A few years later, in c. 1798, Beethoven transferred the second reprise to the second reprise in No. 11 of 12 German dances for orchestra, WoO 13—the meter is 3/4. Finally, Beethoven incorporated the Allemande, also in 3/4, into the trio of his quartet Op. 132.

Let us look at the original version of the Allemande in A major (see Ex. 4.14). It has a simple binary form, each part repeated. Each reprise contains two four-measure phrases, making a sixteen-measure dance, 8+8 measures. The reprises differ strongly. Reprise I has a parallel period that we can label as a+a^1. The phrases start with the same rising arpeggio on I and falling arpeggio on V^7, coming to a half cadence on V, with a slight melodic change in a^1 ending Reprise I. The harmony alternates I and V. Reprise I has the largest melodic range of the dance, two octaves, and the highest note, e^3.

Phrases b and c in Reprise II provide a marked contrast to Reprise I. The b phrase has a descending sequence introducing a secondary dominant, with V^6/ii-ii going to V^6-I, and phrase c makes the final cadence with quickened harmonic rhythm and subdominant chords. Melodically, the two phrases are connected by the predominant half-step motive found at the start of each measure except the last; in four cases the half-step comes by way of a chromatically raised neighbor note which is then cancelled on note 4 or 6, inflecting the melodic line with further chromatic action. The range of part II just barely exceeds an octave and the effective climax in phrase c only reaches a^2.

Example 4.14 The original version of the Allemande, WoO 81, Beethoven-Haus Bonn, BH 114 (c. 1793-94), transcribed by Sieghard Brandenburg

Example 4.15 A modern edition of the revised Allemande (ed. Robert Forster, c 1990, by G. Henle Verlag, Munich, used by permission)

Despite the contrast between the two reprises, some unifying elements exist as well, including the steady surface rhythm in sixteenth notes, the descending scale motive in phrase a that recurs in phrase b and in rising form in phrase c, and the harmonic rhythm with one chord per measure throughout the dance, speeding up only in mm. 14-15 for the final cadence. Further, the V-I progressions in phrase b reverse the I-V alternation in Reprise I.

How did Beethoven treat this modest early dance in the complex style of his last years? First, in the spirit of the *ars combinatoria* Beethoven reversed the original phrase order: phrases a-b-c appear in the order b-c-a.[65] Starting with phrases b and c highlights the half-step motives found in these phrases, and links them with the rising half-steps that dominate the contrapuntal waltz and the basic half-step motive integrating the entire quartet. In the revised version of the b phrase, the half-steps are far less prominent and so this version was less appropriate. The start of the new closing phrase c also picks up the rising tonic arpeggio of a twelfth at the start of the musette, thus integrating the Allemande with the musette as well.

---

[65] For the *ars combinatoria*, see Ratner, *CM*, 98-102; and his basic article, "*Ars Combinatoria*: Chance and Choice in Eighteenth-Century Music," in: *Studies in Eighteenth-Century Music: A Tribute to Karl Geiringer on his Seventieth Birthday*, ed. H. C. Robbins Landon in collaboration with Roger E. Chapman (London: Allen and Unwin, 1970), 343-63. The *ars combinatoria* "deals with the number of different ways in which a given quantity of objects may be arranged according to a given set of conditions" (*CM*, 98).

STRING QUARTET

In a major alternation, the Allemande features extensive metrical displacement, as Beethoven moves the barline one beat to the left so that beat 3 becomes beat 1 (Ex. 4.16). This all-encompassing displacement in both melody and harmony is adjusted back to the normal 3/4 meter, five times at increasingly closer time spans in mm. 147, 171, 191, 199, and 203.[66] The adjustment is effected via an extra beat repetition of the half-step motive from measure 1, beat 3, in the new phrase b, thus adjusting the meter for the cadence on the tonic and creating a temporary four-beat measure.

In addition to metrical displacement, Beethoven plays with the form and key, as well as the number, ordering, and scoring of the phrases, and even the pattern of crescendos. Thus, the entire dance setting is imbued with the spirit of the *ars combinatoria* (see Table 4.12 on p. 332).

The Allemande is no longer organized in binary form but in three large periods I identify as S, S^1, and S^2. The melody actually starts in the dominant key of E major, but a^2 dips down into A major, as its subdominant. S^1 starts again in E, but A major returns permanently with a^4 and the repeated c phrases, thus tonally overlapping S^1 and S^2. S contains six phrases, but S^1 and S^2 have five. The repetition of the phrases both within and among the three periods seems unpredictable. The periods and phrases make the following pattern (see Table 4.12). In S, phrases a and c are repeated, in S^1, only c is repeated, and in S^2, phrase b repeats in place of phrase c, which is omitted. All three periods start, however, with the phrases a-b-a. Beethoven places the new phrase c at the end of S and S^1 to keep these periods open harmonically, since the phrase ends on V, like the old phrase a. On the other hand, he repeats phrase b at the end of S^2 to emphasize closure on the tonic for the dance, since this was the old c phrase ending the Allemande. As a result, the concluding phrases of the periods produce a large-scale V-V-I pattern. The only emphasized cadence is the last, since the motion is unbroken throughout the dance.

Example 4.16 Metrical displacement of the Allemande, return to normal metrical accents, and reversion to metrical displacement (mm. 141^3-150^2)

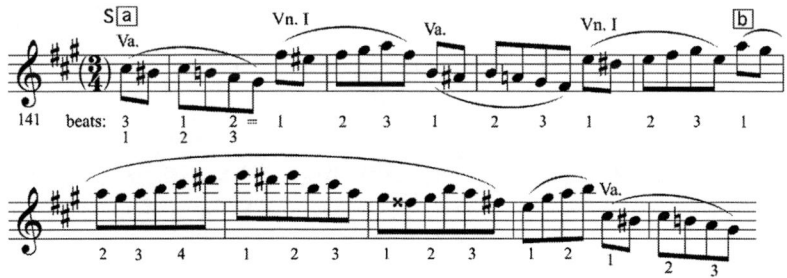

[66] Ratner, *String Quartets*, 268.

Table 4.12 Timeline of the Allemande

	(a)					
S	a	b	a¹	a²	c	c
	141³	145³	149³	153³	157³	161³
	E			A	E	
S¹	a³	b¹	a⁴	c¹	c²	
	165³	169³	173³	177³	181³	
	E		A			
S²	a⁵	b²	a⁶	b³	b⁴	
	185³	189³	193³	197³	201³	
	A					

Beethoven made only one slight melodic change in the new c phrase. He altered the sequential repetition in m. 4 to a simple descending scale by replacing the leading tone on note one by the third degree of the scale—g♯¹ is replaced by c♯² above (in A major). In this way, Beethoven highlights the sequence in the new b phrase, which becomes the only sequence in the dance.[67]

Another aspect of variation concerns the scoring, which differs in nearly every phrase. The scoring of phrase a in general has the greatest variety (see Table 4.13). Each of the six presentations of phrase a contains a different instrumental setting and includes hocket-like dialogues in the subphrases. The most elaborate setting of this phrase occurs at the start of S² (it is a⁵ in the table), where subphrases are harmonized in sixths, sixth chords, and mirror harmony rather than the previous octave doublings, the number of voices being 2-3-2-4. It is the only time in the dance that an entire phrase occurs without accompaniment. All b and c phrases are played by a solo instrument: b, violin I-viola-violin I; and c, viola, violin I, violin I. Only the last appearance of phrase a is heard in violin I solo, and violin I alone performs phrases 2-5 in S² as a culminating effect. These phrases have the longest *crescendo* in the Allemande—8 measures – leading to the only *forte* of the Allemande before a sudden drop to *piano* for the very end of the dance. Phrase b⁴ concludes the dance partly an octave higher and reaches the highest range in the Allemande together with the brief *forte* dynamic.

Reference to the *crescendo* leads to the consideration of dynamics in the dance. The original Allemande had no dynamic indications. Here, the dance starts *pp* for its first three phrases and thereafter has a simple *p* level, enhanced by four highly-organized *crescendos*. The first three *crescendos* end in *piano* as the *forte* culmination is deferred until near the end of the dance. *Crescendos* appear in mm. 153³, 173³, 190¹, and 193¹. The first three decrease in length: 4 mm., 3 mm., 1 m., the second effect indicated as a "poco crescendo." If we omit the short *crescendo* in m. 190, the *crescendo* occurs every 20 measures, the short

---

[67] Beethoven made only a few local harmonic changes, such as replacing IV by V at the start of the new b phrase (mm. 145-46), and especially replacing root position resolutions in the new phrase a by first inversions, so that the leading tone in the bass leaps up to the third of the chord, a typical late freedom in voice leading (see mm. 149³-153¹).

Table 4.13 Different Scorings of Sa

S	a	alternation of va. and vn. I
	a^1	alternation of va. and vn. II+va. (octaves)
	a^2	alternation of vn. I+va. (octaves) and vn. II+vc. (octaves)
S^1	a^3	like a^1 but vc. an octave higher, vn. I higher and paired with vc. in 10ths (in the accompaniment)
	a^4	alternation of vn. I+va. (octaves) and vn. I
S^2	a^5	alternation of vc.+va. (par. sixths and mirror) and vn. I+vn. II+va. (par. sixth chords and mirror)—vn. II+va. (par. sixths and mirror) and tutti (chordal and mirror)
	a^6	vn. I only

crescendo in m. 190 acting as a kind of anticipation of the long *crescendo* of 8 mm. nearly three measures later. The longest *crescendo* of all in the return of the Musette—9-1/4 measures, thus also extends the long *crescendo* ending the Allemande, further relating the sections in this way.

The regular beat of the dance comes from the new staccato quarter notes in the non-melodic parts, a kind of thumping accompaniment that seems deliberately crude in contrast to the lilting melody. Truly, the Allemande is another of those examples by Beethoven of how to make something out of nothing. The variations in texture in the musette and Allemande, and the long metrical displacements in the Allemande especially characterize the late style, when Beethoven achieved a new richness of treatment, particularly in sound and rhythm.

The Allemande ends with a rising arpeggio from phrase c, which overlaps the upbeats to a strange and dramatic N (new) theme in C♯ minor, a shocking interruption of the seeming endless dance. This primitive-sounding theme is set in bare octaves, at first in the low range of the viola and cello. Its long notes in dotted halves and quarters effect a drastic slowdown in surface rhythm and reassert metrical regularity. The theme provides the most extensive minor-mode color in the trio. Though it sounds disrelated thematically, N does contain a descending three-note figure also found in the musette (mm. 208, 216), and the musette starts on the same note ending the N theme, c♯. Set *forte*, with *sforzandos* on the long notes, the eight-measure theme is repeated with the addition of the second violin. The first violin overlaps the start of the repeat with a vastly expanded arpeggio ascending three octaves, which also anticipates the return of the musette seven measures later. A variation of the cadential phrase of N^1 occurs with a change of meter to ¢, recalling such "strategic changes in motion" found in the scherzos of the *Eroica* Symphony (mm. 381-84) and String Quartet Op. 127 (mm. 70-80).[68] These examples introduce an almost violent contrast in expression as well. After N^1, the return of the musette restores a heightened tranquility.

---

[68] For the quotation, see Ratner, *String Quartets*, 269.

The three strongly contrasted elements of the trio—musette, Allemande, grotesque dance— could well fit a dramatic scene in the theater or a ballet. I will close with Theodor Helm's reference to the trio (but surely with the Allemande in mind) from his book on the Beethoven string quartets. Here is his late 19th-century view of this section (he calls the movement as a whole an intermezzo):

> ... the effect of the intermezzo's contrasting middle section at first hearing in the original medium is electrifying, astonishing. We have seen it happen more than once that given the right temperament for the performance of the movement ... a whole audience was swept up with the composer in a sort of Bacchanalian frenzy. [69]

The Third Movement: *Molto adagio-Andante*

The subject of Beethoven and program music is a broad one, needing a comprehensive study well beyond the limits of this chapter. Two of Beethoven's friends and students made well-known remarks regarding Beethoven's often pictorial imagination. In the early biographical volume by Franz Wegeler and Ferdinand Ries, Ries wrote:

> When composing, Beethoven frequently had a certain subject [einen bestimmsten Gegenstand] in mind, even though he often laughed at and inveighed against descriptive music, particularly of the frivolous sort.[70]

Carl Czerny stated:

> "It is certain that, in many of his finest works, Beethoven was inspired by ... visions and images, drawn either from reading or created by his own excited imagination, and we should obtain the real key to his compositions and to their performance only through the thorough knowledge of these circumstances, if this were always practicable. [71]

Czerny also observed that Beethoven "knew that music is not always so freely felt by the hearers, when a definitely *expressed* object has already fettered their imagination."[72] Owen Jander tries to fathom Beethoven's descriptive images in works without title or verbal indications. Most famous is his detailed Orpheus program for the Fourth Piano Concerto (especially the second movement).[73] For his dialogue plan relating to the *Larghetto* of the Violin Concerto, see the reference in Ch. 1, p.50, n. 64.

Of the twelve works with titles (all but WoO 54 were published; see Table 4.14), most reflect Beethoven's words regarding the "Pastoral" Symphony: "more an expression of feeling than painting." Such titles include *Sonate pathé-*

---

[69] Helm, *Beethoven's Streichquartette*, trans. Bent, 255.
[70] *Beethoven Remembered, The Biographical Notes of Franz Wegeler and Ferdinand Ries*, trans. Frederick Noonan, from *Biographische Notizen über Ludwig van Beethoven*, Koblenz, 1838, 1845 (Arlington, VA: Great Ocean Publishers, 1987), 67-68.
[71] Czerny, *On the Proper Performance*, Ch. II, 60.
[72] Czerny, loc. cit.
[73] See his articles "Beethoven's 'Orpheus in Hades': The *Andante con moto* of the Fourth Piano Concerto," *19th Century Music* 8 (1985): 195-212; and "Orpheus Revisited," *19th Century Music* 19 (1995): 31-49.

tique, La Malinconia, Sinfonia Eroica, and *Quartetto serioso* (the adjective found only on the autograph, not in the first edition). Four quartets include titles; seven programmatic examples appear in the middle period and only three in Beethoven's late years. The most pictorial of Beethoven's instrumental works is surely the orchestral work *Wellington's Victory*, or *The Battle of Vittoria,* Op. 91 (1813), battle music in a long tradition extending back to the Renaissance.

Table 4. 14 Programmatic Works and Movements (Excluding Sketch References and Overtures to Dramatic Works)

1. *Sonate pathétique* for piano, Op. 13 (1797-98)[74]
2. String Quartet, Op. 18, No. 6/IV: slow introduction entitled "La Malinconia" (1799-1800)[75]
3. Piano Sonata Op. 26/III: "Marcia funebre sulla morte d'un Eroe" (1800-01)
4. Bagatelle for piano, WoO 54 (unpublished): "Lustig-Traurig" (?1802)
5. *Sinfonia eroica,* Op. 55, including as movement II: "Marcia funebre" (1803)
6. *Sinfonia pastorale,* Op. 68. Each movement has a title: I, "Erwachen heiterer Empfindungen bei der Ankunft auf dem Lande"; II, "Szene am Bach"; III, "Lustiges Zusammensein der Landleute"; IV, "Gewitter, Sturm"; V, "Hirtengesang, Frohe und dankbare Gefühle nach dem Sturm". On the first performance parts and the handbill handed out at the first performance: "Mehr Ausdruck der Empfindung als Malerei" (1808)
7. Piano Sonata *Das Lebewohl,* Op. 81a. Three movements: "Lebewohl," " Abwesenheit," "Wiedersehen" (1809-10)
8. "Quartetto serioso," Op. 95 (1810-11)
9. *Wellingtons Sieg oder die Schlacht bei Vittoria,* Op. 91 (1813)
10. Piano Sonata Op. 110/III, IV. Inscription on movement III: "Klagender Ge sang"; on its return, "Ermattet, klagend"; second part of the fugue in movement IV: "Nach und nach wieder auflebend" (1821-22)
11. String Quartet Op. 132/III: "Heiliger Dankgesang eines Genesenen an die Gottheit, in der lydischen Tonart"—"Neue Kraft fühlend" (1825)
12. String Quartet Op. 135/IV "Der schwer gefasste Entschluss": "Muss es sein? Es muss sein!" (1826)[76]

Like all the main slow movements of Beethoven's late quartets except Op. 130, the *Adagio* in Op. 132 is in variation form. However, it is the only example in all the quartets that follows the variation format developed by Haydn

---

[74] See Elaine R. Sisman, "Pathos and the Pathétique: Rhetorical Stance in Beethoven's C-Minor Sonata, Op. 13," *Beethoven Forum* 3 (1994), 81-105.

[75] See the discussion of Op. 10, No. 3/II (Ch. 2).

[76] The translation of the titles follow: for No. 1, "Sonata in the pathetic style;" No. 2, 'Melancholy;" No. 3, "Funeral march on the death of a hero;" No. 4, "Merry-Sad;" No. 5, "Heroic Symphony, Funeral March;" No. 6, Pastoral Symphony: I. "Awakening of happy feelings on arrival in the countryside;" II. "Scene by the brook;" III. Merry gatherings of the country people;" IV. "Thunder, Storm;" V. Shepherd's Song. Joyful and grateful feelings after the storm;" No. 7, 'The Farewell, Absence, Reunion;" No. 8, "Serious Quartet;" No. 9, "Wellington's Victory, or the Battle of Vittoria;" No. 10, "Threnody—exhausted, lamenting—gradually revived;" No. 11 (see p. 290); No. 12, "The difficult decision, Must it be? It must be!" The translation of the titles in the Sixth Symphony largely comes from Jones, *Beethoven: Pastoral Symphony.*

called "alternating variation" by Sisman.[77] This type of variation movement contains two themes that alternate, creating a form that can be symbolized as: A-B-A¹-B¹-A² (coda). In Haydn's examples, as in Symphony No. 103/II (1795), the themes are usually contrasted in mode and motivically connected.

Beethoven associated this form mainly with the symphony, where examples occur in Symphonies Nos. 3/IV, 5/II, 7/II, and 9/III, as well as in the Piano Trio Op. 70, No. 2/II and this string quartet. In Symphonies Nos. 5 and 9 the second theme is in a distant key a third apart: in No. 5, E♭-C and in No. 9, B♭-D, B♭-G. All movements are slow except the *finale* of the *Eroica*, which utilizes the bass and its treble in a unique transformation of the Haydn model.

Except for the variations in Op. 70 and the Seventh Symphony, both themes are in the major mode, though in the process of variation one of the themes can shift to the minor, as in the Fifth Symphony, first theme (setting in a♭). In the Ninth Symphony, the two themes also contrast in meter and tempo as well as variation technique, as in Op. 132. These two final variation sets thus have much in common, including the contrast of hymn and dance, duple vs. triple meter.

Aspects of Gross Form

Strong contrasts between the two themes reflect their programmatic headings (see the timeline, Table 4.15 on facing page). P is a heartfelt prayer of thanksgiving in chorale style and S a joyful, active, dance-like section that reflects its programmatic inscription "feeling new life." The faster tempo (*Andante* vs. *Molto adagio*) and meter (3/8 vs. c) underscore the change of mood, as does the shift from the mystical Lydian mode to the clear and bright major mode on D. The third relation mirrors such relationships especially in the first movement, and in the Fifth and Ninth symphonies. Further, the themes differ strongly in structure, the through-composed chorale as against a small two-reprise form with concluding (K) section or coda (as Ratner calls it). Variation starts immediately in S where Beethoven varies each of the two reprises rather than literally repeating each unit, an example of double variation so important in the other late variation movements in the quartets Opp. 127 and 131.

Each theme receives one formal variation, intensifying through dissonance and range in the chorale, and rich ornamentation in S, as well as rhythmic acceleration in both themes. The final section, which has been called a fugato by Ratner and coda by Brandenburg, contains features of both. Based solely on the first chorale phrase and transformation of its introductory melody, this intensively imitative section creates the greatest climax of the movement and, one might say, of the quartet itself.

---

[77] See Elaine R. Sisman, *Haydn*, 152-62, 246-49, 254-62, with detailed discussions of Beethoven's Piano Trio, Op. 70, No. 2/II and the *Eroica finale*.

Table 4.15 Timeline: Movement III

Theme A (P): Chorale   Mode: Lydian   Meter: ¢
               (ar)   (ar)   (ar)
| a^0 a | b^0 b | b^{01} c | b^{02} d | a^{01} d^1 | T |
| 0^3 2^3 | 6^3 8^3 | 12^3 14^3 | 18^3 20^3 | 24^3 26^3 | 30 | 30 mm. |

cadences: vi   C:I   C:V   F:I   d:V

Theme B(S): Dance-like Key: D major   Meter: 3/8
Form: two-reprise form with varied repeats (double variation) and closing period

| 1Sa b | $1S^1$ | 2Sa b c | $2S^1$ | Ka a^1 b c c^1 | RT |
| 31 36^2 39 | 47 | 51 55 57 | 67 | 71 75 77 79 | 81^2-84^{2-3} 53 1/2 mm. |

cadences: V   V   I   I   I mod. F

Theme A^1 (with T):   mm. 84^3-114   Variation
Theme B^1 (with RT):   mm. 115-68^3 Variation
Theme A^2 mm. $168^{3.5}$-211   Contrapuntal development and climax

THE CHORALE THEME

The chorale setting, its variation, and its apotheosis reflect Beethoven's deep interest in contrapuntal forms and techniques in this period. The many fugues, fugatos, canons, and examples of non-imitative counterpoint as well as double counterpoint well illustrate this signal feature of the late style, as does the renewed and culminating treatment of variation form.

Beethoven's familiarity with the traditional chorale settings and theoretical writings about it has been thoroughly documented by Brandenburg in his brilliant and rich article, "The Historical Background to the 'Heiliger Dankgesang' in Beethoven's A-minor Quartet Op. 132."[78] Beethoven also suggested working out chorale settings to his composition student, the Archduke Rudolph, to whom he wrote on 1 July 1823: "You should also compose without a piano; and you should sometimes work out a simple melody, for instance, a chorale with simple and again different [figures] according to the laws of counterpoint and even neglecting the latter."[79] This was a prophetic statement, almost a description of Beethoven's approach to the "Heiliger Dankgesang" less than two years later.

---

[78] See *Beethoven Studies* 3, ed. Alan Tyson, 161-91. Many examples are given of sketches for the chorale section and from treatises dealing with chorale settings. The most important of such treatises are by J. H. Knecht, *Vollständige Orgelschule für Anfänger und Geübtere*, 3 vols. (Leipzig: in der Breitkopfischen Musikhandlung, 1795, 1796, 1798) and D. G. Türk, *Von den wichtigsten Pflichten eines Organisten: ein Beytrag zur Verbesserung der Musikalischen Liturgie* (Halle und Leipzig: Schwickert, 1787). These and two other treatises by Türk (1791) and G. J. Vogler (1800) were in Beethoven's library. For Beethoven's use of hymn-like melodies in his late works, see the discussion of Op. 96/II in Ch. 3.
[79] Translations from Anderson, III, No. 1203 . See BGA, 5, No. 1686.

Nearly every aspect of the chorale theme reflects standard procedures (see below). The less typical selection of the Lydian mode may be further explained by its connection with the second key area of the exposition in movement I. Moreover, so many of Beethoven's works in minor move to the submediant major for the slow movement, a preference found also in the Op. 131 quartet for the variation movement.[80] Of all the modes, the Lydian was least popular in the late eighteenth century because of its b♮-b♭ problem. The standard solution to avoid the tritone f-b by lowering the b to b♭ transformed the mode to Ionian, thereby erasing its unique modal pattern.[81]

Beethoven added the reference to the Lydian mode only on the autograph, after the parts were copied,[82] thus clarifying the melodic-harmonic organization of a large part of the movement. The style of the chorale prelude, after all, was associated with organ music, not music for string quartet.

Kirkendale has suggested that the choice of the Lydian mode was influenced by Zarlino's reference to the mode as "a remedy for fatigue of the soul, and similarly for that of the body."[83] However, there are good, purely musical reasons for the choice of mode, as noted above, and, as Brandenburg points out, Beethoven was already a "convalescent."[84]

Beethoven's interest in the modes went back several years, especially to the period just preceding and during work on the *Missa solemnis*, 1818-20. In 1818, he noted on a sketchleaf plans for an "Adagio Cantique" or a "Cantique Ecclesiastique—A pious song in a symphony in the old modes, Lord God we praise thee—alleluja."[85] On another sheet, with excerpts he copied out from fugue treatises, Beethoven wrote: "The devotion in the old church music is divine, I called out, and God allow me to produce it some day.[86] In another entry of 1818, this time in Beethoven's *Tagebuch*, the composer notes: "In order to write true church music, go through all the liturgical chant of the monks."[87] Refer-

---

[80] Some earlier examples are the Piano and Violin Sonatas in C minor, Op. 10, No. 1, Op. 13, and Op. 30, No. 2, the Piano Sonata, Op. 57, and the Fifth and Ninth Symphonies.

[81] Beethoven's interest in the old church style is shown by his copy of a *Gloria Patri* in the Lydian mode by Palestrina. The copy, however, was made from an altered, modernized version with all the b-naturals changed to b-flats by Johann Friedrich Reichardt, who published the work in keyboard reduction in the second volume of his *Musikalisches Kunstmagazin* (Berlin, 1791), 19. See Richard Kramer, "In Search of Palestrina: Beethoven in the Archives," in *Haydn, Mozart, and Beethoven: Studies in the Music of the Classical Period. Essays in Honour of Alan Tyson*, 284-85 and 283-300 for the entire article. Beethoven copied another work attributed to Palestrina, a *Pueri Hebraeorum*, in c. 1826. This significant article considers the available information regarding Beethoven's interest in the church modes in his late period.

[82] Brandenburg, "Historical Background," 167.

[83] Warren Kirkendale, "New Roads to Old Ideas in Beethoven's *Missa Solemnis*," MQ 56 (1970): 677; reprint in *The Creative World of Beethoven*, ed. Paul Henry Lang (New York: Norton, 1970), 175.

[84] Brandenburg, "Historical Background," 167, fn. 9.

[85] Ibid., 169. See also N II, 163.

[86] Kramer, "In Search of Palestrina," 294. Kramer indicates that the leaves may well date from 1818 and 1819 (299).

[87] Kramer, ibid., 299. See also the corrected translation of Beethoven's Tagebuch in Maynard Solomon's *Beethoven Essays* (Cambridge, MA: Harvard University Press, 1988), 294; and his presentation of the German text, *Beethovens Tagebuch*, ed. Sieghard Brandenburg (Mainz: v. Hase & Koehler Verlag, 1990), 121.

ences to Zarlino's treatise also occur slightly later in the conversation books of December 1819 and January 1820.[88] Beethoven did introduce modal writing in the *Missa solemnis*: the Dorian mode for the "Et incarnates est" and the Mixoloydian mode for the *a cappella* "Et resurrexit," references to the two miraculous occurrences in the Mass text.

The treatises that Brandenburg cites show how strongly Beethoven was bound to contemporary practice in the chorale sections. The following traits were standard features: (1) the ideal of simplicity; (2) solemnity; (3) slow tempo; (4) motion in half notes and *alla breve* meter (though Beethoven used C meter); (5) preference for modal melody; (6) the unaltered melody; (7) note-against-note setting in the lower parts; (8) four-part harmonization; (9) use of richly varied secondary triads; (10) use of *crescendo-diminuendo* effects; (11) accompaniment varied from verse to verse; (12) use of brief interludes between phrases, ending with an anticipation of the first note of the chorale. Though it was conventional to present the chorale melodies in uniform half notes, this rhythm of the "Heiliger Dankgesang" also connects with the introduction of the first movement.

Melody and Dynamics (Ex. 4.17)

The chorale melody contains five phrases in the order: a-b-c-d-d^1, the last phrase a varied repeat of phrase four. Each phrase is typically four measures in length. The total range is only an octave but the outer notes are not the expected f^1-f^2 but d^1-d^2, closer to Hypolydian than Lydian, which, however, is usually situated a fourth below the Lydian, its range being c^1-c^2. The irregular emphasis on d rather than on f and c (the final and dominant of the Lydian mode) helps connect the melody with the contrasting section in D major.

Each phrase expands in range as the melody grows in intensity, slightly decreasing in the last phrase:

Phrase a:	d^1-g^1:	4th
Phrase b:	d^1-c^2:	7th
Phrase c:	e^1-d^2:	7th
Phrase d:	d^1-d^2:	octave
Phrase d^1:	e^1-d^2:	7th

The melodic skips also increase in size and number:

phrase	skips
a	no skips
b	two thirds
c	rising minor sixth, third
d	two descending fifths
d^1	one descending fifth, two thirds

---

[88] Kirkendale, "New Roads," loc. cit.

Example 4.17 The chorale sectiion (mm. 1-30)

Here, the last phrase is the most disjunct. All skips are descending except for the first skip in phrase b and the rising sixth in phrase c.

Each phrase starts on a different note (except for the last phrase)—f^1, g^1, e^1, c^2—the highest note occurring at the start of phrases four and five. Relating to the range of each phrase is the rise in tessitura, phrase three being largely between a^1 and c^2, while phrases four and five start on the highest notes, c^2 and d^2, before descending.

Beethoven colors each phrase with a different choice of dynamics. Each phrase begins and ends *piano* (starting *sotto voce* in phrase a) except for the *crescendo-forte* in phrase c, surely the climactic center of the melody. A *crescendo* is indicated mostly from the second note (the first in phrase b) in all phrases except the first. Two examples of the *crescendo-piano* in phrases a and d^1 make dramatic deceptive effects, in d^1 before the *crescendo* in T to the B section. The length of the *crescendo* increases and decreases over the length of the melody.

phrase	length of the cresc.
a	1 m.
b	3 mm.
c	3 mm.
d	2-1/2 mm.
d^1	2 mm.
(T	1 m.)

The longest *crescendos* coordinate with a clear emphasis on C major in phrases b and c, phrase c being the only phrase that rises with the *crescendo*, strengthening the climactic effect. While the chorale melody is not based on Gregorian chant, it resembles the style of chant, as Kirkendale has shown.[89] The half-step opening of Pa, with the notes f-e, connects with the half-step openings in movements I, II, and VI, the half step recurring a fifth higher in Pc.

THE INTRODUCTIONS (see Ex. 4.17)

Each phrase is preceded by an introductory subphrase of two measures. Brandenburg points out that interludes between the stanzas were discussed by Knecht and Türk, and illustrated in great detail by Knecht. The interludes they show, however, are in a typical keyboard style—short and cadenza-like, featuring scales and broken chords—a style quite inappropriate for strings, though Beethoven tried some out in the sketches (see Brandenburg, Exx. 12-14). The imitative style eventually selected by Beethoven is far more natural for the quartet and mood of the chorale section. It may have been inspired by Knecht's examples of fughettas (called Versettes) between phrases in Catholic hymn settings. Unlike the theoretical models, too, Beethoven's phrases appear as introductions starting with the first phrase rather than as interludes after the first phrase.

---

[89] See Warren Kirkendale, "Gregorianischer Stil in Beethovens Streichquartett Op. 132," in *Bericht den internationalen Musikwissenschaftlichen Kongress, Berlin 1974*, eds. Helmut Kühn and Peter Nitsche (Kassel: Bärenreiter, 1980), 373-76.

The introductions, designated by a small o on the timeline (as a^o) contain imitation of the opening melodic figure, strict in some voices (at the unison or octave) and freer in others. All start with a skip, of a rising major sixth at the opening and end, and a descending fifth in between. Varied returns of a^0 and b^0 integrate these units in the pattern: a-b-b^1-b^1-a^1. Thus there are only two forms of the introduction. The b^{01} phrase appears a second below b^0 (on c, not d), and appears twice, first in the cello with rising entries and then two octaves higher in violin I with descending entries. The opening a^0 recurs at the end an octave higher as Beethoven again varies the octave placement of the introduction, the overall pattern being: low-high-lower-high-high. Each introduction has a different continuation, imitative setting, and harmonization (see below). In its last appearance, strettos in the lower parts help intensify the final portion of the chorale. As stipulated by the theorists, the introductions conclude on the same note as the first note of the chorale phrase except at the end when a^{01} moves to the half step below, making a deceptive cadence. The introductions also contrast with the chorale in their steady quarter-note rhythm, legato performance, and lack of dynamic variation except for the *crescendo* in a^{01}.

Beethoven has integrated the introduction with the chorale intervallically. The rising sixth in a^0 recurs as a rising minor sixth at the start of Pc, and the descending fifth of b^0, heard three times, recurs prominently in Pd and d^1. Also integrating the introductions is the rhythmic placement, since all start on beat 3. This is an example of compound 4/4 meter where beats one and three are equally strong, the measure really being 2 x 2/4.[90] The addition of the introduction creates a broader rhythm of six-measure units rather than four, both longer and less regular than the usual chorale settings. The rhythmic simplicity and uniformity are eroded only by the movement in quarters in the lower voices that adds some rhythmic drive to all the cadences except in Pc.

Harmony

This section's most radical feature is Beethoven's use of the pure Lydian mode on F without the b♭ that composers had regularly substituted since the Middle Ages in order to avoid the tritone between f and b. The b♮ affects both melody and harmony and creates a unique spiritual, unearthly expressive language. The resulting effect recalls Beethoven's earlier remarks on the piety and devotion evoked by the old church modes.

As the sketches show (see Brandenburg, Ex. 4), at first Beethoven included the b♭ and only later decided on using the pure mode. Melodically, the b♮ appears only twice, both times in Pc. There it functions as the leading tone of both the note and the key of C. The only dominant seventh available within the diatonic scale is the one on G (together with vii and vii⁶ of C), since the absence of b♭ eliminates the dominant seventh (and vii) of F as well as its IV and ii

---

[90] See Grave, "Metrical Displacement" 25-60; and this writer's "Beethoven and Mozart's Requiem," 472-74. Some late Beethoven examples include the overture to *Die Weihe des Hauses*, Op. 124 (1822) and the fugue in the String Quartet, Op. 131 (1825- 26).

chords. Thus, the chordal vocabulary favors C major rather than F, and this key emerges prominently in Pb (with a cadence on C) and Pc (with a half cadence on G). Beethoven frequently uses both V^7 of C and its inversions as well as vii^6 of C. Otherwise the chord vocabulary consists only of triads and their inversions, treated by Beethoven with considerable variety and modal effects. The center on F is well established in Pa, which, however, ends with a deceptive cadence on d. The only cadence on F occurs in Pd, which comes as a surprise since the final six chords consist of the progression V^7/V-V-I, having a strong emphasis on C. Thus the first four cadences occur on d, C, G, and F chords.

A number of progressions are modal rather than tonal. These include in F, V-vi-V in Pa; in C, vi-iii-I in Pc; and the chords ending Pd^1, where a d-chord initiates a half cadence in the Dorian mode: I-IV-V, the final A-major chord being the only chromatic chord in the chorale section and the pivot into the S theme in D major. There also occurs such non-tonal voice leading as the fifths in contrary motion between the outside voices in Pd (mm. 21^3-22^2), making an uncharacteristic V^7-I progression.

The harmonization of the introductions also plays an important role in the harmonic organization. Thus, Pa^0 alternates C and F chords, establishing the F mode. Pb^0 picks up the d-minor harmony ending Pa and then moves to V^7 and I in C, modulating to the dominant key of C. Pc^0 and Pd^0 are entirely in C. For Pc, this adumbrates the strong half cadence in C after the modal beginning, but for Pd, the harmony is deceptive since the phrase ends in F. Most varied is Pa^{01}, which starts around F, as in the opening, but then moves strongly toward C; however, the resolution of I^6_4-V^7 is to the first inversion of an F chord, making another deceptive cadence V^7-IV^6. The F chord starts Pd^1 and is repeated, but this phrase is thoroughly ambiguous harmonically, as indicated above. The harmonic rhythm of the introductions in quarter notes and often with lighter-weight intervals and inversions contrasts with the monumental effect of the chorale chords. Further, these short phrases end on the weak second beat or elide with the chorale phrase, making a nearly unbroken flow of the larger six-measure groupings.

Sound

The low register of the chorale melody and its chordal setting help to create a serious, contemplative mood. Occasional enrichment of the chords with double stops and open strings intensify their rich, organlike sonority. Note how Beethoven varies the spacing between Pd and d^1 via higher inner voices that serve to produce a brighter sound, preparing the listener for the change of sonority in S.

Beethoven contrasts the imitative texture of the introductions with the nearly note-against-note homophony of the chorale setting. Each six-measure unit is articulated by the reduction of sound to only one voice at the start of the imitative buildup of these subphrases. The entrances of the imitative voices expand the sonority to the culminating entrance of the chorale phrase. The second, fourth, and fifth introductions are placed in the highest register of the section (reaching a^2 and g^2), offering further contrast to the chorale melody.

The Chorale Variation

A single variation of the chorale follows the prescription of the theorists to vary the accompaniment but not the melody (Ex. 4.18).[91] Beethoven places the melody an octave higher in the first violin with rests between the phrases. Thus the melody stands out even more and the total range of sound is greatly expanded. Though the shift in register can be compared to a change of organ manual or register, transferring the melody of a variation an octave higher or lower also occurs in a few of Beethoven's movements, most notably in the quartet Op. 74/II (a rondo) and the symphonies Nos. 7/II and 9/IV. It is thus not at all unique to this movement.

Beethoven relegates the introductions to the lower three parts. They fill in the rests in the chorale melody, and the composer gives them the same rhythmic and contrapuntal style as the accompaniment to the chorale melody. The setting for this variation appears in the first sketches for the section.[92]

Beethoven does not change the basic harmony. He animates the rhythmic motion of the three lower parts, which represent an artistic embodiment of Fux's fourth-species counterpoint of tied notes and suspensions. The accompaniment moves in tied quarters, dotted quarters plus an eighth, two eighths and a quarter note. The cello part is the most active line, and varies rhythmically the original bass line. It moves incessantly in ♩. ♪ and ♪ ♩ patterns, with octave leaps, and frequent crossing of the more sedate viola part. The cello plays in a much higher register than in the chorale setting, which helps produce the brighter sound of the variation. The inner voices are newly worked out and often in a higher register, while violin II especially brings suspensions against the chorale in violin I.

Besides introducing many suspension dissonances of the 2nd, 4th, 7th, and 9th, as well as passing tones and other non-harmonic tones, Beethoven incorporates some irregular dissonances caused by the delay of harmonic resolution. For example, in Pb, the bass part in mm. 94-96¹, the harmony is delayed by a beat (see Ex. 4.18).

Example 4.18 The chorale variation, phrase 2 (mm. 92-96)

---

[91] Brandenburg, "Historical Background," 175-76. The directions for the chorale variation quoted from Türk's *Von den wichtigsten Pflichten eines Organisten*, 103-04, fit Beethoven's variation very closely.
[92] Brandenburg, "Historical Background," 176.

In summary, the variation is more active, more contrapuntal, more dissonant, more unified, and more expanded in range. It thus presents less contrast to S and also acts as a preparation for the most intensive counterpoint, dissonance, and enlarged span of sound in section 5.

Section 5: Contrapuntal Development of the Chorale (A²)

This second, concluding section of 43-1/2 measures is almost 50% longer than the chorale section. As indicated in Exx. 4.19 and 4.20, it contains only two thematic elements, Pa and a transformed Pa° that acts as both the introduction to Pa and its countersubject (indicated as CS in this discussion). The new indication "Mit innigster Empfindung" (with innermost feeling) points to the depth of personal emotion here, not usually associated with the sustained contrapuntal texture of this section, as Ratner observes.[93]

One cannot even call this a free variation since it omits all of the chorale except the first six measures. Beethoven thus departs in this respect from the Haydn model and indeed from his previous movements in this form. The section divides into three parts:

mm. 168^3-182^2 (14 mm.)　　ends with a cadence on D Dorian, m. 182^1
mm. 182^3-202^1 (19-1/2 mm.) climax section
mm. 202^1-211 (10 mm.)　　conclusion

In part 1, the dynamics remain on a low level and the part ends surprisingly with an archaic open-fifth cadence on d, preceded by a V chord on a, with c♯. Four chords make the modal progression on C-d-A-d. Beethoven picks up the half cadence in the Dorian mode ending the chorale section and variation I, and resolves it, another of many examples of Beethoven's long-range connections and resolutions.[94]

Another, more dramatic long-range effect in this movement concerns the transformation of Pa⁰ from the simplicity of the opening phrase to the complex, ornamental, balanced expressive theme emerging as the CS to the entrance of Pa (Ex. 4.19). As we see in this example, syncopations were added in variation I, the neighbor-note decoration at the start of variation II ($Pa^{0.2}$), and the fully developed balanced theme with subphrases x and y only with the entrance of Pa. $Pa^{0.2}$ is first imitated in the three lower voices as in variation I. The entrance of Pa overlaps with the end of the imitation, an overlap with the cello that continues with the entrance of the fully evolved $Pa^{0.3}$ functioning as the CS. The CS provides sharp contrast with its large range of a ninth (c^1-d^2), balanced subphrases, rhythmic complexity, and intensified motion, combining sixteenths, tied notes, and syncopations against the slow-moving half notes of Pa. Heard throughout the section until the last four measures, it is found in all the voices, from low C to d^3, a span of over four octaves. The transformed Pa⁰ has become the personal, subjective theme as against the timeless chorale. It seems to embody the composer's most moving prayer.

---

[93] Ratner, *String Quartets*, 274.
[94] For further examples of such connections, see Ch. 3, 281.

Example 4. 19   The transformation of Pa^0, especially in section 5.

The entire section has been called a chorale fugue[95] but is more like a chorale fugato with CS and strettos (see the outline in Ex. 4. 20). Like a fugue, Pa, notes 1-5, twice alternates on F and C (I and V), combined with the CS in double counterpoint. A fifth, false entry on g^2 occurs in violin II (m. 177^3). All the entries are in stretto, overlapping with the last note of the phrase except for the entry on g^2 which comes against note 3 of Pa. After an extension to the surprising cadence on d, $Pa^{0.2}$ returns, parallel to the start of the section, in an expanded three-part stretto to initiate the main, climactic portion of the section. The complete Pa now appears in the deepest register of the cello on F in a three-part stretto with the first violin four octaves higher, starting on f^3 (after a false entry on c^2, m. 186^3). While the second entry comes just before the last note of the subject, the third entry on V quickly follows after a measure, starting with an octave reinforcement of the low C of the cello, *forte*, in the climax phrase of the movement. Beethoven places a *sforzando* on most notes of Pa in the stretto in mm. 189-93. Pa is combined with an extension of the neighbor-note motive of the CS, the complete CS heard only with the first cello entry. The extension of notes 6-8 in Violin I partially overlaps with the cello in m. 193. Thereafter, the descent from the heights takes place with a free descending melodic line in half notes in Violin I against a rising line in the three lower parts derived from CSy, paired in warm tenths and parallel sixth chords. The *decrescendo* ends *pp* with only two voices—the violins—on a major third, c^2-e^2, in m. 197^3.

---

[95] Brandenburg, "Historical Background, 190; Ratner, *String Quartets*, 273-74.

Example 4. 20 Strettos of Pa in section 5

Two new strettos ensue, fragmenting Pa to only three and then two notes. A third stretto on notes 1-3 essentially in C major occurs between violin II and violin I (mm. 197³-201, though anticipated by violin I, mm. 196³-97³). Entries are on c^2-f^2-c^3-d^3, and the stretto cadences finally on F, eliding with the concluding portion. This ethereal ending fragments Pa to only notes 2-3 (f-e, the motto of the quartet, mm. 202-05), starting on the downbeat and combined with a twofold complete statement of the CS plus CSx. The CS appears at its original pitch and an octave higher in the first violin. A statement of Pa notes 2-6 follows, high in violin I on f^3, and then the final high F chords, *più piano-pp*, the first violin again reaching up to its highest note a^3 before descending to f^3.

This section contains a fugato, four strettos, five versions of Pa, with a final fragmentation to notes 2-3, and two versions of the CS and its fragmentation. This brilliant contrapuntal achievement totally serves the poetic idea.

Much has been made of the very dissonant harmonic setting in much of this section, going beyond the dissonances of the variation section. But how else could Beethoven achieve intensity of expression harmonically since modulation to distant keys and chromatic alteration were excluded? The diatonic dissonance reminds us of some of Stravinsky's Neo-Classic passages. They are achieved through appoggiaturas, tied notes, and non-harmonic tones, including the old suspension-cambiata formula. Let us look at a few of these dissonant clashes:

m. 170³: The first note of Pa, f² in the second violin, is intensified by the g appoggiatura in the viola and cambiata e in the cello, causing a 7th and minor 9th respectively.

m. 172¹: The d² of Pa is treated like an appoggiatura to c in the cello (making a ninth), and creates a second with the tied c² in violin I.

m. 174:   Beat one: The viola in Pa forms a seventh with the tied g² in violin II, which resolves irregularly to a consonance by skip (a frequent device).

Beat two: The passing tone d¹ in violin II produces a seventh with violin I.

Beat three: The seventh between the violins is due to the suspension of e² in violin II, resolving after a cambiata to d², part of the V chord. The entrance on f¹ in the cello makes a major seventh with violin II as well as a diminished fifth with the viola b.

m. 178:   Beat one: seventh between the violins, a¹ in violin I being an appoggiatura.

Beat three: V⁷ of C in the three upper parts against a suspension-cambiata of e-c in the cello, sounding a minor ninth with the f² in violin II. The cello figure persists in mm. 179-80, creating further dissonances on beats one and three (Ex. 4.21).

These dissonances remind us of other dissonant passages in Beethoven, ranging from the Neapolitan ⁶⁄₅ at the climax of the development in the *Eroica* Symphony I, mm. 276-79, to the mingling of V and I chords in the coda of the Piano Sonata, Op. 81a/I ("Das Lebewohl"), and the severe dissonance of the chord opening the finale of the Ninth Symphony, not to say the dissonant counterpoint in the fugue of the Piano Sonata Op. 106 and the *Grosse Fuge*, Op. 133. Every example is different and has a different purpose but all show Beethoven's readiness to go to the extreme with regard to the standard treatment of dissonance in order to achieve an expressive or stylistic goal.[96]

Example 4.21 *Dissonant clashes in section 5 (mm. 178-79)*

[96] For several dissonant passages in the Beethoven symphonies, see the essays on the symphonies by Hector Berlioz. Many nineteenth-century critics ascribed the dissonances in the late works to Beethoven's deafness. See K. M. Knittel, "Wagner, Deafness, and the Reception of Beethoven's Late Style," *JAMS* 51 (1998): 49-82. According to Knittel, such criticism was altered

The largest span of sound in the entire quartet occurs here in the climax section: the low C of the cello to the high g^3-a^3 in the first violin, mm. 192-93—four octaves plus a fifth and sixth.

The S Theme

The contrast posed by the D-major, 3/8 theme is the sharpest in all the examples of Beethoven's alternating variations. First, there is the certainty of a stable D-major tonality as against the ambiguities of Lydian harmony. How does Beethoven relate this theme to the chorale? In previous movements in this form, the connections are clear (see the table below).

Table 4.16 Connections Between P and S Themes in Alternating Variation Movements by Beethoven

Work	Thematic Relationships
Symphony No. 3/IV (1803)	Bass (P) and treble to the bass (S)
Symphony No. 5/II (1804-08)	Similar upbeat in rhythm and melodic contour
Piano Trio, Op. 70, No. 2/II (1808)	Upbeat with a rising third, expanded to other rising intervals
Symphony No. 7/II (1811-12)	Basic rhythm of P (♩ ♪ ♪) maintained in the pizzicato bass part throughout S and occasionally in the melody
Symphony No. 9/III (1822-24)	S uses sigh motive from P

The tempo and meter contrasts between P and S in Op. 132 are far greater than those between the themes in the Ninth Symphony because of the program: the meters ¢ and 3/8 in the quartet versus ¢ and 3/4 in the symphony. While the tempo marks are almost the same, the metronome marks for the symphony indicate only a small difference in the degree of speed. The connections between P and S in Op. 132 are less obvious than the examples listed in the table. As indicated above, the range of P, d-d, relates to the new tonic of S, and the descending melodic line of 1S mirrors the descending start of Pa.[97] In 1S, the octave leaps in melody and bass adumbrate the cello's octave leaps in the variation of P that follows. Most relevant are the descending fifths in the melody of 2S which echo the descending fifths in Pb° (and the two related introductions) as well as Pd. Further, the descending sixths at the start of K (m. 67) and later on in K (m. 76) are surely linked with the memorable rising sixth starting Pa° and recurring at the end of the chorale before Pd¹ as well as in Pc.

Beethoven links the chorale with the *Andante* in the simplest possible way in m. 30 with a *crescendo* and repeated notes on the dominant of D, violin

---

by Wagner's belief that Beethoven's deafness was actually the source of his creative power. However, as the examples I have cited indicate, unusual dissonances occur in Beethoven's music long before the nearly total deafness of his last years, from 1818.

[97] See the melodic reduction in Ratner, *String Quartets*, 273.

I anticipating its starting note. The second transition in m. 114 is modified according to the chorale variation in the lower three voices while violin I continues in half notes like the chorale theme, thus enhancing the continuity between the themes. Now the violin I a^2 rises to d^3, since the theme of 1S moves from violin II to violin I, an octave higher. The retransition to P is about three measures longer than the transition and unchanged in both passages (see mm. 81^2-84^2). The cadence on d, which elides with the retransition, occurs in octaves, without a third or fifth, and can thus easily pivot back to F, moving to V^6 and I. Beethoven reverses the *crescendo* leading to the *Andante* by a written out *decrescendo*—*p, più p, pp*—in the return to the chorale. Here the final note in violin I, c^2, anticipates the first note of Pa° two octaves below.

The retransition picks up the repeated notes ending S (note how they start from beat two), cutting them from three notes to two, and then one note twice heard between a lengthened quarter-note rest. A metrical displacement occurs where the grouping in three is shifted back a beat (see Fig.4.1).

Figure 4.1 Metrical Displacement in mm. 81^2-84, vn. I

The eloquent silences support the metrical shift, low dynamic level, and effect of suspense and mystery.[98] The details of this apparently simple connection again reveal Beethoven's incredible care with every aspect of structure and expression.

In general, the brilliant *Andante* is dazzling after the sober chorale. Much higher and broader in total range, it goes up to the high a^3 by its seventh measure, a high note heard three times thereafter, in contrast to the chorale that reaches the note only once at its climax in A^2 and in its penultimate measure. The theme expresses its title "Feeling New Strength" by several means: by the high notes, and greater fullness and range of sound; by joyful trills, short appoggiaturas, and other short decorations; by an energetic disjunct melody and accompaniment, containing leaps of the octave, seventh (major and minor), and tritone, as well as thirds, fifths, and sixths; by intense activity in the surface rhythm, with its many 32nds and occasional 64ths, and greater range of rhythmic contrasts; upbeat accompaniments in 2S; many more dynamic nuances; and a much richer harmony, including ornamental dissonances of appoggiaturas, échapées, and cambiatas. Despite the leaps, a warm and touching lyricism infuses 2S and K.

---

[98] For Beethoven's use of pauses, see Miriam Sheer,"Dynamics in Beethoven's Late Instrumental Works," 372-78.

STRUCTURE AND VARIATION PROCEDURES

S consists of three periods I have designated as 1S, 2S, and K (Ex. 4.22 on p.352). The lengths are 8+10+8-1/3 measures, and with the double variations 16+20+14-1/3 measures. While the basic periods grow in length, with the varied repetitions of 1S and 2S, it is 2S that becomes the longest and thus most emphasized unit, while 1S and K balance each other. Each period has a contrasting and irregular phrase structure. Beethoven builds 1S (6+2 mm.) on an old descending scale sequence alternating triads and first inversions (familiar to us from Mozart's *Magic Flute*). After a descent from the tonic to the third degree, a two-measure cadence (1Sb) leads to V on the weak beat three (m. 38). The variation of the period ensues which connects to 2S via a move to V^6_5, the first chord of 2S, as the same root harmony holds over. 2S combines three phrases in the order 4+4+2 mm. (a-b-c). 2Sa subdivides 2x2 and x+x^1, as mm. 3-4 vary mm. 1-2. The cadence phrase 2Sc has nearly the same surface rhythm in violin I as 1Sb. The light tonic cadence on a sixteenth of beat three (m. 56) is obscured by a suspension of V over the tonic in the upper three parts while the bass moves on the last note to the dominant, anticipating the start on V in the variation of 2S. Both weak-beat cadences and sustained harmony between phrases, periods, and sections occur in the first and last movements as well, being typical late Beethoven devices. 2Sc^1, however, maintains the tonic on all of beat three (m. 66). Such fine distinctions are also typical of the late Beethoven style, as is the weakened tonic on the weakest beat of the measure.

Unlike 1S and 2S, K builds a long period via immediate variation of phrases a and c, making the following pattern: a (4)-a^1 (4)-b (2)-c (2)-c^1 (2-1/8). The following three eighths on the tonic after c^1 both end K and start the retransition to the chorale. Typical of a cadential unit, K starts with a strong emphasis on the subdominant, with c in the bass and later in the inner parts, as well as a tonic emphasis. Quite unusual is the contrapuntal setting of K, with a contrasting sixteenth-note turn figure in the bass and inner voices (Ka, a^1) and contrasting thirty-second-note lines throughout most of Kc.

The double variations as well as the full *Andante* variation follow tradition in their overall surface-rhythmic acceleration, as smaller rhythmic values, including fast triplets and sextolets, are steadily introduced (see Ex. 4.22). Unlike the chorale, these are ornamental melodic variations with some exchanges between the violins of the main melodic line. Enrichment of the texture occurs with occasional additions of countermelodies (Var. 1, 1Sa^3), integrative details (use of 2Sbr as accompaniment to Kc^3, mm. 163-65^1), steady eighth-note accompaniment to 1Sa^3 (mm. 123-28), and nearly steady sixteenth-note viola and bass movement, with pizzicato (2Sa^3, mm. 141-44).

The use of double variation creates four versions of nearly every phrase, remembering too that each period has phrases and subphrases that vary as well. In the *Andante* variation (B^1), certain features parallel the chorale variation. Like that variation, Beethoven places 1S an octave higher, and he strictly maintains the basic harmonies throughout. The overwhelming impression of motion and ornamentation recalls especially variation 2 in the quartet Op. 127,

Example 4.22 1S, its variation, and the start of 2S (mm.31-50)

second movement.[99] A comparison of the four versions of the cadence of 1S (1Sb) shows how Beethoven enriched each appearance of the phrase in inner voices, rhythm, counterpoint, and melodic divisions. In the three variations of 2Sa, increasing melodic ornamentation and finally bass movement elaborate the phrase.

If we consider the movement as a whole, we see not only the juxtaposition of extreme contrasts but a progression in the chorale settings that relate them more and more to aspects of the D-major theme. Kevin Korsyn makes several important observations in this respect in his discussion of the movement with relation to the famous book by J. W. N. Sullivan, *Beethoven: His Spiritual Development* (1927). He points out, as partly noted above, that the chorale variation already lessens the contrast with S in its expanded range, increased rhythmic movement, use of syncopation, and "greater mobility of the cello part."[100] The fifth, climactic section further assimilates features from S. As Korsyn states:

> "The Lydian material is reshaped, revised, in light of its experience of the D-major sections; the restrictions of the cantus firmus ... are finally overthrown. In their place, the phrasing, registral freedom, and dynamics of the D-major theme take over."[101]

Korsyn also refers to the greater complexity of phrasing, broad spacing, high register, and the final section of closure denied to the chorale twice before. To all these we should add the new lyricism provided by the transformation of Pa^0.

From a programmatic point of view, we may suggest that the "new strength" experienced in S affects the increasing intensity of the song of thanksgiving, which reaches its apex near the end of the movement.

Bartók and the "Heiliger Dankgesang"

Bartók's admiration for Beethoven's music is well known. Many observers feel that the line of development from the late quartets of Beethoven connects directly with the twentieth century and especially the six Bartók quartets, considered today as the greatest twentieth-century works in the quartet genre. According to his student Tibor Serly, "Bartók carried Beethoven's string quartets around with him and read them permanently in his last years."[102]

As noted in the background remarks to this quartet, Bartók may have been influenced by the sequence of movements in Op. 132 as a model for his Fourth and Fifth String Quartets. Another example of a Beethoven model is the "Heiliger Dankgesang," which profoundly influenced the slow movement of

---

[99] As noted by Kerman, *The Beethoven Quartets*, 256.
[100] See Kevin Korsyn, "J. W. N. Sullivan and the *Heiliger Dankgesang*," *Beethoven Forum* 2 (1993): 161-62.
[101] Ibid., 167. Korsyn refers to Sullivan's belief in the "indescribable synthesis expressed in the 'Heiliger Dankgesang'." Korsyn assumes that Sullivan meant that "the primary experiences of the quartet—'exhaustion and defeat' and 'the new life bestowed as an act of grace from on high'—must somehow interpenetrate each other, reaching a coalescence in which opposing attitudes are finally recognized as 'harmoniously flowing from a single stem," 145-46.
[102] See Mark A. Radice, "Bartók's Parodies of Beethoven," *The Music Review* 42 (1981): 254, n.7. This article contains further references to Bartók's knowledge of Beethoven's music and his admiration for Beethoven.

Bartók's Third Piano Concerto, a work composed in the summer of 1945 when Bartók was gravely ill (he died on 26 September 1945 and Tibor Serly scored the last seventeen measures of the third movement). While the main influence pertains to the A section of this A-B-A^1 form, some other features of the later sections also contain links with the Beethoven movement.

Aspects of the Gross Form

The movement is in major, here C major, like the basic major character of Op. 132/III. Its slow tempo, "Adagio religioso," largely 4/4 meter, and chorale melody all resemble Beethoven's model, as does the slightly faster tempo of the B section, "poco più mosso," and the section's sharp contrast to A. Bartók's adjective "religioso," a rare indication in his music, not only confirms the religious style of A but points to the Beethovenian origin of the movement. The variation aspect is seen in the varied return of the A section.

The sectional lengths differ from Beethoven's proportions. A (mm. 1-57) is the longest section of 57 mm.; B (mm. 58-88) is the shortest, being only 31 mm.; and A^1 is shorter by 8 measures (mm. 89-137, including K and KT). The emphasis thus falls heavily on the first chorale section.

Table 4.17 Bartók, Third Piano Concerto/II, Section A

Section A: Chorale.   Key: C   Meter: mostly 4/4

phrase:	Ox	y	x^1	(x) x^2 inv.	z	y^1	Pa	Oy	(ar inv.) b	Oy^{2}inv.	(ar inv.) c	Ox$^{2.1}$
measure:	1^2	4^2	7^2	9^2	10^4	12^2	16	20^2	24	28^2	31	35^2
chord:	C	G	E	F	a	C		G		E		F

	(ar) d	Oz^1	(d) e	Ox^1		
	38	46^2	48	54^2	57	57 mm.
		a		C	e unis.	

The A Section (see the Timeline and Ex. 4.23): Similarities to Op. 132/III

1. Five phrases in chorale style, a-b-c-d-e, harmonized in a mainly chordal texture. A simple rhythm prevails, mainly of half notes and quarters. Phrases a-d, mm. 1-4, have the same rhythm.

2. The phrases are partly interrelated. Pb is a partial inversion of Pa and Pe picks up the neighbor-note motive of Pd and develops it.

3. The phrases grow in range, though slightly irregularly, and then taper off, the ranges being a sixth, seventh, fifth, ninth, octave. Climax notes of the phrases rise as well: a^2 a^2-c^3-d^3-a^3. As in Op. 132, the highest climax notes occur in the last two phrases.

4. Each phrase cadences on a different degree, the tonic reserved for the end: G-E-F-a-C. The cadences are adumbrated in the long introduction, where each phrase centers around chords on C-G-E-F-a-C.

STRING QUARTET   355

Example 4.23 Bartók's Piano Concerto No. 3/II: the five phrases of the chorale melody (mm.16-57)

5. The introductions. Instead of a brief introduction of two measures, Bartók presents a 15-measure introduction, in a five-part string texture (violin I is divisi and the double bass is omitted) together with a single clarinet as background. The imitative texture, diatonic harmony, and rhythmic movement in quarter notes resemble Beethoven. The phrases provide the basic motives used for the imitative postludes after each phrase in quarter notes, integrated like the introductions in Beethoven. A slight variation of the opening phrase returns at the end, also resembling Beethoven.

Differences of the chorale setting
1. The phrase lengths are irregular: 5-5-5-9-7 mm., with a holdover of the final chord via the sustaining pedal for one, two, or three additional measures.
2. The chorale phrases begin on beat one, not beat three, and some simple rhythmic motives in quarters and dotted notes are introduced, most extensively in phrases d and e.
3. Pe is not a variation of Pd but partly derived from it. It is the most chromatic phrase and stresses the flat side of the harmony.
4. The chorale is not in a low but middle-high register.

5. Voice-leading is free, in four-seven parts, and Bartók doubles the melody in octaves in Pc, d, and e in typical piano style.
6. Pd and e are the most impassioned phrases, breaking with the block chords and more restrained harmony of Pa-c.
7. Bartók uses postludes rather than short introductory phrases. His postludes enter a beat after the final chord of the phrase and elaborate the harmony of the chord. They are thus upbeat phrases, not downbeat. Their length also varies from 1-3/4 to 3-3/4 mm., and they are diatonic, contrasting with the richer harmonization of the chorale phrases.

Section A^1

While the chorale is placed in the piano in A, it is transferred to the winds in A^1. As in Beethoven, the texture becomes contrapuntal, the solo given Bachian imitative counterpoint against the chorale phrases, as well as large cadenza-like flourishes after the phrase endings (reminding us of the late eighteenth-century organ chorales as described in the treatises of the time—surely unknown to Bartók). Like Beethoven, too, the melody itself is unchanged except for a final intense climax via a long developmental extension of the last phrase, which starts in the highest string register and is shared among the strings, winds, and piano. Unlike Op. 132, the Bartók movement is connected with the *finale* by a last-minute shift to an E-major chord in the piano.

Section B

Bartók's B sections in his ternary forms often contain high activity and coloristic scoring, with sounds of nature that critics have described as "night music" (as in the slow movement of *Music for Strings, Percussion, and Celesta*). However, here, as Sándor Kovács remarks, it is nature music of "broad daylight," with birdsong—actual birdcalls that Bartók notated during his stay in Asheville, North Carolina.[103] The main motive of section B is called by Bartók "Parting in peace" and may have symbolic meaning. Though a common type of contrast in Bartók's music, this section also offers the sharp contrast with A in every element also found in Op. 132. The highly active texture, large and high range of sound, and use of such devices as trills and short ornaments also appear in Op. 132. The section may well represent the "feeling new strength" of Beethoven as found by Bartók in nature.

The form of the selection is unrelated to Op. 132, being: Sa (mm. 58-71)- a^1 (mm. 72-78)- b (mm. 79-83)-a^2 (mm. 84-88). The rising and falling fourths in section Sa relate to Pa and b, and the repeated notes in section Sb to Pd.

Perhaps Bartók chose the model of the "Heiliger Dankgesang" as a prayer for strength and survival in the last months of his life. Kovács observes that

this music. . . although starting with a disciplined, dispassionate C major, gradually assumes a pathos and emotion rarely found in Bartók's composition[s].[104]

---

[103] Sándor Kovács, "Final Concertos," in *The Bartók Companion*, ed. Malcolm Gilles (London: Faber & Faber, 1993), 545-46; László Somfai, *Béla Bartók: Composition, Concepts and Autograph Sources* (Berkeley and Los Angeles: University of California Press , 1996). 55.

[104] Ibid., 545.

STRING QUARTET

The movement also stands as a final tribute to a composer perhaps closest to Bartók's musical mind.

The Fourth Movement: *Alla marcia, assai vivace*

Breaking the introspective mood of the ethereal final measures of the "Heiliger Dankgesang" is a short march that returns to the key of A, the tonic major. The "Alla marcia" is the only march in the Beethoven quartets but one of the three late marches, each one of which produces a drastic contrast to the preceding movement. Here, the march, in a normal register and energized by typical dotted rhythms, conveys "the confident stride of renewed vigor."[105] In the words of Leonard Ratner, it "represents still one more upsurge of 'new strength'" (Ex. 4.24).[106]

The shock of the contrast, nevertheless, is strong. Philip Radcliffe compares it to the appearance of the march movement in the late Piano Sonata, Op. 101 (1816).[107] This much longer contrapuntal march with canonic trio carries nearly the same heading as the march in Op. 132—"Vivace, alla Marcia (the original German title is: *Lebhaft, Marschmässig*)." It enters after a delicate, lyrical opening movement, producing a shock like that in Op. 132, though less

Example 4.24 The end of movement III and start of the March

---

[105] A. B. Marx, in Helm, *Beethoven's Streichquartette*, trans. Bent, 261.
[106] Ratner, *String Quartets*, 275.
[107] Radcliffe, *Beethoven's String Quartets*, 119.

extreme since the questioning character of the first movement receives in the march a stable, resolute reply, embodied, as so often in late Beethoven, in the contrapuntal style. The third, perhaps most shocking such late example, occurs in the finale of the Ninth Symphony. There, the exalted ending to variation 6, "Und der Cherub steht vor Gott," is followed by the Turkish march that begins with the famous offbeat grunts in the bassoons, contrabassoon, and bass drum, surely Beethoven at his most humorous.

GROWTH AND SOUND

Table 4.18 Timeline: Movement IV

Key: A   Meter: ¢

		(ar)	(Tr)							
P(x-x^1)	|T	K	:||:	T+K	|Px-xm	|P^1	|T^1	K^1	:||:	
1	4^3	7	8^3	9	13	15	18^3	23	24^3	24 mm.
A		E	E:I	E-A	D-A	A	E-A		A:I	

This brief 24-measure march is a type of rounded binary form with an intensified tonic reprise of its main phrases an octave higher, a connection with such procedures in movement III. The phrases here have tiny P-T-K functions. The movement is unified by dotted rhythms and a chain of derivations as shown in the timeline. Though the length of the larger parts is symmetrical—8+16 measures—the inner subdivisions have some irregularities. These include the lengths of P and T+K (3-1/2+4-1/2 measures), so that the final cadences of each part land on the third beat. The simple tonal scheme shows a circular pattern in fifths: A-E-A-D-A-E-A; a surprising shift back to E in the reprise extension of T creates further tonal tension near the end. A special detail is the motivic recombination at the start of Part II. There, a variant of Txm combines with Km—the final cadence figure—to produce a new subphrase. This old device goes back to the earliest years of the Classic style. The small development thus contains elements from all three functions.

Five main types of texture occur in this small movement: homorhythmic in P (but with initial imitation of violin I); canonic motivic accompaniment in T (♩. ♪♩ motive); paired canon at the octave below at the start of Part II (mm. 9-13); unison (mm. 13-14^2); and overlapping imitation (m. 14).

RHYTHM

Most of Beethoven's marches have a straightforward rhythmic style but a few feature rhythmic dissonance and metrical displacement, as the march in *Fidelio*, the march variation in the *finale* of the Ninth Symphony, and this march in Op. 132. One analyst dealing with the rhythmic aspect of this movement is Leonard Ratner.[108] First, Ratner points out the metrical displacement of beats caused by

---

[108] Ratner, *String Quartets*, 275-77.

the fact that the dotted rhythm on beat one in measures 1 and 3 functions as an upbeat to the longer note on beats two-three, which is strongly accented by a *sforzando* on beat two in violin I and becomes the real downbeat. This short-long pattern occurs as well in the lower parts as canonic accompaniment, the long notes creating as many as three downbeats in a row (see mm. 5-6).

Another aspect concerns the irregular beat groups here, as observed by Ratner, which results in the following pattern in the first violin in Parts I and II: [109]

    Part I: 1   3   5   3   4   4   4   6   2
    Part II: 6   2   8   9   3   5   3   4   4   4   4   4   6   2

Finally, taking off from the implied triple meter of the opening, Ratner shows how the march can be turned into a mazurka in a brilliant transformation of the movement.[110]

The march in *Fidelio*, Act I (added in 1806) also transforms the natural upbeat on V into a downbeat, so that in the first three measures the barline is shifted one beat to the right; this makes the beat groups 1-4-4-3. In the final C section, mm. 25-38, the phrases begin throughout on beat 3 in another example of compound 4/4 meter where beats one and three are equally strong.[111]

A further example of rhythmic manipulation occurs in the 6/8 Turkish march in the *finale* of the Ninth Symphony. There, the barline of the introduction shifts over one beat to the right so that beat two functions as beat one. The melodic line of the A sections in the winds is then syncopated against the beat marking bass and percussion instruments, being set on beat 2 rather than beat 1 as well.[112]

Despite the strong contrast made by the march in Op. 132, the dotted rhythm of the march inevitably recalls the march rhythm found in the first movement. Even the appoggiatura figures in P (mm. 2 and 4) have a kinship with similar figures in Pa of movement I. Further, perhaps Vitercik is correct when he observes that the quartet's unifying half-step motive appears even here in the connection between the final melodic f^3 of the third movement and e^1 starting movement IV in the first violin, despite the disparity of registers.[113]

---

[109] Ibid., with some differences from Ratner. Note the increased regularity of the four-beat groups near the end of Part II caused by the extension of T.
[110] See the Mazurka in Ratner, 276..
[111] See n. 90.
[112] The vocal parts are not metrically shifted, however.
[113] Vitercik, "Structure and Expression," 249.

The Fifth Movement [Recitative]

The March connects directly with the recitative via the indication *"attaca subito"* at its end, just as an *"attaca"* marking links the recitative with the *finale*, thus making an unbreakable continuity from the March. The abrupt change of mood is a second shock in connection with the march movement. A two-measure extension of the March's cadential figure (designated as KT) leads directly into the recitative proper (A); the first measure of the extension then reappears before the parallel recitative phrase (A^1). KT modulates at first from a to F, the key in which the recitative starts. Section A quickly modulates to d and half of the short movement remains there until the B section that reasserts A minor as it prepares the key of the *finale* and return to the quartet's tonic key (see the timeline, Table 4.19).

The recitative is in the expressive *accompagnato* style (also called *recitatif obligé*), as are all of Beethoven's instrumental recitatives. The melodic line here appears in the first violin, which acts as the dramatic protagonist, while the lower parts form the orchestral background with sixteenth-note tremolos and chordal punctuation. Like many recitatives, this example opens on a sixth chord ($F:V^6$). Another cliché is the descending skip starting A and A^1. The initial skip recalls the recitative in the Ninth Symphony, entering there with a rising fifth. A third cliché of the recitative style is the use of appoggiatura cadences ending the main sections.

Table 4.19. Timeline: Movement V

Key, modulatory: a-F-d-a   Meter: c and ¢
più allegro
(IV ext.)

KT	A: ax	y	KT^1	|A^1:	a^1x^1	z	zm, ext.
1	3	6^2	7		8	11^3	13
a	F-d						

	Presto ¢		*poco adagio*		
(I/Po)			(I/Pm)		
B: bx	y		z		⌐ attaca
15^4	16	20	21	22	22 mm.
a			V ped.	V cad.	

Though the recitative is an open, modulating form, Beethoven has shaped it into two parallel sections and a conclusion, $A-A^1-B$.[114] The second,

---

[114] This form is proposed by Paul Mies, *Das instrumentale Rezitativ: Von seiner Geschichte und seinen Formen* (Bonn: Bouvier, 1968), 83. See his discussion of Beethoven's instrumental recitatives, 73-85. Another valuable study is by Jurgen Thym, "The Instrumental Recitative in Beethoven's Compositions," in *Essays on Music for Charles Warren Fox*, ed. Jerald C. Graue (Rochester, NY: Eastman School of Music Press, 1979), 230-40. For more general studies see Herbert Seiffert, "Das instrumentalrezitativ vom Barock bis zum Wiener Klassik," in *De Ratione in Musica, Fest-*

longer A section is an intensification of the first: the skip down is enlarged from a fourth to a fifth; the first note lengthened, placed offbeat and *sf;* a new closing phrase is added with increased eighth-note motion and an expressive extension of the cadential appoggiatura leading to the dramatic B unit. A^1 also has a higher tessitura ($b\flat$-c^2 of A vs. f^1-g^2 of A^1) and contains many more performance indications. A also overlaps KT^1 in a tight continuity between sections.

The B unit is approached by an *accelerando*, a *crescendo*, and an upward leap of a tenth to f^3. The climax, placed on beat 4, starts *ff;* and the tempo and meter change to *Presto*, ¢. Beethoven restores A minor suddenly with a dissonant V^0_9, the implied harmony throughout the brilliant descending violin passage of nearly three octaves (f^3-$g\sharp$). All commentators have noted the relationship of this passage to Po in the first movement. After a descending skip of a diminished seventh (the largest of the descending skips here), section B makes the typical cadence on V, with a descending skip of a fourth on i^6_4, a^1-e^1—another cliché. However, this descending fourth also connects with the descending fourth that starts the recitative and the actual notes of the start of P in the *finale*. The surprise is the elaboration of the dominant e^1 with its upper half step, f^1. The ending f-e not only anticipates the notes in the accompaniment of violin II opening the *finale*, but the notes embody the basic half-step motive of the quartet, especially prominent in the last movement (see below).[115]

Besides the integration of the recitative with the first, fourth, and sixth movements already mentioned, there exist some other connections with the *finale* and first movement. These are (1) the rising sixth ($b\flat$-g) in both A and A^1 (octave higher) with the rising sixth e^1-c^2 (minor, not major), on beats two and three of P; and (2) KT recalls the KT phrase in the first movement (mm. 73-74, 188-92), both in rhythm and rising melodic line. The keys too prepare the *finale*, not only in the framing key of A minor, but the large area in D minor, so that the minor mode has an overwhelming presence.

Though the movement is not entitled "Recitative" in the autograph or first edition, it is so inscribed in two early sketches in the Moscow sketchbook.[116] That Beethoven did not in the end call the movement a recitative may be related to the tradition of free performance of the recitative.[117] Beethoven instead carefully controls the dynamics and tempos of the recitative, giving it great flexibility and color. Thirteen dynamic marks occur in this short movement, most of them in A^1. The indications range from *pp* to *ff*, and include three *crescendos* that gradually increase in length. The mark *espressivo* appears near the end of A (together with *ritardando*) as well as *smorzando* at the very end. Beethoven prescribes the variable tempo associated with the recitative, moving from *più allegro* to *Presto*

---

schrift Erich Schenk zum 5. Mai 1972, eds. Theophil Antonicek, Rudolf Flotzinger, and Othmar Wessely (Kassel: Bärenreiter, 1975), 103-16; and David Charleton, "Instrumental Recitative: A Study in Morphology and Context, 1700-1808," *Comparative Criticism* 4 (1982): 149-68.

[115] The same notes link KT^1 with A^1 in violin II (mm. 7^4-8^1).

[116] See the transcriptions in Vjaskova, ed., *The Moscow Sketchbook*, on 6/st. II ("Recit.") and 9/st. IV ("Re").

[117] Mies, *Das instrumenale Rezitativ*, 82. But see the remarks of Karl Holz on the performance of the movement, 292.

and *poco adagio*; he specifies two retards at the cadences of A and A¹, as well as an *accelerando* to the *Presto*. The effect is totally different from the indication "in tempo" that Beethoven applies to the orchestral recitative of the Ninth Symphony (an indication, however, rarely observed). For the function of the recitative movement, see below.

SOME REMARKS ON THE SKETCHES

The sketches for the recitative are revealing. Beethoven at first intended to present a short recitative connecting the third movement to the *finale*, thus making a conventional four-movement cycle. This six-measure sketch in the de Roda sketchbook is largely in D minor and 3/4, and anticipates almost exactly the rhythm of P, m. 1, of the *finale* (Ex. 4.25).[118] This anticipation appears in other early sketches but was altered in the final version so that the recitative avoids the *finale*'s rhythmic pattern. Another early sketch, in Aut. 11/2, starts with a variant of Pax of the first movement,[119] and several sketches anticipate the start of VI/P without the opening accompanimental figure.[120] An early sketch in the de Roda sketchbook shows an approach to the *finale* with eighth-note trill figures that outline the diminished seventh of A minor largely with the basic motives of the quartet, f-e and g_s-a.[121] All these early versions show Beethoven exploring ways of integrating the recitative with the *finale* as well as with earlier movements.

Example 4.25 An early sketch for a recitative connecting the third movement with the finale (de Roda Sketchbook)

The Instrumental Recitative in Beethoven [122]

Table 4.20 Beethoven's Instrumental Recitatives

1. *Die Geschöpfe des Prometheus*, ballet, Op. 43, No. 9; 1800-01; orchestral, oboe solo plus string tremolo; 11 mm.; *Adagio*, ¢, preceded by an *Adagio* 3/4 in E♭; keys: e♭; b♭-f-cV; many dynamics; at start: "con molto espressione"; followed by an *Allegro molto* ¢, c minor, *Sturm und Drang* style.

---

[118] See Vjaskova, ed., *The Moscow Sketchbook*, 23, Ex. 15.
[119] Ibid., 25, Ex. 18a.
[120] Ibid., 27, Ex. 20b.
[121] Ibid., 24, Ex. 16.
[122] See Mies, *Das instrumentale Rezitativ*, 73-85 and Thym,"The Instrumental Recitative." Mies also includes the famous "beklemmt" portion of the Cavatina in the quartet Op. 130 among Beethoven's recitatives.

2. Piano Sonata, Op. 31, No. 2/I; 1802; starts m. 143³; 4+4 mm.; *Largo* ₵ ; keys: d, f-f♯; unharmonized; no dynamic markings but "con espressione e semplice"; preceded by *p* and *pp*; functions as expressive expansion of P in recap.: Pa-Na-Pb-Pa¹-Nb resolving enharmonically into NT (f♭).

3. Piano Sonata, Op. 110/III; 1821-22; starts m. 4; unmeasured with an introduction of 3 mm. in ₵ meter; titled Recitativo: *più adagio, Andante, Adagio, Meno adagio, Adagio* (+ use of *rit.*); keys: a♭-E (*ff*)-a♭V; many dynamic marks, *cantabile, smorzando* at end; followed by "Klagender Gesang" (*Arioso dolente*), in a♭.

4. Symphony No. 9, Op. 125/IV; 1822-24; cello and double bass; length of recit. sections only (including orchestral cadences): 8-6-10-7-12-11-1/4 (54-1/4 mm.); titled "Selon le caractère d'un Récitatif, mais in Tempo;" start of mvt. is *Presto* 3/4; but *rit., Poco adagio* before quotation from second mvt.; twice Tempo 1 *Allegro* after quotation from third mvt. and phrase of Joy theme; keys: d-B♭-g-a-F-B♭-G♭-c♯-D, largely unharmonized; several dynamic marks; followed by the "Joy" theme in the cello and double bass.

5. String Quartet, Op. 132: 1825; 22 mm.; *più allegro* ₵-*rit.-in tempo-rit.-accel.- Presto* ¢, *poco adagio*; keys: a-F-d-aV; many dynamic marks, *espress.* (m.6), *smorzando* (m. 22); followed by the *finale, Allegro appassionato*, lyrical P.

6. String Quartet, Op. 131/III; 1826; 11 mm. (6+5); *Allegro moderato, Adagio*, ₵; keys: b-E-AV; many dynamic marks in mm. 9-11; followed by the lyrical theme of the variation set that follows, *Andante ma non troppo e molto cantabile*.

As the Table shows, the six recitatives make two groups chronologically: two appear in the early middle period, 1800/01-02, and four in the late period, 1821-26. Two occur in piano sonatas, two in string quartets, and two in orchestral works. The longest recitative, of course, is in the *finale* of the Ninth Symphony. While all the examples have been discussed and analyzed in many studies (except for the recitative in the ballet *Prometheus*, which has been neglected) some remarks are added here regarding these examples because of their relevance to the recitative in Op. 132 and their typically wide stylistic range.

Only two include the printed indication of "Recitatif" (Op. 125) and "Recitivo" (Op. 110). Two recitatives, in *Prometheus* and Op. 132, have a sixteenth-note tremolo string accompaniment for nearly all or a good part of the recitative, an old dramatic orchestral device.[123] The only recitatives with several prescribed tempo changes, including *ritardandos* and *accelerandos*, are those in Op. 110 and

---

[123] According to Egon Voss, "Schwierigkeiten im Umgang mit dem Ballett 'Die Geschöpfe des Prometheus' von Salvatore Viganò und Ludwig van Beethoven," *Archiv für Musikwissenschaft* 53 (1996): 31, Melpomene, the Muse of Tragedy, enters the stage in No. 9, where the recitative appears as the second of three parts. The reference to Melpomene occurs in Beethoven's sketches, as does the reference to the death of Prometheus at the end or middle of Part III, a long and stormy *Allegro molto* that follows the recitative. The one critic who discusses this recitative, David Charleton, 153-54, compares it to a recitative in C. S. Catel's ballet *Alexandre chez Apelles* (1808). This example fits Charleton's category of recitatives that give "'life' to silent characters in a ballet."

Op. 132, though such changes can also be found in Op. 125 and Op. 131. Both the recitatives in Op. 110 and Op 132 contain many dynamic contrasts and the indication *smorzando* ("dying away") at the end. The recitative in Op. 110 is unique in being unmeasured until its last cadential eighths.

All the recitatives modulate and end on V or I_4^6 of the key of the following movement except that in the Piano Sonata, Op. 31, No. 2 (see below). The new tonic arrives at the very last moment in Op. 131, as observed by Robert Winter.[124]

Beethoven makes the recitatives in Op. 31, No. 2 and Op. 125 largely or entirely unaccompanied. In Op. 31, No. 2, however, the pedal holds down during each phrase in a unique, coloristic effect. A different coloristic effect occurs in the recitative in Op. 110, which is to be played *una corda* except for the brief addition of *tutte le corde* with the marking < >.

A special consideration concerns the question of derivations in the recitatives. Op. 132 contains one of the richest sets of such connections. In Op. 125, besides the quotations from movements I-III, the opening phrase adumbrates the closing phrase, which itself nearly duplicates the bass recitative starting the vocal portion of the movement. The example in Op. 31, No. 2, contains stepwise motion and sigh motives related to Pb.

All the recitatives but the one in the D-minor piano sonata function as a bridge, a spiritual journey, or, as Thyn prefers, a "mediation" between two dissimilar movements.[125] The recitatives lead to an aria-like theme or movement, or literally to a vocal melody, as in the Ninth Symphony. Kinderman emphasizes the expressive function of the recitative in Op. 132, noting that

> Beethoven has inverted the function of the recitative in the Ninth: instead of opening utopian possibilities, this recitative forces a renewed confrontation with the music of pathos.[126]

The one exception occurs in the D-minor sonata, where the recitatives enrich the recapitulation of the primary key area, the second phrase modulating to the remote key of F minor and joining the new transition enharmonically. Beethoven prepares the recitative phrases by the freer style of P itself, with its unusual tempo and motivic contrasts. The opening of Pa, with its broken sixth chord, actually invites a continuation in recitative style since it represents a typical start to a recitative passage.

As scholars have discovered more and more, the use of instrumental recitative has a long history from the seventeenth century on. Beethoven's own examples influenced many later nineteenth-century composers such as Mendelssohn, Berlioz, and Liszt.[127] As Thym remarks, the instrumental recitatives

---

[124] Robert Winter, *Compositional Origins of Beethoven's Opus 131* (Ann Arbor: UMI Research Press, 1982), 127.

[125] Thym, 237.

[126] William Kinderman, *Beethoven* (Berkeley and Los Angeles: University of California Press, 1995), 297. See also Kerman, *The Beethoven Quartets*, 262.

[127] See Reinhard Strohm, "Rezitativ," *MGG*, 2nd ed., *Sachteil* 8 (1998), 236-37. While the first instrumental recitatives are usually attributed to Johann Kuhnau in his keyboard sonatas *Bibliche Historien* (1700), Seiffert, "Das Instrumentalrezitativ," 104-10, discovered much earlier seventeenth-century examples in a trio sonata "Harmonia Romana" (1669) and in G. B. Viviani's solo violin

represent a type of expression that can only insufficiently be translated into verbal concepts, because they are a pre-verbal or non-verbal kind of communication—through memisis and gesture rather than through words.[128] Beethoven's models for the instrumental recitative may perhaps have been the examples in Bach's Chromatic Fantasy and Fugue, a work he partly copied; Haydn's String Quartet in C, Op. 20, No. 2/II (1772), which he may have known since he copied the E♭ Quartet, Op. 20, No. 1; and Haydn's Sinfonia concertante, H: 105, with its violin recitatives in the finale (London, 1792). This is a subject, however, that requires further investigation.

Op. 132 and Mendelssohn's String Quartet A Minor, Op. 13

Beethoven's use of instrumental recitative had a strong impact on the young Mendelssohn, who was in general strongly influenced by Beethoven in his early years. Important examples of instrumental recitatives occur in Mendelssohn's early Piano Sonata Op. 6/II (slow movement) (1825) and the A-minor String Quartet Op. 13. Mendelssohn undoubtedly became familiar with Beethoven's late quartets as soon as they were published: Op. 127 in May 1827, and Op. 131 in June 1827. As noted above, both Opp. 132 and 135 were published in Berlin in September 1827 (in Paris, August 1827). The first movement of the quartet Op. 13 is dated 28 July 1827 and the end of the *finale* 26 October 1827. It may be possible that Mendelssohn examined the score of Op. 132 in Berlin during the summer of 1827, before the music was published. Otherwise, it is hard to explain certain similarities between the *finales*.[129]

Mendelssohn's fourth movement starts with an introduction in recitative style that has thematic connections with both the recitatives of Op. 31, No. 2/I and Op. 132 (Ex. 4.26a). The first phrase, Oa (mm. 1-8), closely resembles the first phrase in the D-minor Beethoven sonata and is in the same key. In *Presto* tempo and ¢ meter, it is inscribed "ad libitum," its free performance typical of recitative style. Like the sonata, there follows a quick passage in eighth notes, Ob (mm. 9-12), with similar articulations and "in tempo." Oc. (mm. 13-20) appears largely in F major (not F minor as in the sonata) and is succeeded by Ob¹ (mm. 21-28), doubled in length, varied, and leading to the P theme in A minor. The concluding half-step motive on f-e (mm. 25-28) also reminds us of Op. 132. Though it is related somewhat to Oa, Oc starts by duplicating almost exactly mm. 1-4 of the recitative in Op. 132 and 8-1/4 mm. of its bass line (Exx. 4.26b, c). Beethoven's phrase starts in F but quickly modulates to D minor,

---

sonata "Sinfonia Cantabile," Op. 4 (1678). Seiffert adds a long list of Baroque and Classic instrumental recitatives through Beethoven, and Charleton adds five more examples. In the Beethoven list, Seiffert includes the solo portions of the *Andante* in the Fourth Piano Concerto as well as the "beklemmt" passage in Op. 130. Strohm states that the term "Recitativo" occurs for the first time in F. A. Bonporti's *Invenzione da camera*, Op. 10 (Bologna, 1712), violin sonata No. 2. Charleton presents nine categories of instrumental recitatives but omits discussion of a linking function, which he places with "functions allied to those of the cadenza;" nor does he mention in this otherwise excellent article the recitative-aria relationship.

[128] Thym, "The Instrumental Recitative," 234.
[129] See Friedhelm Krummacher, *Mendelssohn—der Komponist, Studien zur Kammermusik für Streicher* (Munich: Fink, 1978), for the most detailed comparison with Op. 132 on 161-66, 190-94, 309-18.

Example 4.26a Felix Mendelssohn, String Quartet in A Minor, Op. 13/IV, introduction (mm. 1-28) and entrance of P

Example 4.26b A comparison between Op. 132/V (mm.3-6) with Mendelssohn's Op. 13/IV (mm. 13-18)

Example 4.26c The bass lines compared

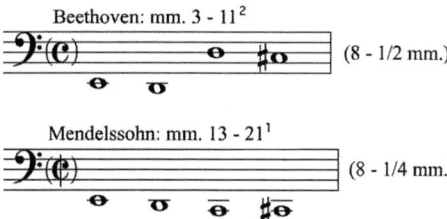

while Mendelssohn modulates to D minor suddenly, after eight measures. Both Mendelssohn recitatives are placed in the first violin accompanied by orchestral sixteenth-note tremolos in the lower parts, as in the Beethoven model. But the excited large leaps ending Oa and c have no parallel in Beethoven.

Mendelssohn integrates the recitatives with the main part of the movement in ways different from Beethoven. Ob returns to conclude P and initiate the transition—but only in the exposition of the sonata-form movement. Most novel is the recurrence of the recitative in the body of the movement. Oa returns at the start of the recapitulation (mm. 239-50), with a new expressive continuation in place of Ob. Finally, a brief new, unaccompanied phrase entitled "Recitativo" precedes the return of the Adagio that opened the quartet (mm. 368-72). This time the Adagio presents a full quotation of the second part of the song-motto of the quartet, "Ist es wahr?," bringing the quartet to an end.

Mendelssohn makes additional connections between the introduction and the *Presto* movement itself. The descending three-note motive in Oa returns as a basic motive in the secondary and closing areas; the descending skip of a fourth in Oc relates to the descending skip of a fifth starting P, resembling Op. 132; and the half-step motive recurs as a phrase link within the long primary theme (see mm. 36, 44, 48).

Perhaps most like Beethoven is the function of the recitative introduction as a mediation between the preceding lighthearted Intermezzo and the climactic finale, effecting a return to the tragic Affect. Besides the clear evidence of the impact of Op. 132 on the young composer, Robert Schumann, in his memoir of Mendelssohn, also notes that even much later in life, Mendelssohn spoke of Beethoven's A-minor Quartet.[130]

The Sixth Movement: *Allegro appassionato*

This impassioned movement is the longest in number of measures in the quartet, 404 mm., though in the performance of the Budapest Quartet it takes only two-thirds of the time of the first movement. Both A minor and major return as the *finale* touches on many of the main keys and some of the expressive states of earlier movements. The intense quality of motion, often with regular four-measure phrases and a regular harmonic rhythm, brings a feeling of resolution to the many tensions in preceding movements. As Ratner so rightly observes:

> Marked irregularities or wide contrasts of motion appear in each of the preceding movements. The finale, on the other hand, maintains its regularity of motion in waltz tempo from the first to the last, with one major change, a shift into Presto at the final refrain and throughout the coda. In terms of pure motion, the finale is a counterstatement to all that preceded it ....[131]

The use of the sonata-rondo plan for the *finale* has a long history (see 51-52). As Cole points out,[132] much time—eleven years—had passed after Beethoven's last example in this form, the lyrical second movement of Op. 90 (1814), a two-movement piano sonata. The basic structure of Op. 132/VI is given in the timeline (Table 4.21).

What are some of the surprises in this movement regarding the sonata-rondo tradition? The list below derives from but expands such features given by Cole in his analysis of this movement.[133]

SURPRISES IN THE SONATA-RONDO *FINALE* OF **OP. 132**

1. Use of the minor mode (only eight examples in Beethoven).
2. The unusual modal inflection in Pb, suggesting the Aeolian mode (see the discussion of P below).
3. Harmonic surprise in the first couplet where the second key area is not in the usual relative major (C major) but the remote G major and

---

[130] Robert Schumann, "Aufzeichnungen über Mendelssohn," Mit Anmerkungen von Heinz-Klaus Metzger und Rainer Riem, in *Musik-Konzepte 14/15, Felix Mendelssohn-Bartholdy* (Munnich: Hans Pribl, Sept. 1980), 112 (Blatt 4). For a study of Beethoven's influence on chamber music of the 19th and 20th centuries, including references to Op. 132, see Reinhold Brinkmann, "Wirkungen Beethovens in der Kammermusik," in *Beiträge zu Beethovens Kammermusik, Symposium Bonn 1984*, eds. Sieghard Brandenburg and Helmut Loos (Munich: G. Henle, 1987), 79-110.
[131] Ratner, *String Quartets*, 280.
[132] Cole, "Techniques of Surprise," 261.
[133] Ibid., 261-62.

STRING QUARTET

Table 4.21 Timeline: Movement VI

Key: a   Meter: 3/4

```
A                                                                        
     (+oh)    (oh)       (Poh, Pby)                              (Ny)   (ar)
                         B
Po    a    a¹    b    b¹   |PTa      a¹ (+Ny)   a²   a³ (Ny ext.)  |Sa   b   |
1     3    11   19²   27²   34        38        42.⁵  46.⁵         51²   57³
a                                                 G                 G    e
```

```
                              A
                   (Kb)    (Pom)
Ka    b    a¹    |KTa    b       |P      |Pbym-o
63³   67³  71³    75³    82²     90       123²
                          (C) a
```

```
C
Pbym-seq.   bym   Pom   dev.   |Pybm seq. inv.                        Pbym |
124         128   132   136    140    144    triple cpt.   148   152   156   160
F           C                         C:V⁷                 G:V⁷  a:V⁹⁰  d:V⁹⁰
```

```
                          A¹    B¹                                 D
(Pom)(+Poh)              (+Nh)                                   (KTb¹)
|RT:   Pom   ax-x¹- xy   |P¹   |PT¹   |S¹a¹   b   |K¹   |KT¹    |1N-fugato    1N+Pax
164    166   168         172    176   191   208²  214³  220³ 232³  243³         264
             d                         a           C     a          F          C-a   a-C
```

```
                          A²       Coda: E (A)
immer geschwinder        Presto
                         (Po¹,Nh)           (Sar)                       (a)
2RT:   Po¹+a¹ m¹-2m¹    |P²       |Pax²   2Na      Pax².¹   2Na¹   b   b¹   |3Na   a¹   |
271                      280       294³    299     302³     307    313  317   320²   324²
(C)a                                        A
```

```
                                           E¹
                    (Po²)                                               (c)
N2Ka   a¹   Pam²   |N3Ka   b    c   |enhanced repeat from Pa².¹        N3Kd ||
328    332  336     340    344  349  351³-400                    401      404mm.
```

the dominant minor, e, S being in both keys. In the recapitulation the keys return a fifth below in C-a, so that Sa is never heard in the tonic.[134] Both the exposition and recapitulation are dominated by the minor mode, while the development and coda feature major keys.

4. Importance of contrapuntal textures throughout the movement. The development exploits free triple counterpoint and melodic inversion (mm. 148-59), while the unexpected D section presents a fugato whose subject combines with motives from Pa (mm. 1-2). Many passages contain linear textures (such as Sa, Kb, P¹, coda-2N). All these examples connect with the intensive contrapuntal textures in movements I-III.

5. Metrical displacement in several passages, especially in Ka, where the barline is moved one beat to the left, and eighteen measures of the development, where the barline shifts one beat to the right (mm. 125-27, 129-31, and parallel passages).

6. The twelve-measure false recapitulation of P in D minor.

7. The final return of P in the high cello range and fast *Presto* tempo.

8. An enormous coda in A major and Presto tempo of 110 mm., more than 25% of the length of the movement. Ending in the tonic major occurs in three other Beethoven rondos in minor (Opp. 18, No. 4, 37, and 95).

9. Appearance of four new ideas in the coda.

10. A long and varied repeat of the coda section (57+53 mm.).

11. In contrast to the traditional sectionality of the rondo style, the movement displays an intensive continuity, characteristic of the quartet as a whole.

The P Theme

This is one of Beethoven's greatest lyrical melodies. He avoids a parallel-period arrangement as in the Violin Concerto and many other Beethoven rondos, even in the Op. 90 sonata. Instead, we find two long continuous periods, each containing eight measures in a two-reprise form of sixteen measures. Each period is repeated, the first an octave higher. Since Pb is also placed in a high register, the total range of the theme is over two octaves, its breadth intensifying the soaring quality of the melody (see Ex. 4.27).

These periods avoid the usual four-measure groupings. Various factors produce a longer continuity, as the repeated e in Pa, mm. 4-5, the descending bass in Pa, mm. 4-8, and the extended sequence in Pb, mm. 1-6.[135] Continuity is further achieved via the *crescendo* in each period that bridges mm. 4-5. In Pa, the *crescendo* starts in m. 3, and declines in m. 6 to *p* in m. 7, while it lengthens in Pb, starting in m. 2. Pb also contains an important *rinf.* in m. 6 that produces a 5+3 phrase subdivision.[136] Variety of structure occurs in Pb, with three two-measure modules in a varied sequence, creating more intense motion toward the final cadence.

[134] See Churgin, "Harmonic and Tonal Instability," 49-51, Kerman, "Beethoven's Minority," 151-73, and remarks in Ch. 2, n. 81.

[135] In discussing P, I refer to mm. 1-8 of Pa (excluding Po) and Pb separately.

[136] In the Eulenberg score, the *rf* is replaced by *sf* in m.32. Another error concerns m.3 and parallel measures, which are slurred in the Eulenberg score but with a staccato on note 4 in the autograph.

STRING QUARTET

Example 4.27   The primary theme (mm. 1-34)

Each period rises in direction to a climax, g^2 in Pa, m. 6 (and g^3 in its repetition) and the more sustained e^3 in Pb, mm. 6-7. The climax in Pa is further intensified by the dissonance of a major ninth on the beat (see below). The rhythmic pattern in Pam unifies the melody, as it returns in Pa, mm. 3 and 6, and Pb, m. 7.

HARMONIC ASPECTS

The half cadence in Pa, m. 8, is not in A minor but C major, a key tonicized in mm. 5-8 of Pa. Note the beautiful progression V^4_3/IV-IV, the g climax making a major ninth against the IV chord in m.6. Because of the prominent g♮, both melodically and harmonically as C:V, one hears a suggestion of the Aeolian mode in Pa.[137] This color is strengthened by the rise of g♮ to a in the bass of Pa, m. 8 (V-V^7-vi of C, vi becoming the tonic of A minor). In the repeat of Pa, the juxtaposition of the G chord with the initial D-minor chord of Pb is decidedly modal, suggesting a minor dominant relationship with the G chord (as in G Mixolydian). The modal color in P connects with the use of the pure Lydian mode in the *Adagio*. These harmonies enrich the long tonic arrea of 47-1/4 measures (with PT).

Five outstanding harmonies in P recur later in the movement as keys—F, C, G, d, and e. The last two are tonicized in the Pb sequence. Surely the return of G as the key of Sa reinforces the Aeolian color, though e is the main key of the rest of the exposition. C and F major return as significant keys in the development, and C as the key of Sa in the recapitulation and even as bVII in the D-minor false recapitulation (m. 171). All these keys are heard earlier in the quartet and their return here is cyclical in effect (see the discussion below on cyclical aspects).

THE ACCOMPANIMENT

The two-measure introduction to P is very appropriate here as a kind of orchestral setting for the aria-like P that follows. Such introductory measures in an *allegro* movement that present the accompaniment before the theme appear in the late quartets also in the second *finale* of Op. 130 in B♭ major—Beethoven's last completed movement—where the accompaniment starts on the "wrong" note, g, for an off-tonic start to the movement on V/ii.[138]

A basic cyclical aspect is the half-step motive f-e, and related motives, which dominates the accompaniment and recalls notes 3-4 of O in movement I (see the discussion of the motive below). The homophonic texture is more than simply melody and accompaniment highlighting the great melody in the first violin. The accompaniment is given many special details. The lower three parts group in contrasting rhythmic patterns, as the cello stresses the downbeat with the exaggerated trochaic rhythm ♩ ♫ coupled with a short *crescendo* on

---

[137] As Ratner, *String Quartets*, 279, observes: "... the finale introduces a folkloric modality in an offhand fashon by canceling the leading tone in a minor mode, and by sliding back and forth between A minor and C major.

[138] The device recalls the introduction to Mozart's 40th Symphony/I. See Glenn Carruthers, "Strangeness and Beauty: The Opening Measure of Mozart's Symphony in G Minor, K. 550," *JM* 16 (1998): 183-99, which concerns Po in Haydn and Mozart.

beats two-three; and the second violin and viola pair in syncopated patterns emphasizing beat two, with an upbeat to beat two in violin II, which carries the half step. Both instruments also contain a *crescendo* sign on beat two. As Ratner points out, the lower three voices create a composite rhythm ♪♩ ♩. ♪, where beat three is heard only in the violin melody.[139] The syncopation produces a restless intensity of its own. It is both a foil to the straightforward rhythm of the melody and a factor in heightening its pathos.

THREE SKETCHES FOR THE PRIMARY THEME

The earliest versions of P were noted down by Beethoven while he was composing the Ninth Symphony. He was considering an instrumental rather than choral *finale*, as shown by the heading for the earliest sketch, "Finale instrumentale." The sketches appear in a pocket sketchbook, Aut. 8/2, probably dated in the winter of 1823/1824. They are transcribed and published by Nottebohm, who dated sketches 1-2 June or July 1823 and sketch 3 in the fall of 1823, dates no longer valid (see Ex. 4.28 on p. 375).[140]

The sketches, written in D minor, the key of the symphony, were later taken up by Beethoven for the *finale* of Op. 132, another striking example of the reuse of earlier ideas in this quartet. Though these earliest sketches seem primitive, they contain several connections with the primary theme of Op. 132. The length of Pa and Pb is the same—eight measures for each phrase. Both Pa and b have the same basic rhythmic motive as in the final version, ♩. ♫ , though it is repeated mechanically through most of Pa. Melodically, Pa, mm. 1-4 of sketches 1 and 3, is nearly the same as the final version, while sketch 2 slightly alters and weakens the contour of the first measure. Pb, which appears in sketch 2, also presents a threefold rising inexact sequence and cadences with a similar motion from the fifth to the first degrees. The repeated quarters ending Pa¹ in sketch 2 and extended at the cadence in sketch 3 were eventually pushed back to mm. 4-5 of the final version.

Perhaps the most revealing is the harmonic aspect since all three sketches show the modal inflection so striking in the final version. The cadence in sketches 1 and 3 occurs on a major IV—G major—suggesting a Dorian relationship or a V/♭VII, as indicated in sketch 3. Indeed, sketch 2 features the flat seventh degree melodically in mm. 6-7, a location similar to the final version. The strong emphasis on G in the melodic line of these sketches, though related to the Dorian mode, seems to furnish the background to the beautiful climax on g in the final A-minor version. Steady harmonic rhythm, basically moving a chord per measure, also resembles the final version and the chords in mm. 1-4 are exactly the same.[141]

---

[139] Ratner, *String Quartets*, loc. cit.

[140] See N II, 180-81; Sieghard Brandenburg, "Die Skizzen zur Neunten Symphonie," in Harry Goldschmidt, ed., *Zu Beethoven 2* (Berlin: Verlag Neue Music, 1984), 128-29; and JTW, 408-10. Brandenburg's dating of Aut. 8/2 is the same as that in JTW. Aut. 8/2 is now located in Kraków, Biblioteka Jagiellońska.

[141] Some of these analytical points are made by Radcliffe, *Beethoven's String Quartets*, 120.

Varied Repeats of P

In the exposition, when Pa and b are repeated, Beethoven varies the setting. He doubles the melody entirely or partly in the viola an octave below, and in Pb, places the bass line an octave higher in two measures (mm. 27, 29). When P recurs after the exposition Beethoven repeats the same layout but with some melodic and harmonic nuances and exchanges of parts. Thus, in Pa, m. 6, second eighth, violin II adds $b\flat^1$, the seventh of the preceding V/IV, giving an even stronger feeling of F major. Beethoven eliminates the repeats in the second return of P(P^1), starting the recapitulation. Pa, returning at the higher octave, is not doubled; the viola has the cello part an octave higher, while the cello carries a varied violin II part, starting with the half step f-e motive, a continuation of the previous half step on $b\flat$-a from the false recapitulation. The step motive is imitated by violin II in dialogue with the cello, thus striking beat three in the accompaniment, now given a composite steady eighth-note motion against the melody. Motion increases in Pb^1 via the addition of eighth-note figures in the second violin. Introduced at the cadence of Pa^1, the figures are incorporated in Pb^1 and expanded from m. 4 to larger groups of five eighths. All these changes plus the cello pizzicato in most of Pb^1 refresh and enrich the theme. Even more, as so often in Beethoven, the start of the recapitulation is intensified, here especially through the high range and increased motion.

The fourth appearance of P, leading to the coda, is the most altered and dramatic. In a *Presto* tempo (after a nine-measure *accelerando*), the dynamic level becomes *forte*, with *sf* accents on the first note of each measure after the first, and violin II and the viola accompany in repeated eighths. Beethoven places the melody in the high cello (Pa being at the same pitch level as the opening of the movement), while violin I continues with its previous eighth-note figure and f-e motive, joining the cello at the higher octave from Pa, m.12^3 (m. 283^3) (Ex. 4.29). The final two measures, however, are truncated as the dominant note e^3 holds over *decrescendo*, and the coda starts softly with a new form of Pa based on 1m.

What is the meaning of the final setting of P? Tempo variations involving a faster tempo setting occur in several Beethoven codas, as in the codas of the "Waldstein" Piano Sonata, Op. 53 (P) and Fifth Symphony, Op. 67 (P, T, K), but it rarely occurs with an entire, continuous lyrical theme. Can we say this is an heroic or defiant transformation, coming after the larger part of a twelve-measure painful passage involving the f-e motive in the high range of violin I? Helm describes the theme as achieving "its most passionate, most fervid expressiveness."[142] Vitercik calls it "explosive,"[143] while Lam states that the f-e climax and *Presto* P produce "scarcely endurable tension, belonging to the world of twentieth-century Expressionism and unparalleled in Beethoven."[144]

---

[142] Helm, *Beethoven's Streichquartette*, tr. Bent, 265.
[143] Vitercik, "Structure amd Expression," 249.
[144] Lam, *Beethoven String Quartets*, 34.

STRING QUARTET

Example 4.28 Three sketches of P for the Ninth Symphony (NII)

Example 4.29   The primary theme (P²) in the high cello, Presto (mm. 280-86)

THE HALF-STEP F-E (OR E-F)

A dominant feature of the movement, especially regarding P, is the falling half step f-e. These notes appear as notes 3-4 of I/O and notes 1-2 of the inversion of O, which combined with I/Pa. Here, it is prominent in the accompaniment to P. Anticipated at the end of the recitative it continues in violin II in the two-measure introduction where the motive is highlighted. It is actually heard 16 times in the first 33 measures, more than half the section. PT verticalizes the motive as a bitter dissonance of the two notes, first as a minor ninth (f^3 in violin I against e^1/e in violin II and the viola, mm. 35, 39), and then reversed in double counterpoint as a major seventh (f in the cello against e^3/e^2 in the violins, m. 43) (see Ex. 4. 30). This function also includes the melodic motive as an inner voice in PTa¹, harmonized within an augmented sixth chord (mm. 42, 44, 46) and minor V^9 (m. 47). In the recapitulation of PT, the f-e dissonance becomes sharper with a two-octave e against f^3 (m. 196) and doubled f in octaves against e^3 (m. 200). Further, the melodic motive appears in the cello for the augmented-sixth progression (m. 195).

The fiercest setting appears in the *Presto* return of P. For 13 measures (mm. 271-82), Beethoven repeats the f-e motive high in the violin, with f^3-e^{2-3},

Example 4.30 PT, showing the verticalized dissonance of the f-e motive, mm. 35-48¹

as five measures in quarter notes accelerate to seven measures in eighth notes. Beethoven stresses the note f, placed as the first note of the figuration, the f leaping down a minor ninth to e, which then rises and later falls an octave. The f-e half step appears on beats one and three and then on one and two (Ex. 4.31). Combined with a long *crescendo* and *accelerando* ("immer geschwinder"), this unit has tremendous power. As a high upper pedal, it sounds against the only motivic development and fragmentation of Pam in the lower parts, and then overlaps for three measures the start of P in *Presto* tempo. This is the climactic appearance of the motive for the entire quartet.

Finally, near the end of each large section of the tranquil coda that follows, Beethoven both recalls and resolves the motive in N3Ka. It is heard in the violin I melody twice in rising form as e^3-f^3 and then twice in major, e^3-$f_{\sharp}^3$. However, Beethoven also recalls the sharp dissonant setting in PT in two ways. In the first presentation of N3Ka (mm. 340-343), f^3 and $f\sharp^3$ sound against e^2 in one of the inner parts. The dissonance is softened by the dynamics, which proceed from a *dim.* in N1Ka to *pp* starting N3Kb. The variation in mm. 389-92 contains new eighth-note motion in the lower parts, the second violin presenting the original falling motive f^2-e^2 and $f\sharp$-e^2 rubbing even more strongly against the slower moving quarters in violin I with major and minor sevenths (Ex. 4.31).

Example 4.31 The accelerando setting of the f-e motive in violin I (mm.271-79), combined with Pam and 2m

OTHER HALF-STEP MOTION

Since half-step motion is unavoidable in melody and accompaniment, only unusual or emphasized half-steps will be mentioned. Many such examples are chromatic leading-tone figures. The rising half-step stands out in PT (see Ex. 4.30), in both inner voices and violin I. On d♯-e, these half-steps both anticipate the final use of the rising form in N3Ka and recall the rising half step that opens movement I (g♯-a). Both rising and falling half steps mark Kb and KTb, preparing the accompaniment of P that follows (KTb has eleven half steps in eight measures).

Example 4.32 The coda setting of 2NK, section 2 (mm.389-93), with the e-f♮ and the e-f♯ motives in violins I and II (in reverse), combining quarter- and eighth-note motion

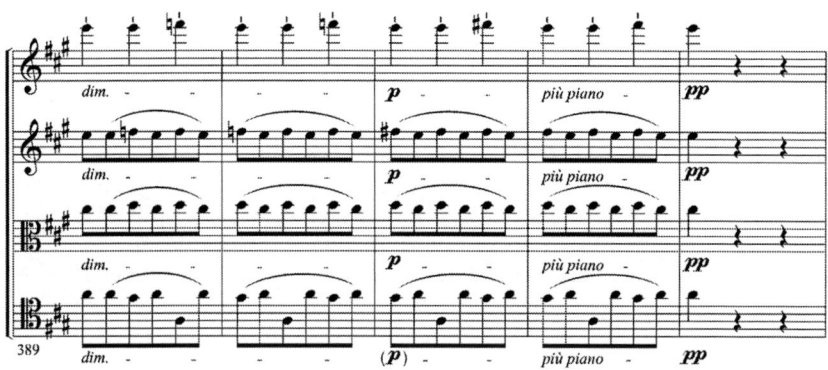

The forceful development focuses on Pbm and is saturated with half-step motion. In two sets of sequences, descending half steps occur alternating in the cello/violin I accompaniment every four measures, while the eighth-note motivic development ornaments rising half steps (Ex. 4. 34 on p. 381). In between the sequences Beethoven inserts a mysterious passage in eighth-note motion whose melodic line also features rising half steps against descending chromatic motion in contrapuntal combination. The final section that both contains and intensifies half-step motion is the fugato, which evolves into the astringent f-e violin part. While some half-step motion continues in the coda, as in the viola bass of 2Nb and b^1 (mm. 313-319), as well as the closing chromatic unison in mm. 348-49 and especially mm. 396-98, it is the highlighting of the half steps in N3Ka that remains the most memorable and significant passage.

CONTINUITY

Despite the more relaxed style associated with the rondo, all the functions and major sections are connected in various ways. Most striking are the following examples:

1. The PT section that functions also as the codetta to P by extending its final two measures, as Ratner points out.[145]
2. The overlapping of the main secondary key, which starts in the middle of S with Sb rather than in Sa or Ka.
3. The extension of Kb^1. Modulating away from the second key, it becomes the first phrase of the transition leading back to P (Kb^1=KTa).
4. The intertwining of the false recapitulation in D minor with the return of P in the tonic, thus linking developmnent and recapitulation (mm. 164-76; see Ex. 4.33). Here P is heard in its original key of d. After the hocket V_2^0 of d, the cello line bridges the section with its continuous

---

[145] Ratner, *String Quartets*, 278.

Example 4.33 The false recapitulation in D minor and start of P¹ (mm.164-79)

presentation of the half-step motive as mournful sighs, first on $b\flat^1$-a^1, then on f^1-e^1. In the violin dialogue that ensues (mm. 168-76), violin II presents Pax in the subdominant D minor, echoed by violin I an octave higher. Its expected c♮ ending, however, is replaced by c♯ and harmonized with a C-major chord, ♭VII, like the end of Pa but without the intervention of the relative major. Violin II then presents all of Pax (mm.1-4) in D minor as if the entire theme would be heard in that key. Violin I again replies, but in the tonic key of A minor, initiating the "true" recapitulation. This return, however, does not seem quite secure —perhaps the dialogue will continue—until the remaining measures

Example 4.34 Half-step motion at the start of the development section (mm. 124-31)

of Pa complete the phrase. Beethoven here achieves a remarkable section of suspense and connection. The octave relationship of the violin dialogue anticipates the recurrence of Pa at the higher octave.

5. The overlap of the first violin part ending 2RT with the final return of P (mm. 276-82; see Ex. 4. 29).

6. The shift to the *Presto* tempo that links the final appearance of P with the coda rather than reserving the fastest tempo for the coda itself, as in the "Waldstein" Piano Sonata, Op. 53/II. This tempo overlap resembles the tonal overlap between S and K.

These dramatic examples complement several shorter examples of continuity, like the imitative overlap between T and Sa (mm. 50-52), and the harmonic connection between the end of S and the start of K via the resolution over the same bass of an unusual augmented sixth chord on V/VI-VI (m. 63). Beethoven also ends the first return of P *forte*, connecting to the loud start of the development (m. 123).

The Coda

This large coda of 110 mm. constitutes more than 25% of the movement. Its sheer length anchors the conclusion, not only for the *finale* but also for the composition as a whole, as in so many works by Beethoven (and also in the Violin Concerto). The turn to the tonic major—A—resolves the expressive tension of both the *finale* and the entire quartet. It also recalls the A major of S in the recapitulation in movement I,[146] of the mainly calm second movement, and the key, though not the mood, of the March. The key also harks back to Beethoven's first conception of the *finale*, which was to be in A major. [147]

A feeling of resolution for the entire quartet stems from several factors, first of all the stable A-major tonality, with only a hint of minor in the f-e phrase and the cadence of section 2. Unlike many Beethoven codas, no tonal digression occurs at the start of the section (as in the *Eroica* and String Quartets, Op. 127/IV and Op. 130/III). The coda resembles the finales of the Violin Concerto, the Fifth Symphony, and Op. 131 in this respect. The quality of resolution is further supported by the largely four-measure phrase structure and varied phrase repetitions which have a stabilizing effect, as do the simple rhythmic patterns and repetitions, especially the ♩ ♩ repeated pattern in 2N.

A basic stabilizing factor is the large-scale repetition of the coda's main section, creating divisions of 57+53 mm. (not counting the upbeats at the start). The repeat was an afterthought and added on the autograph when the moveent had been finished (see Plate 4.II)[148] Varied repetition of section I, beginning from m. 351^3, recalls the process of double variation in the D-major theme of the "Heiliger Dankgesang." As in that theme, the texture is enriched with new doublings and fuller settings. Further, rhythmic motion, mostly in the lower parts, increases to the eighth-note level, especially in 2N and N2Ka, so that overall 32 measures of the varied repetition drive forward with increased rhythmic intensity necessary for a strong conclusion. Unlike the D-major theme, however, only one phrase is slightly ornamented, Pam^2 (mm. 385-88), here in eighths. The varied repetition also provides greater harmonic nuance, especially in 2N and N2Ka (see Ex. 4.35 on p. 384).

Thematically, Beethoven frames the section with derived material, while new themes and new cadential periods enrich the thematic content, a device mentioned in the composition treatise by Anton Reicha.[149] Thus, the coda starts with the lyrical expansion of Pa (m. 294^3-98, a 2+2 sequence), which returns in ornamented form (m. 302^3-06), while a more extensive treatment of Pam recurs *forte* and largely *sf* in mm. 336-39, the sequence mounting scalewise in one-measure modules from a^2 to f^3; succeeding this phrase is the final resolution of the f-e motive (mm. 340-43). The last cadential measures follow these concrete references (344-51, 393-404).

The N ideas are lyrical as well as active and cadential. Most extensive and moving is the lyrical 2N of 17 measures, with its high cello melody and

---

[146] Vitercik, "Structure and Expression," 250.
[147] Brandenburg, "The Historical Background," 164; Vitercik, "Structure and Expression," 251.
[148] See Brandenburg, "The Autograph of Beethoven's String Quartet in A Minor, Op. 132," 283. Brandenburg states that the present coda is actually a third version. Beethoven replaced the first version because of voice-leading changes.
[149] Anton Reicha, *Traité de haute composition musicale*, vol. 2 (Paris: Zetter & Cie., c. 1825), 298. Famous late examples of N ideas in the coda appear in Beethoven's Ninth Symphony/I and III.

STRING QUARTET

PLATE 4.II *Autograph, Op. 132/VI, coda, showing the original ending of the movement crossed out and the Coda repetition starting from m. 351. Staatsbibliothek zu Berlin-Preussischer Kulturbesitz, Musikabteilung mit Mendelssohn-Archiv, Mendelssohn-Stiftung 11, p. 132.*

doubling (see Ex. 4. 35 on p. 384). Interestingly, 2Na twice follows the lyrical transformation of Pam almost as a consequent phrase until its recurrence is lengthened and completed by its own consequent. With the lyricized Pam the lyrical section is 25 measures. This lyrical area returns to the lyricism associated with P but long deferred by episode D and the *Presto* transformation of P.

In considering the structure of the coda, we have mentioned the large-scale sectional repetition, variation process, and framing of the section with derived material. Another element is also at work, the organization of surface rhythm. At first the lyrical section has a motion-rest plan, with the larger values

Table 4.22 Deceleration of Surface Rhythm, mm. 327–47[1]

function	end 3N-N2K	Pam	N3Ka	N3Kb	
rhythmic pattern	♩♪♪♪♪♪.	♩. ♪♪♩	♩ ♩ ♩	♩ 𝄽 𝄽 | 𝅗𝅥 ⌒	♩ ♩ ♩
no. of measures	9	4	4	2	2
measure number	326	336	340	344	346 347

of 2N predominating. After the active area of 3N-N2K, Beethoven gradually decelerates the surface rhythm to the final cadence as follows (see Table 4.22 on p. 383).[150]

The slowest motion coordinates with the softest dynamics, *dim.* to *pp.* The final cadence in N3Kb restores the motion to two impacts a measure, one being a syncopated half (m. 348). Increased eighth-note motion in the sectional repeat alters the surface-rhythmic plan to a large motion-short rest effect.

We should note the emphasis on f♯ in the final cadence of section 1 (m. 346), strengthening the major mode. In the parallel passage of the repeat, however, f♯ is replaced by c♮ in the lowest open strings of the viola and cello (m. 395), dramatically recalling A minor and lengthening the chromatic rise to V (mm. 395-98; Ex. 4. 36). But the f♯ still appears here for a vi chord that comes a measure earlier, replacing the tonic major found in section 1 (m. 394). The c♮ that follows makes a drastic augmented fourth with the preceding f♯, increasing the tension of this remarkable ending to the movement.

Example 4. 35 A comparison of the two settings of 2Na in the coda (mm. 307-12 and mm. 356-61)

---

[150] In Table 4.22, the rhythmic pattern of Pam is in violin I and, I believe, predominant. However, the inner voices continue eighth-note motion, grouped in a 2 x 3 hemiolic pattern based on Pam. Thus both types of motion are combined in this phrase as a transition to the much slower surface rhythm that follows.

Probably the sonority and dynamics strike the listener first of all. The oft-cited ethereal quality is produced by the passages with high cello, the viola functioning as a high and weak bass (mm. 293^4-319). This happens especially in 2N, where the first violin doubles the high cello an octave above, the cello reaching the high $f\sharp^2$, while the viola-bass contrasts on its C-string (see Ex. 4. 35). Another high sonority occurs with the return of the e-f($\sharp$) motive, juxtaposed with the low unison in mm. 347-49, and especially in section 2 with the low $c\sharp$ and chromatic lines in the lowest parts.

Supporting the ethereal effect of the coda are low dynamics on the *piano* level with expressive < > within most phrases. 2N starts *pp* and a gradual *crescendo* starting in m. 326 reaches a *forte* only in m. 336, with *sf* on beat one of the next three measures. The e-f phrase recedes to *pp* before a *crescendo* to *forte* occurs in the unison cadence. The movement ends with a firm *ff* only in the last two measures (mm. 403^2-404).

And so concludes one of Beethoven's greatest works, a quartet that requires and repays the deepest study. It seems appropriate to end this part of the chapter with Karl Holz's report of his conversation with Beethoven after the composer had completed the three Galitzin quartets (partly cited above). While Holz thought the Quartet Op. 130 was the greatest of the three, Beethoven answered:

> *Each in its own way*! Art demands of us that we . . . shall not stand still. You will find a new manner of voice treatment . . . and *thank God there is less lack of fantasy than ever before*.[151]

Integration of the Cycle and Cyclic Form

Throughout the discussion of Op. 132, larger integrative features have been mentioned, which are summarized and further elaborated here.

The traditional concept of "cyclic form" considers only the thematic aspect,[152] and indeed several such examples occur in Beethoven's music, most of all in the late period. Table 4. 24(pp. 390-91) can undoubtedly be augmented by additional examples with further study of this subject.[153] In Op. 132 the themat-

---

[151] Translation from Thayer-Forbes, 982. The German text appears in Lenz, *Kritischer Katalog*, 217: "j e d e s i n s e i n e r A r t! die Kunst will es von uns, dass wir . . .nicht stehen bleiben. Sie werden eine neue Art der Stimmführung bemerken . . . und a n F a n t a s i e f e h l t ' s G o t t l o b, w e n i g e r a l s j e z u v o r."

[152] See, for example, the brief entries in the *New Grove Dictionary* by Hugh MacDonald (the same article appears in both editions) and the *New Harvard Dictionary of Music*. A survey of concrete thematic recurrence between movements in works from Beethoven (only a few examples) to Bartók is given in Günther von Noé, "Der Strukturwandel der zyklischen Sonatenform," *Neue Zeitschrift für Musik* 125 (1964): 55-62. Noé, 146, rejects most of the thematic resemblaces between movements in examples by Haydn and Mozart cited in Karl Marx, "Uber die zyklischen-Sonatenform, zu dem Aufsatz von Günther von Noé," in the same issue as Noé's article, 142-46. For a survey of the topic and consideration of cyclic elements in Haydn, see James Webster, *Haydn's "Farewell" Symphony and the Idea of Classical Style* (Cambridge: Cambridge University Press, 1991), especially the section "Integration of the Cycle," 174-224.

[153] I am excluding references derived from Schenkerian analysis. For an example of this approach, see Keven Korsyn, "Integration in Works of Beethoven's Final Period" (Ph.D. dissertation, Yale University, 1983). Elaine Sisman, "Memory and Invention at the Threshold of Beethoven's Late Style," in *Beethoven and His World*, eds. Scott Burnham and Michael P. Steinberg

Example 4.36 The conclusion of the finale (mm. 383-404)

ic connection of movements is effected through the half-step motive, both rising and falling. Each movement, except movements IV and V (however, see the reference regarding movement IV below) begins with the half step g♯-a (movements I, II) or f-e (movements III, chorale phrase a, and VI, in the introductory accompaniment to the opening theme). Both half steps open movement I: g♯-a-f-e, and half- step motion in general occurs prominently in many figures and figurations. We see too how the first half step g♯-a is emphasized in the opening of the first two movements, while the f-e motive predominates in the latter part of the cycle, especially the *finale*. As noted on p. 359, Vitercik speculates regarding a possible f-e connection in violin I from the last note of movement III, f^3, to the first note of the upbeat to movement IV, e^1.[154] The use of a recurring head motive for each movement is a device associated with the late period, being found earlier in the Piano Sonata, Op. 106 ("Hammerklavier"), 1817-18, and the Ninth Symphony, 1822-24. This device is adumbrated in the Piano Sonata Op. 57 ("Appassionata"), 1804-06, where a neighbor-note motive occurs at the start of movements II (theme and variations) and III, and near the start of movement I (mm. 3-4). The motive is developed in the fast movements as well.[155]

Many other factors besides the thematic integrate the cycle as a whole.[156] These include the thematic and harmonic connections of movements IV-VI; the sectional recurrence in movements I, III, and VI; beginning movements I-V with single tones (movements II and V in unison), "as if Beethoven were moving from either silence into action or using a single tone to bring about a transition from one affective stance to another;"[157] tonal cross reference (see below); contrapuntal textures in all movements except the recitative; in movements I and III cantus-firmus like themes which combine with an expressive, individualized melody (in movement I, the combination of O and Pa; in the third movement, section A², the transformed Pa⁰ joined with Pa); dance rhythms in all movements except the recitative: the march relating movements I and IV, the waltz movements II and VI, and the sarabande in movement III/B.

Tonal cross reference is a basic feature of Beethoven's music, though not unique.[158] It occurs in all works examined in this volume. The main keys of movement I reappear in later movements. Besides the tonic A minor of move-

---

(Princeton and Oxford: Princeton University Press, 2000), 51-87, deals essentially with three works composed in 1815-16 (nos. 8, 9, and 18 on my list). She is concerned with recall of movements and themes, giving in her Table 1 (p. 52) a list of eight works with the heading "Pieces by Beethoven with 'Returns' of Earlier Movements toward the End of the Cycle (nos. 1, 5, 7-9, 11,12, and 18 on my list). Beethoven's use of head motives, and choral examples are not included.

[154] Vitercik, "Structure and Expression," 249.
[155] For the Piano Sonata, Op. 57, see Frohlich, *Beethoven's "Appassionata" Sonata*; for the Op. 106, see the discussion by Tovey, *Companion*, 221.
[156] See Tusa, "Some Factors for Cyclic integration," 153-92, and my discussions in chapters 1 and 2, 9-13, 185-89.
[157] Ratner, String Quartets, 277. See also 272.
[158] Examples can be found in the works of many composers such as G. B. Sammartini, Boccherini, Viotti, Haydn, and Mozart, as well as Beethoven. See also Ethan Haimo, "Remote Keys and Multi-movement Unity: Haydn in the 1790s," MQ 74 (1990): 242-68.

Table 4. 23   Recurrence of Keys Found in Movement I

Key	Movement
a	tonic of mvts. I, VI; end, mvt. V
A	I, recap of S; tonic of II, IV; mvt. VI, coda
F	I, second key area, exposition; related to Lydian mode, III/P; development of II/A, VI; start of V
C/c	I, second key area of recurrence; development of I, II/A, VI; recap of Sa in VI; as c minor, I dev.
d/D	I, exposition, 2Ta; recurrence, NT; V, main part; VI, false recap; as D major, III/S; IV development
e/E	I, recurrence/P; VI, exposition, Sb, K; as E major, second key area of II, waltz and Allemande, IV
g/G	I, development; as G major, VI exposition, Sa

ments I and VI, the appearance of S in A major in the recapitulation of the first movement recurs as the tonic key of movements II and IV as well as the coda of the *finale*. The choice of F major as the second key area of I/exposition links especially with the chorale of movement III. Certainly, the keys of a, A, and F are the most important in the quartet. In addition, other keys appearing in movement I also return in later movements. These are C, d, e, and g. The major-minor exchange of a-A recurs with the other keys except F major (see Table 4.23 above).

Looking most broadly at the tonics of each movement, we find a degree of symmetry, with the Lydian movement in the center flanked by A major, a chromatic third-relationship typical of the late period (X stands for the modulatory recitative; see Fig.4.2)

Figure 4.2   Symmetrical plan of keys in Op. 132
a-A-F-A-X-a   (A)

The cyclic *finale* coda integrates certain basic aspects of the quartet. The key of A major picks up the keys of movements II and IV; the varied repetition of the entire section reinforces the variation procedures of movements I, II trio, and III (especially S); and the half-step motive appears near the end of each section, resolving the minor half-step into the major, as e-f becomes e-f♯.

A final integrative feature rarely mentioned in this connection concerns the treatment of dynamics. On one hand, we find such older devices as changing the dynamic level of P themes from *piano* to *forte*. This occurs with both I/P in the recurrence (from *pp* to *ff*) and VI/P in its final appearance in *Presto* tempo. *Crescendos* are also carefully organized, as in the second-movement trio. On the other hand, the total dynamic span is lower. *Forte* is the basic loud level, while many stretches of *piano, pianissimo,* and *decrescendos* to *pp* appear. Only a few *ff* marks can be found and only in movements I, V, and VI. As noted earlier, Beethoven prescribes only one *ff* for the climax of the coda in the first movement, which ends in *f*, not *ff*. The *finale* contains *ff* phrases only in Ka (2 x 4 mm.), not in the powerful development, and not at all in the coda until the last two cadential measures.

Small nuances on the measure and even beat level are notated, with such markings as < > (see movement II/A), < (accompaniment in VI/P), and > . As Miriam Sheer observes, we discover in "Beethoven's approach to dynamics during his late period [such trends as] sublimation and restraint, long-range planning (found earlier as well), simplicity, subtlety, and increased attention to details."[159]

Let us return to the issue of cyclic form and thematic recurrence within a multimovement cycle. This kind of recurrence goes back to the fifteenth-century Mass, with its single cantus firmus for each movement and head motive (as in Dufay's "Missa se la face ay pale"). In the Classic period, such recurrence is relatively rare except in the music of Boccherini where we find recurring motives, themes, sections, and movements. Indeed, these are the most significant examples before Beethoven and more pervasive than in Beethoven.[160]

Leading Romantic composers used this device in their instrumental cycles, starting with Schubert, Mendelssohn, and Berlioz, in their desire for a more literal and comprehensive integration of the cycle. Perhaps the most important example of cyclic form in the twentieth century occurs in the works of Bartók, including varied returns of complete movements in palandromic form, as found in the String Quartet, No. 4 (1928). The purpose and techniques of integration must, of course, be studied for each composer.

With respect to cyclic form, Beethoven's music undoubtedly wielded the greatest influence on Romantic composers, in particular works such as the Fifth and Ninth Symphonies, and the piano sonatas such as the "Appassionata." Beethoven's concern for the work as a whole was articulated in a well-known letter from the beginning of March 1814 to Friedrich Treitschke, revisor of the libretto for *Fidelio*, regarding Beethoven's revision of the opera. Beethoven remarked: "For my custom when I am composing even instrumental music is always to keep the whole in view."[161]

At least 18 works by Beethoven contain cyclic returns, including three vocal works. Beethoven uses a considerable variety of techniques, encompassing head motives, motives, themes, sections, and movements. Most of these examples—nine—appear in the late period, dating from 1815 to 1826. Eight movements contain a simple recall of a theme or motive, most often from the opening theme of the first movement, as in Opp. 24, 27, No. 1 (recall of the slow movement), 43, 86, 98(recall of the opening song), 101, 110, 131. Other movements exploit a recurring motive in all or most movements, such as the Piano

---

[159] Sheer, "Dynamics on Beethoven's Late Instrumental Works," 359.

[160] See especially my article, "Sammartini and Boccherini: Continuity and Change in the Italian Instrumental Tradition of the Classic Period," *Chigiana* 43 (1993): 185-91; and Timothy Noonan, "Structural Anomalies in the Symphonies of Luigi Boccherini" (Ph.D. dissertation, University of Wisconsin, 1996). For further examples in Boccherini's chamber music, see Ellen Amsterdam, "The String Quintets of Luigi Boccherini" (Ph.D. dissertation, University of California at Berkeley, 1968); Miriam Tchernowitz-Neustadtl, "Aspects of the Cycle and Tonal Relationships in Boccherini's String Trios," *Chigiana* 43 (1993): 157-70; and Elizabeth Yougar, "A Study of the Piano Quintets, Op. 57 (1799), G. 413-18, by Luigi Boccherini" (M.A. thesis, Bar-Ilan University, 1998).

[161] BGA, 3, No. 707: "wie ich gewohnt bin zu schreiben, auch in meiner Instrumental Musick habe ich immer der ganze vor Augen...." The English quotation is taken from Anderson, I, No. 479.

Sonata, Op. 57 and the Fifth Symphony, while the *finale* of the Fifth Symphony also cites a varied version of the concluding section of the scherzo. The recall of the opening themes from movements I-III near the start of the *finale* of the Ninth Symphony is a unique dramatic device, used in addition to a recurring head motive at the start of each movement, as in Opp. 106 and 132. In most cases, these head motives are pervasively developed within each movement as well. The Cello Sonata, Op. 102, No. 1, presents a more complex example involving recall of part of the first slow movement in the second slow movement as well as use of motivic derivations from the initial movement within the two *allegros*.[162] In two examples entire first movements return, as in the Serenade, Op. 8 and the Cantata on the Death of Joseph II. While the return in Op. 8 is literal, in the cantata, the secondary material that appeared in the second key area returns in the tonic, a tonal adjustment we associate with the recapitulation of a sonata-form movement. The return in the cantata may be related to procedures associated with sacred vocal music. This is certainly the case with the reappearance of the Kyrie melody at the end of the C-Major Mass with the text of the Agnus Dei.[163] The table below lists Beethoven's cyclic works chronologically, and adds some details not mentioned in this brief survey.

Table 4.24 Beethoven: Works in Cyclic Form

Instrumental Works

1. Op. 8, Serenade in D for string trio, 1796-97: The opening movement, *Marcia, Allegro*, returns completely, even with the repeats of both sections, at the end of the cycle, which has eight movements.

2. Op.10, no. 3, Piano Sonata in D, 1797-98; The descending tetrachord in the opening of the movement returns at the close of movements II and IV. See 181-82.

3. Op. 24, Violin Sonata in F, "Spring," 1800-01: In the *Adagio*, a five-part rondo, the last return of the refrain (mm. 54-60) is replaced by new material recalling the opening five quarters of movement I, with slight variation. The turn motive of the sonata's opening appears earlier in partial inversion as an ornamental figure in section A (m. 6) and in inversion for section B (mm. 18, 20).

4. In the ballet *Die Geschöpfe des Prometheus*, Op. 43, 1800-01, the opening motive of the Overture's *Allegro* (mm. 16-18) returns toward the end of the *finale* in a fugato section (mm. 193-211).

5. Op. 27, No. 1, Piano Sonata in E♭, "quasi una Fantasia," 1800-01: Ten measures of movement III, *Adagio con espressione* in A♭, return in E♭ in the *finale*, just before the coda (+ new close).

6. Op. 57, Piano Sonata in f, "Appassionata," 1804-06: Each movement contains a neighbor-note motive near (movement I, mm. 3-4) or at the start of the movement (movements II, III). The motive recurs in other functions as well in the allegros, and is heard twice in the first period of the theme and variations of the *Andante*.

---

[162] See Lewis Lockwood, "Beethoven's Emergence from Crisis: The Cello Sonatas of Op. 102 (1815)," *JM* 16 (1998): 301-22.

[163] For returns of opening movements in sacred music, see also my article "Sammartini and Boccherini," n. 24. For the return of the Kyrie melody at the end of the Mass, see Bruce Campbell MacIntyre, *The Viennese Concerted Mass of the Early Classic Period* (Ann Arbor, MI: UMI Research Press, 1986), 121, 515-18, and Figure 10-7, 517.

7. Op. 67, Symphony No. 5 in c, 1807-08. The basic motive that pervades movement I recurs in movements II, III (especially the Scherzo), and IV (S, the development, the coda). In addition, part of the transformed A section (A^2) of the Scherzo returns at the end of the development section of the *finale*, leading to the recap. The section is 54 mm. long (mm. 152-206), and is only partly a direct quotation.

8. Op. 102/1, Cello Sonata in C, 1815: A varied presentation of the first slow movement recurs at the end of the second slow movement (last 7 mm.), and one of its main motives returns in the first part of the second slow movement. A K figure in the cello from movement I returns in II/P, which also recalls in inversion the first four-note motive that opens the sonata. Motives from the first slow movement recur in both fast movements.

9. Op. 101, Piano Sonata in A, 1816: Four measures of the opening theme and its extension (total of 8 mm.) return after the brief *Adagio* in a and connect with the *finale*.

10. Op. 106, Piano Sonata in B♭ ("Hammerklavier"), 1817-18: Each movement opens with a rising tenth or third, followed by a falling third, except the fugue *finale*, which opens only with a rising tenth. In each movement, the head-motive in P is extensively developed.

11. Op. 110, Piano Sonata in A♭, 1821-22: The motive of the rising fourths—$a\flat^1$-$d\flat^2$, $b\flat^1$-$e\flat^2$—found in the opening of movement I (mm. 1-3), returns at the start of the subject in the concluding fugue (mm.1-2). Movements III and IV are also interlocked in the pattern A-B-A^1-B^1.

12. Op. 124, the Ninth Symphony in d, 1822-24: Each movement starts with a descending broken tonic chord; in movements I, II, and IV a broken d-minor chord; in movement III, mm. 3-5^1 (after Po), a descending B♭: I^6 chord outlined in Pa; the broken chord in movement IV appears after a crashing dissonant chord. All the descending chords in movements I-III start on the note d. In both movements I and II, the head-motive is well developed within the movement. In the introduction to movement IV, Beethoven recalls the initial measures of the P themes of preceding movements in search for the "Joy" theme.

13. Op. 132, String Quartet in a, 1825: Movements I-III and VI begin with a half step, g♯-a or f-e, the notes that start movement I.

14. Op. 130, String Quartet in B♭ 1825: Movements I and III start with nearly the same notes, b♭-a-a♭ (movement I) and b♭-a-b♭-a♭ (movement III). Melodic and rhythmic motives from the first movement recur in the later movements as well.

15. Op. 131, String Quartet in c♯, 1826: 2P in movement VII is based on the fugue subject of movement I, using the rhythm of the original but varying the succession of notes, the theme presented as a parallel period. The theme is prominent in the coda as well.

There are other types of connections, as in the following examples from the piano sonatas. In Op. 31/2, 1802, movements I and II both start with rolled chords. In Op. 53, 1803-04, movement I, and the introduction to movement II, the initial measures contain a descending chromatic tetrachord in the bass.

Vocal Works

16. Cantata on the Death of Joseph II, WoO 87, 1790: The opening chorus returns at the end of the cantata with the same text. However, from m. 72 of the original, a change occurs. Material in E♭ is transposed down to c and C. From m. 98 there is a coda-like extension to m. 122 (the opening chorus is 111 mm.). The final orchestral conclusion is very similar but in c minor. Thus, Beethoven rounds off

the cantata in the tragic mood in which it opened, reiterating the word "Death" and Joseph's name. Structurally, the return resolves the opening section which ends in E♭ major. The two large sections together make an exposition-recap form on a grand scale, the sections separated by five intervening numbers.

17. Mass in C, Op. 86, 1807: At the very end of the Mass, after the Agnus Dei, a brief citation is heard of the opening of the Kyrie, but with the text "dona nobis pacem." The citation is 17 mm. long and in the tempo and meter of the Kyrie. The prayer for mercy here merges with the prayer for peace.
18. Op. 98, the song cycle "An die ferne Geliebte," 1816: The opening song returns at the end with a text similar to the last stanza of that song, with further development in a coda-like function (48 mm.).

Some Early Reviews of Op. 132

It is well known that Beethoven's late works were often severely criticized by reviewers, and his deafness frequently blamed for the unusual dissonances as well as for structures and expressions difficult to understand.[164] On the other hand, we also find comprehension and appreciation, though with acknowledgment of the truly new directions these works represent. Of the four reviews concerning Op. 132 reprinted in Kunze's collection and dating 1825-30, three are positive.[165]

In only one of these reviews, appearing in the *Revue musicale* (Paris, 1830),[166] does the reviewer stress a "bizarre conception," "a sometimes harsh harmony," and "vague intentions." He remarks that the quartet's progress is clearest in movements I, II, and VI. That the unique and complex first movement seemed "clear" may be ascribed, perhaps, to the rondo-like returns of the material, the traditional aspects of the exposition, and the distinct contrast between P and S. Like many critics of the time, and even in the twentieth century, the reviewer criticizes the length and "monotony" of the *Adagio*. On the other hand, there is warm appreciation for the "delicious details" in the second movement (called a "Scherzo" by all the reviewers) and the *finale*, "where Beethoven reveals himself entirely."

The German reviews show far greater enthusiasm for the quartet. The *AmZ* review (1825) reports the first public performance of the quartet in Joseph Linke's benefit concert on 6 November. Performed by the Schuppanzigh quartet, Op. 132 was heard between Beethoven's "Archduke" Piano Trio, Op. 97, and Bernhard Romberg's Fantasy for Cello and Orchestra. The review gives many details about the work and praises it throughout.[167] It lists each movement and its key, calling the opening an "Introduction," movement II a Scherzo, and movement V a "Recitative." The trio "captivated" listeners with its "naïve

---

[164] See Robin Wallace, *Beethoven's Critics* (Cambridge: Cambridge University Press, 1986), 41-42; K.M. Knittel, "Wagner, Deafness, and the Reception of Beethoven's Late Style."
[165] See Kunze, ed., *Die Werke im Spiegel seiner Zeit*, 590-93.
[166] Kunze, ed., ibid. The review appeared on 212-213.
[167] Kunze, ed., ibid., 590-91. The review is found in col. 840-41.

PLATE 4.III PETER PAUL RUBENS, LION HUNT (1621). Bayerische Staatsgemäldesammlungen, Alte Pinakothek, Munich.

naturalness, charming color, lovely melodies, and piquant flavoring."[168] As a whole, the quartet is described as "grand, splendid, unusual, surprising, and original."[169] However, the reviewer observes that the music must be heard often and requires study, a statement frequently encountered in reviews of the late works. Also noted is the fact that the prevailing "mournful character" of the music, the "uniformity of the very long Adagio," and "unbearable heat" in the hall were responsible for the fact that the quartet did not make a "general sensation," as expected, considering its success in earlier performances for small circles of listeners. Finally, the reviewer expresses his conviction that this quartet will become popular like the E♭ quartet, which had a lukewarm reception at the beginning. This statement implies a weak response to the quartet at the concert, and it contradicts the report of Beethoven's nephew Karl that the Piano Trio "as well as especially the quartet were much applauded . . . and Linke played better than ever."[170] It seems that Karl exaggerated the success of the work so as not to disappoint the composer.

---

[168] Kunze, ed., ibid., 591:"mit einer naiven Natürlichkeit, mit dem reizenden Colorit, den lieblichen Melodien, der pikanten Würze."
[169] Kunze, ed., ibid., 591: "gross, herrlich, ungewöhnlich, überraschend und originell."
[170] The full statement runs as follows: "Es war unendlich voll, und das Trio sowohl als besonders das *Quartett* wurde sehr beklatscht; auch ging es sehr gut zusamen, und Linke spielte besser als je." See *Ludwig van Beethovens Konversationshefte*, Bd. 8, 182. Wallace, *Beethoven's Critics*,

A brief review of the first editions of the string quartets Op. 132 and Op. 135 appeared in the *Allgemeine Musikzeitung* (1830).[171] The reviewer refers to the "difficult harmonies, wonderful leaps, and attractive passages" here as in the composer's other last works. He concludes that Beethoven was a "great star in the musical heaven," and his works should be studied industriously.

The longest and most wide-ranging review was written by A. B. Marx in the *Berliner Allgemeine musikalischer Zeitung* (1828).[172] This review actually deals with the late quartets in general. In complex, poetic language Marx points to several characteristics and difficulties of these works. He asserts the greatness of the quartets, which are superior to Beethoven's earlier quartets and quartets by other composers. He stresses the new texture in the late quartets, with independent voice leading of the four parts that has not been seen in music since J. S. Bach. Long study is required by the performer in order to join one to the other parts "freely and flexibly." He remarks that the next generation will be able to play this music as easily as performers then played Haydn's quartets.

Marx stresses the emotional and spiritual depth of the music that pours out in a "sea of feeling." He later relates the expressive impact to the "overflowing feeling" in the writings of the German author, Heinrich von Kleist. He compares the complex character of the music to the effect produced by the paintings of Rubens—*The Lion Hunt* or *Sanherib*—paintings that require time for even the practiced eye to fit the many details into the whole. Rubens's *Lion Hunt* (see Plate 4.III) provides a truly shocking analogy to Beethoven's late quartets (also in its violence) and illustrates how even a highly knowledgeable musician like Marx could be overwhelmed by the intricacy of Beethoven's music.[173]

40-42, points out that only after Beethoven died did the *AmZ* publish harsh criticism of the late works. One such example occurs in a review of the Sixth Symphony that also includes Op. 132 (1828, col. 363). It describes the quartet as "very difficult," criticizing "the fatiguing length of the movements and rhapsodic development." Once again it was the "Scherzo" that was most successful.

[171] Kunze, ed., *Die Werke im Spiegel seiner Zeit*, 591-92. The review is in Jg. 1, col. 47-48.

[172] Kunze, ed., ibid., 592-93 The review appears in Jg. 5, pp. 467-68. See also the brief summary of the review in Wallace, pp. 57-58. On 19 July 1825, Beethoven wrote to the music publisher Adolph Martin Schlesinger in Berlin about the sale of two late quartets, Op. 132 and the still uncompleted Op. 130. He also expressed his appreciation of Marx's articles in the Berlin *AmZ*, of which Marx was editor. He wrote: "When turning over its pages I noticed a few articles which I immediately recognized as the products of that gifted Herr Marx. I hope he will continue to reveal more and more what is noble and true in the sphere of art." See Anderson, III, No. 1403 (but misdated July 15-19), and BGA, 6, No. 2015.

[173] For the date of the Rubens painting, see David Rosand, "Rubens's Munich Lion Hunt: Its Sources and Significance," *Art Bulletin* 51 (1969): 29.

SELECTED BIBLIOGRAPHY

Adelson, Robert. "Beethoven's String Quartet in E Flat Op. 127: A Study of the First Performances," *Music & Letters* 79 (1998): 219-43.
Agawu, V., Kofi. *Playing with Signs: A Semiotic Interpretation of Classic Music.* Princeton: Princeton University Press, 1991.
Ahn, Suhnne. "*Quasi come d'un concerto*: Genre, Style, and Compositional Procedures in Beethoven's 'Kreutzer' Sonata." Ph.D. diss., Harvard University, 1997. UM-9721651.
Albrecht, Theodore. "Beethoven's Tympanist Ignaz Manker," *Percussive Notes* 38 (2000): 54-66.
_____ "Franz Stadler, Stephan Fichtner and Other Oboists at the Theater an der Wien during Beethoven's 'Heroic' Period," *Double Reed* 25 (2002): 93-106.
_____ "The Musicians in Balthasar Wigand's Depiction of the Performance of Haydn's *Die Schöpfung*, Vienna, March 27, 1808," *Music in Art* 29 (2004): 123-33.
Allanbrook, Wye Jamison. *Rhythmic Gesture in Mozart: Le Nozze di Figaro and Don Giovanni.* Chicago and London: University of Chicago Press, 1983.
Bandmann, Günter. *Melancholie und Musik: ikonographische Studien.* Cologne: Westdeutscher Verlag, 1960.
Barth, George. *The Pianist as Orator: Beethoven and the Transformation of Keyboard Style.* Ithaca and London: Cornell University Press, 1992.
Beck, Dagmar, and Grita Herre. "Anton Schindlers fingierte Eintragungen in den Konversationsheften," in Harry Goldschmidt, ed. *Zu Beethoven* 1. Berlin: Verlag neue Musik, 1979, 11-89.
Becking, Gustav. *Studien zu Beethovens Personalstil: Das Scherzothema.* Leipzig: Breitkopf & Härtel, 1921.
Beethoven, Ludwig van. *Sonate für Klavier und Violine, G-dur Opus 96.* Faksimile nach dem in Eigentum des Pierpont Morgan Library New York befindlichen Autograph. Munich: G. Henle, 1977. With a "Geleitwort" by Martin Staehelin.
_____ *Konzert für Violine und Orchester, D-Dur, opus 61.* Facsimile ed. Hrsg. und Kommentiert von Franz Grasberger, mit einemVorwort von Wolfgang Schneiderhan. Graz: Akademische Druck u. Verlagsanstalt, 1979.
_____ *Ludwig van Beethovens Konversationshefte.* Bd. 8 (mid July 1825-12 February 1826). Eds. Karl-Heinz Köhler and Grita Herre, with collaboration of Günter Brosche. Leipzig: VEB Deutscher Verlag für Musik, 1981.
_____ *Moscow Sketchbook from 1825.* Ed. Elena Vjaskova. Facsimile, Study, Transcription, and Commentaries. Moscow: The Gnesins Musical Academy of Russia, 1995. In Russian, German, and English.
_____ *Beethoven im Gespräch.* Ein Konversationsheft vom 9. September 1825. Faksimile, Übertragung, und Kommentar von Grita Herre, Übersetzung ins Englische von Theodore Albrecht. Bonn: Beethoven-Haus, 2002.
Biermann, Joanna Cobb, "Cyclical Ordering in Beethoven's Gellert Lieder, Op. 48: A New Source," *Beethoven Forum* 11 (2004): 162-80.
Block, Geoffrey Holden. "The Genesis of Beethoven's Piano Concertos in C Major (Op.15) and B-flat Major (Op. 19): Chronology and Compositional Process." 2 vols. Ph.D. diss., Harvard University, 1979.
Brandenburg, Sieghard. "Violin Sonatas, Cello Sonatas and Variations," in *Ludwig van Beethoven*. Eds. Joseph Schmidt-Görg and Hans Schmidt. Bonn: Beethoven-Archiv and Hamburg: Deutsche Grammophon mbH, 1969, 135-55.
_____ "Bemerkungen zu Beethovens Op. 96," *B-J* 9 (1973-77): 11-25
_____ "Die Quellen zu Entstehungsgeschichte von Beethovens Streichquartett Es-Dur op. 127," *B-J* 10 (1978-81): 221-76.

_____"The Autograph of Beethoven's String Quartet in A Minor, Opus 132: The Structure of the Manuscript and its Relevance for the Study of the Genesis of the Work," in *The String Quartets of Haydn, Mozart, and Beethoven: Studies of the Autograph Manuscripts*. Ed. Christoph Wolff. Cambridge, MA: Harvard University Dept. of Music, 1980, 278-300.

_____"The Historical Background to the 'Heiliger Dankgesang' in Beethoven's A-minor Quartet Op. 132," in *Beethoven Studies* 3. Ed. Alan Tyson. Cambridge: Cambridge University Press, 1982, 161-91.

_____"Die Skizzen zur Neunten Symphonie," in Harry Goldschmidt, ed. *Zu Beethoven* 2. Berlin: Verlag Neue Music, 1984, 88-129.

_____"Beethoven's Opus 12 Violin Sonatas: On the Path To His Personal Style," in *The Beethoven Violin Sonatas: History, Criticism, Performance*. Eds. Lewis Lockwood and Mark Kroll. Urbana and Chicago: University of Illinois Press, 2004, 5-23.

Braun, Joachim. "The Sound of Beethoven's Orchestra," *Orbis Musicae* 6 (Tel Aviv University, 1978): 59-90.

Brinkmann, Reinhold. "Wirkungen Beethovens in der Kammermusik," in *Beiträge zu Beethovens Kammermusik, Symposium Bonn 1984*. Eds. Sieghard Brandenburg and Helmut Loos. Munich: G. Henle, 1987, 79-110.

Brown, A. Peter. *The Symphonic Repertoire. Vol. II. The First Golden Age of the Viennese Symphony: Haydn, Mozart, Beethoven, and Schubert*. Bloomington and Indianapolis: Indiana University Press, 2002.

Brown, Clive. "The Orchestra in Beethoven's Vienna," *Early Music* 16 (1988): 4-20.

_____"Ferdinand David's Editions of Beethoven," in *Performing Beethoven*. Ed. Robin Stowell: Cambridge: Cambridge University Press, 1994.

Busby, Thomas. *A Complete Dictionary of Music*. 2nd ed. London: Richard Phillips, 1806.

Cahn, Peter. "Aspekte der Schlussgestaltung in Beethovens Instrumentalwerken," *Archiv für Musikwissenschaft* 39 (1982): 19-31.

_____"Violinsonate G-Dur op. 96," in *Beethoven, Interpretationen seiner Werk*. Eds. Albrecht Riethmüller, Carl Dahlhaus, and Alexander L. Ringer. Vol. II. Lauber: Lauber Verlag, 1994, 86-92.

Carruthers, Glenn. "Strangeness and Beauty: The Opening Measure of Mozart's Symphony in G Minor, K. 550," *JM* 16 (1998): 283-99.

Charleton, David. "Instrumental Recitative: a Study in Morphology and Context, 1700-1808," *Comparative Criticism* 4 (1982): 149-68.

Chew, Geoffrey, and Owen Jander. "Pastoral," *NGD*, 2nd ed., 19: 217-25.

Churgin, Bathia. "Francesco Galeazzi's Description (1796) of Sonata Form," *JAMS* 21 (1968): 181-99. A slightly revised translation was published in Oliver Strunk, ed. *Source Readings in Music History*, rev. ed., ed. Leo Treitler. Vol. 5. *The Late Eighteenth Century*. Ed. Wye Jamison Allanbrook. New York: Norton, 1998, 85-92.

_____"A New Edition of Beethoven's Fourth Symphony: Editorial Report," *Israel Studies in Musicology* 1 (1978): 9-53.

_____ Review of Sieghard Brandenburg, ed., *Ludwig van Beethoven: Kesslersches Skizzenbuch, Israel Studies in Musicology* 3 (1983): 171-77.

_____"Beethoven and Mozart's Requiem: A New Connection," *JM* 5 (1987): 457-77. Reprint, with additions and corrections, *Min-Ad*, Israel Studies in Musicology Online (Vol.II, 2006): 19-39, and Addenda.

_____"Beethoven's Sketches for his String Quintet, Op. 29," in *Studies in Musical Sources and Style: Essays in Honor of Jan LaRue*. Eds. Eugene K. Wolf and Edward H. Roesner. Madison, WI: A-R Editions, 1990, 441-79.

_____ "Harmonic and Tonal Instability in the Second Key Area of Classic Sonata Form," in *Convention in Eighteenth- and Nineteenth-Century Music: Essays in Honor of Leonard G. Ratner.* Eds. Wye J. Allanbrook, Janet M. Levy, and William P. Mahrt. Stuyvesant, NY: Pendragon, 1992, 23-57.

_____ "Sammartini and Boccherini: Continuity and Change in the Italian Instrumental Tradition of the Classic Period," *Chigiana* 43 (1993): 171-91.

_____ "Exploring the Eroica: Aspects of the New Critical Edition," in *Haydn, Mozart, and Beethoven: Studies in the Music of the Classical Period. Essays in Honour of Alan Tyson.* Ed. Sieghard Brandenburg. Oxford: Clarendon Press, 1998, 181-211.

_____ "The *Andante con moto* in Beethoven's String Quartet Op. 130: The Final Version and Changes on the Autograph," *JM* 16 (1998): 227-53.

_____ "Beethoven and the New Development-Theme in Sonata-Form Movements," *JM* 16 (1998): 323-43.

_____ "Recycling Old Ideas in Beethoven's String Quartet Op. 132," in *Essays in Honor of László Somfai: Studies in the Sources and the Interpretation of Music.* Eds. László Vikárius and Vera Lampert. Lanham, MD: Scarecrow Press, 2005, 229-45.

Churgin, Bathia, ed. *Ludwig van Beethoven. Symphony No 4.* London, Mainz: Eulenburg, No. 414/6820, 1998.

Cole, Malcolm S. "The Development of the Instrumental Rondo Finale from 1750 to 1800." Ph D. diss., Princeton University, 1964.

_____ "Sonata-Rondo, The Formulation of a Theoretical Concept in the Eighteenth and Nineteenth Centuries," *MQ* 55 (1969): 180-92.

_____ "Techniques of Surprise in the Sonata-Rondos of Beethoven," *Studia Musicologica* 12 (1970): 233-62.

_____ Article "Rondo," *NGD* 16 (1980): 172-77.

Cooke, Deryck. "The Unity of Beethoven's Late String Quartets," *The Music Review* 24 (1963): 30-49.

Cooper, Barry. "Beethoven's Portfolio of Bagatelles," *Journal of the Royal Musical Association*, 112 (1987a): 208-28.

_____ *Beethoven and the Creative Process.* Oxford: Clarendon Press, 1990.

_____ *Beethoven.* Oxford University Press, 2000.

Cooper, Barry, ed. *The Beethoven Compendium*, London: Thames and Hudson, 1991.

Czerny, Carl. *Über den richtigen Vortrag der sämtlichen Beethoven'schen Klavierwerke.* Ch. 2 and 3 of Vol. IV of Czerny's *Vollständigen theoretisch-praktischen Pianoforte-Schule,* Op. 500. Vienna, 1846. Eng. trans. as *On the Proper Performance of all Beethoven's Works for the Piano.* London, 1846. Facs. ed. in German, Vienna: Universal Edition, 1963; in English, 1970. Both editions contain excerpts from Czerny's "Memoirs" and "Anecdotes and Notes about Beethoven." Ed. Paul Badura-Skoda.

_____ *School of Practical Composition,* Op. 600. Trans. John Bishop. Vol. I. London: Robert Cocks & Co., 1848?

Dahlhaus, Carl. "La Malinconia," in *Ludwig van Beethoven.* Ed. Ludwig Finscher. "Wege der Forschung," vol. 428. Darmstadt: Wissenschaftliche Buchgesellschaft, 1983, 200-11.

_____ *Ludwig van Beethoven: Approaches to his Music.* Trans. Mary Whittal. Oxford: Clarendon Press, 1991.

de Roda, Cecilio. "Un quaderno di autografi di Beethoven del 1825," *Rivista Musicale Italiana* 12 (1905): 63-108.

Deutsch, Otto Erich. "Beethovens gesammelte Werke, Die Meisters Plan und Haslingers Ausgabe," *Zeitschrift für Musikwissenschaft* 13 (1930-31): 60-79;

with the contents of "Haslingers Ausgabe" reprinted and revised by Alexander Weinmann, in *Beiträge zu Beethoven-Bibliographie*. Ed. Kurt Dorfmüller, 272-79.
Dorfmüller, Kurt, ed. *Beiträge zur Beethoven-Bibliographie*. Munich: G. Henle, 1978.
Eggebrecht, Hans Heinrich, ed. Article "Pastorale," in *Handwörterbuch der musikalischen Terminologie*. Ordner III M-R. Stuttgart: F. Steiner, 1996,11-14.
Elterlein, Ernst von (pseud. of Ernst Gottschald). *Beethoven's Clavier-Sonaten für Freunde der Tonkunst eiläutert*. Zweite Auflage. Leipzig: Heinrich Matthes, 1857, 46-48.
_____ *Beethoven's Pianoforte Sonatas Explained for the Lovers of the Musical Art*. Trans. Emily Hill. Preface E. Pauer. London: W. Reeves, 1875, 43-46.
Forchert, Arno. "Die Darstellung der Melancholie in Beethovens op. 18, 6," in *Ludwig van Beethoven*. Ed. Ludwig Finscher. "Wege der Forschung," vol. 428. Darmstadt: Wissenschaftliche Buchgesellschaft, 1983, 212-39.
Forster, Robert. "Zu Klavierfassung des Violinkonzerts op. 61 von Ludwig van Beethoven," *Die Musikforschung* 36 (1983): 1-15.
Frohlich, Martha, Beethoven's "Appassionata" Sonata. Oxford: Clarendon, 1991.
_____ "Ideas of Closure, Derivation, and Rhythm in the Sketches for the Andante of Beethoven's 'Pastorale' Sonata, Op. 28," *JM* 16 (1998): 344-57.
_____ "Beethoven's Piano Sonata in F Major, Op. 54, Second Movement: The Final Version and Sketches," *JM* 18 (2001): 98-128.
Frohlich, Martha, ed. *Ludwig van Beethoven, Piano Sonata Op. 28, Facsimile of the Autograph, the Sketches, and the First Edition*, with transcription and commentary by M. Frohlich. Bonn: Beethoven-Haus, 1996.
Gemeiner, Joseph. *Menuett und Scherzo: Ein Beitrag zur Entwicklungsgeschichte und Soziologie des Tanzsatzes in der Wiener Klassik*. Tutzing: Schneider, 1979.
Gjerdingen, Robert O. *A Classic Turn of Phrase*. Philadelphia: University of Pennsylvania Press, 1988.
Grave, Floyd K. "Metrical Displacement and the Compound Measure in Eighteenth-Century Theory and Practice," *Theoria* 1 (1985): 25-60.
_____ "Concerto Style in Haydn's String Quartets," *JM* 18 (2001): 76-97.
Greenzweig, Eli. "A Survey of Keys in Symphonies and Slow Movements in the 18th-Century Viennese Symphony," *Min-Ad*, Israel Studies in Musicology Online (Vol. II, 2006): 112-41.
Grove, George. "Beethoven's Violin Concerto," *Musical Times* 46 (1905): 459-71.
Haimo, Ethan. "Remote Keys and Multi-movement Unity: Haydn in the 1790s," *MQ* 74 (1990): 242-68.
Hatten, Robert S. *Meaning in Beethoven. Markedness, Correlation, and Interpretation*. Indiana and Indianapolis: Indiana University Press, 1994.
Helm, Theodor. *Beethoven's Streichquartette*. Leipzig: E.W. Fritzsch, 1885, Op. 132, 267-95. Trans. Ian Bent in *Music Analysis in the Nineteenth Century*. Vol. II: *Hermaneutic Approaches*. Ed. I. Bent. Cambridge: Cambridge University Press, 1994, 238-66.
Henle, Günter. "Ein Fehler in Beethovens Violinsonate?" *Die Musikforschung* 5 (1952): 53-54. Translation and Commentary, Geraldine de Courcy in Letter to the Editor, *Music & Letters* 33 (1952): 276-77.
Hess, Willy. "Beethovens C-dur-Konzertsatz und seine Ergänzungen," *Schweizerische Musikzeitung* 115 (1975): 233-36.
Hickman, Roger. "Romance," *NGD*, 2nd ed., 21: 573-76.
Horsley, Imogene. *Fugue, History and Practice*. New York: The Free Press, 1966.
Jander, Owen. "Romantic Form and Content in the Slow Movement of Beethoven's Violin Concerto," *MQ* 69 (1983): 159-79.

_____ "Beethoven's 'Orpheus in Hades': The Andante con moto of the Fourth Piano Concerto," *19th Century Music* 8 (1985): 195-212.

Johansen, Gail Nelson. "Beethoven's Sonatas for Piano and Violin, Op. 12, No. 1 and Op. 96: A Performance Practice Study." D.M.A. thesis. Stanford University, 1981. UM-8115843.

Johnson, Douglas. *Beethoven's Early Sketches in the "Fischhof Miscellany," Berlin Autograph 28*. 2 vols. Ann Arbor: UMI Research Press, 1980.

_____ "1794-1795: Decisive Years in Beethoven's Early Development," in *Beethoven Studies 3*. Ed. Alan Tyson. Cambridge: Cambridge University Press, 1982, 1-28.

Jonas, Oswald. "Bemerkungen zu Beethoven's Op. 96," *Acta musicologica* 37 (1965): 87-89.

Jones, David Wyn. *Beethoven: Pastoral Symphony*. Cambridge: Cambridge University Press, 1995.

Jung, Hermann (Hans Engel). "Pastorale," in *MGG*, 2nd ed., Sachteil, vol. 7 (1997), col. 1499-1509.

Kagan, Susan. *Archduke Rudolph, Beethoven's Patron, Pupil, and Friend, His Life and Music*. Stuyvesant, NY: Pendragon, 1988.

Kamien, Roger. "Conflicting Metrical Patterns in Accompaniment and Melody in Works by Mozart and Beethoven: A Preliminary Study," *Journal of Music Theory* 37 (1993): 311-48.

_____ "Non-Tonic Settings of the Primary Tone in Beethoven's Piano Sonatas," *JM* 16 (1998): 379-93

_____ "Phrase, Period, Theme," in Glenn Stanley, ed. *The Cambridge Companion to Beethoven*. Cambridge: Cambridge University Press, 2000, 64-83.

Katz, Mark. "Beethoven in the Age of Mechanical Reproduction: The Violin Concerto on Record," *Beethoven Forum* 10 (2003): 38-54.

Kerman, Joseph. *The Beethoven Quartets*. New York: Norton, 1966.

_____ "Notes on Beethoven's Codas," in *Beethoven Studies* 3. Ed. Alan Tyson. Cambridge: Cambridge University Press, 1982, 141-59.

_____ "Beethoven's Minority," in *Haydn, Mozart, and Beethoven: Studies in the Music of the Classical Period. Essays in Honour of Alan Tyson*. Ed. Sieghard Brandenburg. Oxford: Clarendon Press, 1998, pp. 151-73.

Kerman, Joseph, ed. *Ludwig van Beethoven: Autograph Miscellany from circa 1786 to 1799 . . . (the "Kafka Sketchbook")*. Vol. I, Facsimile. Vol. II, Transcription. London: The Trustees of the British Museum, 1970.

Kerman, Joseph, and Alan Tyson. *The New Grove Beethoven*. New York: Norton, 1983.

_____ (with Scott G. Burnham). Article "Beethoven, Ludwig van," *NGD*, 2nd. ed., 3: 73-140. Work-list by Douglas Johnson and Burnham; Bibliography by William Drabkin and Burnham.

Kinderman, William. *Beethoven*. Berkeley and Los Angeles: University of California Press, 1995.

Kirby, F. E. "Beethoven's Pastoral Symphony as a Sinfonia caracteristica," *MQ* 56 (1970): 605-23; reprint in *The Creative World of Beethoven*. Ed. Paul Henry Lang. New York: Norton, 1970, 103-21.

Kirkendale, Warren. "New Roads to Old Ideas in Beethoven's Missa Solemnis," *MQ* 56 (1970): 665-701; reprint in *The Creative World of Beethoven*. Ed. Paul Henry Lang, New York: Norton, 1970, 163-199.

_____ *Fugue and Fugato in Rococo and Classical Chamber Music*. Trans. Margaret Bent and the author. 2nd ed. Durham, NC: Duke University Press, 1979.

_____ "Gregorianischer Stil in Beethovens Streichquartett op. 132," in *Bericht des internationalen Musikwissenschaftlichen Kongress Berlin 1974.* Eds. Helmut Kühn and Peter Nitsche. Kassel: Bärenreiter, 1980, 373-76.

Klein, Hans-Günter, and Douglas Johnson. "Autographe Beethovens aus der Bonner Zeit: Handschrift-Probleme und Echtheitsfragen," in Kurt Dorfmüller, ed. *Beiträge zur Beethoven-Bibliographie.* Munich: G. Henle, 1978, 115-24.

Knittel, K. M. "Wagner, Deafness, and the Reception of Beethoven's Late Style," *JAMS* 51 (1998): 49-82.

Koch, H. C. *Musikalisches Lexikon.* Frankfurt, 1802, facs. reprint Hildesheim: Olms, 1964.

_____ *Introductory Essay on Composition, The Mechanical Rules of Melody, Sections 3 and 4.* Trans. Nancy K. Baker. New Haven and London: Yale University Press, 1983.

Kojima, Shin Augustinus. "Die Solovioline-Fassungen und-Varianten von Beethovens Violinkonzert op. 61—ihre Entstehung und Bedeutung," *B-J* 8 (1971/72): 97-146.

Korsyn, Keven, "Integration in Works of Beethoven's Final Period." Ph.D. diss., Yale University, 1983.

_____ "J. W. N. Sullivan and the *Heiliger Dankgesang*: Questions of Meaning in Late Beethoven," *Beethoven Forum* 2 (1993): 133-74.

Kovács, Sándor. "Final Concertos," in *The Bartók Companion.* Ed. Malcolm Gilles. London: Faber & Faber, 1993, 543-46 (on Piano Concerto No. 3).

Kramer, Richard. "An Unfinished Concertante of 1802," in *Beethoven Studies* 2. Ed. Alan Tyson. Oxford: Oxford University Press, 1977, 33-65.

_____ "In Search of Palestrina: Beethoven in the Archives," in *Haydn, Mozart, and Beethoven: Studies in the Music of the Classical Period. Essays in Honour of Alan Tyson.* Ed. Sieghard Brandenburg. Oxford: Clarendon Press, 1998, 283-300.

Krummacher, Friedhelm. *Mendelssohn—der Komponist, Studien zur Kammermusik für Streicher.* Munich: Fink, 1978.

Kunze, Stefan, et al eds. *Ludwig van Beethoven: Die Werke im Spiegel seiner Zeit.* Laaber: Laaber Verlag, 1987.

Lam, Basil. *Beethoven String Quartets.* BBC Guides. London: BBC, 1975.

LaRue, Jan. "Harmonic Rhythm in the Beethoven Symphonies," *The Music Review* 18 (1957): 8-20; reprint *JM* 18 (2001): 221-48.

_____ "Significant and Coincidental Resemblance between Classical Themes," JAMS 14 (1961): 224-34; reprint *JM* 18 (2001): 268-82.

_____ "Multistage Variance: Haydn's Legacy to Beethoven," *JM* 1 (1982): 265-74; Reprinted with clearer music examples in *JM* 18 (2001): 344-60.

Lenz, Wilhelm von. *Beethoven et ses trois styles.* St. Petersburg, 1852. New ed. by M. S. Calvocoressi. Paris: Legouix, 1909.

_____ *Beethoven, Eine Kunst-Studie. Kritischer Katalog sämmtlicher Werke Ludwig van Beethovens mit Analysen derselben.* 2nd rev. ed. Hamburg: Hoffmann & Co, 1860.

Levy, David B. "The Contrabass Recitative in Beethoven's Ninth Symphony Revisited," *Historical Performance* 5 (1992): 9-18.

Levy, Janet M. *Beethoven's Compositional Choices: The Two Versions of Opus 18, No. 1, First Movement.* Philadelphia: University of Pennsylvania Press, 1982.

_____ "Texture as a Sign in Classic and Early Romantic Music," *JAMS* 35 (1982): 482-531.

_____ " 'Something Mechanical Encrusted on the Living': A source of Musical Wit and Humor," in *Convention in Eighteenth- and Nineteenth-Century Music: Essays in Honor of Leonord. G. Ratner.* Eds. Wye J Allanbrook, Janet M. Levy, and William P. Mahrt. Stuyvesant, NY: Pendragon, 1992, 225-56.

_____ "The Power of the Performer: Interpreting Beethoven," *JM* 18 (2001): 31-55.

Lockwood, Lewis. " 'Eroica' Perspectives: Strategy and Design in the First Movement," in *Beethoven: Studies in the Creative Process*. Cambridge, MA: Harvard University Press, 1992, 118-33.

―――― "Beethoven's Emergence from Crisis: The Cello Sonatas of Op. 102 (1815)," *JM* 16 (1998): 301-22.

―――― *Beethoven, The Music and the Life*. New York: Norton, 2003.

Lühning, Helga, "Das Schindler- und das Beethoven-Bild," *Bonner Beethoven-Studien* 2 (2001): 183-99.

Lutes, Leilani K. "Beethoven's Re-uses of His Own Compositions, 1782-1826." Ph.D.diss., University of Southern California, 1975. UM- 76- 5250.

Luxner, Michael. "The Evolution of the Minuet/Scherzo in the Music of Beethoven." Ph.D. diss., Eastman School of Music, 1978. UM 78 -17, 561.

MacArdle, Donald W. "Beethoven and Schuppanzigh," *Music Review* 26 (1965): 3-14.

―――― "Beethoven und Karl Holz," *Die Musikforschung* 20 (1967): 19-29.

Macek, Jaroslav. "Franz Joseph Maximilian Lobkowitz, Musikfreund und Kunstmäzen," in *Beethoven und Böhmen*. Eds. Sieghard Brandenburg and Martella Gutiérrez-Denhoff. Bonn: Beethoven-Haus, 1988, 147-202.

―――― and Tomislav Volek. "Beethoven und Fürst Lobkowitz," in *Beethoven und Böhmen*. Eds. Sieghard Brandenburg, and Martella Gutiérrez-Denhoff, 203-17.

Mahaim, Ivan. *Beethoven, La Terre Natale et la Trilogie*. Vol. II. Paris: Brouwer, 1964.

Mahling, Christoph-Helmut. "Violinkonzert D-Dur, op. 61," in *Beethoven: Interpretationen seiner Werke*. Eds. Albrecht Riethmüller, Carl Dahlhaus, and Alexander L. Ringer. Vol. I. Laaber: Laaber-Verlag, 1994, 455-71.

Marx, A. B. *Ludwig van Beethoven, Leben und Schaffen*. Berlin, 1859; facs. reprint Hildesheim: Georg Olms, 1979. Rev. ed. Berlin: Otto Janke, 1863.

Marx, Karl. "Über die zyklische Sonatenform― zu dem Aufsatz von Günther von Noé," *Neue Zeitschrift für Musik* 125 (1964): 142-46.

Mason, Donald Gregory. *The Quartets of Beethoven*. New York: Oxford University Press, 1949.

Matthews, Denis. *Beethoven Piano Sonatas*. BBC Music Guides. London: BBC, 1967.

Meredith, William. "Beethoven's Sonata in A-flat Major, Op. 110: Music of Amiability, Lament, and Restoration," *The Beethoven Journal* 17 (2002): 14-29.

Mies, Paul. *Beethoven's Sketches: An Analysis of His Style Based on a Study of His Sketch-Books*. Trans. Doris L. Mackinnon. London, 1929; repr. New York: Dover, 1974.

―――― *Textkritische Untersuchungen bei Beethoven*. Bonn: Beehovenhaus, 1957.

―――― *Das instrumentale Rezitativ: Von seiner Geschichte und seinen Formen*. Bonn: Bouvier, 1968.

Misch, Ludwig. "Fugue and Fugato in Beethoven's Variation Form," *MQ* 42 (1956): 14-27.

―――― *Neue Beethoven-Studien und andere Themen*. Bonn: Beethovenhaus. Munich: G. Henle, 1967.

Monelle, Raymond. *The Musical Topic: Hunt, Military and Pastoral*. Bloomington and Indianapolis: Indiana University Press, 2006.

Morrow, Mary Sue. *Concert Life in Haydn's Vienna*. Stuyvesant, NY: Pendragon, 1989.

Moyer, Birgitte. "Ombra and Fantasia in Late Eighteenth-Century Theory and Practice," in *Convention in Eighteenth- and Nineteenth-Century Music: Essays in Honor of Leonard G. Ratner*. Eds. Wye J. Allanbrook, Janet M. Levy, and William P. Mahrt. Stuyvesant, NY: Pendragon, 1992, 283-303.

Newman, William S. *The Sonata in the Classic Era*. Chapel Hill: University of North Carolina Press: 1963; 2nd and 3rd editions, New York: Norton, 1972, 1983.

_____ "The Opening Trill in Beethoven's Sonata for Piano and Violin Op. 96," in *Musik-Edition, Interpretation, Gedenkschrift Günter Henle*. Ed. Martin Bente. Munich: G. Henle, 1980, 384-93.

_____ *Beethoven on Beethoven: Playing His Piano Music His Way.* New York: Norton, 1988.

Noé, Günther von. "Der Strukturwandel der zyklischen Sonatenform," *Neue Zeitschrift für Musik* 125 (1964): 55-62.

Noonan, Timothy. "Structural Anomalies in the Symphonies of Luigi Boccherini." Ph.D. diss., University of Wisconsin, 1996.

Nordström, Folke. *Goya, Saturn, and Melancholy.* Stockholm: Almqvist & Wiksell, 1962.

Nottebohm, Gustav. *Ein Skizzenbuch von Beethoven aus dem Jahre 1803.* Leipzig, 1880; reprint New York and London: Johnson Reprint Corp., 1970.

Obelkevich, Mary Rowan, "The Growth of a Musical Idea—Beethoven's Opus 96," *Current Musicology* 11 (1970): 91-114.

Plantinga, Leon. *Muzio Clementi, His Life and Music.* London: Oxford, 1976.

_____ *Beethoven's Concertos.* New York: Norton, 1999.

Platen, Emil. "Zeitgenössische Hinweise zur Aufführungspraxis der letzten Streichquartette Beethovens," in *Beiträge '76-78, Beethoven-Kolloquium 1977.* Ed. Rudolf Klein. Kassel: Bärenreiter, 1978, pp. 100-07.

Portowitz, Adena. "Mozart's Early Concertos, 1773-1779: Structure and Expression." Ph.D. diss., Bar-Ilan University, 1995. UM-9544795

_____ "Innovation and Tradition in the Classic Concerto: Mozart's K. 453 (1784) as a Model for Beethoven's Fourth Concerto (1805-06)," *The Beethoven Journal* 12 (1997): 65-72

_____ "Art and Taste in Mozart's Sonata-Rondo Finales: Two Case Studies," *JM* 18 (2001): 129-49.

_____ "The Recapitulation as Climax in the First Movements of Mozart's Early Concertos," *Ad Parnassum* 2 (2003), 7-20.

Radcliffe, Philip. *Beethoven's String Quartets.* New York: Dutton, 1968.

Radice, Mark A. "Bartók's 'Parodies' of Beethoven," *The Music Review* 42 (1981): 252-60

Ratner, Leonard G. "Key Definition—A Structural Issue in Beethoven's Music," *JAMS* 23 (1970): 472-83.

_____ "*Ars Combinatoria*: Chance and Choice in Eighteenth-Century Music," in *Studies in Eighteenth-Century Music: A Tribute to Karl Geiringer on his Seventieth Birthday.* Ed. H. C. Robbins Landon in collaboration with Roger E. Chapman, London: Allen and Unwin, 1970, 343-63.

_____ "Texture, A Rhetorical Element in Beethoven's Quartets,"*Israel Studies in Musicology* 2 (1980): 51-62.

_____ *The Beethoven String Quartets: Compositional Strategies and Rhetoric.* Stanford, CA: Stanford Bookstore, 1995.

Reicha, Anton, *Traité de haute composition musicale.* Vol. 2. Paris: Zetter & Cie., c. 1825.

Reinecke, Carl. *Die Beethoven'schen Clavier-Sonaten.* Leipzig, 1895; 2nd ed. Leipzig: Gebrüder Reinecke, 1897, 26-29.

Riezler, Walter. *Beethoven.* With an introduction by Wilhelm Fürtwängler. Trans. G. D. H. Pidcock. New York, 1938; reprint New York: Vienna House, 1972.

Rosand, David. "Rubens Munich Lion Hunt: Its Sources and Significance," *Art Bulletin* 51 (1969): 29-40.

Rosand, Ellen. "The Descending Tetrachord: An Emblem of Lament," *MQ* 55 (1979): 346-59.

Rosenberg, Richard. *Die Klaviersonaten Ludwig van Beethovens.* Vol. 1. Olten and Lausanne: Urs-Graf Verlag, 1957.

Rosenblum, Sandra P. *Performance Practices in Classic Piano Music.* Bloomington and Indianapolis: Indiana University Press, 1988.

_____ "Two Sets of Unexplored Metronome Marks for Beethoven's Piano Sonatas," *Early Music* 16 (1988): 58-71.

Rostal, Max. *Beethoven, The Sonatas for Piano and Violin: Thoughts on their Interpretation.* Trans. Horace and Anna Rosenberg.Toccata Press, 1985. German edition: Munich: R. Piper, 1981. With Günter Ludwig, "Postscript from the Pianist's Point of View," 189-202.

Rudolf, Max. "Inner Repeats in the Da Capo of Classical Minuets and Scherzos," in Max Rudolf, *A Musical Life: Writings and Letters.* Eds. Michael Stern and Hanny Bleeker-White. Hillsdale, NY: Pendragon, 2000, 123-34.

Russell, Tilden A. "Minuet, Scherzando, and Scherzo: The Dance Movement in Transition." Ph. D. diss., University of North Carolina, Chapel Hill, 1983.

_____ and Hugh MacDonald."Scherzo," *NGD*, 2nd ed., 22: 486-89.

Schenker, Heinrich. *Beethoven's Ninth Symphony.* Vienna, 1912. Trans. and ed. John Rothgeb. New Haven and London: Yale University Press, 1992.

Schiedermair, Ludwig. *Der junge Beethoven.* Leipzig: Quelle & Meyer, 1925.

Schindler, Anton Felix. *Beethoven as I Knew Him.* Ed. Donald W. MacArdle. Trans. Constance S. Jolly. Chapel Hill: University of North Carolina Press; London: Faber and Faber, 1966.

Schmidt, Hans. "Verzeichnis der Skizzen Beethovens," *B-J* (1965-68): 7-128.

Schmitz, Arnold. *Beethoven: Unbekannte Skizzen und Entwürfe. Untersuchung, Übertragung, Faksimile,* Veröffentlichungen des Beethovenhauses in Bonn III. Bonn: Kurt Schroeder, 1924.

Schumann, Robert,"Aufzeichnungen über Mendelssohn," Mit Anmerkungen von Heinz-Klaus Metzger und Rainer Riem, in *Musik-Konzepte 14/15, Felix Mendelssohn-Bartholdy.* Munich: Hans Pribil, 1980, 97-122.

Schwartz, Judith L. "Phrase Morphology in the Early Classic Symphony (c. 1720-c. 1765)." Ph.D. diss., New York University, 1973. UM 73-19,967.

_____"Thematic Asymmetry in First Movements of Haydn's Early Symphonies," in *Haydn Studies. Proceedings of the International Haydn Conference, Washington, D.C., 1975.* Eds. Jens Peter Larsen, Howard Serwer, and James Webster. New York: Norton, 1981, 501-09.

_____"Conceptions of Musical Unity in the 18th Century," *JM* 18 (2001): 56-75

Schwarz, Boris. "Beethoven and the French Violin School," *MQ* 44 (1958): 431-47.

_____ *French Instrumental Music Between the Revolutions (1789-1830).* New York: Da Capo Press, 1987. Ch. IV, "The French Violin Concerto," 163-222.

_____ and Clive Brown (work-list). "Rode, (Jacques), Pierre, (Joseph), *NGD*, 2nd ed., 21: 491-92.

Schwindt-Gross, Nicole."Zwischen Kontrapunkt und Divertimento: Zum zweiten Satz aus Beethovens Streichquartett op. 132," in *Studien zur Musikgeschichte. Eine Festschrift für Ludwig Finscher.* Eds. Annegrit Laubenthal and Kara Kusan-Windweh. Kassel: Bärenreiter, 1995, 446-56.

Seiffert, Herbert."Das Instrumentalrezitativ vom Barock bis zur Wiener Klassik,"in *De ratione in musica, Festschrift Erich Schenk zum 5 Mai 1972.* Eds. Theophil Antonicek, Rudolf Flotzinger, and Othmar Wessely. Kassel: Bärenreiter, 1975, 103-16.

Senner, Wayne M., ed. and trans. *The Critical Reception of Beethoven's Compositions by his German Contemporaries.* Musicology eds. Robin Wallace and William Meredith. Vol. I. Lincoln and London: University of Nebraska Press, in associa-

tion with the American Beethoven Society and the Ira F. Brilliant Center for Beethoven Studies, San Jose State University, 1999; Vol. II, 2001.
Shamgar, Beth. "Dramatic Devices in the Retransitions of Beethoven's Piano Sonatas," *Israel Studies in Musicology* 2 (1980): 63-76.
Sheer, Miriam. "The Role of Dynamics in Beethoven's Instrumental Works." 2 vols. Ph.D. diss, Bar-Ilan University, 1990.
_____ "Patterns of Dynamic Organization in Beethoven's Eroica Symphony," *JM* 10 (1992): 483-504
_____ "A Comparison of Dynamic Practices in Selected Piano Sonatas by Clementi and Beethoven," *Beethoven Forum* 5 (1996): 85-101.
_____ "Dynamics in Beethoven's Late Instrumental Works: A New Profile," *JM* 16 (1998): 358-78.
Sisman, Elaine R. *Haydn and the Classical Variation*. Cambridge, MA: Harvard University Press, 1993.
_____ "Pathos and the Pathétique: Rhetorical Stance in Beethoven's C-Minor Sonata, Op. 13," *Beethoven Forum* 3 (1994): 81-105.
_____ "Memory and Invention at the Threshold of Beethoven's Late Style," in *Beethoven and His World*. Eds. Scott Burnham and Michael P. Steinberg. Princeton and Oxford: Princeton University Press, 2000, 51-87.
_____ "Variation," in *NGD*, 2nd ed., 26: 284-326.
Solomon, Maynard. *Beethovens Tagebuch*. Ed. Sieghard Brandenburg, Mainz: v. Hase & Koehler Verlag, 1990.
_____ *Beethoven*. 2nd rev. ed. New York: Schirmer Books, 1998.
_____ "Pastoral, Rhetoric, Structure: The Violin Sonata in G, Op. 96," in *Late Beethoven: Music, Thought, Imagination*. Berkeley, Los Angeles, and London: University of California Press, 2003, 71-91.
Solomon, Maynard, trans. and ed. "Beethoven's Tagebuch," in *Beethoven Essays*. Cambridge, MA: Harvard University Press, 1988, 233-95.
Somfai, Lásló. *The Keyboard Sonatas of Joseph Haydn*. Chicago and London: University of Chicago Press, 1995.
_____ *Béla Bartók: Composition, Concepts, and Autograph Sources*. Berkeley and Los Angeles: University of California Press, 1996.
Spohr, Louis. *Lebenserinnerungen*. Ed. Folker Göthel. Vol. 1. Tutzing: Schneider, 1968.
Steblin, Rita. *A History of Key Characteristics in the Eighteenth and Early Nineteenth Centuries*. Ann Arbor: UMI Research Press, 1983.
Steinbeck, Wolfram. " 'Ein wahres Spiel mit musikalischen Formen': Zum Scherzo Ludwig van Beethovens," *Archiv für Musikwissenschaft* 38 (1981): 194-226.
Stevens, Jane R. "Theme, Harmony, and Texture in Classic-Romantic Descriptions of Concerto First-Movement Form," *JAMS* 27 (1974): 25-60.
Stowell, Robin. *Violin Technique and Performance Practice in the Late Eighteenth and Early Nineteenth Centuries*. Cambridge: Cambridge University Press, 1985.
_____ *Beethoven: Violin Concerto*. Cambridge: Cambridge University Press, 1998.
Stowell, Robin, ed. *Performing Beethoven*. Cambridge: Cambridge University Press, 1994.
Strohm, Reinhard, "Rezitativ," *MGG*, 2nd ed., Sachteil 8 (1998): 236-37.
Szigeti, Joseph. *The Ten Beethoven Sonatas for Piano and Violin*. Ed. Paul Rolland. Urbana: American String Teachers Association, 1965.
Thompson, Harold. "An Evolutionary View of Neapolitan Formations in Beethoven's Pianoforte Sonatas," *College Music Symposium* 20 (1980): 144-62.

Thym, Jurgen, "The Instrumental Recitative in Beethoven's Compositions," in *Essays on Music for Charles Warren Fox*. Ed. Jerald C. Graue. Rochester, NY: Eastman School of Music, 1979, pp. 230-40.

Tovey, Donald Francis. *A Companion to Beethoven's Pianoforte Sonatas*. London: Associated Board of the Royal Schools of Music, 1931.

_____ "Beethoven's Ninth Symphony in D Minor, op 125–Its Place in Musical Art," in *Essays in Musical Analysis*. Vol. II. London: Oxford University Press, 1935, 1-45.

_____ "Beethoven, Violin Concerto in D Major, Op. 61," in *Essays in Musical Analysis*. Vol. III: Concertos. London: Oxford University Press, 1936, 87-103.

_____ *Beethoven*. London: Oxford University Press, 1944.

Türk, Daniel Gottlob. *Klavierschule*. Leipzig and Halle: Schwickert, 1789; facs. reprint Kassel: Bärenreither, 1962. Trans. as *School of Clavier Playing* by Raymond Haggh. Lincoln: University of Nebraska Press, 1982.

Tusa, Michael C. "Some Factors for Cyclic Integration in Beethoven's Early Music," *International Journal of Musicology* 2 (1993): 153-92.

_____ "Beethoven's C Minor Mood: Some Thoughts on the Structural Implications of Key Choice," *Beethoven Forum* 2 (1993): 1-28.

Tyson, Alan. "Maurice Schlesinger as a Publisher of Beethoven," *Acta musicologica* 35 (1963): 182-91.

_____ "The Textual Problems of Beethoven's Violin Concerto, *MQ* 53 (1967): 482-502.

_____ *Thematic Catalogue of the Works of Muzio Clementi*. Tutzing: Schneider, 1967.

_____ "Notes on Five of Beethoven's Copyists," *JAMS* 23 (1970): 439-71.

_____ Review of the Willy Hess edition of the arrangement for piano of the Violin Concerto, *Musical Times*, 111 (Aug., 1970): 827.

_____ "Sketches and Autographs" in *The Beethoven Companion*. Eds. Denis Arnold and Nigel Fortune. London: Faber and Faber, 1971, 443-58.

_____ "The 'Rasumovsky' Quartets: Some Aspects of the Sources," in *Beethoven Studies* 3. Ed. A. Tyson. Cambridge: Cambridge University Press, 1982, 107-40.

Uhde, Jürgen. *Beethovens Klaviermusik*. Vol. II. Stuttgart: Reclam, 1974.

Vitercik, Gregory John. "Structure and Expression in Beethoven's Op. 132," *The Journal of Musicological Research* 13 (1993): 233-53.

Volek, Tomislav, and Jaroslav Macek. "Beethoven und Fürst Lobkowitz," in *Beethoven und Böhmen*. Eds. Sieghard Brandenburg and Martella Gutiérrez-Denhoff. Bonn: Beethoven-Haus, 1988, 203-17.

Voss, Egon, "Schwierigkeiten im Umgang mit dem Ballett 'Die Geschöpfe des Prometheus' von Salvatore Viganó und Ludwig van Beethoven," *Archiv für Musikwissenschaft* 53 (1996): 21-40.

Wallace, Robin. *Beethoven's Critics*. Cambridge: Cambridge University Press, 1986.

Webster, James, "The Form of the Finale of Beethoven's Ninth Symphony," *Beethoven Forum* 1 (1992): 25-62

_____ *Haydn's "Farewell" Symphony and the Idea of Classical Style*. Cambridge: Cambridge University Press, 1991.

Wegeler, Franz Gerhard, and Ferdinand Ries. *Biographische Notizen über Ludwig van Beethoven*. Koblenz, 1838, 1845. Trans. as *Beethoven Remembered* by Frederick Noonan. Introduction by Eva Badura-Skoda. Arlington, VA: Great Ocean Publishers, 1987.

Weill, Hanna. "The Two Versions of the Adagio of Beethoven's String Quartet, Op. 18, No. 1: Revisions in Dynamics, Harmony, and Rhythm," *The Beethoven Journal* 10 (1995): 60-65.

Wheelock, Gretchen A. *Haydn's Ingenious Jesting with Art: Contexts of Musical Wit and Humor.* New York: Schirmer Books, 1992.

Winter, Robert. *Compositional Origins of Beethoven's Opus 131.* Ann Arbor: UMI Research Press, 1982.

Wintle, Christopher. "Kontra-Schenker: *Largo e mesto* from Beethoven's Op. 10, No. 3," *Music Analysis* 4 (1985): 145-82.

Wolff, Barbara Marenholz. *Music Manuscripts at Harvard.* Cambridge, MA: Harvard University Library, 1992, No. 53, "An die Hoffnung."

Zaslaw, Neal. "Mozart's Tempo Conventions," in *International Musicological Society, Report of the Eleventh Congress Copenhagen 1972.* Eds. Henrik Glahn, Søren Sørensen, and Peter Ryom. Vol.II. Copenhagen: Wilhelm Hansen, 1974, 720-33.

Zenck, Martin. *Die Bach-Rezeption des späten Beethoven.* Stuttgart: F. Steiner Verlag Wiesbaden, 1986.

INDEX OF BEETHOVEN'S WORKS

SYMPHONIES
Symphony No. 1, Op. 21   22, 54n, 102
Symphony No. 2, Op. 36   207n
Symphony No. 3, Op. 55   26, 40, 54n, 103, 112,
    118, 130, 132, 148, 164, 220n, 237, 248,
    255, 261, 281, 333, 335, 336, 348, 349,
    382
Symphony No. 4, Op. 60   10, 41n, 97, 132,
    207n, 237, 266
Symphony No. 5, Op. 67   3, 16, 40, 54n, 71,
    113, 114, 132, 336, 349, 374, 382, 391
Symphony No. 6, Op. 68   61, 196-97, 209, 290,
    335
Symphony No. 7, Op. 92   40, 326, 336, 344,
    349
Symphony No. 8, Op. 93   103, 237, 296-97
Symphony No. 9, Op. 125   40, 49, 114, 127,
    162, 195, 235-36, 248, 252n, 266, 311,
    326, 336, 338, 344, 349, 358, 359, 362,
    363-64, 382, 389, 391

OTHER ORCHESTRAL WORKS
Wellingtons Sieg oder die Schlacht bei Vittoria,
    Op. 91   335
Overture, *Die Weihe des Hauses*, Op. 124   144,
    342

CONCERTOS
Piano concertos, general features   2-3, 21
First Piano Concerto, Op. 15   60, 92
Second Piano Concerto, Op. 19   60
Third Piano Concerto, Op. 37   57-60, 92, 370
Fourth Piano Concerto, Op. 58   3, 10, 16, 73,
    296
Fifth Piano Concerto, Op. 73   16, 44n, 111, 266
Triple Concerto, Op. 56   3, 8, 44n, 92
Violin Concerto, Op. 61, 118, 130, 132, 158, 194,
    195, 230, 240, 252, 261, 277, 281
Other concerto projects, 2

OTHER WORKS FOR SOLO INSTRUMENTS
AND ORCHESTRA
"Romance cantabile," Hess-Green 113
    (unfinished)   49
Romances for Violin, Opp. 40 and 50   49-50

CHAMBER WORKS
Wind Octet, Op. 103   35
Septet, Op. 20   290
String Quintet, Op. 29   9, 49, 120n, 130, 144,
    153, 194
String Quartets
    Op. 18, No. 1   22, 103, 113, 135n, 145
    Op. 18, No. 2   26, 109n
    Op. 18, No. 3   49
    Op. 18, No. 4   370
    Op. 18, No. 5   109n, 158
    Op. 18, No. 6   109n, 148, 335
    Op. 59, No. 1   3, 10, 16, 96, 114, 127,
        146, 178, 237, 283
    Op. 59, No. 2   237
    Op. 59, No. 3   3
    Op. 74   3, 185, 248, 265-66, 344
    Op. 95   185, 231-32, 335, 370
    Op. 127   184, 248, 264, 277, 333, 351,
        382
    Op. 130   102, 195, 237, 240, 283, 290,
        293, 310, 338, 372, 382, 391
    Op. 131   144, 248, 264, 290, 310, 342,
        346, 363, 382, 391
    Op. 132   96, 112, 117, 132, 138, 155,
        194, 197, 230, 233n, 248, 261,
        281, 283
    Op. 133   144, 278, 348
    Op. 135   248, 290, 335, 346
Piano Quartets and Trios
    Quartets, WoO 36   185
    Trios, Op. 1   90, 91
    Op. 1, No. 1   155
    Op. 1, No. 2   92, 328-29
    Trio, Op. 11 (with Clarinet)   248

Trio, Op. 70, No. 1 92, 145
Trio, Op. 70, No. 2 92, 247, 336, 349
Trio, Op. 97 10, 39, 91, 185, 237

String Trios
Trio, Op. 3 118, 290
Serenade for String Trio, Op. 8 181, 290, 390
Trio, Op. 9, No. 3 238

Violin Sonatas
Op. 12 186
Op. 12, No. 1 102, 108n, 248, 264
Op. 12, No. 2 222
Op. 3, No. 3 222,
Op. 23 222, 237
Op. 24 9, 222, 240, 390
Op. 30, No. 1 10, 222, 233n, 248, 251, 261, 264, 280
Op. 30, No. 2 108, 222
Op. 30, No. 3 194, 222
Op. 47 124n 186, 222, 248, 251, 264, 280
Op. 96 10, 91, 107, 111, 132, 155

Violin sonatas, general features, 222

Sonata for Horn and Piano, Op. 17 94

Cello Sonatas
Op. 5, No. 1 9
Op. 69 10, 91, 237, 238
Op. 102, No. 1 391
Op. 102, No. 2 96, 195, 234-35

Piano Sonatas
Op. 2, No. 1 21, 113, 154
Op. 2, No. 2 92, 107n, 108n, 109n, 154, 176
Op. 2, No. 3 102, 107n, 135n, 204, 206
Op. 7 92, 93, 102, 109n, 161, 176
Op. 10, No. 1 107n, 130, 176
Op. 10, No. 2 90, 107n, 108n, 130
Op. 10, No. 3 54n, 320, 390
Op. 13 226n, 335
Op. 14, No. 1 103, 107n
Op. 14, No. 2 93, 102, 176
Op. 22 93, 109n, 154, 155
Op. 26 10, 91, 146, 155, 158, 335
Op. 27, No. 1 3, 91, 390
Op. 27, No. 2 10, 108n, 145
Op. 28 9, 124, 145
Op. 31, No. 2 92, 363-65, 391
Op. 31, No. 3 10, 93, 154
Op. 49, No. 1 154
Op. 53 109, 161, 204, 374, 383, 391
Op. 54 154
Op. 57 3, 16, 39, 40, 108, 109, 113, 127, 132, 252n, 390
Op. 78 10
Op. 81a 13, 112, 335, 348
Op. 90 127
Op. 101 91, 127, 194, 202, 357, 391
Op. 106 91n, 93, 96, 145, 237, 240, 348, 391
Op. 109 127,194, 248, 264
Op. 110 91, 96, 111,127, 194, 202, 209, 240, 321, 335, 363-64, 391
Op. 111 144, 248

Early piano sonatas, general features 90-94

Piano Variations and Other Works
Variationen über ein Schweitzer Lied WoO 64 97
"Righini" Variations, WoO 65 35, 86, 261
"Prometheus" Variations, Op. 35 40, 164, 261
"Diabelli" Variations, Op. 120 237, 261
Bagatelle for piano, WoO 54 335
Fantasy, Op. 77 162
Multicouplet rondos 93-94

CHORAL WORKS
Cantata on the Death of Joseph II, WoO 87 181, 391-92
Choral Fantasy, Op. 80 162
Mass in C, Op. 86 392,
Missa solemnis, Op. 123 Gloria 144

DRAMATIC WORKS
Ballet, *Die Geschöpfe des Prometheus*, Op. 43 362 ,363n, 390
Incidental Music to *Egmont*, Op. 84, No. 7 145
Opera, *Fidelio*, Op. 72, No. 6, March 359

GENERAL INDEX

Agawu, V. Kofi, 294, 296, 316
Agrell, J. J. 289
Allanbrook, Wye Jamison 10n
alternating variation 40, 336, 349
ars combinatoria 330-33
Bach, C. P. E. 100
Bach, J.S. 87, 300, 365
Baillot, Pierre 5-6, 8
Bartók, Béla 290, 353-57, 389
Beethoven, Karl van 287, 393
Beethoven, Ludwig van
    style of performance 88
    views on composition 337, 385, 389
    views on voice leading 315
Bent, Ian 291
Berlioz, Hector 348, 364, 389
Bilson, Malcolm 99, 178n
Boccherini, Luigi 10, 241, 389
Brandenburg, Sieghard 185, 191-92, 222, 245, 249-50, 257, 286-87, 290, 291, 327, 336, 337, 341, 373n
Brendel, Alfred 99
Breuning, Stephan von, and Julie 6
Budapest String Quartet 292
Busby, Thomas 146
calando 151n
Cahn, Peter 124n, 199, 218
Chelleri, Fortunato 289
Cherubini, Luigi 117
Chorale settings 337-39
Chua, D. K. L. 294, 296, 326n
Cibini, Antonia 288n
Clement, Franz 3-5, 9n, 15
Clementi, Muzio 6, 15, 80, 87, 117
Cole, Malcolm S. 51, 59, 60, 69, 94n, 368
Cooper, Barry 184, 327
Cyclic form 12-13, 387-90; table, 390-91
Czerny, Carl 4, 20, 21, 50, 57n, 70n, 83, 86, 88-89, 96, 98-99, 114, 146, 147, 161, 163, 177, 198-99, 244, 250, 265, 272, 274, 288, 334
de Roda Sketchbook 286, 362
dissonance 142-43, 166, 170, 229, 320, 344, 347-48, 376-77, 378

Dahlhaus, Carl 118
Dittersdorf, Carl Ditters von 289
Elterlein, Ernst (*see* Ernst Gottschald)
Endler, J.S. 289
Eskeles, Marie 288n
Fétis, F.J. 5-6
Fischhof Miscellany (Berlin Autograph 28), 119, 120-23, 149-50, 159-60, 179
Forchert, Arno 147-48
Frolich, Martha 89, 124n, 177
Galeazzi, Francesco 20n, 107n, 145, 178-179
Galitzin, Prinz Nikolaus 285
Gottschald, Ernst (pseudo. Ernst Elterlein) 94
Goya, Francisco de 148n
Grave, Floyd, 144, 269n
Haimo, Ethan 387n
harmonic rhythm, 34, 42, 64-65, 135-37, 158-59, 204, 206-07
Haydn, Joseph 93
Works
    Symphony No. 12 10
    Symphony No. 28 15n
    Symphony No. 29 10
    Symphony No. 30 113
    Symphony No. 44 113, 317n
    Symphony No. 45 289
    Symphony No. 60 289
    Symphony No. 85 113
    Symphony No. 88 326
    Symphony No. 97 266, 317n
    Symphony No. 103 15, 40, 93, 336
    Symphony No. 104 29, 113
    Sinfonia concertante, H105 365
    String Quartet Op. 20, No. 1 (5) 15
    String Quartet Op. 20, No. 2 365
    String Quartet Op. 33, No. 1 163
    String Quartet Op. 64, No. 6 (5) 296
    String Quartet, Op.76, No. 2 317n
    String Quartet, Op.76, No. 3 49
    String Quartet, Op.76, No. 4 326
    String Quartet, Op.77, No. 1 113
    Cello Concerto in D, H7b:6 2, 10
    Piano Variations in F minor, H17:6 40
    Piano Sonata H16:36 113
    Piano Sonata H16:49 15

Helm, Theodor 291, 294, 295, 316, 317, 334, 374
Hess, Willy 37n
Hiller, J.A. 249
Holz, Karl 97, 287-88, 291-93
humor 93, 159, 177-78, 240
Jander, Owen 41n, 48-49, 50n, 334
Joachim, Joseph 5
Johnson, Douglas 2n, 112, 119, 123, 327
Johansen, Gail Nelson 215, 234, 268
Jonas, Oswald 81, 257
Kafka Miscellany 119, 123-27, 151-54, 160-61, 179-80
Kamien, Roger 29n, 308n
Kerman, Joseph 112, 123-24, 129n, 294, 295, 318, 326
Kinderman, William 294, 295, 364
Kirkendale, Warren 297n, 300, 338, 341
Kleist, Heinrich von 394
Knecht, J.H. 337n, 341
Koch, H.C. 20-21, 63, 83, 91-92, 104, 146, 230n, 317
Kojima, Shin Augustinus 79-81
Kollmann, A.F.C. 20n
Kramer, Richard 2n, 338n
Kremer, Gidon 37
Kreutzer, Rodolphe 8
Krumpholz, Wenzel 7
Lam, Basil 374
LaRue, Jan xvii, 1n, 16n, 20n, 34, 116, 181n, 207n, 320n
Lenz, Wilhelm von 89, 95-96, 194, 196
Levy, Janet M. 177
Linke, Joseph 287-88
Liszt, Franz 364
Lobkowitz, Prinz Franz Joseph Maximillian 187
Long-range connections 129, 281-82n, 345
Lydian mode 338, 342-343
Marx, A.B. 95, 291, 294, 295, 316, 357, 394
Mason, D. G. 294, 296
Matthews, Denis 177
Mendelssohn, Felix 364, 365-68, 389
Mesto 146
metronome marks
    Opus 61, 83
    Op. 10, No.3 97-99
    Op. 96 197-98
    Op. 132 291-93n
mezza voce 230n
Michaelis, C.F. 177
monothematic form 112, 163, 318
Moscheles, Ignaz 98-99
Moscow Sketchbook 286, 361

Mozart, Wolfgang Amadeus 33
Works
    Symphony No. 25, K. 183 195
    Symphony No. 31, K. 297 15, 130
    Symphony No. 38, K. 504 15, 163
    Symphony No. 39, K. 543, 10, 113, 247, 317n
    Symphony No. 40, K. 550 10, 102, 195, 317n, 372n
    Symphony No. 41, K. 551 15, 29, 309
    Eine kleine Nachtmusik, K. 525 50
    Overture to *Die Zauberflöte*, K. 620 15
    Piano Concerto, K. 271 25
    Piano Concerto, K. 414 10
    Piano Concerto, K. 453 10, 26, 248
    Piano Concerto, K.456 40
    Piano Concerto, K. 466 50
    Piano Concerto, K. 467 25, 39
    Piano Concerto, K. 488 10
    Piano Concerto, K. 491 24, 40, 248
    Piano Concerto, K. 503 57, 59
    Piano Concerto, K. 595 10
    Violin Concerto, K. 216 25
Comparison of Mozart and Beethoven Concerto Styles 24-25
Mozartian features of WoO 5 9
    Clarinet Quintet, K. 581 248
    String Quartet, K. 421 248
    String Quartet, K. 464 317n
    Violin Sonata, K. 379 248
    Violin Sonata, K. 454 185
    Violin Sonata, K.526 185
    Piano Sonata, K. 331 252n
    Piano Sonata, K. 570 113
multimovement cycles 289-90
Newman, William S. 89, 99, 221
Nottebohm, Gustave 71- 72, 81, 191, 220n, 226, 249, 256-257, 327, 374
Obelkevich, Mary Rowan 19
pathotype fugue subject 297-300
perdendosi 63
performance practice, Op. 61 83-84
Pergolesi, G. B. 15n
Petter Sketchbook 191
piano pedal markings 212-14
Platen, Emil 286n, 291, 293
program music 334-36
Portowitz, Adena 22n
Rampl, Wenzel 287
Radcliffe, Philip 357
Ratner, Leonard G., 10n, 15n, 20n, 25n, 59-60, 252, 261, 294-97, 314, 316-17, 319, 333, 336, 345, 357, 358-59, 368, 387

reviews, early
    Op. 61 4-6;
    Op. 10, No. 3 99-100
    Op. 96, 190, 199, 244, 261
    Op. 132, 392-94
    later 19th- century views of Op. 10, No. 3 94-96
rhythmic ambiguities, hemiola, metrical displacement, surface rhythmic organization 35, 42, 45, 109, 117, 132, 137, 144-45, 163, 167-68, 170, 172, 215-16, 234, 319, 326, 331, 350, 358-59, 370, 381, 383-84
Riemann, Hugo 291
Ries, Ferdinand 90
Ries, Franz 7
rinforzando 139-40
rising melodic peaks, Op. 96 194
rondo hybrids 39-40
rondos, multicouplet 93-94
Rode, Pierre 187-90
Rosand, Ellen 316n
Rosen, Charles 294-95
Rosenblum, Sandra P. 89, 140, 198n
Rostel, Max 186n, 245n, 284n
Rubens, Peter Paul 393, 394
Rudolf, Max 155n, 198n-99n, 221, 237
Rudolph, (Johann Joseph Rainer), Archduke of Austria, later Archbishop of Olmütz (now Olomouc) 187, 224n, 337
Sammartini, G.B. 25, 29n, 113 (JC 14, 39), 113n, 195 (J-C 57, 58) , 249n
Schenker, Heinrich 89, 140n, 175n, 176n, 235n
scherzo 236-37
Schindler, Anton 95-146-147
Schlesinger, Maurice 288
Schnabel, Artur 99, 198
Schubert, Franz 389
Schumann, Robert 368

Schuppanzigh, Ignaz 7, 9n, 197, 288
Schwarz, Boris 3n, 8
Schwartz, Judith L. 66
Shamgar, Beth 27
Sheer, Miriam 32, 176, 209
Sisman, Elaine 40, 146, 248, 261, 336
Smart, Sir George 288, 292
smorzando 140
Solomon, Maynard 148, 195
Spohr, Ludwig 188, 191
staccato marks 84, 97, 287
Stadler, Abbé Maximilian 288
Szigetti, Joseph 186n, 198
textual errors and problems
    Op. 61 76, 79-80
    Op. 10, No. 3: II 140n; IV 175-76
    Op. 96 221-22, 276n-77n
    Op. 132 293, 370n
textural variation 15, 300, 310-11, 315-16, 320, 326, 332-33, 358
Thompson, Harold 108
topics (topoi) 9-10, 40, 52-53, 118, 145-49, 155, 158, 177-78, 195-97, 223, 234-36, 245n, 249, 272, 274, 278, 297-98, 316-17, 321, 370, 374
Tovey, D. F. 20n, 26-27, 39, 40n, 51, 59, 89, 103, 129
Türk, D. G. 140, 146, 337n, 344
Tusa, Michael 9n, 181-83
Tyson, Alan 5n, 76n, , 79-81
Viotti, G. B. 2n, 8, 9, 10, 26n, 113
Vitercik, Gregory John 311, 359, 374
Vogler, Abbé Georg Joseph 20n, 337n
Wegeler, Franz Gerhard 148
    and Ferdinand Ries 334
Weill, Hanna 308n
Wheelock, Gretchen A. 177
Wintle, Christopher 142n
Zaslaw, Neal 91

DATE DUE

NOV 1 1 2009